D1432757

CLASSICAL SPIES

Classical Spies

AMERICAN ARCHAEOLOGISTS

WITH THE OSS IN

WORLD WAR II GREECE

Susan Heuck Allen

THE UNIVERSITY OF MICHIGAN PRESS · ANN ARBOR

Copyright © by the University of Michigan 2011
All rights reserved
Published in the United States of America by
The University of Michigan Press
Manufactured in the United States of America
♾ Printed on acid-free paper

2014   2013   2012   2011   4   3   2   1

A CIP catalog record for this book is available from the British Library.

Library of Congress Cataloging-in-Publication Data

Allen, Susan Heuck, 1952–
    Classical spies : American archaeologists with the OSS in World
War II Greece / Susan Heuck Allen.
        p.   cm.
    Includes bibliographical references and index.
    ISBN 978-0-472-11769-7 (hardback) — ISBN 978-0-472-02766-8
(e-book)
    1. World War, 1939–1945—Secret service—Greece.   2. World War,
1939–1945—Secret service—United States.   3. Espionage—Greece—
History—20th century.   4. Spies—Greece—History—20th century.
5. Archaeologists—Greece—History—20th century.   6. Archaeologists—
United States—History—20th century.   7. United States.
Office of Strategic Services.   I. Title.
D810.S7A54   2011
940.86473092—dc23   2011020863

I dedicate this book to the American men and women, classical archaeologists and classicists, and the Greeks who joined them, whose heroic deeds during World War II are here told for the first time.

Acknowledgments

I DREW MY INSPIRATION for this project from the lives of my professor John Langdon Caskey and my friend Clio Adossides Sperling.

I acknowledge with pleasure the generous support of a senior research fellowship from the National Endowment of the Humanities in 2006, a Seeger Fellowship at Princeton University's Program in Hellenic Studies in 2007, and an Andrew Mellon Fellowship at the American Philosophical Society in 2008. Travel-to-conference grants from Providence College and Smith College advanced my research in Turkey and enabled me to conduct interviews at the annual meetings of the Archaeological Institute of America. The AIA's lecture program has helped me access additional archives.

I should like to thank John Taylor and Lawrence MacDonald at the National Archives in College Park, Maryland; Alex Pezzati of the University Museum Archives of the University of Pennsylvania; Natalia Vogeikoff of the American School of Classical Studies at Athens; Jan Jordan at the Agora Archives; Carol Herschenson at the University of Cincinnati; Donald Skemer, Rare Books and Manuscripts of Firestone Library of Princeton University; Erica Mosner, the Institute for Advanced Study, Princeton, New Jersey; and Shelley Lightburn, United Nations Archives; archives in the American Farm School; Anatolia College; California State University, Sacramento; Hoover Institute, Stanford University; Mudd Manuscript Library of Princeton University; New Jersey Historical Society; Rockefeller Foundation; State University of Iowa; University of Cincinnati; University of Minnesota; University of Oregon; and Yale University.

I should like to single out Clio Sperling, with whom I had many good conversations and who permitted scans to be made of her personal photographs, some of which are included in the book. I thank John O. Iatrides and William M. Calder III for their encouragement. The following individuals shared their wartime experiences in Greece or relevant knowledge: Miriam Caskey, Ellen Kohler, Edmund Keeley, Raphael Moizis, Kitty Kyriacopoulou, George Paspati, Harry Tzalas, Kaiti Koumarianou, Nikos Vernikos, Elizabeth Milburn Schofield, Martha Heath Wiencke, Larissa Bonfante, Sara Anderson Immerwahr, William H. McNeill, James Russell, Crawford Greenewalt, James McCredie, T. Leslie Shear, Jr., Alan Boegehold, Emmett Bennett, Eve Harrison, Charles Williams, James Mc Credie, Spyro Cappony, Machteld Mellink, George Bass, Stephen Tracey, Oscar White Muscarella, G. Roger Edwards, Keith de Vries, Zoe Rees York, Gwynneth Giraud, William K. Pritchett, Al Simes, John Coleman, Jack Davis, and Peter Allen. They made it come alive.

I gladly acknowledge the hospitality of friends and institutions: Clopper and Joan Almon, Melissa Hunsicker, Bülent and Elif Becan, Julie Steinmetz, Jeff Clarke, Alain and Brian Giraud, Peggy and Eric Messer, Andrea Pilling, Constance Degerberg, Penny Wilson and Nikos Zarganis, Miriam Caskey, Alexis Phylactopoulos and the College Year in Athens, and Richard Jackson and Anatolia College. I would also like to thank Miriam Caskey, Jack Thompson, Abbott Gleason, Dorothy Emeline Allen, Alan Boegehold, Wendy White, Beth Kiley Kinder, and Morris Nathanson for reading parts of the manuscript and offering their insights. I owe a great deal to Miriam Caskey, but supreme among my many debts is that to my husband, Peter Sutton Allen.

Contents

Abbreviations

ACLS	American Council of Learned Societies
AFHQ	Allied Forces Headquarters, Algiers, Caserta
AIA	Archaeological Institute of America
AMM	Allied Military Mission
ASCSA	American School of Classical Studies at Athens
ASOR	American Schools of Oriental Research
BBC	British Broadcasting Corporation
BMM	British Military Mission
BSC	British Security Coordination
CCC	Civilian Conservation Corps
CSDIC	Combined Services Interrogation Center
CGP	Comprehensive Greek Project
COI	Coordinator of Information, predecessor of OSS
CMC	Cyprus Mines Corporation
EAM	Ethnikon Apeleftherikon Metopon (National Liberation Front)
EDES	Ellinikos Dimokratikos Ethnikos Stratos (National Democratic Greek League)
ELAS	Ethniko Laikos Apeleftherikos Stratos (National Liberation Popular Army)
EKKA	Ethniki kai Koinoniki Apeleftherosis (National and Social Liberation)

FEA	Foreign Economic Administration, United States
FIS	Foreign Information Services, part of COI
FNB	COI and OSS Foreign Nationalities Branch
FRUS	Foreign Relations of the United States. The conferences at Washington and Quebec.
G-2	U.S. Army Intelligence
GIP	Greek Irregular Project
GWRA	Greek War Relief Association
HIS	Hellenic Information Services, known as NIPS in Cairo
ISLD	Inter Service Liaison Department (MI-6 or SIS)
JIC	Joint Intelligence Sub-Committee
JICAME	Joint Intelligence Combined Army Middle East
KKE	Kommunistiko Komma Ellados (Greek Communist Party)
LRDG	Long Range Desert Group, British special forces
LSF	Levant Schooner Flotilla, British special forces
MEIC	Middle East Intelligence Centre
METO	Middle East Theatre of Operations
MERRA	Middle East Relief and Rehabilitation Administration
MI-5	Military Intelligence 5, British domestic security intelligence, SIME
MI-6	Military Intelligence 6, British secret intelligence (SIS or ISLD)
MI-9	Military Intelligence 9, British, escape
MID	Military Intelligence Department
MIS	Military Intelligence Service
MO-4	Military Operations, British, SOE cover name in Cairo
MO	Morale Operations, OSS
MU	Maritime Unit, OSS
OFRRA	Office of Foreign Relief and Rehabilitation Administration
OSS	Office of Strategic Services
ONI	Office of Naval Intelligence
OWI	Office of War Information
PICME	Political Intelligence Committee Middle East
PWE	Political Warfare Executive

RAF	Royal Air Force
R & A	OSS Research and Analysis Branch
RHAF	Royal Hellenic Air Force
RHN	Royal Hellenic Navy
RNVR	Royal Navy Volunteer Reserve
SIME	Security Intelligence Middle East
SAS	Special Air Service, British special forces
SBS	Special Boat Service, British special forces
SD	Sicherheitsdienst (German Security Intelligence)
SHAEF	Supreme Headquarters, Allied Expeditionary Force
SI	OSS Secret Intelligence Branch
SIS	Secret Intelligence Service, British
SOE	MO-4, British sabotage service
SSU	Strategic Services Unit
UNRRA	United Nations Relief and Rehabilitation Administration
UPMB	University of Pennsylvania Museum Bulletin
USAFIME	United States Armed Forces in the Middle East
USNR	United States Naval Reserve
X-2	OSS Counterintelligence

Prologue

IT WAS OUZO HOUR. Archaeologists gathered for the nightly ritual as the sun set across Vourkari Bay on the island of Kea. From the dig house veranda, you could see past Cape Sounion and the Aegean all the way to the Peloponnese with each rocky spine deepening to violet across the blood orange sky.

The evening was deceptively casual, the society highly stratified, a lieutenant parrying and flirting with younger diggers while others silently nursed their drinks. Everyone self-identified according to a code of initials: JLC, JLD, MEC, JLO, GFO, SAH, and JLB, a tradition that stretched back to the early twentieth century at the American School of Classical Studies at Athens, the research home for American archaeologists in Greece. "*Karpousi me makhairi!*" ("Watermelon with the knife!") a gypsy cried as he threaded the lane below the verandah in a tiny three-wheeled truck, stabbing watermelons open in an attempt to sell them to the yachting set crowding into Tasso's taverna. Past the pleasure boats, ruined hulks of the Michalinos Coal Company stood sentry in the distant dark while a disco sent its throbbing rhythms over the inky waves. Then the dig director, Jack Caskey, arrived and poured himself a drink.

Now was the time for tales. One by one the archaeologists fell silent as Caskey spun a yarn about an Albanian Turk who had become valet to the British ambassador in Ankara and sold Allied secrets to the Nazis. Hollywood had made a movie, and books had outed the famous spy Cicero, but Caskey claimed they had gotten it wrong.[1] His eyes brightened as he recalled the beautiful blonde whom he had helped to rescue from the pursuing Germans after she had fingered the World War II spy. The escape involved moonlight and a small fishing boat. I never heard the story again, but I never forgot it. It was the only episode Caskey ever shared of his time in the Office of Strategic Services (OSS), predecessor of the CIA.

Three years later, Jack Caskey was dead. Just before he died, he was honored by the Archaeological Institute of America (AIA) with its Gold Medal for a distinguished career in archaeology, the highest accolade given to an American in our field. When I walked into the award ceremony, I was confronted by a sea of tweed seeming so staid and traditional. Little did I know that in the audience that night were a clutch of Caskey's cohorts who had served with him in intelligence during their youth. What seemed to me like a fusty group was really a tight network of courageous men and women who had climbed out of their trenches to wage their own war against Hitler and help save Greece. These excavators, who had ringed the wartime Mediterranean at exotic ports like Istanbul, Alexandria, Kourion, and Cairo, now stood to applaud one of their own.

I picked up Caskey's thread twenty years later. After a decade as a field archaeologist in the eastern Mediterranean, I had left "dirt" archaeology to study the archaeologists themselves, finding the recent history of the discipline more intriguing than the ancient artifacts. I researched and wrote *Finding the Walls of Troy* (1999) about Frank Calvert and Heinrich Schliemann, who searched for and excavated Homer's citadel. When asked to lecture in memory of Caskey, I decided to follow up on Caskey's war episode.

I had always had a particular interest in World War II lore and had relished Dilys Powell's slim *Villa Ariadne* on John Pendlebury, the British archaeologist-spy who organized Cretan resistance, and William Stanley Moss's *Ill Met by Moonlight,* which featured British special agents kidnapping a German general, the only one so abducted during the war. Since Greece was important to Britain's imperialist foreign policy in the Mediterranean, British intelligence services in the Aegean were long lived, large, and well funded. Later some of its agents, often archaeologists and classicists, wrote autobiographical accounts, and biographies profiled others.[2] Thus, Pendlebury and other British archaeologists acquired iconic status, and the story of British intelligence and special operations in the Aegean became well known,[3] but few of the war narratives mentioned any Americans.

No books concerning other countries' World War II intelligence services in and around Greece have yet appeared; although some of the Greeks involved in intelligence work published memoirs, they generally focus on their work with the British.[4] Only now are researchers probing the role of German and Italian archaeologist spies in wartime Greece. So far, their archives have revealed little about American activities and the role of American archaeologists.[5]

Before I began researching Caskey's secret life, I had thought him too young to have played an important role in the war. To learn more, I turned to the National Archives in College Park, Maryland, which I had found to be a fertile field for other books. On my first day, I discovered that Caskey had not been alone. He had worked with a handful of other archaeologists: Rodney Young, John Franklin "Pete" Daniel III, Jerome Sperling, James Oliver, and Dorothy Cox. Some names I knew well; others I had never heard before, but all were dead.

At this point, the search became an obsession. I brought my tape recorder on pilgrimages to Cincinnati, Athens, Oxford, Cambridge, Izmir, and Philadelphia to interview the archaeologists' spouses, colleagues, and students. At every AIA meeting, I interviewed anyone who could add a piece to my puzzle. Bronze Age archaeologist Sarah Anderson Immerwahr told me that before the war she had dug in Turkey and Cyprus with Daniel (see fig. 11), one of the four OSS "archaeological captains" and the wunderkind of Bronze Age Cypriot scripts and pottery. In the immediate postwar period, after he had supposedly severed ties with American intelligence services, Daniel had died under mysterious circumstances just before his thirty-ninth birthday. Immerwahr believed that he had been poisoned, although she had no idea who might have done it. Archaeologist Ellen Kohler, Daniel's postwar administrative assistant on the *American Journal of Archaeology,* also thought there was "something fishy" about how Daniel died.[6] Daniel had just recruited Rodney Young for the Department of Archaeology and the University Museum of the University of Pennsylvania. Kohler, who had later worked for Young in Turkey and Philadelphia, told me that on Daniel's last trip in 1948, he and Young were scouting for a new site in Turkey. Young was driving the jeep the day Daniel died. Young himself had died in a car crash before I graduated from college, so she recommended I talk to Roger Edwards, who was with them in the jeep. After speaking with Kohler and Edwards, I read Daniel's letters for clues to his demise and first saw his image: a slim, intense, good-looking man whose sad smile was more of a sneer, the corners of his mouth turning downward, his young forehead creased, hardened by war. How had this restless man who sought tranquility, and finally found it on an old Bucks County farm along a winding creek, died so young and so far from home? The mystery remained.

I spoke at conferences in Turkey and Greece so that I might trace the paths the archaeologists trod through the streets of Istanbul, Izmir, and Athens and hunt for the OSS bases. Alain Giraud, a Levantine friend whose ancestors had lived around Izmir for over two centuries, volunteered to be my host, chauffeur, and translator. Together we scoured the coast north of Izmir and the Karaburun Peninsula, passing the ghost towns of once thriving Greek communities that were abandoned in the population exchange between Greece and Turkey in 1922 and frozen in time when the area became a military zone. Alain had been a yachtsman and knew the coast and its inlets well. We scouted for locales that fit the descriptions of Caskey's secret harbors, code-named "Boston," "Miami," and "Key West," where he had sequestered agents before sending them into Axis-occupied Greece. At one nondescript crossroad, Alain paused and said, "I've been here before." More than fifty years earlier, a friend's father had given his teenage daughter and Alain a ride to the beach and stopped to run an errand at a nearby harbor on the way to the families' summer compound. The man was Noel Rees, the head of British secret intelligence in Izmir, and the inlet, unbeknownst to Alain, had been the top-secret British base.

After sleuthing in Turkey, I crossed over to Greece and contacted Caskey's widow, Miriam, in Athens. Surrounded by treasures of a life richly lived, she and I focused on a man long dead and experiences that had occurred before I was born. Miriam generously shared photographs, address books, and memories, but her most precious gift was an introduction to Clio.

I had actually wanted to meet Clio's husband, Jerry Sperling, like Caskey a veteran of the 1930s Troy excavations and one of the OSS archaeologists whom I had chosen to investigate. Nine years earlier, I had interviewed him for my book on Troy, but since then he had died. Miriam said that I might be able to meet his widow; however, although they were close friends, she could not guarantee anything since Mrs. Sperling was a recluse. She and Clio were the widows of best friends, but Miriam, Caskey's second wife, was some twenty years younger. She was Clio's lifeline, calling her every day and visiting often. With great anticipation, I purchased flowers for the visit. Miriam rang the bell and an unseen hand buzzed us in. As we climbed the steps to the second floor, a door opened just enough to shine light into the dark stairwell. A tiny birdlike woman appeared, elegantly dressed and coifed. She and Miriam embraced, and then I was introduced.

Clio hesitated to speak. Then, enunciating every English word precisely, she told me a little about herself. Jerry had been her second husband. Her first husband had been Greek. "His name?" I asked. "Adossides." "Not related to Anastas Adossides?" I asked again. "His son," she replied. I told Clio that both Adossides père and Jerry Sperling appeared in my book on Troy and gave her a copy. She began to warm. I looked around the room for Trojan mementoes, but saw none. Instead, a majestic grand piano occupied pride of place. Clio's taste was modern. Unlike Miriam, she kept the past locked away in her mind. "How did you meet Jerry?" I asked. Clio balked and told me that this was her story and that she wanted to take it to the grave. Then, glancing furtively at Miriam, she slowly let out that she had met Jerry in Cairo, where she worked at the OSS Greek Desk for the American archaeologist Rodney Young. Beginning around teatime, Clio shared her photographs and talked until long after sundown about those "perfect years" of her life.

That was in June 2002. Thereafter, each time I visited Greece, I sought out Clio. For me, each encounter opened a precious window on history. For her, the effort of dredging up the past and reliving so many intense experiences must have been excruciating. Although these reflections sometimes awakened fond visions of youthful frolicking, they also resurrected horrible nightmares of long-buried loss.

In the intervening years, Miriam was my go-between with a shopping list of names, dates, and places that I needed to clarify. In the autumn of 2006, as Clio lay wasting away in Athens, she agreed to let me record her story. When I arrived in 2007, her voice was so faint as to be inaudible, but she still proved to be my most compelling witness. At what was to be our last meeting, Clio divulged new aspects of her story that again led me back to Rodney Young, with whom she shared her wartime adventures in Albania. Later that summer, I followed their footsteps.

Young turned out to be the key, but as I tried to learn more about this shadowy figure, I found that he was an intensely private person who had left no personal papers. Undaunted, I continued to sift institutional archives in Princeton, Philadelphia, and Athens.

I began piecing together each of the archaeologists' stories, wondering what motivated them to get involved in espionage and what they had accomplished. I expanded my lens to include the men *and* women who had worked together on behalf of Greece and the United States in Washington, Princeton, and the Mediterranean. Since these archaeologists had played such a significant role informing U.S. policy, why had the *History of the American School of Classical Studies at Athens* (Meritt 1984) said nothing about their OSS involvement? Was it a conspiracy of silence? One member of the School told me to keep quiet and said I should never publish this book. As I questioned my generation of archaeologists about their predecessors, I was struck by how many scholars knew little about what their professors had done in World War II.

Time after time, I returned to the National Archives. When I had first encountered the overwhelming OSS records, some 4,000 cubic feet of files had been declassified. Under the guidance of John Taylor, intelligence expert, and Lawrence MacDonald, a classics-trained archivist, I searched and searched, but found the cumbersome organization difficult to plumb. Now instead of digging trenches, I excavated the OSS archives. Once, as a dirt archaeologist, I excavated horizontally, opening up a site to one period and examining the architecture and contemporary relationships. But OSS was organized vertically. So, as an "archival archaeologist," I conducted vertical soundings, looking at the history of each base stratified through time, month by month through the course of the war. Then I repeated the process for the different OSS branches concerned with Greece. Only then could I begin to piece together the relationships between bases and branches, examining their part in the Mediterranean mosaic.

Sifting through the archaeologists' paper trail, I found the stratigraphy disturbed, but not by burrowing rodents or roots as in "dirt" archaeology. As each OSS base closed down its operations, it wrote its own history and boxed its documents for Washington. After the war, each branch compiled its respective history for the historian of OSS. When the Central Intelligence Agency (CIA) was created in 1947, OSS files were forwarded there for sorting. CIA archivists cherry-picked reports marked "Restricted," "Secret," "Top Secret," "Most Secret," and "Eyes Only," according to their degree of confidentiality. They retained the more sensitive materials for reasons of national security, declassified only the most harmless documents, and surrendered them to the National Archives. In so doing, they broke up the "primary" undisturbed context of many of the files and only made a partial record available to the public. Periodically, the CIA released more sensitive records, but pulled, retained, and boxed separately the most secret materials. Thus, documents generated by the Greek Desk became scattered, with the result that some, boxed by release date, are now sandwiched between unrelated (but equally sensitive) files having to do with OSS in China and

Burma. The CIA released additional material in 2004 and, in August 2008, opened 20,000 OSS personnel files. Unlike potsherds, the bread and butter of "dirt" archaeologists, the files were not mute, so I was able to discover their original contents, but, in archaeological terms, this disturbance or "secondary" context made reconstructing the past far more difficult.

With each round of declassifications, I searched for the secret account that matched the tale Caskey had told. Eventually, I uncovered each of the archaeologists' files. In them, I found tantalizing references to a "delicious" report that Caskey had fired off in late April 1944. Did it concern Cicero? Because Caskey had marked it "Eyes Only," after they read the document, they had to burn it, and each assured him that he had done so. Again and again I hit a brick wall. Then I unearthed a bound volume containing copies of all of my professor's reports and correspondence, prepared in 1945 shortly before he returned to Washington. As I thumbed through the tome, I finally hit pay dirt: "Operation Honeymoon," and my heart raced as I devoured Caskey's account of his evacuation of the fraulein who had figured in Cicero's tale.

Until now, the American archaeologists' intelligence work in World War II Greece has remained a well-kept secret, largely unknown by the public.[7] Each of the OSS recruits swore never to keep a diary and not to divulge his or her wartime actions. Many carried their secrets to the grave. Most of the documents that I have used to weave this narrative have only recently been declassified and have never been published. This is the first account of archaeologists at war who formulated and managed the first major American intelligence service in Greece. Trained to interpret the classics, they knew the land, languages, and people through long years in the trenches. Thus bound up with modern Greece and its way of life, these American men and women put themselves in harm's way to save the country and people they loved. They put their scholarship to work for the United States, gathering secret intelligence, planning missions, and managing intricate networks of spies who penetrated into Axis-occupied Greece until they became operatives themselves.

ONE

"On the Rim of a Volcano"

OCTOBER 28, 1940, DAWNED CLEAR and bright over Mt. Hymettus. Nine men gathered on the summit, though it was a military zone and Greece's fascist dictator, General Ioannis Metaxas, had just declared war. Rodney Young dwarfed the others. Once the Cary Grantish darling of New York debutante balls, Young had spent the last eight summers excavating in and around Athens with this band of men. He stood erect in his excavation uniform: a tawny long-sleeved shirt open at the neck, cuffs rolled up, and jodhpurs tucked into tall black boots, his dark hair bleached and his smooth skin leathered by the Mediterranean sun. Young savored the god's eye view over the Athenian plain between Mt. Parnes, Mt. Pendeli, and the ships in the bay off Phaleron. A haze hung over the city, with the Acropolis and Mt. Lycabettus rising above the morning mist. At the base of Lycabettus lay the American School of Classical Studies at Athens.

Young's Greek workmen grabbed their tools and headed to the trenches. They believed in the value of archaeology for their country. Greece was a young nation in spite of the antiquity of its civilization and had grounded its modern identity in its ancient past. Metaxas promoted archaeology as a "patriotic duty" and a bridge between that glorious era and the troubled present. He staged youth rallies using ancient temples as backdrops and sent antiquities, fundamental to the country's image, as "ambassadors of the nation" to the 1939 New York World's Fair. After all, Greece's classical pedigree helped legitimize the century-old nation-state.[1]

For a fortnight, Young's men had been digging from dawn to dusk on the broad back of the mountain. Around a stone altar and in dumps from

8

Fig. 1. Rodney Young at the Agora, 1947. (Courtesy of the Penn Museum, by Alison Frantz, film #184893.)

earlier excavations, they had found pottery painted with intricate geometric patterns and with incised Greek letters spelling out an early form of Zeus and confirming an ancient account of the mountain's altars to the father of the gods. Some workmen descended into a cavish cleft. Penned in, they could see only the soft black earth through which they dug, the walls of

Map 1. Greece with insets of Athens and Attica

the cleft, and the sky. Soon baskets brimmed with fragments of ancient drinking cups and jugs left by thirsty farmers who prayed for rain and looked to clouds clustering on Mt. Hymettus as a sign. Urgently, they gathered bones in the ashy earth from animals sacrificed to win the god's favor. The clang of trowels pierced the thrum of the diggers' banter and the peaceful tinkling of goat bells in the distance.

The men had left the American School on foot at six that morning, but when they were about halfway to the monastery of Kaiseriani on the lower slope of Mt. Hymettus, sirens had started to wail. Perhaps Young considered it a false alarm. In any case, he did not take it seriously. His work came first. Ignoring the noise, the men trudged on.

Since Metaxas had declared martial law with the approval of Greece's King George II on August 4, 1936, the dictator had abolished the parliament, banned political parties, and made himself the sole ruler of Greece. Then he purged the government and armed forces. Republicans had lost their jobs and fled into exile to escape imprisonment, and the traditional wrangling between them and the royalists had festered underground. Not all Greeks approved of their government. But over time, Metaxas repealed martial law and led the fractious country reasonably well, while retaining absolute power.

Would Metaxas sidle up to Hitler or cast his lot with the British? Over the years, Metaxas had cultivated friendly relations with his fellow fascist dictators, modeled his repressive regime on Mussolini's, and made Greece economically dependent on Nazi Germany. His royalist cabinet included some of Greece's leading Germanophiles, who were avowed fascists. Rumors circulated that "fifth columnists," a clandestine wave of Germans or German sympathizers working as advisors, middle managers, and nannies, had poured into Athens, infiltrated important households and industries, channeled Nazi propaganda into Greece, and forwarded information about Greece back to Berlin.[2] No one could predict what the dictator would do, and what Metaxas decided now would determine the fate of Greece.

The men did not have to wait long for the answer. Late-arriving youths had joined Young at the monastery. They brought bad news. Special newspapers announced that at three in the morning the Italian ambassador had handed Metaxas an ultimatum. It demanded authorization for Italian troops to occupy unspecified strategic points in Greek territory. To this call for Greek surrender, Metaxas had shouted "Okhi!" ("No!"). Greece was at war with Italy.

Young was not surprised at the Italian outrage. For a year, he had distrusted the Italians—ever since Good Friday, April 7, 1939, when they had invaded Albania. At that time, everyone worried that the Italians would press south into Greece. To stop them, Britain and France had declared that they would support Greece if it were attacked, and the British fleet had showed the flag at the Greek island of Corfu, just seventy miles from Italy and three from Albania. Mussolini backed off, but Metaxas kept a watchful eye on the Italian troops near Greece's northwestern border.

Nevertheless, a year later Young dug as usual. On October 28, 1940, knowing the country was at war and not registering the gravity of the situation, Young went up to the site anyway. Young was arrogant. Since he had already come so far, he might as well get on with it. The show must go on. Not knowing when he would return, Young wanted to finish his work and bring down his tools and artifacts, which he hoped would date to the age of Homer.[3]

About half an hour after he began, Young heard a strange droning. From the northwest, Italian planes roared toward Athens, approaching Mt. Parnes on the far side of the city and dropping bombs that ignited the parched oak groves flanking the airfield protecting the king's summer palace. Pluming flames shot skyward, and a halo of fire soon crowned the slopes where lightning flashes once signaled the need to send offerings to Delphi. Other bombs fell by the sea, and staccato antiaircraft guns flashed and barked from the hills of Athens as Greek planes rose to engage the enemy. The men had a grandstand seat and were momentarily transfixed by the spectacle. Within minutes, the planes were gone. Although they were exposed in a military zone within spitting distance of Athens, Young still did not call it a day, so the workmen tidied their trenches and packed their finds. Around two in the afternoon, the bombers returned and pounded the naval base at Salamis, causing smoke to silhouette the Acropolis. Then, like a bull, Young stomped the ground and bellowed that it was time to go.

From the mountain's bald summit, the encumbered men began the one-and-a-half-hour trek back to the city, lumbering along the scrubby shoulder, crushing thyme and terebinth underfoot. After forty-five minutes of slogging, they descended into a copse of cypress and sweet-scented pines fed by a sacred spring above Kaiseriani. Pressing on, they passed through the suburbs, where they learned that Metaxas had again declared martial law, this time ordering a general mobilization and exhorting his people:

> Greece is not fighting for victory. She is fighting for glory and for honor. She has a debt to herself to remain worthy of her history. . . . There are times in which a nation, if it wishes to remain great, gains by being able to fight, even if it has no hopes of victory. . . . The moment has come for us to fight for the independence, the integrity and the honor of Greece. . . . We shall now show whether we are really worthy of our ancestors and of the freedom won for us by our forefathers. Let the entire nation rise as one man. Fight for your country, your wives, your children, and our sacred traditions. The struggle for all has begun.[4]

Stirred by these words, the crew hiked the rest of the way to Athens, where they learned that enemy planes had bombed Eleusis and Corinth and killed civilians at a market in the city of Patras. Church bells clanged, and the ceremonial cannons of Mt. Lycabettus boomed. The government declared a state of siege and called up thousands of reserve firemen and police. Athenians filled the streets. Schools had closed, and children ogled the skies hoping to see enemy aircraft. Older girls volunteered as Red Cross nurses, while older boys rushed to their regiments shouting, "We will throw them into the sea!" Paramilitary youths distributed handbills and pasted war posters on walls. Men who had been summoned for military duty hurried to their mustering stations. At every street corner, Young's workers read the conscription notices and scattered to enlist at their own mobilization points.

Young soldiered on alone through the crowds, his ears ringing with the news, "Eenai polemos, eenai polemos!" ("It's war; it's war!"). When he reached Vasilissis (Queen) Sophia Avenue at Evangelismos Hospital, Young found pandemonium. Police blocked his normal route and demanded to see Young's papers for Metaxas had barred aliens from the center of town between Mt. Lycabettus, the Acropolis, and Omonia Square. When they saw that Young was an American, they let him pass and bawled *"Zeeto Ameriki!"* ("Long live America!"). Their enthusiasm was contagious, and the normally reticent archaeologist yelled back *"Zeeto Ellas!"* ("Long live Greece!"). An irrational euphoria took hold of the Greeks. Athens erupted and roared with delight. A sea of people carried pictures of the king and Metaxas. Waving American, British, and Turkish flags, they undulated by the respective legations and surged down to Syntagma Square, cheered by screeching crones and women with bawling babies. Elsewhere a procession of people wielding flags, makeshift signs, and banners poured down Panepistimiou (University Street), where students who had not yet enlisted begged their professors to let them volunteer. Streets rang with the din of regiments marching. Conscripts in khaki uniforms and civilian clothes sang the national anthem, and the applauding throng screamed "Zeeto Ellas!" Bystanders rushed in and heaved soldiers onto their shoulders shrieking, "Death to the macaroni eaters!" Athenians cheered the troops and guns as they rounded the corner by the elegant arcade of the Grande Bretagne Hotel and entered Syntagma Square. There the flows converged and swelled before the Tomb of the Unknown Soldier and the old palace, now the Greek Parliament building. There commandeered cars, trucks, taxicabs, and buses painted with "Athens-Tirana-Rome" paraded, packed with young men shouting and singing as they prepared to head north and defend the border. Everything on wheels was rolling to Albania.[5]

Foreign journalists packed the bar of the King George Hotel at Syntagma, astonished by the unanimity among the Athenian politicians. Although some differed about the course Metaxas had chosen, all favored going to war. Instead of arguing along the usual royalist-republican lines, all supported Metaxas, who, with a single word, *okhi,* had united the country. The newsmen marveled at the Greeks' confidence in their ability to rebuff the Italians since, at that point in time, the Axis had won every major battle fought on European soil.[6] Next door, the top brass of the Greek military streamed in and out of the Grande Bretagne, which they had taken over as Greek General Headquarters early that morning.

The Italians had invaded western Greece from their chief stronghold of Koritsa, Albania's second largest city, only twenty miles west of the Greek border. Their northern thrust targeted Salonika with the intention of cutting it off from Central Greece, while another penetrated from Albania's Adriatic shore to cut off the island of Corfu, seize the coast, and threaten the western Greek city of Yannina. Fortunately, the Greek army had already moved troops to block these traditional avenues of attack.

Young ascended the slopes of Mt. Lycabettus heading for the School. Not until seven that evening did he reach the walled compound that the Americans shared with the British. After unlatching the massive iron gates,[7] he discovered on the front door a torn sheet of paper on which was penciled, "Notice. The American Legation has telephoned that Americans should not go into town until further notice. G. P. Stevens, 8 A.M. October 28, 1940." Gorham Stevens, the School's director, had already cabled the School's managing committee in the states, reporting, "Since 7 o'clock this morning there has been a state of war between Greece and Italy." Then he closed the School.[8]

The academic enclave that Young called home had housed Yankee excavators for over half a century. Young had first come eleven years ago, fresh from Princeton, eager to be trained on the School's excavations. Now he climbed to the top floor of the main building, where his room opened onto a roof terrace. Down below, the lush garden hummed with British archaeologists and classicists. In the distance, Mt. Hymettus glowed purple-blue, dominating the horizon as the city's ecstasy resounded. No one slept that night. Everyone was in the streets, blaring horns, climbing lampposts, brandishing flags, and screeching themselves hoarse.

In the dark, Young must have considered his options. Up to this point, he had not been particularly patriotic nor much concerned with politics. Rather he had played the game, dutifully following his father to Princeton and continuing his studies in graduate school, the *cursus honorum* or prescribed path to academic achievement. Nothing suggested that he would step out of that line.

How had Young come to this moment when everything changed? Since 1933, he had dug in the ancient Agora (marketplace) at the foot of the Athenian Acropolis. As the civic center of the ancient city, it had great symbolic value to the Greeks. Being the cradle of democracy, the site also conferred cultural capital on the nation that excavated it. The United States, as the preeminent twentieth-century democracy with a history of romantic philhellenism, was heavily invested in the excavations, financially and ideologically. They were sponsored by the School, funded by John D. Rockefeller, Jr., and directed by T. Leslie Shear of Princeton. At the Agora, Young and his colleagues had found buildings, inscriptions, and pottery showing that the area had been used for millennia, but they privileged the time of democratic Athens' golden age, the fifth century BC. This was good copy, and the *New York Times* ran several features on the American work there.[9]

Block by block, they had labored, building an edifice of American scholarship on Greek soil. Young's Princeton roommate, Eugene Vanderpool, along with Virginia Grace, Arthur Parsons, and Margaret Crosby, supervised trenches. Epigraphers Benjamin Meritt, Sterling Dow, and James Oliver deciphered ancient inscriptions, while registrar Lucy Talcott organized and catalogued the finds and Alison Frantz photographed them.[10] They had all been well trained, at Harvard, Princeton, Yale, Bryn Mawr, Radcliffe, and Smith, and, over time, cohered into a tight band of friends who counted on each other to get the job done.

The excavators took responsibility not only for the scientific, but also the more mundane practical aspects of the work, such as removing the remains of modern houses, vast quantities of earth, and large blocks of stone and marble in order to reach the ancient ruins. To reconstruct the site, they had to be efficient and observant, scrutinizing their trenches, updating field notebooks daily, and synthesizing the results in weekly reports. Each reported to Shear and, with the help of a single foreman, supervised, inspired, and ran herd on gangs of ten to fifty Greek workmen, who performed the

Fig. 2. The Agora excavation team, 1933. *Back row, left to right,* P. de Jong, Arthur Parsons, Eugene Vanderpool, Mary Z. Pease, James Oliver. *Middle row,* Joan Bush (Vanderpool), Elizabeth Dow, Virginia Grace, Gladys Baker, Homer Thompson. *Front row, left to right,* Lucy Talcott, Benjamin Meritt, Josephine Shear, T. Leslie Shear, Dorothy Burr Thompson. (Mauzy 2006, Fig. 239. Courtesy of the Trustees of the American School of Classical Studies at Athens.)

physical labor and whom they treated paternalistically, referring to them as their "boys." All the while, the archaeologists sank deep roots into the land of Greece.

Outside the excavations, Young cleaved to Gene Vanderpool and fellow Princetonian Alison Frantz, whom he affectionately called "Old Horse." She and Lucy Talcott adopted Young and organized tennis matches, barbecues at Cape Sounion, outings to Mt. Parnes and the beaches of Attica, junkets to Delphi and the islands, and dinners under the stars on their roof terrace overlooking Mt. Hymettus, Mt. Lycabettus, and the sea. Amid endless rounds of luncheons, teas, and dinners, they attended formal evenings at the homes of Carl Blegen, the excavator of Troy; Anastasios Adossides, the

Fig. 3. The Agora excavation team, 1934. *Back row, left to right,* Dorothy Traquair, Sterling Dow. Middle row, Alison Frantz, Rodney Young, Eugene Vanderpool, James Oliver, Arthur Parsons. *Front row, left to right,* Joan Bush (Vanderpool), Lucy Talcott, T. Leslie Shear, Josephine Shear. (Mauzy 2006, Fig. 240. 2008.18.0262. Courtesy of the Trustees of the American School of Classical Studies at Athens.)

School's business liaison; and Lincoln MacVeagh, the U.S. minister (ambassador) to Greece, whose daughter participated in School excavations. In time, several members of the Agora team intermarried, but Young and Frantz remained single and forged a deep friendship that endured through revolutions and coups.

In 1939 the archaeologists had read the signs of approaching war, but ventured to Greece anyway, to shovel that last spade of earth before it was too late. Some shuttled from excavation to excavation: After a week digging with Young on Mt. Hymettus in the spring, "Trojan" Blegen launched new excavations at Pylos in southwestern Greece. Pete Daniel excavated at Kourion on Cyprus, feeling as if he was "on the rim of a volcano" that might erupt any minute and joking nervously about using Hellenistic tombs as bomb shelters in case of war.[11]

When Mussolini invaded Albania in April 1939 and had his submarines patrol the Italian-held Dodecanese islands off southwest Turkey, the British Royal Navy beefed up its presence in the Ionian Sea. The U.S. State Department recommended that Americans leave Greece, and one Agora archaeologist packed up her children and household possessions and left at once. Blegen aborted his new excavations, liquidated his old ones at Troy, and visited American excavators on Cyprus. Meanwhile, Metaxas's director general of Greek antiquities, Spyridon Marinatos, dug the site of Thermopylae, where the Spartans once defended Greece, as propaganda fodder glorifying Greek patriotic sacrifice.[12]

The U.S. legation (embassy) in Athens issued instructions for those who stayed, devising an emergency telephone tree and recommending that all American citizens purchase gas masks, find a safe house, and remain at home in case of sudden crisis. Most secured a refuge outside Athens where they kept an emergency food supply.[13] Frantz and Talcott leased a seaside bungalow that they jokingly called their "country estate" and there entertained Young with chess and *Princeton Heralds,* the university's newspaper. Vanderpool moved with his wife and three small children out to a house at the foot of Mt. Pendeli and dug a shelter in the garden. Parsons and his wife took a similar house closer to Athens in the saddle between Pendeli and Mt. Hymettus, but most of the American archaeologists left Greece, including Rodney Young.

German scholarship and the German Archaeological Institute (DAI), the counterpart of the American School and the AIA combined, had long dominated classical archaeology and philology. The German government funded the DAI and used it to legitimize the country's foreign policy. As part of its nationalist propaganda promoting the 1936 Berlin Olympics, glorified in Riefenstahl's film *Olympia,* the government also reopened the Olympia excavations. This was not lost on American archaeologists, who had often undertaken graduate work in Germany and loathed to take a stand against it. But when Hitler annexed the Sudetenland in 1938, Benjamin Meritt (fig. 2), Young's Agora colleague, resigned his prestigious membership in the DAI in protest.[14]

Back at Princeton, Meritt became active in politics and targeted the sluggish American government, which was split between isolationists and those who supported Britain. For months Meritt, who worked at the Institute for Advanced Study under the same roof as Albert Einstein, argued for

U.S. readiness and global responsibility. After Mussolini's invasion of Albania and the outbreak of war in Europe, Meritt wrote his senator and congressman, advocating national defense, total preparedness, and U.S. support for Britain and France to ensure that Germany was defeated on the other side of the Atlantic.[15] But President Franklin Delano Roosevelt, then up for reelection, demurred.

Young's Princeton classmate, George McFadden, behaved as if nothing had happened and, after digging on Cyprus in 1939, blindly headed for the Bavarian Alps, where he and a male companion used to lounge all summer in bucolic splendor, enjoying the glitterati at Berchtesgaden. There they honed their German while Aryan athletes worked out at sports facilities for Hitler Youth, and Hitler entertained luminaries at his nearby retreat, "Eagles' Nest." But soon after arriving, McFadden was greeted by news of Hitler and Stalin's nonaggression pact. He managed to slip out through Switzerland on August 31 and, despite being interrogated and strip-searched at the border, reached Paris. There he met Young's former Columbia professor, William Dinsmoor, who, as AIA president, had just been treated at German government expense, along with 599 other scholars (no Jews), to "a dance on the volcano," the sixth International Archaeological Congress held in Berlin.[16] Dinsmoor and McFadden seized two of the last berths on the *Ile de France,* scheduled to depart the next day. After a twenty-four-hour delay caused by the Nazi invasion of Poland, the blacked-out vessel set sail for New York as war broke out in Europe.

In 1939, Young had chosen to do nothing. The U.S. government had responded to the outbreak of war in Europe by remaining neutral and sticking its head in the sand, and Young had followed suit, dutifully returning to Princeton to prepare for his oral examinations and defend his dissertation. By New Year's Day 1940, Young had received his doctorate. The next step on the career path was to publish his dissertation and secure a teaching job.

Not everyone followed that path. After war had been declared in Europe and the School placed on a wartime basis, Young's best friends had defied Washington's admonitions and had stayed in Greece. Gene Vanderpool decided to weather the storm since it was difficult to move his young family, and Alison Frantz refused to be "haunted by things undone." Together they dismantled the Agora museum and packed things for safekeeping. Frantz wrote her mother in Princeton once a week and retreated to her refuge by the sea "where it is so peaceful that it is hard to believe that the world is falling apart all around us." From Frantz's mother, Young caught glimpses of life in Greece. Metaxas had sent Greek troops to the Albanian border and then pulled them back to defuse escalating tensions with Italy. Optimists at the American School, observing the dwindling coal supply, ordered an extra shipment, while pessimists, expecting Athens to be bombed, painted twenty-foot-high apotropaic "USAs" on the roofs of the School's buildings and debated turning one into an American Red Cross Hospital. Gorham Stevens, who had led the School's equivalent in Rome during World War I, canceled the School's customary trips to archaeological sites and, instead, had a gas-proof bomb shelter constructed under the marble colonnade of the School's Gennadius Library. Frantz bucked up her courage and got on with her work, but felt the effects of the British blockade of Germany as imports disappeared from the shops. Sugar, coal, and gas were rationed; meat was available every third day; bread was made of beans; and the proportion of coffee to weeds shrank daily. Yet Frantz most lamented being deprived of her friends, whom she called the "exiles," "caught" on the "wrong side of the Atlantic." She dismantled their apartments, sent them artifact photographs so they could work in the States, and lived from day to day. By October, few letters were getting through.[17]

Frantz chirped that there were "quite a lot of British here," but their archaeologists transferred to work "of a more pertinent nature," that is, intelligence. Among those mobilized was Alan Wace, the Cambridge don, excavator of Mycenae, and close friend of Blegen's who knew the Albanian border terrain and dialect well from having conducted a year of archaeological research in that region. As director of the British School at Athens in World War I, Wace had been seconded to the British legation chancery, where he coded and decoded telegrams and directed relief for British Levantines fleeing Turkey. They, in turn, provided him with military intelligence on their way to British Egypt. After Gallipoli, Wace launched Britain's "passport control office" and compiled lists of suspect persons to combat the casual passage of spies between Greece and Egypt.[18] At the outset of this war, he quietly took up residence at the British School with his American archaeologist wife and daughter, lectured on Mycenae to the Americans, and segued back to intelligence. Wace worked for MI-6, an elite secret intelligence-gathering operation, handling covert information and counterintelligence in enemy-occupied and neutral countries. "Passport control officers" were MI-6 station heads. In this role, Wace scanned international communications and monitored enemy intelligence organizations.[19] Meanwhile, German archaeologists did the same.[20]

Britain spun webs of alliances just as it had during World War I. This time, the British bound Greece and Turkey in a mutual assistance pact, but after being enemies in the nineteenth century and during four twentieth-century regional wars, the Aegean neighbors were uneasy allies. Still, both were unprepared for more bloodshed and steered a neutral course. So war did not come to the Aegean in 1939.

In fact, Frantz wrote that it was hard to convey how normal life had become.[21] Soon the stateside archaeologists regretted fleeing. Impatient to return to Greece, they discovered that the State Department had recalled or invalidated all passports for European travel and discouraged casual excursions. Nevertheless, Young secured a passport and sailed for Greece in January armed with coffee, film, and plum puddings for Frantz. He knew that coming to Greece was a gamble, and his initial experience bore out his anxieties. He spent thirty-three days at sea dodging U-boats and over a week at Gibraltar, detained by British security, before finally arriving in Greece. But it was a gamble he had been willing to make. Just the thought of digging made his fingers "itch." When Young finally arrived, Frantz greeted him, and Mts. Hymettus and Lycabettus shone with a "delicious frosting" of snow.[22] Young loved Greece, and it had become more of a home to him than Princeton.

Eventually, most of the archaeologists crept back to Greece. When Shear announced at the end of February that he would come and dig again, Young and Frantz rejoiced, but kept one eye on the international situation. Virginia Grace went sight-seeing in Lebanon and Palestine and returned to excavate classical and Hellenistic tombs with McFadden at Kourion, writing that Cyprus seemed untouched by the European war, spring was glorious, the sea was warm enough for swimming, and the orange groves were in blossom. But while Shear was crossing the Atlantic, Russia invaded Finland, and Germany attacked Norway and Denmark. After that, the U.S. legation formed a safety committee, and the men of the American colony met regularly. Frantz, Young, and Talcott only left town to go to their safe house. Now and then, they heard rumors from someone with "inside information," but most of their news came from the BBC. No one knew what to expect, but Frantz reassured her mother that the war would not reach them for a long time.

When Shear arrived on April 26, the Agora team set to work. In the first week, a certain listlessness prevailed. One colleague wrote that Athens was very quiet "and, as always under the fascist regime, orderly and efficient.

Neutrality is the chief wish of everyone . . . in this most wretched year of our Lord 1940." MacVeagh apprised Roosevelt that they were all "living under the sword of Damocles."[23]

Then on May 10, Hitler unleashed the Nazi blitzkrieg, and the German army invaded Holland, Belgium, and Luxembourg. That afternoon, the British prime minister resigned, bringing Winston Churchill to power. In spite of legation warnings that U.S. citizens should leave while they could, Shear insisted on working until war made it impossible. He lectured at the School and gave a tea where he, Stevens, and Parsons were photographed with the Greek king on May 11. Two days later, the German army invaded France, and on May 15 the Dutch surrendered. The next day, Roosevelt asked the Senate and House of Representatives to approve almost $900,000,000 for the U.S. armed forces, and Shear announced that the Agora team would fold up "the business." Immediately, the archaeologists crated their artifacts and shipped them to the National Museum, placed their records in the Gennadeion bomb shelter, and sent duplicates to Princeton to protect them from impending war. By May 23, seventeen of the seventy-two Americans who wanted to leave had fled.

William Dinsmoor resigned his twenty-six-year membership in the DAI and wrote that he regarded it "as a blot" on his record. His gesture provoked international repercussions. Numerous DAI scholars, including the president and director in Athens, were members of the Nazi Party. German archaeologists in Athens were ordered to sever relations with American colleagues. Meanwhile, Meritt, a member of the British Academy and honorary member of the Athens Archaeological Society, demanded that the United States cease its "pretense of friendly relations" with Hitler, expel all German diplomats from the United States, and recall American envoys in Germany.[24]

When Belgium surrendered on May 28, 1940, and the British Expeditionary Force commenced evacuating over 300,000 troops from Dunkirk, Americans began to realize that they could no longer hide behind France and Britain. Whereas a 1939 poll had declared that 82 percent of Americans thought that France and Britain would defeat Germany, a more recent one indicated that most felt the opposite. "Belief in security" soured into a "dread of tomorrow." MacVeagh reported to Roosevelt that "the prestige of the Allies was gone forever," and both Italians and Germans considered Greece "their own particular meat."[25]

This time, the legation did not need to advise Americans to leave Greece.

With wireless reports of parachute landings and air bombardments, the size and speed of the German advance grew hourly more horrifying. Archaeologists scattered. Three Canadians residing at the American School fled overland via Istanbul, Iraq, and India on their way to the Pacific.[26] Shear flew to Italy and caught a ship that passed Gibraltar just before June 10, when Mussolini teamed up with Hitler and declared war on England. The next day, the Italians advanced on British Egypt and began bombing the Royal Navy's principal port at Malta, which remained besieged for the next two and a half years.[27] Mussolini pledged not to drag Greece into the conflict, but few believed him. Meanwhile, the U.S. consul general worried about the proliferation of Italian "fifth columnists," air attacks on Athens, and a land invasion from Albania.

Frantz and Talcott dismembered a decade of their lives and crated their precious possessions. As she looked for a ship, Frantz tried to placate her mother. "If we should be unable to get away, there will be no cause for alarm because . . . if there is any trouble, this country will not resist at all. If there should be a few days' of unpleasantness, we will be in one of the three country refuges." Frantz reported ten days later, "No one in Athens expects the unpleasantness to last more than a few days."[28] Then the Germans marched into Paris.

By the time Shear reached New York, France had fallen and the Turkish government had declared a state of emergency and partially evacuated Istanbul. Despite Britain's poor showing in Scandinavia and Western Europe, Greece had remained pro-British, but German influence increased enormously. On June 20, BBC radio reported that the Italians had sunk or bombed five or six Greek ships that week. Virginia Grace stopped digging to tend wounded British soldiers being evacuated to Cyprus from North Africa. On June 23, Grace returned to Athens to share a cabin with Talcott, the Waces' eight-year-old daughter, and Frantz, who were evacuating the next day on the *Excalibur,* the last American ship to leave Greece. When the authorities refused to take the English child without her American mother, Grace gave her berth to Wace's wife so mother and daughter could flee.[29]

Approximately ninety nervous Americans (archaeologists, businessmen, diplomats, and their dependents) lingered in Greece. Of the Agora team, only Young, Vanderpool, Grace, and Arthur Parsons, now assistant director of the School, decided to stay. The School braced itself for an uncertain future and cut the number of its Greek employees. Adossides transferred his office from the Agora to the main building. The legation posted

Map 2. The Central and Eastern Mediterranean with missions, radio stations, and secret harbors once indicated with pushpins, OSS Maritime Unit, 1944. (Courtesy National Archives. Enhanced with place-names added by author and inset details of Attica, Crete, Cyprus, and the west coast of Turkey.)

signs in four languages that the School was under the protection of the U.S. government, the British secretly asked the Americans to take over the British School in the event of war, and the Gennadius bomb shelter stayed open day and night.

Young determined to continue life as usual. After "pottering away" on research, he rode his motorcycle up to northern Greece for the summer hike of the Royal Alpine Club on the island of Thasos. There he met a soft-spoken outdoorsman who divulged that he was General Nikolaos Tsipouras, World War I veteran and former governor of Attica who had married an American, traveled widely in the States, and sympathized with England and France. They chatted over campfires about Greece's fascist dictatorship and wondered how long Metaxas could publicly ignore Italian planes violating Greek air space and the bombing and sinking of Greek ships. Young did not know that Metaxas was privately girding himself for battle, mustering men for a month's training with modern weapons, and fortifying the mountains facing Bulgaria not an hour north of Thasos.[30]

Mussolini struck again on August 15, a national holiday marking the Orthodox Festival of the Dormition, when the Virgin Mary ascended to heaven. Thousands of Greek pilgrims had converged on the Cycladic island of Tinos, hoping for cures from the healing shrine's miraculous icon, when an unidentified submarine slipped into the harbor, blasted a quay crowded with pilgrims, and torpedoed and sank the *Elli,* a Greek ship lying at anchor with all her dress flags flying. Although the strictly censored press said little, outraged Greeks talked of nothing else. The army established no-fly zones in the north and specified forbidden areas throughout the country. On August 23, King George II called an emergency meeting of his ministers and generals, and Metaxas mobilized Corfu, the Ionian Islands, and the northwestern province of Epirus.

By September, almost all of Europe was under German control, and war inched toward Greece.[31] On the sixth, MacVeagh wrote that "the whole country is on a war footing." Within a week, the Italians had invaded Egypt. Coal prices doubled and gas rationing resumed. When Russia swallowed part of Rumania, fewer than 300 miles north of Greece, Turkey agreed to help Greece protect Thrace and Salonika. Most American archaeologists, including Virginia Grace and Parsons and his wife, abandoned their houses and moved into the School for security. At the end of the month, BBC radio announced that Germany, Italy, and Japan had signed a military alliance.[32]

By the time Virginia Grace decided to get out, it was almost too late. All escape routes to the west were cut except that by rail to Geneva and bus to Lisbon. McFadden telegraphed her and Blegen's friend Bert Hodge Hill, the former director of the School and excavator of Corinth and Cyprus, and invited them to dig at Kourion. Hill demurred, but Grace, the last American archaeologist to leave before Greece was plunged into war, acted. On October 5, the day after Hitler and Mussolini met at the Brenner Pass to plan their next move, she took the train to Istanbul. There, she caught another to Alexandretta (Iskenderun), where McFadden arrived on his yacht and whisked her off to Cyprus.[33]

Up to this point, Young, Vanderpool, and Hill had remained independent, but now Young grudgingly moved into Grace's penthouse. In defiance or denial, Young requested permission to reopen Blegen's excavations on Mt. Hymettus, but his timing was terrible. Two days after Grace left, the Germans seized Rumania's Ploesti oil fields. No longer did Hitler need Stalin's oil. Now he could conveniently barge the fuel up the Danube or transport it by train. Within a week, Germans raised the swastika over Bucharest. Mussolini canceled air service between Albania and Greece, sending large military units to the Greco-Albanian border, and bands of Albanian recruits, at the instigation of the Italians, secretly crossed into Greece to harass border villages. Gorham Stevens applied for protection to the U.S. legation. Meanwhile, the Greek War Ministry, worried about attracting "German lightning" (blitzkrieg), worked around the clock, and civilian safety preparations intensified. The legation offered its building as a meeting place for the American residents and extended the lease on its refuge, the Hotel Diana on the slopes of Mt. Pendeli. MacVeagh confided in his diary that Greece should "be ready now for an Italian attack with German permission" and braced for an invasion on October 26, the Greek holiday of St. Dimitrios, noting superstitiously that after the Good Friday invasion of Albania and the sinking of the *Elli* on the feast of the Dormition, it seemed as if Mussolini favored attacking on religious holidays. But nothing happened. Many agreed that it was too late in the season, and *Il Duce* would wait till spring. No one noticed that the eighteenth anniversary of Mussolini's march on Rome was approaching. It fell on October 28, 1940, two weeks after Young had begun to dig.[34]

Amid the din that night, Young had to confront what role he might play in the drama unfolding around him. Congress had just passed the Selective Service Act requiring all male citizens between the ages of twenty-one and thirty-six within the continental United States to register with their local draft boards. On "R Day," just after he had begun excavating on Mt. Hymettus, over seventeen million American men registered to secure first-call duty ratings. As an American in Greece, Young was exempt until he returned home. Yet since his mentors were all World War I veterans, he must have felt obligated to serve. He may also have felt torn between allegiances to Greece and the land of his birth. U.S. Army Lieutenant Dinsmoor had satisfied both loyalties by serving as assistant military attaché to the U.S. legation in Athens during World War I, engaging in part-time intelligence-gathering while conducting research on the Acropolis.[35] But the United States had recalled its attaché in 1939.

In choosing to remain, Young had, in fact, cast his lot with the Greeks. His Greek friends, colleagues, and workmen had been conscripted, and Tsipouras would be one of several generals leading the Greek army. Perhaps in the heat of the moment, Young thought of Byron and the American phil-hellenes who had fought alongside the Greeks in their War of Independence and considered a more active role of that nature. For once, taking no action seemed untenable.

On the morning of October 29, troops left for the northwest frontier. Lucky soldiers embarked on ships or whatever other conveyance they could find, including American School vehicles, requisitioned by the Greek army, while others walked as many as 300 miles to the front for lack of transportation. Troop movements blocked main highways leading out of Athens, and train after train pulled away from the Athens station headed north. Metaxas had mobilized 600,000 men—one-tenth of the Greek population. In the rush to defend the country, farmers abandoned their fields before planting next year's crops. Most massed west of the city of Florina (acquired by Greece only in 1913), unaware that the main Italian invasion force had secretly crossed the precipitous Pindus Mountains, which controlled the main pass into Central Greece.[36] When finally apprised of the situation, General Alexander Papagos, the Greek commander in chief who had considered the mountains impassable, ordered the only division guarding them to hold its ground and fight to the death.

Mussolini's strategy might have worked well at a different time of year, but October was too late for such a plan. The following morning, clouds gathered on Mt. Hymettus. In northern Greece, it was raining heavily. Snow had already fallen in the mountains. Winter lay ahead.

Those left behind in Athens hunkered down for the duration, storing water in case bombs destroyed the Marathon Dam. They covered windows with dark paper, painted headlights blue, and marked curbs white to guide night traffic. To confuse enemy pilots, police camouflaged landmarks like the tiny white chapel on Mt. Lycabettus and the Olympic stadium. When asked for news by reporters from the *New York Times*, Greek command barked, "Operations are proceeding satisfactorily." Metaxas met secretly with Athenian newspaper owners and editors to solicit positive stories to bolster the fighting spirit of their countrymen and ordered that expressing defeatist, alarmist, or critical opinions was a court martial offense. Italians crowded into their legation for safety, and their foreign minister moved in with his German counterpart. Many, including MacVeagh, fled to the countryside. On the night of the twenty-ninth, a dangerously full moon rose over Mt. Hymettus, rendering the city vulnerable to nocturnal attack. After nothing happened and the air-raid alarms subsided, Stevens cabled the managing committee, "ALL WELL, NO DAMAGE, NO DANGER THUS FAR, REASSURE SHEAR."[37]

On October 31, the fourth day of the war, prospects looked bleak. Italian troops had seized several border towns in northwestern Greece; Italian planes continued to bomb Patras, and others, camouflaged with Greek insignia, targeted Salonika.[38] Relations with Berlin reached "an extremely delicate state," and all communications between the two governments ceased. The Greeks "quietly, but closely" watched the 800 Germans residing in Athens and over 2,000 others in Greece, not including German "tourists." The government forbade all aliens to appear in the streets after nightfall or to travel from one city to another without a special permit and banned photography—even on the Acropolis. Stevens learned that the Italians had bombed Corinth, where Bert Hill was working, and tried in vain to telephone him, but the lines were down. Rumors flew that Metaxas had begged Italy to treat Athens as an open city in order to protect its civilians and historic monuments, and threatened that if the Italians bombed Athens, the British would bomb Rome. MacVeagh apprised FDR, "Our present situation is uncertain."[39]

International aid failed to materialize, and uneasiness spread as the Greeks realized that they would be fighting alone. Nazi propaganda hinted that Mussolini's attack was merely the prelude for a German drive through Turkey to create a Berlin-Baghdad corridor linking Germany with the oil fields of Iraq. So, fearing Nazi and Soviet retribution, Turkey decided not to risk war and only agreed to protect the Greco-Bulgarian border to free up Greek troops for Albania. Meanwhile in London, the British Foreign Office, under constant German bombardment since July, maintained that Britain was giving Greece "all possible aid," though none arrived.[40]

Throughout Europe and America, people read of Greece's brave struggle, but still expected the nation to collapse. The BBC quoted the British air marshal who said, "The Greeks are a brave people and though they can't win, will go down fighting." Although the Italians had destroyed sixty Greek villages and left thousands of refugees, Greek morale remained high, and newspapers urged the Greeks to remember the courage of their ancestors in the 1821 War of Independence.[41] Then news reached the School that on Sunday, November 3, the Greek army had held the line in Epirus and seized the advantage. Instead of waiting to enlist in the U.S. Army, Young volunteered for active military service with the Greek forces.

It was a brazen decision for this coddled child of the gilded age. The heir to the Ballantine Ale fortune had grown up in his grandmother's opulent mansion in Newark, New Jersey, surrounded by classically inspired sculptures, vases, and architectural flourishes. As a pampered youth, he was accustomed to New York cotillions, European tours, and summers at the family's sprawling rural estate while 75,000 workers labored in the brewery. He had enjoyed an elite education, at his father's knee, at St. Paul's School, and Princeton. After earning a masters degree in Classical archaeology at Columbia, he had attended the American School in Athens before returning to Princeton. But Young's father had planted seeds in fertile soil. Aside from his love of Horace, Henry Young, in his capacity as president of the local chapter of the American Red Cross, also imparted the lesson of noblesse oblige, helping others, and relieving suffering. Thus, spurred by birthright and circumstance, Rodney Young stepped out of line to help the Greeks.

TWO

Leaving the Ivory Tower

YOUNG WAS THE FIRST AMERICAN who volunteered to fight alongside the Greeks against Mussolini. However, the xenophobic Greek government refused to accept foreigners in the army and turned him down. Instead of sulking or remaining inactive, Young considered relief work. American School archaeologists had engaged in it since the nineteenth century, including men he knew, like Carl Blegen and Bert Hill. Thinking along the same lines, Gorham Stevens requested permission for School staff to work with the Red Cross. One American wrote to the Greek government, "Consider us as members of the same Greek family and use us where you think suitable."[1]

Arthur Parsons, the School's assistant director, wanted to start a courier service to bring medical supplies to the front while his archaeologist wife suggested that the School contribute an ambulance to the Greeks. Young embraced the idea. Ernest Hemingway had driven an ambulance in World War I, and his novel *A Farewell to Arms*, about an American driving an ambulance for the Italian army, had been published the year Young graduated from Princeton. Moreover, Young's professor George Elderkin had driven one in France. Since it would take less time to build one in Greece than to ship it from the States, an embassy staffer found a GM truck chassis, and Young volunteered to raise the cash required to purchase and transform it, but he wanted to drive the ambulance.[2]

On November 5, Young cabled Princeton professor Edward Capps, who had organized the archaeologists working for the American Red Cross in Greece after World War I. The former chair of the School's managing committee had clout. He had served as U.S. minister to Greece during the glory days of Greece's greatest statesman—republican Eleftherios Venizelos. Young asked Capps to solicit School trustees, alumni, and friends to fund ambulances that the School would give to the Greek Red Cross. Capps turned to Ben Meritt, who urged immediate action.[3] Already on October 28, Meritt had demanded that his congressman seek U.S. aid for Greece, writing to U.S. Secretary of State Cordell Hull that

> the unprovoked attack made upon Greece . . . calls for a vigorous expression of sympathy on the part of the United States. This small land, with the history that lies behind it, was an inspiration to the men who framed our own constitution and patriotic Americans played an important part in the establishment of Greek independence. . . . if we are ever to lodge an effective protest anywhere, now is the time to do it. . . . If this administration can think of nothing effective to do, we consider that it will have failed in a great moral obligation to mankind. . . . I urge that in the name of the great Democracy of the west a strong protest be made against the wanton Italian assault on the little democratic state in the Balkans, and that all possible moral and material support be extended to Greece in her brave resistance to the invader.[4]

Working with the American Hellenic Educational Progressive Association (AHEPA), an organization founded to promote Hellenism in the United States, Meritt marshaled thousands of Greek-Americans nationwide to protest against Italian aggression to the State Department. Young's proposal would put the School "ace high" with the Greeks. So Meritt drafted a letter to the trustees and agreed to support it even if they refused.

MacVeagh cabled the trustees that their gift would be gratefully accepted, but instead of rallying to the cause, the trustees balked. The chairman of the board considered Young's action "impetuous." Others waffled. Thinking "eventual Greek defeat . . . inevitable," they did not want the School associated with "the defeated political party." Lukewarm at best, they counseled delay and "a perfectly neutral attitude." Leslie Shear appealed to the "honor of the School" and demonstrated how Young's proposal could benefit both it and Greece, cautioning:

> if the totalitarian powers should prevail and Italy maintain permanent control of Greece, let none of us have any illusions as to the fate of the American School. . . . If they control Greece, American archaeologists will work no more in that country. But if the totalitarian force dominates the world, the youth of America will have too much serious work on hand to spare any

time to anyone for archaeological research. Let the American School rise to its privilege and opportunity and give all possible moral and material support to this friendly and pitiable little nation in the hour of its dire peril.[5]

Young did not wait for the trustees to act. He cabled his father for an advance, which he sent at once. With the cash, Young commissioned Athena Motorworks to build the ambulance.[6] Nor did Meritt wait. As a former student, visiting professor, and associate director of the School, he appealed to alumni and elicited their support. Meritt published his letter to Hull in a widely circulated Greek-American newspaper and sought photos to engage American hearts. "The whole country has for the past year been so anxious for . . . victory that such photographs would do more than anything to keep up the morale of an aroused public opinion."[7]

The impatient Princetonians formed the American School Committee for Aid to Greece and guaranteed the ambulances themselves. Capps, Shear, George Elderkin, Meritt, Hetty Goldman, Alison Frantz, Lucy Talcott, and Oscar Broneer among others met in Meritt's office at the Institute, assumed all of the overhead costs, and volunteered to raise the necessary funds. Frantz and Talcott would publish a book and donate the proceeds. To achieve their goal, the Princetonians organized a benefit concert at which Meritt's little sons would usher, dressed as Greek evzones in the black vests, white blouses, kilts, stockings, and red-pompomed shoes worn by the heroic soldiers of the Greek War of Independence whose descendants, elite mountain troops, led the present fight.[8]

While American archaeologists scrambled for cash, the Greeks fought to save their country. A single Greek regiment struggled to hold the heights and defend the Pindus Mountains guarding the Metsovo Pass that led into Epirus and Central Greece. Greek reinforcements arrived after a forced march and took their positions at night, climbing mountain paths inaccessible by mules and hoisting artillery with ropes. Forced to abandon supplies in favor of speed, the exhausted men survived, thanks to leadership, morale, and rusks of bread known as *paximadhia*.[9]

Then the Italians faltered. One division lost its way and fell back. The jubilant Greeks attacked, shrieking their battle cry, "Aera!" Supplied by old men, women, and children with food and munitions bound to their backs, the Greeks advanced along ridges, narrow passes, and uplands, ascending peaks 4,000 to 8,000 feet high. They encircled the invaders, who lost contact with each other in the parallel mountain valleys and retreated to avoid being surrounded. The Greeks pursued and ambushed the Italians until even Mussolini's crack troops broke ranks and fled, abandoning their equipment and forcing the rest of the Italian army to fall back into Albania. Soon the whole world knew of the "miracle of the Pindus."[10] Instead of collapsing, the Greeks had resisted and reclaimed their territory. After two weeks, the only Italians left on Greek soil were prisoners of war.

The Greeks took advantage of the Italian retreat, seized the offensive, and invaded western Albania. A handful of pilots flew reconnaissance runs and guided troops to grab the high ground west of Florina where the borders of Greece, Albania, and Yugoslavia met. Then the Greek army pressed on, advancing from peak to peak. The older soldiers had literally been down this road before. In the last thirty years, the Greeks had repeatedly conquered and relinquished the Albanian province (which they called "Northern Epirus" and alleged was Greek).

At last, the Greeks had the trophy city of Koritsa in their sights. After shelling it, General Georgios Tsolakoglou captured the city on November 22. Again Greece erupted with joy. In Athens, a seething, flag-flourishing crowd massed in Syntagma Square chanting, "We want Tirana! We want Tirana!" Others shrieked, "On to Rome!" In front of the blacked-out Parliament building, they listened to King George II and Metaxas and thanked God for their victory. Across the country, church bells clanged, and Salonika cafes offered free drinks to all. The Greeks had proven that the Axis could be defeated. It was the first Allied land victory in Europe in over a year.[11]

After watching France knuckle under to the Nazis, Americans marveled at the heroism of the Greeks, acknowledged America's debt to them, and embraced the brave nation. They flocked to support Greek relief organizations, such as the New York-based, Rockefeller-funded Near East Foundation, the Committee for the Restoration of Greece, and the Greek War Relief Association, founded by Spyros Skouras—the Greek-American movie mogul of Twentieth Century Fox.[12] Philhellenes revived the American Friends of Greece, which promoted cultural ties between the two nations, publicized war news, and sold books to raise money.[13] Not only the *New York Times* and *Los Angeles Times,* but even the *News Sentinel* of Fort Wayne, Indiana, headlined Greece. Covers of *Time* carried images of the king and General Papagos in front of the Parthenon. The cover of *Life* depicted an evzone bugler before the Athenian temple of Olympian Zeus. Roosevelt, who had just won reelection, took notice and pledged aid through Lend-Lease, which gave him the power to transfer, sell, exchange, or lend equipment to any country defending itself against the Axis powers without sacrificing U.S. neutrality.[14]

General Tsolakoglou moved his headquarters to Koritsa, where he found Mussolini's occupation drachmas and propaganda in Greek for an Italian victory parade in Athens. Instead of stopping for winter, Tsolakoglou pressed north and west. When he demanded reinforcements, the Cretans responded and abandoned their island to fight in Albania. The Greek crown prince visited the front and rallied the men. On December 4 the Greeks captured Pogradets, twenty-seven miles northwest of Koritsa on Lake Ochridha. In the south, they conquered the Adriatic coastal strip facing Corfu and pressed north to Argyrokastro, the regional capital, which they took on December 8. The Italians retaliated by bombing unfortified Corfu on Christmas and killing 400 children who had gathered in the town square to open presents dropped by British fliers. Condemning this atrocity, Metaxas congratulated the army and praised his people. He had knit them into a "force" with "only one party, one class, one purpose," the Albanian campaign being the "national intoxication." By the end of 1940, Greece again controlled "Northern Epirus."[15] To celebrate, Metaxas cut the *vassilopita* (the kings' bread for Epiphany) with one piece for Koritsa and one for Argyrokastro, the two bases from which the Italians had launched their invasion, and hoped they were finally Greek for good.[16]

Greek cartoons and posters mocked Germany's Axis partner. In Athens the Germans faced off with their British enemies at chic restaurants and American-style ice cream parlors like Maxim's and Zonar's. Under the table, both sides jockeyed for position, and their intelligence agents relayed situation reports to their respective governments. Rumors circulated that the Germans were abandoning Athens, the Luftwaffe had failed to subdue Britain, and the British were chasing Mussolini's troops out of Egypt. But Berlin bided its time, censoring news of Mussolini's botched invasion and awaiting the outcome.

So far, Greece had few combat losses, but as winter descended in the mountains, casualties mounted, and the death toll rose. On the northern front, Greeks perched at altitudes as high as 6,000 feet in crude shelters, snow caves, and tents with one blanket, half cotton and half wool. They died more from hunger and exposure than combat, fighting the enemy over food and shelter. Winners scored stone huts or supply dumps while losers starved or ate mules that had gone lame or died. Cold became the Greeks' chief enemy. Feet froze and "swelled up so that men had to take their shoes off and could not get them on again." Without ambulances, only the ambulatory stood a chance of survival, so some walked barefoot for miles to get help. Those who were left behind either lit fires that attracted Italian bombers or hid in the dark to sleep and die.[17] At home Greeks were told to pray for snow to cover the corpses. It came early and fell continuously.[18]

Greek women managed relief work, acquiring and staffing hospitals and hospital trains to bring casualties south. When the first trains reached Athens, crowds showered them with flowers, but each returnee made clear the human cost of the struggle. Soon endless trains and ships ferried thousands of frostbite victims with gangrenous legs requiring amputation. To handle the surge of wounded requiring long convalescences, women transformed children's clinics and private schools, such as Athens College, into military hospitals. These they staffed with Greek Red Cross volunteers.[19]

Elli Adossides, matriarch of a prominent republican family, answered the call. She had engaged in relief work with her sister during four wars between 1912 and 1922 and worked arm in arm with Carl Blegen after World War I. Since then, her husband, Anastasios Adossides, had worked at the American School (fig. 7). He notified the School's committee in Princeton that when the first ambulance was ready, Greek General Headquarters requisitioned its tires, rendering it useless.[20] Adossides reported that the front desperately needed doctors and nurses, so instead of other ambulances the committee decided to fund Red Cross canteens, which Elli Adossides volunteered to set up and manage. They would offer first aid to Greek soldiers in Albania, evaluate casualties, and prioritize evacuation for the severely wounded most likely to survive. With hot food and other comforts, they would also cheer the sick and wounded on their way from the front to Salonika.[21]

The indomitable Elli Adossides planned to take her sister, Irene "Tuna" Hadzilazarou, her daughter Bessie, and daughter-in-law Clio, women who climbed Mts. Parnes and Parnassus for sport.[22] Clio had married the Adossideses' eldest son, Costas, the slim, dark-haired boy next door who encouraged her passion for piano as she did his for flying. Clio was a protégé of one of Greece's greatest conductors and loved Mozart, Debussy, Beethoven, and Chopin.[23] She acted as her husband's navigator in a series of competitive flights over Germany, France, and Switzerland connected with the Berlin Olympics, where they won the bronze medal for Greece. The German press lionized the dashing pilot and his beguiling bride, and the cou-

Fig. 4. Elli Hadjilazarou Adossides and Bessie Adossides. (Courtesy Clio Sperling.)

ple dreamed of circumnavigating the globe. But by the time the national heroes returned to Athens, Metaxas had transformed Greece into a fascist dictatorship. Then war intervened, and Costas enlisted. Clio had been playing a concert on Corfu on the eve of the Italian invasion and, by the time she reached home, Costas had already joined his air force squadron. Rather than dwell in the past, Clio faced the future with his kinswomen, repeating, "You can't go back. Don't go backwards. Go forwards."[24]

Bundled up for winter, the Adossides women trundled north in troop trains, passing refugees and ruined villages. In Koritsa, they trudged up slushy basalt-cobbled alleys past Ottoman houses, a toppled minaret, Catholic and Orthodox churches, and staring Albanians. They found the Greek camp sprawled in a city park along a tree-lined avenue with cypress spires etched sharp and clear against December's snowy sky. Elli and her sis-

Fig. 5. Clio Adossides, 1934.
(Courtesy Clio Sperling.)

Fig. 6. Costas Adossides and trainer plane. (Courtesy Clio Sperling.)

ter reported to headquarters and volunteered to go where they could be most useful. However, Tsolakoglou did not want Greek women on the front in an official capacity or in the mountains near the troops. Instead, paramilitary youth would handle the canteens, and the women could work at the hospital across the street that he had commandeered for his troops. The only hospital on the northern front was in desperate need of doctors and operating at twice its capacity with less than one nurse for forty patients. Wounded soldiers lay everywhere.

Elli wrote home about Tsolakoglou's refusal to let them open the canteens as well as the lack of supplies, organization, and preparedness to handle the large number of frostbite victims and amputations. Thanks to these briefs from the front, the archaeologists reacted with flexibility and speed to the army's changing needs and decided to postpone the canteens in favor of stockpiling supplies. Adossides glowed as funds arrived from Princeton. Soon the School resembled a medical supply warehouse with portable X-ray machines, ultraviolet lamps for the treatment of frostbite victims, wheelchairs, pneumonia jackets, thermometers, and hot water bottles, drugs like antipneumonia serum and morphia, novocaine injections and ether. Staff amassed warm clothes, flashlights, barber's tools, and cases of canned milk. Whatever luxuries existed went to the soldiers. Village women wove wool bought by the School into blankets and knitted sweaters and socks while cityfolk made crutches, canes, wheelchairs, and wire cages to keep scratchy wool from raking the soldiers' frozen feet. Meanwhile, School and legation wives formed the American Bandage Circle, cutting and rolling hospital dressings and bandages in the legation drawing room. Stevens gave Sunday Acropolis tours to British officers, while archaeological couples translated nightly broadcasts of Athens radio for Americans back home. To feed the soldiers' children, Gene Vanderpool and his wife Joan opened a soup kitchen in their home.[25]

Greek Red Cross drivers loaded the School's 1927 Chevy with medicines, equipment, and supplies and drove it to Yannina and Salonika, but the army still needed ambulances to transport the wounded. Young waited while MacVeagh begged the king to intercede on behalf of the School's ambulance. After New Year's Day the tires were returned. MacVeagh asked Metaxas to accept the vehicle "as a precious witness to the love of the Greek people which is felt by Americans who habitually live and work among them," and "Rodney Young an ardent American Philhellene" as driver. General Constantinos Maniadakis, Metaxas's minister of national security, approved Young, and Metaxas replied that the gift was

> particularly moving, coming as it does, from those of our American friends … who, having shared our moments of happiness and peace, have hastened to prove their sympathy and love in this hour of stress. . . . my warmest thanks to the [School], whose admiration for the Glory that was Greece has broadened to include Her sons now fighting for the same ideals which have inspired their ancestors and Mr. Rodney Young, whose gracious offer of his services I deeply appreciate.[26]

On January 5, Stevens ceremoniously presented the ambulance, with Young at the wheel, to the Greek Red Cross of Salonika and spoke of the "special sympathy which members of the School feel toward the Greeks, whose history they study and whom they have the opportunity to know at first hand." A cross protected the ambulance's roof. Inscriptions named the vehicle as the gift of the School, and on its sides images of intertwined American and Greek flags crowned red crosses. MacVeagh's wife christened it "Iaso" after the ancient Greek goddess of healing.[27] Afterward, Young packed it full of equipment, supplies, and woolen socks and shirts, flannel pajamas, slippers, and bales of woolen clothes from Americans and British in Greece. A *New York Times* reporter interviewed him as the first American to take an active part in Greece's war. Young responded that he simply "wanted to serve Greece in her present struggle." Yet as Young left for Salonika the next day, Stevens noted that his "eyes blazed like the eyes of the dragon in Siegfried."[28]

By that time, the Greeks were just about spent. Deep snow halted their advances in northern Albania. Further south, where weather was milder, the Greeks scored their last conquest at Klisura on January 10, but found the prize burned, pillaged, and deserted. Beyond Klisura lay a gorge that controlled the road to the Adriatic coast and Albania's oil fields. To reach the oil, they had to take the gorge. But this bitter victory would be the Greeks' last. Instead the Italians retained control, and bombed undefended Greek cities.[29]

Concern mounted in Athens. Unity broke down under the burden of increasing casualties. Hospital and troop trains burned olive wood because they had no other fuel. The Albanian campaign had drained the country's coffers. Relations between the Greeks and the British soured. Although Churchill had pledged help, he had given little. The Greek king complained

Fig. 7. The ambulance *Iaso* in front of the Gennadius Library. *From left:* Anastasios Adossides, Arthur Parsons, Lincoln MacVeagh. Rodney Young in driver's seat. Gorham Stevens, *far right.* (Meritt 1984, Pl. 8a. Courtesy of the Trustees of the American School of Classical Studies at Athens.)

that the British had not sent the numbers of divisions they had promised. In fact, Metaxas had vetoed British land forces because he feared antagonizing Hitler. He wanted air support, however, and, in exchange, gave Britain permission to establish naval and air bases on Crete. For a month and a half, the Royal Air Force (RAF) had secretly contributed planes and pilots, but too few to be effective, and, by early January, evacuated most of the planes to protect Egypt. On January 10, General Sir Archibald Wavell, the one-eyed British commander in chief of the Middle East theater, came to Athens for damage control.[30] Washington and Berlin watched closely but remained neutral.

Six months earlier, Churchill had sent a Canadian millionaire to Manhattan to cement ties between Britain and the United States, train American and Canadian spies, and root out enemy penetration. At Rockefeller Center,

William Stephenson opened a "passport control office," the cover for MI-6, also known as the Secret Intelligence Service (SIS) or ISLD (Inter-Service Liaison Department). MI-6 came under the British Foreign Office and handled political intelligence, security, and counterespionage. In America, MI-6 became known as the British Security Coordination (BSC).[31] To gain the president's ear, Stephenson targeted William James Donovan, a Wall Street lawyer who had earned the moniker "Wild Bill" as a World War I hero. FDR sent him to London to report on "fifth column activities" and whether Britain could survive the Blitz. Donovan returned, convinced of Britain's need for American support, and lobbied hard to get it.[32]

In January 1941, Roosevelt sent Donovan on a Mediterranean fact-finding mission to assess the conduct of the war in Greece and impress upon the Greeks the overwhelming support being given to FDR's foreign policy. Stephenson orchestrated everything and accompanied Donovan to London, where Churchill asked the American to encourage Greece and Yugoslavia to resist by promising them arms shipments.[33] Escorted by Churchill's personal representative and British intelligence officers, Donovan inspected British defenses at Gibraltar, Malta, and Egypt's Western Desert. On January 15, he flew to Athens in a British plane, accompanied by the commander in chief of the British air forces in the Middle East, and was billeted by British handlers at their legation. MacVeagh briefed Donovan and presented him to the king and Metaxas, to whom Donovan promised farm equipment and fighter planes as Churchill wished.[34] Then he addressed the men of the American colony about recent developments at home. The British arranged trips to Belgrade, Yugoslavia, and Sofia, Bulgaria, where they wanted him to convince the Balkan rulers to join a united front to resist the Germans, but after Donovan departed, the same rulers, playing both sides against the middle, flew to Berchtesgaden.[35]

On his way south, Donovan stopped in Salonika, where he dined with Charles House—head of the American Farm School and wartime American Red Cross in Greece. The Princetonian led an important delegation, including banker Alexandros Koryzis, who chaired the Greek War Relief Association in Greece. They had just returned from the front, where they gauged conditions from Messolonghi to Koritsa and debriefed the Adossideses. The delegation returned by way of Salonika, where they encountered American relief worker Meverette Smith and Rodney Young, who was driving for the Greek Red Cross, dodging bombs and transferring wounded soldiers from trains to field hospitals while he awaited permission to proceed to the front. House reported stripped villages, insufficient lines of communication, and suffering that could not be exaggerated.[36] Donovan wanted to see the Albanian front for himself in order to give FDR accurate intelligence. At first aid stations from Koritsa to Klisura, Donovan met Greek soldiers who cheered for Roosevelt. He returned to Athens outspoken in praise of the army, its generals, and morale, but bemoaning "the bitter weather which freezes everything but their heart," the "tortuousness" of Greek communications, and inadequate transport.[37]

That day, Young proceeded to Albania and may have driven Donovan. Once Young arrived in Koritsa, the Adossides women got permission to operate their canteens and became the first nurses to serve north of Koritsa. Young drove them, eyeing the "leaden sky," mountains "veiled in cloud," and fields deep in water. He stopped at Lesnitza, a hill town held by the Greeks, three-fourths of the way north to Pogradets. There they found a house that served as the field hospital and picked their way through foot-deep mud, past a small cemetery with makeshift wooden crosses. Inside, doctors offered them tea in the same room as a shrouded amputee on his stretcher. The sickly sweet smell of rotting flesh emanated from the operating room with its tables laden with gleaming instruments, basins, and stoppered bottles and doctors with sleeves rolled up and bloodied aprons sawing off gangrenous limbs. Upstairs, convalescing soldiers watched pails catch water dripping from the patched roof. When they realized that an American had come to help them, they cheered for Roosevelt and America while distant artillery boomed. While soldiers built their Red Cross huts, the sisters sprang to work, knowing "what had to be done and how to do it."[38]

That week, all were startled by news from Athens that on January 28, at the height of his popularity, Metaxas had died. With one stroke, the country was "decapitated."[39] Greek High Command fragmented, and generals disagreed on how to proceed. Recently back from the front, Donovan witnessed the turmoil. MacVeagh brought him to meetings with the king and General Papagos to discuss who should succeed Metaxas as prime minister. The king appointed Alexandros Koryzis, who met with Donovan before the American left for Turkey and the Levant. When Donovan returned to Washington, he advised FDR that Hitler would spare Greece if he thought the Balkan countries remained united against him.[40]

The first of the School's four canteens opened in late January, and from then until April 10 welcomed 55,000 soldiers through their doors. Each facility provided shelter for one woman, isolated in separate locations in the mountains just behind the front. Each dispensed medical supplies, first aid, and food to the wounded whom Young drove to the hospital in Koritsa. Their establishment and maintenance was the most important wartime achievement of Meritt and Capps's committee and eventually became a joint Greek-American operation with the help of the Greek Red Cross.[41]

Young pitched camp with Elli Adossides at a strategic crossroads two miles below and northeast of Lesnitza on the track to Jerava. Their three-room canteen had plank walls, isinglass windows, and a tar paper roof. It leaked, and everywhere the wind whistled through the planks, but it was home and "seemed warm and cozy compared to being out in an Albanian winter."[42]

Beyond lay the war zone. A supply depot stood across the track from the canteen, protected by artillery wedged into ravines and gullies. The soldiers named their guns, which Young and Elli assisted in firing and upon whose shells they inscribed messages for Mussolini. Young recorded the daily rhythm: "vehicles of every description—buses, old trucks, taxis, and open touring cars" brought army munitions and food from Florina and Koritsa. Men unloaded them by day, and "after dark, more vehicles appeared, coming back from Pogradets and the front to take supplies up to the lines. Strings of horses and mules; two-wheeled carts; four-wheeled wagons, old buggies—everything but wheelbarrows." They moved "silently, without light," because Italian artillery controlled the heights and coastal plain, and the slightest glow or murmur of a motor could provoke a fatal artillery barrage. "Every night they came, between eight and nine o'clock, in wind, rain, or snow, nearly three hours each way through the mud."[43] Many muleteers had colds or influenza since their clothes often did not dry for ten days at a stretch, and almost all suffered from dysentery, yet intoned their mantra, "The supplies must get through." Young marveled at their courage and fortitude as they drove their animals six days a week, slept in tents made by buttoning two ponchos together, and hauled food and munitions through craggy wilds and roadless mountains to the front.

Young and Elli Adossides bantered with the men, gave them cigarettes, hot tea and brandy, dried figs and chocolate, and gathered them round their stove. The drivers, warmed by Elli's hearty smile, shared war stories, joked about the Italians, and offered them Italian hand grenades, rifles, bayonets, knapsacks, first aid kits, and a machine gun as souvenirs. They plotted to

Fig. 8. Clio Adossides in white apron and head scarf, with Greek Red Cross colleague and soldiers in Albania. (Courtesy Clio Sperling.)

steal enough musical instruments from abandoned Italian houses in Pogradets to organize a band and serenade them.[44]

At another shack Clio met soldiers who sought respite from the war. Crawling with lice, they marveled to see the pretty nurse in her Red Cross uniform—petite and delicate like a bird. The slender beauty wore her lush black hair parted to the side and softly gathered into a bun so as not to interfere with her work. Sometimes the Greek soldiers brought Italian prisoners with them and called, "Adelphi! [Sister!] We have an Italian. Please serve the Italian first." Elegant and erect in bearing, Clio graciously ladled hot sweet cocoa, her long, delicate fingers clasping the warm mugs before releasing them to the wounded, who had often walked for days to reach her canteen. She boosted the soldiers' circulation with milk and cognac and soaked their feet to save their legs. "It was a cruel war," and Clio suffered along with the soldiers. She, too, lost toes to frostbite, but did not complain.[45] She must have dreaded the nights, but if Clio was frightened, she never let on. Lonely, she tried to keep warm, fully dressed and huddled under woolen blankets. Only once in more than four months did she see her husband Costas, who surprised her while flying a reconnaissance mission.

Rodney Young was her lifeline. Silhouetted against the sky and snow, Young cut a majestic figure when he arrived at her door. He toured the four canteens weekly, bringing supplies from Florina that her father-in-law had forwarded from Athens and luxuries, such as coffee, sugar, beans, cheese, sweetened condensed milk, cocoa for the wounded, jam, honey, chocolate, and cigarettes (which had long ago disappeared from stores), as well as shoes, woolen socks, and blankets.[46] Young made Clio forget the war. In his convivial company, her brown eyes twinkled, and her smile erupted into laughter as she savored his wordplay, calling those who helped at the British canteens in Athens "monastic egg friars." He regaled her with tales of a bearded soldier who by lamplight looked like he had stepped out of a Byzantine icon, and a hysterical young officer in shock who laughed and cried at the bandaging of his hands, which he had burned while picking up a live grenade for a souvenir. Clio boiled them steaming cups of pale gray coffee sweetened with syrupy milk. "He was wonderful. It was like having a big brother in the group. Always at night I made bread pudding because I always had bread and milk and I got eggs from the village."[47] But all too soon, Young climbed into the ambulance, and Clio was alone again.

Young thought he would never die. Fearlessly he shuttled back and forth to the front north and west of Koritsa, through valleys, past stone huts, and onto a track that zigzagged up to the high mountains where the Cretans were.[48] He passed by those whom he had not reached in time, picked up others, and hauled them down from the mountains. Young's ambulance was designed to carry him, four soldiers lying down, and four sitting up, but Young gave lifts to anyone and, on one occasion, squeezed in thirty-five people. Happy not to be walking, the soldiers often sang, and Young joined in with gusto in his deep, booming voice.[49] Serious cases he ferried to the base hospital in Koritsa, which he supplied with books and magazines, oranges, and cigarettes. Less critical cases—cuts, boils, blisters, mule bites and kicks, colds, and dysentery—he dropped at the canteens, which he supplied along the way, bringing the sick and wounded at the dressing stations.

Young tried to reach home before sundown. There Elli, a stout mother of four, lavished her nurturing instincts on Young, mothering him and reporting to her husband, "Rodney is peeling potatoes and onions for stew." After supper, Young wrote his reports, while outside the snow fell on the endless supply trucks and muffled the sounds of their arriving and being unloaded in the dark.

In late February, Arthur Parsons, who was to take over as director of the School, and Gene Vanderpool, who left his pregnant wife and three small children, drove north to supply the canteens. They reported news from Athens: the AIA and the American School Committee had sent funds to the department of antiquities to bolster morale and encourage the survival of intellectual life. Although chaos had diminished academic life, the Athens Archaeological Society (presided over by the king) maintained a degree of decorum. Its members met every other week seemingly oblivious to current events, listening to Gorham Stevens wax eloquent on the Parthenon's "Sills of the Grilles in the Pronaos and Opisthodomos" and debating whether "The Curve of the North Stylobate" was a circle or a parabola.[50] Parsons and Vanderpool unpacked woolen sweaters, socks, leggings, gloves, helmets, and pajamas as well as candy and medical supplies, such as rubber sheeting, washcloths, doctors' smocks, sterilizers, and bandages. They returned with Elli's cards to her husband.

> In a corner of our barracks which serves as a canteen, Rodney Young sleeps in a loft, in the middle of a heap of dried figs. Since yesterday he is more at the front for transporting the supplies of the canteens. On the route, the drivers often call to him "Hey comrade, deviate a little" or else "Hey, my brave, come give me a slap of the hand." Rodney never refuses. *IASO* is the most popular automobile on all the front. She transports heaps of people, the sick, the wounded, the exhausted soldiers, and even more the stronger, solid ones who break down. The car is always in motion.[51]

In spite of their victories in Albania, most Greeks suspected a threat from the north. Greek High Command, conditioned by decades of aggression, feared Greece's traditional enemies, the Bulgarians. Together Greeks, Turks, and Yugoslavs eyed their neighbor's Germanization with alarm.[52] Bulgaria had much to gain in exchange for offering Hitler a conduit to the Turkish chrome he needed for his war machine. The Bulgarians stood to recover all of the territory that they had lost to Greece after World War I. By February, Germans constituted 90 percent of hotel guests in Sofia, and railroad cars full of German weapons for the Bulgarian army were rolling south to Bulgaria. On March 1, German troops crossed the Danube, and tanks rumbled into Sofia.

To protect Greece from the Germans, Prime Minister Koryzis turned to the British. General Wavell appointed Lt. Gen. Sir Henry Maitland Wilson commander of the British campaign in Greece. On March 3, Secretary of War Anthony Eden of Britain met with Greek High Command. Macedonia and Thrace were placed on full alert. To help defend them, Wilson began sea-lifting British Expeditionary troops from the deserts of North Africa, and Greek parks and vacant lots sprouted soldiers as convoys snaked north. Wearing gas masks in frozen Macedonia, the troops dug a series of fortified positions that stretched from Florina to the Aegean coast, known as the Aliakmon Line. After the German military attaché in Athens notified Berlin of the deployment, German troops advanced south to the Rhodope Mountains, Bulgaria's border with Greece. Meanwhile, the U.S. secretary of state advised American diplomatic staff and relief workers to withdraw from Salonika.[53]

On March 9, the Italians mounted their last full-scale offensive in Albania. Yet even with Mussolini himself present and fresh recruits, it failed, and the Greeks inched westward, emboldened by British air strikes. Although an Italian attack destroyed most of the RAF's planes, when the smoke cleared, the Greek army still held one-third of Albania. But the Greeks were caught between the Italians to the west and the Germans in the northeast. In their rush to pursue the Italians into Albania, the Greeks had recklessly ignored their 100-mile border with Yugoslavia, trusting their northwestern neighbor to shield them from the Germans.

On March 25, Greek Independence Day, Greeks were stunned to learn that the Yugoslavian prime minister and the foreign minister had agreed to let the Nazis pass through their country. Monastir Gap, the traditional invasion highway from Yugoslavia into Greece, lay undefended fewer than twenty miles north of Florina. Although a British-backed coup three days later caused Yugoslavia to side with Greece, it bought little time. With the Monastir Gap defenseless and few Greeks left in Greece to guard it, the Germans simply waited for the snow to melt.

Altitude made all the difference. In the mountains where snow lay nine to twelve feet deep, the Greek soldiers gazed on Albania's oil fields, but could not reach them. Near the Yugoslav border, a half-crazed drunken Greek dragged one gun from place to place nightly so the enemy would not think he was alone. On March 22, the muleteers who supplied him stopped at Clio's canteen twelve miles from the front and invited her to come along. At the Serbian monastery of Osios Naum, the gunner served them dinner with food scavenged from houses abandoned by the Italians. Afterward, Clio looked out over opalescent Ochridha, whose waters had once yielded eels, carp, and trout for the sultan's table. As she admired the rising of the new moon and the reflected lights of Pogradets, somebody shattered her reverie and pushed her to the ground to shield her from a grenade, thrown by an unknown enemy, that exploded a few feet away.

In less than a week winter gave way to spring. When the weather cleared, Italian planes returned to bomb and strafe exposed Greek positions. On March 27, the sun shone in a cloudless sky, and the tall mountains rose dazzling white above the valley. The spring fields near Jerava were green and dry at last. That afternoon, Rodney Young and Elli Adossides were standing at the canteen, serving and joking with Greek soldiers. Young heard the droning then spied the plane. There was no time to run before the bombs began to fall, so he glanced at *Iaso*. It was close, but looked more like a target than cover. Instinctively, he and Elli dropped to the ground.

Dirt rained. One bomb exploded about twenty feet away. The shock of the explosion blew out *Iaso's* windows, and shrapnel punctured its steel doors as gunners strafed it with bullets. A bomb fragment struck Young low in the back and splinters pierced his thigh. After the planes departed, he rose in shock, caked with spring mud. A deep voice rumbling up out of his chest asked Elli, "How are you?" "I'm all right," she replied and asked him the same. "I'm wounded," Young whispered, then passed out in a pool of his own blood. Elli staunched the wounds with her apron while soldiers gently rolled over the unconscious archaeologist. Shrapnel had pierced his ruptured abdomen and perforated his intestines. Like Sleep and Death raising Zeus's mortally wounded son on the ancient Euphronios krater, soldiers lifted Young. They loaded him onto a stretcher and shoved it gently into the battered ambulance. Then Elli took the wheel and sped to Koritsa, where she secured morphine and a good surgeon.[54]

In Athens, the archaeologists were celebrating the allied coup in Yugoslavia and the RAF's destruction of the Italian fleet on March 28, when Charles House telephoned the American School. He had just read in the Salonika paper that Young had been wounded. That night the news traveled by wireless to the *New York Times*, which ran the story the next day. Meanwhile, House drove to Koritsa hospital, where Young lay unconscious and in critical condition after a long and serious operation had removed fragments lodged in his thigh and stomach. The doctors doubted whether he would survive. That evening Tsolakoglou left the front to come to his bedside and, acting for the king, decorated Young with the War Cross while Clio and Elli Adossides looked on.

The next day, the Athenian newspaper claimed, "New American blood is now added to that shed in 1821 for Greek independence."[55] Cables flew across the Atlantic as American archaeologists inquired about Young's condition. Arthur Parsons sped to Koritsa in Adossides' sedan. On March 30, he reported that Young was responding to treatment.

THREE

Flight

FOR A FORTNIGHT, Elli and Clio Adossides persevered. Elli drove the wounded men to the Koritsa hospital and checked on Young. Occasionally, she continued to Florina, where she placed some on night trains for Salonika. There was no heat in the cars, but men with gangrened or frozen feet and legs felt less pain without it. Sometimes Clio went down to the dressing stations to receive the wounded men. Otherwise Red Cross trucks came to get them. On those days, they asked volunteer nurses to accompany them. When Clio did, the soldiers asked her to sing the *Hymn to Liberty* from the Greek War of Independence, and she complied until they droned the national anthem into a dirge. Clio protested, "It should be joyful." But there was little joy in the Albanian mountains.[1]

At the beginning of April, the Germans bombed the Greek positions, rattling the bottles in Clio's canteen. When the young Greeks heard the strange whistling, they "disappeared like rabbits," but Clio reassured them that she would not flee, and slowly they returned. A young soldier with his face blown off marveled, as Clio soaked his frostbitten feet, that "the girl from Athens" had stayed with them.

With Yugoslavia tenuous and the Germans in Bulgaria, Greek prospects looked bleak. Arthur Parsons dared not linger more than a week at Young's bedside. When he began to improve, Parsons felt that his own place was in Athens. He regretted abandoning Young in Koritsa with its roofless Ottoman houses, blown-out windows, and bombs falling in the streets, but it was too soon to move him, so Parsons returned to Athens alone. He reached the capital just before Greece's new prime minister, Koryzis, received an ultimatum from Hitler's emissary.

After deciding to invade Russia, the Führer realized that he first needed to subdue his southern flank. Hitler would not tolerate the British foothold in the Balkans. He relied on the area for oil, cereals, and livestock. Greece and Yugoslavia supplied half of the ore he needed to produce aluminum. Already the British dominated the Mediterranean from Egypt, and its navy held Gibraltar, Malta, and Cyprus. He would not let Churchill have Crete. By occupying Greece, he could keep Britain out of the Balkans, launch attacks against the British in the eastern Mediterranean, and supply General Erwin Rommel, who had just arrived in North Africa. He envisioned a pincer movement with one arm reaching down through the Balkans to North Africa and the other stretching eastward to the oil fields of Iraq. On March 27, the day Young was wounded, Hitler postponed his attack on Russia in order to secure Greece, a costly decision that would delay his primary offensive.

On Sunday, April 6, 1941, German forces invaded Greece and Yugoslavia. For three days, they bombarded Belgrade, then took the railroad terminus at Monastir and poured through the undefended Gap. Moving toward Florina, the Germans wedged themselves between the Greeks in Albania and their homeland. They attacked Greece simultaneously in three spots, using blitzkrieg tactics to startle and disarm the Greeks. Even with British help, the Greeks were no match for the German juggernaut, which vastly outnumbered the Allies and had better equipment.[2] First, German bombers annihilated what remained of the Royal Hellenic Air Force. Then they blasted a tank path south along the Vardar River, the second traditional avenue of attack from Yugoslavia, sixty miles east of the Monastir Gap. Two days after the invasion began, German panzers converged north of Salonika. At six in the evening of April 8, the Greek army loaded the last train with as much ordnance as it could carry and fled Salonika, abandoning mountains of munitions and supplies to the Germans. Reverberations of artillery volleys and the detonation by Greek and British troops of supply dumps and airport oil tanks rattled the windows of Salonika.[3] Brilliant flames illuminated the smoke shrouding the sky as the doomed city fell silent, and heavy rain in the night could not extinguish the fires.

The Turks, who had pledged to monitor the Greek-Bulgarian border and stand by Greece, did just that; they stood by. Terrified of Germany, they did nothing. To defend the country from the Bulgarians, the Greek army had constructed a mini-Maginot, known as the Metaxas Line, just south of the border from Salonika to Thrace with over ninety miles of tunnels, observatories, gun emplacements, and bunkers. However, the German mountain troops, like their Italian colleagues in the Pindus, crossed peaks the Greeks thought impassable and surprised them. Further east, they bypassed the fortified line altogether, as they had the original Maginot, and easily occupied Thrace. To the north, Greek defenders at Fort Rupel guarded the Doiran Pass and the Struma River valley where the Bulgarians had attacked Greece in World War I. Withstanding two days of continual German air and panzer attack, they surrendered only when their commander ordered them to do so. Afterward the Nazis broke through, descended along the Struma, and severed 15,000 Greek troops in Thrace from the rest of their army. The American Red Cross and Greek War Relief delegation monitoring relief in Thrace, led again by Charles House, crossed the Struma just before retreating Greeks blew up the bridge.[4] When the Greeks and British exploded the bridge over the Vardar (west of Salonika), the booms resounded as "final notes in a brilliant but tragic symphony," and at dawn on April 9 Salonika surrendered to the Germans.[5]

America watched as the Nazis swarmed into Greece and set up their command headquarters at Anatolia College on a hill overlooking Salonika and their intelligence operation at the nearby American Farm School, both U.S. institutions. Expecting the inevitable, workers at the American School in Athens scrubbed the *USA* off its roofs. Archaeologists agonized over Rodney Young, languishing in Albania somewhere between the Italians and the Germans, and likewise the ruination of their lives' work. Leslie Shear reflected,

> We write and talk and plan just as if there were not a strong possibility that no School or Agora or anything else civilized in Greece would be in existence on May 10 next. We are in despair over that onrushing horde of gorillas. Will anything be able to stop them, and will we over here be eventual victims also. The whole prospect is too horrible.[6]

After the fall of Salonika, Greek and British defenders focused on withdrawal, but the Greeks could barely communicate with British headquarters and lacked motor transport. Again, the German panzers outmaneuvered British Expeditionary forces, whose vehicles could not handle the terrain.[7] Spread too thin to defend the Aliakmon Line, the Allies kept giving way, scavenging petrol and luxuries like tobacco, cigarettes, and jam from abandoned supply dumps before British Special Forces blew them up and headed south. On April 11, morale began to crack as a result of hordes of refugees, merciless bombardments, and the collapse of Yugoslavia.

The Greeks were still pressing westward in Albania when they got word of the fall of Salonika. In a state of shock, the Greek High Command hesitated for thirty-six hours. Then, at 9:30 on the morning of April 12, it finally ordered the Greek army in Albania to retreat for "reasons of supreme national interest." Again the Greeks would relinquish Koritsa—bitter fruit. At the thought of having achieved so many victories and endured such suffering in vain, some troops disbanded in disbelief. The generals scrambled to muster those who could walk to join the defenders on high ground near Mt. Olympus south of Salonika, but there was no time to reach the home of the ancient gods. By the time they arrived at the Pindus, the Nazis had occupied Florina, fewer than forty miles from Young's hospital bed.[8]

Elli Adossides got word to evacuate and broke the news to the soldiers. She loaded food and medical supplies into the ambulance, picked up her kin and a homeless Salonika boy, and proceeded up the tree-lined avenue to the iron gates of the Koritsa hospital where Rodney Young lay. She climbed to the second floor where wounded littered the Lysoled corridors. Hospital staff hoisted the sedated archaeologist onto a stretcher and carried him down the stairs to *Iaso*. No matter his condition, she would get him out before they were trapped. She sped out of town past standing water and greening fields, to the bear-prowled hills of Greece.

Elli chose a western route and hurried south, just ahead of the retreating army. Mountain roads adequate for the ambulance were few and winding. Around Yannina, the traffic swelled and slowed with converging troops, horse-drawn wagons, mules, and trucks bound for Athens. That night, Elli paused to rest at the Red Cross Hospital in Yannina, where the women guarded the wounded archaeologist before continuing south past Dodona. At Arta, planes bombed the retreat, which started and stopped and slowed again. At the crossroads port of Amphilochia, Clio and Young boarded a hospital ship traveling through the Ionian Sea to the Gulf of Corinth. After crossing the gulf by night ferry, Elli skirted the southern shore and crossed the bridge over the Corinth Canal, met the boat at the port of Loutraki, and pressed on to Athens.

On the night of April 13, the women delivered Young to the Greek Red Cross Hospital on the outskirts of Athens. The next day, Shirley Weber, the Gennadius librarian and fellow Princetonian, visited Young and read aloud scores of congratulatory telegrams from the United States and *Princeton*

*Herald*s containing accounts of Young and Princeton's relief efforts, quoting headlines, "Capps and Shear Assume Lead in Local Work to Aid Greece" and "Alumnus wins War Cross." One began, "[Class of] 1929 on the Greek Front," and spoke of "Rod" volunteering to fight with the Greeks, being rejected, and driving night and day for the Red Cross. Weber told him that the *New York Times* had run four articles on him in two weeks and read the headlines, "Bomb Injures American," "Greeks Decorate Young," "Young taken to Athens," and "Greece honors Jersey Volunteer."[9] After returning to the School, Weber reported that Young was comfortably ensconced: "Rodney is cheerful, and though very modest, seems inwardly pleased at the kindness showered on him by everybody. The Legation people, especially Mr. MacVeagh have exerted themselves to the utmost."[10]

Other news was not so rosy. Although the Greeks and British Expeditionary forces defended the Olympus Line, which stretched from Kastoria to the Aegean and held the Germans at the strategic Olympus Pass, a tank battle raged in the plains west of the mountain. In one week, the Germans had advanced a third of the way to the capital, and Athens was in a state of anarchy. Early on, a lucky bomb had struck a British munitions ship, which exploded, destroying eleven other vessels and most of the Piraeus harbor installations, shattering suburban windows twelve miles away, and rocking Anastasios Adossides and his neighbors "as if they had been blown out of their beds." Since then, antiaircraft guns banged endlessly, while unopposed German planes scattered bombs and mines like seed along Attica's coasts and hit British planes on the runways at Phaleron. The constant air-raid alarms terrorized the population into living underground, and the bomb shelter under the Gennadius Library became very popular. For this reason, MacVeagh designated the School as the rallying point for the American colony, and the American Bandage Circle moved its operation there. Meanwhile, Eugene Vanderpool, who worked with the American Red Cross, guarded the Agora despite the fact that his wife had given birth to their fourth child just days before the invasion.[11] Moonlight only multiplied the bombing opportunities and extended the hours into "nights of hellfire."[12]

In the second week of the invasion, rumor outran the German advances. "Fifth columnists" spread false tales that Mt. Olympus had fallen. Then the Germans sent advance troops to cut the north-south railway linking Athens and Salonika. Others breached the Olympus Line and encircled the sacred mountain while a patrol climbed the summit to honor Zeus with a swastika. When word spread that the Germans controlled Mt. Olympus, Greeks, already cowed by rumor, were devastated.

Panic erupted. No one knew where the front was or if it would hold. In the west, massive waves of refugees roamed the Pindus, where whole villages were burning. For three days, seasoned British soldiers held the Pinios Gorge south of Olympus in order to protect the way south to the critical transportation and supply dump at Larissa. Troops from Macedonia and Thrace funneled along the north-south coast road littered and clogged with burned-out trucks and broken-down vehicles, abandoned artillery carts, and other debris of the retreating army. One unit proceeded only twenty-three miles in nine hours because of unrelenting and unopposed air attacks, which left craters twenty yards long that the men filled with "dead mules riveted with castaway Greek rifles" so that the men and equipment could pass. Looking over their shoulders, the Greeks and British Expeditionary forces bought precious time by defending a position by day and abandoning it by night, as they ceded one historic pass after another in "a succession of Thermopylaes."[13] Southward through the plains of Thessaly the Germans pursued some fifty thousand soldiers along the coast road to Lamia and the Brallos Pass until they reached a narrow gap between 500-foot cliffs and the sea. There, at Thermopylae itself, the Allied defenders held the line.

Defeatism spread as the fighting neared Athens and the German planes dive-bombed and machine-gunned military targets as well as schools, hospitals, and hospital ships and trains. For protection, Young was transported one last time, to Evangelismos Hospital in the shadow of the American School, where a handful of Americans could monitor his treatment and visit him more easily.[14] There he remained in a long room with tall windows opening onto the same view over the city and Mt. Hymettus that he had enjoyed from the School.

Riots erupted among tired soldiers and outraged students as troops swarmed into the refugee-swollen city. Civilians could not understand why the army had collapsed so quickly. Meanwhile, Nazi propaganda sowed rumors that the British had poisoned drinking water from the Marathon reservoir with typhoid bacilli, and residents scoured markets for food and water.

Chaos reigned. The Yugoslavian king and government arrived in Athens to find Greek cabinet ministers packing. On April 17, Greek General Headquarters began burning documents, and the government destroyed its codes. The next day, Prime Minister Koryzis committed suicide with a gun in one hand and an icon of Our Lady of Tinos in the other. It was Orthodox Good Friday. The Greeks fasted, but blackout restrictions banned their customary candlelight procession. Once again, the weak king, a mere figurehead under Metaxas, took over for a dead prime minister and struggled to form a government.

Further west, Greek troops in Albania trudged day and night through the mud and snow on roads choked with traffic backed up for as much as ten miles, struggling to reach the Metsovo Pass, leading to Yannina and Thessaly. After a week of freezing rain and snow, April 20 dawned clear. Orthodox Easter, the Greeks' holiest day, fell on Hitler's birthday that year. As if to celebrate, the Germans bombed the Yannina Red Cross hospital, blowing up doctors, nurses, and patients in the operating room.[15] Yannina and Metsovo fell together, cutting off the remainder of the Greek army in Albania. For three days, the High Command in Athens wanted to continue the struggle while its field generals wanted to quit. The king, never a popular leader of the Greeks, told his people to "take heart in the inextinguishable American torch of Liberty." Meanwhile without informing the king or Papagos, General Tsolakoglou, the hero of Koritsa, capitulated to the Germans and signed an armistice agreement that decreed that the Greek troops must lay down their arms.[16]

In the third week of the invasion, MacVeagh's prophecy of "another Dunkirk" came to pass.[17] On April 22, the U.S. legation destroyed its codes and confidential files. The British burned their documents and gave the order to evacuate the mainland. For roughly a week, truckloads of troops were dropped on the beaches of Attica and the Peloponnese, where they were picked up by fishing boats, yachts, and merchant vessels, shuttling to Crete by night while the Santorini volcano erupted. At the same time, the Nazis sunk over twenty vessels, including one with 800 Australians and British as well as Greek civilians. Thousands were left stranded at the southern port of Kalamata. Meanwhile, demobilized Greek soldiers walked day and night back to Athens, where they arrived homeless, hungry, thirsty, and ill clad, suffering from sepsis, anemia, hemorrhages, tetanus, gangrene, and infectious diseases. Some who had suffered compound fractures, left untreated, had deformed limbs, and thousands were amputees. Others had severe head and chest injuries. Fit soldiers wanted to evacuate with the British, but even Cretans struggling to get home to defend their island were refused.

Rather than remaining with their countrymen, the Greek leaders absconded. At dawn on April 23, King George II fled to Crete with his British mistress and his new prime minister, Emmanuel Tsouderos, a Cretan republican once exiled by Metaxas whom the king recalled after Koryzis's suicide. General Papagos resigned as Greek commander in chief, and the rear guard at Thermopylae pulled out the night of April 24. General Wilson departed on April 25, crossing the Corinth Canal just two hours before the Germans bombed two fully loaded Greek troop trains, and Nazi paratroopers stormed the bridge.[18]

That week, Clio visited Young daily. He lay inert while she related tales of their escape and conditions in Athens. Heavily armed police kept order in the city amid widespread looting of abandoned British camps and public employees vacating their posts. Elli Adossides continued her relief work at various Red Cross hospitals using the School's truck, brought Young home-cooked food, and presented him with the jagged shell fragment pulled from his gut. Both women were at Young's bedside when Crown Prince Paul came to decorate him with the Greek War Cross for bravery in the name of his father the king.[19]

When the Germans broke through Thermopylae, the British told Costas Adossides to scuttle his planes. Adossides refused and insisted on flying them from Phaleron to Crete, the only way he and Clio could evacuate together. The British maintained there was not enough fuel, but Costas disagreed. When the British ceded permission, Clio joined him, and together with his squadron they flew to Maleme, Crete.

In Washington, President Roosevelt expressed unequivocal support for Greece, but did nothing. Two days after the surrender, Stevens cabled the United States, "Americans staying on. All well." Thereafter, the air-raid sirens stopped, and an anxious and unnatural silence enveloped the city. Athens went "behind its shutters," and MacVeagh witnessed "the death pangs" of a nation.[20]

On April 27, one month after Young was wounded, the mayors of Athens and Piraeus handed over their cities to the Germans at the Parthenon Café. The Germans ordered all Athenians to remain indoors and marched through empty streets to the Grande Bretagne, where they established their headquarters. Later that day, they commanded the evzone guard, responsible for protecting the Greek flag on the Acropolis, to hoist the German one in its place. When he refused and, instead, leaped to his death like the Greek heroes in the War of Independence, wrapped in the Greek flag, Nazi troops raised their swastika over what Hitler called "the symbol of human culture,"[21] and German nationals, who earlier that month had holed up in the DAI, began to celebrate.[22]

Young witnessed the impact of the German occupation.[23] Evangelismos, one of the best hospitals in the country, felt the brunt of German policy. Within twelve hours of their arrival in Athens, the Nazis had stripped it of bedding, bandages, and medical supplies. Soon it ran out of "iodine, alcohol, X-ray plates, gauze, and cotton and was using benzene and tannic acid for antiseptics, paper for cotton, and old bed linen for gauze." Because the Americans were noncombatants, the Germans suffered Young to stay. In the next room lay the ill permanent undersecretary in the Ministry of Foreign Affairs whom the Nazis had arrested and placed at Evangelismos under a twenty-four-hour guard.[24] Other Greek patients they turned out to fend for themselves. From all over the country, sick and wounded Greeks had nowhere to go, so Elli Adossides converted the Marasleion School, just up the hill from Evangelismos, into an emergency hospital for Greek veterans and staffed it with Greek Red Cross nurses. To supply it, she relied upon the American Bandage Circle and Edward Capps's daughter, who had marshaled Greek women to produce clothing and other woven goods for the war. Elli Adossides and her sister, speaking flawless German and wearing Red Cross uniforms and a "full panoply" of World War I decorations, made their daily runs, picking up and distributing Red Cross supplies to makeshift hospitals.[25] Thus, they managed to save *Iaso* from Nazi clutches despite the Germans requisitioning all vehicles.

German troops wasted no time subduing the rest of the mainland. With the Italians, they appointed Tsolakoglou to form a quisling government on April 30. Other generals joined his puppet regime, and Maniadakis, Metaxas's security czar, arrested republican officers and gave them to the Gestapo as a pledge of support. Aside from collaborators, the Germans prohibited Greek officers and soldiers from entering the central triangle of Athens between the Acropolis, Lycabettus, and Omonia Square. Yet Stevens cabled the chair of the managing committee on May 7, "Everyone well. Properties in good order. Americans planning to return to America at Legation's advice."

One by one, islands fell to the Germans, but the British still held Crete, the only hope for Greece. Six months earlier, they had agreed to defend it and secretly occupied the island. But while the Cretans fought in Albania, the British did little to fortify Crete or improve the roads along the north coast linking its strategic cities of Iraklion and Khania, so that without the

Cretan soldiers, the proud island lay virtually defenseless. Then within a fortnight, British command established its headquarters just north of Suda Bay. Between a wall of snow-capped mountains and the sea, 16,000 exhausted British Expeditionary troops and 9,000 Greek soldiers camped on a narrow coastal plain stretching from Khania to Maleme airfield, seventy miles to the west.[26]

For a month, all was quiet in mainland Greece. Young lay in Evangelismos Hospital, and Clio and Costas lived at Maleme, Costas with his squadron among RAF pilots and Clio alone in an abandoned shack near the airfield's runway. Meanwhile Nazi troops made the 1,000-mile thirteen-day trek from Germany to Athens, where they bivouacked around airfields just evacuated by the Greeks and British. Across town at the Grande Bretagne Hotel, German generals planned the invasion of Crete.

The British knew from Ultra, their decoded German signal intelligence, that the enemy would invade after May 17, but they did not know how or when. In the second week of May, Clio heard three loud, long blasts that signaled that the Germans had taken the island of Melos, just north of Crete. Each subsequent morning around eight o'clock, a German reconnaissance plane flew over Maleme, followed by intense bombing raids, known as "the daily hate." To save his planes, Costas and his squadron moved them into the olive groves.

May 20 dawned clear. That morning, 2,000 German planes took off from Greek airports bound for Crete. They arrived in three waves, one before dawn, another at eleven o'clock, and a third in the afternoon. Clio was awakened by the din of the first raid and grabbed breakfast during a lull. Then just after eight, she heard an "angry throb" of engines. She looked up and saw a "black cloud" of German planes. When they began strafing and bombing the landing field, she hid in the shadows behind a little church.[27] Large dust clouds hung in the air. Bamboo thickets, vineyards, and olive trees obscured vision beyond the airfield. Then paratroopers and gliders crash-landed on the rocky hills. Defending troops at the airfield's northern edge repulsed attacks from the beach. But those to the west were besieged, and confusion engulfed the scattered pockets of men who could not communicate with each other or British headquarters.

While Maleme was still in British hands,[28] Costas and his squadron took off with Clio and flew seventy-one miles east in the early afternoon to the Iraklion airfield, not knowing it was the Germans' next target. Again, they hid the planes in the surrounding olive groves. Then at four in the afternoon, German planes began strafing and bombing, and, just before 5:30, paratroopers descended around the airfield and south and west of Iraklion. Fierce fighting erupted west of the walled city. There British archaeologist and vice consul John Pendlebury, who doubled as intelligence agent, charged with recruiting and preparing Cretan resistance, was captured, identified by his glass eye, and shot.[29]

King George II and Prime Minister Tsouderos fled after spotting the first gliders and paratroopers, which landed only a few hundred yards from Knossos, where Pendlebury, who had excavated there for years, had billeted them at the villa of British excavator Sir Arthur Evans. Unable to contact Allied command or his skeleton cabinet in Athens, the king and his entourage moved west, ascended the foothills, crossed mountains, and spent the night in a cave guarded by shepherds, before making it down to the coast of the Libyan Sea. On May 23, the British spirited them away on a boat bound for Egypt. The king, who had already spent twelve years exiled in England, proclaimed,

> We leave Crete for the time being and proceed to British territory. . . . It is the only course which enables us to carry out the duties imposed on us. . . . [to] work in closest cooperation with the British government, and share with the gallant British people . . . the efforts they are making with the support of the great American people for the triumph of the cause of freedom and democracy.[30]

Because the British would not allow him to pass his exile on Cyprus, and the Egyptian king forbade him to form a government in noncombatant Egypt, George II soon moved on.

Across the north coast, the Germans pounded Crete's defenders. At Maleme on May 25, they were shot at from all directions, and by the next night reduced to rabble. Evelyn Waugh later recalled the road, "densely filled with walking men interspersed with motor vehicles of all kinds, lightless also, moving at a walking pace. Some of the men were in short columns of threes, fully equipped, some were wounded, supporting one another, some wandered without arms. . . . Most did not look up." By the light of a young moon, flames licked a British oil tanker and illuminated Suda Bay.[31] After Iraklion suffered its heaviest bombing raid, the British converted Evans's villa into a military hospital. Clio witnessed long lines of miserable soldiers, and dogs fed on unburied bodies, but the proud city still refused to fall.

On May 27, the Royal Hellenic Navy withdrew to Alexandria, and the British again ordered retreat. The only escape led across the mountains and the Libyan Sea.[32] Again, the British would not transport the Greek soldiers who had fought alongside them and wanted to continue doing so. Again, they told Adossides to scuttle his planes and evacuate south by submarine or the armored cruiser *Averoff*. Again, Adossides resisted.

Adossides insisted that he and his squadron would fly to Egypt. When the British said there was not enough fuel, Adossides said he would go anyway. He and his pilots brought the hidden planes up to the runway, but no one would come onto the field and give them gasoline. After Clio bartered a British breakfast of eggs and bacon in return for gas, the British accepted. While they were refueling, German bombers hit two of Adossides' planes. Dust billowed in the dark, but three remained. The British added two unmarked ones and said, "If you're brave enough to do it, we'll join you."[33]

They were lucky. With the help of a tail wind, in about three hours Clio saw the coast of Africa. A shell pink beach and figure-of-eight lagoon at Marsa Matruh signaled the gateway to British Egypt, only 168 miles from Alexandria. For millennia, Aegean sailors had sought its harbor as a landmark. Now it was the terminus of a single track railway, a lifeline for British troops stationed in the Western Desert. Further west was Cyrenaica (eastern Libya), where they and the Italians had been chasing each other back and forth for the last nine months.[34] To the south lay the impassable Qattara Depression, and to the east El Alamein, the desert way station of Rameses II at the narrowest and most defensible point between Tobruk and Egypt. Marsa Matruh radioed Cairo, "Planes approaching. Allow them to fly to Alexandria." Frenetic searchlights combed the sky as Costas's squadron neared the mouth of the Nile.[35]

After landing, they entered Alexandria, which they found crawling with British soldiers and Greek refugees. Egypt had become the hub of Allied intelligence in the Mediterranean overnight as governments of occupied countries fled and geared up their secret services there. To be ready for the evacuation, Alan Wace and several other British archaeologists had skipped Crete altogether and gone directly to Alexandria, where they met and debriefed British troops at the quays before they flooded into the city.

The next day, Costas and Clio Adossides were driven to Cairo, where Costas contacted a prominent Greek republican connected with a branch of British intelligence charged with conducting sabotage, known as MO-4 or the Special Operations Executive (SOE).[36] Then Costas and his squadron, notorious for having flown their own planes out of Greece, reported to an RAF base at Helwan outside Cairo. After being brought to full flight strength as one of four Hellenic Anson squadrons under the British for operations in North Africa, they moved to a desert base at Dhekela outside Alexandria, and Clio returned to nursing at Alexandria's Greek hospital.[37]

As the war in Europe spread across the globe, President Roosevelt declared "an unlimited national emergency" for the United States on May 27, insisting in his fireside chat on vigilant defense of the Western Hemisphere and increased patrolling of the Atlantic. But he still would not ask for a declaration of war.[38] Three days later, Crete fell to the Germans.[39] On June 15, FDR closed the Axis embassies and consulates in Washington and gave the expelled diplomats and consular staffs one month to get out. MacVeagh had already left Greece and strongly urged all Americans to do the same, but German authorities stalled, "pending questions of a major political nature," and convinced the remaining Americans that they would be kept as hostages.[40] When it was announced on June 19 that Turkey had signed a nonaggression pact with Germany, the Turkish ambassador fled Athens. Many expected the Germans to strike British Cyprus and the Suez Canal, their gateway to India. Instead, on June 22, the Nazis with 4,500,000 Axis troops invaded Russia. Hitler gambled everything on the subjugation of his former ally, but because of Greece, he was six weeks behind schedule.

To prevent the Nazis from severing their land route to Turkey and their pipeline to Iraqi oil, the British invaded Syria in early June. While Costas and his squadron hunted submarines off the coast and escorted convoys, the Germans responded by bombing Alexandria. Yet within a month, the British secured Syria. Although the king and many Greeks fled for South Africa or London, Clio knew that Egypt's hospitals needed nurses, so she continued her Red Cross work. While tending the wounded, she often thought of Young.

Rodney Young had remained at Evangelismos, listed as a "serious invalid." Gradually, he began to interact with the staff. In Albania, he had learned a good deal about the Greek order of battle from soldiers he had picked up on his rounds. Well placed to learn about the occupation from the Greeks' point of view, Young questioned veterans and caregivers from his hospital bed. They talked despite a German decree of three months' imprisonment for discussing the war or criticizing the occupation. Some were optimistic, relating how defiant compatriots traced Churchill's *V*'s for victory on the dusty windshields and hoods of German and Italian vehicles and chalked them on sidewalks, streets, café windows, and train cars to boost morale even though by these actions they risked death. One nurse recounted how she had written eighteen *V*'s on the three-block stretch between her house and the hospital. Defiant Greeks protected British soldiers in spite of generous rewards for handing them over to the Germans or the prospect of being shot if caught.

> Almost everybody one knew in Athens was sheltering British . . . Not only the rich, but also the very poor . . . one Greek girl, a hospital nurse who had a New Zealander in her home, [answered]: "As long as we have one potato, we can cut it in half."[41]

At the same time, Young heard many Greeks denounce the king and his politicians for desertion. Uncertainty coupled with the enormity of the Greek defeat stymied their remaining politicians. Angry soldiers and veterans who had been ordered by their superiors to surrender felt betrayed. While the futility overwhelmed others, Communists gathered on Mt. Olympus.

Among Young's informants was AP correspondent Wes Gallagher, who had interviewed Tsolakoglou. The general justified his role in the occupation government as necessary to carry out the demobilization and get food to Athens. After the Nazis told him that they would not allow the Italians to occupy Greece, the general had proclaimed over Athens radio that "everyone should join in giving thanks for the resurrection of Greece and stop fighting for foreign interests." Instead, the Germans carved Greece into three sectors, keeping Salonika, Athens, Piraeus, Western Macedonia, Eastern Thrace, central and western Crete, and three strategic islands—two near the entrance to the Dardanelles, and Chios, west of Izmir—for itself. Bulgaria got Eastern Macedonia and Western Thrace, which they treated as annexed, beginning a program of ethnic cleansing. When the Germans announced that the Italians would occupy and administer the rest of the country, including Athens, the Greeks were outraged. But lacking a credible state and functioning infrastructure, Tsolakoglou and his cronies were powerless. Young wrote, "Such bitter things were constantly and commonly said in Athens both against Tsolakoglou and the Metaxas governments as could not have been believed by anyone of mental balance." The Greeks despised the Italians and treated them "with a queer mixture of condescension, derision, and pity—as toward an invasion of some sort of helpless and clumsy beetles, . . . harmless and dirty." But "the Germans have earned for themselves, after their repeated announcements that they came to Greece as friends, a hatred that will last for many years—in fact, it is unlikely that its memory will ever be forgotten."[42]

Athens could not support its swollen population. Two-thirds of the working class was unemployed. Not counting the sea of soldiers flooding into the city, Athens and Piraeus housed one-fifth of all Greeks. Their slums and shanty towns accommodated refugees from the north, many of whom walked the streets selling sacks of matches, figs, cigarettes, and old clothes. Yet still German officers turned Greeks out of their homes on no more than five minutes' notice.[43] To make matters worse, the Germans systematically stripped Greece of its mineral resources and its liquid and financial assets. Before they left for the Russian front, German soldiers looted houses, villages, farms, and vegetable gardens under the guise of "requisitioning." Italian occupiers' food speculation and profiteering led to anarchy, and Germans and Italians shot each other. Meanwhile, the British blockaded Greece in accordance with Churchill's policy of preventing resources from reaching the Axis. In so doing, they further deprived the Greeks of food and other necessities.

At the end of June, Young finally left the hospital because of food shortages. Doctors warned him of malnutrition and the lack of drugs and medical supplies and advised him to leave the country. To recover, he had to have an adequate diet, but that was no longer possible in Greece.[44]

As the deadline for the departure of the diplomats approached, the U.S. legation and consulate closed, and essential diplomatic personnel moved into the School, now guarded and marked as "the American Legation Annex." They celebrated the Fourth of July in its once lush gardens, now a tinderbox of dry leaves. On July 14, the twelve American diplomats and their dependents evacuated on a plane sent from Rome. With them went all official protection. Getting them to America required intricate international choreography. They and sixty-four Americans in Italy and their pets boarded a special train bound for France, but fifteen miles from the border the Italians held them hostage for four days while their Axis counterparts from the United States crossed the Atlantic to Lisbon. Once the Axis officials arrived at the neutral port, the Americans were permitted to leave Italy and embark on a French train to Spain. Only after they and 250 American diplomats from Berlin had reached Portugal safely did Americans in Lisbon release the Axis officials and their families, whom they had held hostage on the ship. On July 25, jubilant crowds of resident Germans and

Italians welcomed their countrymen to Lisbon as the Americans boarded the same ship for home.[45]

Leslie Shear awaited the passengers at the New York docks, but the archaeologists were not among them. The consuls confirmed only that the Italians had promised to allow another forty-five Americans to leave Greece for Lisbon in the next three weeks. They reported that Greece was in "a progression toward famine." The Germans had devoured everything, "as if a horde of locusts had worked their way across it inch by inch." Although Axis propaganda trumpeted occasional food distributions by the Italians, people were collapsing in the streets "from hunger, or lack of resistance to other ailments."[46]

As a total evacuation of Americans in Athens appeared imminent and the American archaeologists planned their exodus, a handful remained intransigent. Among them was Bert Hill, who had survived the German paratrooper attack in Corinth and protected the American excavations there until he was forced to return to Athens. He would safeguard Blegen's home at 9 Ploutarchou (Plutarch Street) even though he was forced to billet a German consular official who wired his telephone directly to the German consulate and the Red Cross. Once Young determined that he could do no more for Greece by remaining, he decided to return to the United States, convinced that America was now Greece's only hope. Yet he would not evacuate without Vanderpool. On July 19, unable to risk being jostled in the suffocatingly crowded wood-burning buses with people riding the roofs and luggage racks, Young bicycled eight miles north of Athens to convince his friend to leave with his family. But Vanderpool Child Feeding was keeping the children of Greek soldiers from starving. Thanks to a grant from the Near East Foundation and the American School Committee, after buying a goat for milk and planting their yard with vegetables, Joan, the mother of four, gave 250 children a warm meal, clothing, and medical supplies daily and the chance to see a doctor once a week. Even though cholera had broken out in Piraeus, the Vanderpools refused Young's plea to escape, because lives depended on them.[47]

The State Department confirmed on August 10 that thirty-seven of the Americans stranded in Greece had been flown to Rome. The Webers left on July 23. The U.S. secretary of state cabled with particular concern for Young, who reached Rome "in good health" on July 25. Arthur Parsons, director of the School since July 1, entrusted it to Anastasios Adossides for the duration of the war and left with his wife and mother-in-law on July 31. By August 7,

Young reached Lisbon. He wrote Clio that he was coming back and waited for Parsons and Weber. They would leave on the American Export Line.[48]

At the same time, Winston Churchill left Scotland shepherded by U.S. destroyers guarding the strait between Iceland and Greenland. While Churchill's convoy sailed for a historic meeting with FDR, the archaeologists steamed home. Both groups crossed a treacherous Atlantic patrolled by Nazi submarines. Amid rumors of British promises ceding Eastern European territory to Russia and pledges to governments-in-exile in London that violated the American ideal of self-determination, Churchill met with FDR off Newfoundland and established common peace aims canonized in the Atlantic Charter, signed on August 14. The first three principles stipulated that neither nation sought territorial gain from the war, that all territorial changes had to accord with the will of the peoples concerned, and that both countries respected "the right of all peoples to choose the form of government under which they will live; and they wish to see sovereign rights and self government restored to those who have been forcibly deprived of them."[49] It would take three years to discover how tremendous an impact these lofty and contradictory ideals, interpreted differently by Churchill and Roosevelt, would have on Greece.

FOUR

From Relief to Intelligence: Forging a "Grecian Formula"

AFTER ALMOST A MONTH AT SEA, Young arrived in New York in early September and presented himself for registration, but the draft board examined and rejected him as 4F because of his wound. So he indexed Agora finds with Frantz in Princeton and devoured the *New York Times* for news of Greece, but the bleak reports made him "want to play the ostrich and not think about it at all." The British blockade had worsened Greece's food shortage, and the Germans exacerbated it by sending wounded soldiers from the Russian front to recuperate in Greece. Refugees reaching Egypt claimed: "Hundreds of deaths from starvation have already occurred in Athens . . . and twenty to thirty cases of fainting in the streets from hunger . . . daily." Joan Vanderpool described two-year-olds who weighed fewer than twenty pounds, and headlines screamed: "BABIES ARE STARVING." In America, Spyros Skouras, the president of Greek War Relief, was trying to break the British blockade by shipping food via Turkey. Meanwhile in the mountains of Greece, a "cauldron of revolt" was simmering as Greek guerrillas banded together to fight the Axis occupiers.[1]

Young read in the *New York Times* and *Washington Post* that Roosevelt had appointed William Donovan the coordinator of information (COI) in Washington. He would "collect and assemble data on 'national security' from the various governmental agencies and analyze and collate this material for the use of the President and other top officials." His organization would also engage in "counter-espionage operations . . . sifting truth from misinformation." Before this, the State Department and armed forces had had a monopoly on foreign intelligence. But now COI attracted an impressive intellectual cohort, including the president of Williams College, a Harvard professor, members of the Institute for Advanced Study, and Roosevelt's speechwriter, who produced radio news for occupied Europe. Later the *Times* backpedaled, claiming that Donovan was just "a liaison man, and not in actual command of intelligence," which the State Department, War Department, the navy, and the Army Air Force handled.[2] In fact, Donovan's enigmatic title obscured his true mission—to create a top-secret global intelligence service for the United States in charge of secret intelligence gathering, special operations, counterespionage, sabotage, psychological and guerrilla warfare, and other subversive activities.

Donovan's fledgling organization had to become operational immediately. To launch this immense covert undertaking, he drew on William Stevenson and the British Security Coordination, which had been operating for over a year in the United States and would be COI's liaison with British intelligence. Donovan's personal contacts in the law profession and the Fight for Freedom Committee walked into top jobs at COI. To find additional men, Donovan scoured the government's "Roster of Scientific and Specialized Personnel," which noted American scholars' geographic and linguistic expertise. Then he prowled the national research councils, such as the American Council of Learned Societies, and academia for individuals with area-studies skills. These he funneled to Washington for Secret Intelligence or Special Operations, identifying as officer material anyone who could speak, read, and write foreign languages, especially if they had lived in the country whose language they spoke.[3]

Young surfaced as an authority on the Greek occupation. On October 28, 1941, the first anniversary of the Italian invasion of Greece, Young told his story publicly. He spoke at the Grand Central Palace, a cavernous exhibition hall in New York City and the largest army induction center in the country. Two weeks later Young addressed an audience in Newark, where, after relating his adventures as a volunteer ambulance driver, he spoke of his wound. "I was standing . . . at a field canteen serving the Greek fighting forces when we sighted planes. We flopped when the bombs started to fall. One of them landed 20 feet from where we were and a fragment struck me in the back." No doubt stung by the army's rejection, Young looked out on the comfortable Americans for whom the war was still far away and added, "In spite of what I went through if there was a boat leaving for Greece I would take it tomorrow."[4] In a letter circulated to American School alumni Young described Greece under the occupation. He declared that "the antiquities seem to be the only things in Greece which are to be protected from looting." Young objectified the Nazis as "vermin" and lamented that Greece had been "blighted and polluted," noting that after the war it would need "a thorough fumigation and purification . . . particularly on the Acropolis." He grumbled bitterly that German archaeologists in Greece were the only ones "in no danger of starving" and recounted how one had volunteered to guide the paratroopers who had attacked the Corinth Canal. According to Young, they were "fifth columnists" who "had all been doing their duty over a period of years beforehand as patriotic men."[5]

Americans were terrified of "fifth columnists" and suspected foreigners in their midst, either born abroad or first generation, who constituted one-quarter of the American population. Yet the State Department realized that it could tap these immigrants for intelligence to help inform its foreign policy and increase national security. So Donovan instructed Dewitt Poole, the head of Princeton's School of Public and International Affairs, to extract political information from foreign nationality groups in the United States to guide the Department of State. Using the Institute for Advanced Study as cover, Poole planned COI surveillance of immigrants. He would study each group's foreign language press and radio transmissions, interview its refugees and political leaders, and monitor its members' private correspondence. To do so, Poole needed nonpartisan academics who combined a "working command of the language with a broad historical and general cultural background," an understanding of "current movements of political life," and "a complete familiarity with the foreign political situation."[6]

Two weeks after Pearl Harbor, Poole's Foreign Nationalities Branch (FNB) went operational, and he recruited Meritt as a part-time consultant to screen the press and radio programs and glean information on the shifting political alignments of Greek-Americans. Soon all branches of COI turned to FNB for expertise on Greece. By the end of January, Meritt was cooperating with several COI divisions, spending five out of seven days in Washington and commuting to New York. There he translated Greek documents and interrogated prominent Greek refugees, including well-informed dignitaries.[7]

A year earlier, one of Ben Meritt's colleagues had predicted that the war would "invade the classrooms of [American] colleges [and] rustle the thumbed pages of [its] scholars."[8] Now it came to pass as Meritt transformed his office at the Institute for Advanced Study from a sanctum of epigraphic "squeeze cabinets," whose shelves held impressions of ancient inscriptions, into a secret research center on modern Greece and Greek-Americans. After subscribing to Greek and Greek-American newspapers and magazines for the FNB, Meritt recruited volunteers from Princeton. First among them were Leslie Shear, who, being over sixty, was too old for active service, and Rodney Young. They both began by listening to radio broadcasts in Meritt's office, where they read, translated, and analyzed articles in the Greek press. Meritt submitted their reports not only to Poole, but also to COI's Research and Analysis Division, whose staff did not know Greek. Soon Young became dissatisfied with his desk job and working with Princetonians who seemed "too old, too fat or too wheezy to be of much use." Young wanted action. Discouraged by his lack of military prospects, he grew morose, confiding to a colleague, "the sooner we all die, the better."[9]

Then Meritt asked them to compile special reports for FNB, steering him away from relief toward intelligence. While Shear reported on the geography and economics of Greece and amounts raised by Greek War Relief, Young focused on the country's political movements.

Only someone who had lived under the occupation could understand the volatile situation. Young kept expanding the scope of his report, consulting key individuals and gathering and weighing sources to craft a balanced account. In the end, he produced a massive analysis of the puppet government and conditions in Greece under the Axis Occupation. The stakes were high. The previous summer, a German officer had told him that "there were twice as many people in Greece as the new order wanted and by the time the war was over, . . . the rich would be poor . . . [and] the poor would be dead."[10]

Young also reported on the brewing political crisis between Britain and the Greek king and his cabinet. However, he did not know that as he wrote a British intelligence team had botched a secret operation in Greece and been caught by Italian occupation police, who found the leader's list with the names of his Greek contacts, most of whom were prominent Athenians. Among those compromised by him was Panayiotis Kanellopoulos, a liberal economics professor from Athens University who had remained in Greece as a liaison with British intelligence, hoping to lead a resistance sympathetic to the monarchy and the government-in-exile. Kanellopoulos escaped to Egypt, and others went underground, but the Italians still arrested, tried, and executed fifty individuals.[11] Others were caught helping British agents escape, including the Adossides' daughter and son-in-law, who were imprisoned and brutally interrogated.[12] Greeks, long smoldering at being abandoned by their king and government, were outraged. In reaction, many moderates gravitated to the left, and leftists and communists increasingly dominated the guerrillas resisting in the countryside. Moreover, anti-British sentiment was fed by British censorship that concealed the devastating economic impact of the blockade by maintaining that no one was starving in occupied Europe in spite of refugee reports to the contrary.[13]

In early March, Shear heard from Anastasios Adossides, who was struggling to run the School under the occupation. After months of writing unanswered letters to the chair of the managing committee, Adossides wrote to Shear in desperation. He assured him that Greece had not forgotten the debt it owed to America.[14] To keep the Germans from requisitioning School buildings, Adossides offered one to neutral Swiss diplomats as a residence while Gorham Stevens remained in the other along with a Swedish Red Cross Mission. In order to pay the staff despite spiraling inflation, Adossides stopped drawing a salary, sold his car to raise cash, and noted, "when a ship is sinking, the captain is the last to leave."[15]

Adossides described the disastrous winter of 1941–42. In Athens, fifteen inches of snow had fallen and owners of olive groves had felled their trees for fuel. At the American dig in Corinth, looters had stripped the site and museum, not for antiquities, but for precious fence posts and doors, pulleys, chains, and locks that they could burn or sell, while at the Agora excavations Athenians had burned fences and gathered wild greens that grew among the ruins for food, so that the site was "in danger of literally being excavated a second time."[16] *Poena* (hunger or famine) stalked the land. Along with tuberculosis, it created thousands of widows and orphans, and Athens became "the abode of hordes of destitute, starving people." There were no animals, no seed, no manure for fertilizer, and no tools to work the soil. Whereas a plentiful grape harvest had sustained the Greeks during the first summer of the occupation, now there was nothing left. Food disappeared from stores, so Adossides allowed the School's starving guards to grow vegetables in the garden. Hospitals accepted only those patients whose families could feed them. Soup kitchens, like that of the Vanderpools, had sprouted across the nation, and even in the Agora, where Adossides gave employees and their children a daily portion of cooked food to keep them alive.[17]

Wraith-like Athenians wandered through the streets whispering "Peenao" ("I'm hungry"). Hundreds collapsed and died daily. The Agora typist starved to death, the pot mender threw himself down a well in the excavations, and the emaciated carpenter was in critical condition. Adossides expected that most Greeks would not live to see the next winter. Already between 100,000 and 200,000 Greeks had died, many shoveled into anonymous graves. The Greeks endured these trials silently, but the spiritual torture of having to view others in distress was unbearable, and the country was in grave danger of emerging from the nightmare "utterly broken economically, physically, and morally."[18]

Soon a bell jar descended upon occupied Greece and silenced direct communications with the outside world. Refugees who escaped to Turkey, Cyprus, and Egypt brought harrowing tales of conditions in Athens. Former *New York Times* Athens correspondent Alexander Sedgwick covered the story from Beirut, and his colleague, Cyrus Sulzberger, who had married Sedgwick's Greek niece, interviewed refugees who recounted hearing "the quiet thud that signifies the fainting or death of a passerby." Dead bodies littered the streets, covered with handkerchiefs to distinguish them from the living.[19] The International Red Cross arranged a sort of *kinder transport* for 9,000 Greek children to be evacuated to other countries while desperate Greeks fled to Turkey on small boats, one of which sank in the islands, drowning 209 women and children.[20]

Adossides' letter galvanized Meritt and Young. Young submitted his tome, and Meritt forwarded it to Washington, where he spent more and more time. Meritt agreed to monitor political movements throughout southeastern Europe and assess their impact on respective foreign nationality groups in the United States. To find more readers, he recruited archaeologists and classicists: Alison Frantz, her companion Lucy Talcott, Shirley Weber, and others from the School and Agora who lived near the Institute. Eventually, he amassed a network fluent in Albanian, Arabic, Bulgarian, Czech, Dutch, German, Irish, Italian, and Lithuanian, many of whom he drafted through the elite East Coast Archaeological Club.[21] For Italian, he marshaled the Institute refugee art historian Erwin Panofsky, Helen Wace, and Agora epigrapher James Oliver, who wrote special reports on Italian Communist newspapers and antifascist societies. Meritt turned to Cypriot archaeologist John Franklin Daniel III, who consulted on that island's key individuals and institutions. Later, Meritt expanded the operation to include professors, known as the Harvard Defense Group, and scholars at twenty universities, such as Minnesota, Cal Tech, and Wisconsin. These stay-at-home consultants (many of whom were women) contributed to the war effort by interviewing key individuals, scanning the press within their respective language groups, and obtaining raw intelligence on political sentiments, cross-currents, and subversive activities that they analyzed and funneled to Princeton. Meanwhile, Shear took over Meritt's office, appraised the interviews, often biased or dishonest, and wove them into reports that were intellectually sound and as objective as possible.[22]

Young began "fishing" for a job in Washington. Rumors circulated that he was going to Syria, and he considered driving an ambulance in North Africa or writing propaganda in Smyrna (Izmir), but preferred to do something for Greece. While Young waited for his next assignment, Meritt moved to Washington to take over the Chancery Division of the FNB. There he oversaw the Herculean collection and processing of all field intelligence. Meritt also supervised the creation and dissemination of top-secret policy analyses for Donovan and the secretary of state, comprehensive area studies, notes targeting specific issues or significant changes of public opinion, and reports on public meetings from members of the Field Study division who attended them.[23] Since COI was placed under the supervision of the Joint Chiefs of Staff, Meritt worked with the Treasury, State, and Justice departments; the army; the navy; the Board of Economic Welfare; and the Maritime Commission. He also maintained the area files of Slavic, Latin, German, and Miscellaneous Languages (including Greek) and monitored the political movements of thirty-six U.S. foreign nationality groups, hiring Agora registrar Lucy Talcott to bring order to the inchoate Chancery, which Young nicknamed "the Augean stables."[24]

By mid-April, Poole's staff had read Young's report. One called it "the most thorough and complete job [he] encountered anywhere"; another rated it "of greatest importance to their work" and circulated it around COI and the State Department, whose political advisor on European Affairs praised Young as "alert" and possessed of "too much spirit to remain inactive."[25] While Americans tried to chart their course in occupied Greece, they used Young's report as their foundation study. It landed on the desk of Lt. Col. Ulius Amoss like manna from heaven.

Amoss had been Poole's first hire at FNB, even before Meritt. He, too, had dedicated decades of his life to Greece, but he was no academic. In-

Fig. 9. Ulius Amoss. *Man's Magazine,* December 1955: 2, 8. (Image courtesy of Special Collections and University Archives, UO Libraries.)

stead, like Young, Amoss had worked in relief, setting up the Salonika YMCA as chief of the YMCA military mission to the Greek armed forces after Greece's war with Turkey ended in disaster and population exchange. He had been given every philhellenic award that the country could offer. For his services to Greek refugees and veterans, King George II had decorated him with the War Cross, and the Greek General Staff had made him an honorary colonel, its highest honor for a foreign civilian. Later, he launched an import-export business, represented numerous Greek relief organizations in the United States, and founded the North American Committee of Friendship and Cooperation with Greece. As its executive director, Amoss inspired the philanthropy of university presidents, a former U.S. minister to Turkey, the Greek ambassador to the United States, and President and Eleanor Roosevelt, all the while relaying information to Washington. Poole had brought Amoss in as a "consultant" to organize the Field Study division of FNB and set up and direct its Balkan desk. In this role Amoss gathered maps and plans for a comprehensive survey of Greek military, naval, and air installations, FNB's first major study, which was praised by Army intelligence. Moreover, he assembled a blacklist of Greek political undesirables and a "Secret Report on the Collapse of Greece" that Poole circulated to the State Department and FBI. Later Amoss met with Donovan himself. Thus Amoss and Merritt led FNB and COI to focus inordinate attention on Greece.[26]

Amoss used his personal ties to establish U.S. diplomatic contact with the

Greek king, the fourth monarch of an occupied country to take up residence in London. With King George II was Amoss's old YMCA colleague, Stavros Theofanides, the king's personal deputy and confidante and minister of the merchant marine, who recommended establishing a Greek "fifth column," using key Greek-Americans or forwarding them to COI for Secret Intelligence and Special Operations. Theofanides wanted to garner support for Greece in the United States. Although the British tried to block his passage, Amoss delivered Theofanides to Poole and insisted that he be protected.[27]

Thereafter, Theofanides guided Amoss through the minefield of Greek politics and dealings with the cabinet, which included royalists and republicans, like Prime Minister Emmanuel Tsouderos. Theofanides promised Amoss direct access to the king and Tsouderos as well as the prime minister's communications with the Hellenic Information Service (HIS). Theofanides also proffered equal access to the facilities of the government-in-exile in Cairo and the prime minister's own intelligence network. Tsouderos communicated through his covert deputy (part of a secret governing committee near Athens) and agents throughout occupied Greece, all of whom were independent of British channels. In exchange, Amoss arranged for Theofanides to meet with Donovan (unbeknownst to the king), as Greece's intelligence liaison with the United States, and set up the Greek Office of Research and Information for the Western Hemisphere (a cover for Greek intelligence) with himself as director general. It was Amoss who persuaded Donovan and Roosevelt to approve the Greek government-in-exile as an ally.[28]

In February, while Meritt was becoming more and more enmeshed in FNB, Amoss (who had once attended a Greek army sabotage and spy school in Salonika) helped Major David Bruce found COI's Secret Intelligence (SI) Division and indoctrinate its first recruits. Donovan had Amoss commissioned a colonel in the U.S. Army and gave him the task of formulating an SI plan for Greece.[29] Amoss drew up a blueprint for SI and Special Operations known as the Greek Project. His goal was to ensure accurate and quick exchange of information between Washington and Greece, give proof of American interest in the occupied country, encourage resistance, and coordinate and expand Greek guerrilla groups already carrying out acts of sabotage and demolition.[30] Theofanides had given him a Greek assistant, but Amoss wanted an American.[31]

Young was just the man for Amoss. He was one of few individuals outside the Greek army who knew some of the generals in the occupation's puppet government. Young knew the Greeks' military potential and believed that they would unite in anticipation of an Allied invasion. He understood the country's complex politics, the tenuous state of the monarchy and government-in-exile, and the political divide that separated the Axis-controlled cities from the mountains where the guerrillas roamed free.[32] Moreover, COI division heads praised Young as a "star . . . too good to miss."[33]

When Amoss summoned him to headquarters in late April and offered Young a slot in his SI plan for Greece, he accepted on the spot. In early May, Young moved in with Meritt, who was shuttling between Washington, Princeton, and Baltimore in the "rather strenuous business of hour by hour struggling for democracy."[34] Young was grateful for the "little Athenian nucleus" in the "madhouse" of Washington. Everyone at COI was on tenterhooks: General George Strong of Army Intelligence distrusted Donovan and wanted to disband his upstart organization altogether. Instead COI was simply reorganized. On June 13, 1942, it split into the Office of War Information (OWI), devoted to propaganda, and the Office of Strategic Services (OSS).[35] Donovan became director of OSS, whose mission was to collect, analyze, and disseminate information bearing on national security. Remaining under the jurisdiction of the Joint Chiefs of Staff, OSS was to gather, evaluate, and analyze intelligence in support of the war against the Axis powers and plan and execute operations in support of intelligence procurement.[36]

Young worked for SI, which handled information-gathering and espionage in theaters of operations across the globe under the umbrella of the Intelligence branch. It comprised and was closely allied with Poole's FNB, Research and Analysis (a group of historians that collated and evaluated intelligence for distribution to government organizations), and Counter-intelligence (which guarded OSS security). While the branches were porous, the strengths of FNB and SI compensated for the weaknesses of R&A, particularly in respect of Greece, and Young and Meritt often pooled information.[37] Later the different branches became carefully guarded and embattled turfs.

On Greek Independence Day, March 25, Meritt and Young heard King George II's wireless broadcast from London wherein he announced that he had taken command of hundreds of royalist officers, the remnants of the Greek military in Egypt and Palestine, reconstituted as the Free Greek Forces. To placate the growing power of the Left, he pledged to liberalize his cabinet, remove the fascist ministers loyal to Metaxas, and support a constitution and democracy in place of the prewar dictatorship. Then the king announced that he would visit Washington to secure financial support. However, several leaders opposed his return until a plebiscite could be held in which people could decide whether or not they wanted him back, and the emergence of rival resistance groups with competing postwar visions complicated the issue of who should hold power when hostilities ended.

Faced with the king's imminent arrival in the United States, Theofanides worried that the king's plummeting popularity might harm Greece's image in the eyes of Americans and scotch his mission. To gauge Greek-American sympathies about the king before and after his visit, Meritt sent Corinth archaeologist Oscar Broneer on an FNB reconnaissance trip to St. Louis, Chicago, Boston, Toronto, and New York. Meanwhile, other archaeologists conducted interviews, and Alison Frantz monitored the Greek-American press, which she found openly hostile to the king because of his tolerance of Metaxas's dictatorship and retention of the dictator's men.[38] But by the time he came to the United States, the king had replaced the offending ministers.

King George II arrived on June 10, 1942, the first monarch to visit Washington since the war began in 1939. What ensued was a carefully orchestrated public relations blitz for Greece. First, the king met with President Roosevelt to discuss the prospect of Lend-Lease. After laying a wreath at the Tomb of the Unknown Soldier, he made a nationally broadcast speech from Mount Vernon and addressed the Red Cross. One day before the creation of OSS, he held a press conference arguing for U.S. aid to Greece. On June 15, he addressed the Senate and House of Representatives. Then he and Prime Minister Tsouderos ran the gamut of embassy receptions and social and speaking engagements, zigzagging for weeks between Washington, Philadelphia, Montreal, and New York, where they met Mayor Fiorello Laguardia, Harold Vanderbilt (honorary chairman of the Greek War Relief Association), Spyros Skouras, Archbishop Athenagoras, and William Dinsmoor, who had known the king as a prince twenty-five years earlier. The king spoke to press clubs and the Council on Foreign Affairs, prayed with thousands at the Hellenic cathedral in New York, and addressed 2,000 Greek-American members of AHEPA. On his last night in New York, he dined with members of nine philhellenic institutions, including the YMCA, the American School, and the Near East Foundation. After likening the ancient Persians to the Nazis and Xerxes to "the Hitler of that ancient day," his host vowed that America would repay its debt to Greece and help secure peace in the Aegean.[39]

Back in Washington, the king and the prime minister attended a luncheon hosted by Meritt where Young occupied the seat of honor between them. Amoss met secretly with Theofanides and Tsouderos, State Department agents, and the FBI about monitoring Greek dissidents and tailing former fascist cabinet members who had sought asylum in the United States. On the day after OSS was formed, Young and Amoss got down to business with Theofanides and Tsouderos. Young reported that the prime minister acknowledged verbal attacks on the king and large numbers of Greeks who opposed him and the government-in-exile. Yet Tsouderos argued for unity for the sake of the peace.

Tsouderos asked for tangible signs of American sympathy and participation. He wanted the United States to set up a secret one- to two million-dollar fund to support the escape of Greeks to the Free Greek Forces and the postwar reconstruction and rehabilitation of the country. He also desired the United States to leverage Greece's postwar union with the Dodecanese, "Northern Epirus," and the largely Greek-speaking island of Cyprus (then a British colony).[40] In return, he pledged the OSS his complete cooperation, including biweekly intelligence reports and the use of men from the Free Greek Forces as OSS agents.

Tsouderos explained the structure of British intelligence, a triumvirate of secret information, operations, and propaganda, fragmented into non-cooperative bureaus rife with jealousy and internal rivalries. He gave Young and Amoss lists of all British intelligence personnel in Cairo and Greece. Then he criticized their agents as ineffectual, dangerous, and cavalier in their treatment of the Greeks.

During his discussion of the British, Tsouderos dropped a bombshell. First he praised the top-secret SOE training school on Mt. Carmel near Haifa in Palestine where Greek and British agents drilled for sabotage and special operations in occupied Greece. Then he damned its lack of security and propensity for fatal accidents, one of which one had claimed the life of Costas Adossides. He had been on active duty when the RAF asked for pilots to test new planes. The new planes climbed and swooped fast, but the British wanted to try out new defensive tactics. Costas volunteered and moved to Palestine. On May 13, they asked him to perform dangerous maneuvers in midair. Adossides agreed, but during the test the plane did not respond. By the time the British told him to bail out, he was too low. Eyewitnesses saw Adossides jump, but his parachute caught the propeller and wound him round it. Then, his plane went into a vertical free fall and crashed. The British hushed up the disaster and buried the Greek hero's mangled body without a funeral. Thus, Young heard of the death of Clio's husband and Elli's son and, in the midst of dispassionate reporting, slipped and used the diminutive, "Costaki," the only indication of his intimacy with the family whose loss he officially recorded in the minutes.[41]

Fortunately, the king's visit was a public relations coup for Greece. Wary of the Atlantic Charter, Roosevelt made no promises regarding the postwar settlement of disputed lands. However, he and the king signed the Lend-Lease Agreement.[42] Later Tsouderos and King George II left to review the Free Greek Forces and shore up the king's image in Egypt.

By the end of June, Donovan approved what was then called the Comprehensive Greek Project, authored by a committee including Amoss and Young. They justified America's backing Greece militarily because it offered a viable Allied invasion route into occupied Europe through the Balkans, a lever to swing Turkey toward the side of the Allies, a buffer against further Axis penetration in the eastern Mediterranean, and a staging point for operations in Italy and Yugoslavia. Washington needed prompt and reliable information on the location of enemy troops and military installations. From Greece, Allied bombers could strike at and sabotage the Ploesti oil fields in Rumania, which were pumping nearly 3,000,000 tons annually, one-third of Hitler's oil.

They argued for American autonomy in political intelligence on Greece. Churchill and the Foreign Office backed King George II, cousin of the king of England and Churchill's fellow Mason, but the Greeks disliked the British meddling in their domestic affairs, suspected British imperialism, and did not want a "client king" foisted upon them. Because of the mutually exclusive agendas of the British and the Greek government-in-exile, America had to sort out its own course of action with the Greek political factions. While OSS maintained contact with the king and cabinet through normal diplomatic channels, it would observe relations between them and the British and monitor all propaganda "designed to forward the restoration of the King." America, being predisposed toward self-determination, should ensure that "the people inside Greece must be allowed to make the decision" about their postwar government.

> Many refugees from occupied countries, and even the leaders in the countries themselves, are almost more interested in winning the civil war that may follow the present struggle, than in winning the war itself. It is the duty of the United States and Great Britain to forestall and as far as possible pre-

vent any such civil wars, or even political uprisings . . . and riots and that governments acceptable to the majority of the people may be set up as soon as possible after the period of chaos that will follow the withdrawal or slaughter of the Axis occupying forces. There is no use trying to force on any people a government not acceptable to the majority. The Greek political situation is very delicate; the people cannot speak for themselves, and we must allow the government-in-exile to speak for them. But when they can speak for themselves, they must be given the opportunity of rejecting or endorsing their present spokesmen.

Amoss foresaw expanded U.S. influence in Europe and argued that "the United States will wield the greater importance armed with complete and accurate knowledge of facts and conditions. . . . The United States must have their say in the establishment of the new Europe, and in view of the record of consistent failure . . . of the 'Great' European powers . . . it would be well that the United States had the greatest say." Regarding politics, he wrote, "Questions of High Policy do not come near the scope of an S.I. officer, but the number of Americans who are intimately identified with and who know Greece by instinct rather than by intellect are so few that when such an officer chances to have a Greek assignment, he is compelled to recommend conference and action beyond and outside his line of duty."[43]

Americans based in Cairo and known as "the Greek Desk" would control the OSS intelligence network for Greece. Cairo would be its operational field headquarters since it had the largest Greek population outside of Greece and an American military presence. Initially, Lieutenant Commander Joseph Leete, former professor at the American University in Cairo, and Lieutenant Turner McBaine USNR, a San Francisco lawyer who was among Donovan's earliest hires and his personal assistant, handled Greek concerns in Cairo.[44] Eventually, Amoss would coordinate SI and Special Operations, preside over supplies and American soldiers for Greece, and communicate with an administrative Greek Desk office in Washington that would supply Cairo. Under him, Young would direct the Greek Desk SI and recruit its agents.

At the outset, Amoss and Young had to depend on their allies. Between the Greeks and the British, they preferred to work with the Greeks. Kanellopoulos, as vice premier, minister of war, and head of Greek intelligence (HIS), would be the Greek Desk's contact in Cairo, and its agents would have letters of introduction to him.[45] Through him, Greeks in Egypt would help the OSS with bureaucratic matters, while the Orthodox Church would provide it with a network of havens throughout the Balkans.[46] To begin with, Amoss and Young would recruit their field agents from the Free Greek Forces, who would be vetted by HIS and the Greek military security service. Yet since HIS was linked with British intelligence, it had a royalist bias. To avoid its operatives having divided loyalties and reporting first to the prime minister or withholding information unfavorable to it, OSS would use only those Greeks recommended by Tsouderos or known by Amoss or Young.[47]

In the long run, Amoss and Young wanted to be independent of HIS. For this reason, they preferred to recruit and train Americans and Greek-Americans. Amoss had already compiled a report on the latter: tracing their immigration histories, occupations, and economic statistics. Moreover, he had induced the Greek Orthodox archbishop in North and South America to conduct a census encompassing all Greeks in America, screening parishioners, with the name, age, skills, languages, and military experience for males of military age, 80 percent of whom were bilingual. Some would form a commando battalion or occupational group for Special Operations engaged in sabotage, raids, and resistance activities behind enemy lines, while others with special skills and education, such as radio operators, mechanics, sailors familiar with Greek waters, pigeon trainers, artists, photographers, and Italian speakers would become SI field agents.[48]

Amoss and Young planned to get agents in by parachute or submarine, expecting the United States to provide planes and the Greeks a submarine. If not, the Greek Desk could use the cheaper and much slower method of caiques, Greek fishing boats with motors and sails, from Izmir and overland trekking from Istanbul. For their lifeline to Cairo, they considered every type of communication, from high-tech radios to secret writing with invisible ink and carrier pigeons but, in the end, settled on radios in the cities and hand-operated wireless sets for those imbedded with the guerrillas in the mountains.[49]

Once inside Greece, SI agents would assess the Greeks' morale and physical condition to discern their continued ability to resist. They would contact the local organizations and guerrilla units that could offer agents asylum and support. Young suggested recruiting agents from relief workers and Greek Red Cross doctors, nurses, and food distribution assistants, since only they could travel. As guides, he recommended recruiting agents from the walking clubs, regional representatives of the Greek Archaeological Service, and workmen from American excavations: they were loyal, intelligent, and inconspicuous. In addition, agents could call upon employees of U.S. businesses, such as Standard Oil, American tobacco companies, and engineering firms, as well as alumni of Anatolia College, the Farm School, and Athens College.

With its head start, OSS considered the Greek Desk a valuable template for other countries' missions. Young foresaw that the greatest challenges would be for SI to maintain independence from the British and to function smoothly with Special Operations, with which it overlapped and was mutually dependent. Young preferred that SI and Special Operations be completely coordinated, but if not they had to be utterly separated with clear parameters for each. SI would establish the networks, nurture the guerrillas who were by far the most successful agents of resistance in Greece, establish liaisons and radio hubs, and guide the operatives who would harass the enemy in tandem with the guerrillas. They would distribute arms, food, and drugs within each group, and conduct special operations, fomenting armed and passive resistance, sabotage, and demolition. Special Operations would reciprocate by transporting SI agents to Greece. But for the time being, Young had to find the right staff.

FIVE

Recruiting the Four Captains

BY THE END OF MAY 1942, Rodney Young had submitted a list of names
to Amoss of people who had lived in the Eastern Mediterranean and knew
its languages. Because the job required loyalty and a delicate balance of
teamwork and self-reliance, he chose archaeologists he knew well, Americans whose linguistic abilities, ingenuity, integrity, and personalities fit the
needs of the Greek Desk. His once and future colleagues hailed from three
principal excavations: the Agora, the University of Cincinnati's dig at Troy,
and the University of Pennsylvania's at Kourion, the only American expedition on Cyprus. All were WASPs, connected with the American School and
elite Ivy League universities. The men were in their early thirties and scram-
bling to find the best way to serve their country, but each had a marriage de-
ferment, so none had been drafted.

At the top of Young's list was James Henry Oliver, Jr. (figs. 2 and 3) who
was already stringing for Meritt. A week after Young signed on to work for
Amoss, he sounded out Oliver following the School's managing committee
meeting. Jim was a gangly, immaculately dressed New Yorker with prema-
turely thinning hair and an "Archaic smile" similar to the pursed-lip grins of
early Greek statues. The Yale man had earned his doctorate in classics and
archaeology and studied in Germany, Rome, and Athens, where he and
Young had dug together for eight years at the Agora. Oliver had also worked
in an oasis in the Western Desert of Egypt, where he had studied inscriptions on the walls of a Greek temple and learned some Egyptian Arabic and
Berber. He taught history and epigraphy at Barnard College and had just

finished the spring term. While deciphering Agora inscriptions at Leslie Shear's country house in New Hampshire, he received Young's offer.

Young promised Oliver an important job with a "whiff of danger" that required his particular strengths and training. Not only would he engage in intellectually stimulating work, but also be with men he liked in an area he knew and loved. Oliver wished "to be absorbed in the war effort." Although the U.S. Naval Reserve had offered him a post in Pensacola, the patriotic archaeologist was still looking for the right "pigeonhole." Espionage and intelligence promised relief from routine and sounded glamorous and fashionable, especially compared to the infantry. Oliver's Egyptian and Berber suited him best to Alexandria, which would handle traffic to and from Greece and work closely with Cairo. Young wanted someone he could count on with sound and mature judgment, who could share the responsibility for the Cairo hub. Oliver fit the bill; he was level-headed, careful, thorough, and detail oriented. Young valued his breadth of interests and infectious enthusiasm. Oliver's interviewer described him as "intelligent, quite reserved, observant, accurate and very painstaking" with "a good deal of nervous energy." His fluency in Modern Greek, Italian, French, and German was also excellent training for cryptography. When Young proposed an assignment in the Near East, Oliver accepted forthwith and reported for duty on June 30.[1]

For Turkey, Young needed at least two agents: one in Istanbul and the other in Izmir. Istanbul was the center of Allied intelligence services in Turkey, and its agent had to cooperate with them and the Turks. He needed to know Greek and Turkish and have contacts in the city. He would be smuggling missions overland through Thrace to the guerrillas and oversea from the Dardanelles and the Gallipoli Peninsula to northern Greek islands and the Thracian coast. Young chose Jerome Sperling. While earning his doctorate in archaeology at the University of Cincinnati with Carl Blegen, the slim, sandy-haired Greek scholar had dug at Troy, where he had acquired an unparalleled knowledge of the strategic straits by tramping through the Troad hunting for archaeological sites. After five seasons of digging, the athletic topographer could read and speak Turkish, Greek, German, French, and Italian. Moreover, he could read Ottoman Turkish in its Arabic script and had collaborated with Turks and coauthored a book in Turkish. He taught archaeology at Yale and had recently led a Yale expedition to southwestern Greece. In May, Young had casually inquired whether Sperling would consider going to the Near East. Although he was married

Fig. 10. Jerome Sperling.
(Courtesy Clio Sperling.)

with two young sons, Sperling came to Washington to be interviewed by Amoss and, after requesting leave from Yale to work "on a special problem," accepted "in a somewhat effervescent state."[2]

The coastal emporium of Izmir, directly opposite Athens, was paramount for making contacts inside Greece and extracting information. Greek refugees fled there because only at Izmir did the railroad come down to Turkey's western coast, and they hoped to ride it to freedom in Syria, Palestine, or Egypt. The Turks frowned on these rogue Greeks and interned thousands in a large camp near the city. Izmir's agent had to protect and debrief refugees to glean fresh intelligence. From them, OSS would get practical details, such as regional dress and proper stamps and seals for the identity papers that agents would need to carry. He would also recruit promising ones to go back in as agents. The Izmir officer required all of Sperling's skills as well as knowledge of Bodrum, the Greek islands, and the Dodecanese. He would have to interact smoothly with Sperling and with the British and Turkish services and supervise a Greek War Relief volunteer of independent means who would secure visas and papers for refugees in return for information.[3] As yet, he left the Izmir post unfilled.[4]

Beirut was next in importance. Its representative would recruit SI field agents from the Free Greek Forces while smuggling operatives into Turkey and refugees from Turkey into Syria. To do this, the candidate needed Greek, Turkish, French, and Arabic as well as a familiarity with the countryside. Stumped, Young left the post blank.

Last was Cyprus whose agent would gather information on Greece and British postwar intentions for the island. John Franklin Daniel III was clearly the man for this job. The Ann Arbor–born professor's son was legendary for his knowledge of Cypriot topography and dialect. Educated at Berkeley and in Germany and well traveled in France, Greece, Egypt, and Turkey, "Pete" had known Young from the Agora. Daniel was the peerless wunderkind of Late Bronze Age languages like undeciphered Cypro-Minoan or ancient Akkadian and Hittite, all of which would be excellent training for cryptography. After over five years of living and excavating on Cyprus, the intense, ruddy-faced archaeologist knew more about the island (its British and Cypriot colleagues, government officials, and residents) than any other American scholar. Daniel taught at the University of Pennsylvania and was the assistant curator of the Mediterranean Section of its University Museum. Egyptologist John A. Wilson, former director of the Oriental Institute of the University of Chicago, trustee of the American Schools of Oriental Research (ASOR), and chief of OSS's Special Information Division, had recommended him to Meritt, and for months Daniel had supplied FNB and William L. Langer, chief of R&A, with the names of useful, well-placed Cypriots and companies, like Harvey Mudd's Los Angeles–based Cyprus Mines Corporation.[5]

For each location, Young suggested archaeology as a cover. Curiously, none of the archaeologists was troubled by Young's suggestion to use his profession as a cover for espionage in the countries where he dug. For Istanbul, Young suggested affiliating with the Byzantine Institute's excavations at Haghia Sophia or Blegen's from Troy, whose finds were stored in Istanbul, or education (using Robert College, the American missionary school on the shores of the Bosphorus whose president, a former COI man, was looking for teachers). For Izmir, Young suggested either commerce (in tobacco or dried fruit) or archaeology, since America had had excavations nearby at Sardis and Colophon. The archaeologists' quick acquiescence is

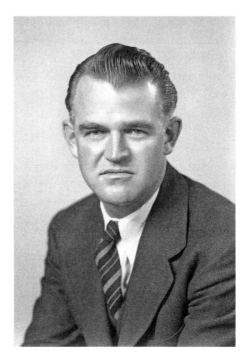

Fig. 11. John Franklin Daniel III.
(Courtesy of the Penn Museum,
film #24137.)

all the more surprising since the well-renowned anthropologist Franz Boas
had publicly excoriated scholars who had done the same in World War I,
charging them with "prostituting science by using it as a cover for their activities as spies." Moreover, military intelligence circles held that, as a cover,
archaeology was suspect, because the British and Germans had so overused
it in the last war. Unless one specialized in field surveying or traveled exten-
sively as part of one's work, just "membership in such an expedition entitled one to a firing squad without the delay of a trial."[6]

Unaware of this, each archaeologist excitedly set about putting his affairs in order. Soon they would leave everything behind for the opportunity
and privilege of using their talents to help their country and Greece.
Though none of the assistant professors signed on to OSS for the money,
intelligence work also represented a welcome jump in salary.[7]

Young contacted Clio Adossides, whom he hoped would join them.
Her world had collapsed. After Costas died, she felt lost and moved into
the hospital where she worked. Each day, the war drew nearer. Alexandria
had been under permanent blackout for two years—ever since Italy had

declared war on England—and many residents had long since devised bomb shelters for themselves, some in ancient Roman cisterns. By mid-June, it seemed like one long ghastly battle in the desert. Air-raid sirens became so regular that Clio could practically set her watch by them, and bombers provoked a sweep of searchlights and barrage of antiaircraft guns, leaving shrapnel clattering in the streets and sparkling explosions in night skies followed by red tracer bullets resembling a "gigantic display of fireworks."[8]

Roughly a month after Costas's death, the pattern changed. On June 21, Tobruk, a port eighty miles west of the Egyptian border, fell to the Germans along with 35,000 captured British, South African, and Indian troops. Although the fortress had withstood a 241-day siege the year before, it did not last twenty-four hours against Rommel, whose army raced eastward into Egypt, covering 100 miles in two days and sparking a run on the banks. Wounded soldiers poured into Clio's hospital and overflowed into others in Palestine. To bolster confidence, Churchill, who was in Washington conferring with FDR, told Congress on June 26 that the British would make a "last ditch" stand at Marsa Matruh. Rommel attacked it the next day. On June 29 when the news came of its capture, British forces sounded the El Alamein alarm: three long blasts, just like at Maleme. Within minutes, the crowded harbor emptied and the Royal Navy's Mediterranean Fleet fled to Beirut, Port Said, and the oil port of Haifa. That evening, bombing raids intensified over the deserted streets of Alexandria.

By June 30, Rommel had advanced another seventy-five miles, stopping just outside El Alamein, the key to Egypt, just seventy miles west of Alexandria. There, motorized vehicles were limited to a thirty-five-mile strip between the sea and a vast impassable depression in the desert. On Wednesday July 1 at three in the morning with the help of a full moon, Rommel attacked. The night before, German bombers had made so many raids on Alexandria that the harbor was full of dead fish from exploded bombs. By breakfast, the train station was choked with evacuees. Everyone was fleeing. Billowing clouds of smoke blossomed over the British Consulate as employees torched their records rather than leave them for Rommel.[9] The doctors evacuated the hospital, dressed their patients as civilians, and embarked on a hospital ship flying a Red Cross flag even though the one before had been sunk. They advised Clio to leave, but even though her best friend left with them, Clio refused. Other people warned her to go to the shelters, but she ignored them also and climbed to her room over the empty hospital where from her bed she could hear the El Alamein guns and the German planes "flying very low over the sea, throwing their bombs on Alexandria." Explosions lit up the night like day, but Clio was tired and did not care. She "had nothing, no one, no house, no money, nothing."[10]

The next morning Clio took the train to Cairo to get Costas's ring and watch, which he had left with Greek friends when he entered British service. Being a nurse, she traveled first class, terrified by "Arabs" climbing onto the roof and clinging to the walls outside her window. Overhead, she could hear the RAF pounding Rommel's troops at El Alamein while trucks and troop carriers obscured by dust clouds streamed toward Cairo from the Western Desert, littered with unburied bodies, past the British encampment that stretched along the desert road. By the time she arrived, a "pure vertigo of panic" had gripped Cairo, and people were running everywhere. As in Alexandria, the air was thick with the smoke of burning files, and a "black snow of charred documents fell from the sky." The rumor circulated that the British were deserting, fearing Rommel would enter the city direct from El Alamein.[11] Women and children evacuating for Palestine, Eritrea (Ethiopia), or South Africa flooded the train station. Then just before curfew descended, Clio was ordered to Suez for evacuation.

On the banks of the Canal, Clio sat stranded without food, waiting for three days to join the hospital ship that was scheduled to pass through. Suddenly, like a mirage, the hospital doctor and the two male nurses appeared and told her that the ship had been rerouted to Haifa. Meanwhile, frenzied evacuees offered bribes for berths on the *Averoff*, which was sailing for South Africa full of Greeks, some of whom would continue on to London. Costas's uncle encouraged her to come to South Africa and start a new life, but she refused. Clio wanted to see what would happen.

The doctor insisted that she evacuate with them to Palestine and commandeered an abandoned car whose keys were still in the ignition. The nurses took another car in case one broke down. Out of the hell of Egypt they passed General Wilson's fallback defenses, crossed the wastes of Sinai, and entered Jerusalem, where they made their way to a monastery in the old city. The men slept inside, while Clio was issued a blanket and joined women on the roof. Later, they continued on to Haifa, where they found her friend, the hospital staff, and patients glistening with sweat at a detention camp. Palestine under British Mandate seemed an insulated, privileged enclave, and Clio breathed a sigh of relief, as she and her friend planted a *musmulla* tree for the refugees.

In Washington, news from Libya and Egypt blasted America's false optimism. Already Japan controlled most of the Pacific. No parades or fireworks marked July 4, 1942. Instead, FDR called for "unceasing toil in the fight for freedom in this dark hour." Meanwhile, Amoss cautioned, "We must . . . use stratagem, and . . . be frugal in civilized scruple. We are in a nasty business, facing a nastier enemy." The Greek Desk moved into Room 1274 of OSS Headquarters in Q Building. Young's team wore a special security badge, acknowledged that all information connected with OSS was "Secret," and swore an oath never to divulge it.[12] Meanwhile, Young met in New York with Leslie Shear, Harry Hill, and Homer Davis of Greek War Relief, Laird Archer of the Near East Foundation, and several Greeks to focus optimistically on postwar reconstruction.[13]

Amoss and Young still had to fill the slots for Izmir and Beirut. Archaeologist John Caskey had volunteered for the air force or Naval Reserve. That spring, the Army Air Force had passed him to Military Intelligence while the Naval Reserve considered him for intelligence in Turkey under the cover of an exchange professor. Jack Caskey was a second-generation classical archaeologist, reared in the shadow of the American School, where his father had served under Bert Hill and his parents had met and married. His father had been curator at the Museum of Fine Arts, Boston, for over thirty years. Jack had learned Greek, German, and French from the cradle, had attended Choate and followed his father and grandfather to Yale. After seven seasons at Troy, he spoke and read Turkish fluently and had made ten trips to Europe, where he had traveled widely, even to Belgrade and Sofia. Caskey had earned his Ph.D. under Carl Blegen at the University of Cincinnati in 1939 and joined his mentor on the faculty, where he taught classics and archaeology. His application took a month to clear COI security, whereupon Amoss flagged it, summoned him to Washington in mid-July, and offered him a job "so exceedingly secret and hush-hush" that it "smacked of intrigue." Thrilled that the OSS required his training and experience, Caskey accepted on the spot.[14]

Then Young contacted Dorothy Hanna Cox. Being female, she did not fit the mold, but Talcott had alerted him that Cox might be game "for work of various kinds." She was single, well-heeled, and well educated—in Switzerland and at Bryn Mawr, the American School, and Columbia, where she had earned a second degree in architecture. Cox had already broken gender barriers as excavation architect and assistant director for Blegen and Hetty Goldman, both of whom praised her drafting skills and powers of

Fig. 12. John Caskey, 1944.
(Courtesy Miriam
Caskey.)

Fig. 13. Dorothy Hanna
"Hiram" Cox. (Courtesy
Mary Schmitz Santen.)

observation. Moreover, Cox seemed suited to working with refugees. She had lived through the 1922–23 exchange of populations when Greece was overrun with refugees, an experience that imbued her with tremendous compassion for the Greeks. Having served as a nurse in France with the American Expeditionary Force during World War I and dug for over twenty years on both sides of the Aegean and Cyprus, Cox was used to toughing it and familiar with relief work. As a result, she spoke fluent Turkish and Greek and flawless French. Cox was fifty, graying, and not robust, but promptly accepted Young's offer and reported to Washington. Although fewer than a third of OSS employees were women and only 20 percent of those received overseas postings (mainly as secretaries, librarians, or file clerks), Amoss nabbed her as reports officer because of her background in relief and her languages, especially French.[15]

Young also contacted Meverette Smith, the relief worker from Salonika. Meanwhile, Meritt recommended Charles Edson, an epigrapher whose knowledge of Macedonia was unparalleled. Edson, a Harvard Ph.D. who taught ancient history at the University of Wisconsin, had spent two years at the American School on behalf of the Prussian Academy of Sciences in Berlin, covering western Macedonia on foot in search of inscriptions. With a 1B draft rating, he was "willing to serve in any capacity and in any part of the world in which he might be thought useful." Young thought Edson "very Harvard," but vouchsafed him with Amoss, who approved him in mid-July. However, while Security cleared Edson, the army drafted him as an infantry private and sent him to boot camp. He would have to wait.[16]

Amoss requested commissions for his men (being a woman, Cox was not eligible). He wrote to the surgeon general that Young was "indispensable," even if the job proved fatal, but the army was adamant and rejected Young, fearing that his wounds might become reinfected. So Young and Cox remained civilians. Within a month, the others were commissioned captains in an advanced OSS unit serving the Cairo headquarters of the United States Armed Forces in the Middle East (USAFIME), and thereafter they were known as "the four captains."[17]

None had any previous experience in espionage, so from July to September they took turns in SI training and manning the office. After three days of screening, medical examinations, and inoculations at the Old Navy Hospital, they left in pairs for Lothian Farm, a sprawling estate in horse country twenty miles southeast of Washington, known by insiders as RTU-11 or "the Farm" and by outsiders as a place where the army tested equipment.[18] Oliver and Sperling were followed by Young and Amoss's assistant, Ronald Pearce; Caskey and Daniel, and finally Cox. For four weeks they lived without surnames, attending informal lectures from dawn to late at night in cohorts of fifteen, after which they were invited to parties to see if they would drop their guard. The spying smorgasbord entailed information on cover, subversive warfare, and security as well as organizing field desks. They learned how to report communications, naval, and air intelligence; identify German army and air ordnance and vehicles; interpret psychological and police reports; and recruit and handle agents in the field. They crammed army organization, codes, communications, counterintelligence, interrogation techniques, and police methods. They drew and interpreted maps, transposed letters in a unique cipher that they memorized in verse so as to be free of incriminating evidence, and composed ordinary letters carrying enciphered messages. They learned how to shoot a gun, engage in close combat, and defend themselves through lying and bribery, use invisible inks, and install listening devices. Meanwhile, they watched movies, embarked on "missions" to Philadelphia and Baltimore, and visited Aberdeen Proving Grounds (where the army tested munitions) to identify U.S. military equipment.[19]

At the end of each session, Dr. Kenneth Baker, the psychologist who directed OSS Schools and Training, evaluated each prospective agent's personality to discern his or her ability to withstand stress, what activities best suited him, and whether he could perform what was expected of him. Baker recommended Young "without reservation. . . . he will turn in a commendable performance . . . no matter what task you assign to him. He is thoroughly sold on his job." An independent evaluator wrote, "A good man with a splendid background for this work. He ranks with the best we have had in general all-around ability. His familiarity with his territory is exceptional, and he has the contacts . . . he is definitely grade A." Baker also recommended Cox "without qualification" and praised "her loyalty, cooperation, and all-around reliability." She was "intelligent, agreeable, easily teachable, and should be very useful." She had demonstrated her capacity to adjust to unforeseen circumstances by coping with the unsatisfactory living accommodations. She was "very persistent and devoted to duty," "a natural for the project to which she [had] been assigned," and would produce "careful and painstaking work." Like the best spies, Cox was "quiet and nondescript" and did not draw attention to herself. Meticulous in her dress and her work, the cranky spinster admired order and precision. Men worked well with her, accepted her on an equal footing, and respected her position and judgment, unlike other women whom Baker had encountered. Other evaluators wrote that her "work at the school compares favorably with that of most of our good men students," but her atrocious spelling might affect her ciphers.[20]

That this process was not merely a rubber stamp is indicated by less positive evaluations. Baker ranked Caskey "well among the top men," yet noticed "a natural hesitancy . . . to engage in certain operations until he is absolutely sure of himself," adding "his general lack of aggression is not lack of physical courage." Another evaluator wrote that Caskey "seemed to be too concerned with what he should do or say if and when he was caught by the enemy." Regarding Sperling, Baker wrote that "it is difficult to predict how useful Jerome will be in the field because his operation is going to be seriously hindered by the fact that he is overly tense and serious in an attempt to be profound and cautious. . . . This trait produces a slowness and deliberateness . . . [that] gives Jerome away even to the most casual observer." He was sure to be exposed by "the aura of mystery which appears to surround everything he does . . . Jerome will very soon come under suspicion because of this secretive and overly cautious way he has of doing even the most commonplace things." At the same time, he noted that Sperling was "likeable . . . both cooperative and capable of individualized effort . . . unusually intelligent." Of Sperling, the other evaluator wrote, "studious and . . . cautious. . . . A worrier—will lay all his plans with the greatest of care, and will really work hard . . . will approach his job with the attitude of a scientist."[21]

Sperling had good reason to fear since the entry of enemy spies into neutral territories, like Turkey, was illegal. To resist attempts to break them under interrogation, Caskey and Sperling had to be able to "live their covers," shields on which depended their security and success. That summer, they abandoned archaeology and scrambled for semiovert government posts, such as consular officials; naval, military, and commercial attachés or observers; Lend-Lease officials, or representatives of the U.S. Treasury and Agriculture departments. They hoped to be special advisors or assistant military attachés for Laurence Steinhardt, the U.S. minister to Turkey, but Sperling was placed under OWI and Caskey under Lend-Lease, requiring him to cram U.S.-Turkish commerce.[22] The United States channeled over 10 percent of American aid to Greece through Greek War Relief, so Cox chose it as her cover and trained for ten weeks under Homer Davis at their Fifth Avenue office.[23]

In Allied territory—Cyprus, Syria, Lebanon, and Egypt—conditions differed. Young (who was going to Cairo) wanted a position with the *Baltimore Sun*, but the editor rejected him lest he jeopardize legitimate journalists in the field. Those going to Cyprus and Alexandria were to be army officers serving as military observers, but this ruse did not work for Cyprus because it had no U.S. consulate. So Daniel—who insisted upon using expedition property and securing an excavation permit—would have to communicate through archaeological channels rather than a diplomatic pouch. Young suggested that his OSS documents might be "casually inserted among the conventionally locked records and data of the University of Pennsylvania excavations" and paid through Penn.[24]

While they sorted out cover, Britain's struggle against Rommel resulted in a stalemate. A breathing space of several months followed while life settled back to a semblance of normalcy, and most of the British returned and referred to the July 1 panic as "Ash Wednesday" or "the Flap." In spite of this, occasional German planes bombed Cairo by moonlight, although as an open city it had immunity under international law. U.S. Army General Lewis Brereton, who had arrived in late June, prepared to deploy ground forces in the Western Desert, but in fact contributed only bombers. Then General Bernard Montgomery took command of the British army in North Africa, and the eventual showdown between him and Rommel occurred under a full moon in late October, two years after Mussolini's invasion of Greece. For eleven days, the outcome hung in the balance until, between November 3 and 4, Rommel retreated. Within a week, General Brereton became USAFIME theatre commander and took over the Ninth Air Force, whose mission was to gain air superiority, cut Rommel's supply lines, and support Allied ground troops. General George S. Patton and the American army landed near Casablanca for the Allied invasion of North Africa, Operation Torch, whose goal was to rid North Africa of Axis forces, a prerequisite for invading southern Europe. Finally on November 15, 1942, British church bells, silent for three years, rang out the victory of El Alamein. As the British struggled west to join the Americans, the Allies set up Allied Forces Headquarters (AFHQ) at Algiers under General Dwight D. Eisenhower.

In Greece, SOE commandos had planned to cut Rommel's supply lines using the anticommunist republican resistance group EDES. Demolition expert Brigadier General Eddie Myers and twenty-four-year-old classicist Christopher Woodhouse had parachuted into Greece in October but got lost trying to find the guerrillas. EAM/ELAS (a rival group of communists and socialists formed the previous autumn) learned of the plan through

SOE contact General Euripides Bakirdzis ("Prometheus" in Salonika) and insisted on participating. On November 25, the Anglo-Greek team attacked and blew up the Gorgopotamos Bridge near Thermopylae, disrupting all north-south rail transport. Although they were too late to influence El Alamein, the successful sabotage galvanized Allied morale and strengthened both guerrilla factions.[25] Buoyed by the spectacular result, the British decided to leave their agents in the mountains embedded with the guerrillas as the British military mission in order to undertake additional sabotage.

Meanwhile, Clio put the past behind her and embraced the future. Between the two El Alamein battles, friends invited her to live with them in Cairo. Once there, she got a job with Greek intelligence through Kanellopoulos. Clio was commissioned a lieutenant in the Royal Hellenic Air Force and worked in the section devoted to general, military, and political intelligence, where her knowledge of German and Morse code, acquired for flying in the Berlin Olympics, made her valuable.[26] Around her, royalist officers handled liaison with Allied secret services for escapes and contact within enemy-occupied territory. Different branches selected personnel and caique crews for secret action and controlled counterespionage, investigations, and blacklists and monitored radio broadcasts in Greek.[27]

Clio blossomed in Cairo. Beneath a thin British veneer, the Arab metropolis swarmed with life. Unlike blacked-out Alexandria, Cairo was an exotic paradise and Shepheard's Hotel like a movie set, teeming with rich refugees, war correspondents in khaki chic, and officers from occupied France, Greece, Yugoslavia, and Poland. Thousands of British, Australian, Indian, South African, and Canadian troops, and some Americans, were quartered in and around the city. Hundreds of military cars and vehicles jammed streets filled with white-robed Bedouins sporting crimson fezzes. Clio moved to the Anglo-Swiss Pension, which housed a congenial group of British officers and Wrens (British female naval officers) who serenaded each other every Sunday on a Leningrad piano on the roof. Clio's balcony faced a cloister where nuns scurried to vespers while towering masts of feluccas on the Nile floated above the gardens. Every morning before breakfast, she swam at the English Sporting Club on Gezira Island. Then she worked from seven till two and returned for a swim and lunch. After siesta, she attended chamber music recitals or took lessons from an English poet. She counted Lawrence Durrell, of the British Information Office in Alexandria, a friend.[28] Every fortnight, she could fly gratis to Jerusalem in order to visit Costas's grave and stay at the glamorous King David Hotel. But often

Fig. 14. Clio in Giza. (Courtesy Clio Sperling.)

she preferred to explore Cairo, enjoying the minarets overlooking the vast city to the desert, the brown Nile and its emerald delta. A young Greek soldier, whom she had met in Albania, was serving with the American army and gave her a gun to protect herself. At night, the Nile blazed from the glittering clubs and *thés dansants,* and Clio went out at all hours.[29] Thus, began "two or three perfect years."[30]

In Washington, Meritt soared through the ranks of FNB, but the other archaeologists were caught in the cross fire between OSS and the military.[31] For three precious months, they remained stuck at their desks, meeting members of Donovan's inner circle: David Bruce, SI chief; General John Magruder, just back from China; Lt. Col. Florimund Duke, chief of Southeast Europe SI; and Colonel Ellery Huntington, Donovan's close friend and Special Operations chief.[32]

In November, Sperling sketched plans for Special Operations in Greece and the Balkans. Amoss, Duke, MacFarland, Young, and Sperling discussed a "South East European Undertaking." From a field headquarters in Cairo, it aimed to complement work by other allies to secure intelligence, destroy or demoralize the Axis invaders, encourage inhabitants' will to resist, lay a basis for subversive operations in neutral and allied territory, and prepare for zero hour. They would continue these undercover activities for at least six months after the end of the war or until canceled by the U.S. government. British experience showed that espionage was best performed by residents of the countries in question, and so they decided to keep American personnel in an executive capacity and not have them crossing in and out of Axis territory. Relief continued to be an important part of the plan for Greek operations.

Although the geographic desks were originally conceived as a unity, in the autumn of 1942 they were separated into SI and Special Operations so that whichever got going first could get to work. "Heads of the geographic desks would be able to participate in both SI and Special Operations, but mention of the dual function was to be omitted." The archaeologists, who controlled these bases, would be considered SI with any subversive functions they might acquire granted only on the basis of oral or private understandings. They constituted the lowest link in the chain of command with a knowledge of SI and Special Operations missions. It was also agreed that, although Istanbul would fall under Cairo, it would enjoy quasi-independence.[33]

While OSS stalled, Amoss launched the Greek Irregular Project (GIP). The top secret operation had a minimal paper trail so it could never be traceable to the OSS since the "methods to be used and the persons employed could not possibly be acknowledged officially or passed through security." Amoss introduced the archaeologists to Colonel Demetrios Xenos, Maniadakis's former director of sabotage and secret intelligence for combined military operations, whom the U.S. Army approved to recruit and train a Greek-American battalion. Through his cover as chief of Alien Control, Xenos became the UN's Greek intelligence liaison and second to Theofanides in the GIP.[34] Officially sponsored by Theofanides and the Greek government-in-exile and approved by Donovan, the GIP enlisted diaspora Greeks "to collect data and information" and engage in "espionage and underground activities" that the U.S. government funded through the National City Bank of New York at roughly $10,000 per month. One of these was Theofanides' former employer, Prodromos Bodosakis-Athenasides, an Asian Minor Greek who had made a fortune in the arms industry and had considerable ties with Metaxas' government and the German munitions manufacturers. Amoss's liaison Ronald Pearce would establish agencies in the most useful Greek centers, approve recruitment, and supervise operations. Leon Melas, aka L. C. Miles, would manage the New York office, and FNB undercover men, including AHEPA president George Vournas (fig. 18), would funnel him information.[35]

In GIP's global underground, Greeks worked with Greeks. A field agent established European information channels and got Axis intelligence, while Greek-Americans from New York, Chicago, and San Francisco operated as cutouts, or undercover men abroad, interviewing refugees for information from Axis Europe via the "Greek grapevine."[36] GIP agents reported German reprisals, increased Axis presence in the Cyclades, Greek army officers hiding on Mt. Taygetus in the southern Peloponnese, Jews paying to escape the occupation, epidemics of typhus and yellow fever, and the sabotage at Gorgopotamos. They reported on the anticommunist EDES, the leftist EAM/ELAS, and the Evvia guerrillas who worked with them. Chief among them was Melas's cousin, HIS Captain Alexander Melas (Heinrich Schliemann's grandson), who worked with a band of Epirot guerrillas known as the "American Legion." Melas advised on bombing objectives in Greece and on Crete for General Brereton of the Ninth Air Force in Cairo.[37]

The GIP worked with RHN Captain Athenasios Zangas of HIS, who built up, operated, and controlled an intelligence network in Athens, an "underground railroad" to move men and mail from Khalkidiki to Salonika, and a caique service in which he partnered with Greeks at the British consulate in Izmir. Zangas's boat left Turkey for Piraeus weekly with blackmarket produce, hiding GIP ammunition and arms for resistance groups from whom Zangas got information on Greek and British plans in Greece and documented the rise of Communists on the mainland. The Italian authorities took the butter, cheese, olives, and other food and helped Amoss's men unload the grenades, bombs, and assorted side arms in broad daylight. The boat returned with British veterans and Greek refugees.[38]

Although Amoss had great hopes for the GIP, Young remained skeptical about an intelligence operation American in name and financing but under Greek control. To be successful, the GIP had to rely on the Greek government-in-exile, but it was becoming clear that Amoss's confidence in it was misplaced, as FNB reported the Greeks' increasing ambivalence if not opposition to the king and his government, and Tsouderos could not deliver.[39]

Holding the archaeologists back damaged their morale. In November, they learned that Anastas Adossides had died, and the Germans had arrested Gene Vanderpool and interned him in a Bavarian concentration camp.[40] AIA trustees met at the Metropolitan Museum of Art in New York, where Dinsmoor laid plans for the protection of monuments, works of art, and architectural remains of Europe and Africa exposed to the devastation of war and recommended the establishment of American archaeological schools in Turkey and Egypt.[41] Before the end of the year, Meritt prophesied that postwar Athens would resemble the nineteenth century with no tools, equipment, or labor, and they would have to wait years to excavate again. Discouraged, he returned to Princeton to prepare a Civil Affairs Handbook for Greece for R&A. Carl Blegen succeeded him at the FNB Chancery, and Alison Frantz (who had transferred from R&A and replaced Lucy Talcott) was promoted to senior political analyst. As Harvard archaeologist Sterling Dow arrived to take over the Greek Desk's gloomy Washington office, his colleagues tried to stay motivated.[42]

Military men who disliked having civilians at the heart of wartime planning and operations besieged OSS. Donovan sparred with Military Intelligence, and rivalries paralyzed OSS. Finally, in mid-December the Joint Chiefs of Staff authorized "expert advisors" to consult with SOE and MI-6 on SI and Special Operations in the Middle East. But precious time had been lost, and only Cox reached Cairo in 1942.[43]

SIX

"Playing Ball" and Striking Out with the British

BY JANUARY 1943, the playing field had changed. More than two years had passed since the world focused on Greece's heroic stand against the Axis. Before El Alamein, Donovan had seemed willing to grant anything and everything Amoss wanted, but after the invasion of North Africa, America's priorities lay elsewhere.

Churchill and Roosevelt met at Casablanca and decided to intensify Allied operations in the Mediterranean. Pressured by Stalin to open a western front, they disagreed on where to invest their effort. Churchill wished to gain access to Turkey's massive mobilized army, open a new supply route to Russian allies, and eliminate the costly treks through the Arctic and the Persian Gulf. He proposed to invade Greece and the Balkans via Turkey and the Dodecanese, all within the British-controlled Middle East theater of operations. Roosevelt and Eisenhower, however, preferred to attack in the west, keeping the U.S. troops already in North Africa in American hands and away from the eastern Mediterranean. The Americans prevailed, and the die was cast for an invasion of Sicily. Yet Churchill remained undaunted. Perhaps to redeem his disasters in Gallipoli and Greece, he secretly traveled to Adana, Turkey's fifth largest city, where, in a private train car, he and General Wilson tried to lure the Turkish president to the Allies' side. Even when Ismet Inönü hedged his bets and would not budge, Churchill refused to give up, a tenacity that would have grave repercussions later that year.[1]

The staff of the Greek Desk labored in the dark. Unaware of changes in

Allied strategy, Amoss flew to London to coordinate the Allied invasion of Greece. Amid barrage balloons and antiaircraft crowbar showers, he and Colonel Huntington met with the Tsouderos and the Greek king.

Amoss encouraged the king to move to Cairo within sixty days to be near his troops, since the longer he lingered in England, the more he lost credibility with the Greeks. Unaware that the move to Egypt was Amoss's idea, the British gave the king permission to leave, but warned him against notifying the Yanks. British cooperation with the Americans had decreased along with the German threat to Cairo, and in 1943 they regarded their ties with their "cousins" as more "familial than operational."[2]

They planned three separate attacks: an overland invasion across Turkey and Thrace to Bulgaria and Rumania, a secondary action through Italy, and a third through Greece. For the latter, Tsouderos, being a Cretan, promised to orchestrate a Cretan revolt simultaneous with a sabotage mission organized by Amoss. After an Allied aerial and surface invasion, the Greek government would return to Greece. But while they plotted in London, they learned of problems in the Greek alliance with SOE. Kanellopoulos's chief agent, Colonel Ioannis Tsigantes, had been working with SOE when someone betrayed him. Double-crossed in Athens, he was assassinated by Italian occupation police, who subsequently purged other resistance leaders. Alex Melas escaped by going into hiding, but others were arrested and executed. The Greek caique service collapsed, and those who had worked with SOE defected to Amoss and the GIP.[3]

Within British ranks opinions diverged on how to proceed in Greece. The Foreign Office began to throw its weight behind the anticommunist EDES guerrillas and withdraw backing from the growing ranks of leftist EAM/ELAS with whom a marriage of convenience grew less appealing.[4] Their political agendas clashed for EAM/ELAS wanted to liberate Greece, achieve independence, and create a provisional postwar government that could elect an assembly and determine the form of the constitution, rather than submit to the British and restore the king. Independently, the British Military Mission (BMM) recommended that the Greek king agree to a plebiscite before returning. The Foreign Office, refusing to believe that the king was so unpopular, pronounced the advice rash and widened the gap between Churchill, Wilson, and SOE.

In early February, Amoss flew to Cairo. There OSS would handle all intelligence from the occupied countries of southeast Europe and the Middle East, a region encompassing the eastern coast of Italy to the western boundary of India and from Libya to Eritrea, roughly equivalent to the British Middle East theater. Less than a year earlier, Colonel Huntington had set up an American radio station there and left Lt. Turner McBaine to organize communications as liaison officer with the British, dealing with MI-6 and HIS. General Brereton, whose Ninth Air Force pilots were responsible for bombing the Athens and Salonika air bases, was commanding officer.[5] He gave Huntington permission to develop OSS Cairo on February 15, and Col. C. B. Guenther arrived to take charge.

Stalin's recent victory over the Germans at Stalingrad sounded a wake-up call in Washington and London. Months earlier, Amoss had portrayed Eastern Europe as "a natural empire" of occupied countries where the United States might build an espionage system bordering Russia from Poland to the Balkans and Turkey. Concerned about America's postwar policy in the Balkans, Amoss, as OSS chief of southeast Europe operations, volunteered to use the GIP as a stay-behind network in Central and Eastern Europe providing political intelligence on Stalin and economic information not available to the State Department. Greece, the most southerly country in the region, could serve as a deterrent to Soviet postwar expansion. "The presence of Allied forces in Southeastern Europe might serve as a check on possible Russian moves after the collapse of Germany. A Balkan front would serve at the same time as a prop and check to Russia."[6]

While the archaeologists waited in Washington, Amoss used his GIP network to gather intelligence on secret Greek cabinet meetings and subversive army activities.[7] Unbeknownst to the Greek king or Tsouderos, Amoss had hired the chief of Secret Criminal Police in Egypt and, through a semisecret servants' guild, got access to files on every foreigner who passed through Egypt, including head of the SOE Cairo, Lord Glenconner. The chief could perform search and seizure, get intelligence on Axis prisoners, and have anyone tailed by Arab boys. By March, Amoss segued into investigating smuggling and spying in Jerusalem and amassed an arsenal of pistols, ammunition, submachine guns, and dynamite.[8]

By then the Washington log jam had begun to break. To avoid U-boats in the Atlantic, Captain Jack Caskey shipped out from San Francisco in mid-February and reached Egypt, via Australia and India, in a month and a half.[9] Three weeks after Caskey departed, a blacked-out troop ship steamed past the Florida Keys and entered the sub-infested Atlantic zigzagging south to Accra and hugging the coast of Africa to the Cape of Good Hope. On it were Rodney Young, Pete Daniel, Jerry Sperling, and Jim Oliver, although the archaeologists were advised not to travel conspicuously as a group or at the same time.[10] While the archaeologists were at sea, the Greek king and prime minister returned to Egypt, igniting insurrection among republicans in the Greek army, who took over several brigades in the Alexandrian barracks, demanding the removal of fascist officers and protesting the return of the king before elections. As a result of the British arrest and internment of thousands of Greek soldiers, Kanellopoulos resigned. The Greek violence confirmed British resolve to support the unconditional return of the king. But it shocked and bewildered the U.S. State Department, which fumbled its response. After a month, the archaeologists docked at Capetown and sought out Lincoln MacVeagh, then serving as U.S. minister to South Africa, who briefed them on current events in Egypt. Then Sperling flew north via Nairobia and Khartoum, and Young, Daniel, and Oliver journeyed up the east coast of Africa on a munitions ship, wondering what they would find in Cairo.

The government-in-exile regrouped. Tsouderos, who opposed the immediate return of the king after liberation, signed a secret manifesto demanding a plebiscite. Then he appointed several liberal ministers, one of whom was Sophocles Venizelos, the son of the great statesman who had been living in New York.[11] OSS agent Alexander (Alekko) Georgiades was assigned to Venizelos. Months earlier, the son-in-law of the owner of the *Washington Post* had spotted the naturalized Greek in a South Dakota army camp and recommended the air force private for the Greek Desk. As a result, Georgiades was pulled out of line, given a gun and a sealed envelope, and told to report to Washington. There Young met him and pronounced the correct password, whereupon Georgiades handed over the envelope and was taken to Q Building in a chauffeur-driven limousine. Then Sterling Dow sent Georgiades to be trained and ordered him to accompany Venizelos to Cairo. Meanwhile, Amoss worked behind the scenes to ensure that the new cabinet would include Theofanides, the backbone of the GIP.[12]

As a result of the recent troubles, Amoss urged Donovan to observe caution with their British counterparts. OSS must not only collect its own political intelligence, but also actively spy on its British allies, "whose collateral interests [did] not entirely parallel" those of Washington.[13] SOE regarded sabotage as its prerogative and was determined to control OSS Special Operations. But Huntington and Guenther advised Donovan on March 28 that SI must be kept independent.[14]

That day Caskey showed up in Cairo. OSS Cairo. still awaiting approval by the Joint Chiefs of Staff, was crammed into two ground floor rooms at the American Consulate. McBaine was SI chief and Amoss the executive officer and deputy director of operations.[15] Amoss sized up Caskey as "a lone wolf, . . . temperamentally reserved and scholarly, rather than a man of action." After briefing him, Amoss acknowledged that Caskey's patience, tenacity, and analytical mind suited him best for military intelligence and the processing and evaluating of intelligence as an attaché. "Caskey has been somewhat miscast as the head of an operating organization. He is a scholar and a diplomat, a reserved person who gets along well with people because he abhors wrangling, but is primarily more interested in understanding than doing." Although Caskey lacked "great drive" and "preferred not to" assume larger responsibilities, Amoss believed him capable of doing so. As events unfolded, Caskey was thrust into circumstances that pushed him to snap judgments and heroic actions.[16]

Caskey, a Boston Red Sox fan, looked forward to "playing ball" with the British. This was a British theater, and he had to play by their rules. Exploring pyramids and souks, Caskey waited in vain for the other archaeologists. Then he cleared his travel plans and secured a jeep. On April 15 Caskey mounted his "chariot" for Turkey, like pharaoh setting off to fight the Hittites.[17] Armed with letters of introduction, Caskey crossed the Suez Canal and "bowled along" through the white sand wastes of the Sinai, captivated by the historic landscape. He admired World War I General Allenby, who studied the Bible like a history book and won his greatest battles following the routes of earlier conquerors. Near the frontier police post at Asluj, where Allenby had led the cavalry charge against the Ottomans, Caskey picked up an English major whose corps was preparing for a special operation. He spent the night in Gaza royally entertained by the Englishman with the "personal service of a batman, excellent food and drink, and a genuine binge." The camp's intelligence officer gave him a British military map of Palestine with routes were color-coded in red, yellow, blue, and green. Although asked to destroy it after use, Caskey kept it for army intelligence.[18]

"Galloping through the Middle East," Caskey watched for sites and antiquities along the way. He entered the Holy Land through the Negev, passed Beersheba, and ascended to Jerusalem past the Mount of Olives. Skirting the walls of the Old City, he passed the Jaffa Gate and stopped at the American School of Oriental Research, where the director, archaeologist rabbi Nelson Glueck, an old friend and Cincinnati alumnus, gave him tea, dinner, and a bed for the night. Since 1930, Glueck had been surveying the Transjordan and had made a reputation by discovering King Solomon's mines north of Aqaba. Early on, John Wilson had recruited Glueck for Near East SI. For over a year, Glueck used survey archaeology as his cover, mapping the Negev and Transjordan from Aqaba to Irbid while he created an Arab-American intelligence network.

Caskey, looking very "GI," left Jerusalem. He passed British military establishments in the Judaean Hills, the supply depot for the entire Middle East theater. At Tel Aviv he headed north along the Via Maris, the coastal highway of pharaohs' armies, where to the east the recently fortified bastion of Mt. Carmel protected Haifa's oil refineries. Everywhere building projects revealed new sites. Barely pausing at the chalk promontory marking the Lebanese border, Caskey visited the Phoenician sites of Tyre and Sidon at sunset before speeding through the dark to Beirut. At the bar of the fashionable Hotel Normandie, Caskey met officers from British Royal Navy who welcomed him and pledged their support. Over drinks, W. A. (Sandy) Campbell, a friend of Young's from Princeton who dug at Antioch and Seleucia and handled OSS in Alexandretta, warned Caskey that the Turkish border was thick with British soldiers.[19]

Two days later, Caskey headed east, threading the pass through the snow-capped Lebanon Mountains and descending to the Beqaa Valley, where he had "a brief run around the ruins" of the gargantuan Roman temples at Baalbek before dining at the British officers' club. In the valley Caskey encountered hundreds of trucks carrying massive guns toward Beirut, British military bases, RAF and Royal Engineers installations, and internment camps brimming with Greek refugees. From Baalbek, he followed the Orontes River north, passing Krak des Chevaliers and a monumental tell that loomed over a medieval city of cobbled alleys and towering wooden water wheels. Due east across the desert, Caskey's professor had excavated on the banks of the Euphrates. Further north, Rameses II had faced the Hittites, and Alexander had bested the Persians. But Caskey's route led to Aleppo, so he headed past camel-colored hills for the crusader fortress crowning the tell that commanded the plain between the Orontes and Euphrates Rivers.[20] He checked into the Baron Hotel, whose guestbook read like a who's who of English archaeologists and spies—Gertrude Bell, Max Mallowan, Agatha Christie, T. E. Lawrence, and Sir Leonard Woolley. The following day, the U.S. consul provided lunch and a tour of a mosque containing remains of the Roman temple upon which St. Helena, the mother of

Constantine, had built a church marking the tomb of John the Baptist's father. Caskey had to forgo Woolley's and Lawrence's sites and Campbell's excavations at Antioch, for this was the end of site-seeing.

Caskey shed his uniform and jeep and prepared to leave the safety of the British zone.[21] He continued north on the Baghdad Railway. At the Turkish border, a menacing inspector pulled him off the train for an expired visa and vowed to return him to Syria. Since his own mother had once been imprisoned in Istanbul on the same ruse, Caskey knew that such threats were not unusual. Yet the next day, the Turks stamped his passport and let him proceed. He took the afternoon train to Adana, which straddled the major east-west road through malarial plains once held by the Hittites. After sniffing around for antiquities, Caskey caught the Taurus Express, the slow train for Ankara that jerked and snorted along a stretch of track laid by the Germans in time to supply their Ottoman allies fighting the British over Iraq oil fields in World War I. At dusk the train climbed through the snowy Taurus Mountains at the Cilician Gates and passed within yards of the route once trod by the Persian army, Alexander the Great, St. Paul, and the caravans of the First Crusade. During the twenty-six-hour ride, Caskey met American teachers from Robert College who had been on "holiday" (with X-2) in Palestine and Syria and an Englishman inspecting army depots who told him that Turkey was "fairly *stiff* with British . . . doing various jobs under thin cover."[22]

The British "octopus" had drawn on a wellspring of experience not only from World War I, but also the centuries-old Levantine community of British nationals fluent in Turkish and Greek (still sizable and well placed in shipping, trade, and banking) and familiar with the coasts and offshore islands from years of yachting. Under Major General Allan Arnold, the military attaché, and Colonel Harold Gibson of MI-6, they formed the backbone of the Inter-Service Balkan Intelligence Center at Pera House. In this massive former embassy in Istanbul, they coordinated British espionage, monitoring Germans near the Rumanian oil fields and Russian designs on the Turkish straits and British oil fields in Mesopotamia. Meanwhile, British intelligence officers, identified as archivists, assistant military attachés, and information officers, also crammed the British embassy in Ankara.

Caskey arrived in the Turkish capital on April 24. At the U.S. legation's Easter egg hunt the next day, he met staffers and downed American fliers who had traded their planes for freedom of movement. The military attaché billeted Caskey at his flat, an unofficial boardinghouse for migratory attachés and transients.[23] After two days, Caskey revealed himself to his Lend-Lease boss; Lieutenant Commander George Miles, assistant naval attaché (ONI); and the Seager brothers: Cedric, U.S. Air Force lieutenant and assistant military attaché in Istanbul, and Ewart, who worked in Ankara.[24] Born in Istanbul, the Seagers were Levantine Englishmen fluent in Turkish and Greek who had climbed most of the mountains in the Balkans and walked across Anatolia from the Mediterranean to the Caucasus. They left Turkey in 1935, when laws forced foreigners out unless they took Turkish citizenship. After marrying American sisters, they became U.S. citizens. Amoss had recruited Cedric to collect military intelligence and plan Special Operations for Central Europe, and Caskey would collaborate with Ewart.[25]

Caskey soon left for Istanbul and Izmir. He shared a first-class sleeper with a courier who was transporting the U.S. diplomatic pouch. On the morning of May 1, the Anatolia Express pulled into Haydar Pasha Station on the Asian shore of the Bosphorus. As Caskey crossed the historic waterway, the silhouetted domes and minarets of Haghia Sophia and Sultan Ahmet were just emerging on the horizon from the morning haze. On the European side, Caskey hailed a cab for Tokatlyan's Hotel in the foreign enclave of Pera. He called on Burton Berry, the recently arrived U.S. consul general—a former Standard Oil man who had bounced around U.S. legations from Bucharest to Athens to Rome in 1941 and now led the State Department's Balkan Reporting Unit, which processed intelligence from Greece's northern neighbors. First on Caskey's agenda was meeting Lanning "Packy" MacFarland, Donovan's World War I friend and chief of OSS Istanbul, but the Chicago banker was in Cairo "supervising" developments in Yugoslavia, his true area of expertise.[26] Caskey needed 225 pounds of gold to commence operations. It had to be obtained on the black market, as bank accounts were closely watched. So Berry and vice consul Richard Gnade "asked no questions" and, thanks to a helpful attaché, by four that afternoon, Caskey got the gold. With it, he slipped out through the Sea of Marmara, where he noted fifteen Danube barges suspiciously hugging Prinkipos Island.[27]

Caskey reached in Izmir on May 3 and reconnoitered. Worried that the United States had "arrived on the scene far too late," he began laying the groundwork for a base and building bridges with other services[28] Caskey knew that he had to get "a . . . green light from the Turks," who could and would block any major enterprise that they had not sanctioned. He also required the cooperation and backing of British intelligence, which was firmly established, well organized, and in full control. In Izmir alone, their personnel exceeded eighty with competing branches coexisting uneasily in the annex of the British consulate, adjacent to the Anglican church in the European section known as Alsanjak or the "Point."[29]

Caskey's counterpart, the linchpin of the British operation, was Nöel Rees, known as "Hadzis"—an impeccable Englishman in gray flannels and Royal Harwich Yacht Club blazer who had been born into the Levantine community of Boudjah near Izmir. His family had resided there for generations, racing yachts in the bay and horses at the hippodrome. From shipping offices in Izmir, Alexandria, and England, they had supplied Lord Nelson's fleet in the Battle of the Nile and British troops in the Crimea and World War I. Afterward, they moved their operations to Alexandria, where Nöel grew up, married a Greek, and managed the business. He worked well with Greeks and spoke Greek fluently, but no Turkish. Connected socially with the Greek crown prince, he was a royalist, ready to return the king to the throne whether the people wanted him or not.[30] When war broke out, Rees became British consul on Chios—supplying military and naval intelligence on the Italians in the Dodecanese and along the Turkish coast. After the Germans occupied the island, he and his wife and daughter fled to Turkey in a caique and landed at the end of the Karaburun Peninsula. Thereafter, he occupied his family's baronial house surrounded by vineyards and decorated with trophies of the hunt—antlers, stuffed animals, and a bear that held a tray for visitors' cards. He commuted by train or Rolls Royce to Izmir, where he became British vice consul and head of MI-6, controlling a large staff of Levantines from the first floor of the British consulate. Prominent Greek refugees, such as British consular officers of Samos and Mytilene (Lesbos), and Rees's former Chiot employees, worked for him, interviewing refugees, briefing and debriefing caique captains, and administering his operations.

Rees and Michael Parish, a British escapee from the Battle of Crete who recuperated with him in 1941, hatched the idea of operating a rescue service (MI-9) to get British evacuees from occupied Greece to Cyprus and Alexandria via Turkey. To do so, Parish commandeered a fleet of yachts and caiques purloined by the British Royal Navy. For a safe haven, Rees and Parish convinced the Turks to make the Karaburun Peninsula off-limits to all but the British and established their secret base at Cheshme three hours west of Izmir, where Rees himself had landed in 1941 (see map 2). Turkey's territorial waters extended up to three miles off shore, roughly half the distance to Chios, the nearest Greek island. For over a year with the help of

Captain Zangas of HIS (through whom the GIP exchanged arms for intelligence), Rees and Parish rescued their countrymen and four-fifths of the 15,000 Greeks of military age who escaped after December 1941.[31] Their service came to a halt, however, in March 1943 when two Nazi spies posing as refugees alerted the Germans, who pressured the Turks to shut down the clandestine port. Afterward, Rees sacked Zangas.[32] Lest General Brereton lose the intelligence chains that had guided the bombers, Amoss ordered GIP files transferred from the British Consulate to H. Lanning Williams, ONI agent and shipping advisor at the U.S. consulate, and planned to revamp Zangas's service for OSS.[33]

Eventually, the Turks allowed the British to resume operations on a smaller scale. Henceforth, all boats had to be cleared with the Milli Emniyet, Turkey's secret police, security, counterespionage, and military intelligence service. The Emniyet performed most of the country's intelligence tasks, maintained files on all foreign residents and tourists through *tezkeres* (residence permits), and monitored strategic coastal areas. While performing their other duties, its army of agents and port workers, train porters and conductors, concierges and bellhops, waiters and clerks, and translators watched for foreign spies.

Rees moved the Cheshme operation to the fjord of Khioste, conveniently near his seaside villa within the 200-year-old Levantine compound at Lidja. Captain Alexandros Levides of the Royal Hellenic Navy (RHN), a Venizelist who had left Greece after the murder of Tsigantes, operated his own rescue network and became HIS's chief liaison officer with Parish and Rees.[34] From Khioste, MI-9 caiques sailed to Greece three times a week on three main escape routes, from the Peloponnese near Monemvasia, at the island of Evvia (just north of Athens), and the Khalkidiki peninsula at the southernmost beach of the monastic realm of Mt. Athos. From there, they took refuge at Khlioste before sailing south. They stopped at a small inlet north of Bodrum near the ancient oracular temple to Apollo at Didyma, the last shelter before the perilous voyage through the ten-mile Kos Channel, a three-mile-wide strait between the Greek island and Turkey. Then they rounded Cape Krio, skirted the islands of Simi and Rhodes, and began the long, lumbering "thresh" along the south coast of Turkey, an "open leg" of sea with hundreds of bays and fjords to Kastellorizo, an island fewer than two miles from Turkey.[35] After passing Cape Gelidonia, they headed for the safety of British Cyprus.

SOE or Special Operations Executive represented the third major branch of British intelligence at Izmir. Its head, David Pawson, a prewar businessman in the Balkans, did not get on with Rees. Pawson concocted flamboyant sabotage missions, poached on Rees's bases, and compromised their security until he developed his own base on Rees's private island at Egrilar. As a Venizelist sympathizer, Pawson also clashed with Rees over politics, and their quarrels complicated operations for their Greek staffs. Although Caskey liked Pawson and his politics, he trod lightly among his feuding "Bretannic cousins."[36]

At the American consulate, Caskey found his Trojan teammate, Dorothy Cox, who had reached Turkey five months earlier in the guise of a civilian relief worker. Upon arrival in Egypt, she had spent ten days under cover of Greek War Relief questioning Greek refugees on military, political, and economic subjects and then visited refugee camps at Moses' Wells, a bleak oasis in the Sinai nine miles south of Suez, and in Aleppo and Beirut. Then she proceeded to Ankara, where she found fellow numismatist George Miles. The British chief of Middle East Relief and Rehabilitation advised Cox that she could only be of use by working under him in Cairo, but his attempt to keep Americans out of Izmir backfired. She established herself there as quickly as possible and independent of the British. On December 31, 1942, Cox received clearance from the Turks, revealed herself to Ellis Johnson, the U.S. vice consul in Izmir, and Amoss's ONI contact, Lanning Williams, and set to work.

Cox was sixteen years Caskey's senior. Rather manly in appearance, she dressed conservatively in a long skirt, dark jacket, buttoned-up shirt, and tie, with her brown hair concealed under a black, broad-rimmed hat. To keep her from standing out as the only woman in a man's world, OSS colleagues addressed her as "Hiram" in correspondence and referred to her with the masculine pronoun. Cox was the reports officer, responsible for extracting information from Greece. Opinionated and sympathetic to Greeks, she did not like Turks or their language, a prejudice no doubt acquired on American excavations near Izmir in 1925 after the exchange of populations made ghost towns of the formerly Greek villages. Young suspected that she might have been doing intelligence work even then. She submitted weekly reports to the Greek Desk in Washington and, in return, requested feedback and supplies, such as military maps for interrogations. Meanwhile, bureaucrats underpaid her, thinking that as a female civilian she was only a secretary, and Dow never acknowledged receiving her reports. In her first five months she received no supplies or communications whatsoever.[37]

Yet Cox was confident, smart, and able to function on her own. Absolutely fearless, she interviewed refugees, most of whom left for political or military reasons; enemy deserters; and special agents. Because the Turks did not allow them to land and either imprisoned or sent them back, the British landed Greek refugees by night, furnished them with papers or collective passports, and had them surrender to the nearest police station. They arrived in Izmir on Sundays and satisfied formalities with the Greek and British consulates on Mondays. Cox got a crack at them on Tuesday and Wednesday and had her interviews transcribed for the noon pouch by Thursday.[38] She was a good listener: her gray eyes and empathetic smile encouraged refugees to talk, and they gave her "an inexhaustible and ever-changing supply of sources." Cox was a shrewd and immediate judge of character and minutely described them while respecting their anonymity, although she admitted that "sifting out the truth" was one of the most difficult things she ever tried to do.[39]

From January to March, she single-handedly tried to match Rees's operation, but the British "held too many trumps." When the Turks clamped down, her stream dried up. Officers were put up in a pension and allowed to go about freely, but other evacuees were interned in a *khan* (inn) and only allowed to leave on official business. No longer could the Greek officials pick the men they wanted to bring out.[40] Sometimes the republican Greek consul tipped off Cox that the British were expecting "several lots." Other times, he kowtowed to Rees, who confined and interrogated important officers for hours, took written statements, and shipped them back to Cheshme. As a result, Cox, who thought Rees was "shortcircuiting" her because he did not like her "milking their goats," saw a fraction of the men and got only part of the picture from those who often were ignorant of foreign political or military intelligence. Even so, Cox reported everything to Cairo, Washington, and ONI.[41]

The Greek refugees provided a constant source of friction between Cox and Rees. Rees forwarded them according to their politics, culling royalists for Greek resistance work or the Free Greek Forces and shunting the republicans to internment camps, where they wasted away in the Syrian desert. Some hoped for better treatment from the Americans and sought out Cox, who insisted that Caskey accept them so she could interview them. But fearing that refugees might endanger his secret operation, Caskey refused to get involved and avoided the escape business altogether.[42]

Cox also clashed with Rees, because she was outspoken and her politics were diametrically opposed to his.[43] For Cox, it was "impossible for any but supermen or super morons to be neutral." She sided with the radicalized republicans and leftists. She sympathized with EAM/ELAS and reported military intelligence on ELAS's increasing sabotage and guerrilla activities as well as intelligence on EAM, its political wing. In the name of the Red Cross, Cox smuggled funds, food, clothes, and medical supplies to the guerrillas in exchange for information. She distrusted International Red Cross personnel and suspected the neutrality of four IRC colleagues who were assigned to the islands around Izmir, believing the Swedes to be pro-Allies and the Swiss "little better than Axis agents." She dismissed the Greek Red Cross committee on the Greek island of Mytilene as a "social club" of the "rich and socially select" and accused its board of profiteering and not sharing the island's oil surplus with the rest of Greece.[44]

When Caskey took charge of Izmir, he smoothed the waters between Cox and Rees. Then, because Young had still not arrived, Caskey charted his own course. After chastising Dow for ignoring Cox, Caskey insisted on regular communication between bases. To facilitate this, Ambassador Steinhardt gave him his own radio and telegraph code, identifying Caskey's cables as coming from "HECTOR." Ellis Johnson offered him a "swank" office on the upper floor of the Izmir consulate. There he could string radio antennae (fifty to seventy-five feet of wire pointing toward Cairo) away from the scrutiny of passersby.

Caskey took to Izmir, frequenting casinos offering local imitations of "Vermut," "Votka," "Kanyak," highballs, and martinis; and enjoying restaurants and nightspots where he could drink raki (the Turkish equivalent of ouzo) and Turkish beer. He stayed at the Izmir Palas, which he described as "a hive of gossip," and quickly met employees of the American Tobacco Company, the staff of the American girls' school, and the Levantine community. Izmir offered a level of independence unattainable at any other Greek Desk post. It would prove the most profitable field base, and Caskey was an ideal choice for it. His previous work with Cox helped him establish an efficient office and good records while, thanks to the archaeological mafia, he had clear channels of communication with and support from Istanbul, Cyprus, Cairo, and Washington. His Greek enabled him to interface with Greek colleagues. He cultivated useful officials in the Greek consulate who worked at Khioste and had been associated with the GIP. Thanks in part to a beloved Scottish stepmother, he was an Anglophile, well equipped socially and intellectually to work with the British. Having been "brought up in the Blegen tradition," Caskey did not share the British bias against Turks. Instead, after years at Troy, he liked them and made allowances, thinking that one accomplished more that way. Caskey hired Blegen's foreman as his all-purpose *kavass* or doorman, handyman, dragoman, and courier. Fluent in Turkish, Caskey could communicate directly with the Emniyet. He wanted "tickets to the ball game" and planned "to go all the way with them." "Playing ball" was fine as long as he could preserve his own initiative and effectiveness.[45]

Caskey turned to his primary task: establishing an OSS port for a caique service to and from Greece. Through MacFarland, who finally appeared in mid-May, Steinhardt, and Istanbul MI-6, Caskey secured the cautious cooperation of the Emniyet. All agreed that OSS needed a separate port, so MacFarland, the Emniyet, and Istanbul MI-6 convened in Izmir with Caskey, Pawson, Rees, Levides, and the Izmir Emniyet chief, a colonel in the Turkish army. After the Istanbul entourage impressed upon Rees, the Greeks, and the U.S. naval attaché the necessity of giving Caskey complete cooperation, Rees invited the Americans to tour his bases, workshops, and communication centers. All concurred that to avoid surveillance, Caskey's port should be far from Izmir in a military zone, approachable on land or by caique only by authorized persons. To "sweeten" the Turks, they allowed Emniyet guards to collect duty on imported oil, gas, arms, and ammunition while maintaining security.

Caskey hoped to get a port by late May, but predicted that it would take thirty to sixty days to secure equipment and transportation and make it operational. MacFarland asked Amoss for radios, maps of the Turkish coast, and caiques to make nightly dashes to the Greek islands and the long run to Cyprus as well as a heavily armed one "for destructive purposes."[46] MacFarland promised to organize everything in Ankara and urged patience but did not produce, and Amoss focused on the GIP: working with Mossad, the Jewish intelligence service, and meddling in Greek politics.[47] Meanwhile, Rees claimed that the OSS would never get a port and tried "to put a spoke in their wheels," and then Robert Parker, OWI chief in Istanbul, got wind of SI bases, wanted his own, and botched the process.[48] By the time Young and the "archaeological captains" arrived in Cairo, Caskey had collapsed from stress.[49] Finally, on June 18, Caskey met in Ankara with the Emniyet chief, who allowed him to proceed, insisted that he be independent of the British, and advised him to keep his operations compact so as not to draw attention. This satisfied Caskey, who understood that Turkey could not jeopardize its neutrality by showing support for the Americans.

Instead of playing ball, Caskey played "catch up." It became clear that between the allies lay a deep divide of ambivalence and competition. Rees seemed to thwart his every move. Likewise, Caskey got little from Levides, who was, after all, "Rees's man." Turf battles erupted between them. One OSS agent later described the British attitude as "that of a jealous elder husband when another younger man pays attention to his younger wife."[50] Rees eyed Caskey's aggrandizement with irritation and accused him of stealing agents by paying them better, but Caskey replied that they preferred his politics. When Rees did release agents to Caskey, such as Lieutenant Commander Stamatopoulos, deputy director of HIS Izmir, Caskey never knew to whom they bore allegiance.[51]

SEVEN

"Preparing the Underground Railroad"

RODNEY YOUNG FINALLY REACHED CAIRO after a two-and-a-half-month voyage. He had left Washington with high expectations and promises of support, but it was May 19, 1943, over a year and a half after Pearl Harbor.[1] Rommel's Afrika Corps had surrendered in Tunis, and Cairo was celebrating the victory of Operation Torch and the capture of 240,000 Axis soldiers. Roosevelt and Eisenhower had placed Greece on the back burner, and in Aqaba Wilson was conducting a dress rehearsal for the Sicily landings. Donovan made trips to Cairo to buttress his field men, bolster their acceptance by their theater commanders, and acquaint Washington with their needs, but he, too, focused on the west.

Yet OSS Cairo, just authorized by the Joint Chiefs of Staff, was expanding. It had abandoned the crowded consulate for a villa next to the Greek legation. Stephen Penrose, Young's equivalent at Near East SI, discovered Turner McBaine "presiding in solitary splendor over the entire top floor . . . all but one room of which was devoid of either occupants or furniture." SI was "surrounded by quantities of echoing space."[2]

Young found a dysfunctional family and organizational chaos. Navigating between his bosses' clashing agendas was like sailing between Scylla and Charybdis. McBaine focused on Athens, knew no Greek, and required a Greek national, Dimitri Petrou, to handle personnel and keep him abreast of breaking political developments.[3] Meanwhile, Amoss focused only Special Operations, the GIP, and its part in Tsouderos's invasion. Steering his

Fig. 15. OSS Cairo. Rustem Pasha. (Courtesy National Archives.)

own course, Young labored to knit their hand-me-down agents into his own teams.

Like McBaine, Young was given a bare room to establish the Greek Desk. With him were Sperling, Daniel, and Oliver. After Sperling left for Istanbul, Young kept Daniel and Oliver in Cairo to help him set up the office. Clio Adossides joined them to interview Greek refugees and handle cipher and cables. She worked in the code room, translating all interviews and field intelligence into English and checking paraphrases and translations from English into Greek.[4] As he cast about for helpers, Young rediscovered Alekko Georgiades. As part of Tsouderos's invasion, Alekko would go on a GIP sabotage mission to Crete, to accompany Kapetanios "Y" (Petrakogiorgi), a Cretan guerrilla leader who claimed to lead 500 men whom he called "Donovan's Band," organize sea contact, and guide parachute drops in central Crete.[5] In the interim, however, Georgiades helped Young: reporting on troubles in the Greek camps, getting propaganda leaflets printed, and combing Cairo for "theatricals": suitcases that looked as if they had weathered the black market, clothes from Greece or Greek labels to sew into other garments, paper for identity cards, and forgeries of German, Italian, and Greek stamps and seals. He and Young hatched the agents' code names. Young became Pigeon; Caskey, Chickadee; Oliver, Owl; Sperling, Sparrow; Cox, Thrush; and Georgiades, Gander. When Young's Princeton classmate Lt. George McFadden turned up in Cairo as a naval attaché, Daniel, who had dug with him on Cyprus, recommended they snap him up even though he had no OSS training. Against his better judgment, Young consented. He had known McFadden since prep school and considered him "naïve, obstinate, and insecure." But he knew that McFadden had "compensating virtues," namely his schooner, the *Samothrace*. Although McFadden worked for Special Operations, Young christened him Daffy for his aptitude and because he would work with Daniel ("Duck").[6]

Then Young began recruiting in earnest. The best field agents and guerrilla liaisons were military men: able to command respect, hardy, and willing to rough it in the mountains. The British tried to block his using Greeks in Greece and even Greek-Americans, but Young insisted that his agents know Greek. Special Operations had already snagged most Greek-Americans for a commando battalion, and Young already had almost all of the Americans he wanted who knew Greek, so he recruited Greeks in spite of the British. Hiring Greek-speakers in Egypt cost less and speeded the process. Furthermore, most of them were experienced, having already worked for the British, HIS, or both. Zangas and Melas funneled agents to Daniel for interviews, and Young matched them to missions. Meanwhile, HIS ran security checks and vetted their politics regarding "the king business," an issue that Young considered "the root of most . . . trouble."[7]

Aside from his Greek Desk responsibilities, Young interacted with other Americans in Cairo: at the embassy, OWI, Greek War Relief, the Allied Military Liaison at USAFIME headquarters, and the Joint Intelligence Collection Agency (JICAME), which was charged with transmitting military intelligence to the U.S. Army, Navy, and theater commander.[8] Young's wide circle of friends made the task easier. As the American liaison for Greece with British intelligence, Young encountered British School acquaintances from Athens, including Ellis Waterhouse, advisor on Greek affairs at the embassy; Major Tom Dunbabin of SOE; and Alan Wace, who edited and disseminated British intelligence reports, provided British missions to the

Fig. 16. George McFadden.
(Courtesy John McFadden.)

Fig. 17. The *Samothrace*, Paul
Gotch Photograph Album.
(Courtesy Michael Haag.)

Aegean with forged passports and ships' papers, and volunteered to help Young. Indeed, Young's cordial relationships with the British archaeologists of MI-6 (known in Cairo as ISLD, Inter Service Liaison Department) inclined them to a noncompetitive relationship (unlike Izmir), and they opened their "blackbooks" to him.[9]

Communication reached Young by means of personal correspondence, routine base reports (the "weekly bilge"), and raw intelligence that Caskey and Cox translated, hand-copied, and sent under their code names by the slow, safe diplomatic pouch. Breaking news arrived via cables and radio transmissions, which then had to be decoded by the Cairo message center. All of this Young digested and relayed to Sterling Dow (see fig. 3) in his own weekly reports and correspondence. Caskey and Cox repeatedly asked Young for direction in intelligence-gathering because reporting was laborious, snags in communication rendered SI stale, and all intelligence was rated according to reliability and freshness.

From the safety of Q Building, Dow put "true facts under the right noses," apprising Donovan of field intelligence that the Greek Desk gathered and relaying what Cairo and the satellite bases needed. Theoretically, Dow also communicated with each base, but the oh-so-secret Dow insisted on sending correspondence only by personal courier, sometimes resulting in four-month delays.[10] With a revolving fund of $200,000, Dow was to procure and ship supplies and staff, but these traveled slowest of all since they first had to be approved by theater commander General Wilson and, once okayed, were often bumped by military needs. Shipping space was tight, and sailings infrequent. Moreover, waiting for space took almost as long as waiting for approval. To staff the Washington office, Dow recruited his former students: Gerald Else, a Harvard classicist, one of the last Ph.D.s to have written a Harvard dissertation in Latin. Dow so impressed on him the need for security that Else actually burned his job offer letter. Else began by procuring maps and other supplies.[11] Dow also hired Margaret (Missy) Crosby, an Agora archaeologist from Bryn Mawr and Yale, who edited and routed reports on Greece to Donovan and the State Department.[12] Meanwhile, Charles Edson, Dow's fellow graduate at Harvard, ASCSA alumnus, and colleague, who had been working on Greece for R&A since February, was compiling reports on Greece.

In early June, Sperling reported to Young that he had reached Turkey by the newly completed coastal railway along the Via Maris, distracted en route by "the most wonderful looking habitation mounds." Sperling spent two days in Ankara, where he visited the Hittite Museum and the temple of Augustus with an old Turkish colleague, who had since been promoted to director of the Department of Antiquities. There Sperling met German archaeologists who he assumed were intelligence agents like himself.[13]

At the American embassy Sperling encountered Agora archaeologist Virginia ("Tiggie") Grace (fig. 2), who regaled him with her experiences from the winter of 1940 to mid-April 1942, during which she had dug with McFadden on Cyprus until they fled to Alexandria. There she had met McFadden's uncle Judge Jasper Brinton, head of the Mixed Courts in Egypt and president of the Archaeological Society. McFadden had shipped the *Samothrace* to Mombasa and left to enlist. Grace had remained in Egypt, clerking at the American consulate. On the eve of the "Flap," before all nonemergency staff evacuated to Khartoum, Grace had buried the Agora index in a Giza tomb along with the records of the Harvard Pyramids Expedition, whose director, George Reisner, had just died at his camp beside the Great Pyramid.[14] From July to September, she worked and smoked nonstop at the U.S. consulate at Asmara in the former Italian colony of Eritrea. She enjoyed wartime clerking and compared it to "the system" at the Agora. Looking after items marked "Secret" reminded her of curating the Agora's gold artifacts. Grace visited archaeological sites at leisure and found the 8,000-foot altitude intoxicating. Upon returning to Cairo, she found that Harvard was still excavating and ran into archaeologists W. S. (Bill) Smith and Sandy Campbell, who were headed to Syria. After requesting reassignment to Beirut, Grace was sent as a file clerk to the U.S. embassy in Ankara. From her tower room, she looked out over the dusty capital on the Anatolian steppe and the grim mountains beyond, deploring the city as "hot in summer, cold in winter" and complaining of shortages, even of Turkish cigarettes. Colleagues suggested that the embassy's emblem should be crossed cocktail glasses, and journalists claimed that the "screwdriver" was invented there to make the "votka" palatable. To cheer her, Sperling encouraged her to learn Turkish so she might join the Greek Desk.[15]

On June 4, Sperling pulled into Haydar Pasha Station, excited to be in Istanbul establishing the Greek Desk. He loved cloak and dagger and dressed the part of a "spook," slouching in a trench coat and referring to himself as "the inscrutable mystic" Russo-Chinese "Sper ling H.H. = Hush Hush Stinkovich."[16] Thinking OSS resources limitless, he requested secretaries and staff, but Young had none to give. Soon Sperling discovered that he was "more or less out on a limb."[17] No one was in control at the lax OSS headquarters in the American Consulate in Pera, later nicknamed the "Yale Club of Istanbul" for its social atmosphere and alumni from Old Eli. Security was lax. The day before, Sperling's office-mate arrested someone at gunpoint for buying information from one of the Levantine clerks. Moreover, all mail from Ankara to Istanbul or Izmir went through the U.S. embassy, which turned it over to Turkish postal workers on the train who met consulate employees at either end. To top it off, when Sperling established his cover with the American News Service (a front for OWI), scanning newspapers and monitoring radio programs for Greek intelligence, he discovered that the British regarded OWI as the least secure branch of American intelligence, and an OWI colleague had just penned the popular nightclub song "Boo boo, baby, I'm a spy!"[18]

In Cairo, Young became mired in unexpected OSS bureaucracy. Cox was the only one sending in Greek intelligence. The rest were consumed with setting up the machinery and losing sight of their purpose for being there.

Young focused on "preparing the underground railroad." Envisioning an Aegean offensive, he planned to channel a pipeline of agents following ancient sea lanes from Egypt, to Cyprus and Izmir, and into enemy-occupied Greece. Although Amoss had wanted Zangas and the GIP to run the caique service, Rees threatened to withdraw British cooperation if Zangas returned to Izmir. So along with their SI work the archaeologists had to set up and administer the caique service. Doing so required nautical expertise, and OSS Cairo had none—not even a Maritime representative, and, of the archaeologists, only McFadden had much sailing experience.

To begin with, Young needed to find "holding points," intermediary stopping places where he could hide his agents for twenty to thirty days until he was ready to send them to Greece. One had to be on the North African coast, so Young sent Oliver to reconnoiter the Western Desert and Cyrenaica. As he scouted locations for OSS bases, Oliver viewed the landscape through archaeological lenses and allowed them to cloud his judgment. He set out on the desert road past the Faiyum and the Wadi Natrun, where the ancients had harvested salt to mummify their dead. At the coast, he veered westward, past El Alamein, minefields, wire entanglements, and burnt out vehicles. At Marsa Matruh, Oliver passed the road to the oasis where Alexander the Great had once been recognized as a god. He crossed the Libyan border and pressed on into Cyrenaica, speaking Berber and Egyptian with the Sanusi Bedouin and Italian with educated Libyans while surveying the devastation of Benghazi and Tobruk, where wrecks still lay in the clear green water of the harbor. He wrote of Hellenistic and Roman sites whose state of preservation exceeded that of houses just abandoned by the Italians and plundered by British troops. Site museums had been looted by fleeing Italian archaeologists and then stripped of doors and windows by the locals. In contrast to these modern ruins, Oliver found Tolmeta, the partly excavated site of ancient Ptolemais east of Benghazi, unscathed, and recommended it for Special Operations, although its wells remained booby-trapped, and errant camels and donkeys were still stepping on occasional land mines and blowing themselves up. Oliver pronounced the site of ancient Cyrene, for which the province was named, a "spectacle . . . in a class all by itself." Young hoped to place him there, so Oliver saved Cyrene for an SI base for agents going into western Greece and Crete, although its 500-mile distance from Cairo was impractical.[19]

Young also needed a stepping stone between Alexandria and Izmir. Before going into the Aegean, all British vessels called at the Cypriot port of Kyrenia, which faced Turkey, fifty miles to the north, and the eastern and southern ports of Famagusta and Limassol, which lay about 150 miles from Beirut. Meanwhile, flights connected Cairo with Nicosia, the island's capital, and RAF flying boats took off from the Great Salt Lake on the south coast near Episkopi village, where Daniel had excavated for the University of Pennsylvania at the site of ancient Kourion. MI-9 deposited Greek refugees at internment camps and then returned to Greece bearing agents and supplies.[20]

Young sent Daniel to Cyprus on reconnaissance. He stayed with British archaeologist and Civil Affairs officer A. H. S. "Peter" Megaw, who, after junkets to Kyrenia and Stavrovouni monastery, introduced Daniel to the top military, administrative, and maritime brass, including Major LeFroy, the chief of General Staff Operational Intelligence and MI-5. Daniel's cover was with Allied interrogations, and so he would work closely MI-5 interrogators from Egypt, charged with guarding the island's security, grilling the refugees for information, and ferrying the most promising candidates to Alexandria to be interrogated. Daniel had to find caiques, so LeFroy escorted him to Famagusta to charter boats and crews, helped him acquire caiques and get them overhauled, and offered to take Daniel's crews on a dry run to Izmir before going solo.[21]

Daniel also had to a locate a secure OSS transshipment base, where agents and goods, such as dynamite, could be off-loaded, kept "in cold storage," and then reloaded, either for the Aegean or Alexandria. The British wanted it enclosed by barbed wire, guarded, and commanded by a U.S. army officer. Although Young had hoped that McFadden could handle it to free up Daniel for the Dodecanese, the British had blacklisted McFadden as commander of OSS Cyprus.[22] So Daniel laid plans for his own operation, which had to balance security and isolation against transportation and communication. LeFroy leant him a vehicle to survey the island. Following a tip from Megaw, Daniel found a Turkish village in the foothills of the Troodhos Mountains on the outskirts of which lay "Metamorphosis Farm," a two-acre apple-growing estate with a good spring, a concrete irrigation vat deep enough for a pool, and open fields secluded by forests of Aleppo pines and sycamores that he could enclose with barbed wire.[23] Once the home of a boys' school that had closed during the Depression, it was owned by a friend of Megaw's and could hide as many as thirteen agents. Covered porches surrounded the main house, which had living room, dining room, kitchen, three bedrooms, and bath, while the smaller building provided overflow with another two rooms and a bath. Two other candidates lay on the major east-west road near Limassol on the south coast. The once impregnable Kolossi Castle built by the Knights Hospitaller and Templar was an empty shell, but offered plenty of space for a covert base.[24] To the west was McFadden's commodious villa, the Penn dig house in Episkopi where Daniel had spent years. Because the latter two could not be isolated, Daniel, who privileged security, chose Metamorphosis.[25]

Next Daniel needed to find a port in which to receive and moor caiques. Ideally, this would double as the holding point, but not in the case of land-locked Metamorphosis Farm. Daniel considered Karavostasi, a sheltered harbor on the Bay of Morphou in northwestern Cyprus twenty-five miles south of the former Penn excavations at Lapithos and near the site of ancient Soli, the capital of one of the island's nine classical kingdoms from whose temples the British had quarried stone for Port Said.[26] The Cyprus Mines Corporation used Karavostasi for processing and exporting the copper ore from which the island took its name, and so a railway and a good road linked with Nicosia and Famagusta.[27] The harbor also had clear views of the Turkish coast, roughly 150 miles to the north, and a sea lane leading west to the Aegean. Moreover, the U.S. companyp promised to overhaul Daniel's caiques and volunteered a temporary slip and another under construction that could serve as a repair area and emergency refuge.[28] But Karavostasi had considerable traffic and could never be secure. So Daniel again opted for security and chose remote Pissouri, a deep sandy bay on the southwest coast twenty miles west of Paphos. It had spectacular views to the south and east and a ridge that paralleled the beach and restricted access from the nearby fields. Daniel would enclose a 200-square-yard area including one warehouse, some smaller huts, and a jetty with barbed wire. But he had to wait for Middle East theater commander General Wilson to grant permission.

From mid-June rumors circulated about the opening of an Aegean front. Edson reported, "Everybody is expecting from moment to moment an Allied landing in the islands and in Crete." Sources reported "Cretan population is in full effervescence, its civilians mobilized." Despite massive arrests in Athens and Piraeus, the Greeks' morale had risen to a fever pitch, and they transmitted all BBC broadcasts from mouth to mouth within hours. An Associated Press journalist expected "hell to pop loose" any day.[29] On July 1, the day that Daniel arrived in Cyprus, disturbances broke out in Athens and Salonika. Tsouderos expected the imminent invasion of Crete and secretly telegraphed leaders in occupied Greece and advised the king that his government would submit its resignation following its return to Greece to enable general elections for a national assembly. Even the U.S. State Department finally spoke up, noting that the United States wished to avoid the impression that it wished to impose the king under the protection of an Allied invading force. Then on July 4, King George II declared on Cairo Radio that six months after liberation the Greeks could decide the fate of their government. That day, Brigadier General Eddie Myers of the British Military Mission, who, after Gorgopotamos, had blown up two other bridges with Greek guerrillas, convinced EAM/ELAS to cooperate with the BMM and other guerrilla bands and set up a joint headquarters in the mountains, bringing the resistance groups together in an unstable union under the BMM and formally recognizing ELAS as an Allied force.[30]

They did not know that they were victims of a well-wrought deception, Churchill's "bodyguard of lies" to make Hitler *think* that the Allies would attack Greece. All around the eastern Mediterranean, the British had labored to make their numbers seem greater than they were. In Egypt, they hired Greek translators and interpreters and conducted amphibious trainings, planted agents in the islands, and sent decoy radio signals and administrative orders.[31] On Cyprus, they set up a bogus division whose troops, divisional signs, and inflatable tanks and trucks, displayed for the benefit of enemy agents on the ground, prompted German photographic missions to fly over the island. The Germans were prepared. Amid daily arrivals of men and materiel, they had evacuated villages by the Corinth Canal and barred all but military traffic from it. Salonika resembled an immense entrenched camp; troops packed into former refugee shanty towns; airfields bristled with German fighter planes and troop transports; and residents had been evacuated from the harbor so that fuel could be stockpiled there. Meanwhile, throughout the Aegean the Germans had strengthened coastal defenses and enforced strict blackouts while Italian subs prowled the Dodecanese, Volos, and the Evvia Channel and destroyers policed the Macedonian shore.

Also expecting the invasion of Greece, the Izmir Emniyet suddenly offered Caskey three ports: Aivalik, opposite the Greek island of Mytilene about seventy-five miles north of Izmir, Chandarli, thirty miles south of Aivalik, and Kushadasi, fifty miles south of Izmir. All were far from the British and Karaburun. Exhilarated, Caskey christened them with cryptonyms according to an internal logic reflecting his East Coast upbringing—"Portland," "Boston," and "Miami"—and imagined "a whole row of ports each with its own fleet setting out nightly on its errand of mercy."[32] The Emniyet representative recommended starting at Kushadasi, a picturesque port two hours south of Izmir, and drove Caskey to the small harbor, sheltered by a fortified islet and headland. Greeks once inhabited it, but their red-tiled, whitewashed houses, abandoned in World War I and again in 1922–23, had crumbled to ruins. Its anchorage boasted a quay with a small marine repair shop and a crane to offload oil drums and bales of supplies. Meanwhile, a good road to the north connected it with the site of ancient Ephesos at Seljuk, where OSS could use a telephone for emergencies. Near the Kushadasi quay stood the City Hall, the customs house, and telegraph office.[33] Behind and above the caravanserai (fortified Ottoman palace) perched Emniyet headquarters. Because of his commercial cover, Caskey chose the customs house as his office. In a second-floor room, furnished from the Troy dig, Caskey would organize his first covert base.

On July 6, ships crowded into Alexandria's harbor. There and at other North African ports, liberty ships, hospital ships and liners departed at four-minute intervals. Yet instead of an overture to the invasion of Greece, the Aegean excitement shrouded events in the central Mediterranean, where intensified air attacks riveted attention and tension escalated. The die was cast. The United States was beginning to pull American troops out of Egypt in preparation for Sicily. On the night of July 9, Allied armadas set sail, and U.S. paratroopers dropped in the dark. The next day, 3,000 landing craft, 160,000 men, and 600 tanks hit the beaches near the site of ancient Gela. The Allies had invaded Sicily.

The Italians were not the only ones caught off guard. Young was stunned and wondered what would happen to the invasion of Greece. Young panicked and cabled Daniel to return at once because Georgiades, his right arm, had just left for Istanbul. By the time Daniel reached Cairo almost a week later, Young was running up and down "like a squirrel in a cage."[34]

Young was desperate. On top of the chaos in Cairo, Sperling reported trouble with MacFarland, who could not manage the Istanbul office and its Balkan agent networks. So MacFarland snared Sperling and loaded on work, forcing Sperling to function as his reports officer, writing up Balkan field intelligence; act as MacFarland's cipher clerk, coding and decoding his correspondence; and do scut work for other OSS branches. MacFarland made Sperling his liaison with British intelligence, and, because he knew no Turkish, MacFarland demanded that Sperling act as his liaison and interpreter in all Emniyet negotiations: weekly summits on the setting up of naval bases, rental of ships, engaging of crews, and planning of operations. Entangled and exhausted, Sperling had "done nothing but develop gray hair" and begged Young to get Grace transferred to Istanbul.[35]

Young got angry. From the beginning, the relationship between OSS Cairo and Turkey was flawed, with overlapping authority. Turkey was neutral, and so it had no OSS representation in Washington or Cairo. Because MacFarland badgered him for everything, Young reasoned that Istanbul should be under him, but MacFarland refused to acknowledge dependency and invented his own system of code names using flowers, instead of Cairo's birds. Contested agents on the Greek Desk answered to both, so that Sperling was "Basil" to Istanbul and "Sparrow" to Cairo, while Georgiades likewise answered to "Aster" and "Gander." To further confuse the situation, Caskey self-identified by different nicknames depending on whom he was addressing and often referred to colleagues only by number, so that even Young needed "occult science" to figure it out.[36]

Sperling wrote that Georgiades was moving into eastern or Turkish Thrace, a wasteland like the Karaburun Peninsula that had been repeatedly devastated, evacuated, resettled, and finally declared a military zone. As "Gander," Georgiades would work as an interpreter at the Greek consulate in Edirne (Adrianople), strategically located in the Evros River Valley, known as "the Triangle," a wild, desolate region wedged between Bulgaria, Greece, and Turkey. From the frontier city, astride overland routes from Istanbul into those countries, Georgiades was to establish both safe routes for SI and procure intelligence through border runners. MI-6 had failed to penetrate Evros from their old bases at Enoz and Ipsala on the Turkish bank of the river, and so the British encouraged Geordiades to develop a regular cross-border courier service. A courier who had survived being attacked by Turkish guards while guiding agents across the frontier volunteered to escort Georgiades across and put him in touch with the Evros guerrillas, but warned him that Greeks at the consulate were working for MI-6, that the Gestapo had just purged the previous cell of thirty-four Greek agents, and that MI-6 planned to use Georgiades to neutralize the very guerrillas on whom he was to depend for hospitality and contacts.[37]

Caskey had his own difficulties setting up his secret harbor "Miami" (Kushadasi), trying to scrounge caiques, a car, and fuel, as well as proper papers for men and boats, radios and operators. To stockpile supplies, Caskey rented storerooms from the Emniyet.[38] He hired George Manoudis, who spoke fluent Turkish and had worked in the Greek gendarmerie and British intelligence, as his base chief and hoped to recycle Greek refugees as agents. MacFarland advised him to "keep a stiff back up," but did not understand Turkish customs. Caskey knew, from being Blegen's right-hand man at Troy, that "For the pleasure of doing business," he had to pay off the local Emniyet man, who, according to reputation, had to be "very liberally sweetened."[39] To avoid dependence on the Turks, Caskey looked to expand his operations into the Aegean islands, but to succeed, he needed caiques.

Meanwhile, Young struggled single-handedly to launch his first mission, "Settler," whose two Greek agents were to pave the way for the rest. They were bound for Athens to procure and export forging materials, buy and send out a "legal" caique, and inform McBaine's Athens mission about safe routes, police regulations, curfews, and forbidden zones.[40] Settler would report information on air-raid results and targets for Brereton's pilots, as well as military intelligence and shipping news.

But Young, too, needed transportation. Originally, he had hoped to use Brereton's planes or fast motorboats, but General Wilson had ignored the request. OSS had just started a Maritime Branch that was to handle all boats and boating operations, and so McBaine had requested that it send personnel to develop the caique service, but when Lt. Jack Taylor arrived to set up Maritime in mid-July, he came alone and empty-handed. Without overt U.S. military activity in the eastern Mediterranean, OSS could not provide maritime training and tactical assistance, nor could it conduct the marine sabotage because it lacked high-speed craft. Ironically, it considered a knowledge of seamanship nonessential.

In late July, Young swallowed his pride and asked the British to transport his agents. They agreed to do so, but only from Beirut. Panos Morphopoulos, who had just arrived to chronicle the Greek brigades interned in Syria for SI, was to accompany his agents there. However, because he had come under a *Newsweek* cover but unaccredited, he could not leave Egypt. Meverette Smith ("Melvin"), Young's relief colleague whom he had earmarked for the Greek Desk in Beirut, had still not left the States.[41] So Young escorted them to Beirut. The motley crew attracted attention with a uniformed driver, Young in civilian dress, and two agents in khaki with their rubber dinghies in plain sight.

By the time they reached the Royal Navy base on July 25, Mussolini had fallen from power. Italians were pulling down statues of their former dictator, and the Italian king declared martial law while he formed a new government under Marshal P. Badoglio. He assured Berlin of Italy's continued allegiance and simultaneously sent surrender feelers to the Allies. Meanwhile, Wilson froze transportation in the eastern Mediterranean, marooning Young's agents.[42]

Young lost patience, for everyone who wanted anything came to him. Yet he had not foreseen the delay and had no one to cover for him, nor had he authorized anyone to make decisions in his absence. After depositing 500 pounds in gold sovereigns (more than $10,000) and a couple million occupation drachmas in the MI-6 safe, Young summoned Oliver to chaperone the men and returned to relieve Daniel. Meanwhile, his agents chilled for two weeks in Beirut while MI-6 coached them and gave them identity papers and pistols.

When Young returned to Cairo, he learned that the GIP had collapsed. For weeks, Amoss had struggled to keep it intact under MacFarland and Caskey, but Young and McBaine, tired of his intrigues, disapproved and feared that it would sink the Greek Desk.[43] Finally, Donovan had terminated the GIP and recalled Amoss.[44] With his Byzantine empire in ruins, Amoss returned to Washington. Henceforth, Young answered only to McBaine. Unfortunately, Amoss had already summoned George Vournas to be a GIP liaison in postinvasion Greece (fig. 18). Young was steamed at being saddled with the outspoken Greek-American president of AHEPA, named him "Vulture," and described him as "a large and pretentious personality not meant for intelligence." Tsouderos had tried to block Vournas, fearing his impact on the Greeks in Egypt. However, along with his brother-in-law Lt. Chris Petrow, Vournas also brought Young his first letter from Dow in almost five months.[45]

Young opened the precious communication. Instead of giving direction on intelligence-gathering, the ominvorous Dow asked for everything, from information on British political schemes to restore King George, to Greek telephone exchanges and central telegraph offices.[46] Upon reading that Washington considered the Greek Desk "unproductive," Young exploded and suggested that if Dow intended to send anything, he should try to get it to Egypt "in time for this war, not the next."

> In this game one has to grit one's teeth and take chances. . . . By not sending us planes and speedboats with which we could get people quickly into occupied territory, WASHINGTON HAS FORCED ON US THE SLOW METHOD AND EXPENSIVE ONE. . . . How in hell can we produce anything until we get people into Greece? . . . we get no backing from Washington and the theatre commander. . . . We have not been doing what we were sent here to do—get information—but rather have been setting up the machinery to do it. . . . tell the people in Washington, Donovan himself if necessary, to put up or shut up. . . . typical of the Washington attitude . . . Let the British do all the work! And then be disagreeably surprised to discover (too late) that they have surprisingly looked to their own interests and not to ours. Many of us here feel that we would like to be turned loose with a machinegun in Washington.[47]

Knee-deep in chaos, Young begged for more staff. He was spending more than five hours a day at the typewriter because he had no secretary. In trying to write one letter, Young counted seventeen interruptions and threw up his hands in frustration.[48] His desk was a foot deep in paper and the message center "crammed and jammed and sunk" under the weight of "nebulosities from Washington." The "boys in the ivory tower" (at Q) talked big, but seemed impotent. Else proposed "to pull a scoop or two" on their "Imperial cousins," but provided cigarettes instead of radios, cameras, and transportation. And when long-awaited supplies did arrive, such as Caskey's sea charts, they blew his cover in crates stenciled "Office of Strategic Services, Izmir."[49]

Washington did not understand the realities of the field; out of touch, Dow and others surveyed the panorama to make "the tesserae . . . fit their mosaic."[50] The gulf had to be bridged. Since the end of May, Young had begged Dow to come to Egypt, but Dow, who had a family, had not wanted to risk Atlantic travel. Now Young could no longer cope. "Exasperated, exacerbated and almost extinguished," Young wrote that he needed someone "P.D.Q." McBaine cabled Dow to send someone immediately. Dow suggested Sergeant Charles Edson, but he had not yet been trained. Finally Dow agreed to come if Edson or Else would replace him in Cairo and Margaret Crosby take over in Washington until he returned to "Queue."[51]

Else recommended Young pursue an "inch by inch policy," moaned that they were "very small fish in a big pool," and claimed that Maritime would tackle transportation. Dow tried to mollify Young by writing "confidence in all of us is high" and promising "a plane and a submarine for each on Christmas morning."[52] But Washington's shift in priorities meant that Young waited in vain. After the invasion of Sicily, Brereton's planes and U.S. submarines went up in smoke like pipe dreams, and personnel and supplies flowed west to the invading troops rather than east to Cairo. As a result, Young's idealism eroded, ground down between the millstones of Britain's control and meddling and Washington's ignorance and indifference.

Young reported that Greek elation evaporated after the invasion of Sicily spotlighted the Allies' second front. Though U.S. planes dropped Young's propaganda leaflets during their bombing raids, and the BBC appealed to the Greeks to remain calm, the landings on Sicily appeared to slam the door on Greek liberation hopes in 1943. Again violence erupted among the Greek brigades in Egypt. Dodecanesians were disenchanted with the British, who refused refugees a role in any future occupation of the islands, and students demonstrated in Athens. Few believed the king would keep his word.[53]

Finally, Wilson lifted the transportation freeze, and McBaine arranged for Settler to proceed to Greece on an MI-6 submarine. It left on August 9 with the operator cradling a trick Shell-Ellas oil tin designed to hold several kilos of oil in the false top and precious radio in a secret lower chamber. A week later, the agents disembarked off Attica posing as fishermen with their gold sovereigns sewn into special nylon belts, 32 caliber pistols, and "Q" pills, small glass vials containing a lethal dose of cyanide. Three Greeks met them and arranged safe housing, but the mission did not begin well: leaking oil had destroyed the radio, and security police arrested and executed one of their contacts for attempted sabotage. They were marooned and incommunicado in the heart of enemy territory.[54]

Sicily fell to the Allies on August 17, the opening day of the Quebec Conference where Roosevelt and Churchill hashed out plans for the invasion of Italy. With Mussolini deposed and Sicily taken, Churchill argued for an

Aegean offensive, but again Roosevelt hove to the west, where General Eisenhower insisted on focusing Allied forces. Even in the event of an Italian collapse in Greece, Eisenhower and Roosevelt only agreed to support small raids and unopposed landings. Instead of backing Churchill, they limited Allied activities in Greece to strategic bombing and support of the guerrillas, stating that only if Rhodes could be won cheaply should it be pursued. Otherwise, it must be deferred in favor of victory in the west. In spite of Roosevelt's rebuff, Churchill pressured General Wilson to "foment Balkan disturbances." As early as August 2, Churchill ordered him to marshal British Expeditionary Forces for a real assault on Rhodes and the Dodecanese, especially Kastellorizo and Kos.[55] Because the men and equipment he needed to mount the offensive were committed elsewhere, Wilson proposed to occupy the islands by means of a "piratical war" like that organized by British special agent "Assyrian Myres," who had terrorized the Turkish coast in World War I.[56] As Settler left the safety of Beirut harbor, Wilson's troops were already drilling on Cyprus.

Wilson secretly marshaled a task force of commandos that would moor and strike at the islands from Turkey. These volunteer battalions, which the OSS archaeologists dubbed "rara boys," were the descendants of the raiders led by John Myres (RVNR), "the Blackbeard of the Aegean," who gathered intelligence while conducting sabotage and wrote a secret handbook to the Dodecanese that the World War II raiders consulted. Like him, they fell under the jurisdiction of the Royal Navy. They were based in Beirut, Famagusta, and Haifa, their bewildering names reflecting the chaos of July 1942, when the British retreated and regrouped after El Alamein. The Long Range Desert Group (LRDG) commandos reinvented themselves as an amphibious force and operated from submarines and motorboats in the Aegean. The Raiding Forces Middle East comprised the Levant Fishing Patrol and the Levant Schooner Flotilla (LSF) whose leader, Lieutenant Commander Adrian Seligman, had circumnavigated the globe on a windjammer before the war and patrolled the east coast of England in 1939. From his floating headquarters, he and the Flotilla transported the others on schooners and caiques outfitted with tank engines. Major the Earl George Jellicoe commanded the Special Boat Service (SBS) from a Crusader castle near Haifa where they drilled on land, sea, and in the air, often spending the mornings skiing on Mount Carmel and the afternoons swimming in the sea in "an ecstasy of fitness and sense of mission." From Limassol on Cyprus, they entered the Aegean, eventually mooring their headquarters southeast of Bodrum at the so-called English Port, a buccaneers' lair cluttered with all manner of vessels, from ketches to kayaks, near where Myres had operated in 1915.[57]

Young prepared his own men in Cairo, billeting them first in the "palace," a Garden City villa that he shared with Daniel and Oliver. After several security breaches by loose-lipped Greeks who bragged in bars about their missions, Young decided to build a camp in the desert, but found that the Royal Navy used his area for target practice.[58] OSS Special Operations had chosen Tocra (ancient Taucheira) near Benghazi as a holding point, but Young opted for a headland near Marsa Matruh, about 140 miles west of Alexandria—far more secure than Cairo and less than half the distance to Cyrene.

At Ras el Kanayas Young established a combined SI and Special Operations training school known as Area A, after its model outside Washington (which was to fund and staff it). Young aimed to provide systematic training, although ironically, the trainees were more experienced than the trainers. Most were veterans who had operated in occupied territory and needed to learn enough English to be indoctrinated with OSS codes and procedures. In the first lot of agents and radio operators half were Greeks who had fought in the Albanian campaign and, frustrated by the indolence imposed upon them in Egypt, wanted to return to their homeland to fight. The rest were Slovene, Serb, and Albanian POWs, only one of whom spoke English.[59] Without instructors, Young improvised. To train radio operators, he recruited George Chrysostomas, a Greek-American communications expert whom he met on the voyage from the United States. Oliver pitched in, recruiting and training agents. He cobbled together a makeshift SI course, taught cipher (where one uses a phrase whose letters would be substituted to code telegrams), security, cryptography, and reporting in Greek, Italian, and English, and also supervised Italian POWs held at the camp. Amateur at best, the operation lacked the most basic supplies and equipment, such as maps and cameras, and McBaine had to beg for German magazines to help agents identify enemy weapons and uniforms.

Oliver tried to follow the Washington curriculum. Before sunrise, he had the men do gymnastics. After breakfast, the classics professor lectured on reporting, corrected and supervised code exercises, and taught the mountaineers to swim. Over lunch, he edited their work and handled the PX or exchange. In the afternoons, he taught security measures while Chrysostomas trained the radio operators. Following a swimming lesson, they dined together and then played volleyball or watched American movies that Oliver translated into Greek. Occasionally, he took them on excursions and had them write up reports that he translated into English. Afterward, those who needed parachute and commando training transferred to the SOE facility on Mt. Carmel.[60] Meanwhile, Oliver discovered a cave where he excavated Roman pottery in his spare time, a far cry from gathering SI.

After the close of the Quebec Conference on August 24, General Wilson finally granted permission to open the Cyprus base. Forthwith Daniel departed, activated his British and Greek contacts, hired his excavation foreman for counterespionage, and began stockpiling furniture, food, fuel, and first-aid and port supplies.[61] But the distances between the port (Pissouri), base (Metamorphosis), and repair area (Karavostasi), and the lack of public transportation linking them with McFadden's villa, created serious logistical problems, so Daniel required cars for himself and the base as well as domestic staff. These he requested from Young, who had none.[62]

Tired of waiting for Washington, Young asked McFadden to use his 150-ton schooner the *Samothrace,* which was then transiting the Suez to be used as a training vessel for refugee scouts. McFadden chartered it to OSS after Young insured it for $50,000 and paid a $1,500-a-month premium. He had it refitted to ferry Greek Desk agents and supplies back and forth between Cyprus and Alexandria and staffed it with two Greek naval officers. The ninety-two-foot yacht was not ideal. It required a nine-man crew, not including McFadden, who came with it, although he could neither skipper the vessel nor command the crew's confidence. But less than ideal was better than nothing, so Young left McFadden lolling about on the deck at his Royal Yacht Club slip in the Western Harbor of Alexandria, where the dilettante entertained his relatives, the Brintons, and Daniel, and his skipper hosted Lawrence Durrell and Elizabeth Gwynne (David), who worked for the British Ministry of Information and notified Allied intelligence circles about the vessel.[63]

In the interim, Young prepared two missions, both of which would ride the *Samothrace* as far as Cyprus, where they would be sequestered until transshipped to Izmir.[64] The Brigand mission was bound for Piraeus to acquire a "legal" caique and report on naval installations and shipping intelligence. Crayon, meanwhile, would head to Mytilene to monitor shipping in the northern Aegean and set up communications with Athens and Salonika via caiques that the Nazis sent to get olive oil from the island. On August 25,

Young assembled both groups in Alexandria. There they met McFadden, port officers for Caskey and Daniel, and ten armed U.S. military police and a radio operator for Daniel. Young gave each travel papers with a false name and destination, foreign currency, drachmae, and "Q" pills, wished them luck, and returned to Cairo.[65]

Young felt "twisted into the shape of a corkscrew," trying to run Cairo and Alexandria and get the agents trained and into Greece. At the same time, Young felt obligated to report on the "complicated and delicate Greek political snarl" that was developing in Cairo. That month, Eddie Myers had stunned the Allies by flying from a clandestine air strip in the Greek mountains to Cairo with a delegation of guerrilla leaders. Myers intended to initiate constructive dialogue and forestall interband rivalry by establishing British military liaisons in the mountains and guerrilla liaisons in Cairo and facilitating communication and coordination between the resistance, the Greek government-in-exile, the Greek general staff, and the British.

But Myers's timing was terrible, and the mission backfired. The presence of the guerrillas in Cairo aggravated tension and exposed a widening gulf between them and the British, forcing Reginald Leeper, the British ambassador to the government-in-exile, to support the king with one hand and EAM/ELAS with the other. After two days, discussion deteriorated into an ugly row over the postliberation role of the king. Myers told King George II that his return to Greece would foment civil war. The guerrillas further affronted him by insisting that he remain outside Greece until the people had voted on the fate of the monarchy and whether he should return. They wanted representation in the government, but Tsouderos and the king rejected their demands, the Foreign Office terminated the discussions, and Myers was relieved of his command. Afterward, the guerrillas demanded that the king sign a statement that he would return to Greece only after a national plebiscite invited him back, but when Tsouderos and the cabinet pressed him, the king ignored his July 4 concessions and cabled Churchill and Roosevelt (who were still in Quebec). Churchill adamantly supported the king. General Wilson (along with Myers and the head of SOE Cairo) favored the guerrillas' demands as the only way of achieving cooperation in Allied military strategy, since they were, after all, a representative group, proportionally matching their Greek constituencies, with four from leftist EAM/ELAS and one each anticommunist EDES and another group. Then on August 22 FDR and Cordell Hull responded to the king's telegram, declaring that they had no objection to the British policy of supporting the government-in-exile until the defeat of the enemy. Without authorization, Leeper had Wilson order the guerrillas to return to Greece at once. Instead, the guerrillas protested and refused to board the plane. When Tsouderos tried to open discussions, Churchill and the Foreign Office declined, and the ordinarily obstinate king became intransigent. Weeks went by. Instead of bridging the gap, the British widened it and polarized the situation.[66] Meanwhile, as Greeks looked to America to take a leadership role, the United States assumed a subordinate position rather than formulate its own policy toward Greece.

During the diplomatic stalemate, Young met with the representatives of the liberal politicians, but otherwise stayed out of politics. He believed that the Greeks should be able to choose their postwar government, but that in the meantime, they must honor the legitimate one. He felt that reporting the Greek political dilemma emerging in Cairo was of utmost importance and demanded the closest attention and astute judgment in separating fact from fiction. This *should* have been the responsibility of the U.S. ambassador to the Greek government-in-exile, Alexander Kirk, who instead espoused a policy of disinterest and aggravated the situation by insulting the Greeks publicly.[67] On top of this, Vournas, who had been warned to stay out of Greek domestic politics, meddled instead and met with the Greek guerrilla delegation. Fearing that Roosevelt was not getting an accurate picture of the crisis, Young suggested that Vournas lobby in Washington to reappoint MacVeagh to Greece.

McBaine felt the hot breath of failure on his back. Young and the others had guilty consciences that they had managed to procure so little SI, yet he wrote Washington, "The links in the chain are all forged and falling together." As his agents prepared to leave for Greece in early September, Young wished that he, too, might to be free to go.[68]

After a week of waiting, Young's agents secured British permission to leave Alexandria harbor and crossed to Cyprus on the first solo Greek Desk venture. In two days, they showed up at Pissouri, which Daniel had christened "Cincinnati." Because Young had neglected to notify Daniel of their day of arrival, the landing was a fiasco. Despite orders not to let anyone above decks upon arrival, McFadden rushed ashore, everyone else followed, and Daniel arrived to find utter mayhem. Daffy, whose code name proved apt, spoke Greek to those whom he had been told only spoke English and blew their covers. Moreover, since Dow had not sent the barbed wire, Daniel could not keep agents and officers from mingling with random bystanders. While Daniel was transporting agents to Metamorphosis, McFadden's cook smuggled a letter ashore to his wife, who, in turn, arrived with the whole family to see papa and, let in by the port guard, was screeching "Agapi, agapi!" ("Love, love!"). Fortunately, Metamorphosis was more successful. Local Turks thought the farm a German prison camp and flooded it with fruit for the poor inmates, a cover Daniel had not considered. Daniel begged Young never to send the flighty and irresponsible Daffy back, even at the risk of jeopardizing future funding of the Kourion excavations by antagonizing their sole patron. Hobbled by another British shipping ban, the agents and officers remained at the farm for a fortnight, most of which the sailors spent drunk until they boarded a caique bound for Izmir.[69]

EIGHT

≈≈≈

"Entering the Danger Zone": The "Samos Show"

IN EARLY SEPTEMBER 1943, the Aegean remained quiet.[1] While Young scrambled to prepare missions and waited for Dow to arrive, Sperling went so deep undercover that he "almost vanished," and Caskey expanded his empire along the Turkish coast. The Emniyet had granted Caskey secret harbors further north, from Chandarli ("Boston") to Aivalik ("Portland"). Further north, "New Orleans" on the Evros delta, "Cardiff" (Kum Kale) on the Asian shore of the Dardanelles, and Tenedos ("Bristol"), the Turkish island off the Troad, could handle traffic for Macedonia and Thrace. To these they added Arslan Bournu ("Key West") just south of Kushadasi, extending Caskey's reach 150 miles as the crow flies, though bays, fjords, and peninsulas more than doubled the distance. However, without transportation the espionage network remained grounded. Caskey suspected increased action on the nearby Italian-occupied Greek island of Samos, but he could not investigate it without boats. Caskey begged Young for gold to buy his own vessels and quipped that the only gold he had ever seen was that which he himself had scrounged "back in Middle Minoan I." Unaware that Cairo was initiating its own Maritime Unit to handle the traffic, Caskey pressed Rees, who finally begrudged him an old tub from Egrilar.[2]

At five in the afternoon on September 1, Caskey, with the Turks' blessing, sent his first field agent to Samos to hunt for agents and caiques. George Manoudis, Caskey's base chief at "Miami" (Kushadasi), gave the agent let-

ters of introduction and a crew borrowed from the Greek and British services.[3] That night, they moored the caique at the end of a long uninhabited
peninsula below Mt. Mykale. The next day, the agent rowed a skiff across
the mile-wide Samos Strait. Italians greeted him with eighteen grenades
when he approached an island guard post, and Caskey's agent returned fire.
After killing one Italian and wounding another, the agent beached the boat.
That night, he celebrated on an "imperial scale," but forgot to notify Caskey,
who feared for his safety. The next day when Manoudis grilled a caique full
of refugees arriving at Kushadasi, they divulged that Samos had been quarantined and a Fascist legion was hunting down guerrillas. Manoudis seized
their caique and searched for the lost agent, but an Italian patrol fired on
him and took him prisoner.[4]

Events were breaking fast. Lincoln MacVeagh arrived in Cairo as the new
U.S. ambassador to the Greek government-in-exile, bringing Arthur Parsons as his political analyst. On September 3, the Allies crossed the straits of
Messina and set foot on the Italian Peninsula. Five days later on September
8, 1943, the Italians signed an armistice, and Eisenhower announced the
Italian capitulation on the six o'clock BBC evening news. According to the
terms of surrender, the Allies agreed to treat Italy leniently, but Italian ships
had to surrender weapons to the Allies, and POWs had to be released, but
not to the Germans. In addition, all Italy and Italian-held territory were to
be opened to the Allies.

While American Lt. Gen. Mark Clark led the Allied invasion of Italy at
Salerno, Young, at his desk in Cairo, speculated about moving his operation
to Brindisi on the west coast of Italy. There he would be only sixty-five miles
from Greece instead of 600. He became almost cheerful as he wrote Crosby
in Washington that he expected to spend the winter in Athens doing SI and
"laying PIGEON eggs."[5]

The question on everyone's mind that night was, "Who would get to the
islands first?" Churchill lusted after the Aegean "island prizes." "Improvise
and dare," he cabled his chiefs of staff on September 9, "This is the time to
play high."[6] British intelligence personnel from Izmir reached out to beat
the Germans to the Italian archipelago. In Cairo, the British military focused on Rhodes, the plum of the Dodecanese, but British agents in Izmir
looked to what was at hand. Without clearance and ignoring communiqués
urging him *not* to operate in enemy territory, Michael Parish acted unilat-
erally. To secure Samos, he organized a triumvirate consisting of himself,
David Pawson, and Alex Levides.

As Izmir's U.S. intelligence chief, Caskey wanted "tickets to the ball game" and cabled Cairo and Istanbul for permission to join them. Caskey was not impulsive and refused to leave his station without it. Young requested permission of acting Cairo chief Lt. Col. John Toulmin, a suave Choate-Harvard banker from Boston, who replied that it would take a long time and why not just go anyway. Young responded to Caskey pointing out why he should not, but fantasized that night about Caskey and Daniel setting up a Samos base. Meanwhile, MacFarland dispatched Sperling to Izmir to investigate. For five days, Young languished in suspense, and Caskey kept the "bold, dangerous, and quite unauthorized" mission "utterly and bitterly secret," thinking the British might be court-martialed.[7]

On the night of September 8, the Anglo-Greek team, unwilling to delay and compromise their mission, grabbed Pawson's wireless operator to ensure their ability to communicate and abandoned Caskey in Izmir. To avoid the Italian motor launch that patrolled Samos between dusk and dawn, they set out at sunrise on September 10, crossed the sixty miles between Cheshme and Samos, and put in on the uninhabited southwest shore of the island. There they met a guerrilla contingent and awaited clearance to proceed. Runners announced that the guerrillas had armed a large village where British and Greek flew flags side by side, and the Italians were withdrawing from outlying garrisons to Vathi, the main town and commercial harbor in the northeast.

While Italy declared war on Nazi Germany and thousands of Germans marched into Rome,[8] the Anglo-Greek crew edged along the southern shore of Samos. On the morning of September 11, they approached Tigani, a quiet harbor whose red-tiled, whitewashed houses clustered around a quay where fishermen repaired their nets and tended their boats. The Allies feared a clash between the disgruntled Italians and the guerrillas, for the Greeks could not imagine that perverse fate had transformed their enemy into their ally overnight, and the Italians, fearing reprisals, would surrender only to the British. Pawson telegraphed Ankara that Major General A. C. Arnold, British military attaché, should accept the surrender, but added that Levides was prepared to take control on behalf of the Greek government should Britain not be interested. Meanwhile, Pawson ordered the Italians to take them to their commander in Vathi, nine miles to the north, to enforce order and put the island in a state of defense in preparation for Arnold's arrival. Then, Pawson demanded surrender from General Mario Soldarelli, the head of the division that controlled all of the Italian-held Dodecanese except Rhodes. Ready to resist the Germans who had abandoned him at El Alamein, Soldarelli surrendered 10,000 Italians on Samos to Pawson and dispatched the most militant Black Shirts (a volunteer paramilitary security militia loyal to Mussolini) to Ikaria, which had also surrendered. Then Soldarelli transferred civil authority to the Samians. That night, he and the British dined together in the officers' mess.[9] The trio had indeed "played high." Their daring had won the island cheaply. Churchill would be pleased.

While Pawson, Parish, and Levides celebrated, British Special Forces prepared to beat the Germans to Rhodes. On September 9, they moved up from Beirut and took Kastellorizo.[10] The next day, the Allied combined chiefs of staff approved a low-cost occupation of Rhodes, under pressure from Churchill (who ignored that the invasion had been canceled at Quebec and reported that on Rhodes Italians were resisting the Germans). On September 9, Jellicoe left Cairo for Rhodes with an interpreter and a five-page letter of introduction from General Wilson to Admiral Inigo Campioni, the commanding officer and governor of the Dodecanese. After his pilots lost their way, Jellicoe returned the following night and parachuted into Rhodes. A stiff breeze separated the descending men. Defending Italians, mistaking them for Germans, fired on them, and Jellicoe's interpreter broke his leg. Thinking himself about to be captured, the twenty-four-year-old earl ate his letter. At two in the morning, Jellicoe's captors arranged an interview for Jellicoe with Campioni, whose 35,000–40,000 troops, although widely dispersed across the island, vastly outnumbered the small garrison of 7,000 Germans who were concentrated in the capital of Rhodes on the northeastern tip of the island. But during the lost day, the Germans had captured the airfields and cut communications between the commander and his men. When Jellicoe admitted that British reinforcements would not arrive for six days, Campioni vacillated. While the earl napped, the Germans moved in and gave Campioni an ultimatum. Upon waking, Jellicoe found that he had lost the advantage and fell back to Kastellorizo, where he regrouped and gathered commandos to take other islands.[11]

On the night of September 10, British infantry from Malta, SBS commandos, and paratroopers parachuted into Kos and garrisoned the island. Wedged between Turkish peninsulas, it controlled views to Bodrum and Knidos and the islands of Samos and Kalymnos. Once home to Cleopatra's treasury and the Knights of St. John, Kos now boasted one of the best airfields in the east Aegean. When Jellicoe arrived on September 13, islanders greeted his fleet with flowers as if part of a Theokritian idyll. But Kos was only one-fifth the size of Rhodes and not nearly as strategic.[12]

At one in the morning on the clear, moonlit night of September 12, Pawson, Parish, and Levides left Samos with an Italian brigadier general[13] and headed south in a fast Italian motor torpedo boat past silhouetted islands. In fewer than two hours, they approached Leros. No lights illuminated the islets and dangerous rocks that lurked at the island's perimeter below the inky waves. In the early morning dark, they entered the fjord leading to Lakki, which during World War I had been a British Royal Navy base and which the Italians had refortified as Porto Lago, known as the "Corregidor of the Mediterranean" after the impregnable Philippine stronghold. Upon arrival, the Anglo-Greek trio hit a snag. Admiral Luigi Mascherpa, the Italian commanding officer, was away. The officer in charge placed them under guard in a clammy ammunitions bunker and met privately with the Italian brigadier while the trio anxiously awaited dawn. After being released from their subterranean cell, they contacted the Greek bishop and the guerrillas, who pledged their support. Pawson entered the town and found no Germans, while Parish and Levides reconnoitered the airfield, 300 yards away, and discovered 3,000 Italian troops and coastal defenses. Antiaircraft guns ringed the vertiginous *kastro* towering over the isthmus at the heart of the island. The officer in charge reported sufficient food stores for four months and claimed that he could repulse any attack except a major infantry landing. Pawson doubted his allegiance, but thought that he might accept a small British garrison to hold the island and "stiffen resistance." Without securing a commitment, Pawson, Parish, and Levides raced back to Samos that morning and requisitioned the best house in Vathi. That afternoon, Admiral Mascherpa reached Leros in time to receive Jellicoe, whom he wined and dined before the young earl returned to Kastellorizo.

Shortly after Pawson returned to Samos on September 12, German headquarters in Athens ordered Soldarelli to hand over the island. German spies were already on Samos and Leros, stirring Italians to resist. Meanwhile, in Pawson's absence, two divisions of Black Shirts arrived from Rhodes with instructions to sabotage the cease-fire. With Pawson, Parish, and Levides present, the Italian carefully replied that Samos was under British control. Then he cabled his superiors in Italy that he still held several islands in the Cyclades, the Sporades, and Dodecanese. That afternoon, General Arnold left Ankara for Izmir, and Pawson ordered Italian guards to free Manoudis, who found Caskey's agent and caique and returned them to

Izmir. The agent gave Caskey his first intelligence from enemy-occupied Greece, and Caskey proudly passed it to Young. Both Young and MacFarland apologized for being "too late on the Samos show" and discouraging Caskey's participation in the British mission.[14]

The British had taken Kastellorizo, Kos, Kalymnos, Leros, and Samos without resistance, yet everything hinged on Rhodes. In spite of Churchill's August 2 order to organize the expeditionary force and proceed with the secret invasion of Rhodes, General Wilson had dithered and frittered away thirty-seven days. But time was running out.

Meanwhile, Daniel waited for missions and tried to get information. However, the British wanted no leaks to prejudice operations. They kept Daniel in the dark about troop movements, and British interrogators from Egypt refused him access to interned Italians.[15] Daily from dawn to midnight, Daniel ricocheted from Pissouri to Metamorphosis Farm, to Limassol and back again before bedding down in Nicosia. At Pissouri, his coast watchers saw a small, heavily armed convoy moving north, and, in Famagusta, he himself saw the British loading paratroopers.[16] Daniel knew from the British army buildup and clear-outs on Cyprus that Allied military action was occurring in the Dodecanese. Yet in spite of the "steady stream of small stuff going up," Daniel thought the British were still only attempting to create a "nuisance."[17] He had had no inkling of the grand offensive.[18]

Even on Samos the British hold was fragile. Whereas elsewhere in Greece the Italians had surrendered their weapons to ELAS, in the Dodecanese islands they had not. As the British tried to ease tensions and unite the new "allies," guerrillas began attacking outlying Italian garrisons. Pawson asked Soldarelli to disarm the carabinieri, the Black Shirts, and 1,500 armed fascists, so that he could arm the guerrillas, who had only 300 guns among them. He asked the Greek bishop to head the island's civil administration, and to help maintain order, he recommended bringing in the Samiot battalion fighting with the British in the Middle East.

That day, the BBC recklessly announced that German commandos had rescued Mussolini from his mountain prison and brought him to Berlin. The news electrified the Black Shirts, and Soldarelli requested help from British forces on Leros to diffuse the crisis. He knew that without help his disheartened Italians would mount only a token resistance. Fearing a Black Shirt rebellion or German attack, Soldarelli wanted to remove the fascists before they could stage a coup. That night, the bishop fled to his mountain monastery while Soldarelli and his staff likewise retreated to their aerie, and the harbormaster lay off the Turkish coast with the Italian archives, ready to evacuate. When the Germans cabled Soldarelli about the allegiance of the Leros garrison, the Italian replied that it stood by him.

On September 15, Rees purloined one of Caskey's caiques at "Miami," conveyed General Arnold to the edge of Turkish territorial waters, and transferred him to another boat, which ferried him to Vathi. The general was shocked to find Samos defenseless, lacking coastal artillery and antiaircraft guns. He cabled Cairo about developing an airfield to accommodate British and American fighters and parachute dropping ground southwest of Tigani, but time was short. From SOE's base at Egrilar, he requested rifles and uniforms for the guerrillas, reasoning that, without their help, the Allies could not hold the island for more than forty-eight hours.[19] Asking repeatedly for emergency support from Kos, Arnold prepared to negotiate with Soldarelli's Italians, who were demanding repatriation and transport, enticements already proffered by the Germans.

That night, the BBC announced that Mussolini and Hitler were dining together at Nazi headquarters in East Prussia. Mussolini had returned to power and reestablished Fascism in northern Italy. Furthermore, he demanded that Italian forces ignore any previous orders, as they were again under his command and allied with the Germans. He threatened death for any Italian bearing arms in German-occupied zones. Outraged by the BBC broadcasts, Soldarelli wanted them censored. He promised not to let the Germans land, but could not guarantee the response of the island's fascist troops. If the Black Shirts revolted, he would negotiate with them, not fight.[20]

To reinforce British Special Forces, paratroopers dropped onto Leros on September 14. On September 15, General "Squeaker" Anderson, leader of the Rhodes assault force that had been training in Cyprus, arrived on Samos. The royalist Greek Sacred Brigade followed on the sixteenth along with Jellicoe's second-in-command. That day, forty-five British commandos from Kos and Leros removed the Black Shirts from Samos to the island of Ikaria thirty miles to the west. With that, Samos quieted down, and Arnold departed after instructing Parish to remain on the island until British suzerainty had been established and to transfer his MI-9 operation from Khioste to Samos. Meanwhile, caiques ferried supplies for the Royal Engineers developing the Samos airfields and over 2,500 Allied soldiers reached Leros by destroyer, submarine, schooner, and launch.[21] But all avoided Rhodes, where heroic Italians resisted the Germans and held the airport for five days, awaiting Allied reinforcements.

British successes excited Allied euphoria. Energized, Young dispatched the *Samothrace* twice in one week, once with a field agent for Salonika and fuel for the caique fleet, the other with Maritime staff. In Izmir Caskey ("Chickadee") and Cox ("Thrush") cabled a series of intelligence reports. When MacFarland and Young heard that the British had incorporated Samos into their zone of military operations, they felt it was safe enough for Caskey to "look the ground over" for SI opportunities and bases. MacFarland wrote that the Italians would surely surrender the rest of the islands they occupied and the mainland south of Olympus, and Young counseled Caskey that operations might immediately shift to Greece.[22]

They did not know that the tide in the Aegean was turning against the Allies. The Germans on Rhodes had expected an attack since August and increased security. They had already begun bombing Kos and Leros, and the Black Shirts on Ikaria were attacking the local guerrillas and threatening to deliver Soldarelli's islands to the Germans. Against orders, on September 18 Pawson, Parish, and Levides left Samos with Soldarelli's second-in-command to quell the Black Shirt revolt. They proceeded with caution and reasoned with the commanders who pacified the dissidents. Then the trio edged back along Ikaria's northern coast. With Samos silhouetted against the setting sun, they stopped for a siesta and supper and tied up to rocks in a horseshoe-shaped bay on the barren island of Fournoi.[23]

Ironically, that day Caskey had requested permission to tour Samos from General Arnold, who advised him to come to Vathi on September 20. It was a risk. Caskey knew the entire Greek Desk operation, and his capture would have been disastrous, but he went anyway. Even the Emniyet skipped the usual formalities and let him go.[24] Internally, SOE warned against officers going to Samos, but did not share the information with their American allies.

Caskey drove south with Stamatopoulos, the deputy director of HIS Izmir, to "Key West," which lay south of Kushadasi on the southern tip of a headland once inhabited by Greeks. Since the population exchange, it, too, had been evacuated and off limits to all but a plainclothes Emniyet agent who operated a customs office a quarter of a mile away. Caskey parked the car near a clutch of hovels clustered around the mouth of a gorge. Then he threaded a path between bushes and olive trees, perfect for hiding beached boats. Beyond stretched the peacock-blue Aegean.[25]

Caskey stepped from the shingle into his new caique and sailed past Mt. Mykale into the historic strait. Here ancient Athenian triremes had destroyed the Persian fleet, a Samian patriot sacked the Ottoman navy, and fewer than two weeks ago the Italians had caught Manoudis.[26] From their islet lookout, Turks fired their "customary greeting" of several shots in the water. Halfway across, Caskey donned his army uniform and penetrated the enemy-occupied Aegean.

Caskey raised the American flag as he entered Tigani harbor. He was the first American on reconquered Greek soil, and islanders crowded in to get a look at him and his American uniform, the first they had ever seen. Caskey surveyed the ancient capital that once was the pride of Polykrates, a sixth-century BC tyrant celebrated by the Greek historian Herodotus. For over a decade, Polykrates controlled the sea with his private fleet. He had given Samos three of the engineering marvels of the ancient Greek world: four miles of fortifications, harbor installations, and a 1,000-yard-long tunnel under the city to serve both as a secret sally port and aqueduct that piped water from a mountain spring.[27] After Polykrates, the opportunistic islanders had waffled in their politics, switching sides nine times in 120 years after deserting the Greeks for the Persians in 494 BC. In 1913 the Samiots gained their freedom from Turkey, and although the Germans had established themselves there archaeologically,[28] Caskey hoped that the islanders would stand firm with the Allies.

The Italians hung back as Caskey awaited the staff car sent to bring him to General Arnold, who had returned to Vathi when Pawson and Parish did not return. Arnold understood the meaning of cooperation and invited Caskey to live at British headquarters on a spacious terrace in the upper town. At the officers' mess overlooking red-tiled roofs that stepped up the slopes of the harbor, Arnold briefed Caskey on the tactical situation, gave him carte blanche to open an OSS base, and volunteered one of the six Italian staff cars to facilitate his reconnaissance.

That night, Caskey reported to Young that Samos was a powder keg. Its military goulash included Soldarelli's division (whose artillery regiment was necessary for defense against the Germans), one Fascist legion, 500 armed guerrillas, and fifty British officers and men, but no one expected Soldarelli's men to fight hard if the Germans attacked, and one had to keep the peace between the sullen and dangerous fascists and their guerrilla "allies" who defended the west of the island and still clamored for guns. Meanwhile, the Samiot civilians, 3 percent communist, 5 percent royalist, and the rest republicans, were insulted that their former occupiers remained armed. They wanted weapons of their own, and Caskey supported having Greeks defend the island. In spite of the need for reinforcements, Arnold refused to bring in Greeks because of the danger of "political troubles." Expecting trouble, the British brought over tons of aviation fuel from Kushadasi and enough food to feed 4,000 troops for eighteen days, since Churchill refused to let them fight for their own country.[29]

By the time Caskey bedded down for the night, rumors flew that Pawson, Parish, and Levides had been sunk and drowned attempting to capture Ikaria.[30] In fact, they had been betrayed by their Italian captain. When the loyal Italian heard Il Duce's broadcast from Berlin, he bided his time while Pawson pacified the rebels. Then he pulled a gun on the British while they were napping. Soon British intelligence confirmed that the trio had been taken to the German-held island of Syros. The next day, SOE agents thronged Izmir in a vain attempt to ransom the captives before they were transferred by sea plane to Piraeus, but they were too late. German military transport whisked the captives to Averoff Prison in Athens and then flew them to Gestapo headquarters in Salonika.[31] Caskey had dodged a bullet.

With British intelligence services in turmoil, Caskey pounced on the opportunity to beat the British at their own game. For once, he was "a jump ahead of MI 6" and SOE. Needing to find and staff another base, he picked out a small protected bay on the Gulf of Vathi and christened it "Cuba." A mile outside and east of town, the three- or four-caique anchorage was safer than those on the funnel-shaped fjord that led to the main harbor, which the enemy might target. One house provided offices, bunks for agents, and space for a radio; another, storage. Stamatopoulos began lining up staff: a wireless operator and the chief of police and his lieutenant. He set up a smaller base to the northwest, where Piraeus boats called, and another in Tigani at the house of an old man who had spent six years in Chicago.

For once, caiques were ripe for the picking. Arnold gave Caskey one that was large and fast enough for piratical purposes, and Stamatopoulos rounded up three others that would become the workhorses of Caskey's private fleet. Arming them was critical because of the region's shifting politics. The innocent trader pose once used by the British would no longer suffice; if Caskey's "boys" were caught, they would have to fight it out. Again Caskey turned to Arnold, who told him to take anything he wanted from the depot. Caskey grabbed Italian carbines and cases of grenades.[32] Buoyed by great prospects, he left Stamatopoulos in command and returned to Turkey on September 23.

To his dismay, Caskey found "Miami" a mare's nest "of madhouse insecurity." He vented on Young that in his five-day absence, Young's agents had arrived unannounced. No one had bothered to tell them how to contact Caskey, and Manoudis had kept them in "the cooler" without him. The new Services and Personnel branch was to supply missions Brigand (Piraeus) and Crayon (Mytilene), but since they spoke no Greek, they could not provision the agents properly and dispatched them without navigation compasses and functional radios.[33] To make matters worse, the British had compromised "Miami." Caskey longed to transfer his operations to Samos. While he operated from Izmir, the Emniyet would deal only with him, necessitating a constant five-and-a-half-hour round-trip commute from Samos to Izmir, whereas on Samos, Caskey could streamline the transport and supply of his "two ring circus," omit the Turks altogether, and recruit Greek deckhands directly. Meanwhile, Cox could remain in Izmir to handle the diplomatic pouches from Cairo.[34]

To the Greeks' surprise, within a week of General Arnold's arrival, the British imposed a military government. Henceforth, all Allied activities came under British command, including OSS. This was not the outcome that the Greeks had anticipated from liberation, and they were outraged to trade one foreign occupier for another. Instead of allowing them to govern the liberated islands, the British would permit a Greek civil administration only on Samos and retained veto power over it.[35] The Greeks felt hobbled and betrayed. Caskey feared a Greek exodus and wrote Young that the Samiots "howl for guns and curse the British."[36]

Greek and British relations were at an all-time low. For the first time since Young had arrived in Egypt, the Greeks were united in their disgust for the British. Young sympathized with them politically and reported to Caskey that in their dealings with the Greeks the British had surpassed even the general stupidity of the U.S. State Department. Fierce anti-British rumors flew among the Greeks in Egypt where a "tromokratia" (government of gossip) flourished.[37] In occupied Greece, popular support had increased the ranks of the leftist EAM/ELAS from 2,000 in March 1943 to 12,000 by the end of summer. Resistance spread like wildfire when the islands were freed. Now EAM/ELAS threatened not only the Germans, but also more conservative Greeks under General Napoleon Zervas, who had committed the anticommunist EDES to side with the British and reinstate the king.

The crisis had been brewing since the guerrilla delegation left for Cairo. By mid-September when it returned empty-handed, knowing that the British would force the return of the king, and after the British established their occupation government on Samos, tension reached the breaking point. EAM/ELAS lost all hope for dialogue and capitalized on the Italian surrender by taking POWs and stockpiling their weapons. As a sop to the United States, the British War Cabinet transformed the British Military Mission into the Allied Military Mission (AMM) by suffering Americans to join them in the mountains.[38] Although EAM/ELAS was persona non grata with the British Foreign Office, the Allied military commanders needed EAM/ELAS to harass German troops in the Balkans while Allied armies pressed northward through Italy. So the British tolerated it as a necessary evil while trying to control and contain it. But the chasm between the guerrilla groups deepened, and in weeks would fracture the nation.

Caskey moved the compromised "Miami" operation to "Key West," where not even docks betrayed the base. When the Cyprus caiques arrived, Caskey's men rowed dories out to unload agents and supplies and then hid them and their cargo beneath the trees as the caiques headed south. Manoudis managed the base, consisting of two buildings hidden in a vineyard and olive grove. One stored supplies; the other, a four-room farmhouse, served as mess for the caique crews, who ate on the ground floor and lived upstairs in a dormitory facing the sea with a radio shack next to an office with two extra bunks.[39] Additional agents slept under the trees. After provisioning the missions and sending them back to Vathi and off to Piraeus, Caskey returned to Izmir.[40] He worried that increased traffic to Samos would damage his relations with the Turks since Greek and British politicians and military began using "Key West" to leave and enter Turkey without passports, examination, and customs control. Under German pressure, the Emniyet closed all Allied traffic to Samos.[41]

After pacifying the Emniyet, Caskey, exhilarated, settled into Samos. He expected that the move would be permanent and sent for his winter uniform, gas mask, tin hat, and overcoat.[42] Young was thrilled and congratulated Caskey, releasing him from Cairo's tangle of red tape, delays, and snafus and encouraging him to recruit his own men locally. Young called Caskey's three-ring circus between Izmir, Kushadasi, and Samos a "Cerberus show" after the three-headed dog that guarded the gates of the underworld. The archaeologists pored over Young's weekly accounts of Caskey's triumphs. Sperling coveted Caskey's independence, his camaraderie with Cox, and the atmosphere reminiscent of their Trojan "alma mater." The captains remained at their posts, but wanted to get in on the action. At least in Samos, everything seemed to be "breaking well," and they were at last accomplishing what they had given up everything else to do.[43]

In September 1943, the top OSS Cairo personnel migrated west, following the troops. In a week and a half, the Allies had taken Sardinia, Corsica, Bari, and Pompeii. As soldiers moved up the boot of Italy, OSS responded. The center of gravity shifted to southern Italy, and Donovan arrived to address the turmoil. Colonel Guenther moved to new Allied headquarters at Caserta, outside Naples, which was taken on October 2, and Toulmin replaced him. McBaine moved to Brindisi, and Steve Penrose became head of SI.[44]

No one knew what would happen with the Greek Desk. Sterling Dow had just arrived. He took over Alexandria as Young's dispatcher and paymaster, exchanging gold for local currencies and dealing with Greek couriers. Buoyed by harbingers of peace, Young hoped that all or most of the islands would soon be free. If the Greek Desk packed up, perhaps he, too, could move to Samos.[45]

Young talked of abandoning Cyprus, which was too far east for the current center of gravity, and moving the caique base to Kastellorizo ("Havana"), which was on a more direct route from Alexandria to the Dodecanese and Samos and had a better harbor. Kastellorizo, a halfway station, would provide food, water, emergency repairs, and the last briefing before enemy territory. Since July Daniel had entertained the idea of setting up a base in the Dodecanese or at Bodrum to watch German freighters along the coast and the Italians, but the Emniyet had blocked American surveillance there, since Turkey was still supplying Germany's steel industry, which used chrome from Turkish mines to fortify tank armor and gun barrels.[46] After Bodrum fizzled, Daniel volunteered to command "Havana" or penetrate Rhodes.[47] From his interrogations of Greek refugees and boatloads of Italians fresh from Rhodes, Daniel reported to Young that Rhodes was in chaos. Italian residents sabotaged planes and air force munitions dumps to keep them from the Germans. Its Greek residents wanted to cooperate with the Allies, but the Germans had taken their weapons, leaving them free but disarmed until they deported them as laborers to Germany. Daniel planned to work with a handful of Italian refugees from Afando, just south of the island's capital. Its residents agreed to enter the mined harbor to bring out officers with maps and plans. On Afando's broad unmined strand where caiques could be beached, Daniel proposed to plant a caique base facing Cyprus.[48] But Young told him to sit tight.

By the beginning of October, the Allies had taken other islands in the Dodecanese. Young told Caskey to capitalize on the fluid situation, so he diverted the Crayon mission from Mytilene to the Cyclades, where circulation was fairly easy. After establishing a safe house on Tinos, Caskey's agent Vassilios Koskinas left on a reconnaissance tour to see which islands were free of garrisons and patrols.[49]

The British asked Cox to provide relief for the wounded Samiotes who needed vitamins, medicines, and supplies. Cox begged Greek War Relief for support, but knowing how long its appropriations took to get to the field, she borrowed $6,000 from the Ottoman Bank in her own name. With the money, OSS loaded 7,000 cubic feet of dehydrated potatoes, onions, and tomato juice onto an RAF plane and the *Samothrace* to be transshipped on Cyprus and ferried north by caique for Cox's project. Caskey planned to have Cox offer relief with one hand and "gather dope" with the other. Confident that liberation was at hand, Young wanted to know the general situation on Samos regarding politics, food, and medical supplies, thinking that Samos could provide a test run for postwar relief in Greece.[50]

However, despite the ease of conquest, the allied occupation of Samos remained tenuous. Rhodes was the key and sticking point. Without Rhodes or Turkey, all conquests remained insecure. One or the other was necessary, and, because Wilson secured neither, the Dodecanese campaign faltered. In fact, his strategy was doomed from the beginning, for his opponent was not some rival corsair, but Hitler himself. The day after Jellicoe had approached Rhodes's Italian commander, the Germans had demanded and secured the Italian surrender with the added persuasion of dive-bombing Stukas. Daniel's intelligence was stale. In less than a week, the Italian troops on Rhodes had capitulated to a German force one-fifth their size, and Nazi troop carriers began streaming south from Piraeus. Once the Germans had a lock on Rhodes, they organized their own assault force.

Churchill's hoax, designed to make Hitler expect a major Allied invasion of Europe through the Aegean, backfired, for the Germans believed him all too well.[51] Whereas Hitler's advisors counseled him to abandon the islands, cut his losses, and save his troops and equipment for engagement elsewhere, the Führer feared the political fallout of another defeat and refused. Instead, the dummy brigades stirred him to reinforce his troops. Wilson set his feigned invasion for October 26. Then, after the enemy had been led to expect it, Churchill actually ordered him to carry it out. To please his deluded prime minister, Wilson cabled Churchill his barebones plan to wrest

Rhodes from the Germans, but the invasion force comprised a rough, rag-tag assortment of men and equipment insufficient to the task.

Churchill cabled Eisenhower for help, but Ike refused to commit resources to the scheme. and continued to focus on a successful outcome in Italy, where the Allies were hard-pressed. Unprotected British supply and troop ships, harassed and crippled by German bombers, snaked up the Turkish coast from Cyprus and Egypt so slowly that by the beginning of October, only 2,700 men, twenty-seven guns, and seven vehicles had reached the Aegean. Of these, 1,500 British (infantry and two RAF squadrons) guarded Kos, while commandos swelled British presence elsewhere. Still, Wilson shied away from Rhodes.

Despite great heroism, the lucky, reckless days of the Dodecanese Campaign were over within a month. Leapfrogging from island to island, Hitler's force again caught the British off guard and seized the southeastern Aegean. On October 2, a German naval convoy hiding at Suda Bay steamed north from Crete and veered east toward Kos, where they landed undetected.[52] At five the next morning, German commandos began knifing sentries at the airfield. Pilots, roused from sleep beside their planes, sounded the alarm too late. Visible at dawn off the coast, landing craft were joined by paratroopers who dropped onto the airfield as Stukas dive-bombed the waking garrisons. After knocking out the telephone exchange and all communications, they struck the town and the harbor. Then the island fell as Hitler beat Churchill to his own invasion.

In just two days, the British lost Kos and their only Aegean airstrip for Allied fighters. British agents sent in as demolition squads did double duty by evacuating stranded Allied troops. By October 5, the Germans had taken 600 British POWs while the rest fled pell-mell for asylum in Turkey. Meanwhile, the victors showed no mercy to their erstwhile allies. After executing the Italian commander and over 100 of his officers, they ferried the remaining 2,500 Italian soldiers and their equipment to Piraeus for internment and storage.[53]

Early that day, an OSS caique arrived at Vathi. It lay off Samos, where guns were ordered to fire on craft approaching after dark, and then docked at "Miami." On it were agents: Caskey's long-awaited assistant, Lt. John Savage, a Greek-American who had taught for years in Greece and Turkey at Athens College and Robert College; and Lt. Jack Taylor, the new OSS Maritime chief. Taylor visited Caskey's bases. Toulmin wanted him to take over the caique service and establish advanced bases with Vathi preempting "Key

West" and "Havana" replacing Cyprus. After delivering emergency food and medical supplies for civilians to the archbishop and fuel and arms to the British, Taylor regaled Caskey with their "trial by fire," as they had passed dangerously close to

> a beautiful RAF attack from eight miles off [Rhodes] and later, four miles off Kos, we witnessed eight Junkers 88s dive-bombing, strafing, and sinking a destroyer. One plane pulled out of a dive in our direction and gave us a long machine-gun cannon blast, following a single bomb 50 yards to starboard. No casualties. Continuing through the three-mile-wide Kos Strait, we witnessed leisurely dive-bombing and naval shelling on Kos city by Junkers 88s and the Nazi invasion fleet of 15 vessels. No fighter defense, and light ack-ack made it pitiful.[54]

Then Taylor left. He traveled at night through the Samos Strait, fired upon by both British and Turks. After delivering a British doctor to Leros, Taylor sheltered off the Turkish coast and returned to Alexandria.

After listening to Savage and Taylor, Caskey's confidence in the British evaporated. He wrote Young that he could get no official news. Devastated by the collapse of Kos, he thought that the Germans already had Leros. Fearing that Samos, too, would fall, Caskey organized a stay-behind officer to report on a possible German invasion and occupation and procedures for the immediate evacuation of caiques.[55] He stipulated that all Cyprus caiques must fly the Turkish flag, report to the Emniyet, and claim to be in its service. One day, he demanded that they call first at "Miami" instead of Vathi and, the next, he flip-flopped and ordered them to anchor off "Key West," and only those with "innocent" cargo proceed to "Miami."[56]

The loss of Kos betrayed Churchill's impotence. On October 7, Churchill cabled Roosevelt for help, but FDR stood behind Eisenhower in opposing Churchill's ill-conceived stratagem, which diverted troops and equipment from the major Allied offensive in Italy in exchange for what he called a "minor objective." Roosevelt knew, as did Churchill, that the capture of Rhodes entailed a concomitant push to Athens that was unwise, if not downright irresponsible, to undertake without the means to follow it through. FDR saw Churchill's "Balkan Front" as a morass into which he refused to be sucked. On October 9, without Roosevelt's support, the desperate Churchill ordered Wilson to "storm Rhodes." The LRDG launched two missions into occupied Rhodes. After they fizzled, Churchill cabled FDR, warning that the complete abandonment of the Aegean would result in its becoming a "frozen area with most unfortunate political and psychological reactions."[57] But FDR's support of Greece did not extend much farther than a schoolboy's enthusiasm for its ancient inhabitants. Whatever philhellenism he had felt in 1940 and 1941 paled before the task of saving the world as he knew it from Hitler's clutches. Greece was a pawn to be sacrificed. Roosevelt had his eyes on the big picture, which did not include Greece.

Wilson cabled Churchill that the "Rhodes plan as it stood was on such a scale as to incur the risk of failure" and referred to the British liberation of the islands merely as their "tenancy in the Aegean." Even the division that Churchill begged of Roosevelt was insufficient, and sending any more would jeopardize not only the assault on Italy, but also the future Operation Overlord, the invasion of Normandy. Wilson believed that he could hold Leros and Samos only if the Turks cooperated, and he warned that evacuation of the Leros garrison would be extremely difficult. Still, Churchill refused to let go. Unless he got Turkey's permission to use its airfields to regain Kos, the fate of Leros was "sealed." After he threatened FDR that he would advise Wilson to evacuate the garrison, taking with them as many Italian officers and men as possible and destroying the guns and defenses, FDR and Eisenhower ponied up some fighter planes. With these the Allies managed to sink part of a German convoy but only delayed the inevitable.[58]

To make matters worse, Greek resistance leaders, expecting the mainland to be liberated, became discouraged by the loss of Kos. They saw that when the war was over they would again be saddled with a government against their will, this time imposed by the British. Anger boiled over, and on October 9, the countryside erupted into civil war. Armed with Italian weapons, ELAS assaulted its rivals, destroyed the military wing of a smaller resistance group, and pinned the EDES guerrillas to Epirus. Each side dug in and, in the end, stalemated while British airdrops kept EDES alive.

Then an unexpected lull blanketed the Aegean. Again the British froze all transportation. By night, their commandos swept the seas, slapping limpet mines on the hulls of German ships, and, by day, hid off the Turkish coast while the Germans mined the Kos Channel, bombed vessels arriving from Cyprus, and turned to their next island prey. All hung in a delicate balance. Instructions changed almost daily as once-free channels were patrolled by the Germans. Daniel instructed all caiques to sail directly to Cape Gelidonia, hug the Turkish shore, and pass Kos only at night.

By this time, the British were simply hoping to hang on. Until the danger of attack receded, they forbade Caskey to send ciphers, records, radio station, or women to Samos. So Caskey would not let Cox leave Izmir. Prophetically, Young wrote Margaret Crosby, acting chief of the Washington office, that he hoped that Caskey would not get all set up in Samos only to have the island snatched back by the Germans and reported an unconfirmed rumor that Cox might already have been captured.[59]

Not knowing that their president set such low stock in the Aegean, Young labored to get men and supplies north while the weather held. Speed was critical, but the *Samothrace*—fully loaded with sardines and soup for the Samiotes, rations for Daniel, and ammunition for Caskey—remained docked in Alexandria, stalled for almost a month by engine trouble, German subs, and the British shipping ban.[60] Young worried that the Samiotes might not receive Cox's humanitarian shipment when it finally arrived and plotted how to disperse or hide it from the Germans. Finally on October 18, the *Samothrace* set sail with missions Gasoline (Khalkidiki) and Oracle (Amphissa, Parnassus, and Delphi). This time McFadden brought guests along for the ride. When they reached Cyprus, Daniel cabled Cairo about the security breach, "Daffy intolerable . . . Tell him we are at war. He hasn't heard." The time had come to get rid of Daffy and his yacht.[61]

As the OSS caique left Cyprus and steamed northward bearing agents through the Kos Channel, past Allied raiders stalking their prey by night and German bombers patrolling round the clock and pinning them to the Turkish coast, a crisis brewed in Istanbul. MacFarland insisted on controlling all OSS personnel in Turkey. Young balked, and MacFarland flew to Cairo, where he, Young, and Dow hashed out their respective jurisdictions and agreed to cooperate and share responsibility for Caskey, Sperling, and Georgiades. Yet MacFarland refused to sign the agreed-upon memorandum and left for a pow-wow in Washington.[62] Insulated by distance, Caskey consolidated his empire, sailing back and forth between "Cuba" and "Key West." Like Polykrates, he acquired more and more vessels for his fleet, especially small fast ones "for piratical uses." Unable to send Cox to Samos, Caskey dispatched Savage as adjutant supply officer and base supervisor in Vathi with a wireless set to facilitate communication. Young and MacFarland promised Caskey support and gave him independence, assuring him that it was *his* "show."[63]

In mid-October, Young got permission to open "Havana."[64] Despite the danger, Daniel still wanted to command it. He fantasized about getting "hot dope fresh" from the German-held islands and longed for a "lurid future . . . up north." As Daniel prepared to move west, Young again cabled him to wait. General LeFroy, hospitalized on Cyprus with wounds from the Aegean debacle, discouraged Daniel, confessing that Kastellorizo was "frightfully congested," and the British were"ready to pull out."[65] On October 25, Daniel cabled Young that Simi and Kalymnos had fallen to the Germans and Kastellorizo was "precarious," but Young was loath to cancel the new port. "Havana"'s advantages still outweighed its drawbacks. Toulmin had given Taylor command, but he was leaving for Italy, so Special Operations loaned Chris Petrow to Maritime to cover it and British military maneuvers on Kastellorizo. Young was worn down from haggling over fiefdoms. Defusing squabbles with Maritime over the control of bases and caique service exposed the arbitrariness of Donovan's bureaucratic branches.[66]

Young felt out of touch with his original colleagues and their operations. He did not relish thrashing things out with MacFarland, but needed to see Sperling's situation firsthand. Young had not seen him since May and had not laid eyes on Caskey since January. When Lt. Charles Edson arrived in Cairo in late October to take care of Reports and Personnel and Captain Gerald Else appeared to handle supply and reporting, Young felt that Dow could manage without him.[67] He decided to visit the satellite bases, hoping to hitch a ride on the *Samothrace,* but Toulmin forbade it as too dangerous. For staff officers or civilians doing staff work, flying over enemy territory or taking unnecessary risks of being captured were court-martial offenses. The British believed it was "unwise to have a man of Caskey's knowledge of organization even in Samos." Manning an advanced base was the job for an agent (like Petrow) who could blow only his immediate contact, rather than the whole cell.[68] Young and Caskey knew too much and, if caught by the Germans, might be made to tell all.

On November 3, Dow took over the Greek Desk for a month so that Young could visit his field officers. Young rode in a convoy as far as Aleppo where he and his vehicle boarded a train for Turkey. First he visited Sperling in Istanbul. Then they met with Georgiades at a safe location halfway to Edirne where they discussed SI preparations for sabotage in Evros by Special Operations's Chicago mission.[69] Afterward, Young hoped to cheer Sperling with a trip to Izmir and Cyprus with Caskey and Daniel.

While Young was in Istanbul, Churchill cabled Wilson to "cling on" to Leros and Samos at all costs.[70] SBS commandos were split between the two islands, and British reinforcements kept arriving by destroyer from Cyprus and Egypt, but without Allied air support, the troop carriers were sitting ducks. To protect them and regain "a foothold in the Aegean," Churchill requested permission to use Turkish airfields on November 7. Making no headway, he instructed Foreign Secretary Anthony Eden, at a conference of Allied foreign ministers in Moscow, to feel out Stalin with regard to "opening the Dardanelles and the Bosphorus."[71]

As Young prepared to visit Caskey's operation with its secret harbors and caique service, the situation was extremely tense. Dow warned Caskey of the danger of "friendly fire" and ordered Daniel to hold all caiques in Cyprus until advised by Izmir. Caskey muttered darkly that the Greek Desk had "lost" contact with its first three missions: Settler was mute; Crayon was stranded in the Cyclades; and Gasoline's advance agent had not returned. So Caskey hesitated to send on Gasoline's radio operator and agents for Oracle, who had arrived in Izmir on Halloween. "Sure that something big was in the air" and "watching for signs," Caskey sealed his letter to Dow. He left the office early that afternoon and headed for "Miami" and "Key West" to see "the boys" who had been in his care for almost a fortnight.[72]

About one that morning, Caskey heard "all hell break loose" to the southwest. It went on for hours. Returning by car to Izmir, he still heard the roar. The Greeks in his office optimistically said that it was the Allies taking Kos, but Caskey feared otherwise.[73]

Allied agents had reported a buildup of German planes around Athens and troops and equipment in Piraeus while the Germans hid their amphibious craft and rehearsed landings off the Attic coast at Lavrion and Kea. Then on November 11—Armistice Day—the anniversary of Germany's humiliating surrender in World War I, these vessels and troops steamed by moonlight for Kos and Kalymnos. From Kalymnos, it was just over a mile to the beaches of Leros, whose Allied garrison, consisting of 3,000 British, including SBS under Jellicoe, and over twice as many Italian defenders, had endured almost fifty days of air strikes. For the last week, they had been "softened" by continuous bombing in the early morning and evening. Even the storks abandoned their perches in the exposed antiaircraft gun emplacements garlanding the *kastro*'s heights. Although British intelligence warned Jellicoe to expect an assault the following day, troops scattered in isolated pockets across the island played cards in their slit trenches.

Two months earlier, the Italian officer in charge had advised Pawson that only an infantry invasion could take Leros. At dawn on November 12 it came to pass. The Germans began landing on the west and northeast coasts to rid the Aegean of its last defensible Allied bastion. At noon, 600 German paratroopers dropped west and southeast of the main town in order to divide the defenders while Messerschmitts dived and strafed to cover them. Allied commandos tried to "mow them down" to prevent them reaching their weapons canisters. Fighting was "unbroken" and "tough," but varied throughout the island, which was plagued by poor communication. That night a gale forced Samos reinforcements to turn back. More paratroopers jumped the next day. Eyewitnesses described how they wriggled and jerked "like grubs on fishhooks," thudding or bouncing on the rocks when their chutes failed to open. Others "fell to their death with a Roman candle of silk streaming tautly above them," and soon bodies littered the drop zone and dangled from power lines.[74]

On the moonless night of November 13, a destroyer bearing fresh troops threaded the rocky channel by dead reckoning to land a 380-strong detachment of the royalist Greek Sacred Brigade, "encumbered with every weapon of death—grenades slung all over them, knuckle-duster knives, submachine guns, automatic pistols, and even butchers' cleavers." Grim street fighting followed in Lakki. No house remained intact, and the carnage was described as "Thermopylaean."[75] Early on the fourteenth, the LRDG's commanding officer was killed, and communications failed. The British naval base, just across the isthmus from Lakki, destroyed its signal books before collapsing. As Jellicoe scavenged food and ammunition, the Allies were still holding out and fighting back. Then Stukas from Rhodes, Crete, and the Greek mainland converged on the forlorn island.

By then, Caskey in "nightmare ignorance" suspected the worst. He reported to Dow that Leros might have already fallen. "If Leros, then quite possibly—though not certainly—Samos." He had received only one brief radio transmission from Vathi, followed by silence. Finding Dow's responses "very cryptic and darkling," Caskey insisted on printed orders on procedure for the military attaché, should Samos also fall.[76]

For several days, BBC omitted news of Leros. Then, after holding out for five days, Allied resistance collapsed, hammered by German bombardment and a final bitter fight on November 16 when the besieged headquarters finally capitulated. On November 18, Churchill's special naval appointee in Ankara came to Izmir to organize the evacuation. Ironically, the flotilla sent to supply the British garrison ended up evacuating it, ferrying stragglers to asylum on Turkey's shores for four successive nights. When the veil of silence was lifted, the Allied world was shocked to learn of the Allied defeat. It marked the first major German victory of 1943, and the Nazis insisted on unconditional surrender, capturing 3,000 British and 5,000 Italians, including Admiral Mascherpa. Of the four Allied infantry divisions on the island, only 250 men escaped.[77] Another Gallipoli.

For Samos, the handwriting was on the wall. Its garrison had held out longest, but after Leros, Samiotes lived in constant danger of bombardment and invasion, and life became untenable. For a week, all communication with the mainland was broken. Allied commanders ordered troops to withdraw from the Aegean, The Germans occupied the nearby islands of Fourni, Ikaria, and Patmos, and refugees began pouring out of Samos.[78]

November 18 was the low point for the Greek Desk. The Germans surrounded Samos, occupying the nearby islands of Fourni, Ikaria, and Patmos. Then the Germans turned their guns on Vathi. On November 18, the long-feared attack on Samos commenced. Like birds of prey, Stukas circled and dived on Vathi's fjord, releasing their bombs on the last Allied port in the Aegean. Waves of Junkers 88s glided unopposed toward their quarry. Strikes punctuated surreal interludes of peace as residents scrambled for cover. Some troops hid in the Tigani tunnel, others in the monastery of Panaghia Spiliani, where caves had once concealed patriots in the War of Independence. Caskey's hair grayed overnight as he set up a stay-behind radio station, and his assistant, John Savage, was wounded.

On November 19, Caskey opened an envelope from the British consulate marked "PERSONAL MOST SECRET." General Arnold had been ordered to evacuate the British troops and Greek Sacred Brigade from Samos that night. On top of this, he had to evacuate some 200 Greek civilians whose support of the Allies compromised them with the Germans. Arnold asked Caskey for help and confessed that he could not get accurate figures, but estimated that 500 persons needed to be evacuated. Others reported thousands.[79]

Caskey agreed. He reported to Lieutenant Commander Adrian Seligman of the Levant Schooner Flotilla, who briefed him at Kushadasi. That night Caskey provided caiques and crews. It was cold and dark as the overloaded vessels bore away troops packed shoulder to shoulder, over hatches and decks, toward asylum at Kushadasi. There they anchored just long enough to disgorge their cargo before heading back on another run to Samos, where desperate men and women queued at the quay till dawn.

Young was just completing his tour of the bases. Never could he have foreseen how dramatic his timing was. He arrived in the midst of the maelstrom and pitched in at "Key West," while the wounded Savage directed the withdrawal of all OSS personnel and caiques from Samos during the nocturnal evacuations of November 20 and 21. Caskey pressed everyone into service, evacuating seventy-five British officers and men, 400 of Soldarelli's soldiers, most of whom were destined for British internment camps in the Middle East, soldiers of the Greek Sacred Brigade, and Greek civilians. At the quay, Turkish officers made them surrender their rifles and sidearms while General Arnold arranged to send the exhausted British and Greek soldiers on to Syria and Lebanon by train. In the distance, German boats prowled the strait as the Nazis took Samos.[80]

At least the evacuation had succeeded: all British, American, and Greek troops reached safety as well as all compromised Greek civilians and a large proportion of the Italians. Caskey spent several days mopping up operations and departed with Young. In the aftermath, Lieutenant Savage was awarded a Silver Star. British generals Arnold and Wilson lavished praise on Captain Caskey for the efficient and effective evacuation of the troops by caique. Ambassador Steinhardt and Brigadier General R. G. Tindall, U.S. military attaché in Turkey, also commended Caskey and his team. For once, OSS earned kudos from their British "cousins." Only Churchill was silent, never acknowledging the contribution of OSS in his bitter narrative of the Dodecanese campaign.[81]

Churchill's gamble failed because he never secured his main objective, Rhodes.[82] Wilson's improvised defense of the Kos, Leros, and Samos ended in their costly sacrifice. The invasion of Rhodes never materialized, and the Dodecanese Campaign ended in disaster. Without air support, the British Royal Navy, 350 miles from Alexandria and Cyprus, lost half of its Mediterranean fleet: thirty-two cruisers, destroyers, submarines, coastal craft, and minesweepers sunk, crippled, or captured. Of the 282 aircraft flown, 113 were lost. Of the five British battalions that entered the battle, 3,000–4,000 were killed, wounded, or taken prisoner, including Pawson and Parish. Tons of supplies and matériel were abandoned to the Germans, and the British navy was on the brink of mutiny. Wilson wrote the prime minister, "When we took the risk . . . , it was with our eyes open, and all would have been well if we had been able to take Rhodes." But Churchill refused to acknowledge his flawed strategy and accept blame, responding that, like Wilson, he had been fighting with his "hands tied" behind his back. He wrote his chiefs of staff that Eisenhower had drawn an "imaginary line" east of Italy that relieved him and his armies of all responsibility for the Dalmatian coast and the Balkans. He advised Anthony Eden on how to respond in Parliament to questions, such as, "Have we not learned the lessons of Crete?"[83] But it was he who had failed to learn.

Churchill met with Ismet Inönü, president of Turkey, and pressed him to allow the RAF to prepare and use airbases in southwestern Turkey so they could strike at Axis targets, but Inönü, unimpressed by the recent British performance in the Dodecanese, demurred.[84] Winter gales descended. The rougher the waves, the quieter the theater. The repercussions rippled out to the archaeologists for, as Churchill predicted, the impact of British evacuations froze operations in the Aegean, and the Emniyet clamped down on Allied operations and canceled all voyages north.

NINE

"Oriental Endurance" and the "Somber World of Snafu"

ON THANKSGIVING DAY, NOVEMBER 25, 1943, Caskey and Young abandoned Izmir and headed south for a tête-à-tête with Daniel. In Washington,
representatives of forty-four countries sketched out a blueprint for economic assistance to war-devastated European nations through the United
Nations Relief and Rehabilitation Administration (UNRRA). Meanwhile,
in the shadow of the pyramids, Roosevelt and Churchill feasted on turkeys
at the Mena House and plotted their strategy for dealing with Stalin, whose
armies had trounced the Germans in Russia and were pushing them back
across Eastern Europe. To accommodate their victorious ally, they moved
the conversation to Tehran where, from November 28 to December 1, they
nailed down plans for the invasion of Normandy.

With respect to Greece, the Allies committed only to keeping "the
Balkan pot boiling."[1] Roosevelt did not mind if Wilson's commandos kept
German forces pinned down in the Aegean and distracted Hitler from concentrating fully on the defense of Italy and the Eastern Front, but he would
sanction no invasion or much fighting in Greece, where civil war raged in
the mountains.[2] To quiet the factions ravaging the countryside, Churchill
advised the Greek king to appoint a regent and agree to remain abroad until after a plebiscite, but the king refused. When pushed by MacVeagh to
meet with George II and try to persuade the king to agree to a plebiscite,
FDR maintained that "the best way to handle Yugoslavia and Greece would
be to build walls round them and let those inside fight it out, and report

when all was over who was top dog."[3] Roosevelt, who had tired of Churchill's machinations in Tehran, instead foiled what he saw as Churchill's colonialist pretensions, reversed the policy of his own diplomats, and paternalistically advised the king to resist the British and stand his ground.[4]

From Turkey's Mediterranean port of Adalia (Antalya), Young and Caskey passed huddled boatloads of British, the last stragglers from Wilson's task force, as they crossed over to Karavostasi. In Nicosia, Young discussed turf wars with the British, MacFarland, and OSS branches: Special Operations, Maritime, Personnel and Services. Finally, the archaeologists charted the future. Among their priorities were establishing communications with their missions, opening a gateway or bridgehead to mainland Greece via the island of Evvia, and an understanding with the EAM/ELAS guerrillas, and accommodating Maritime within their caique service.[5] To do so, they had to rethink the whole operation. After touring Daniel's bases, they decided to consolidate everything at Karavostasi, where they could hire Greek crews and stockpile supplies with the help of the Cyprus Mines Corporation. The CMC had given them two rent-free buildings within sight of the harbor to use for supplies and "cold storage." It was only one hour from Nicosia, and so Daniel could drive over at night and load and unload agents unobserved.[6] Since Dow wanted to be home for Christmas, Chris Petrow would take charge of Alexandria. In an attempt to streamline operations, Caskey agreed to launch future missions from "Boston."

After a few halcyon days, they departed, but it was not smooth sailing. Caskey's caique exploded as it left Kyrenia. Caskey brushed off the incident, hopping a British caique to Mersin, where he ran into Gerald Calvert, an old friend and nephew of the first excavator of Troy, who got him a berth on the Ankara train. Rattled at the close call, Daniel had the captain arrested, believing the sabotage was related to mounting tension between the Greek Cypriots and the British concerning the postwar status of the island.[7] Meanwhile, Young returned to Cairo only to find that the Emniyet had frozen transportation.[8]

Fortunately, in southern Italy and the Adriatic, the Allies were making important military gains. General Wilson relocated to Algiers and succeeded Eisenhower as supreme Allied commander of the Mediterranean theater, and, by extension, all OSS operations. As the pendulum swung to the west, the former head of Area A took charge of the OSS beachhead at Bari that focused on Yugoslavia, Albania, and "the Adriatic world." Turner

McBaine headed SI, Jack Taylor Operations, while Hollywood star Sterling Hayden, "John Hamilton," ferried agents across the Adriatic.[9] Oliver followed them to Bari and set up a satellite base to handle northwestern Greece.[10] It, too, was rising in importance, since Special Operations had dropped a medical mission to minister to the guerrillas and the Allied Military Mission.

Bari was a windy, rainy mess of nightmare shortages and empty shops, and residents had no food, clothing, electric lightbulbs, or fuel. So Oliver was thankful for C rations and Spam. On the afternoon of December 2, fewer than two weeks after he arrived, thirty ships loaded with food and supplies crowded into the harbor. After dinner, German planes began bombing the convoy. Whatever ships did not receive direct hits were blown up by their neighbors. Within minutes, the port was an inferno of violent explosions, the most serious being a munitions ship whose detonation shattered Oliver's windows and buckled shutters all over town. Those who coped with the 800 injured discovered the ship's highly classified cargo: mustard gas. Over 10 percent of those exposed to it died. GIs who had been pulled from the water and survived were blinded by the poison-saturated oil slicks. No hospital facilities existed in the newly freed sector, and all medical supplies sank with the sinking ships.[11]

Surrounded by suffering, Oliver envisioned thousands of Balkan nationals eagerly volunteering as spies, but most preferred to be transferred to Egypt. Instead, after touring all the concentration camps and prisons of southern Italy, he found that no Greek officer was willing. Security was difficult in Bari, where hordes of released prisoners and internees swarmed the streets. Oliver's first mission fizzled because an agent from Cairo got cold feet, thinking he had been recognized.[12] So when Oliver finally recruited nine Greeks from Algiers, he resolved to house, train, and exercise them and keep them occupied at night. He devised animal cryptonyms, using "Rhinoceros" for himself and "Black Camel" for his assistant, American School classicist Lt. Richard Treat Bruère, who had been seconded from ONI in Tunis, where he had interrogated German POWs after the surrender of Rommel's Afrika Korps.[13]

Across the Strait of Otranto from Bari lay Corfu, which the British had not yet penetrated, with its deep harbor considered a likely point of embarkation for the German withdrawals. Oliver saw his chance and planned the "Alcinoos" mission. He recruited and trained a Greek from Corfu who had crossed the Adriatic in a caique and reported that the Germans had not yet occupied Erikousa (Fano) and Merlera, midsea islands northwest of Corfu. The man agreed to go back to Erikousa as an agent, survey and reconnoiter Corfu, and approach Greek officers who claimed to be establishing a guerrilla operation there. He would persuade them to accept a radio operator whom the OSS would infiltrate and who would collect information on German equipment, installations, numbers, and disposition that he would verify. However, without transportation, Oliver's agent languished for months, flummoxed by the moon, winter gales, destroyer sweeps, and British obstruction. While the Allies stormed the beaches at Anzio and the Russians reached Poland, Oliver and Bruère twiddled their thumbs and busied themselves as Reports officers for the Albania Desk, translating its agents' reports since they had none of their own.[14] Eventually, Gerald Else became Oliver's liaison with Cairo, recruiting five missions in Egypt and escorting them to Bari by plane or boat.

As the Greek Desk network expanded and launched more missions, personnel and agents multiplied from eight to eighty in six months. Young moved Area A to the "palace," a villa near the pyramids where the school reopened with a proper director by Christmas 1943. Proximity to Cairo decreased security, but improved contact between Young, Edson, Else, and the students. Theoretically, each archaeologist could follow a student through his entire training, visit regularly, and give individual attention. Edson replaced Oliver, interviewing refugees to find SI recruits, training them, sleeping there, and showing American movies to improve the men's English and keep them at the base, but students still complained that the program was weak and disorganized.[15] A nine-day English-language curriculum attempted to prepare them for intelligence-gathering. Eventually, Edson dropped the course in close combat, small arms, mapping, and demolition in favor of a more realistic approximation of field conditions although he had not been there himself. Cognizant of the resistance politics in Greece, Edson monitored students' biases and discouraged divisive discussions. Increasingly the Desk favored using Americans to avoid being mired in political sludge, but the pool remained largely Greek speakers. Edson tried to fill gaps in experienced agents' knowledge and technique while culling those who suffered from anxiety or chronic fatigue.

Meanwhile, operational control for Greece, Turkey, and the upper Balkans remained in Cairo, as did the Greek Desk. Through the Anglo-Greek Committee, the British ambassador to Greece and representatives of MI-6, MI-5, MI-9, SOE, and HIS rewarded royalists and blacklisted leftists as politically undesirable. It purported to establish protocol and enhance interservice cooperation, although to Young and Else, who also attended, it was only a rubber stamp. Otherwise, the Cairo routine varied little. Else handled the new missions: arranging ciphers, wireless supplies, caique transportation, ID cards, and travel orders. Petrou and Edson interviewed the Greeks, and Adossides gave agents going into Greece a gold coin to help her family get food.[16] Called "Colonel" around the office, she labored in the code room and checked all translations of intelligence into Greek. Just before Christmas, someone walked into her office and called her "Clio." Surprised that he knew her true name, she mused, "This must be one of the boys." It was Jerry.

"To break away from slavery in Istanbul," Sperling had volunteered to "prowl" about Thrace or Macedonia "under the benign 'cover' of archaeology," but a smallpox outbreak quarantined Evros, and Bulgarian mine laying between the island of Samothrace, Alexandroupolis, and the Evros River made reconnoitering by sea inadvisable. Because his operations were blocked, Sperling spent eight days in Cairo and saw a good deal of Clio Adossides but, being a married man, confided nothing about her in letters.

Sperling informed Young and Toulmin that he had secured Emniyet permission for a top-secret base at the entrance to the Dardanelles through which passed all Black Sea shipping. Because of the sensitive nature of the straits, "Dublin," on the island of Imbros, would be modest and unofficial, but from it, Sperling could monitor North Aegean shipping and the Thracian coast and open both to SI caiques as far as Salonika.[17] It would handle "local boats" between Evros and "Boston." To access it, Sperling would found a sea-runner service at "Cardiff," the Turkish port of Kum Kale near his old archaeological site in a military zone on the Asian shore of the straits opposite "Dublin."[18] With Toulmin's consent and financial backing for "Dublin," Sperling returned to Istanbul. But he could not plan the new base on top of his MacFarland work. So the battles between Cairo and Istanbul resumed. Donovan advised MacFarland to release Sperling, but instead he piled on work. Meanwhile, Sperling begged Young to get Virginia Grace as his assistant.[19]

On January 6, 1944, Young's first mission, Settler, wished him "Happy New Year!" from Athens, his first message carried by boat from occupied Greece. Within a month, Settler's collected military and political intelligence came pouring in. It had organized a network to cover the railroads, the airports, Piraeus harbor, and the meteorological observatory in Athens.

Since U.S. forces would take part in the reoccupation of the Balkans and undertake feeding in Greece, Young asked Settler to gather economic information for postliberation relief and rehabilitation. He wanted information on Ioannis Rallis, prime minister of the third occupation government, which had further polarized Left and Right and instituted the "Rallides," four Greek security battalions that had been terrorizing Athens. Rallis had recruited them before the civil war erupted from a coalition forged by an MI-6 officer, Archbishop Damaskinos, and Evert, the head of Athens police, with EDES and conservative republicans. Rallis used them to combat EAM/ELAS, whose population swelled with disaffected republican and EDES resistance fighters. The battalions' numbers had increased, and after being trained by the SS in the autumn, they replaced the Italian occupation forces in Athens.[20] Young cautioned Settler that OSS did not "intend to interfere in Greek internal affairs, but to let the Greek people choose for itself what kind of government it wants after the war. At the same time we are interested in how they feel in general, and about the various organizations which are at work in Greece."[21]

Young depended on Caskey's operation in Izmir, which had mushroomed into a large organization. Caskey forwarded most of Young's missions, among the more important of which were Stygia to Evvia, Byzantine to Athens, Floka to Florina for economic, military, air, and naval intelligence, and Horsebreeders to Volos for military and economic intelligence. He also organized his own missions, such as Dago to Leros and the Dodecanese, using Italian refugees from Samos whom the British had rejected. Early in 1944, Caskey, too, heard from agents in occupied Greece. He received reports from Oracle at Amfissa and Delphi; Despot at Andros; and Emerald, his stay-behind mission on Samos. To monitor the Italian refugees around Izmir, Caskey used an Italian count with the rank of lieutenant colonel who functioned as his assistant military attaché.[22]

In January 1944, Donovan proclaimed that henceforth Maritime would direct all boating operations. His decision, meant to release the archaeologists from drudgery, displeased them since they did not wish to relinquish command of the fleet that they had worked so hard to gather and set afloat. Moreover, Maritime's officers were a mixed bag (from Washington, or hired locally from military police, the armed guard at Port Said, or other OSS branches), and few spoke Greek, the only language spoken by the majority of agents and crews. Furthermore, Maritime men, often accompanying the sailings of one and a half to two months, could not communicate with the crew and left operating the caiques to the Greeks, whose experience trumped their own. In the end, because of the language barrier, the archaeologists still had to do much of the work, without having authority.

Nevertheless, once Maritime secured sufficient staff, financial support, and vessels, the caique service thrived. Steve Bailey, a reports officer who succeeded Taylor as chief, cooperated with the British so that crews could get supplies and repairs en route at Famagusta or Haifa and insisted on knowing all sailings so that he could inform the proper authorities lest Allied planes target the boats.[23] He grouped the boats into three fleets. The southern one braved the Mediterranean between Alexandria and Cyprus and supplanted the *Samothrace*. The largest supply caiques, between 40 and 185 tons, were slow but more reliable.[24] Cyprus managed the central fleet, which had vessels of middling size, twenty to forty tons, and sailed from Cyprus to Turkey. "Boston" ran the northern fleet with small fast boats of eight to twenty tons, which darted from Caskey's secret harbors ferrying agents through the deadly Aegean.

Greeks, Dodecanesians, and Cypriots controlled the caiques, which needed only half a schooner's crew. Three or four sailors from the same island manned the boats, whose captains usually owned them and plied the same waters before the war as fishermen, traders, and smugglers. Like ancient mariners, they stayed close to shore and eschewed broad stretches of open water. They were not trained mechanics, but knew the prevailing and seasonal winds, so that when newly installed tank engines broke down, they could rely on sail like their ancient counterparts. In exchange for the risks involved, sailors generally earned a good wage, and captains, who rented their vessels to the OSS, often profited from smuggling Jews or black market goods. Although some talked too much, and others liked the bottle, most were loyal to the Americans.

Maritime headquarters were in Alexandria, the point of departure, major repair station, and source of supplies. Chris Petrow managed its makeshift operation in the Western Harbor, which grew to include a warehouse, a villa housing Petrow and transitory agents, and a pier next to the *Samothrace* inside the Royal Yacht Club at Ras El Tin. Petrow ensured that supplies arrived where and when they were needed (with accurate manifests) and informed the field promptly of all ship movements.[25]

Young and Bailey got along well and bundled missions and supplies. Caiques left Alexandria laden with bales of clothing, weapons, and food, often on the hoof to keep it fresh. Beer and cognac helped pass the time, as the

Alexandria to Cyprus leg took about fifty-four hours. Lambs were slaughtered on board with blood running all over the deck. The crew prepared morning tea and afternoon coffee on a wood stove as well as two hot meals a day of stew and rice or meatballs and potatoes. But agents had to get used to the roll and vibrations as well as noxious fumes and the swinging boom, and nausea often set in soon after they left Alexandria and headed into the wind in a heavy sea. The captains, who navigated with a compass, usually hit the western tip of Cyprus right on the nose. By the time they reached it, the men were eager for land, but waited until dark to disembark to avoid detection.

After leaving Cyprus, they sailed all night until late afternoon the following day when they anchored for the night in a well-sheltered harbor adjacent to a Turkish lighthouse at Trasania (Trianisia), southwest of the twinkling lights of Adalia. In the Mediterranean, the caiques flew the Turkish and Americans flags while sailing and dropped the Turkish one as they came into port, where payoffs in the form of American cigarettes, aspirin, and quinine sweetened the local officials, who looked the other way. They continued along the south coast, setting sail again at dawn, past Cape Gelidonia, whose treacherous rocks had claimed many ships over the millennia. Hugging the coast past Fenike, the caiques threaded their way between tiny islands only fifty to one hundred yards from the mainland. Opposite Kastellorizo, they anchored near Kash or continued to a small bay hiding an extremely well-protected harbor near an island cluster called Tarsanades, where ghostly Roman arches marked the site of ancient Patara.

At dawn the next day, they pressed on past Fethiye Bay (the chrome port where German freighters lurked), Seven Capes, and the Marmaris straits. In rough weather, they ducked into the British base at Apothika, on Doric Bay near Cape Alyro in late afternoon. Its narrow-mouthed, well-protected harbor opposite Rhodes opened to a cluster of huts sheltering refugees and a base manager, who sometimes offered them fresh snails and pigeon pilaf. Several caiques with machine guns mounted on their decks anchored there. On a promontory, a small Turkish military observation post housed five or six uniformed sailors and soldiers who sometimes asked to know one's nationality. All knew of the American bases at "Miami" and "Key West."

From dawn to dusk, the caiques inched north along the coast of the enemy-occupied Aegean, flying the Turkish flag if they saw Germans and the Greek flag if they saw Turks. By evening, they reached the tip of Cape Krio at a small harbor with a lighthouse near the ancient site of Knidos. Two or three huts housed a Turkish military observation post, the only sign of life. The following dawn, the caiques broached the Gulf of Kos, where they could travel only by day and watched for enemy torpedo boats, keeping their weapons ready, either camouflaged or buried under provisions. Usually they gave Kos a wide berth and hugged the Turkish coast, passing Bodrum, whose harbormaster was pro-German and hinterland was rife with Nazi agents and sympathizers. That afternoon, they reached Gümüzli, a British anchorage with ancient ruins run by a helpful island Greek. At the Samos Straits, a rifle shot signaled the need to check in with onshore Turkish officers who might want a lift into Kushadasi. Thenceforth, caiques hugged the shore until they reached "Key West," whereupon Manoudis walked them through Turkish customs.[26] If they put into Kushadasi, they stayed below deck until dark, when they were ushered to the officer, photographed for an ID, and given 1,000 drachmas.

On the last leg of the journey across the enemy-infested Aegean, the caiques darted about as *peiratika* (piratical boats). Their captains sailed by the stars, pumped with adrenalin. By day, they slept under camouflage or in sea caves to avoid being seen. As the sun sank and temperatures cooled, crews quickened, for this was the hour to set sail. In port, these black market caiques passed as legal, camouflaged with sugar, soap, wheat, and cheese.

"Key West" continued to handle southern traffic,[27] but Caskey opened "Boston" as a more secure alternative. The harbor lay on a windy peninsula fifty miles northwest of Izmir, southeast of Mytilene, and about forty miles southwest of ancient Pergamon. Just south of Chandarli at a beach known as Reshadiye or Rasadia on Rema Bay, it was in a military zone patrolled by Turkish soldiers. The small fishing village consisted of ten houses, a *kaffenion*, and Turkish customs building. OSS occupied a defunct olive oil factory whose dirt floor reeked of stale oil and was home to long-tailed rats "as large as cats." The first floor housed thirty-five cots, a mess hall, gun room, storage room, kitchen, and carpenter's shop. Above and accessible only by ladders was a radio shack with antennae strung toward Cairo, and a room used as an office and dormitory for the four regulars stationed there.[28] "Boston" was, in fact, Caskey's only truly secret harbor and became his main base, commanded by Lieutenant Savage, with a communications officer in charge of all the Turkish bases, a Maritime radio operator, and general assistant. In time, it housed ten Americans and fifty Greeks who serviced and repaired caiques and warehoused supplies ferried north from Cyprus. The northern fleet moored here, and the excellent harbor became the final staging point for all missions headed for occupied Greece.

While Caskey opened "Boston," Cox went to Egypt. It was her first rest in a year, and she went sightseeing in Luxor. In Cairo, she discussed Greek War Relief and devised a plan whereby Americans would be first to offer the Greek islanders postliberation relief. Then she enlisted Donovan's support to stockpile food, medicine, and clothing in Izmir. He urged U.S. minister Lawrence Steinhardt to back her plan and reminded him that he had once called Cox "the best man we have in Turkey."[29]

Around this time, American School archaeologist Gladys Davidson joined the Istanbul consulate under the cover of Greek War Relief, replacing Homer Davis as the State Department's special assistant in Greek matters. Davis passed through Izmir with his wife Marjorie, listed as a clerk. Cox moved her office to her quayside apartment. Her Greek assistant prowled bars and coffeehouses for newcomers, sized them up, and brought them to her. Caique captains corralled others, who provided useful information and tended to be more expansive in the unofficial atmosphere of her apartment. "Under the influence of a Turkish coffee and cigarettes, especially American, they told what they knew and drew maps, diagrams, etc." Groups of three gave the best results. In that relaxed setting "where they could come, sit, imbibe coffees, smoke, and occasionally in the evening take an oozo," they talked.[30] Cox also used her flat as an OSS boardinghouse. "I give them bed and breakfast or if they are rundown or ill or something, other meals." It became a convenient depository for

> a couple of Americans who ought not to be seen or three or four agents or crew members. . . . a tucked away propeller shaft (or even 2) brought to Izmir to be repaired, a couple of battered army rations, radios, or a choice of 45s, 38s, and a Baretta for an agent to choose from. Men came there for lessons in code ciphering. And groups who leave together for the bases are often collected here and depart from my back door.[31]

In early February, Virginia Grace began working as Sperling's code clerk, assuming his former tasks of ciphering and deciphering messages and translating field reports from Greek into English. Sperling was elated at the "windfall." Imagining that he, too, might soon command his own empire, he virtually cooed about his bases: "Dover" (Istanbul) and "Bristol" (Tenedos). Soon he would open and staff "Cardiff" and "New Orleans."[32] Young tried to place Meverette Smith ("Melvin") in Izmir to help Cox, but got bogged down arranging her passport and visa.[33]

Hoping to build bridges between OSS branches, Young agreed to place Special Operations agent Captain James Kellis of the Army Air Force as a liaison with the Evros guerrillas in exchange for intelligence. Quiet, soft-spoken, and of medium build, the Greek-American had worked six months in Cairo, where he had conceived of the Chicago mission, to sabotage the rail transport of chrome from Turkey to Germany.

Early in the war, the Turks had worried that the Germans might invade Turkey at Edirne, only two hours from Istanbul, so they destroyed their only rail links with Europe. But after the countries signed a nonaggression treaty and trade agreement in 1941, Germany had pledged weapons in exchange for Turkish chrome, and the Turks rebuilt the bridges.[34] Since then, they had shipped approximately 135,000 tons of chrome either by barge up the Danube or by rail. By the spring of 1944, over ten trains a day carried ore or passengers between Turkey and Germany, where the Reich stockpiled chrome to protect its war machine. The line forked in Turkish Thrace with one branch passing through Bulgaria and the other through Greece.

The State Department asked Kellis to go to Istanbul to assess the plan's feasibility. So Sperling met the Greek-American at Haydar Pasha station. Ever the "spook," Sperling wore a trench coat and extended his bejeweled hand. Seeing the flash of a ruby ring, Kellis followed Sperling into a black sedan. When Kellis's radio operators arrived, Sperling met them in similar fashion.[35] They would work closely with Georgiades, or "Gander," in Edirne, code-named "Pittsburgh" after Georgiades' home in the United States. Cairo gave top ratings to his intelligence. Gander had crossed the river frontier between Greece and Turkey four times, thanks to the local Emniyet agent who transported his supplies, gave him a special password, and allowed him to dress in a Turkish officer's uniform. Georgiades provided photographs and operational intelligence for four railroad bridges that crossed the Evros from Svilengrad just across the Bulgarian border to east of Alexandroupolis in Greek Thrace. Kellis had given them code names consistent with that of the Mission: "Chicago," "Cicero," "Milwaukee," and "Joliet" and hoped to blow up two of them.[36]

However, Georgiades' main job was to obtain SI from Evros, the Sorcery mission. Over the course of four months, he also met with guerrillas in the Rhodope Mountains and the Evros valley to glean intelligence and coordinate resistance against the Germans, and Virginia Grace supplied him and handled his reports. British sources passed him pouches for MI-6 in Istanbul and tried to replace the leftist guerrillas with those loyal to the Greek

Fig. 18. George Vournas, "Vulture" (center in tuxedo) and the Chicago mission to Evros at AHEPA Convention in Washington. *On left, front row:* Captain James Kellis. *Left to right, back row:* Michael Angelos, George Psoinos, Spiro Kapponis. (Courtesy Spiro Cappony.)

government-in-exile. Repeated purges had polarized the guerrillas into a radicalized ELAS in the mountains and a cowed conservative one to the south. Georgiades tried to mediate between them and restore harmony. OSS had instructed him to refrain from politics, but Georgiades clearly admired the guerrillas, who lived communally in primitive conditions, sharing guns, caps, and sweaters and weapons that belonged in a museum. He offered them medical help and warm clothing in exchange for accepting Kellis; they, however, preferred guns. His contact, a rogue communist guerrilla leader, became more and more violent, dispatching death battalions to purge Evros of collaborators, black marketers, and political rivals and terrorizing the local population. Kellis arrived during the reign of terror when he declared war on all English sympathizers. In February 1944, Georgiades' ELAS contact was apprehended by an ELAS leader who tried, condemned, and executed him under trumped-up charges to get him out of the way. To infiltrate the Chicago mission, Georgiades had to negotiate all over again with the new man. The longer Kellis and his men waited, the lower their morale sank.[37]

Although Oliver, Caskey, and Sperling were promoted from captain to major in February, the promotions did little to ease Sperling's troubles with MacFarland. Cultivating "Oriental endurance," Sperling wrote Young cryptic letters about the "wolves" at the Istanbul consulate, which he called "the Istanbul animal cage" and "a madhouse of intrigue and counter-intrigue." He reported that MacFarland was plotting a hostile takeover of Greek Desk agents in Turkey and had hired someone to be his "eyes and ears" in Cairo. Eventually, MacFarland's interference and hoarding of Georgiades' written reports led to a showdown. MacFarland stormed down to Cairo, and he and Young had their third row.[38]

That month, Churchill reopened negotiations with Turkey and again asked Inönü to allow the Allies to use Turkish airfields. Franz Von Papen, the German ambassador to Turkey, found out about the plan and threatened that if Turkey were to agree, Hitler would bomb Istanbul.[39] When Inönü rejected Churchill's scheme and declared that Turkey would not enter the war on the side of the Allies, the British withdrew their military mission.

Immediately, the Turks blocked all operations in Thrace; they refused to let Georgiades' agents back into Evros and prevented him from crossing the Evros for months. "Cardiff" collapsed, and the only way to supply Evros was through "Dublin" and "New Orleans," but the islands were "closely watched," and German sea and air patrols made contact "very difficult" between Izmir and Khalkidiki (where thousands of Germans swarmed into the Cassandra Peninsula). Sperling wrote that "guerrilla action remains confused." Sick of "bureaucratic dyspepsia" and being "tied down" to an office, Sperling confided to Caskey that things were moving, but "slowly and through mazes of guile" and, regarding "Dublin," there was "not much cheer."[40] Meanwhile, Kellis was marooned in Istanbul, caught in the larger game of cat and mouse between Turkey, Germany, and the Allies. Although OSS was not to spy on its host country, Sperling put Kellis's operators to work, gathering intelligence at Istanbul's port and train station, where they noted the time, day, and number of shipments and bribed a Turkish official to get their manifests as more chrome reached Germany.

OSS relations with the British were on thin ice. Cairo gossiped that Rees was trying to liquidate Caskey's operation.[41] When the British asked to use "Dublin," Sperling refused. Young's agent on the Gasoline mission to Khalkidiki was in desperate straits, with no radio operator. He had sent intelligence along with a plea for help with a British boat in December, but Rees impounded the files rather than forwarding them to Caskey. So the agent waited, stranded in the mountains. When British agents on Evvia asked an agent from Brigand to carry their mail, he had done so, not knowing that the mail was anti-EAM. As a result, the EAM guerrillas in control of the island had captured him and held him hostage for seven weeks. When they released Young's agent, he tried to reach an agreement between them and OSS, but was prevented by a German security sweep. When he finally reached Izmir and relayed his story, Caskey blasted his British "ally" and confessed that he found himself "swinging strongly toward EAM."[42]

At that point, Ensign "Johnny" Athens (Maritime), who had recently arrived to manage "Boston," wanted to see some action and decided to go to Evvia to negotiate with the guerrillas for the free passage of OSS agents and mail. He left his post on February 23 and sailed for Evvia with a Dr. Green who was supposed to minister to the Evros guerrillas for Kellis's Chicago mission, but because the doctor could not proceed north, he went to Evvia instead.[43] There they contacted the guerrillas and, in exchange for medical supplies, tried to establish OSS points of entry, dropping grounds for supplies, and permission to open a Maritime base and bring out downed Allied pilots. Athens's mission was helped by a cease-fire reached between EDES and ELAS just before he arrived. On February 29, the Allied Military Mission (AMM) brokered an agreement at Plaka near Yannina whereby the guerrillas accepted a "cessation of hostilities" and both sides exchanged prisoners and hostages. Confining themselves to the territory they held on the day of the Plaka Agreement, each faction promised to fight only the Axis occupation forces and secretly signed on to "Noah's Ark," the AMM's plan for the liberation of Greece.[44]

While Athens was negotiating with EAM on Evvia, Georgiades risked his life crossing the Evros border and zigzagging between the guerrillas and Sperling to organize and train resistance groups from Evros to Mt. Pangaion to collect information for the OSS. The winter's purges had polarized the Greeks in Evros. Because of his good relations with the guerrillas, Georgiades alienated his pro-British Greek "allies" at the Edirne consulate, who did not trust the ELAS communists. Georgiades called them "vultures" and imagined that in his absence they violated his secret files.

When the Emniyet suddenly gave the Chicago mission the go-ahead, Kellis and his radio operators embarked on their so-called medical mission without the doctor. On March 22, Georgiades' assistant picked them up in a black sedan. At Edirne, Georgiades outfitted them with rifles, ammunition, and horses. After being delayed five days by snow, they finally set out with ten Turkish border guards. Knowing of a recent ambush and sensing that the Turks were stalling, Kellis feared betrayal and sent them off at gunpoint. That day, Emniyet relations deteriorated for good.

As the agents hiked downriver, the situation worsened. The Germans had guards posted every two miles along the border, heavily armed cavalry rode between them, and motorized patrols prowled the area's few roads. On March 29, the agents rowed across the Evros into Greece in a flat-bottomed wooden boat. German patrols were already hunting for them, so Georgiades led them on a five-hour march to the mountain headquarters of the ELAS guerrillas. In their lair, Kellis and Georgiades negotiated cooperation with the new chief and his band, called the "Capetanios." OSS would provide guns if they agreed to use them against the enemy rather than other Greeks. They agreed and Kellis recruited ten former Greek army officers to discipline the unruly throng. After finding a suitable cave, Spiro Kapponis set up his wireless and began sending messages to Cairo, using his own distinctive style and signature, his Gary, Indiana, high school fight song.

While Kellis and the Chicago mission were settling into guerrilla life, Alcinoos mission returned to Bari with the first Allied intelligence from Corfu in over a year and the first Allied communication with the island in five months. It had made contact with EDES on the island. Alcinoos reported that the Germans were fortifying Corfu.[45]

Just as Young was feeling good, Maritime's relations with SI blew up in his face. When Athens and the doctor finally returned to "Boston" after a month's absence, Caskey ordered Athens to remain at his post. But the truculent ensign defied him, insisted on delivering his intelligence directly to Cairo, and deserted his post.[46] Caskey complained that Athens had absconded, leaving a leadership vacuum that resulted in mayhem and unprepared mission crews making dangerous runs into occupied territory. Caskey judged the differences "irreconcilable" and dragged Young into the fray.[47]

Meanwhile in Cairo, Athens reported to Toulmin that he had been wildly successful. The swashbuckling ensign had dealt with EAM Central Committee and painted a moderate and reasonable picture of the guerrillas, far less black than the conventional one. Within a month of the signing of the Plaka Agreement, EAM opened routes on Evvia to SI and allowed the first courier to cross unmolested as a gesture of friendship. Instead of reprimanding Athens, Toulmin promoted him and transferred the new lieutenant to Special Operations. Because the lack of a clear chain of command caused unnecessary confusion and friction, on March 27 Toulmin, tired of quibbling, gave Maritime sole charge of the boats and their bases.

That day, Toulmin wrote Young that he had officially transferred Sperling, Georgiades, and their Greek Desk operations in Turkey from Young's jurisdiction to MacFarland's. Fed up with "the Istanbul circus" and the "cat-and-dog fights," Young cabled his resignation to Washington, explaining that he felt "personally responsible" for the men.

> The reason that this desk has functioned at all is because Caskey, Sperling, Daniel, Georgiades, Edson, Else, & Co. have mutual confidence in each other's judgment, and want to get a job done together. Caskey has worked himself nearly to the point of exhaustion not on any military orders, but because he wants to get the job done and not to let down Hiram and Savage and Pete and me. We in the office here are supposed to work an eight hour day; we work a ten hour day because that much time is needed to get the work done—so that the recruiting and training, equipping, sending off, communicating, and supplying of bases may be done. There is no necessity for this along military lines. We could work eight hours, then say the hell with it, that's all we are paid for, and go and sit in Shepheard's bar for the rest of the day, and nobody could object legally or militarily. . . . [They needed] UNIFIED MILITARY COMMAND UNDER ONE HEAD.[48]

In preparation for his departure, Young began a history of the Greek Desk. He recommended as his successor Daniel or Vanderpool (if he could be got, trained, and delivered within a month) or Sherman Wallace (an American School alumnus who had succeeded Dow as head of the Washington Greek Desk when Dow resigned in February). Toulmin accepted Young's resignation, but ignored his recommendations. Instead he championed the head of Area A as Young's successor. Fortunately for the Greek Desk, Donovan countermanded the "offensive MacFarland arrangement" and rejected Young's resignation. Young reconsidered, and his resignation was "overlooked." Without him, the Greek Desk would collapse, and Else would request immediate transfer. Even with him, its key players were beginning to crack. "Consistent failure was not good medicine."[49]

Smoldering Greek political enmities also reignited. EAM formed the Political Committee of National Liberation (PEEA) and appealed to Tsouderos "to realize the imperative national needs and make an effective contribution to the formation of a government of national unity."[50] When the Greek armed forces in Egypt realized that the king would not agree, republican politicians expressed allegiance to EAM and its committee. On March 31, they presented Tsouderos with an ultimatum demanding the formation of a national unity government along the lines of the committee and warned that delay meant civil war. When Tsouderos refused, mutiny erupted. The king asked the British to intervene and arrest the demonstrators. Churchill was appalled and sought backing from Roosevelt, who reprimanded the Greeks for their "pettiness" and advised them to focus on their "glorious past." Tsouderos resigned, and the king appointed Sophocles Venizelos. The British threatened to deny Greece a place at the peace conference if he did not end the mutiny. After almost a month without foreign support, the mutiny, exacerbated by British mishandling, collapsed. The British court-martialed its leaders and interned more than 10,000 in concentration camps in the Sudan and the Western Desert and the Free Greek Forces disintegrated.[51] Venizelos resigned within days. Afterward the British and King George II replaced him with the republican George Papandreou.

Emboldened by news of Russian victories and German defeats, Hungary decided to defect from Axis control. Lt. Col. Florimund Duke, OSS's southeast European chief, parachuted into Hungary to help the resistance, but due to leaks in MacFarland's operation, German sympathizers were expecting him. They arrested and handed him over to the Nazis who, on March 23, marched into Budapest.

Turkey continued to walk the tightrope of neutrality between Germany and the Allies. The United States left its military mission intact, but revoked its Lend-Lease agreements with Turkey. The Emniyet responded by canceling "Dublin." As Soviet troops entered Rumania to capture Hitler's oil fields, Turkey realized that its increasing isolation left it more and more vulnerable to its arch enemy, Soviet Russia.

TEN

~~~~~

Operation Honeymoon

IN EARLY APRIL 1944, Young felt that the archaeologists were "gradually being overcome by a sort of creeping paralysis." No one felt he had any authority. In Cairo, Young was coping with the aftermath of the mutiny and the Greek political crisis. To discover the true intent of EAM/ELAS, SI would partner with the Labor Desk. Together they would send the Pericles mission. It would be the first to enjoy the privilege of free passage on Evvia. Young warned Caskey that its agent would soon arrive at "Boston."[1]

Young's letter was still en route on April 15 when Caskey stepped out into the cool night air, heavy with jasmine. Caskey was agitated and looked out to sea. That afternoon, representatives of General Arnold, the British military attaché, and MI-5's internal security officer had asked him to assist them in a top-secret mission.[2] Caskey was to receive a most important guest—a fraulein of twenty-five, the daughter of an old-school Berlin diplomat who had had numerous postings abroad. In 1936 she had moved to Cleveland, Ohio, where her father had served as consul general for five years.[3] Reports varied about his allegiance to Hitler. Word had it that he had displayed a life-size portrait of Hitler in his office and the swastika in his home in suburban Shaker Heights, spoken at rallies of German-Americans, and supplied the German military attaché in Washington with data and clippings about Cleveland industries and civil defenses.[4] Yet his daughter later maintained that he was adamantly anti-Nazi.

Nele Kapp had enjoyed the life of an American teenager, making friends, going by her Americanized name of Cornelia, and perfecting her English in a private high school and at Case Western while her two brothers remained in Germany.[5] When the U.S. government closed all German consulates in July 1941, the Kapps returned to Germany. Nele did not adjust well and studied nursing to avoid factory work.[6] After her father accepted a posting to Italy and before joining her parents,[7] Nele made an extensive tour of Germany and became well informed about conditions there. With the invasion of Sicily, Herr Kapp was reassigned as consul general in Sofia, Bulgaria, and Nele followed, working as an embassy secretary while her brothers fought on the Russian front. According to one account, an OSS agent in Ankara contacted her to spy for the Americans, letting it slip that her Ohio boyfriend was with the OSS in Ankara.[8]

The Allies bombed Sofia in November and December 1943, killing thousands, destroying hundreds of homes and offices, shutting down water and electricity, and feeding fires that ravaged the defenseless city. During one attack, a German embassy employee from Ankara met the Kapps in the air-raid shelter of Sofia's German embassy.[9] The shell-shocked girl asked her father to allow her to recuperate in Turkey, where she secretly hoped to defect.[10]

To get her to safety, her father asked the man about work.[11] Impressed by the efficient, well-dressed woman with long blond hair, "a true 'Gretchen,'"[12] the Ankara representative mentioned an opening and recommended her for the post. The commercial attaché in Ankara needed someone trustworthy and of an unimpeachable background to fill a confidential position as temporary secretary and cipher clerk. Apparently, she struck him as outspoken in her support of National Socialism as the only hope for Germany, and her father's excellent record with the diplomatic corps, coupled with her family's standing in German society, recommended her, so Ankara hired her in less than a fortnight.[13]

A very different young woman presented herself in Ankara early in January 1944. By that time, Kapp had endured yet another bombing raid and suffered a nervous collapse—her eyes were glazed, her hair disheveled, and her skin was gray.[14] She lived in perpetual fear and took sleeping pills and drugs to assuage her nerves.[15] In this way, she survived, plodding through translating, taking dictation, and answering the phone in the commercial attaché's office.

Like most attachés, Kapp's boss at the German embassy in Ankara, Austrian Ludwig Moysich, actually worked in espionage, as *Obersturmbann-führer* in the SS and chief of the Ankara Sicherheitsdienst (SD) under

Hitler's intelligence czar, Ernst Kaltenbrunner.[16] Ironically, Kapp reported that security in Moysich's office was surprisingly lax. Four days after she arrived, the shapely secretary had a key to her boss's safe.

Soon Kapp began an affair with a good-looking young pilot named Gustav Rengers, who had deserted from the Luftwaffe and roomed in a building where an employee of the British embassy resided.[17] She later told Caskey that she first offered to turn over secret information to the British embassy in Ankara, but had received a noncommittal response.[18] Perhaps she had asked for too much in return, or perhaps the British had not taken this young German with an American accent seriously. Their loss.

Kapp had then gone to a German-Jewish dentist in Ankara and asked to be put in contact with an American.[19] She met an U.S. foreign service officer who, conveniently, also had a toothache.[20] Was he her young Clevelander? Richard Gnade, special liaison to Ambassador Steinhardt and Third Secretary at the U.S. embassy in Ankara worked for military intelligence. To him she pitched the same offer, proposing to swap Nazi secret information in return for a pledge to help her escape from Turkey to America.[21] She claimed that she and her father were anti-Nazi[22] and promised to make shorthand copies of the German documents at the office and then transcribe them at home. She brought Rengers and asked the United States to get him out as well.[23]

Gnade communicated her offer to Steinhardt and returned the following night. Kapp gave him the documents she had copied. Gnade informed Rengers that the U.S. ambassador was willing to stick his neck out for Kapp alone. To her he made her no promises, but welcomed her information.[24] Then Gnade handed her over to the military attaché.

Early in her tenure at the German embassy, Kapp received an odd telephone call from a brusque and rather presumptuous gentleman who muttered, "Pierre speaking." His cocky manner roused her suspicion. She had no way of knowing that for months this had been his code of address when contacting her boss.[25] Nor did she know that the voice was that of Elyesa Bazna, a notorious spy whose handiwork had for six and a half months reached Hitler's desk.

In the first month of his employment as the British ambassador's Turkish valet or *kavass,* the observant servant had penetrated security at the embassy. First the swarthy valet located the black box in which his oblivious employer kept his most important papers. Then he made a wax impression of its key and had a duplicate fashioned. With this, he removed top-secret documents, photographed them with a Leica and a 100-watt bulb screwed into the sitting room lamp, and replaced them without notice. He sold the resulting film for £20,000 sterling in cash to Moysich, who promptly forwarded it to Berlin. Von Papen, the German ambassador, nicknamed the spy Cicero after the Roman orator since his prolific documents were so "eloquent." They gave Hitler briefs of the Moscow, Cairo, and Tehran conferences, disagreements between Churchill and Roosevelt over the European invasion route, and British attempts to pressure Turkey into joining the Allies.[26] Those that he offered to Moysich that January afternoon foretold a massive bombing raid later that week on Sofia where Kapp's parents were.[27]

When Kapp began to spy for the Americans is unclear. According to one source, she began delivering intelligence by the middle of January, according to another, mid-March.[28] She worked without pay, copying documents in the evenings and handing the copies to a representative of U.S. Military Intelligence, including her boss's cables to Berlin and lists of Nazi spies working throughout the Middle East.[29] It is also not clear when Kapp connected the paper Cicero with the voice of "Pierre."[30] She told Gnade that on certain Fridays her boss got very excited and locked the code room. When "Pierre" phoned, the office staff had to clear out. She knew it concerned the British.[31]

SI in Berne had known of Cicero since late December, when a German agent Fritz Kolbe, aka George Wood, divulged copies of top-secret documents to Allen Dulles, the head of that OSS office.[32] Dulles tipped off his British counterpart to the Ankara leaks at New Year's and relayed the information to Roosevelt, who cabled Churchill on January 15.[33] After Churchill complained about "the leaky conditions," the Foreign Office in London sent its assistant head of security and a detective to Ankara. They arrived the day that Bazna first spoke to Kapp as "Pierre."[34] Independently, the American military attaché shared Kapp's information with Steinhardt, who advised notifying the British.[35] Again they were told of the leaks, this time that an agent was giving the German embassy information of top importance and that every fortnight the Germans transmitted this information by code to Berlin. Ironically, although a British assistant military attaché checked for bugs and tightened security,[36] Cicero remained on the loose.[37]

In early February, an Istanbul Abwehr (military counterintelligence) agent and his wife went over to the Allies. Hitler reacted by abolishing the entire division and consolidating German intelligence under Himmler. Their well-publicized defections strained Kapp's boss, but gave her hope. Sperling reported that the Nazis were "boiling mad" and that he had been warned to watch out for "itchy trigger-fingers."[38] Then the diplomatic scene in Ankara quieted down as Germans and Turks watched with horror the approach of the Russians.

At the beginning of March, Cicero made his last delivery. After that, the British ambassador went on a three-week leave. So far, his "valet" had received £300,000 sterling, or 2.3 million Turkish lire. He returned to the German embassy to collect the balance of money owed him for photographing 130–150 telegrams in 400 images on forty to fifty rolls of film, the last containing documents that referred to Operation Overlord, the Normandy invasion.[39]

Then the pattern suddenly changed. Moysich instructed Kapp and the other staffer to await a phone call every Saturday afternoon from a man who would say in French, "Mr. Moysich is expected for poker tonight at the same house." She was to reply "Mr. Moysich regrets that he cannot come." But no call came.[40] When the other staffer became ill, Kapp took on her work, going through embassy mail that arrived every evening by Berlin courier in a special envelope marked "STRICTLY CONFIDENTIAL TO BE OPENED PERSONALLY" by Moysich. On one occasion, classified mail was mixed with the batch to be opened by the office clerk. In it, she found three secret documents, one of which concerned Cicero and made it clear that he worked at the British embassy. That night she copied them.[41]

Like Cicero, Kapp played "a . . . subtle, psychological game."[42] Her task was to establish Cicero's identity. By late March, she felt she had as much information on him as it was possible to obtain.[43] She knew he was a servant at the British embassy and, although she did not know his name, she believed she could establish which he was. Moreover, she had obtained the German diplomatic cipher as well as copies of secret documents, in which she read of an American spying for the Germans, increased Allied military aid to Turkey, and Germany's attempts to stop the rash of defections.[44]

When the original secretary returned to work, Kapp lost her privacy, control, and access to mail. Stymied at the brink of discovery, she returned to routine translation, frustrated and completely distracted. Feigning hysteria to mask her fear, Kapp imagined "in a state of frantic anxiety, almost of terror" that the other woman was watching her and that her superiors suspected her. Although Moysich thought her "out of her mind," he only suspected that she was having a nervous breakdown.[45] He wrote Herr Kapp, who had transferred to Budapest in March after the German occupation of Hungary,[46] but his wife was ill so he could not collect her until after Easter.[47]

Meanwhile, Moysich was beside himself because Cicero (who had decided to end his espionage career) had not contacted him.

Nearing the breaking point, Kapp needed to get out fast. She had asked Moysich to hire Rengers. Worrying that the flyer had talked too much and jeopardized her safety, the Americans gave her "Q" pills, just in case.[48] On Monday, April 3, she requested leave to be with her family over Easter (when her brothers would be home from the eastern front) and promised to complete all of her work by April 6.[49] After Kapp had secured leave, she quieted down and, as a cover, sought presents for her parents. Moysich took her shopping and by bizarre chance chose the same store where Cicero was purchasing a dress for his mistress. Eyeing the attractive young woman, the "valet" offered to interpret as she purchased lingerie.[50] Despite frequent phone conversations, she did not recognize him when he stood before her, translating her measurements to the shop girl behind the counter. Once she had even followed him in the night as he called on her boss, but it was dark and she had not gotten a good view.

On April 5, Moysich was distracted by breaking news that the Russians had besieged Odessa and Sevastopol in the Crimea and had just entered Rumania. At the same time the Americans and British were conducting round-the-clock raids on Rumania's Ploesti oil fields. Germany's situation looked hopeless. Moysich was so eager to be rid of Kapp that he bought her ticket for the April 6 overnight train to Istanbul, which connected with the next morning's courier plane for Berlin on which the ambassador himself had reserved her seat.[51] When Moysich announced this seamless itinerary, Kapp suspected treachery. Later that day she bumped into Cicero at the Ankara Palace Hotel, but she was again oblivious, being in the company of a young man with whom she appeared to be on "intimate terms." The furtive "valet" fancied that that same young man had given him and Moysich a hair-raising nocturnal chase.[52] This time, the Turk panicked and expunged all traces of Cicero's activities.[53]

Kapp called the Americans on the morning of April 6 and told them that her boss had ordered her to take the Istanbul train that night and fly on to Berlin.[54] After saying her good-byes at the office, she went home to pack. Moysich went to see her off on the Istanbul train. So did Rengers.[55] Moysich had heard rumors that they were having an affair and, when she did not appear, interrogated the ignorant pilot.[56] Then he rushed to her flat, but found it empty. At midnight, Moysich checked the train, bound for Adana. No luck. He suspected suicide, but when the German embassy suggested that she might have defected, Moysich put a price on her head, ordered that she must be found "dead or alive," and offered a large reward for clues to her whereabouts.[57] After "an avalanche of excited signals," he alerted agents across the country to watch all means of transportation. But they were not quick enough.[58]

Kapp fled on the afternoon of Maundy Thursday—April 6, 1944. According to her own report, she went to the young man from Cleveland, who worked for the OSS, and demanded asylum. Hitherto the Americans in Ankara had kept Kapp's work secret, but as soon as she abandoned her post, they alerted British authorities. Perhaps they wanted to protect her, but she herself claimed that they wanted to present the British with a fait accompli.[59] The embassy resolved to send her to Cairo, where the authorities could decide what to do with her. The problem was how to get her out of the country and safely to Egypt.

The American military attaché gave the job of getting the young woman out of the capital city to his assistant, Lieutenant W. Ewart Seager. First he had to make her disappear. In order to do this, Gnade picked her up at her apartment at three that afternoon and drove her to Seager's flat. She was moved three times that first night, and finally hid for a week in a flat that belonged to two American secretaries from the U.S. embassy. The girls cropped her platinum blonde hair and rinsed it in henna till it was black. Seager gave her the uniform of a Wren, or British nurse. At one point, she left the apartment with the OSS man, whom she had encountered at the Ankara Palace.[60] Cicero saw them, recognizing first the young man, then the walk of the slim nurse. He informed Moysich of her whereabouts and demanded his reward.[61]

But Seager was too quick. Like his brother Cedric, who had masterminded the Abwehr defections in Istanbul, Ewart was a Levantine Englishman who had been born in Istanbul before emigrating to America and earning his U.S. citizenship.[62] Seager operated like a native and knew the Turkish transportation system. He drove to the station alone, expecting the Taurus Express, and remained there for approximately five minutes. The northbound train for Istanbul and southbound for Syria and Baghdad arrived simultaneously. He hopped on the southbound train, moving through the cars, and then jumped out and into the northbound train before it left the station. He dodged into an empty car, the entrances to which the conductor was locking as his followers began searching the southbound train.

He had arranged to have a rowdy group of embassy employees go to the girls' flat, pick them up (including Kapp and her luggage), and drive to the first stop that the northbound train made at Ayash. He would jump off the train, grab Kapp, and get her on it in a matter of minutes. In order to keep the conductor from locking the doors and ruining his scheme, the fast-talking Seager took him into his confidence, with the help of a wink and *baksheesh*. He explained, showing his passport, that he, an American citizen, had just gotten married, and that his bride and the wedding party had missed the train, having been conducted to it separately, according to a quaint American custom. The conductor cooperated, allowing Seager to jump off and nab Kapp and her trunks before he locked both doors and the train got under way again.

Kapp, who was by now wearing "smart New York clothes and fairly heavily made up . . . like an elegant young American," was in a bad way, "clutching tablets in her hand the whole time." Sleeping pills or cyanide? Seager gave her a loaded gun, which she kept on her person at all times. He had brought a bottle of Scotch along and offered her a "thick slug," but it did not sit well. No sooner had they lain down on their separate berths than she announced that she was going to be sick. He went outside while she retched. The complicit conductor came up to the "bridegroom" and assured him, "Don't worry too much; they're often like that on the first night." Instead of continuing on to Istanbul, where they would have been caught, they got off at six in the morning at the railroad junction of Balikesir, an important Turkish military center near a British camp where RAF engineers had been supervising the construction of Turkish air bases. Upon arrival at the provincial station, the "newlyweds" were met by a British officer, who dropped them at the camp, where they spent the night.[63] The next morning they were driven by truck to Izmir.

They arrived in the late afternoon of April 15 at the British consulate. Rees had just submitted his resignation for reasons of declining health, but still interrogated Kapp. Although he had managed thousands of escapes, Rees refused to help, maintaining that the difficulties under present conditions seemed to him insurmountable. Seager recorded him saying, "That girl is a German. I'll have nothing to do with her. The only good Germans are dead Germans."[64]

And so they came to Caskey. The Izmir representative of the British military attaché and security officer told him about the girl and asked him to give the fugitive and her escort asylum until they could get her out of the country.[65] Caskey agreed. He was curious and up to the challenge, fluent in German thanks to his German-American mother and his father, who had been raised in Dresden. He offered the honeymooners Cox's quayside apartment, and they gratefully accepted. The last year's comings and goings of Greek refugees, Americans, and an occasional whore provided the perfect cover for the night's guests. No one would bat an eye.

Caskey was used to hiding "bodies," but none as hot as this. Although Kapp was seriously depressed and her nerves completely shot, Caskey, who always had "an eye for the ladies," could see that she was still a knockout. Because of her mental condition, Kapp could not be left unguarded and required round-the-clock supervision. So Caskey and his radio operator, a sergeant named Romeo, served as armed guard outside her door while "bride" and "bridegroom" spent the night.[66]

The next day, Caskey had them removed to one of the suburban British enclaves that surrounded the city. It was Greek Easter. There, within the high walls that separated the British villas and their gardens from the rest of the population, the honeymooners enjoyed tea in comfort, natural beauty, and relative security. They would need their strength.

The British security officer suggested sending them with a throng of Greek refugees who were traveling overland by train to Aleppo in Syria, but Caskey knew better. The exhausting trip would take days and present too many chances for detection and exposure, especially at border security, an ordeal even under normal wartime conditions. Word had gone round that the Germans had already posted agents at Adana, where the couple would have to change trains, as well as the frontier. So that journey looked excessively risky, even with a resourceful groom.

Late that night, the British called on Caskey again. The American offered to engineer her escape in an OSS caique from "Boston" and made preparations "in astonishingly short order."[67] To ensure success and Turkish support, he insisted on notifying the Emniyet.[68] It proved to be a good decision.

Honeymoon would be a joint Anglo-American operation.[69] Caskey, Seager, and the British security officer laid the plans. A young British officer, recently returned from a tour of duty in enemy-occupied Greece, would replace Seager as Kapp's escort.[70] At a quarter past ten on the night April 16, he, Caskey, and an Emniyet officer left Izmir. They met Seager and the girl outside town and sped north, arriving at Caskey's secret port at half past one.

The unsuspecting base was brimming with agents in transit for the Horsebreeders, Pericles, Byzantine, and Chicago missions. Through a fault in communications the base had not been notified of the top-secret operation, but the groggy men hove to. Some would never forget the stunning young woman who stepped out of the long black sedan and was whisked away in the dark. While two men stocked the caique, the Greek captain checked the engine, and his crew hoisted its sails. By four in the morning on April 17, the *Mary B* slid silently away from the shore under sails bathed in moonlight.[71]

Later that day, Savage drove to "Key West" to meet the caique and provide any additional assistance before it braved the treacherous waters of the southwest Aegean.[72] The boat arrived at one in the morning on the eighteenth, took on more provisions, and passed four precious hours, waiting for an opportune moment to slip through the Samos Strait. Every hour's delay compounded risk. It sailed at five. The day dawned perfect, and the caique averaged a little over six knots in spite of a slightly damaged propeller. After half a day at sea, they put the perilous Kos Channel behind them, and even Kapp recovered her spirits.

In their wake, a steamer loaded with German agents from Istanbul arrived in Izmir. Ostensibly they had come to inspect the chrome mines east of Bodrum, but the following afternoon the German consul general's private Mercedes was also seen heading south.[73] Were they part of the stakeout or coincidental? In the week that followed, both of Caskey's ports attracted unwelcome attention. German consulate cars passed "Boston" with "uncomfortable regularity." One afternoon, the Mercedes stopped outside the gate of "Key West." While four passengers were "busily picking daisies," another inquired about the collection of caiques anchored off shore. Meanwhile, the British security officer in Izmir received daily reports of German agents watching the railway traffic at Adana, including a hunchback.[74]

Although Izmir was known to be a point of egress and hotbed of Allied activity, Caskey managed the escape without hindrance, knowledge, or even suspicion of unauthorized persons. Newspapers in Turkey shouted the disappearance of the embassy secretary on April 19 and recounted the Germans' feverish attempts to recover her. Overnight cables flew to London, New York, and Cleveland, where articles announced Kapp's defection.[75] By the time the *Cleveland Plain Dealer* ran the story on April 24, the Turks had officially stopped shipping chrome to Germany.[76]

Kapp had entered the world of the Greek Desk at just the right time and added "a little luster" to life in Izmir. Young read in Caskey's weekly report of Operation Honeymoon, one "bright spot of efficient smooth cooperation in a somber world of snafu." Yet even there Caskey withheld "Details too secret to be given . . . until fingers be uncrossed at news of successful completion."[77] Daniel signaled from Cyprus on April 22 that the *Mary B* arrived with Caskey's "married couple . . . in fairly good form." But Kapp was decked out in her Sunday best and halfway to shore before Daniel could turn her back. Word had gotten round, and the whole island knew they had come. That night, Daniel gave them a shower, hot meal, and a good night's sleep before turning her over to MI-5, which billeted her in a military hospital and then flew her to Cairo for interrogation.[78] Caskey notified Seager of her safe arrival at Karavostasi. And the Levantine thanked him heartily for "the mad, glad news" and reported that the many photographs he had taken on the "interesting journey" had come out "more than well . . . despite broken propellors [*sic*], Greek Easters, irate Security men, and Lord knows what other obstructive forces." Seager hoped to use them to "achieve the ultimate ambition of [his] life to collect the reward for [his] ward," and awaited news from Kapp herself.[79]

Caskey had reason to be pleased. Honeymoon had been praised "a superbly efficient and successful operation." With his part in the affair successfully concluded, Caskey fired off an "Eyes Only" to his chums in Istanbul and Cyprus that they were to destroy immediately after reading.[80] To Young in Cairo, he sent a top-secret account of the escape of the young German woman who, working for the Americans, had infiltrated the German embassy as confidential secretary and cipher clerk and turned over secret and valuable information to American military intelligence. Kapp had taken considerable risks to acquire and pass on information to the Americans, and he had, in turn, protected her. While she was wanted "dead or alive" by the Germans, his crew had managed her escape and gotten her out of the country. Caskey knew that Kapp would divulge valuable information in Cairo and suggested that Young use her in a propaganda campaign to erode German morale and encourage others to defect.[81]

Thus, the Greek Desk played a critical role in the demise of Cicero, one of the most notorious spies of World War II, and boosted OSS morale. Seager congratulated Caskey on the superb coordination and noted that it was "not altogether unsatisfying that we should have made this, perforce, almost an all-American affair from start to finish, at a time when we few Americans are reputed to be quite inept at skullduggery."[82] The U.S. military attaché in Ankara congratulated OSS Cairo for the "difficult and risky assignment," almost entirely carried out successfully by Americans, and

Whitney Shepardson, Donovan's new director of South Europe SI, extended his "official and personal thanks" and praised with warm admiration "Mr. Caskey's report of Miss Kapp's odyssey . . . this feat is a most encouraging sign of the maturity of our organization . . . well-deserved fruits of the Greek section SI."[83] The Greek Desk had proven that the Americans could hold their own.

ELEVEN

The Birds Began to Sing

AFTER A YEAR IN CAIRO, Young was sick to death of politicking. He remained deskbound, his elbows sticking to the table, his flock flown to Greece, his office flooded with their cabled chatter. Thrush continued to be most prolific, then Gander, but Dodo (Despot mission to Athens), Grackle (Settler to Athens), Loon (Oracle to Amphiṣsa), Seagull (Crayon to the Cyclades), Pheasant (Phalanx to Salonika), also joined the chorus. To process the warblers' chorus, often written in Greek, Margaret Crosby had joined Young as reports officer in Cairo, now a "rear headquarters," and Columbia classicist Moses Hadas of R&A digested and distilled her work for R&A in Washington.[1]

Everyone sensed that the end was near. With Russians marching south, Young expected the Germans to withdraw fast. For months, his agents had monitored the harbors and railroads of occupied Greece waiting to transmit news of the German retreat. Meanwhile, Allied sabotage teams remained poised to strike at the enemy's communication and transport channels. Young wanted to go in, too.

In May, the birds notified Young that the Germans would evacuate southern Greece if the British let them go unopposed. As the troops began their withdrawal, curfews permitted circulation only during daylight, and forbade gatherings of more than five. Churches could only open for half an hour on Sundays, and only food shops could open at all. The British declared the Peloponnese a "zone of operations" on May 20. Young received troubling reports that in March the security battalions had begun to persecute their own countrymen and targeted the communists. Grackle reported that as the Germans destroyed railroads and bridges in the Peloponnese and the SS pulled out of Kalamata, their Greek fascist protégés replaced them and policed the local population. In April, when all German construction ceased, the security battalions swelled with the unemployed and criminals paid with food and cash. A state of siege developed in Athens, as the Germans began disarming the capital's security batallions, and some deserted to ELAS.

Penguin contributed intelligence on George Papandreou, the post-mutiny prime minister of the Greek government-in-exile. Employing EAM's rhetoric, Papandreou fashioned himself "a crusader for national unity" and held a conference in Lebanon from May 17 to 20 in order to form a representative government and meet the demands of the mutineers. Among the twenty-eight delegates were Venizelos, Kanellopoulos, and the head of ELAS. But this was no independent Greek affair. The British staged and monitored it, placing their ambassador to Greece, Reginald Leeper, between Beirut and the conference hotel. MacVeagh refused to participate in the sham proceedings where Papandreou, with his audience captive and Britain behind him, cornered the EAM delegates and blamed them for the March mutinies and the civil war. EAM's leaders in Greece tried to advise their representatives in Lebanon, but the British withheld their messages. By proffering a ray of hope that King George might finally step aside, Papandreou secured an agreement and began to form a "Government of National Unity" with the king's blessing. The majority of the Cabinet took their oaths of office on May 24. When EAM/ELAS threatened to abstain from endorsing the Lebanon Charter and joining Papandreou's government, the British Foreign Office asked the Americans to intervene. The secretary of state refused to become embroiled in Greek domestic politics and, observing the Atlantic Charter, which guaranteed self-determination, demurred. Disgusted, Young wondered why he "*ever* believed that Washington could do or would do what they promised."[2]

Meanwhile, Evros grew increasingly dangerous, and Young worried about Georgiades. After Sperling asked to be transferred, the Emniyet had him followed and arrested his manservant "Jeeves," a Turkish Jew whom they interrogated and accused of espionage. Police inspectors stopped Georgiades' assistant and grilled him about "a tall blond American named 'Jermi Sperlin.'" Gander reported that the Germans increased their forces from 400 to 4,500 and intensified their terrorist tactics in Evros, in response to the increased guerrilla activities. The Nazis terrorized civilians, surrounding and searching villages, seizing hostages from the local population, and posting guards at bridges, rail lines, and river crossings formerly used by Gander's couriers.[3] In spite of this, OSS managed back to back arms drops, and guerrillas flocked to the Chicago mission. Because of the sealed border, Lieutenant Athens went in by sea, landing a caique loaded with marlin submachine guns, rifles, automatic weapons, ammunition, and explosives at "New Orleans" on the Evros delta. With U.S. support, they became the best armed guerrillas in Greece. After weeks of training, they were ready to sever the rail links between Turkey and Germany.[4] Kellis targeted "Milwaukee," a 210-foot span just across the Bulgarian border at Svilengrad that Gander had reconnoitered. On May 29, nine loaded freight and two passenger trains passed over the bridge. Later that day, with the help of more than 170 trained guerrillas, Kellis and Lieutenant Athens mined the bridge with 1,400 pounds of plastic explosives. At quarter past midnight on May 30, Kellis lit the fuse. Within minutes, it exploded and the structure collapsed. With the guerrillas acting as decoys, Kellis and Athens began a forced march back to their hideout. To the south, a smaller group blew up "Joliet," a one-hundred-foot-long concrete and steel railroad bridge at Antheia on the Greek fork east of Alexandroupolis. Then Gander evacuated the Chicago mission, after it achieved the most spectacular OSS sabotage in Greece. They stopped rail traffic between Turkey and Germany, leaving 690 carloads of German-bound freight marooned just inside the Turkish border, but the chrome shipments had officially ceased a month earlier.[5]

In the ensuing weeks, Gander and Sparrow apprised Young of Turkey's mounting concern over the advancing Soviets, and Turkey began to realign itself in a hesitant process of severing ties with Germany. From May 27 onward, the Emniyet prohibited travel around Evros, the Dardanelles, and Aydin Province to facilitate their own troop movements and blocked roads between Izmir and "Key West." The Emniyet, skittish about the OSS's arming of leftist guerrillas and communists for sabotage so near its border, ordered the Edirne base closed and Georgiades removed on the pretext that he was known to the Germans. Any future work there would have to be limited to SI. They did not know that two members of the Chicago mission remained behind.

The Turks were not the only ones concerned about the power of the EAM/ELAS guerrillas. For months, the deputy chief of staff for American command in Cairo had understood that EAM/ELAS was "by far the single most dominant factor" in Greece, but its intentions, the extent of its con-

Fig. 19. Chicago mission packing plastic composition C-2 explosives to blow up the bridge at Svilengrad. (Courtesy Spiro Cappony.)

tacts with the Soviets, and its stance vis-à-vis hard-line communists remained unclear. He knew that the British "Empire-builders" had "tragically mismanaged the Greek situation," and did not think it "wise" for the United States to follow British policy "blindly" and give Churchill a "blank check." Balkan developments would condition life for the next generation, and America could not allow the British to "make a mess of the post-liberation phase and of the peace."[6] Therefore, he wanted an accurate unbiased picture of the motivations and plans of EAM/ELAS. To get it, he contacted the Labor Desk (an SI branch that recruited U.S. agents sympathetic with the Left to gather intelligence from leftists in occupied countries). The mission was aptly named Pericles after the statesman-general of democratic Athens in the fifth century BC. When conceived six months earlier, Pericles was a three-phase mission combining aspects of SI and Special Operations, but by the time it reached the field, it was to gather political and military intelligence on EAM during the occupation. Then during withdrawal, it would organize raids to seize German documents, coordinate transportation and communication paralysis, and penetrate behind German lines. In the postliberation phase, it would focus on political, economic, and psychological intelligence, establish a base in Athens, and decide upon key operational points with EAM.[7]

He apprised Young of Pericles since Young would be responsible for infiltrating and supplying the mission, which otherwise would be kept secret—even from the British. To penetrate EAM/ELAS, they chose Lieutenant Costas Couvaras, the Cairo Labor Desk assistant. The naturalized Greek had studied at Anatolia College, come to the United States to study at Cornell University at age twenty-three, and gone into journalism. Young christened him "Plover," but Young mistrusted Couvaras because he displayed insecure behavior in Alexandria and attempted to woo his men away from "Boston" to go to Greece and shoot Germans.[8] Couvaras had arrived on Evvia on April 29 and spent a week with barefoot guerrillas during elections.[9] After touring villages that had recently been pillaged and burned by Rallides, he crossed to the mainland with the guerrillas and began a seventeen-day trek due west, skirting the plain of Thessaly and snowy Parnassus to the headquarters of the central committee of EAM in the mountains of Central Greece at Karpenisi.

There the guerrillas reigned beyond the reach of the occupation. Couvaras told the EAM leadership that the Labor Desk wanted to establish close ties with them and develop intelligence networks using their men. He asked them to help him create more OSS routes in order to collect material from different parts of the country. Like Georgiades, Couvaras was quite taken with the guerrillas. They saw saw their chance and provided him with everything he wanted: their own political and military intelligence, newspapers, and proclamations. What they lacked was fast communications and money. Plover confirmed by mail and radio dispatches that EAM was "the real power in the whole of Greece." In return, he asked Cairo for rifles, machine guns, and ammunition, as well as food, clothing, shoes, and medicines because the Germans forbade the International Red Cross to distribute aid to the guerrillas. He and Tomtit, a Jewish lawyer from Cincinnati posted on Evvia for the Stygia mission, waxed poetic about the guerrillas as patriots, fighting against dictatorship from the left and the right. They wanted the Allies to hold and supervise an immediate, "really fair election with the Allies backing the winner." To them, "Americans are tops—almost like Gods."[10]

Tomtit wrote Young that Caskey wanted to arm ELAS and had authorized Cox to request Cairo to load a caique with Italian rifles, ammunition,

Fig. 20. "The welcoming party." Evvia guerrillas. Pericles mission to EAM Central headquarters in Karpenisi. (Photo by Costas Couvaras. Copyright held by Department of Special Collections and University Archives, The Library, California State University, Sacramento.)

and "any arms of any description" and send them to Evvia. Young agreed in principle, but blocked the arms shipment even though the OSS had sent arms to the guerrillas for Chicago mission. Instead, he rebuked Caskey by saying that they were in intelligence, not Special Operations. "To keep up their morale, and perhaps buy their help in some intelligence ventures," Young was, however, willing to send EAM clothes, pills, and food from army and Red Cross stores. He was

all for arming ELAS to the utmost if only to spite the foolish British policy . . . but the arms are not accessible to us and SO can put them into Evvia only with the consent of MEHQ. . . . British policy is completely wrong. . . . rather than a few arms in the hands of extremist leaders . . . get enough into the hands of the sensible elements so that they can defend themselves and stop being terrorized. . . . [However,] we cannot lay ourselves open to charges of having armed guerrillas independently . . . it could jeopardize the whole position of SI.[11]

Plover sent Young three dispatches in May, documenting German and security battalion raids, resulting in 400 executions and twelve burned villages in the Peloponnese and 500 deaths in Athens. He warned that the Rallides pillaged, burned villages, and raped Greek women while claiming to have the backing of the Allies in order to rid Greece of communists. In Karpenisi, they were hated more than the Germans. Couvaras denigrated evacuee reports saying that they did not represent the real Greeks since most were middle-class professionals and former army officers, embittered about the rising power of the impoverished Greek majority who disliked the king and the old politicians because they had abdicated responsibility.[12]

After the BBC broadcast news of the Allies marching into Rome on June 4 and, two days later, landing at Normandy, Turkey began to waffle. The Emniyet hedged, saying that Georgiades should simply let things quiet down, rather than close the base entirely. But Sperling had had enough of "the same old squirrel-cage." He flew to Cairo two weeks later, and with his departure, all Greek Desk operations in Istanbul ceased.[13] Meanwhile, the Greek government wanted pro-ELAS Georgiades out of Edirne since they were skittish about his relations with the guerrillas.

Three days after D-Day, the birds crowed over "nervousness" among German troops and security battalions. Plover chronicled the Germans fighting EAM over the new harvest in Central Greece, pulling their troops out of Thessaly, and replacing them with the Rallides, who were bringing their families from the countryside to Athens for safety. To create an illusion of power, the Germans faked troop movements and camouflaged cars with plywood to resemble tanks. Dodo (Despot) wrote that the Germans had replaced the Salamis guns with dummies. All along the rail line to Salonika, troops were putting their luggage by the tracks and emptying ammunition and supply dumps. To cow the Greeks into submission as they loaded men and matériel bound for Yannina, Germans destroyed villages and towns. At Distomon, they executed 500–700 civilians.[14] Terror reigned in Athenian suburbs. But instead of attacking the Germans as they had agreed at the Plaka Conference, Zervas and the EDES let them slip away with their weapons and supplies and used their British-supplied weapons to reopen the civil war by turning on their fellow Greeks.[15]

In spite of their attacks, EAM/ELAS remained strong. Elated over the news from Normandy, the guerrillas prepared to launch their own offensive against the Germans to support the D-Day invasion and the Russian push. Plover reported that ELAS vastly outnumbered the German troops, which, by the end of June, EAM estimated at 10,175 in Epirus, 9,650 in Thessaly, and 3,900 in Central Greece. But ELAS lacked weapons and ammunition. Unable to fight against the Germans by day, ELAS bayoneted them by night for their weapons. They could get weapons and ammunition no other way because Britain and America gave them nothing. Plover wrote Cairo that "ELAS wonders why the Allies at this critical moment do not supply and use ELAS in more active war operations." While EAM used Couvaras as their mouthpiece, he tried to discover their true intentions. He reported that EAM's position was pro-Russian, but they did not distinguish between one ally and another.

> EAM policy now is not the communist policy of old. Also the EAM movement is a mild left wing movement in comparison with the other Balkan liberation movements. There is no talk at all . . . about making Greece a Soviet Republic or connecting it with a federated Balkan state.

Instead, the guerrillas talked of a "popular democracy" in the future, uniting prewar Greece with the Dodecanese and Cyprus, but the leaders were neither interested in taking power by force nor willing to let anyone else do it. Plover echoed EAM's indictment of the British and their Greek cronies from the right-wing democrats, royalists, and former fascists to the anti-communist EDES and security battalions who had ravaged Evvia.[16]

On June 12, Papandreou declared that the king would not return before a plebiscite declared him chosen by the people. At the same time, he invited EAM/ELAS delegates to a Greek Unity Conference in Cairo. EAM was bitter, blaming Tsouderos for sentencing EAM for the spring mutiny. In exchange for joining the government, EAM demanded a statement from the king, a public denunciation of the security battalions, blame for the first round of the civil war to be placed on EDES and Zervas, a retraction exonerating EAM, and amnesty for those sentenced. In addition, EAM insisted upon six out of fifteen ministry chairs, and a clear statement of what had been agreed upon in the Lebanon Charter. Papandreou refused.[17]

Like the Delphic oracle prophesying from Mt. Parnassus, Plover foresaw the future from his mountain. After the conference collapsed, he wrote,

> The break of the talks at Cairo will have bad results for Greece. Here are two forces working hard one against the other. On the one side EAM on the other most of the old politicians together with the 100 percent Quislings and their reactionaries . . . an unhealthy situation. . . . Today Greek is killing Greek and the fight among them will intensify . . . and will turn into a civil

war when liberation comes. . . . All forces of reaction, special interests, old politicians, fascists, German collaborators, and some of the capital of the country have unified with the one purpose of beating the EAM . . . they have stayed inactive for too long and then they let the initiative on national leadership pass to the radicals that comprise the EAM.

Fomented by the Germans, the division among the Greeks deepened after the break of the unity talks. The security battalions intensified their anti-EAM activities, and EAM responded in kind in order to consolidate its position prior to the German evacuation. Daily raids plagued Athens and Piraeus as the Germans cleaned out resistance in Western Macedonia, killing civilians and burning and looting villages and towns. Meanwhile, the British supported EDES, and the Right prepared to take over the government. Couvaras predicted that the strife would lead to a long and bloody conflict and asked, "What is more logical to expect than a civil war?"

Plover continued that the Germans had changed their rhetoric, proclaiming themselves the protectors of Greece and Europe against the Bolshevists and the Slavic danger. Many Greek politicians swallowed German propaganda, "grabbed the anti-communist flute and started playing the German tune," collaborating with the enemy and "clothing their detestable action in patriotic garments." Lest Washington be complacent, he warned, "The subject of EAM against the politicians and security battalions has an international aspect. . . . The internal strife becomes one of Russia against England." This, he prophesied, was "the first seed for another war."[18]

Over a year after Charles Edson filed his first report on the Jewish deportations in northern Greece, the State Department asked Young to determine the whereabouts of American Jews in Greece because the War Refugee Board (WRB) wanted cooperation in rescuing them. The Germans had deported over 50,000 Jews in Thrace and Salonika to Poland or Germany in March 1943, and in September they had tried to deport Athenian Jews. Only after they deported the Jews of Yannina on Greek Independence Day 1944 did Washington pay attention.

Young knew that EAM and profiteering caique captains had smuggled Jews to Turkey after provisioning missions and gathering mail. In Thrace, Georgiades had operated an underground railroad to get Bulgarian Jews to Istanbul before Moses, the Zionist service that helped Jewish refugees escape and shared intelligence with OSS counterespionage, took over.[19] MI-9 had suspended its Jewish transport and wanted the Jews to found their own caique service because it was "straining relations" with the Emniyet, which frowned on Greek Jews arriving in Turkey and prevented boatloads of Jewish refugees from landing. When Berry demanded information on the Jews and asked Caskey to help evacuate them, Caskey balked[20] and replied that, because of the attitude of the Turkish government, he was not "prepared or authorized to engage in escape operations." When Berry "threatened to make damaging comments in a report to the President," Young volunteered to form the Gorgon mission to look into the "fuss about the Jews."[21] He preferred to send money to Athenian Jews or support them hiding in the mountains rather than deal with the messy business of "squealing" and seasick women and children. If the WRB got Emniyet clearance, he would provide caiques, but Berry never pursued the suggestion.[22] Eight hundred Greek Jews escaped that summer, but not because of Young or Caskey.

In Karpenisi, Couvaras planned to develop an independent American intelligence system throughout Greece. Using EAM/ELAS personnel, assistance, and protection, he would set up twelve American-led groups of thirty to fifty men, commanded by a leftist American officer, and mail routes from Athens to Evvia and from Karpenisi to the Peloponnese, Athens, Epirus and Macedonia in return for OSS funding and supplies. Couvaras's boss discussed the opportunity with Toulmin and Penrose, Cairo's new head of SI. He recommended that it "be made the cornerstone of all SO operations in Greece." Furthermore, he suggested that "all available Greek Desk American personnel . . . be placed in Greece immediately through EAM facilities and protection. . . . With a broad infiltration of SI . . . into Greece, the latter could be used as an Advanced Base for operations into Bulgaria and Rumania."[23] Couvaras's boss cabled the plan to Donovan, but Toulmin wrote that "hazardous political repercussions with the British and Greeks" would result if the Americans were to assist ELAS. He killed the plan before it left Cairo, cabling his disapproval to Donovan and Shepardson. With the exception of chronicling the aims and intentions of the EAM Central Committee, other aspects of the Pericles mission were, by this time, redundant. SI teams were already producing adequate coverage for Greece, and larger operations in the Aegean were by that time unnecessary. As a result, Donovan rejected the plan.[24] Stunned, Couvaras refused to believe that the United States refused to act and begged OSS to send ammunition and equipment to EAM. He was outraged that Allied policy permitted the Germans to escape unopposed while they committed unimaginable atrocities against EAM/ELAS and unarmed Greeks. He could not ask favors and give nothing in return, so he begged OSS to send food, supplies, medicines, clothing, and shoes for the guerrillas and personal weapons for the chiefs who guaranteed his safety.[25]

In many ways, Pericles replicated Young's Greek Desk. By July, Young had over twenty missions in Greece from Mani to Macedonia. Despot on Andros transported agents, supplies, and mail to Settler and Brigand. In the southern and western Peloponnese, Helot (Kalamata) opened communication from Gythion, Leonidion, Monemvasia, and Katakolon and sent back political intelligence: collaborators hung on lampposts and clubbed to death by Germans and security battalions as well as the settling of personal grudges between the battalions and ELAS.[26] The Athletes mission handled the Olympia area. Ajax covered Aetolia (Agrinion to Gulf of Arta); Elephant dealt with Epirus and Napoleon Zervas's EDES headquarters; Gasoline (Salonika) and Phalanx (Khalkidiki) gathered naval intelligence shipping requirements and information on Salonika airfields and the location of German minefields.[27] Emerald was Caskey's stay-behind network on Samos, providing full and daily coverage of the German occupation.[28] Helios for Cape Krio and Knidos collected military intelligence on shipping and air movements for MI-6.[29] Dago was Caskey's marine reconnaissance mission to the Dodecanese, and Lucian set up an intelligence service on port activity, Gestapo, and military intelligence on the Leros defenses.[30]

Oracle covered Delphi and Amphissa. It kept track of shipping on the east-west road along northern coast of the Corinthian Gulf and watched the small ports from Itea to Nafpaktos and north to Agrinion. From its perch, Oracle also maintained contact with the ELAS guerrillas on Mts. Parnassus and Ghiona, who informed on troop movements along the highway and railroad from Athens to Salonika.[31]

More than any other mission, Horsebreeders already provided just the kind of military intelligence that Pericles envisioned. It was a successful three-man SI team that had reached the central Greek port of Volos in April and got on well with EAM guerrillas, who helped them extend their scope and contacts until their vast network controlled the Thessalian Plain. They had trained 250 pupils in sabotage and established a network of 500 subagents in cells of ten to twenty. The leader maintained telephone contact with scattered positions. Two watched northbound automobile and train traffic; another gathered military and economic intelligence and followed all shipping to and from Volos harbor and from Evvia to Salonika, and a second radio operator on the island of Skiathos reported on Piraeus-Salonika shipping through the Skiathos Straits, enabling Allied bombers to clear the Aegean of German shipping. With the help of EAM, they also placed another radio operator in the central Greek city of Lamia to cover troop movements through that railroad hub. Horsebreeders emphasized military information on battle order and gathered economic intelligence for the Foreign Economic Administration (FEA), UNRRA, and the Allied Military Liaison (AML). Despite the British attempts to block them, the agents managed to document the times, quality, and quantity of war matériel and troops passing throughout the towns and cities. Their sub-agents watched each town, city, airport, port, and railroad station. Some got maps and plans of airports and ports, while others devoted themselves to sabotage and slipped sand and emery dust into the grease boxes of trains on the Athens-Salonika run. In return, Horsebreeders rewarded its workers with OSS blankets, food, shoes, clothes, and antimalaria drugs.[32]

Although Bari was generally speaking a bust, Oliver sent two missions in this phase of the operation. Alcinoos to Corfu provided critical intelligence on the doubling of the German garrison and refortification of Corfu. This helped prevent a British amphibious invasion that would otherwise have ended like the bloodbath in the Dodecanese. Molossos parachuted into the Pindus and watched the road through the Metsovo Pass. Both were provisioned by a caique named *United States of America.*

While Else serviced the Bari missions, Young hatched a scheme for OSS postliberation intelligence for Greece that came to be called the "Young Plan." He argued that postliberation intelligence in Greece was essential to American interests. His object was threefold: (1) to secure "through American channels" economic and political intelligence from selected strategic areas such as borders, ports of entry and exit, communication arteries, and cities where "sectional feelings, traditional with the Greek people, schisms and political parties prevail"; (2) to establish a permanent intelligence network; and (3) to provide a transmission of information to be used in the formation of American policy entirely secure from foreign observation.[33] Young predicted that "in this period of uncertainties, independent, uncolored, secret information regarding Greek internal and international affairs will provide a basis for the formulation of U.S. policy not only toward Greece and her neighboring Balkan states, but toward other larger powers which have interests in those states."[34] His "potential customers," the AML, UNRRA, the American embassy, FEA, and Greek War Relief, would require fast intelligence on war damage, economic conditions, and the political crisis. Since they could not get their own facilities running quickly, he recommended that they use his reservoir of Greek-speaking Americans "in the neighborhood." As the Germans withdrew, SI would transfer intelligence-gathering from Turkey and Cyprus to Greece. In the absence of any prospectus from Washington, Toulmin embraced Young's plan and laid it before Donovan, who approved it in principle.[35]

An advance base in Athens would act as hub and maintain direct contact with the "customers" as well as Greek ministries and OSS field representatives. Young would find an office that Else would set up. Then Young would focus on reconstruction, getting information from the Greek Red Cross and the Ministries of Health, Agriculture, Public Welfare, and Communications, while Maritime would land the operatives and supply the bases. Young would address shifts in population, condition of water supplies, roads, bridges, railroads, and ports. He would determine where food, fuel, and clothing were most urgently needed and could be stored, what diseases plagued the people and which drugs and medical supplies would eradicate them, the number and locations of burned villages, and the state of relief organizations, such as the Greek Red Cross, the Swiss-Swedish mission, the Agricultural Bank, and their distribution centers and storage facilities. To move the supplies, he would assess the condition of available vehicles and repair facilities. To get the Greeks back on their feet, he would determine the state and nature of agriculture, the availability of seed and animals, what factories and machinery had survived in the cities, and the state of labor, raw materials, quarries, and mines. To deal with the political crisis, he would investigate the plans of the various political parties and their leaders, the strength and composition of the guerrilla factions, and surviving means of mass communication. Then his agents would root out the German stay-behind networks.[36]

Young would lead the Young Plan, incorporating all branches of OSS in a staff of seventy, consisting of fifty-eight American officers, enlisted men, and civilians, as well as three Greek radio operators and Greek civilians, including women, such as Clio Adossides, whose families could "look after them." Using the "archaeological *ouija* board," Young arranged his colleagues geographically. Thirteen field missions would cover the countryside by jeep or motorcycle along with a radio operator. Jim Oliver and Richard Bruère of Bari would cover Epirus from Yannina. Vassos (chief of Area A), Charles Edson, and Jay Seeley would cover Central Macedonia from Salonika. Jim Kellis and Alekko Georgiades would cover Eastern Macedonia and Thrace from Alexandroupolis and Kavalla. Sperling would take the Western Peloponnese from Patras. "Pete" Daniel would handle Central Greece and operate from ELAS headquarters at Lamia. Chris Petrow and John Fatseas (Helot) would cover Lakonia and Messenia from Kalamata and Sparta. Jack Caskey would take charge of the islands with the help of Savage, Cox, and Lieutenant Athens.[37] Young also planned to cover western Greece, Western Macedonia, the eastern Peloponnese, Thessaly, and Crete. After initial intelligence-gathering, each mission would help with regional reconstruction, relief, and military government while maintaining liaison with other Allied intelligence agencies.[38]

The Young Plan was to be a two- to six-month bridge between wartime espionage and a permanent stay-behind network. This suited the archaeologists who had promised to return to their classrooms after demobilization. Furthermore, they were "too well known to the Greek authorities with whom they have been collaborating for the past year, to be able to set up and run a postwar undercover organization in Greece after the war." Instead, they would "maintain existing contacts, spot new ones, suggest channels, methods, and objectives for later work, and chart the means for avoiding pitfalls."[39] Young and his staff would recruit and train Greek personnel as agents, put them undercover, and send them into occupied Greece. The archaeologists would guide "the establishment of a permanent secret intelligence network in Greece," but for reasons of "long-range security," there could be "no apparent continuity between the present organization and such a network." Young suggested that (among other institutions) "the Archaeological School in Athens" could serve as "permanent and plausible cover for American intelligence men."[40]

Initially, Young and Penrose wanted to place the American intelligence network under cover of Greek War Relief. Unfettered by ethical qualms about combining espionage with relief, they cabled Washington with their top-secret solution. They chose George Skouras, brother of the founder of Greek War Relief, as a figurehead who could facilitate recruiting and as the organizer and identifier and reconciler of guerrilla groups. He could deliver Greek War Relief facilities without question or suspicion and had the money immediately available. Skouras could also control the movement of Greek War Relief personnel and have them sent where Young felt he could get the best information. But by the time Skouras arrived in Cairo, OSS was forbidden to use Greek War Relief as cover, and Toulmin had vetoed relief work itself as outside the OSS mandate. The movie mogul's brother was stuck.[41]

After severing Skouras's formal contact with OSS, Young agreed to keep him on their rolls. So Skouras worked with the Special Projects office of OSS that organized the Simmons mission to investigate a new German secret weapon, a radio-controlled glider bomb that, by mid-June, the Germans were launching against southern England. George Skouras masterminded the mission from Cairo. According to London, the flying or "buzz bomb" was housed alternatively in planes at Maleme, Athens, Salonika, and Kalamata. The mission, of critical importance to the American air force, was to determine its presence in the Balkans, organize a raid with guerrillas to secure the control mechanism, a pamphlet on it, or the bomb itself. Referring to the V-1 as the "baby," OSS agents responded to a general inquiry in May 1944 about whether the bombs were present in Athens or Salonika. Pheasant reported that a new type of bomb was to be sent to Salonika. After hearing that a bomber carrying it was grounded at a Greek airport, Washington hounded Young, for the War and Navy departments would stop at nothing to get intelligence on the deadly weapon. So Young and Skouras chose agents to find it.[42]

Meanwhile, senior OSS officials decamped for Italy. Toulmin moved to Bari as OSS deputy director of the Mediterranean theater under Allied Forces Headquarters (AFHQ) in Caserta and stripped Cairo of personnel. Those remaining behind keenly felt the resulting dislocations and each departure's farewell "Scotch on hot nights."[43]

Daniel, waiting for the Germans to withdraw, wanted to be in on the show. Up to now, only Caskey had seen action. Finally Daniel abandoned Cyprus for the Dodecanese, where he opened "Havana" as a mobile base on a schooner with an operational caique on the Helios mission shuttling between the islands to procure intelligence. After exploring the Knidian Peninsula, it dropped him at Aphrodite's shrine. Daniel notified the British of the OSS caique, established its recognition signals, and sent it on a reconnaissance tour. As the caique proceeded to Rhodes on the night of June 24, it was sunk by "friendly fire," trigger-happy British raiders who ignored its signals and opened fire, killing four of the six Greek crew and passengers. Young ordered a major inquiry. He had had it with "gay young men . . . running wild and shooting whatever." Feeling vulnerable, Daniel established his base on Turkish soil and from there reported on German shipping and reinforcements on Rhodes.[44]

Sperling midwifed the Young Plan and expanded its personnel to a stable of eighty. When it learned of news of the Germans' systematic persecutions and the resulting communist flight to the mountains, royalists' enlistments in the Rallides and security forces, and fighting and riots in the streets of Athens, Washington's interest increased somewhat. The American Contingent of the Military Headquarters for Balkan Affairs at USAFIME Headquarters considered postliberation SI essential. The State Department advised Donovan that it wanted American personnel to remain in Greece as a "watchdog." But it insisted that "no American agencies become involved or appear to become involved, directly or indirectly, with Greek domestic policies or factional disputes." OSS could operate throughout Greece and gather intelligence both from EDES and EAM/ELAS, provided they undertook "only intelligence work, together with such special operations" as were approved by Wilson, the supreme Allied commander for the Mediterranean. Yet, despite the interest, OSS did not increase its commitment of personnel to the Young Plan. Toulmin set a maximum number of fifty in the stripped-down version, then christened "Young Plan Jr." Sperling argued that the Young Plan could help win the peace, but neither Washington nor the OSS gave the idea a very high priority. They were planning only for the immediate future.[45]

Then on the night of July 25, a Soviet military mission parachuted to EAM headquarters at Karpenisi. Plover scooped the British and detailed the mission's personnel, purpose, and reception by the guerrillas. He radioed Cairo that Colonel Popov of the Soviet mission to Tito had come with three Greek-speaking Yugoslav partisans to ascertain ELAS's military strength, and EAM had received them warmly. The news electrified Cairo. Moderate elements in EAM hoped this would quell the extremists and guide EAM to a unity government.[46] The EAM rank and file hoped the Soviets would send military supplies, but the Russians stayed only a week and did not discuss aid. After learning that a Soviet mission had parachuted into the Greek mountains, Washington pounced on every dispatch concerning the Russian mission, devouring any documentation of Soviet aid to EAM. Young had been wrong about Pericles. Couvaras produced excellent material on EAM's strength, composition, and leadership, its organization of a national council, and the Soviet mission. However sympathetic it was to the Left, Pericles got the first independent intelligence on EAM and its Soviet guests, and the State Department disseminated it widely.[47]

Three days after the Soviet mission arrived, Young and Sperling circulated a revised blueprint of Young Plan Jr. In it, they turned over the islands to Maritime for supply and transport, preferring the archaeologists to focus on the mainland.[48] As violence escalated in Athens, Toulmin, as Balkan area commander, responsible for Cairo, Bari, and Istanbul, insisted on War Department approval before sending any Americans into postliberation Greece. The British demanded that all SI agents operate in uniform, thus forcing them under the aegis of the Allied Military Liaison, which they controlled. Likewise, they wanted all OSS communication coming out of Greece to be channeled through the AML, so news could be "filtered, censored, expurgated and decontaminated" before it reached the outside world. The American Section of the AML, however, insisted on independent communications.[49] While SOE pressured Young to confide his secret plans, the identities of his agents, and their areas of operation, they disclosed none of theirs to him.

Amid the excitement, the archaeologists were burning out. Young wanted to go to bed for three months. Caskey collapsed after learning of the death of his father. The aggressive young men coming through the pipeline made him feel like "Caspar Milquetoast." He was ready to step aside and "let his "hotter blooded staff tear into Greece and do big things." Moreover, Cox was downright ill. Prolonged stress had compromised her health, making her anemic, inefficient, and confused and causing her dark hair to go white and fall out. Alarmed, Young prescribed a month of pills and rest. But Cox was losing patience. She wanted to go to Greece with a doctor and kept droning that OSS's contribution had been zero and that she wanted to do something before it was all over, but Caskey could not function without her. As Thrush, the interrogator, Cox remained superb and unmatched, but she was consumed with processing the intelligence flowing in from the field. As a consequence of frustration, Cox bullied her Greek War Relief assistant, Theochares Stavrides, and Virginia Grace, who had come from Istanbul and was relegated to secretarial duties because she could type and file. Grace also translated, ciphered, interpreted, and edited intelligence. Moreover, she learned to keep cash accounts and produced a weekly summary of all caique movements. Caskey relied on her energy, versatility, and scruple, but she irritated Cox and feared her.[50]

On August 1, 1944, Young wrote, "This is my birthday. I am 37. I have 39 grey hairs of which I blame 18 on Maritime, 9 on Security, 5 on Labor, 4½ on MacFarland, and ½ on the Germans." The other two he attributed to Amoss. By now, his problems with his Istanbul nemesis were history. With the Russians approaching the Aegean, the stakes became too high for amateur politicking and Toulmin had replaced MacFarland. Scrutinized for months by OSS counterintelligence, "Packy" was found to be "indiscreet," talking "too much and to the wrong people," too "casual in bearing" and in his "private conduct," and "lacking in those business qualifications necessary to lead" OSS Istanbul.[51]

As summer dragged on with the Germans still controlling Greece, the Pericles mission became more strident. Plover accused the EDES and the British of letting the Germans leave unmolested. He chronicled mobilization decrees and movements of security battalions and German troops, and noted three trainloads heading north with bound German soldiers, guarded by SS, and four transports off Messalonghi with 5,000–10,000 troops. July estimates recorded around 100,000 Germans still in mainland Greece. But the German juggernaut had collapsed. By the first of August, stragglers in Athens were selling their cars, arms, and clothing. They stripped Piraeus of supplies and airports of their searchlights. German troops funneled west out of the Peloponnese or north through Athens, where trainloads of soldiers arrived, and twice as many departed for the north, some full of automobiles. The Germans instituted a draft to bolster their numbers for the western front, but in Greece it failed miserably. Some Germans even surrendered to EAM rather than endure evacuation and more fighting. Throughout the country, they were in motion, camouflaging their withdrawals as they headed north and west for Yannina. A 2,000-car convoy moved through Epirus toward the Albanian border while Zervas permitted them to leave quietly. They were getting away scot free.[52]

Pericles documented how EAM/ELAS turned against their British "ally" for not helping them attack the Nazis, for meddling in their internal affairs, and "dealing with Greece as if it were a colony." After the arrest of an agent who knew Couvaras's mission, EAM worried that the British might discover its whereabouts. It abandoned Karpenisi and moved its headquarters southwest of Salonika. Sure enough, on August 7, security battalions attacked Karpenisi, blew it up, and burned it that night. When EAM asked the British for arms to counter the assault, British archaeologist Col. Nicholas Hammond (AMM) replied that he was "not in a position to give any help." In exchange, ELAS raided Florina and blockaded the Germans in their houses and blew up the railroad, airport, and fuel tanks. The Germans and Rallides responded by releasing a reign of terror in Athens, where they blockaded an area and called the people to gather in an open space. When they assembled, the Nazis would begin to shoot, killing some and taking others hostage. In one area, they shot seventy-four and transported 8,000 to

Germany. Meanwhile, the Rallides justified murdering their fellow Greeks by claiming their crusade only targeted communists.[53]

Tomtit reported that 3,500 Germans and security battalions had rampaged through Evvia to eradicate EAM. "The grim rapers" fought over the harvest, illuminated by the glow of burning villages. They marked unburned houses with *Xs* to signify "CHI," the ultra right-wing political faction, and after destroying the homes of communists, the security battalions plastered the walls with propaganda and signed their handiwork "EDES." The agents warned that any attempt by the Allies to "play ball" or even protect them would be disastrous. Husbands scavenged charred grain, and women wandered hysterical with remains of prized family relics. In some, 90 percent of the shell-shocked inhabitants were living in fields. In towns, the looting was every man for himself. Meanwhile, the Nazis shipped the islanders' possessions to Germany, including clothing, food, bedding, dowries, and money, marked "gifts from the Greek people." The locals had only one thought as they hid in the mountains—revenge.[54]

In spite of the devastation in Greece, world news inspired growing optimism. Stix could hardly believe it was almost over and asked for a copy of *Stars and Stripes* so that he could follow the Cincinnati Reds' baseball season. In expectation of liberation, he began building up a retsina reserve. Everyone was saying "Athens in September."[55]

Meanwhile in Evros, the members of the Chicago mission who remained behind enemy lines with the guerrillas kept harassing the Germans.[56] Although the Germans brought in reinforcements and carried out reprisals in the villages, they could not dampen the Greeks' morale. Volunteers swelled the guerrillas' group to almost 2,500. After a quiet summer, they began attacking German garrisons, taking prisoners, and pushing west of Kavalla. To prevent the German withdrawal to Salonika, they stole horses, blew up depots, and sabotaged railway lines, freezing all rail traffic north, south, east, and west.[57] Then they accepted an SI team for Bulgaria, named Springfield to mesh with the Chicago mission's Midwest logic. It parachuted at night into a field marked by bonfires, and ELAS led it safely across the border.

Finally, the Turks took a stand out of fear of Stalin and in order to situate themselves on the victors' side. On August 2, Turkey forbade German shipping in its territorial waters, then enforced the decree by blocking the movement of all merchant and passenger vessels between the Dardanelles and Antalya, including OSS caiques. This cramped conditions at "Boston," where stalled agents piled up and got rowdy. At the stroke of midnight, Turkey broke diplomatic relations with Germany. Von Papen fled on August 5, and the German colony followed suit. Soon 2,000 Germans in Turkey would be evacuated or interned as hostile aliens.[58]

The OSS was ready to move into Greece. Penrose hoped to establish the Greek Section in Athens by early September, and the AML bet on the first or fifteenth. Finally they were "on the last lap." On August 8, Young confided in Caskey that all persons not condemned to be "chair-borne" were on seven-day notice and urged him to "hang on grimly to the end." Yet burdened by "the immense weight of indifference and stupidity" among the OSS branches with which he still had to contend, Young had lost the will to do so.

Wanting to get back to relief work, his original inspiration for action, Young accepted a job as special assistant to Laird Archer, chief of the UN-RRA mission for Greece. He was, after all, far more interested in helping the Greeks than in continued OSS paper pushing. Young wrote Caskey that he was not abandoning them, but through him they would have "unofficial and inconspicuous" connections with someone in a high place ready to help. Again, his timing was terrible.[59]

Army officers who had no love for the "bad eyes brigade" (SI) were beginning to dominate OSS. In Washington, the OSS Planning Group revisited its objectives for Greece. The Middle East commander in chief demanded an outline of OSS postwithdrawal or surrender activities. The Allied Military Mission—SOE and OSS Special Operations men (in Operational Groups made up of Greek-Americans)—would activate the mission called Noah's Ark, destroying lines of communications and conducting sabotage to hinder and harass the Nazi withdrawal. Then the AMM would secure control, bring about order, and institute relief measures in order to aid the Allied military commanders and, if the enemy surrendered, convey to them the orders and terms of the theater commander. America had promised air support for 10,000 British who were to maintain order in Athens upon liberation, but the British wanted U.S. ground troops and informed OSS Cairo that without them it was impossible for the AMM to carry out their orders. Yet they revealed no specifics to OSS about numbers of soldiers to be deployed or whether troops would be used outside Athens. The OSS Planning Group claimed that the Combined Chiefs of Staff's restriction of the participation of U.S. armed forces in the Balkans to relief and rehabilitation wreaked havoc with the servicemen in the Young Plan, but Penrose realized that it was irrelevant and cabled Donovan for approval.[60]

Amid the confusion and mixed signals, Donovan and General John Magruder, his deputy director of intelligence, met at AFHQ in Caserta and agreed that the Young Plan must have complete independence. To avoid seeking permission from USAFIME or AFHQ (which would automatically involve the British), Donovan insisted that its operations be clandestine—with personnel in civilian clothes. Penrose needed USAFIME permission to procure supplies, equipment, jeeps, and fuel and quietly requested it. Unfortunately, Brigadier General Percy Sadler, the American head of the AML, immediately alerted the British, who insisted on complete control and a reduced OSS presence. Out of a total Balkans staff of sixty-three, including Yugoslavia and Albania, established by General Marshall, the number of personnel for Greece was halved to twenty-five. Even Toulmin protested that the number was grossly insufficient, but Donovan acquiesced.[61]

As the Allies liberated Paris on August 25, Toulmin appointed Colonel Harry S. Aldrich as chief of OSS Cairo. Qualified primarily by the old-boy network, Aldrich (AMM China) had served under General Magruder. Thus, a Mandarin linguist assumed control of OSS Cairo with little knowledge of Greece or the eastern Mediterranean. He agreed to use "suitable personnel" already in the field, but insisted on terminating the Young Plan arbitrarily on January 1, 1945.

TWELVE

Liberation and the
"Dance of the Seven Veils"

AS YOUNG PREPARED TO LEAVE CAIRO, the Red Army's advance cat-alyzed events in Greece. Word that Soviet troops had trapped the German Black Sea fleet, captured the Ploesti oil fields, and secured the surrender of Rumania alarmed the Germans. They convinced Hitler to approve a secret withdrawal from Greece before they, too, were trapped.

Liberation had begun. The Evros guerrillas declared August 29 their D-Day: 10,000 Greeks gathered, and church bells tolled as the guerrillas en-tered the first town where women and children disarmed the Germans without firing a shot. Simultaneously, the guerrillas attacked and captured town after town. Gander reported that as throngs shouted "Zeeto Ellas! Zeeto EAM! Zeeto Amerikanoi!" the people of Evros freed an area as large as Normandy.[1]

Finally, EAM agreed to participate in Papandreou's provisional govern-ment.[2] Its delegation flew to Cairo, capitulated unconditionally, joined the National Unity government, and moved to Naples. The Bulgarians declared war on Germany as Stalin's troops crossed the Danube on September 5 and invaded Bulgaria.

Young began killing missions and readying the agents who would ac-company him on Niki I (Victory), the first wave of the Young Plan. Leaving Gerald Else in charge of the Greek Desk in Cairo, Young changed his code name from Pigeon to Dove and departed Alexandria on September 5.[3] Af-ter a rough forty-seven-hour crossing with seasick agents, two jeeps, tons of gas, spare parts, personal gear, equipment, and rations, Young reached Cyprus. There he met with Daniel before they each left for the Aegean.

On September 8, a pro-Soviet coup toppled the Bulgarian government, and partisans occupied Sofia. With that, the British of the AML finally implemented Noah's Ark, the scheme they had devised months earlier to harass the German withdrawal using the united guerrillas of EDES and EAM/ELAS. Worried about creating a military vacuum and unwilling to trade a German occupation for a communist one, the British had consciously delayed engaging the Germans. Instead of uniting the guerrillas, they played the factions off one another, bartered with the enemy and security battalions, and allowed thousands of German troops and tons of matériel to escape Greece. But they were not alone. Young's agents told how ELAS commissars in Larissa also refrained from attacking the retreating Germans, saving their men and precious tanks for more important battles as Amoss had envisioned two years earlier.[4] High in the Pindus Mountains, "the American Lord Byron," Oliver's radio operator on the Molossos mission, signaled the German withdrawals on the Albania road, and Noah's Ark (the guerrillas combined with SOE and OSS Special Operations Greek-American groups) streamed into the breach.

Moses Hadas (R&A, Cairo) sent a distillation of four months' observations on Greek affairs to Washington. To arrive at a balanced picture, he polled representatives from a broad spectrum of Greeks in Egypt. Even moderate Greeks resented British interference in their country's internal affairs and felt that it constituted an "intolerable diminution of Greek sovereignty." EAM sympathizers accused the British of panicking and arresting persons without charge for "security reasons," distorting news for press releases under the pretext of desiring "a 'safe' Greece," deleting derogatory comments about Papandreou and any praise of EAM's achievements while engaging in "extremely severe censorship." Hadas was concerned about Britain's "ambiguous attitude toward the Rallides, an indifference to denouncing them, and Papandreou's silence on the subject." He perceived a unanimity within American and British circles, deploring British policy on Greece that seemed to "lead inevitably to the chaos and bloodshed of civil war." When asked by Hadas "how a government could persist in a policy which its competent experts disapproved, they [the British] laid blame on the Foreign Office." Overt frictions between the Russians and British had become apparent in late spring. As the Red Army approached, a fear of the "Slavic Peril" and Greece "being surrounded and oppressed by more numerous and more powerful Slavic neighbors" increased until the Russian mission to EAM in July fomented concern among Greeks and British about Russian designs on Greece itself.[5]

Meanwhile, Young spent the night of September 8 at Cape Gelidonya on the south coast of Turkey and the following one at Kastellorizo, where he stopped for a last-minute briefing before entering the Aegean. Delighted to experience the caique service from an agent's perspective, he sailed north as Germans evacuated Lesbos and Chios. Young reached "Key West" on September 12, the day the American army crossed the Siegfried Line into Germany. Aldrich flew to Izmir to confer with Young and Caskey on the future of the Young Plan. Caskey suggested OSS might "spy secretly on British and Greek activities" from his Turkish bases. Aldrich toured them and formally recognized Caskey as chief of each. But for Caskey, the recognition was bittersweet, since Aldrich also notified him that as soon as the islands were free of Germans, he must advance west into Greece.[6]

The Young Plan had to choose a leader. Of the original four captains, Sperling would handle Macedonia, Daniel would cover the Dodecanese, and Oliver was abandoning the theater. That left only Caskey, who had earned the position of chief, but was tired and preferred the islands, which were no longer part of the picture. Young wanted his assistant, Gerald Else, to succeed him because he knew the drill and was still fresh.

Young Plan agents walked a tightrope between Donovan's desired independence (operating undercover and armed in civilian clothes) and security (operating overtly in uniform under British control). Toulmin, Aldrich, and Penrose disagreed with Donovan's decision, but enforced it. Yet if the men were caught while any Germans were still in Greece, they would be shot on the spot for operating covertly. In a sea of British officers, uniforms would make Young Plan agents vanish in the crowd. So Young compromised by wearing khaki with a U.S. patch on the collar, bringing storm flags so his jeeps could fly the Stars and Stripes.[7]

While agents reported on the German withdrawal, Young radioed those on Evvia to be ready for his arrival. On September 17, the day marking the formation of a true Greek Government of National Unity, Young sailed out of "Boston" on a fast caique, but he did not get far. A fierce north wind forced him to land only twenty-five miles away on Mytilene. Flying the American flag that evening, he entered the port of Plomari. The harbor was black with people, and more flowed down from every side street. Through mobs of enthusiastic shouting people, Young and his men went ashore, the first Allied persons to appear since liberation. After two hours of pumping the local EAM committee for information, Young reported to Cairo that its members (doctor, lawyer, schoolteacher, olive press owner, and harbormaster—the richest men in the village) defied the stereotype, being "nothing very wild and raving in the little red brothers line." After refusing a banquet (since they were to *bring* food, not consume it), they were marched behind Greek, American, Russian, and British flags back to their caique, where they spent a peaceful night, guarded by a member of ELAN (ELAS's naval wing). The next morning, townspeople brought baskets of walnuts and "grapes as big as plums." Young lunched in the garden of the olive press owner, who produced two bottles of Scotch that he had been hoarding to share with the Allies at liberation. They spent two hours over Scotch, walnuts, and tales of the German occupation in this idyllic setting, surrounded by vineyards and olive groves. Afterward, the men feasted on chicken, mashed potatoes, lamb, pasta, and "regiments of fried eggs, eggplants, grapes, and peaches." Then guerrillas transported them to the upper town. For miles, barefoot yelling children followed their honking truck, which was only stopped by another shouting throng carrying a banner inscribed, "WELLCOME WORLTS SAVVERS." From balconies, Young was showered with rice, perfume, and minced flowers, seated, and given ouzo while the mayor's wife sang and her son fiddled "America" and the Greek national anthem. A crowd escorted Young and his men to the church and the mayor's house, where they were given coffee and then returned to the port. That night, Young distributed medical supply kits and sacks of clothes to the doctor and the secretary of the committee.

They left at sunrise and got soaked heading dead into the wind. After four hours, they had only reached the anchorage of Sigri on the northwest tip of Mytilene, blown north of the 39th latitude, which the British had declared off limits. There they were hosted by another local EAM committee (more communist than the last), which presented them with fig raki, cubes of bread, and *keftedes* (meatballs). Hunks of roasted sheep were served with pasta and chased with new red wine and watermelon. Over coffee and apples, they listened to political speeches against England, the king, and Papandreou. Passed from one committee member to another, they were plied with fig brandy or Bols Cocktail Punch, described by Young as "sluggish red ink," and returned to their caique. Fearing being delayed by more "crushing hospitality," they rose early the next day and prowled about the town, noting cartoons of guerrillas slaying Germans, EAM, ELAS, and KKE slogans, and crossed Greek and Russian flags. Then hoping that the wind had died down, they weighed anchor.

They set off due west across a running sea. Passing north of the central Aegean island of Skyros retching and soaked, they turned south. Young noted two German planes flying north from Athens, but the Germans did not notice them.

By midmorning on the twenty-first, Young had reached Pili on the north coast of Evvia, where he disembarked. He was met by a handful of sleep-deprived agents who had scanned the eastern horizon for over a week expecting his arrival. Immediately, Chrysostomas, Young's radio operator, telegraphed Savage to send on the jeeps while Young presented the EAM regiment with sacks of clothes, cases of medical supplies, and lubricating oil. Then Young holed up in the local church and celebrated with agents John Calvocoressi and Tom Stix, who warned him that the Germans and security battalions were still on the island and opposite the narrows separating Evvia from the mainland, whose shore, main road, and railroad were "full of Huns." "Calvo" later recalled that Young was "evasive" about his future plans, concealed his transfer to UNNRA from them, and had an "aversion to frank talk and love of mystification." Impatient, Calvo joined the guerrillas in the mountains while Young waited for his jeeps and deliberated his next step.[8]

Young was energized to be back on Greek soil and "10 years rejuvenated" by the familiar fragrances of thyme and heather, pine and the sea. With nothing that smacked of Cairo, he reflected, "this is the life," after swimming in the Aegean for the first time in four years. He could not wait to raise the Stars and Stripes over Blegen's house at 9 Ploutarchou and tackle the reconstruction of Greece.[9]

Ten days later, Young was champing at the bit. The day before, a dozen fierce seventeen- to eighteen-year-old guerrilla girls marching in uniform and demanding arms and shoes had "invaded" his camp. Their leader told of Jews hiding in Athens and Evvia and presented Young with a letter for Mrs. Roosevelt. Later that afternoon, the caique with the jeeps arrived with clothes and shoes for the Ellas mission and ten tons of food and medical supplies. To avoid the Germans and security battalions, Young decamped for the island's southernmost port of Karystos. Delayed by a thunderstorm, they stopped to offload the girls and sacks of clothes for the EAM regiment into rowboats and leave a generator and gas for another agent down the coast. Then they headed south into the dangerous Salonika sea-lane, although good weather made it seem "like a Sunday excursion."[10]

On October 1, they reached Karystos, where they uncorked a bottle of raki and slept on their first beds since Izmir. Hung over, Young dreaded the round of banquets that threatened to recommence the next morning, but dutifully received the local EAM committee before unloading the jeeps. He planned to reconnoiter the ports of Stira and Marmari, where he could spy heavy shipping traffic bound for Chalchis, Volos, and Salonika. Meanwhile in Alexandria, Sperling handed his responsibilities to the recently promoted Captain Charles Edson and loaded his own caique with guns, ammunition, tons of medical supplies, and clothing for Niki II, the second wave of Young Plan, consisting of himself, George Skouras, Dimitri Petrou, and Chris Petrow.[11]

On October 8, the day after Sperling departed, Young was still on Evvia, reporting on battalion raids and German shipping, surrounded by waiflike children and sallow middle-aged women. He lingered for two more days, frustrated by inaction and intermittent radio contact with Cairo whereby he missed the news that his father had died.

While Young was incommunicado, the pound hit 165 billion drachmas. Furthermore, the British betrayed no sign of their intentions, so that Else despaired that he could not think of "any way of fucking up the fate of poor Greece that has not been tried in these last few weeks." With Edson as the official historian of OSS–Middle East and Sherman Wallace writing up the history of SI Washington, Else reflected that "we are passing out of the present and into the past."[12]

Finally, Cox conducted postliberation island relief work. She figured that if she, "a poor, frail woman with no political ax to grind," could deliver medicine, clothes, and blankets immediately, the United States could gain "enormous political capital" and keep the British cornering the market on relief and wielding it as a weapon to get a "political stranglehold on the Greeks." Her plan once encompassed the whole country, distributing 500 tons of food and bales of clothing warehoused in Cyprus, over a sixty-to ninety-day period. While Sperling cautioned against trying to entangle intelligence-gathering with relief, nothing had happened, and Cox had watched her relief scheme be repeatedly downsized until Aldrich cut it by 90 percent. Dispirited, Cox had asked to be replaced by Margaret Crosby or Gladys Davidson Weinberg. But after liberation began, she finally managed to undertake reconnaissance missions "Salaminia" to Mytilene and "Mastic" to Chios. Then Cox hoped to dispense supplies to the mainland before engaging in relief and intelligence-gathering under GWRA cover in Athens as "a fine and fitting end" to her OSS career.[13]

Forced to compromise, Else guided Young Plan Jr., nicknamed by Cairo SI chief Steve Penrose as the "Dance of the Seven Veils" because Allied Forces Headquarters (AFHQ) in Caserta had stripped away layer after layer of its operation until it was bare. Caserta had halved its personnel and ordered them undercover. The Young Plan's veils, "most diaphanous of covers," represented the multiple ruses under which it was forced to function. Else scrambled to arrange positions as assistant military attachés in the embassy, advisors to UNRRA, or Military Liaison (ML), the only approved reasons for Americans to be in Greece. He and Penrose met with Laird Archer, head of mission for UNRRA Greece, who needed personnel and offered Caskey acting directorship of the Cyclades. They and Young advised Caskey to take it and Cox to go into the islands with UNRRA or Greek War Relief, hoping she would share intelligence and consider herself OSS in spirit, but the organizations got cold feet. The archaeologists were too well known to fool anyone. Moreover, the military liaison and UNRRA offered only temporary positions, so Else decided to avoid combined allegiances, although he worried that the British might try to evict those whom they could not control.[14]

As the Young Plan shrank, the mission and character of Caskey's proposed island base changed from an SI field operations center on Syra ("Bermuda") to "Elba," a Maritime outpost on Tinos. Caskey still wanted to direct "Elba," using Cox and Savage for relief and SI missions. He considered Grace as reports officer and sent her on a dry run to Mytilene, where she gathered intelligence and forwarded it to Cairo and Izmir. Else also considered placing Petrow as an undercover UNRRA "field observer" or a "scout in the islands and main ports, reporting on naval and shipping matters."[15] Instead, Aldrich appointed Petrow head of "Elba," answering only to Aldrich, who would administer it apart from the Young Plan. Savage would be Petrow's SI assistant, with Cox either flitting about the Aegean on small missions or going home. Although Savage wanted Grace (who had worked with him at "Boston") as his reports officer, collecting information and directing missions, Else insisted that she return to Cairo. Thus, Aldrich scuttled Caskey's plan and scattered his team.[16] Aldrich needed Caskey, one of the two highest-ranked officers in SI, to be a field operative on the mainland, whose importance far outweighed that of the islands. Aldrich insisted Caskey leave Turkey as soon as possible either for Salonika or Athens. The Young Plan could not afford to waste him in the Cyclades; he and Sperling had to assist or replace Young since no one knew whether Young would keep "one foot in the business" or for how long. But Caskey was preoccupied with trying to close "Boston," which was still overcrowded with American and Greek staff and trapped transients. Meanwhile, Else remained in Cairo.[17]

While Young waited on Evvia, the British met with rival guerrilla leaders in Caserta. In concert with the Greek Government and the British ambassador, they agreed in late September on postliberation command and issued detailed operational orders. General Ronald Scobie would direct British Expeditionary forces, invading Greece from the southwest, capturing airfields and moving toward Patras. From his headquarters at Lamia, General Sarafis of ELAS would command all of Greece with the exception of Attica, the Peloponnese, Epirus, and various islands. In return, he agreed to serve under Scobie and evacuate all ELAS units from Attica or put them under the command of royalist General Spiliotopoulos, who would take charge of Athens and Attica (along with Wilson, Scobie, and Stawell of SOE). Spiliotopoulos was to command the region north of the Corinth Canal and harass the Nazi evacuation while safeguarding public utilities and harbors, especially the Marathon Dam. Meanwhile, General Zervas of EDES would command Epirus, Corfu, and Paxos from his headquarters at Yannina. Only with Sarafis's cooperation could he conduct operations further north.

The Greeks would reestablish law and order in their respective regions while government-designated civil officials and British liaison officers persuaded the security battalions to surrender, leave with the Germans, or give themselves up, disarmed, to the Greek military commanders. The security battalions were to stay in their barracks to be disarmed and guarded by the British, and guerrilla commanders pledged that the prisoners would not be harmed. It sounded plausible on paper, but although EAM ordered its leaders to comply, it was unhappy that the Greeks were not united under their own general.[18] Again the Americans refused to get involved: instead, the U.S. Army cut personnel in the Balkans, MacVeagh opted to remain in Cairo, and Penrose insisted that the Greek Desk should stay with the embassy.

During the nineteen days that Young spent on Evvia, he and his agents contributed critical military intelligence on the German withdrawals. The

Nazis airlifted their island garrisons and mined channels between Aigina and the Peloponnese to protect thousands of soldiers and hundreds of cars and vehicles heading north to Salonika by sea. Dodo crowed that the last Germans would evacuate Athens on September 27, and Loon reported that they had already left Amphissa. About 15,000 headed for Lamia in motorized columns, while another 2,000 marched alongside. Pheasant reported that a steady stream flowed northwest from Yannina and Larissa. Molossos in the Pindus related how for three days, the Germans forbade civilians to circulate in Yannina while they destroyed their equipment and threw it into the lake, and thousands of troops and vehicles threaded the Metsovo Road to Koritsa. From Florina and Monastir, they passed north of Lake Ochrida to the Adriatic. Trains brought troops east of Salonika north to Kilkis, whence they crossed the Doiran Pass into Bulgaria. Seagull reported that the Cyclades were clear except for a few small garrisons, and Chickadee (Caskey) noted that the Germans had turned Samos over to Italian fascists and fled on the night of September 28. On October 2 and 3, trains still left Athens loaded with cars, motor vehicles, and antiaircraft guns. Then the Germans towed defunct freighters, railway cars, and engines to Corinth and sank them on October 5 to block the canal. Broiled and Roast Pheasant reported that the Rallides were secretly joining EDES and encouraging armed peasants to attack the communists, although they claimed that when the Allies arrived, they would turn on the Germans. Roadrunner wrote that each night forty transport planes left Athens heavy with fuel and matériel.

Gander's mission to Evros reported constantly, in spite of mounting danger from communists and evacuating Bulgarians, until the Russian occupation of Bulgaria, when Georgiades closed his operation. Frank Wisner, who inherited Istanbul from MacFarland, transferred Georgiades back to the Greek Desk on September 15 because he wanted him to penetrate Bulgaria, but instead Georgiades crossed into Greece.[19] On October 6, Gander reported the arrival in Evros of Russian soldiers, who said claimed that they had come to free Greece.

On October 9, Churchill and Stalin met in Moscow. Over lunch they divvied up the Balkans in what later became known as the "Percentages Agreement." Scrawled by Churchill on the back of a napkin, it promised Britain 90 percent control of the affairs of Greece in exchange for Rumania and Bulgaria. They split Yugoslavia and Hungary down the middle.[20] That day, over one hundred flights departed Salonika for Germany.[21]

The speed of the final evacuation caught the Allies off guard.[22] Noah's

Ark had trouble sabotaging the mass withdrawals and breaking into the heavy troop formations. Horsebreeders and other SI field missions helped the seven Greek-American Special Operations patrols imbedded with the guerrillas. As a result, they killed 349 Germans, wounded 196, took 105 prisoners, attacked fourteen trains and six garrisons, and destroyed thirty-four cars, sixty-one trucks, and eleven locomotives, losing only two officers and one enlisted man.

A week after Kanellopoulos disembarked at Kalamata, the British secured Patras.[23] On October 10, they took Corinth. That day, Young left Evvia with Stix and Chrysostomas. They crossed to the tiny beach at Kaki Thalassa between Sounion and Marathon, on an inhospitable stretch of coast once guarded by German machine gun nests, and spent that night at a nearby monastery. The next morning, Young hired a car and investigated the Attic hinterland, carelessly sending his things by boat to Porto Rafti, where he would meet the jeeps.[24] He found the once fertile landscape barren, and the Germans had blown up the bridges from Lavrion to Athens and blocked the road with uprooted telephone poles. After securing the jeeps, Young crossed the plain of Marathon. Skirting Mt. Hymettus at dusk on October 11, he could see an unnatural glow over the naval base at Salamis. That night, Young used Pterodactyl, the code name reserved for highly classified communications or when the agent was in mortal peril. He announced that Colonel Tsigantes of the Greek Sacred Brigade had arrived with General Turnbull of the British Raiding Forces. The next morning, Young heard explosions in Piraeus. The Germans had sunk ships to block the harbor and sabotaged quays and wharves, and were destroying the gunpowder factory, power plant, and radio stations throughout Attica. Last, they took down the swastika on the Acropolis. When Young walked into Athens on liberation day, October 12, 1944, they were still withdrawing from Piraeus and the suburbs, selling their clothing and bicycles as they departed. At seven that evening, Young stopped to inquire if the Germans had really gone. After being told yes, he spied some in uniform just across the street and "scrammed."[25]

Several of Young's flock covered the events in Athens that day. Loon noted that seven trains left with troops and equipment. Dodo wrote that

> at 0945 hrs. the Germans laid a wreath on the Tomb of the Unknown Soldier in the presence of the Mayor and the authorities. . . . The people showed monumental dignity (staying away from the area). As soon as the Germans

had left, they rushed forward and furiously tore the wreaths to bits in order that the sacred memorial to the struggles of the Greek nation for freedom should no longer be defiled.

People kissed and church bells rang. The city was liberated from the Nazi yoke, everywhere the buildings were decorated with bunting and Greek and Allied flags, and people celebrated in the streets.[26]

Dove cabled Cairo. The night before, the Germans had ceased demolition, abandoned all defensive efforts, and declared Athens an open city. Although battles raged between the Greeks and security battalions, they decreased by the hour as the security battalions deserted.[27] Young found the School unscathed but crammed with Swiss. It was hard to believe that ten days earlier bullets had whistled through the trees of the garden, grenades had exploded in the streets outside its walls, and pieces of shell had landed on its roofs.[28] From the School, Young walked down Ploutarchou Street and, after considerable knocking, roused Bert Hodge Hill, who welcomed him and offered him a place to stay. After swapping stories, Young bedded down for the night.

The next morning, Young established the provisional Athens Desk at 9 Plutarchou (see map 1). As the first American to enter liberated Athens, Young was besieged with requests. Floods of people wanted jobs, favors, money, food. Others wanted to give information, send messages, or establish their U.S. citizenship or their stance vis-à-vis the Greek political factions. People assumed that Young could do the work of Athens College, the consulate, American School, American Legion, Near East Foundation, and a large employment bureau. Soon he looked back nostalgically to the peaceful days in Cairo. He wrote Shear that his head felt like "scrambled eggs," and his life resembled those of mythical figures pursued from all sides until they escaped by turning into something else. Young wished he could do likewise.[29]

Young had imagined that he would be turned over to UNRRA when he got to Athens and only devote overtime to OSS. Instead for three chaotic weeks he was swamped with OSS duties, closing out occupation-era missions, settling agents' claims, collecting, storing, or forwarding to Cairo no-longer-needed equipment, and returning caiques to their owners. He tried to streamline operations, combining the radio networks of his various Athens missions. Some would continue, like Settler, which had infiltrated a German stay-behind cell in Athens, and Horsebreeders and Fleece, which

Fig. 21. "From Galaxidi to Athens," Pericles mission. (Photo by Costas Couvaras. Copyright held by Department of Special Collections and University
Archives, The Library, California State University, Sacramento.)

monitored the Athens-Salonika transportation corridor. Others, like Helot,
he needed to rebrief and dispatch to the Peloponnese, and the northern
missions, Phalanx, Gasoline, and Floka, were still covering the German
withdrawal. Young also coordinated the postliberation networks, such as
Elephant which headed north to join EDES's headquarters at Yannina after
Zervas liberated Corfu on October 13. Costas Couvaras of the Labor Desk's
Pericles mission was moving to Athens to cover political developments with
EAM.

From Cairo, MacVeagh tried to turn Roosevelt's attention to Balkan issues. He wrote that Yugoslavia and Greece might be "small potatoes" in the
typical American view of foreign affairs, however, he stressed the future importance of the region, that the Department of State classified with Africa
and the Near East rather than Europe. He focused on the need for a new approach in light of the failing British empire. "The future maintenance of the
Empire depends on how far England consents to frame her foreign policy in
agreement with Washington, and how far we in our turn realize that where
that Empire, so important in our own security, is most immediately men-

aced." Viz à viz "British fumbling in the Balkans," MacVeagh quoted an OSS SI report declaring that compromise with EAM was the most one could hope for. "British political maneuvering has failed. . . . England has lost ground and will not be able to regain it in the future."[30]

Young cabled military, economic, and political intelligence to Cairo. He told how retreating Germans had blown up the Shell oil refinery at Eleusis and prepared the royal palace at Tatoi for demolition, then left the outskirts of Athens on the fifteenth, burning, pillaging, and killing as they made their way north. In their wake, the Greeks began to clear away land mines. That day, Young cabled Cairo that the main British force had landed at Phaleron, followed by a smaller one that escorted Papandreou's provisional Greek government to Athens. They entered the city on the seventeenth, accompanied by General Scobie, Reginald Leeper, Noel Rees (who had joined Scobie's staff), and Major Dudley Bennett, his successor at MI-6 Izmir.[31] That day, the Greek flag flew again over the Acropolis. Afterward, the British headed for the Grande Bretagne, where MI-6 had set up their headquarters, roped off the area, and allotted space for over 500 agents who would descend on Athens within two weeks.[32]

While the Greek government marched into Athens, Calvo waited for a signal from Young. Calvo approached a security battalion evacuating across the mountains on Evvia, thinking they were guerrillas. Realizing his mistake, he shouted, "Don't shoot, we are Americans!" One fired anyway and shot him through the lungs, dragged him for 200 yards, robbed him of his papers, gun, and shoes, and left him to die. News of Calvo's hemorrhage and peritonitis revived in Young nightmares of his own recovery, including the insatiable thirst that he could not slake for fear of infection. Posthaste he dispatched a doctor and nurse from Evangelismos Hospital, armed with drugs and ice to save Calvo. Then Young returned to the work at hand.

Within a week, Young found 9 Ploutarchou unsuitable. It was not well located for an office and too small for a billet, having only a dining room, Hill's sitting room, and two other rooms on the ground floor. It worked when there were five people, but soon there were eight, and Young's team overwhelmed the house. Young had agreed to provide Hill with food and firewood in return for shelter and servants, but did not want to impose on the old man, who preferred to have only friends, like Young, Sperling, Daniel, Ralph Kent, and Caskey, staying there.

Young considered the Agora, but hesitated to go there. When he did, he found its excavations reasonably intact, although battling Greeks had riddled its houses with bullets, killing at least eight men. Refugees had squatted in its vaulted tombs, and several had starved and died there. Most of the staff had survived, although some were "little more than skeletons" and others mad from misery or ostracized for being pro-German. Although it was available and full of furniture, Young dismissed it as "out of the way, shabby, and primitive."[33]

Thinking that Young was studying problems of economics and propaganda, Antonios Keramopoullos (director of the Greek Archaeological Service) mentioned that he had three buildings at his disposal: the German Archaeological Institute (DAI), symbol of German intellectual prowess and *Kulturpolitik,* the Italian School's director's house, and one used by the German Academy. He offered Young gratis whichever he pleased. Young chose the DAI, centrally located about a mile from British Headquarters at 1 Fidiou (Phidias Street). He relished "the idea of taking over the building which has been the center of German spy work for our own." Unlike the German soldiers, who had largely respected archaeological sites during the occupation, the German archaeologists had "dug when and where they pleased." Unbeknownst to Young, more than a year and a half earlier, Louis Lord, chair of the American School's managing committee, thought the Germans should forfeit the building, its library, and photographic collections as war reparations.[34] Young commandeered the massive neoclassical structure. It was strongly built with three stories, and its vast roof provided a good view of the city. Young allocated space; had the plumbing overhauled; hired servants; set up supply, mess, transportation, and pouch systems; and put security procedures in place while the British installed telephones. Finding that the evacuees had stripped "the quondam German spy headquarters" of everything but the "bedbugs,"[35] he borrowed furniture from the Agora offices. Soon the second floor housed the billet and mess, and the third, offices. The roof had a shack with a small but complete radio station and message center.

When OSS Special Operations Major Wines, the former senior American officer of the Allied Military Mission, returned unexpectedly in November, Aldrich appointed him liaison officer with the British in Greece. By acquiescing with his superior British Colonel Woodhouse, chief of the AMM, Wines had for six months maintained good relations with them. However, despite their initial help, the British tried to stymie and control the OSS in Athens. U.S. policy demanded that "a minimum of American military uniforms be visible in Greece," but without the protection of uniforms, those driving OSS jeeps had them stolen by the British.

At this point, the archaeologists finally became operatives. Only after liberation did they begin to use most of the skills they had acquired at the "Farm" outside Washington. After Aldrich met Daniel on Cyprus and terminated the agreement with the Cyprus Mines Corporation, Daniel released all Cyprus staff, except those guarding the supplies warehoused for the Young Plan. Then he returned to the Aegean for the liberation of the Dodecanese, terminated "Havana," and prepared for his next mission.[36]

On October 17, Niki II docked at "Key West" on its way to Athens. Two days later, it stopped at Tinos, where Aldrich wished Petrow to confer with Caskey regarding the island base. Assessing its lack of shelter and distance from Athens, Petrow rejected it. After waiting for Caskey, who did not show up, he continued to Kea on a tip from his caique captain, and on to Athens. Meanwhile, Caskey had set out on a humanitarian trip to earthquake-stricken Mytilene. After missing Petrow on Tinos and Kea, Caskey caught up with him in Athens. Later that day, Caskey joined his godfather, Bert Hill, at 9 Ploutarchou, where the throng assembled with Young. He agreed with Petrow on Kea as the best location for "Elba" and signaled Aldrich. Caskey knew he was good at military intelligence, but he lacked the necessary confidence to be a field operative. What Caskey knew best was desk work. The next day he and Young discussed the directorship of Athens, but when Caskey found that it had an unclear agenda, he did not want to get embroiled there.[37]

On October 24, Caskey returned to Kea. He found it a perfect hideaway. It was the nearest Cycladic island to Attica, only five hours from Athens, just east of Evvia, and only forty nautical miles from Piraeus. From the sea, its promontories appeared deceptively barren, yet it was fertile and had many springs. At the top of a hill overlooking the deep all-weather harbor of Vourkari, a principal haven in Ottoman times, an observation point surveyed the whole stretch of sea from Evvia to Cape Sounion and beyond. Before the war, the Michalinos Company had operated a lucrative coaling and watering station for passing freighters. During the occupation, Axis forces had used its warehouse and jetty as a covert staging area, but stripped all glass and metal from the buildings before evacuating.

After Caskey returned to Turkey, the owner of the Kea property turned it over to the Americans rent-free. Petrow raised the Stars and Stripes over the stone house that would serve as headquarters, wireless room, mess, and officers' and visitors' quarters. To whip the base into shape, Petrow hired lo-

Fig. 22. Kea, "Elba." Michalinos Coaling Station and Relief Distribution, November 25, 1944. (Courtesy National Archives.)

cal laborers, paying them with flour, sugar, and beans.[38] On October 26, he began receiving enlisted men and caiques that ferried 300 tons of food, clothing, base supplies, and equipment from obsolete "Boston." Three days later, Petrow opened "Elba."[39]

That week, Colonel Paul West (Special Operations) was in Athens to assess Noah's Ark with SOE. After recommending the withdrawal of virtually all Special Operations men from Greece, he had begun evacuating them. Then on October 24, West returned to Cairo.[40] Over dinner, he alerted MacVeagh to the widespread unemployment and hunger he had witnessed and expressed his opinion that Papandreou should concentrate on "bringing down prices and bringing in food." Inflation was out of control: firewood cost a billion drachmas and coffee and eggs at the Grande Bretagne cost over a trillion. West predicted serious trouble if the drachma were not promptly stabilized and supplies made available. The maintenance of public order rested largely on the local gendarmerie, many of whom were former members of the security battalions. Because the British had dispatched their meager troops to harass the German withdrawal and left Athens in the hands of an Indian division, West foresaw serious "social consequences." ELAS had violated the Caserta agreement by refusing to place its men in

Athens under Spiliotopoulos, and maintained a covert battalion in civilian dress. Meanwhile, throughout Greece EAM was keeping its organizations not only intact, but actually increasing them. West predicted that its leader would only cooperate with Britain while British forces were in the country. Afterward, the picture would "change sharply." Moreover, the Russian Colonel Popov was back in Athens "as a military observer." West considered "ridiculous" the notion that there was any "powerful sentiment in King George's favor," and told MacVeagh that "the king's best chance to return with British military protection had already passed." Alarmed at West's assessment, MacVeagh cabled Washington, but when the State Department demanded answers, MacVeagh had left for Athens. So it made Donovan account for the gloomy state of Greek affairs. He, in turn, contacted Aldrich, who despite his power was not well informed. Rather than supporting West, Aldrich tried to reassure Donovan. Aldrich considered postliberation Greece unimportant. He suggested that MacVeagh was only partly correct and that, considering FDR's views, OSS should stick to the New Year's date for closing out the Young Plan.[41]

Penrose knew better and insisted that Athens be supported. With Jim Oliver decamping for reassignment or repatriation and MI-6 having moved all its people to Athens, there was no need to keep a Greek Desk operating from Bari.[42] Everyone should be concentrated in Athens, where the needs were acute. Like Young, Penrose believed that OSS's "difficulties were largely self- generated." Preoccupied with turf wars and security, OSS was "so imbued with the hush-hush policy that it will not let its right hand know what its left is doing," insisting that Greek intelligence be processed in Cairo even though the Young Plan's chief customers were all in Athens. As a result, SI's intelligence had to be sent to Cairo for processing only to be returned to Greece and delivered to the customers. Penrose imagined one day "Young having to meet MacVeagh on a street corner and slip him a batch of reports under a newspaper!"[43] Something had to give.

On October 31, George Skouras set off on a photographic and intelligence tour of the Peloponnese with two SI field agents.[44] General Benjamin Giles (USAFIME commander) had given him a movie camera and film to make a photographic survey of war damage in Greek villages that the War Department planned to use for commercial purposes. It provided Skouras's cover for an SI economic survey. For ten days, they photographed the destruction of bridges, beginning with the Corinth Canal.

They documented German atrocities in village after village where, because the Germans had even destroyed the olive presses, fruit hung on trees long after it should have been picked. After traveling to Gythion, Skouras circled north by jeep and mule, documenting a lack of food and clothing, shelter, medicine and caregivers, farm equipment and draft animals. Then he climbed for four hours to reach the village of Kalavrita, where less than a year ago the Germans had punished the village for the nearby loss of seventy soldiers. There, the "men-less ghostlike women" related to him the events of December 13, 1943.

> The Germans arrived five days before the town was burned. The officers and non-commissioned officers, billeted on every home in the town, proceeded to create a friendly feeling by playing with the children and showing pictures of their own, thus getting the names and age of all members of the family. On the fifth day, all the males from 12 to 95 were called to the square of the town and ordered inside the schoolhouse. The women were called and ordered into the other side of the schoolhouse, which was then locked. The Germans set fire to every house in the town, and as the fire was raging the men were marched to the mountain top where, at a specific spot, they were mowed down by hidden machine guns. The Germans then gave the coup de grace with their revolvers to those who were not yet dead.
>
> Simultaneously, the school in which the women and children were locked, was set on fire. The flames, the smoke, the screaming of the women and children, created a scene which the writer is incapable of describing, even though he heard the story from several women who lived through that hell.
>
> . . . an Austrian officer, seeing a woman jump from a window, was moved and opened the main door, thus freeing the women and children. He paid for his act with his life. The tortured frenzy of the women as they emerged from the school caused hilarious laughter on the part of the Germans, who told the women that their men were up the hill. The poor creatures ran to the place and found a pile of dead bodies and literally a stream of blood running down the hill. The Germans having killed all the animals and destroyed all the implements, the women had to drag their men down to the cemetery . . . and dig graves with their hands.

Skouras photographed the area and recorded that 983 men and boys, two children under twelve, and three priests were killed.[45]

While Skouras covered the Peloponnese, Young made sure that most of the staff were installed at 1 Fidiou and Calvo safe at Evangelismos Hospital. Young resigned on November 1 and began working at UNRRA, recruiting

Fig. 23. Staff of OSS Athens. On left Margaret ("Missy") Crosby and Gerald Else. George Emanuel, Pauline Manos, and Theochares Stavrides. (Courtesy Clio Sperling.)

Elli Adossides and American and British archaeologists. Sperling took control of OSS Athens while awaiting Caskey. When on November 2 Caskey informed Aldrich that he was not interested in directing OSS Athens, Aldrich appointed Captain Gerald Else and dispatched him by plane on November 5.[46] Else assumed his duties immediately, aided by his yearlong apprenticeship in Cairo.[47]

After meeting with Shepardson at AFHQ in Caserta, Penrose arrived in Athens and consulted with Else and Young. They planned the Athens office and met with members of the Greek government and OSS's chief customers, including MI-6. Then they discussed all continuing field missions in the Peloponnese, Thessaly, Epirus, and Macedonia, and Young introduced Else to MacVeagh. For Else, it seemed like one continual conference. A skeleton crew of SI, Finance, Security, R&A, and counterintelligence agents and enlisted men would work double jobs to close out obsolete missions by Aldrich's mandated deadline of January 1. Steve Bailey, Else's successor in Cairo, set up the Reports Office, which Margaret Crosby took over on November 9, wading through almost a month's backlog of agent reports on economic and political intelligence and translating, typing, and mimeographing them for Cairo, Caserta, London, and Washington.[48]

Aldrich conferred with Petrow at "Elba." Because of the dangers from floating mines and British raiders, Aldrich ordered all but seven caiques cashiered at Chios. To supply OSS Athens, Aldrich struck a deal with the Royal Navy to ferry as many as fifty tons every ten days, but the British would only deliver to Piraeus. After scouting with Petrow for a base there, they chose an anchorage east of Piraeus at Kalamaki to serve as "New Elba," should Kea be abandoned. While inspecting "Elba," Aldrich listened to disgruntled Communications officers who denigrated Caskey's administrative abilities. Late on November 9, Caskey received a telegraphed order to come to "Elba" for an emergency conference. Furiously trying to close his bases and waiting for Cox to return from one mission and leave on another to Lemnos and Pelion, Caskey left Virginia Grace in control. Buffeted by gales, he reached "Elba" the morning of November 13.[49]

Aldrich interrogated him on his repeated delays and ordered him to close out his missions on Samos and Leros, dismiss the caiques, shut down the Turkish operation, remove equipment from "Boston" to "Elba," and return to Athens at once.[50] Caskey wanted to pay the hungry crews in food, but Aldrich told him to pay them in gold. Caskey also wanted to give them certificates of service since the British had established a boilerplate solution with the OSS Maritime chief. The British gave their agents a cash bonus, food, certificates of participation, and employment, and allowed them to keep their arms. Although OSS generally awarded certificates, Donovan, Shepardson, and Aldrich vetoed these in Greece because of "political considerations." Only to Papandreou's government would they certify that the men had worked for the OSS. Caskey argued that OSS was obligated to help them find employment if only to prevent their compromising continuing missions, but Aldrich refused, lest OSS be drawn into the escalating political troubles.[51] After Caskey assured Aldrich that he would finish in two days, they agreed that he would pursue a reduced SI operation in the islands. That evening, Caskey retraced his path and Penrose and Aldrich returned to Cairo.

On November 18, Young and Sperling left for Salonika, two days after Clio Adossides reached Athens.[52] Over the course of a week, Young and Sperling closed down missions in Lamia, Volos, Larissa, and Trikkala and collected their intelligence reports. Then Major Sperling took charge of Salonika, which the British had occupied on October 31. There he set up an office and contacted General Euripides Bakirdjis of ELAS and Georgiades, who had spent several weeks collecting intelligence at the Evros border before picking up his jeep in Alexandroupolis. After conferring with Sperling, Georgiades drove Young through eastern Macedonia, Thrace, and Evros to observe conditions.

Personnel were still arriving in Athens during the last two weeks of November. After finishing the history of the Greek Desk, Captain Charles Edson joined the Athens office on the twenty-second. Meanwhile in Istanbul, Thomas Karamessines loaded a station wagon with a portable radio and transmitter, arms and ammunition, first-aid supplies, bedrolls, and food for four. As the head of OSS counterintelligence (X-2 or "double-cross") for Greece, the twenty-five-year-old Columbia graduate entered Evros on November 22 and made his way to Athens, where he was to prepare postmilitary coverage of the Middle East. He and his men arrived on the twenty-fifth, and Young put them up at the Agora, where Yale professor Bradford Welles, Edson's roommate and chief of X-2 in Cairo, briefed them.[53] Others arrived by British convoy bringing jeeps and trailers. By late November, the Young Plan was complete.[54]

The situation was tense. Karamessines, tipped off by Settler, had arrested a cell of German stay-behind agents in Athens. To keep a lid on boiling emotions, General Spiliotopoulos, the military governor, had forbidden outdoor meetings and demonstrations. He opened cinemas to show American prewar movies, but no Greek could afford the price of admission—a bar of soap, two packages of cigarettes, or 40 billion drachmas. Spiliotopoulos called in all arms, but EAM refused to comply and instructed its people to deliver them to EAM arsenals rather than to the police.[55] Then Karamessines learned that General Wilson had decided to arrest all those carrying arms without authority. General Scobie told EAM members of government that the terrorist activities must stop. Else reported that Prime Minister Papandreou had declared that the EAM-controlled police would be abolished by December 1 and EDES and ELAS by December 10. But EAM demanded guarantees that the rightists would not dominate the political and military reorganization.[56] Everyone felt a crisis brewing.

Skouras proceeded north with Lieutenant Stix and met with General Sarafis in Lamia. Proceeding to Volos, Skouras picked up an agent from Simmons. Finding the Salonika road impassable, they drove to Larissa, then detoured west to Trikkala and Kalambaka, passing mountain villages, one of which had been burned six times. Crossing the Vardar by ferry since the bridges had been destroyed, they continued past Anatolia College, where Austrian intelligence officer Kurt Waldheim had been stationed, to the mountain village of Khortiatis. There Skouras documented the fate of sixty women and children (including some infants) who had been "forcibly locked in a bakery [and roasted alive in the enflamed structure], which was fired on from all sides. Machine guns were so placed that any escaping through the fire would be shot down." Skouras could not believe his ears, but later confirmed every detail.[57]

While in Salonika, Skouras and the Simmons agents investigated the airfields in vain for any trace of the Germans' secret weapon but the mission to discover the whereabouts of the German buzz bomb had failed because it arrived too late.[58] Skouras interviewed General Bakirdjis while Lieutenant Stix contacted the Greek Red Cross concerning the fate of the city's Jewish community, 80 percent of whom (over 43,000) had died at Auschwitz. They returned by way of the burned-out former EAM headquarters at Karpenisi, and made a pilgrimage to the village of Distomon, where survivors showed Skouras the victims' graves and told him of the June massacre.

> The town had been visited by a German force, including Gestapo (?) men who . . . found that there were Andartes [guerrillas] about. They stayed long enough to have lunch and drinks, and departed, leaving behind a small garrison. . . . [after] a fight with the Andartes . . . [in which they] suffered some casualties. . . . They returned to Distomon, and the commander, in an almost hysterical way, ordered all the inhabitants to stay in their houses, and then directed his soldiers to enter the houses and slaughter every living thing. 234 people were butchered, 117 being women and 54 children, mostly infants.[59]

Then Skouras returned to Athens with the first intelligence from the north. He reported that the only political differences between the north and south were some support for the king in the Peloponnese and a Communist majority in the north. Strongly, he advised that no fair elections could be achieved without American oversight.[60]

Oliver crossed from Bari to Corfu to visit Alcinoos and to Santi Quaranta on the Adriatic Coast of Albania. From there, he reached his Molossos agents in the Pindus Mountains, who had been waiting since September for the British to fly them out. At each stop, Oliver settled accounts and gathered reports. By Thanksgiving, November 25, 1944, he was making his way to Athens.

On November 19, Major Caskey had still not closed "Key West" and Izmir. He cabled his resignation to Cairo because of "irreconcilable differences" and asked to be reassigned.[61] Then he placed Grace in charge, after admonishing, "No souvenirs." Caskey made one last visit to "Key West," which he evacuated abruptly, bringing men and caiques to Vathi to keep the Turks from looting the base. At midnight on the twenty-second, he sailed for Chios, where storms delayed him for thirty-six hours. Behind in Izmir, Grace finished the process. She spent three days burning papers, settling accounts, and clearing the premises. Although she, too, had wanted to go to Athens, she deposited leftover funds in Istanbul and caught the Ankara plane to Cairo.[62]

On Thanksgiving Day, Caskey arrived at Kea and learned that Aldrich had closed the port. From the quay in front of the Michalinos wharf, Caskey witnessed Petrow distributing surplus supplies of OSS food, blankets, clothing, and shoes to impoverished island residents, 90 percent of whose children were barefoot (fig. 22).[63] In gratitude, islanders donated 400 eggs, several hundred pounds of fresh almonds, and over thirty chickens, which Petrow gave to the Red Cross hospital in Athens. To facilitate British deliveries, Petrow moved "Elba" to Kalamaki ("New Elba"), although being six miles from Athens and twelve from Piraeus, it was far from ideal. Once it opened on November 29, all supplies had to be trucked from Piraeus, off-loaded, stored, and then reloaded and trucked into Athens.[64]

Oliver and Caskey reached Athens on November 27 and made straight for 9 Ploutarchou. As agents flowed into Athens from Turkey and Egypt, others, such as Cox, reached the diminished quarters of the Greek Desk in Cairo. Cox was awaiting transport home when Virginia Grace arrived with the last Izmir reports, still hoping to join Crosby as a reports officer in Athens.[65] Major Wines was writing up the evacuation of Special Operations personnel before returning to the United States. Of the Special Operations teams, only Dr. Robert Moyers's medical mission remained in Greece, distributing medicine and supplies to destroyed villages near Karpenisi.

At this point, Penrose advised Else that the Young Plan should not be "disestablished" until some kind of civilian representation was in place under embassy cover. Shepardson agreed. Although Aldrich acknowledged that the termination date for the Young Plan must depend on their customers' needs, he continued to insist that Else close it out by New Year's Day. Colonel Edward Glavin (Balkans SI chief at AFHQ in Caserta) discussed the Young Plan with its customers: its duration, the number of its personnel, the balance between its release of missions and acquisition of intelligence, the value of said intelligence, and its relation to other U.S. intelligence possibilities. Penrose alerted Else that Glavin's view of Greek affairs was undergoing a sea-change. Now he viewed it as "a feather in the Italian cap," thinking that "the Greek plum" belonged in "Caserta's fruitbowl," and warned Else to watch out.[66]

On November 28, Penrose requested an immediate review of Aldrich's arbitrary January 1 terminus, claiming that "the psychology in Athens was all wrong." Following Aldrich's orders, Else was more concerned with withdrawing than acquiring intelligence. Since British political intelligence continued to be "channeled by their political policy" and "not wholly satisfactory to Americans," OSS needed to bridge the gap.

Penrose believed that as long as their customers wanted their services, they should remain. They did. The Americans in ML and UNRRA were "practically screaming for intelligence," and the embassy needed independent reporting on EAM, EDES, and British and Russian activities concerning Greek domestic problems. MacVeagh and the State Department valued the Young Plan's economic intelligence on relief and rehabilitation and counterintelligence on the German penetration of Greek industry. Most critical were Edson and Else's daily conferences on the governmental crisis, the gist of which Else relayed to MacVeagh while Edson met with General Sadler (AML) and lower-level embassy officials, such as Arthur Parsons and Harry Hill. Shepardson needed to show Else his support. Because "the possibility of post-war intelligence operations" required "a continuity of production," Penrose insisted that the Young Plan overlap with its successor intelligence network to avoid a hiatus in service. Moreover, with so many U.S. servicemen in Athens that they had taken over a hotel, the time had come to drop the "fiction" that America had no military connection with Greece.[67]

But MacVeagh wanted more—intelligence he could control, an OSS man on his staff to do "permanent intelligence work" and "supervise intelligence operations in Greece." Else suggested Carl Blegen as MacVeagh's OSS man "to canvass the situation and arrive at a definite policy for OSS activities in Greece based on realities of the developing political situation." Blegen had been angling for a way back to Greece since January 1942. He began his OSS career with FNB in September of that year by following Meritt into heading the Greek Section, then Miscellaneous Languages, then the Chancery. In each position, Alison Frantz worked at his side as a political analyst. While indexing part time for Meritt at the Institute for Advanced Study, Frantz had begun working as one of his volunteer readers for FNB, moved to R&A, and then joined Blegen in 1942. They had edited the *Kingdom of Greece* monograph to which Shear and Young contributed. Then in 1943 they drafted a tome entitled "Foreign Nationality Groups in the United States: The Greeks," as an exemplum for others to be written on each of the more important foreign language groups in the United States. For the last two years, he was the foremost political analyst of Greece in the United States.[68] MacVeagh agreed. On November 29, Glavin cabled Donovan to keep the Young Plan intact and send Blegen to supervise "the future of OSS/SI activities in Greece."[69]

That evening, Young and Georgiades returned from eastern Macedonia and Evros with Gander's mission reports. When they arrived at 1 Fidiou, Young found that Clio, Edson, and Dimitri Petrou had closed out six missions (Oracle, Gorgon, Athletes, Ajax, Emerald, and Despot).[70] Meanwhile, Sperling had dismissed four (Phalanx, Gasoline, Iron, and Floka); and Caskey and Daniel had cashiered four more (Crayon, Emerald, Archangel, and Helios). They had cleared a quarter of the field agents and hoped to finish by Christmas. The building overflowed with twenty men on camp beds without sheets, mattresses, or pillows. Despite the primitive conditions, it was a jolly sight. Pleased that the Desk had survived so well without him, Young skirted Mt. Lycabettus to Kolonaki. At 9 Ploutarchou, he found Daniel, who had just reached Athens, and Caskey and Hill ensconced beside the fire, just like the old days.

THIRTEEN

Things Fall Apart

ON DECEMBER 3, 1944, the winter sun rose over a ravaged Athens. Avenues empty of cars brimmed with impoverished citizens peddling American cigarettes, pushing overburdened carts, or just standing around. The once jubilant residents who had celebrated the end of the Nazi occupation wondered if life would ever be normal. As winter approached and conditions deteriorated, elation gave way to fear of different enemies.

Buildings were tagged with graffiti, and splashy signs defaced walls. Some welcomed the British and the Yanks while others declared allegiance to sparring political factions ranging from Communists to royalists. Demonstrations were not uncommon. The chief ground for hope of peace was the realization that violence would end in mutual destruction. Or would the royalist British and the EAM avoid an impasse? It seemed a fragile temporary state of affairs.[1]

Caskey had been in Athens for almost a week. Disgruntled and exhausted, he thought he had seen the best and worst that war had to offer. He had evacuated spies, survived bombardments and endless bureaucratic snafus with British and rival American services.[2] After a valedictory voyage across the Aegean, Caskey had come to Athens to check on his godfather. That done, he was ready to go. Everything had changed. Oliver had already left Cairo. Daniel had departed to gather intelligence in Western Macedonia, where he had hiked in the thirties. Young was engulfed in the shadow world of relief and rehabilitation. And Sperling was in Salonika coping with the aftermath of the occupation as EAM police began settling scores, arresting and killing collaborators. Gerald Else a classicist from the prairies of South Dakota, was in charge now.

That morning, Else cabled Donovan for direction. Washington expected him to close out the six-week-old base and all missions by the New Year, but this seemed neither advisable nor possible. Else was tired of stopgap measures and wanted his agents protected by cover. British commander in chief General Ronald Scobie's proclamations to the guerrillas ordering the ELAS demobilization had provoked the EAM ministers to resign from the government, and EAM mobilized its reserves. It was a standoff; EAM controlled the countryside, and the British were concentrated in Athens. Those in the know expected the British to marshal the Greek armed forces from the Middle East, to augment the Greek police, reactionary royalists (CHIites), and security battalions.

As the birds began squawking, Else gleaned disturbing information. Awk, Gander, Glafyx, Buzzard, Black Bustard, Shrike, Penguin, Peacock, Plover, and Grouse noted increased tension. Kingfisher reported that the Volos Greeks were outraged that the British had garrisoned their city with Gurkhas, who had fortified their billet with barbed wire to keep out the Greeks, and accused the British of withholding food to press their royalist agenda. Starling cawed that for over a week Patras had been plagued by leftist demonstrations of children, teens, refugees, and factory and dock workers although the majority of residents hewed to the right. Elsewhere in the Peloponnese, 7,500 national guards deserted to ELAS. That morning, Major Daniel (Duck) was heading north in an American jeep flying the Stars and Stripes. He reported that EAM had planned to strike at the Lamia electrical plant the night before, but called it off and now all was quiet on the Athens-Lamia road.

Sperling (Sparrow) reported that the numbers of workers marching in grim formations had increased, as had spokesmen for the unemployed. "Vociferous pro-Russian elements" protested the British demobilization of ELAS.[3] That night, megaphone men and bell ringers led Salonika crowds through outlying streets, demanding that ELAS be retained and Prime Minister George Papandreou be ousted. They continued past midnight, tearing down Scobie's posted proclamations. The next morning, a high officer in ELAS advised the British that it would not tolerate interference.

Colonel Glavin cabled Donovan and Cairo that Caserta command considered the present transition period in Greece "highly important." He was "anxious that nothing be done precipitately which might prejudice or preclude future SI activities of potential value to the Athens embassy, State Department, and other government agencies."[4] He recommended that Penrose get to Athens at once. Independently, Else requested that Penrose come and assess the situation, but he was departing for Washington, where he would work with SI chief Whitney Shepardson, and the acting head of the Greek Desk was leaving for Italy.[5]

Everyone knew there was going to be a demonstration. A source high up in the Communist Party had told Plover that there would be an EAM rally that morning. Cognizant of the touchy state of affairs, the group had requested and received permission to march with preapproved slogans, such as "Down with the government of civil war"; "Unity government is needed"; "All traitors should be arrested"; and "Food for the people." As far as EAM was concerned, the demonstration was to be peaceful, and it would do nothing to start a clash. Leaders had ordered participants not to bear arms and ELAS to be on guard in its Athens barracks. The Left stood united, hoping to avert bloodshed, but if force were used, EAM would meet it.

Again, the British acted provocatively. On December 2, they stationed tanks in Syntagma and "on all sides of Omonia" Square and paraded others through the villages of Attica. Moreover, they ordered gendarmes in Athens to take up arms.[6] Then, the night before the scheduled demonstration, Papandreou's interim government changed its mind and revoked its permission.

Caskey left 9 Ploutarchou at about ten the next morning and headed for Syntagma Square (map 1, inset). The neoclassical Parliament building, designed as a palace for the Bavarian first king of Greece, commanded the tree-lined square and faced the Acropolis, a reminder of the city's democratic past. Streets named for queens, kings, and philhellenes circumscribed the square's central Garden of the Muses. Queen Amalias Boulevard passed before the Parliament and the immured Tomb of the Unknown Soldier and circled the Grand Bretagne Hotel on a corner of the square opposite the Parliament. Then it became University Street, later renamed for Eleftherios Venizelos, the liberal statesman who often opposed the Greek kings of foreign blood. Even the square's architecture and nomenclature evoked Greece's contested politics, its ideal of independence, and reality of dependence and foreign domination.

Caskey crossed to the Grande Bretagne. The demonstration was gathering peacefully in the working-class neighborhoods on the far side of the Acropolis between Athens and the port of Piraeus where EAM was head-

Fig. 24. Athens, 1944. (Photo by Costas Couvaras. Copyright held by Department of Special Collections and University Archives, The Library. California State University, Sacramento.)

quartered. Caskey could hear the throng long before he saw it. The skittish British-backed Greek police, unprepared for the size of the multitude that stretched down the street in a column for about a quarter of a mile, hurriedly cordoned off the square to prevent the crowds from reaching it. At Amalias, the demonstrators realized they had been blocked, and the crowd grew restive. A small contingent snaked down side streets. From their position in front of British Headquarters at the Grande Bretagne, Caskey and Arthur Parsons saw the crowd approach the square from the Street of the Philhellenes.[7] To their left, Police Headquarters stood at the corner of Sophia and University streets. From a distance of about twenty feet, Caskey watched events unfold.

By about 1045 hrs on Sunday morning, 3 Dec., crowds were demonstrating in Constitution [Syntagma] Square, Athens. Police cordons were near the Grande Bretagne Hotel, in front of the Palace, and at Police HQ. The crowd was excited, but good-natured until the police showed bad temper at about 1100 hrs. The police threatened the crowd with their carbines and subma-chine guns. One British armoured car was parked outside the Grande Bre-tagne and two others were in the Square. At about 1105 hrs the main body of the procession arrived at the Square from the south, i.e. via Amalia Blvd, singing, carrying Greek, British, American, and Russian flags, and placards. There was a large percentage of young men and women at the head of the procession. The police barred the street at the NE corner of the square and fired toward the crowd at about 1110 hrs. Aim for the most part was just above the heads of the crowd; rapid fire continued for about 90 seconds. All demonstrators lay prone from the moment of the first volley. At about 1115 hrs, they began to rise and disperse. During the preceding three to five min-utes, there had been two or three loud reports, presumably from hand grenades. At about 1115 hrs [*sic*] one man from the crowd threw a grenade; he, and possibly others were shot down at point-blank range. As crowd withdrew, a minimum of twelve (positive count, incomplete) bodies lay in the street. Source believes there were 15 to 17. Most of these appeared dead. Among them were at least two young women. Bodies were carried to the side of the street by civilians. An ambulance arrived promptly to take some of them. Source saw three or four seriously wounded being helped away. Friends of the casualties were hysterical.

Men with American and British flags approached the police and dared them to fire; there were no shots just then. Sporadic firing toward the Square followed from Police HQ. There was a disorganized crowd in the Square, concentrating near the KKE HQ on the south side. Two more British ar-moured cars joined the one outside the Grande Bretagne. A British military vehicle failed to stop and pick up wounded (or dead) bodies at the signal of a bystander. There were gestures of anger. Forty to fifty people gathered around an English major, expostulating. There was no indication of vio-lence from or toward any British troops.

At about 1200 hrs, Source observed a parade coming around the Grande Bretagne and moving SW on Bucharest St toward Constitution Square. The crowd was singing and shouting; it was astonishingly good tempered, except for a few with placards stained with blood of the victims. These climbed onto parked cars and showed the stained placards.

Fellow Cincinnatian Lt. Stix also witnessed the events and amplified the previous account.

By noon, British armoured cars were supplemented by ten Sherman tanks. Four of these blocked off Kifissia St and the entrance to Police HQ, and by maneuvers broke up demonstrations. The other tanks covered the entrances to the Palace. A policeman emerging from HQ was surrounded by a crowd who took his rifle from him, turned it over to the captain of a British tank and let the policeman go.

The crowd was not anti-British. Their placards read "Scobie does not represent the views of the British government" and "Independence." British Tommies passing while the shooting was going on were applauded. As the crowd passed the Grande Bretagne they started cheering for Roosevelt and then proceeded to demonstrate enthusiastically in front of the United States Embassy.

The reaction of a British Tommy was: "Why do they want to go and shoot down unarmed women and children?"

Chief of Police Evert, interviewed at Police HQ immediately after the shooting, said that the crowd had fired first and that the police had answered in self defense. He stated that his orders were not to fire unless the police were fired on or unless someone tried to take their arms away.[8]

Figures for the dead vary widely from seven to twenty-one, as do those for the wounded—from twenty-six to 150. Clearly there was great confusion. Rumors circulated about Americans "disarming some members of the police in front of the Grande Bretagne after the police fired."

Couvaras was also on hand and reported a small orderly crowd at first. He entered the Grande Bretagne around eleven o'clock. From a first-floor balcony facing the Tomb of the Unknown Soldier, he confirmed that the demonstration was "entirely peaceful." He added that at a quarter past eleven the police were ordered back. "They withdrew instantly for about twenty to thirty paces and started firing," exactly at the corner of King George and University streets, twenty to forty yards from where he stood. Some people "started jumping down into the Garden of the Muses" or hiding behind balustrades. The official report excised the following paragraph from Couvaras's text.

Looking directly below, saw a policeman firing with his rifle pointed into the crowd. About ten minutes after the firing started by the police, source saw a hand grenade exploding at the empty space between the crowd and the police, but nearer the police. Cannot tell by whom the hand grenade was thrown. Several minutes after the shooting started, the bursts from automatics became less heavy and the crowd made several attempts to get away. The first attempts were unsuccessful because the police every time they saw somebody standing up, started firing again. However, little by little the people running managed to leave the spot of the shooting and got into the Garden of the Muses below. In the end only the dead or wounded remained on the spot of the shooting. . . . firing lasted for about half an hour: it was very heavy only for the first 10 minutes, but the police went on firing from inside the court yard of their police bldg. until an American and a British newspaperman went inside the police building. Soon after that firing ceased. In addition to rifle and automatic firing, source heard a number of shots fired from heavier weapons coming from the direction of the old palace and that of the ministry of war.[9]

Then the transmitted version continued.

At about 11:45 hrs, 3 Dec (i.e. about half an hour after the first shooting) megaphones called the crowd to gather at Constitution Square. As the people gathered waiting for their leaders to speak from the offices of the Communist Party, they were shouting the following slogans: "Down with the civil war government"; "Down with the killers"; "Independence"; "Let the people do what they want." The cry "Roosevelt, Roosevelt" was heard very often.

At about 12:30 hours speakers started talking to the people from Communist Party HQ. . . . The crowd was heaviest at this time.[10]

The following section was deleted from Plover's original report when the processed version was excerpted and transmitted to Washington and Caserta:

Around 12:30 tanks in force appeared coming from Kiphissia St. These tanks first stopped at the corner where the shooting took place, and then went on pushing through the crowd until they formed a cordon all around Constitution Square. . . .

Planes appeared in the skies, flying very low. They were pursuit planes and light bombers, and stayed in the sky from 12:00 to 14:00.[11]

Then the transmitted report to Washington and Caserta continued:

About 1315 hours the crowd knelt and sang a funeral march. The crowd, about 50,000, started breaking about 1330 hours, going in different directions. A large group formed on Kiphisia Blvd. and headed toward the American Embassy. The demonstrators stood in front of the Embassy for about 15 minutes shouting "Roosevelt, Roosevelt"; "America, America"; "Independence"; "We don't want a new occupation"; "Down with the killers' government." This demonstration then passed Papandreou's home, shouting "Death to the killer," "Down with the civil war government."

Source saw blood in front of Papandreou's house. The policeman there said that somebody had thrown a hand grenade which killed the grenade thrower and also wounded a policeman. The people who had been there earlier, however, said that the police had fired on the crowd as it was marching peacefully toward Constitution Square. Source and one person pointed to the police officer who gave the order to fire. Source and an American newspaperman noticed that the police were very embarrassed by questioning and annoyed by what the crowd had said of the shooting. It was admitted by both the police and the crowd that a number of people were wounded and killed.[12]

That was all it took. Once ignited, the orgy of assaults, vandalism, abductions, and executions spread throughout Athens. OSS agents in other parts of the city heard shots fired in Piraeus. From the Agora, X-2 reported that CHI-ites were attacking ELAS from the south and moving from Observatory Hill to the Philopappou Monument. Meanwhile, British snipers fired on ELAS from the Acropolis.

Around two o'clock, British paratroopers cleared Syntagma Square, but the crowds reassembled around the working-class area of Omonia Square. Those at 1 Fidiou found themselves in the thick of the action. Margaret Crosby apologized that her day's reports did not quite measure "up to the Washington standards." She tried to write, edit, and dispatch the dittoed reports as quickly as possible, but it was " a bit difficult to keep anyone at work with shouting mobs parading under the windows and airplanes missing the roof by some 20 or 30 feet . . . [and] disturbances such as . . . stray killing."[13]

That night, electrical company employees went on strike. While the city smoldered in the dark, Crosby and Else labored by candlelight. Several birds called in. Their news was grave, yet not without hope. Sparrow reported that although the political atmosphere in Salonika was tense, the city was quiet. There were no ELAS police or armed guards on the streets, and the British were posting special sentries. Kingfisher chronicled a gathering of 30,000 in Volos. The secretary of EAM called for the continued existence of its army and the ouster of Papandreou, but not civil war.

On December 3, 1944, the world that the archaeologists had tried so hard to save was destroying itself. Else, a student of ancient Greek tragedy, found himself embedded in a modern equivalent. Meanwhile, the British continued to exacerbate the situation. Through go-betweens in the darkened city, the British requested an interview with ELAS commanders in Athens. ELAS officers withdrew outside the city limits to meet the British, who asked them to surrender their weapons. In order to avoid conflict with the British, the officers complied, whereupon the British imprisoned them. Without them, the leaderless ELAS ranks rearmed.

The next day, the narrow lane that led from University Street, past 1 Fidiou, and up Mt. Lycabettus to ELAS territory became a field of fire. From their perch, ELAS sniped at traffic on University Street. Cross fire limited movement and hit OSS headquarters several times. A large slug embedded itself in the wall of the message center two feet above the head of an OSS radio operator, and across town at the American School in British-held Kolonaki, MacVeagh reported that bullets shattered the windows and snipers were firing from Evangelismos Hospital.[14]

No longer could OSS agents move through the streets safely as civilians. Thinking that Greeks would not harm Americans, Else ordered staff members into uniform with the American flag on their sleeves. MacVeagh concurred. "The peaceful liberation of Greece which was the basis for . . . civilian clothes did not exist." Rather, it was "a state of siege." Else would decide whether weapons were necessary to protect agents' lives, but for the time being, he forbade them outside the building to prevent "OSS personnel being accused of incidents." To maximize vigilance inside, Else placed a twenty-four-hour armed watch of four four-man teams that rotated duty every fourth day. Each had a new man guarding the entrance who switched on for two hours and off for six.[15] In the days that followed, shells dropped within fifty yards of 1 Fidiou. OSS personnel were ordered to stay in for their own safety and only left the building on business with a specific purpose and written permission from Else.[16] Else did not want to risk lives.

Nor did he want to remain isolated. Such conditions curtailed contact with the usual customers and delayed the delivery of supplies from "New Elba." When Else finally established telephone contact with General Sadler and Laird Archer, MacVeagh was nowhere to be found.[17] With the building surrounded, OSS intelligence was limited to telephone and personal observation. Edson suggested that all they needed to do to write up intelligence was to open a window and listen.[18]

All of a sudden, Washington began paying attention. On December 6, Donovan cabled them to remain at their posts. The Greek mission had to be established with great care under uncertain conditions. Henceforth, the Athens team could not be treated as other city teams. It had to be "handled in a very special manner." Donovan demanded that "nothing should be done that would in any way disrupt the operation."[19] All field sources were to be briefed on complete coverage of the civil strife.[20] To protect the Young Plan's independence, Cairo would continue to supply Athens and process its reports and communications, and Else could under no circumstances share details on Young Plan communications and activities with AFHQ.

Else made siege preparations in the fortress-like OSS headquarters. To supply provisions, Chris Petrow dodged bullets from "New Elba" to 1 Fidiou by jeep, a route that the British only traversed by convoy or armored car. By the end of the first week of December, OSS Athens had stocked enough food and supplies to last three weeks to a month.[21] An intercom connected the front door with the "war" room. Thanks to a generator, they had uninterrupted radio communication and lights in the lower hall, dining room, kitchen, and "war" room, where the "Nocturnal Council" screened, edited, and evaluated intelligence before batting it out in cables. They laid in batteries, field telephones, extra radios, flashlights, and candles in case the generator died and installed loudspeakers on the roof corners should they find themselves in the middle of the battle and emergency radio equipment on the billet floor should the roof become unusable or breached. At the same time, Else considered fleeing to Kea, and asked that the caiques be readied for emergency evacuation.[22]

The X-2 agents also found themselves in the battle zone and evacuated the Agora for a position opposite the Grande Bretagne. In the process, they revealed themselves to MI-6 and, afterward, were reduced to updating records and conducting security checks on embassy employees for MacVeagh.[23] Both X-2 and its British equivalent suspected that Germans were fomenting the violence in Athens and watched closely for evidence to that effect.

On December 6, Alexandros Svolos, one of the EAM-affiliated ministers who had resigned, contacted Papandreou to announce that EAM and the Communists would join a government under liberal Themistoklis Sofoulis in order to stop the fighting, but Papandreou refused to step aside and Churchill advised waiting.[24] The day before, Churchill cabled Ambassador Leeper that the Athens troubles were a "mob uprising" and telegraphed Scobie, "We have to hold and dominate Athens.... Do not hesitate to act as if you were in a conquered city where a local rebellion is in progress." On December 6, Churchill cabled General Wilson that Greece was of "paramount political importance" and advised him to send reinforcements. Meanwhile, British planes strafed the city and shelled the leftist suburb of Kaiseriani, and the army deployed mechanized troops and Rallides against

ELAS.[25] Velouchiotis, the scourge of the Peloponnese whose code name "Ares" bespoke his warlike blood hunger, was marching toward Athens with his ELAS troops, and a second ELAS division was already fighting in the southeast suburbs of Athens. The situation continued to deteriorate.

Both sides were "trying to ring Americans in." On the seventh, high-placed EAM officials appealed to Britain, the United States, Russia, and France for an inter-Allied commission to find a solution where both sides could save face. On the eighth, the BBC broadcast Churchill's speech to the House of Commons where he professed that British and Americans were "united in present policy" and that their armies would see that order was established. Those who knew better begged Else to correct the record. Apoplectic, he cabled Cairo demanding that, because of "high echelon policy involved," someone at a high level respond to Churchill's gross misrepresentation, designed to make the United States "co-responsible for the military situation." He wanted to evacuate, but Donovan told him to stay put; counteracting Greek broadcasts was not OSS's job. Even the anglophilic MacVeagh wrote FDR that the British were treating the "fanatically freedom-loving country . . . as if it were composed of natives under the British Raj."[26]

Where ELAS ruled, Americans were greeted with cheers and smiles. Duck reported being "at the top of the EAM heap in Kozani and Florina"; Sparrow saw General Bakirdjis frequently; and Gander related ELAS activities from Kavala and Thrace. Other OSS agents announced no problems in the cities of Patras, Tripolis, Larissa, Volos, and Yannina.[27]

OSS experienced difficulties only in contested areas, but there was no uncontested British territory. Of the two British "strongholds," even the British admitted that ELAS held most of Piraeus. The other area was between Kolonaki and Syntagma where, on the ninth, ELAS moved machine guns to the corner of the Parliament building, fewer than 500 yards from the Grande Bretagne, and began firing at a British convoy. After dusk, unidentified snipers targeted two OSS agents on their way back from the Grande Bretagne, perhaps mistaking them for British despite their large American flag. That afternoon and the next morning, shooting erupted and the guerrillas landed mortar shells just in front of the Grande Bretagne. For three days, planes strafed the National Gardens behind the Parliament building where ELAS troops hid, and casualties from British overshooting claimed ten times more civilians than ELAS.[28]

At OSS headquarters, Crosby wrote her Reports counterpart in Cairo noting "fewer bullets going by the building today . . . definitely not helpful, especially for proof-reading. . . . bullets . . . in our backyard." Meanwhile, Georgiades' jeep had been shot at twice, once while he was in the British- and police-controlled area, the other time by mistake when he had forgot- ten a flag for his unmarked jeep, drove from Fidiou Street into ELAS terri- tory, and was fired upon by snipers. When they realized it was an American officer, they cheered and brought Georgiades a U.S. flag to protect him.[29]

Else bemoaned "the lack of effective contact between the government, the British, ML, UNRRA, etc., on the one hand and EAM-ELAS on the other." Only the OSS talked with all sides. Three agents provided day-to-day coverage of the Battle of Athens and political reports (from EAM/ELAS, Greek government, and rightist circles). Several Greek sources covered the politicians accessible at the Grande Bretagne or within a block or two ra- dius where almost all non-EAM political activity took place. However, Else disparaged this "so-called 'political world'" as a small, ingrown clique of old gossiping politicians that seemed more and more ineffectual.[30]

Beyond this might as well have been another country. The British had abandoned the provinces and pulled in their men to the large coastal towns, making no provision for contact with ELAS. In spite of being surrounded by it, OSS only had intermittent contact with ELAS through Couvaras, who braved the streets and the thick of bullets to confer with its leaders. His in- telligence was invaluable, though his leftist bias complicated its analysis. Al- though OSS coverage in Athens was restricted and had limited contacts elsewhere, by mid-December, OSS became the chief source of intelligence on EAM-ELAS. Crosby churned out its reports at an alarming speed, 131 in fifteen days, almost 90 percent of which were political. Accusations emerged that OSS was leftist. The Greek Desk thought that the charges had been planted by the British or their agents. But OSS did have consistently more and better intelligence on EAM/ELAS than the British and was the only outside group in direct contact with them. It had become the *only* link between most of Greece (outside of Epirus) and the outside world.[31]

For the present, an unexpended well of goodwill toward America and all things American kept them safe. The Greek public had still not grasped that the impotent Americans had turned over the whole business to the British. From the number of petitions that the Greeks were trying to get to MacVeagh through OSS, even their leaders had either not quite realized the true nature of the situation or did not want to. MacVeagh made it clear to Else that he would not entertain the petitioners. However, after broadcasts like Churchill's, people were beginning to question the Americans and their policies. If the British policy of lumping the United States with the British through passive association persisted, then it would endanger the safety of Americans in Greece. Since all OSS field agents were known to EAM/ELAS leaders and the local Greek population as Americans or in American service, they would need to be replaced.

Releasing Greek nationals active on field missions against the Germans became a crisis. Some radioed that they were penned up in Volos; others arrived by British ship or RAF bomber from Salonika and more trickled in Athens from Larissa.[32] By midmonth, Athens had processed and discharged all but three of the field missions. Beforehand, however, each agent had to write the history of his mission and account for his equipment and finances. Only at OSS headquarters could they do this without danger. And where could Else release them safely? Letting the Greek agents go in Athens was "tantamount to forcing them into the civil war and, in some cases, exposing them to direct danger from one side or another."[33] Two local Greek agents could not even cross town for processing, and another agent resigned lest his partisanship embarrass OSS. In the end, due to the closure of the banks, inability to secure enough occupation currency, and " chaos in the Greek government's departments," OSS insisted on discharging the rest in Egypt, where they could serve "their country honourably not having to kill fellow Greeks."[34]

On the tenth, Donovan issued a directive extending OSS-Athens until further notice and freezing the Young Plan staff at thirty-three, to which X-2 and "Elba" personnel added another eleven men. Donovan specified that they should now concentrate on political intelligence and agreed to attach future OSS personnel to MacVeagh's office. Finally, he reassured Else to remain where he was, doing exactly what he was.[35]

Else tried to focus on intelligence and penned a long and candid letter to Cairo, describing the "lamentable" British military effort in Athens and excoriating the "inflexible" British for the

> bumbling way in which they have handled the whole affair. Having come into Greece without sufficient forces even to hold a square mile of Athens securely, they continue to act as if they were masters of the situation. They have not yet even given up the contention that they are here only to support the "constitutional" government, not having heard that George II abrogated the constitution in 1936, while at the same time they have on two crucial occasions vetoed agreements reached by the government itself which might have forestalled actual hostilities. The first time was when the government

agreed that *all* Greek armed forces, including the Mountain Brigade, would be dissolved. Papandreou himself agreed to this, but Scobie forbade it. The second time was when Churchill forbade Papandreou to resign. Negotiations were already well along for Sofoulis to take over—God knows, a poor enough solution, but a Greek solution, and the Communists would have stayed in the government. . . . The net effect of their political efforts is that they have a "government" which represents nothing, not even all of the B. G., and a prime minister who has lost any possibility of doing anything. The only possible way one could begin a constructive political discussion now—except that it's too late—would be to discuss how the left parties can be brought back into the government, and who shall replace Papandreou.[36]

Else blamed British "intransigence" for the tragedy. "In spite of violent proclamations and brave talk," he believed that ELAS did not have its heart in the fight. From the beginning, they had said that they did not want to fight the British, but needed to maintain their hold on the country. Without support from the Russians or Tito, ELAS could not fight more than a "sniping war," engaging in house-to-house fighting against the British, and if they went back to the mountains, they might never regain their hold on the towns.[37]

Yet Else thought that both sides had lost sight of the prostrate state of Greece before the shooting began and placed "their own power above even the elementary relief of misery." It was winter and there was neither fuel nor shoes. Wielding food as a weapon, the British would not allow stores of flour to be distributed to ELAS-held areas in Athens and Thessaly, and EAM, which controlled Piraeus and the dockworkers, ordered strikes so that ships could not be unloaded. Meanwhile, no food had been distributed in Athens since the fighting erupted, and people starved. Hospitals lacked food, and children, mothers, and old men wandered the streets, even in the midst of shooting, searching for morsels.[38]

Else was disgusted that the United States sat back and washed its hands of the matter. The country could give millions of dollars and collect millions of pieces of clothing for the poor Greeks, but would

> not lift a finger to take the necessary steps to get the food and clothing to the people who need them. . . . one kind of action is humanitarian and the other is political, and in our blessed sheltered Utopia we haven't learned that the two are tied up together. . . . Greece will not be fed or clothed until political action is taken by somebody. . . . The crying need is for somebody genuinely impartial to guarantee to each faction that the other will disarm, to bring

the two sides back into the government and stand over them [until they had found a solution to the debacle].[39]

Months earlier, MacVeagh had suggested a regency under Archbishop Damaskinos, but no one had listened. Else wished MacVeagh would act, but knew that he did not have the authority.

On December 11, Field Marshal Harold Alexander telegraphed Churchill that British forces were beleaguered in the heart of Athens with only six days' rations and supplies. He begged for reinforcements and permission to bomb sections of the city. That day, an American journalist published Churchill's leaked telegrams to Scobie and enflamed the U.S. public. Churchill sought FDR's support, but the president replied that he was constrained by "the mounting adverse reaction of public opinion" and advised Churchill to prevail upon the Greek king to accept a regency and agree not to return until he had been signaled to do so by a plebiscite. Harry Hopkins cautioned Churchill that American public opinion toward the British was "deteriorating rapidly." Churchill complained that British "prestige and authority in Greece . . . [were] undermined by the American press."[40]

Every trip outside OSS headquarters represented real danger and required careful consideration, with the result that it became isolated from its field agents and received no mail from Cairo. The most dangerous territory was the mile between 1 Fidiou and the Grande Bretagne, in the so-called Papandreou Free State. Ironically, someone had to run the gauntlet between the two to fetch and return those OSS personnel not billeted at 1 Fidiou, such as Margaret Crosby and Clio Adossides, who were billeted at the School and at the Grande Bretagne, until Else pronounced it too dangerous to risk fetching them. Crosby wrote, "The nights I have stayed down here at the office I have tried to act like a dragon. Actually, I have spent most nights. . . . went home . . . to Loring Hall [the American School residence] in a temporary lull . . . forgot pajamas."[41] Else considered evacuating them, but they wished to stay, so from the eleventh onward, he accommodated them at 1 Fidiou. But Cairo vetoed sending any additional women, including Virginia Grace. Although Else briefly regained his humor and quipped that life in Athens was "variegated but not dull," within three days the situation had deteriorated and he allowed trips only when and where necessary.[42] OSS headquarters was now swollen with men and women "living, working, and eating together" and Greek agents who could not be discharged. Else wrote that he enjoyed "large families, but this one is taxing the building."[43] After one month in liberated Athens, Else was ready to leave.

Along with being isolated from their "customers," OSS lost touch with Rodney Young. They heard from Clio that he was driving UNRRA trucks and negotiating with the guerrillas for the safe passage of food and supplies. When she had volunteered to deliver medical supplies behind the EAM/ELAS lines, Young had driven her as far as he could down Syngrou Avenue in his UNRRA vehicle. She then walked the rest of the way, armed only with her Red Cross uniform. Later the area was sealed and for three days she could not get out.

Young was hard at work. As Laird Archer's special assistant, Young helped set up UNRRA personnel at the Hotel Acropole across from the National Museum. American School archaeologists, including Mary Pease, John and Suzanne Young, and British School archaeologists Edith Eccles and Mercy Money-Coutts, engaged in relief work. Gene Vanderpool, who had recently been released from a German concentration camp, was returning to Greece to join them. Meanwhile, British archaeologist Lt. Col. R. F. Hoddinott, UNRRA's chief of Balkan intelligence who was formerly of SOE, also recruited. Relief workers were arriving from Cairo when the fighting began. They vowed to operate in all of Greece or not at all, but on account of the danger in Athens, on December 12 Archer evacuated all but ten observers to Cairo. Among those who stayed was Rodney Young.

In Egypt, at first the rest visited training, internment, and refugee camps, established a staff room for meetings, and gathered weekly in Archer's room to hear policy developments and news of Greece.[44] Then, as time dragged on, Archer organized a party at the pyramids, camel rides at Memphis and Saqqara, and "King's College," a temporary university at the King's Hotel with language classes, current affairs, and intelligence on Greece to keep them occupied.

Sperling and Daniel enjoyed considerably more freedom of movement in Macedonia. Every night, they cabled political intelligence to Else. The U.S. Embassy rated that on EAM-ELAS as unsurpassed.[45] Meanwhile, Lt. Jay Seeley of R&A submitted weekly digests of political and economic affairs, biographical files on Greek VIPs, and periodic analyses of the current political situation, in addition to gathering and forwarding maps, newspapers, and government reports and publications for R&A in Washington.[46] He had just returned from two weeks in Salonika, where Sperling arranged for him to interview the U.S. officers of the Allied Military Liaison, UNRRA's chief for Macedonia and Thrace, and British military officers. He also spoke with bankers, businessmen, industrialists, and members of the major political parties, and held conferences with EAM leaders, General Bakirdjis, and other ELAS representatives, who gave him copies of German maps. Seeley ascribed the causes for the civil war to Britain's support for Papandreou, its veto of demobilization promises, premature ultimatum, and rigid policy without sufficient troops to back it up. He also blamed the lack of trust between EAM and the Right, each of whom suspected the other of trying to grab power. His only solution was for Papandreou to resign and the Greeks to run their own government, and postpone dissolution of ELAS until the new army was strong.[47]

Meanwhile, the Battle of Athens continued almost without interruption. On December 16, the same day that the Germans surprised the Americans in what later became known as the Battle of the Bulge, ELAS forces attacked the British in the Athenian suburb of Kefissia. At RAF headquarters, they killed some and took others hostage. The British diverted three divisions from Italy to try to control the killing spree that they had unleashed. British and Greek troops "cleared" the southern and eastern approaches to the city, but around Omonia Square and OSS headquarters EAM-ELAS held firm. Hesitant to invest in the archbishop as regent, Churchill cabled Field Marshal Alexander on the seventeenth to let "military operations to clear Athens and Attica run for a while," but Alexander replied that Churchill should find "a political solution."[48]

In spite of grave dangers, occasional traffic between Athens and Cairo continued. After waiting two weeks for a lull in the hostilities, Christian Freer, the new head of the Greek Desk in Cairo, arrived. Petrow brought him to 1 Fidiou and back to "New Elba" with discharged field agents bound for Egypt where they would join the Combined Hellenic Intelligence Service. So far OSS had led a charmed life in Athens, but Freer observed that "American casualties [were] only a matter of course."[49]

To brighten Christmas in Athens, Freer sent one hundred pounds of turkey and trimmings. The staff counted their blessings, an act that proved premature. Several got inspired to solve the civil war. Joseph Rudas, chief of the Message Center, and Lieutenant Nickles, head of Security, went out with Else's permission to invite members of all constituencies to their Christmas Eve party. As they approached a guard post that night, British sentries opened fire and wounded both peacemakers. Nickles was shot in the back and through both legs and was evacuated to Bari for treatment. Rudas, however, died of his wounds on Christmas, another OSS victim of "friendly fire."[50]

The night before, Churchill realized that only something dramatic could save Athens and decided to go there himself. On Christmas morning, he and Foreign Secretary Anthony Eden arrived at Kalamaki Field, less than a mile from "New Elba." Only a person of stature acceptable to both sides was capable of uniting the Greeks, and Churchill had come to propose Archbishop Damaskinos. While British planes strafed the city, Churchill met for three hours with Alexander, Leeper, and Harold MacMillan before climbing into the armored car that would take him to Piraeus and his accommodation on the HMS *Ajax*. That evening, Churchill entertained the Greek archbishop and invited him to chair a conference the next day. On December 26, Churchill entered the armored car with a loaded pistol, his private secretary ready with the driver's machine gun as they sped to the British embassy. At six that evening, Churchill, Eden, and Alexander, MacVeagh and the French and Russian ministers met with Damaskinos and Greek politicians. As soon as the proceedings were under way, the foreign diplomats departed and let the Greeks deliberate. Discussion continued without result until the twenty-eighth, when Churchill and Eden withdrew for London. After they left, Rodney Young and the UNRRA observers were ordered into uniform and put under the Military Liaison. That day, the Greeks unanimously backed a regency under the archbishop. Yet Churchill still had to broker a deal in London with the Greek king. On December 30, King George II agreed to appoint Archbishop Damaskinos regent for one year and wait until after a plebiscite before he returned to Greece.[51]

On January 4, 1945, Archbishop Damaskinos swore in republican prime minister Nicholas Plastiras. A week later, a truce to take effect on January 15 was agreed upon. The cease-fire ended a monthlong reign of terror known as the "Dekemvriana," in which whole neighborhoods that had survived the war were destroyed and as many as 10,000 people killed. Yet Margaret Crosby observed, "Life goes on day after day the same. . . . Today is very quiet in our neighborhood . . . the British have been clearing the area east and north of here. . . . We continue to live very well in the German School. . . . I get up to Loring Hall every five or six days, ostensibly to get clean clothes, but actually more interested in the slight break. If I get some time off Sunday, I can get some fresh air and exercise walking the circle of the Gennadius Library. There is an excellent roof here, but not allowed to use it for fear of stray bullets, mortars, etc."[52]

Young remained at 9 Ploutarchou with Bert Hill, Ralph Kent (ONI), and a naval attaché, waiting for his UNRRA colleagues to return. Elli Adossides worked for him in Displaced Persons, locating deported Greeks in Germany. Her son Alekko and Bessie's husband, George Trypanis, also worked for UNRRA, while Mrs. Hadjilazarou distributed clothes and Bessie Adossides worked for the Greek Red Cross. Meanwhile, Young worked on the release of British hostages. He recounted an early December visit from Agora archaeologist Homer Thompson. Thompson had joined the Canadian navy, which lent him to the British Royal Navy for Mediterranean Naval Intelligence in Bari. While going to visit a Greek archaeologist at one of the foreign schools, he passed through ELAS territory and was taken hostage. Quickly released during the lull before he returned to work, Thompson was able to visit the Agora, where, Young observed, "a lot of mortar shells landed in the dig . . . [and people] were still gathering greens." The open space was "a sort of no-man's land under continuous fire." A communist sharpshooter controlled the railroad tracks. ELAS was around the bullet-ridden temple of Hephaistos, where before liberation the Chi-ites had built a makeshift wall between the columns. Meanwhile, the British were on the opposite side, behind the ruins of the Stoa of Attalos.[53]

Young wrote Thompson the latest archaeological news. Hill and Gladys Weinberg, embassy librarian, had been up to the Acropolis during the cease-fire and reported that the Parthenon was chipped and discolored black from tracer bullets, with loose blocks dragged here or there to make fortifications. Mortar shells had landed on the roof of the National Museum, and the front façade looked "as though pepper had been scattered over it—lots of chips from the columns, discolored by bullets." Young had continually requested both sides to respect it and was glad the damage was not worse. He had seen the Vanderpools, who considered moving into town, but with the roads still mined and planes flying low overhead and stray bullets and trigger-happy people all about, they decided it was safer to stay put.[54]

Cox wrote that she had asked to be placed on leave without pay. On her way to New Haven, she stopped to see Meritt, Shear, Goldman, and Frantz.

Princeton's opinion on what you and the Trojans are doing is pretty much the same as yours. The person with the really hush-hush and thrilling job is PT [Peter Topping] who plans commando raids. Asked what our friend from Minneapolis [Blegen] was doing, I said I couldn't say "you see people around, but I didn't ask." Someone said OSS, but Shear said that was impossible, if there was any connection there he would know.

The AIA had canceled its 1944 annual meeting, but its council convened at the Metropolitan Museum of Art, where the New York Society had hosted a symposium, "Europe's Monuments as Affected by the War." William Dinsmoor, who was leading the Monuments Commission for the protection and salvage of works of art in European war areas, gave the keynote speech and exhorted AIA members to drive "the barbarian enemy from the sites and monuments which his presence has so long desecrated."[55]

In Athens, silence shrouded Rudas's death. No one mentioned it in private correspondence, and notice appeared only in Else's official weekly report. Uneasy about the "undefined status of OSS," MacVeagh wanted OSS to regularize intelligence duties in Greece by having its top man in Greece on his own staff. He still favored Blegen for this position, but Blegen was not yet free. So Else and Edson continued as his temporary OSS liaisons. But Glavin demanded immediate clarification from Donovan, while General Sadler and MacVeagh recommended that Else be removed as unfit for command of OSS Athens for violating Sadler's instructions and held him responsible for Rudas's death. Sadler wanted a more senior and experienced officer to take over, but none was available.[56]

Daniel came in from the field to support Else who admitted in the interim that the "political game . . . doesn't even tempt my palate anymore." Epigrapher Charles Edson, devoted to surveying Macedonian inscriptions before the war, was conducting reconnaissance in Salonika and cabled intelligence as "Eagle." He returned to Athens "lyrical" over the discovery of an intact Hellenistic tomb and found it was his turn to lead the Athens base.[57] Edson took control on January 9. Four days later, Else returned to Cairo to consult with Aldrich on reorganizing Athens. Major Dudley Bennett (Rees's Izmir successor and chief of Athens MI-6) had told Edson that the position of OSS in Greece was "tenuous." The makeshift solution could not continue. OSS in Greece had shrunk to only fifteen agents, not including X-2 and the staff of "New Elba."[58]

With General Sadler's permission, Lt. Robert Moyers, the OSS Special Operations doctor, continued his work to gather medical intelligence in ELAS territory. There he located 1,500 British hostages, including 288 seriously wounded who had been captured in the December raid of the RAF headquarters in Kefissia. They were at a makeshift camp and badly in need of medicines, food, clothing, and blankets. According to Young, most suffered "from neglect rather than active ill-treatment." Moyers secured ELAS permission to parachute supplies into the camp. On January 20, he brought two ELAS representatives to Athens to confer with the British concerning a prisoner exchange. ELAS allowed him to arrange the delivery of prisoners to an exchange point at Volos. After General Scobie designated Moyers as his representative and delegated all authority north of the truce line to him and his assistant, Moyers organized the transfer with the approval of MacVeagh and Sadler. On January 24, he evacuated 1,015 British prisoners to Volos and released them into British custody.[59]

Toward the end of January, Glavin decided that direction and responsibility for the Greek Desk should be transferred from Cairo to Caserta, where it could be scrutinized by AFHQ. Gerald Else moved to Caserta to lead it, and Margaret Crosby followed him there to process the Greek reports.[60] Else wrote that, so far, the U.S. had been an

> inconspicuous observer . . . , devoting at least as much time to relief and rehabilitation programs as to politics. . . . [They had succeeded partly] because our cousins have not taken us seriously. . . . One of the strongest cards in our deck is the general unspoken conviction among Greeks and British in Greece that Americans are too naïve, too easy-going, or too disinterested to engage in real espionage. We want at all costs to foster this only too well-founded impression.[61]

Else prepared a blueprint for a permanent espionage network in Greece and recommended that no effort be spared to set it up. He did not recommend using Greek-Americans or the American agents still in Greece, who were "tired and stale," having operated continuously for almost two years in the Mediterranean. Nor did he entertain hope for finding Greeks who would be willing to spy on their fellow citizens for a foreign country. Success in that would depend on U.S. foreign policy. Instead, Else suggested seeking out academics with "flexibility of mind" who already had cover established in Greece. "Any young archaeologist would be likely to welcome a year or two or three at the American School in Athens, if he were assured of the means." Yet he confessed that doing so would put the candidate in an ethically compromised situation since "many deans and professors would be scandalized at the notion of mixing intelligence work with higher study." For this reason, he suggested the young American secondary school teachers who taught at Anatolia College and Athens College.

Recruits should be indoctrinated in recent European, especially Balkan . . .
and Greek history, above all in the period of the Metaxas dictatorship and
the German occupation; in the present international situation—the
Mediterranean, Russia, Turkey, the Balkan question, Anglo-Greek relationships; . . . in our own (?) Balkan and Near Eastern policy . . . . [and European]
economic interests in the Eastern Mediterranean. . . . The problems of a
small country like Greece are in large part international problems, and . . .
the internal disturbances are often the result of external influence.

Else recommended no fewer than four to six months of training, careful
briefing as to what was wanted and for whom, and a six-month settling-in
period before anything was expected. Once normal conditions prevailed, he
foresaw that the United States would require coverage only from Athens
and Macedonia.[62]

Else cautioned against locating OSS "too far under the wing of the Embassy" since MacVeagh sought to control information coming out of his
domain, and his communications "might not square with others' ideas of
full and free reporting." He viewed MacVeagh as an "American representative in a British protectorate. His personal views did not necessarily coin-
cide with the official British position," and several times he criticized
"British tactics and attitudes." But "he could do or say nothing that would
rock the boat." Nor would he brook any suggestion that the "cousins were
employing less than completely straightforward tactics" or anything that
"smacked of spying on the British." MacVeagh's sympathies were with the
British and the government rather than with EAM and the Communists.
Else mused that MacVeagh and his intelligence officer might even end up "a
mutual embarrassment."[63]

For a week in early February, Churchill, Roosevelt, and Stalin conferred
in Yalta. On the way home, Churchill stopped in Athens, where, at nearby
Varkiza, General Scobie, the Greek foreign minister, and the secretary of the
Communist Party (on behalf of EAM/ELAS) signed an agreement on February 12, calling for the restoration of civil liberties, lifting of martial law, a
partial amnesty, demobilization of armed bands, trials for collaborators,
creation of a nonpolitical national army, and a plebiscite to be held within
the year at which the Allies would send overseers to verify the validity of the
elections.[64] Again the United States did not participate.

By then, it was agreed that the Greek Desk's move to Caserta was ill-
advised. Donovan cabled that it should remain under Cairo.[66] Processing
would return to Athens since Caserta was ignorant of Greek matters and

had garbled the Greek reports. After it had cleared its last personnel, inventoried and processed its files, shipped important documents back to Washington and destroyed the rest, the Greek Desk in Cairo would be abolished and the Athens office would stand on its own.

Crosby and Edson were at the end of their tether. Crosby, whose health had been wrecked by stress in December, asked to be sent home, but waited weeks to be discharged. Edson begged Cairo to replace him. Athens needed someone without "preconceptions and prejudices" who could see things from a different point of view and apprehend new tendencies and developments, but no one was available, so Christian Freer, who had supervised the Desk from Cairo, became Edson's executive officer. To support Edson, Crosby agreed to return to Athens for a maximum of two months, but insisted they find a replacement.[66]

Sperling, Daniel, Georgiades, and Couvaras remained as operatives, the former three "undercover on an economic survey" in the border zone of Macedonia and Thrace (the most disputed and important areas) and the latter in Athens. They related a growing strain on all sides and an increasingly marked difference between Right and Left, which was openly espousing communism. Daniel reported that British policy hoped to starve EAM into submission, but it was resisting with the result that most of the population blamed EAM for their hunger and the balance of power had swung against the Left. Because EAM's chief support came from Slavo-Macedonians and refugees, Daniel predicted that ELAS would escape over the border when the going got tough and take hostages with them.[67]

In early March, Young and Gladys Weinberg made a Sunday pilgrimage to Mt. Hymettus. On the climb, they passed the Kaiseriani monastery, which had been struck by British shells. From a distance, the mountain resembled "a newly-shaven German pate," and Young was discouraged to find that it had been "shaved as bare as a billiard ball, all the shrubbery stuff cut down and the roots dug out for fuel." Young reported to Blegen that their archaeological site had survived "somewhat bedraggled and washed-in." The same was true for the Agora, which seemed untouched, with a "bumper crop of nettles," and in all its 150 wells, Young added drily, "not one murdered body was found in January."[68]

On March 25, the whole city turned out to celebrate Greek Independence Day, the first since liberation. Some OSS staffers covered the parade while others gauged popular opinion. Edson remained at 1 Fidiou, where he alone handled administration and operations, while Clio Adossides and

Dimitri Petrou processed agents' claims in Cairo.[69] Edson could only attend to the most urgent matters. He needed someone with judgment, local knowledge, and formal training to replace Margaret Crosby on Reports and hoped to persuade Alison Frantz, Sherman Wallace, or Gladys Weinberg to take the job.

After helping with yet another difficult transition, Crosby, who had labored for two straight years as Reports officer and acting chief and was valued as a "tower of strength as well as a splendid companion and tireless fellow worker," was leaving. To bid good-bye, she and Clio climbed Mt. Hymettus with Couvaras, Freer, and Pauline Manos, Young's former secretary. The next night, Crosby's last, they climbed the Acropolis by moonlight. Then Crosby departed for the United States and an extended leave.[70]

The world situation was changing radically. Roosevelt died on April 12 and Vice President Harry Truman took over the presidency. Later that month, Mussolini was executed and Hitler committed suicide. Stalin, however, was thriving.

FOURTEEN

~~~~~

"Playing a Dangerous Game"

WHILE THE WORLD FOCUSED on the cease-fire on the western front, Rodney Young fought for his life in Greece. On May 5, 1945, the vessel carrying him to Syra to relieve the UNRRA's Cyclades regional director capsized and most passengers were lost at sea, including a member of the Swedish Red Cross. After five hours in the water Young was saved, but the article recording it barely made the *New York Times*. During his three days of recuperation, Germany surrendered and the Allies declared victory in Europe. Buoyed by the good news, Young turned his attention to negotiating with the guerrillas. Young's American School colleague, Oscar Broneer, now executive vice president of Greek War Relief, made his first trip to Greece in six years to get an idea of conditions and was overwhelmed with the magnitude of the destruction.[1] Although the war in Europe was over, in Greece a different sort of war was emerging.

Amid the tumult, Washington's neglect of Greece handicapped future possibilities for SI. Aldrich's parsimonious policy that forbade helping former Greek personnel and their dependents left destitute at the time of liberation and the Dekemvriana had caused widespread dissatisfaction and earned OSS the reputation of "having let people down." Edson worried that some agents felt so badly treated that they "would injure American intelligence if they could" and constituted a "security danger to future clandestine operations by OSS in Greece."[2]

Daniel DeBardeleben, OSS chief of Southeast Europe SI, replied that "the importance of Greece so far as the war is concerned has decreased greatly." Sherman Wallace explained that few in Washington wanted any SI from Greece. Instead the State Department, Edson's chief "customer," was mainly interested in Russian intelligence and Communists.[3]

As the "Cold War" evolved, Greece became important once more. By late May, even the U.S. Military Intelligence was "showing interest," and Donovan prolonged OSS operations in Athens indefinitely. Soon Greece was no longer a backwater, and the State Department and SI/Washington craved intelligence from the critically situated country. By the summer of 1945, the position of Greece was without recent parallel; the country's northern border had become the frontier between the British and Russian spheres of influence in the Balkans. This magnified the importance of the small nation beyond that suggested by its population, its natural resources, or its geopolitical position controlling the Aegean and the approach to the Turkish Straits. Edson recognized that Greece, "lying squarely at a point where British and Russian interests converge," would henceforth be "a political pressure area." As Else had predicted, because the Greek Left was pro-Russian and the Greek Right was pro-British, even internal Greek politics had important international implications, and the success or failure of political entities in Greece could alter the balance of power in the southern Balkans and the Middle East. This circumstance made internal Greek politics much more important than they appeared, and the United States would need to be "continuously and accurately informed" about them by sources under U.S. control and direction. Because it would be difficult to base American SI operations inside countries within the Russian sphere (including Hungary, Rumania, Yugoslavia, and Bulgaria), Greece became crucial for SI penetration of Bulgaria and southern Yugoslavia. Moreover, it was the only place in southeast Europe (aside from European Turkey) where American and British services could operate with any degree of effectiveness without being completely clandestine.[4]

Shepardson informed Aldrich that keeping an intelligence service in Greece, "a natural meeting point for conflicting ideologies," had become a matter of "major importance" to Washington at least "until the end of the Japanese war and very possibly for a considerable period after that." Shepardson was monitoring the flight underground of Axis capital, as well as military activity on Greece's Bulgarian, Yugoslavian, and Albanian borders. The State Department was interested in all political matters that might have a bearing upon the development of British or Russian policy. Finally, the United States "permanently and definitely committed to obtaining intelligence from Greece" and "operations of the unit in Greece . . . of vital concern to the home base." For this reason, Shepardson sent his own deputy, DeBardeleben, to head Cairo's SI.[5]

Ironically, aside from Cox (and occasionally Caskey and Young), only with the liberation of Greece did most archaeologists produce their own intelligence.[6] When they did, it was highly valued and widely circulated. In this new phase, the classical archaeologist-operatives contributed the bulk of SI. When Washington asked them to focus on political intelligence, Sperling and Daniel, who had longed for something substantial, were primed. Sperling wrote, "I thrive on opportunities and responsibilities and am as ready now as in the beginning to work without halt."[7]

Months earlier, the Americans had begun keeping certain intelligence from their allies. OSS Cairo had warned its staff to stamp "CONTROL" on SI reports not meant for "non-American" eyes.[8] Thus, the archaeologists circulated only the less sensitive items to colleagues in foreign services. However, to their American customers they reported that the Greek government had not upheld the Varkiza agreement; that few collaborators had been brought to justice; and most who were tried had been acquitted. By contrast, guerrillas who had fought to regain their country's liberty were persecuted and executed. As OSS liaison for the U.S. consul general in Salonika, Sperling informed MacVeagh that the persecution of EAM-ELAS by the National Guard or unofficial groups tolerated by them had caused an estimated 2,000 members of ELAS to seek refuge in Albania. Hundreds had fled Evros for Bulgaria, where they were interned in a concentration camp. Throughout Greece, right-wing vigilante gangs, known as the "White Terror," exacted retribution against EAM/ELAS. British agents were allowing the royalist and reactionary groups in northern Greece to propagandize with force of arms for the return of the king and were committing acts of terrorism against EAM. But the Greek government was not alone in ignoring the terms of the treaty. Daniel told of ELAS sending motor vehicles to Monastir in Yugoslavia (just ten miles north of the Greek border) rather than surrendering them to the British and hiding over half of its 100,000 guns "in mountain storage places." To satisfy the treaty, they turned over only the bare minimum to the British. Meanwhile, Sperling reported that ELAS had smuggled arms across the Bulgarian border to Sofia by private car and that the British had uncovered 7,000 weapons ELAS had hidden in a cache only twenty-five miles northeast of Salonika.[9] In Western Macedonia such persecution sparked a revival of ELAS.

Sperling scouted the northern frontiers from Florina to the Turkish border, while Daniel covered the Prespa region where Greece, Yugoslavia, and

Albania met and established clandestine intelligence chains and networks into Albania and Yugoslavia and throughout Macedonia. Sperling reported to MacVeagh, "Salonica rumors that Great Britain and Russia would soon go to war with each other." Since Red Army units were stationed in Bulgaria, Sperling and Daniel focused on Russian infiltration into the border regions. Sperling discovered that Russians had been imbedded with ELAS for eighteen months in Macedonia, but had since retreated first to Skopje (seventy-five miles north of the Greek border in Yugoslavia) and then to Sofia, where they maintained contact with ELAS. Meanwhile, Daniel found that a cell of Russians had toured Epirus with ELAS in September 1944 and "promised arms and ammo" that did not materialize. Evidently, only Tito had sent arms. All in all, their observations suggested that Stalin was observing the "spheres of influence" agreement with Churchill, an arrangement still unknown.[10]

Daniel and Sperling also kept an eye on Macedonian separatists who exploited the rather porous postwar borders. Daniel monitored those outside Greece, who agitated for an autonomous Macedonian state. Meanwhile, Sperling chronicled brigades that the Bulgarians had readied in Sofia and massed in Yugoslavia at Skopje. They planned to use them against Greeks in Greece in order "to unite Serbs, Bulgars, and Greeks perhaps to join Yugoslav-Bulgarian or Balkan communistic federation." Sperling advised MacVeagh that the danger came more from Bulgaria than Yugoslavia. He had discovered that the organization worked mainly in the Bulgarian language and was closely allied if not synonymous with the Okhrana (an armed Bulgarian secret police organization active in Yugoslavia; Sperling and Daniel proved that it also operated in western Greek Macedonia). In the Greek frontier region, it claimed that union with Bulgaria had "an even greater urgency than plans to advance communism." At the same time, Daniel sent subagents to Monastir and frequently crossed into Yugoslavia, gathering so much intelligence that he regarded himself as OSS's Yugoslav Desk. MacVeagh commended his reports as "highly useful." His highly valued assessments of Tito and Yugoslavia as well as other regional information would figure prominently in the Cold War years.[11]

Sperling and Daniel did not shrink from the dangers they confronted; rather, they thrived on them. When polled about their intentions for future work, both replied that if they could work where they were, do exactly what they were doing, and not be reassigned elsewhere, they would continue indefinitely. Wallace encouraged them, reporting that "State is tired of pink tinge of Hadas accounts of 'White Terror.' . . . They want the cold dope from you gentlemen in the field, something Pterodactylian or something from the Bald Eagle [Edson] himself." Washington wanted SI, not R&A's reportage.[12] They recognized that the archaeologists' small-scale "overt" missions had contributed "really useful and valuable intelligence to the Balkan picture as a whole," and OSS London headquarters praised Athens for the "most complete coverage of any mission." But it only hinted at what was possible.[13]

Increasingly, the exclusively overt operations ran into difficulties and yielded diminishing returns. Daniel, Sperling, and Georgiades were far too well known to handle true undercover work. Georgiades was also a marked man. He had operated for thirty months, crossed the Turkish border fourteen times into Greece and twice into Bulgaria, bringing tons of medical supplies to the Greek guerrillas and evading German and Bulgarian guards. He had exposed Bulgarian spies in Turkey and Evros and produced a continuous flow of intelligence. Georgiades had alienated Greeks at the Edirne where his presence after the occupation was unwelcome to those Greeks in power as well as the British. High Greek officers, the bishop, and nationalist leaders decided to arrest Georgiades on his next trip to Evros for apparently trumped up hearsay about his being a Communist. Edson ordered him not to return there, but remain in Salonika and Central Macedonia.[14] Intimidated by Greeks and British allies, Georgiades decided in July to return to the United States.

The United States had to monitor the situation carefully and get its permanent network in place. Instead of locating agents at the embassy, where they would be "suspected of intelligence activities," Edson preferred Athens College or the American School of Classical Studies as cover for persons "carefully selected, . . . thoroughly trained and briefed," but advised that they "should be infiltrated into their jobs quite without the knowledge of the institution." For northern cover, he suggested positions with the American Farm School, Anatolia College, American tobacco companies, the Near East Foundation, or UNRRA. Meanwhile, Sperling and Daniel set up small cells of informants to expand their geographical coverage.[15]

Edson was exhausted and worried that he would "crack up." After six months as Athens chief, he could not go on. He wanted to get out of the country as soon as he could and be assigned "somewhere else." After recommending Karamessines (X-2) or Sperling as his replacement and warning that U.S. field missions were "likely to encounter incredible difficulties and possibly actual danger," Edson left to direct Greek R&A in Washington.[16]

When Edson departed, Christian Freer took over as chief of OSS Athens. Remaining at the German Archaeological Institute became awkward, and so he vacated the DAI for a more secure, nondescript flat on Rigillis Street, just a five-minute walk down the hill from the American School.[17] Sperling became chief of SI and reshuffled the teams working the northern frontiers from Western Macedonia to the Turkish border. Daniel moved between the Rupel Pass and his base at Florina.[18] He discovered unsettling evidence of inordinate interest in his activities by government security forces and Macedonian separatists. The East Macedonian National Guard arrested one of Daniel's civilian informants. Bulgarian Okhrana agents assassinated another, and one Okhrana agent, apprehended by the Guard, revealed that a Macedonian autonomist terrorist band had targeted Daniel for assassination. Daniel admitted that he had been "playing a dangerous game" and took precautions.[19] But he continued to submit frequent reports on the secret plans, attitudes, relations, and activities of Yugoslav, Albanian, and extremist Greek political parties and organizations in northwest Greece.

Less than a month later, the United States dropped two atomic bombs on Japan. With the joyful announcement of Japan's surrender and the end of the war in the Pacific, nostalgia swept through OSS and many wanted to return home. Young was ready to resume his "natural" work and notified UNRRA that he would be leaving on November 1. Sperling requested leave to see his wife on personal matters. Not so Daniel, who developed new information sources on peripheral areas of Albania and Yugoslavia that MacVeagh commended as "highly useful."[20]

But the struggle for control of Greece persisted. MacVeagh wanted OSS to continue its surveillance of the northern frontier, the country districts, and the extreme Left and Right. To help guide him in the uncertain political terrain, MacVeagh requested comprehensive and deep studies of political topics and trends.

Carl Blegen remained the ideal choice. Between his acceptance and his arrival as cultural attaché at the U.S. embassy in Athens, the Greek government invited the United States, Britain, and France to send observers to monitor and verify the validity of the elections and plebiscite to determine the fate of the king, according to terms of the Varkiza agreement. On September 19, they accepted. Carl Blegen would pave the way for the Allied observers. To prepare, Blegen requested that OSS Athens compile biographical sketches of the top 200 political figures in Greece for the State Department and Military Intelligence, a project that consumed X-2 and the Athens office until the end of the year. Then in October, Blegen returned to 9 Ploutarchou.

That month, President Truman terminated OSS. However, his executive order did not spell an end to American espionage overseas. To prevent a hiatus in intelligence gathering, the "shadow-land" SI was reconstituted as the Strategic Services Unit (SSU) of the War Department under General Magruder. R&A and X-2 were temporarily preserved under the umbrella of the State Department, with the former known as the Interim Research and Analysis Service (IRIS). Classicist Moses Hadas, who had been in charge of Greek R&A in Cairo, came to Athens, cloaked as SI because MacVeagh wanted no R&A men in Greece. Thomas Karamessines, chief of X-2 in Greece, which had been headquartered since February at "New Elba," became MacVeagh's other man.

Of the archaeologists, only Sperling and Daniel remained at their posts in Greece. They produced reports consistently rated as "definitely valuable" and "timely" by Military Intelligence and the State Department. But pressure was building; Sperling complained of being followed, and Daniel heard for the fourth time that persons were "looking for an opportunity to liquidate him." The Athens chief punned that Daniel was a "sitting duck" and wanted him to pull out of Florina to canvass other areas. But Daniel continued to report on Yugoslavia and Sperling on Bulgaria.

While doing so, the archaeologists surveyed at the postwar landscape and jockeyed for excavation opportunities. Anxious to return to archaeology, but reluctant to leave government service, Sperling approached De-Bardeleben about undertaking future excavations for the University of Cincinnati in the Troad and for Yale in the Peloponnese and inquired whether he "could be of any use . . . during either project?" DeBardeleben responded that his "service would be considered most valuable and eagerly accepted." So Sperling remained on active duty, volunteering to "use such fieldwork as a kind of cover." DeBardeleben replied, "We can certainly arrange for you to undertake the archaeological fieldwork you desire. . . . It should prove advantageous to the organization as well as to you." Satisfied, Sperling went home for Christmas.[21]

In January 1946, the SSU was renamed the Central Intelligence Group, still controlled by the War Department. Sperling returned from the States a lieutenant colonel, moved into 9 Ploutarchou with Blegen and Hill, and took over the Athens station, now entitled the US Economic Research Unit.

He and Karamessines worked on Blegen's biographies with several agents, including Clio Adossides, listed as administrative assistant and operative. Meanwhile, Young, awarded a Bronze Star for his OSS service, was "fishing around" for a job at Penn or Princeton.[22]

On January 8, Blegen's FNB assistant, Alison Frantz, boarded a flight bound for Paris, Rome, and Athens. Six out of the ten passengers were members of the American team of the Allied Mission for Observing the Greek Elections (AMFOGE).[23] Frantz joined her friends at 9 Ploutarchou, where she and Blegen interviewed interpreters and developed a crash course on Greek history, geography, and politics for the indoctrination of hundreds of Americans, military and civilian, who would serve on the Allied mission. A month later, they convened in Naples, where she and Blegen delivered the lectures and later underwent training in first aid, map-reading, conditioning, and instruction on driving and repairing jeeps. While they were there, they managed to visit the archaeological site of Paestum in the height of orange blossom season and dine before an open fire at the American Academy in Rome in a banquet hall "banned to the ladies" when Frantz had studied there twenty-one years earlier. Later that month, they returned to Athens and took up work in the former Italian embassy. Spring was in the air. Poppies dotted Mt. Lycabettus and anemones blanketed the countryside as 240 three-man teams headed to Athens, Salonika, Patras, Tripolis, and Iraklion, where they would monitor registration, conduct surveys, investigate complaints of intimidation, observe the political process, and count the ballots for elections to be held on March 31.

While electrical strikes plagued Athens, everyone wondered if the elections would actually take place. When they did, the Left abstained, and so the Right won. Instead of bringing peace, the elections only begat more conflict as the royalist government intensified its violent repression of the Left and the Left responded in kind. While Europe licked its war wounds, Greece raked open old sores and created new ones.

Daniel completed his "masterpiece" of Macedonian reconnaissance. Eager to escape the death threats, he abandoned the north to cover the Dodecanese, an equally sensitive area, because of its desire for union with Greece. After submitting several reports on the Dodecanese, Daniel left by Liberty ship in June.

MacVeagh wanted the American School to resume the Agora excavations as a symbol of American support for Greece. Money talked, and despite the Greek government's two-year ban on excavations because of unsettled conditions, the Agora secured a special permit for the summer of 1946. On May 18, Young and Crosby returned to dig at the Agora, where they were met by teammates Vanderpool, Parsons, and Homer Thompson, appointed the acting field director after the death of Shear in the summer of 1945. Young stayed with Blegen and Hill, where he heard Grace's archaeological work publicized on the Voice of America, the mouthpiece of the former OWI. After analyzing and editing the observers' reports and preparing the final AMFOGE publication, Shirley Weber had returned to the Gennadius Libary and Blegen to the University of Cincinnati.[24]

Sperling reported that in Thrace the situation was "deteriorating considerably" with regard to internal security and exacerbated by progressively harsher measures against the Left by the government. "One hears . . . that the Greeks are riding towards another civil war."[25] He prepared to dissolve the Athens operation. But U.S. Military Intelligence wanted him to stay on, rating his reports on the Greek elections and other political developments "definitely valuable" and commending their impartiality; they needed still more information on Macedonia, which they viewed as "one of the foremost political hotbeds in Europe."[26] In order to be in New Haven by mid-September to resume his teaching post at Yale, he abandoned his post, but before leaving Greece, he married Clio Adossides.[27]

Epilogue

DURING WORLD WAR II, occupied Greece fell under the umbrella of the Middle East theater of operations, which the British controlled. Thus, Britain's imperialist vision dominated activities in this sphere, and American foreign policy deferred to Britain's. However, during the postliberation period, the American foreign policy makers slowly shed the shackles that bound them to England. They were able to do so, in part, because of independent political intelligence provided by Rodney Young and the archaeologists of the OSS Greek Desk.

What inspired Rodney Young to set aside his archaeological research and participate in the war was the desire to relieve suffering. As a result of his years and shared experience of suffering with the Greek people during the occupation, Young had, from the first draft of the "Greek Project" onward, combined relief with intelligence gathering. It formed an important part of his vision for the Greek Desk and his postliberation intelligence blueprint, the "Young Plan." Eventually, it caused him to abandon OSS to concentrate on the relief and reconstruction of Greece with United Nations Relief and Rescue Administration (UNRRA).

To be sure, Young's primary motive was military—to rid Greece of the Germans. Yet Young was not omniscient. He expected direct U.S. military involvement in an invasion of Greece that never occurred. Because of the passivity of the United States in the Mediterranean arena until the successful conclusion of Operation Torch in 1943, Young's logic and that of his original superior, Col. Ulius Amoss, was colored by that of their dominant ally, Britain, and the Greek government-in-exile.

The chief problem—the lack of a clear U.S. foreign policy for Greece and the Balkans—affected the strategy of the U.S. military and, eventually, OSS. Despite Greece's importance to Donovan and predominance in the early days of COI, after January 1943 and the Joint Chiefs of Staff's subsequent refusal to deploy U.S. troops in the Aegean, Greece plummeted on the list of priorities in the American war effort. Because the United States did not have imperialistic aspirations in the eastern Mediterranean, as did Britain, it had never been vitally interested in Greece.[1] In fact, Washington had no ulterior motives for a deeper commitment to Greece other than exploiting certain commercial opportunities. Having only recently emerged from isolation, the United States, in spite of an active Greek-American population, did not have Greece on its radar screen and would not commit troops there. "The area to the east of the Adriatic was regarded by American strategists with something akin to the superstitious dread with which medieval mariners once contemplated the monster-infested reaches of Western Ocean."[2]

In many ways, America's dilemma was rooted in the mutually exclusive aims of the Atlantic Charter, wherein the signatories, the United States and Britain, eschewed territorial ambition in occupied countries and promised to return prewar rulers to their rightful positions while respecting the right of the occupied peoples to self-determination. The United States was interested in supporting democracy over monarchy, and Churchill's support of the Greek king over the wishes of his people was a thorn in Roosevelt's side. Because of America's antiroyalist tradition, Greeks looked to the United States for leadership, but Roosevelt generally deferred to Churchill and turned a deaf ear to Greece. This conundrum partly stemmed from the lack of an effective ambassador for the occupied country and begat apathy and ignorance. As a result, Roosevelt did not take Greece seriously. Despite his investment of MacVeagh as minister to the Greek government-in-exile in September 1943, the president subsequently declared Greece "a minor objective" in the greater context of global war and compared Yugoslavia and Greece to fighting dogs. Moreover, his paternalistic treatment of King George II betrayed his disregard of the gravity of the political crisis in December 1943.[3]

In spite of a lack of leadership from Washington and its diplomatic representative in Cairo, Young did not shy from grappling with the internal political dilemmas that beset the country. Indeed, his first major intelligence assignment was to analyze the political movements in occupied Greece. In August 1943, Young set aside his other work to apprise Washington of the crisis with the British Foreign Office, the Greek king and his cabinet, and the guerrilla delegation in Cairo. He adhered scrupulously to the principles of the Atlantic Charter yet realized from the beginning that the "king business" was the root of all troubles.

Initially, Young and the other archaeologists approached intelligence-gathering as disinterested researchers, largely without political bias. However, over time their letters make clear where each stood politically. Despite their individual politics, their firsthand experience of British arrogance, bias, and bullying and the heroism of the Greek guerrillas conditioned them. Thus, most came to sympathize with EAM/ELAS as a people's movement formed to resist the German and Italian occupation, which Churchill's intransigence polarized and later demonized in the British-controlled press.

FDR's and Washington's dismissive attitude toward Greece haunted the Greek Desk, and trickledown inertia took its toll. As a mouthpiece for Washington, Young warned the archaeologists and field agents to uphold the tenets of the Atlantic Charter and avoid politics. In the words of Dorothy Cox, the British

> had a definite policy with which we were in rather nebulous agreement, but [we] had no clearly defined policy of our own. [This became an acute problem during interrogations.] It was never possible to give any definite answer as to the opinion of the United States and what America was doing about the Atlantic Charter, a question which arose weekly. At all times it was necessary to defend to some extent the rightist attitude of Great Britain as that of an ally with whom we were cooperating. We could only say that our immediate objective was to win the war and that the United States had no desire to interfere with the internal politics of any nation. While making my usual excuse to one astute politician, saying Greek politics was after all a purely Greek affair, he interrupted to say, "Oh no, it is a British affair."[4]

In his postliberation memorandum to the Joint Chiefs of Staff, Donovan justified the creation of the Greek Desk to provide "exclusively American information sources and to cover areas that, for political reasons, were inaccessible to the British." He credited it with infiltrating thirty intelligence teams that covered the main railway lines, harbors, and ports and reported on German shipping, troop movements, and military installations.

> Especially valuable were units in Evros, East Thessaly and Evvia, areas in which British intelligence coverage was inadequate. Intelligence from simi-

lar teams, placed en route between Athens and Salonika, to RAF squadrons based in Egypt led to the almost total destruction of German shipping in the Aegean.[5]

It is remarkable that Donovan focused solely on the wartime military benefits of the Greek Desk's information. For by the time of his memorandum, the political ramifications of American intelligence from Greece were far more far-reaching than its military intelligence. Although the blueprint of the East European Section of OSS had raised the specter of a Soviet-dominated Balkans as early as spring 1942, the lethargic United States remained in denial, rejected involvement, and invested its capital elsewhere. Young argued for the independent American analysis of secret intelligence from Greece to provide an information stream free from British bias. In this he was successful, despite continual attempts by the British to sabotage American occupation-era secret intelligence production and to frame what Washington saw of the Greek dilemma. For OSS autonomy in Greece, specifically in the realm of political intelligence, threatened the British Foreign Office.

Young had warned against the United States allowing imperialist Britain to do all the work and reap the political consequences. Once he reached Cairo, Young's interest in relief-driven intelligence did not rule out his ability to produce keen analyses of the complex political issues confronting Greece, but his rare but insightful reports on the guerrilla delegation and the British Foreign Office went unheeded. Caskey, Cox, and other SI agents also teased out the nuances of political intelligence, but Washington ignored their warnings of British mishandling of the guerrillas and the political polarization that ensued. The result was a postliberation bloodbath.

For John Caskey and Dorothy Cox, relief was equally important, standing as they did at the Aegean terminus for most Greek refugees and having regular contact with Greek sailors who braved death to transport their agents. Relieving suffering took on greater importance for them than for others who were more insulated. It was exactly this compassionate approach that caused the rift between Caskey and the head of OSS Cairo that led to Caskey's resignation. Again and again several of the OSS archaeologists echoed Young's desire to offer of relief as an engine to fuel intelligence. However, their interest in relief was not shared by OSS colleagues who had not lived among the Greeks and often ignored the archaeologists' requests.

Thus, tons of food and clothing earmarked for OSS relief projects, transported laboriously from Alexandria and stockpiled on Cyprus, remained there after the liberation of Greece due to OSS inefficiency and Washington's sluggishness. And as a result, the archaeologists only accomplished a fraction of the good works that they envisioned.

Young, however, never gave up on his vision of pragmatic philhellenism. With the premature liberation of Samos, he began to amass data to help with the relief and rehabilitation throughout Greece that would be of use after the eventual German withdrawal. In February 1944, he authored the only U.S. plan for postwar intelligence in Greece in which OSS archaeologist agents would disperse throughout the country, sending military and political intelligence to Athens as well as economic intelligence to aid in the reconstruction of the country. The initial phase of the Young Plan would bridge wartime conditions and the establishment of a permanent postwar intelligence mission. Yet, although the commanding officers in Cairo requested a plan from Washington, by late December 1944 William Langer and Sherman Kent had still not generated one. Thus, the Young Plan became the postwar blueprint for a permanent U.S. intelligence network in Greece. During the postliberation period, confusion resulted from a continued absence of a clear U.S. policy toward Greece and the tacit U.S. acquiescence to British policy. This ambiguity of OSS's status endangered the overt archaeologist-agents who worked under difficult conditions. Yet their flexibility, in part made possible by their long-standing relationships, helped them to surmount the frustrations and meet the challenges inherent in Washington's ambivalence.

As late as April 1945, Sherman Wallace, head of the administrative arm of the Greek Desk in Washington, reported that the army was "bored with SI Greek intelligence." And nothing had "happened in Greece since October 12, 1944 to make the army regret its previous decision not to share in the occupation of Greece." Nor was there more interest among Foreign Service customers. He added, "no more than four Greek SI reports [even got] above the lowest echelon at State."[6]

But during the course of World War II, both Greece's stature and that of the United States changed. By the end of the war, America had emerged as a world power, and Greece, situated on the fault line between U.S. and Soviet spheres, had become central to the emerging struggle between the Eastern and Western blocs in the Cold War.

In the confusing and dangerous months following liberation, Young abandoned the OSS to concentrate on the relief and rehabilitation of Greece through the United Nations Relief and Rehabilitation Administration. For those archaeologists who remained as operatives in Greece, political intelligence-gathering became paramount. During and after the Dekemvriana, they provided the only credible information on Greece outside the narrow confines of the British zone. The archaeologists' ability to deliver objective political intelligence bridged the gap between Left and Right. It informed diplomats in Athens and Washington of much more nuanced events occurring in Greece than the censored British press reported. Moreover, OSS had unique access to intelligence concerning EAM that British and American consumers alike ignored at their peril.[7] In subsequent months, the OSS archaeologist spies dared death, not against the Germans, but in the difficult-to-navigate vortex of Greek domestic politics, suspicious Turks, Macedonian separatists, British "friendly fire," and Bulgarian secret police.

The threat was real. The end of the war marked a watershed in U.S. relations with Greece. The archaeologists' labors to apprise Washington of Soviet interest in the Balkans, British imperialism, and domestic turmoil and political chaos in Greece, although often ignored in the course of the war's distractions, helped to awaken and inform America's postwar interest in the country. At this time, Gerald Else, Charles Edson, John Franklin Daniel, and Jerome Sperling helped shape U.S. policy by educating those who eventually made it. By the time the last of the "archaeological captains" left Greece in September 1946, the United States had completely changed its outlook on the country.

Those who wished to influence U.S. public opinion sought out intellectuals whom they knew from wartime Washington to do it. Carl Blegen was hired to write a volume for the Harvard University Press on Greece and the United States under the associate editorship of the former head of OSS Research and Analysis for the Mediterranean that would contextualize the country, U.S. relations with it, and future problems envisioned for those relations. The work was essentially propaganda and, fortunately, never published.[8]

In September 1946, Greece finally held the long-awaited plebiscite to determine whether George II would return from exile. As a demonstration of support, the American School reopened, and Young took one of its two students through guerrilla-held territory on a site trip to Delphi and Corinth on the back of his motorcycle. After a brief stint with the U.S. Information

Service, Alison Frantz succeeded Blegen as cultural attaché at the embassy. One of very few AMFOGE members who also observed the national referendum, Frantz wrote to her mother, "No one has any illusions about the outcome. It will probably be technically honest, in that the King won't get 107% of the votes as he did last time, but only the very brave republicans will dare to vote."[9] As expected, the "predetermined" plebiscite, held on September 28, favored constitutional monarchy, and so King George II returned to Greece. However, fewer than six months later, just after celebrating a Te Deum in the national cathedral on the occasion of Greek Independence Day, he died of a heart attack.

The king was succeeded by his son Paul who inherited a country that had lost 75 percent of its forests and 23 percent of its buildings (400,000 destroyed). Of its population of 7,000,000, 8 percent had died, a death rate ten times higher than that of the United Kingdom. If one considered the casualties of the civil war, it rose to almost 10 percent.

In 1947, sentiment in the United States was strongly sympathetic to Greece. While Blegen consulted for the State Department in Washington, Young returned to the Agora excavations. That year he saw a gargantuan version of his vision of relief combined with political expediency take shape in the form of the Marshall Plan for Greece, under which the formerly isolationist United States lavished billions of dollars to help Greece raise itself from the devastation of World War II.[10] As a part of the agenda aimed at helping the Greek economy, the American School promoted archaeological tourism.[11] *Life* magazine did a story on AMFOGE and the Agora excavations. Oscar Broneer, U.S. head of Greek War Relief and acting director of the American School of Classical Studies at Athens, supervised *Triumph over Time,* a documentary on the School and the recovery of postwar Greece, produced by Margaret Thompson with help from School trustee Spyros Skouras's movie studios.[12] Meanwhile, Frantz became a liaison for the American Mission for Aid to Greece (AMAG).

Arthur Parsons, the director of the American School largely in absentia from 1941 to 1946, had already left the embassy to work as the acting U.S. representative to the United Nations Special Committee on the Balkans (UNSCOB), established by the UN Security Council. Headquartered in Salonika, it was to investigate alleged violations of the northern frontier of Greece with Yugoslavia and Bulgaria. In particular, it investigated whether the Greek guerrillas received aid from Albania, Yugoslavia, and Bulgaria and the claim that Greek children were being abducted to the north.

On September 18, OSS alumnus Allan Dulles helped to found the Central Intelligence Agency and attracted a flock of former OSS agents and operatives, including SI colleagues who had long and productive intelligence careers, such as Frank Wisner of OSS Istanbul, who shepherded OSS Secret Intelligence in postwar Germany with Richard Helms as his deputy. Later they guided U.S. postwar intelligence: Dulles and Helms directed the CIA, and Wisner became its chief of plans (sabotage and subversive operations). Those who answered the call in Greece included Thomas Karamessines (OSS Counterintelligence), who established the Greek Central Intelligence Agency (KYP), and Christian Freer, who had succeeded Else and Bailey as acting head of the Greek Desk in Cairo in 1944, served as executive officer for Charles Edson, and succeeded him as head of the Athens base in July 1945, where he had worked closely with Sperling, Daniel, Clio Adossides, and Karamessines.[13]

By 1948, Freer was in charge of the fledgling Athens Station of the CIA. That year, the archaeologists returned despite the raging civil war in Greece. Archaeology remained central to them and to U.S. foreign policy. Blegen wrote that archaeology offered "one of the easiest and most direct channels through which Greece can assure herself a tide of good will, along with moral and material help, from all the enlightened world."[14] Rodney Young addressed the open meeting of the American School and attended a tea for the king and queen. Meanwhile, Parsons was in the north with the UN Boundary Mission.

One day after attending a May 7 UNSCOB meeting in Salonika, George Polk, the outspoken Middle East station chief for CBS, disappeared. A week later his bullet-ridden body was found trussed and floating in Salonika bay.[15] Immediately, the assassination-style murder became a cause célèbre, and American journalists hired Donovan's law firm to investigate the murder of their colleague who had died on the job. Donovan brought Lt. Col. James Kellis of OSS Special Operations' Chicago mission, with whom Young had worked in Cairo. General George Marshall, then U.S. secretary of state, suggested Rodney Young as a good intelligence contact for the investigation.[16] Furor and accusations of responsibility for the crime threatened to derail international relations between the United States and Greece as well as Soviet Russia at the time when the United States was investing millions of dollars in Greece as a bulwark against Communism.[17] Some feared war with Russia. Meanwhile, by the end of the year, both Arthur Parsons and John Franklin Daniel were dead.

Working to salvage relations between the United States and Greece, U.S. cultural attaché Alison Frantz and American School director Carl Blegen joined forces to help launch the Fulbright Scholarship Program in Greece, the second in the world and the first in Europe. This cultural exchange, meant to promote cultural relations between the United States and Greece, counted Eugene Vanderpool and OSS alumni Young, Lucy Talcott, and Margaret Crosby among its first fellows.[18]

The American archaeologists who worked on the Greek Desk labored on behalf of their own country as well as their adopted home. Through their relief work and pragmatic philhellenism at the beginning of the war, they bonded not only with the Greeks in Greece, but also with the Greek-American communities in the United States. Not just ivory-tower intellectuals, those men and women who accepted the challenge of gathering and directing U.S. intelligence on Greece in World War II were committed not only to resuming their own work and way of life abroad, but also to helping the suffering inhabitants of their host countries. Little did they imagine, when they were digging the ancient ruins of Homer's Troy and Pericles' Athens, that they would someday turn their knowledge of modern Greece to practical use in wartime. But when Mussolini attacked their adopted homeland and then Hitler conquered it, the excavators stepped out of their trenches and into the line of fire because of their emotional ties to modern Greece. Readily they offered relief to Greeks in the Albanian mountains and later banded together to provide intelligence to the OSS. Leaving wives and children behind and abandoning hard-won teaching posts at America's top universities, the archaeologists of "the greatest generation" turned their backs on predetermined paths and embraced certain danger and uncertain outcomes. It was their close teamwork that helped them function in the field in spite of almost insuperable difficulties of supply, equipment, and manpower. Each, stuck at his or her base, desperately wanted action, the chance to be an operative, but the archaeological captains were too valuable to be lost, caught, or killed and had to remain at their posts and anchor the program. Finally, with the liberation of Greece, they saw the action they craved.

What were the valuable qualities which the archaeologists brought to espionage? Christian Freer assessed those of Trojan archaeologist Jerome Sperling, who gathered intelligence from all parts of Greece, but particularly Eastern Macedonia and Thrace from 1944 to 1946, where his proficiency in Turkish and Greek "proved most valuable." Freer rated his performance "superior" and his work "really outstanding." Many of the qualities that Freer deemed exceptional are those of a good field archaeologist.

> As an SI operative Major Sperling's production has always been large, and almost always of high quality. As time passed and he gained experience, his reports became still better. His preciseness, his objectivity, his logical development of ideas and his clarity of expression all combined to enhance the value of the intelligence which he obtained as a result of his highly alert and inquiring mind, his intellectual honesty, his great attention to detail, his indefatigable willingness to work, and his readiness to expose himself to discomfort if not to danger. There can be no doubt that Major Sperling has proved to be much the best SI operative we have had in Greece since the liberation; he has produced far more than any other operative, and his reports have generally been of higher caliber than those submitted by others.
>
> In addition to his accomplishments as an SI operative, Major Sperling has throughout given ample evidence of an exceptionally cooperative spirit, a capacity for teamwork which has included the ability to subordinate himself gracefully to others of lesser rank, and the greatest conscientiousness and devotion to duty.[19]

When they returned home, several of the archaeologists were lionized in newspapers and boardrooms.[20] As the OSS archaeologists returned to their academic lives, the adjustment was not a seamless one. Several maintained their ties to Washington, and at least one abandoned archaeology altogether for government employment. The remainder devoted the rest of their careers to archaeology in the field and classroom. They came through the war with their relationships intact and became leaders in their academic fields nationally and internationally. Those who worked in Greece or on its behalf forged deeper relationships with their Greek colleagues—relationships that bore fruit in excavations on both sides of the Aegean in the following decades. In some cases, archaeologists excavated sites that they had discovered in the process of intelligence-gathering during the war. In others, they switched direction or country, based on wartime experiences.

After the Polk Affair, however, what began, for Young, as a desire to save Greece and the Greece took on a more sinister tinge. As the archaeologists headed back to their countries of research in the postwar era, their war work was not discussed. As the CIA grew more aggressive during the Cold War, intelligence work in general was something to be distrusted. What the archaeologists had done during the war became "hush-hush" and the stuff of legend.

Elli Adossides was supported by the American School until her death in 1972. She remained close friends with Rodney Young and Carl Blegen. In 1953, a bench was dedicated in memory of her husband Anastasios in the newly landscaped Agora, and in 1954 she was invited to plant a tree near the Hephaistion where his office once stood. She wrote a diary of her war years and showed it to Blegen before her death, but it has not yet been found.[21]

As a colonel in the Ninth Air Force, Ulius Amoss (1895–1961) arranged transportation to France in August 1944 for David Bruce, head of OSS London, and served as director of the Balkan Desk for Information and deputy chief of staff, U.S. Ninth Air Force. After his discharge in 1946, he formed the International Services of Information Foundation (ISI or INFORM), a nonprofit, privately owned and operated intelligence service whose purpose was to collect and disseminate information from overseas countries. Since INFORM was a CIA "commercial cover" operation, he worked for CIA's OSS Istanbul veteran, Frank Wisner. Fearing a Communist takeover of the United States, he invented a different kind of organizational structure, Leaderless Resistance, which has since been widely used by activists of all sorts and is of great interest to U.S. Homeland Security. He also formed the U. L. Amoss Syndicate in 1948, which in turn invested in other corporations. One product that he discovered, promoted, and distributed was the hair-restorative Grecian Formula.[22]

From 1948 to 1949, Carl William Blegen "CWB" (1887–1971) served reluctantly as director of the American School of Classical Studies at Athens, during which time he labored to bring the Agora Museum into the Marshall Plan's program to restore the Greek economy by rebuilding its museums.[23] After one year, he returned to the University of Cincinnati and concentrated on building up its modern Greek collection. From 1950 to 1958, he published four volumes on the excavations at Troy, one of which was coauthored by Caskey. From 1952 to 1969, Blegen excavated at the site of Pylos where he had begun digging in 1939. He retired from teaching in 1957 and returned to Greece. Blegen was chosen as the first gold medalist of the AIA in 1965 and was awarded the gold medal by the Society of Antiquaries in London a year later.

After returning to Washington in December 1944, John Langdon "Jack" Caskey "JLC" (1908–81) was recruited to serve as an SI operative in Germany by Richard Helms.[24] Before the German surrender, Caskey directed intelligence from OSS London and entered Germany within two weeks of the surrender. From May 1945 until April 1946, while under cover of public relations (press and radio) for the Office of Military Government in the American Sector, Caskey was actually the SI chief of Munich and, after September 1945, attached to the U.S. Seventh Army and commanding officer of the Munich detachment charged with supervisory SSU operations for Bavaria. He directed the political intelligence section and worked with special sources, nicknamed "Crown Jewels," including the minister of Bavaria, handpicked by spymaster Allen Dulles, as well as army intelligence and internal security officers, churchmen, academics, civil servants, and other political figures who were as clean as possible. Caskey spearheaded ARTHUR Mission, which vetted these individuals to set up a network of German spies working for the United States in Germany until the closure of the Munich detachment in April 1946, when he departed, leaving behind 6–8 confidential sources, 30–40 vetted contacts for future operations, and one organized SI network.[25] Caskey was awarded the Legion of Merit in May 1946 for his war work in Izmir. Afterward, Dulles recommended Lieutenant Colonel Caskey for intelligence work in Branch "A," proposed that he be sent to the Middle East with the State Department in Izmir, Ankara, or Iran (Tabriz), and assigned him to the Turkish Desk in Washington. Just before the fall semester, Caskey decided to return to academia, and Dulles wrote "postpone action for present—of possible use undercover later on."[26]

Caskey returned to the University of Cincinnati's Department of Classics, but two years later was chosen as Blegen's assistant director at the American School. He succeeded Blegen as director in 1949 and held the position for a decade, an unusual honor for one who had never formally studied there. After conducting excavations for the School at Lerna in the Peloponnese, Caskey returned to Cincinnati, assuming the chairmanship of the Department of Classics formerly held by Blegen. In 1955, he presided over the dedication of the new Agora Museum, the Stoa of Attalos, and was decorated with the Greek Order of the Phoenix by King Paul. After a year at the Institute for Advanced Study in Princeton, Caskey commenced excavations at Ayia Irini, a site on Vourkari Bay on the island of Kea, and he used the former OSS base "Elba" as his dig house. He subsequently divided his time between Kea and Cincinnati.

Dorothy Hanna Cox "DHC" (1892–1978) returned in 1945 to New Haven, where she worked as curator of coins in the Department of Classics at Yale University and also worked at the Institute for Advanced Study, where she assisted Hetty Goldman, excavator of Tarsus. In 1946, she became book review editor of the *American Journal of Archaeology* under Pete

Daniel. In the 1950s and 1960s, she assisted Young as architect and numismatist at the Gordion excavations as well as on an archaeological expedition to Balkh, Afghanistan, in 1953. That year, Cox published a volume in the Gordion excavation series and later retired to her farm in Cheshire, Connecticut.

Margaret "Missy" Crosby (1901–72) returned to the United States in 1945. From 1946 to 1972, she divided her time between the United States and excavating at the Agora in Athens, where she was a generous patron. In 1956, Crosby was decorated by King Paul, and in 1964, she coauthored a volume in the Agora excavation series. She continued working at the Agora until her death.

In June 1946, Lt. Col. John Franklin "Pete" Daniel III "JFD" (1910–48) was awarded a bronze star for "courageous, meritorious, and outstanding service against the enemy." He returned to civilian life, resumed teaching at the University of Pennsylvania, and assumed the editorship of the *American Journal of Archaeology,* the flagship journal of the Archaeological Institute of America, a position he held through 1948, when he became professor of Classical archaeology at the University of Pennsylvania and curator of the Mediterranean Section of the University Museum.[27] The university committed substantial resources to the program in Classical archaeology and asked Daniel to find a desirable ancient Greek site in the eastern Mediterranean and commence excavation. Daniel weighed Sardis, Gordion, and a site along the southern and western coast of Turkey near where he had worked during the summer of 1944.[28] At the same time, he worked to establish an American research school and Fulbright program in Turkey and applied for the first Turkish Fulbright Scholarship to cover an archaeological survey either from Antalya to Fethiye and Bodrum or between Kushadasi and Chandarli (the latter two the locations of Caskey's secret harbors). Daniel hired Rodney Young as his assistant or associate curator in February 1948 and, on September 10, sailed for Cyprus to finish his last season at Kourion. Then he, Young, and a School fellow went prospecting for a University of Pennsylvania dig site and chose the mythical King Midas's city of Gordion.[29] It was on that expedition that Daniel died unexpectedly on December 17, 1948.

Lt. Col. William Bell Dinsmoor "WBD" (1886–1973), chief of Committee for the Protection of Cultural Treasures in War Areas (the monuments commission) and president of the AIA, was one of a group of architects, painters, sculptors, archivists, librarians, historians of art, civilians, and military who drafted a memorandum to FDR on December 8, 1942, about protecting European monuments. Dinsmoor and Francis Taylor, director of the Metropolitan Museum of Art in New York, drafted plans for the protection of monuments, works of art, and art historical remains of regions of Europe and Africa exposed to the devastations of war. The Harvard Defense Group, organized by Meritt, handled the monuments and collections of Greece. Volunteers and scholars began by tracing city maps with drafting done at the Frick Museum. In August 1943, the American Commission for the Protection and Salvage of Art Historical Monuments in Europe provided city maps for bombing squadrons and troops in the field. After the war, Dinsmoor returned to the American School as annual professor.

Sterling Dow (1903–95) resumed his teaching at Harvard University in February 1944. In 1946, he was elected president of the Archaeological Institute of America and served through 1948. As president of the AIA in 1946, Dow recommended that a civilian advisory group be established to provide liaison with the Division of Military Information and Intelligence. The AIA would participate through the American Council of Learned Societies (ACLS).[30] In 1947 and 1948, he (on behalf of the AIA) worked with Young and Daniel to start an American School in Turkey and planned to take over the former German School in Istanbul for that purpose,[31] but Daniel's untimely death derailed the project. Dow, who had served OSS in Cairo and Alexandria, also joined other OSS alumni, including John A. Wilson (OSS), and William "Bill" Stevenson Smith (ONI), to found ARCE, where Smith served as the first director.

Capt. Charles Farwell Edson "CFE" (1905–88) worked as a political analyst and chief of the Europe-Africa Division of R&A under Sherman Kent. Then he returned to the University of Wisconsin in Madison, living a monkish life, studying Macedonian epigraphy, a passion that he shared with his British colleague Col. Nicholas Hammond of the Allied Military Mission, who had spent the war in Epirus with the guerrillas. Edson published his magnum opus on Macedonian inscriptions in 1972.

Capt. Gerald Frank Else "GFE" (1908–82) taught for nine years at the State University of Iowa before moving in 1957 to the University of Michigan, where until 1968 he chaired the Department of Classics. A superb administrator, he elevated it to one of the best in the United States. He also founded the Center for the Coordination of Ancient and Modern Studies at Michigan in 1969 and directed it until his retirement in 1976. In addition, Else became president of the American Philological Association from 1963 to 1964. As such, he participated with the ACLS to establish the National Commission of the Humanities, which recommended the establishment of a National Humanities Foundation, created in 1965 as the National Endowment for the Humanities.

Mary Alison Frantz "MAF" (1903–95) excavated a Byzantine church within the confines of the Agora in 1954 and continued as Agora photographer until 1956. She became visiting member at the Institute for Advanced Study in Princeton and, in 1971 and 1988, published volumes on the Byzantine and Late Antique remains in the Agora.

Thanks to Benjamin Meritt, Virginia Randolph Grace "VRG" (1901–94) secured a fellowship to work on stamped amphora handles from the Agora at the Institute for Advanced Study from 1945 to 1948. She earned one of the first grants offered by the America Research Center in Egypt, and her work was broadcast on the Voice of America, the wartime propaganda tool of the Office of War Information. Frantz retired to Athens, where she continued her work at the American School until her death. In 1989, she was awarded the AIA gold medal for her pioneering work on Greek amphorae.

Moses Hadas (1900–66) continued teaching at Columbia University, where in 1956 he was named the sixth Jay Professor of Greek, the university's oldest chair, created in 1839 and named for the first chief justice of the Supreme Court. He devoted his prolific energy to producing surveys of Greek and Latin literature and translating Greek and Latin classics, Hebrew poems, and German historians into English for a wide audience.

While OSS agents were debriefed at the Congressional Country Club, Nele Kapp (1919–?) was flown to Washington. For two months, she was interned in New York as an enemy alien since she had no papers and had worked at a German embassy. "Kept under observation and treated like a criminal," she was "subjected to terrible shock treatment" usually reserved for the mentally ill. She was released only because Ambassador Steinhardt intervened while trying to pinpoint the German mole in the American Embassy, mentioned in one of the documents that Kapp had copied from Moysich's safe.[32] Then Kapp was transferred to an internment camp in Bismarck, North Dakota. She corresponded with contacts in Washington, trying to get word of Rengers, whom she had left behind in Ankara. Eventually, she learned that he had died.[33] After that, Kapp waited tables in Chicago and boarded with a German couple. FBI agents paid her weekly visits, and she eventually married one, William Gorman.[34] Two years after the end of the war, her father died, after being forcibly retired following his daughter's dishonor. To cope with guilt and depression, she drank. Finally, Kapp moved to Southern California, where she had two children, divorced, found religion, sought alcohol treatment at Salvation Army alcoholics meetings, and died in obscurity.[35]

Lt. George H. McFadden "GHM" (1907–53) returned in 1945 to Cyprus, where he continued to fund the University of Pennsylvania Expedition to Kourion and, in 1946, recommended that the University Museum appoint Rodney Young as a curator of its Classical Section or director of the museum.[36] His own excavations at Kourion were cut short when he died in a sailing accident off the coast of Cyprus within view of the site.

Benjamin Dean Meritt "BDM" (1899–1989) continued as kingmaker in the field of classics and professor of Greek epigraphy at the Institute for Advanced Study in Princeton. In 1974, he coauthored a monograph on Athenian inscriptions in the Agora excavation series.

Maj. James Henry "Jim" Oliver, Jr. "JHO" (1905–81) worked as head of the German and Scandinavian unit of the SI reporting board for SSU from 1945 to 1946, when he returned to civilian life. He then taught at Johns Hopkins University. In 1957, he was named the Francis White Professor of Greek, a position he held until his retirement in 1970. Throughout his Hopkins career, Oliver served as editor of the *American Journal of Philology*, and, like Else, he later served as president of the American Philological Association.

After the war, Arthur Wellesley Parsons "AWP" (1900–48), director of the American School in absentia (1941–46), worked as senior political analyst for the U.S. embassy in Athens. In July, Gorham Stevens urged him to serve as the acting U.S. representative to UNSCOB to investigate alleged violations of the northern frontier of Greece with Yugoslavia and Bulgaria. Reluctant to accept the dangerous job, he resigned from the Foreign Service and served with UNSCOB until his untimely death on September 29, 1948.[37]

T. Leslie Shear "TLS" (1880–1945) retired from FNB in 1944 and was succeeded by Rodney Young's brother-in-law, Richard Lindabury. Shear died on July 3, 1945. In 1967, his only child, T. Leslie Shear, Jr., followed in his father's footsteps and became a professor of Classical art and archaeology at Princeton University and the director of the Agora excavations.

Clio Philippidou Adossides Sperling (1912–2007) worked for the Athens Station until 1946, when she moved to New Haven. She continued to give concerts and teach piano, following Sperling in his peripatetic government career and climbing mountains regularly until very late in life. She participated on excavations in Elis in 1968 and at Troy in 1988, but otherwise had little to do with archaeology.

Lt. Col. Jerome Leroy "Jerry" Sperling "JLS" (1908–97) returned to civilian life and resumed teaching at Yale University, but became disenchanted by academic life. He was appointed a fellow at the American School of Classical Studies at Athens for 1947 to 1948, but did not serve since he was recalled to active duty to serve on the Allied electoral supervisory commission in Greece. He was awarded a bronze star as "the outstanding intelligence operative" of the Athens Desk, "frequently exposing himself to personal hardships and to physical danger from anti-American elements." Abandoning archaeology, Sperling served on the U.S. Army General Staff, Balkans–Middle East Division, from 1947 to 1949. From 1952 to 1966, he served with the U.S. Foreign Service Reserve in Greece, Saudi Arabia, and Washington. In 1968, he participated in rescue excavations at Armatova in Elis. Upon retirement from government employ, he lived in Athens, teaching for the College of Wooster (in Greece) and the College Year in Athens and serving as archivist at the American School from 1974 onward. He authored two archaeological publications in the 1970s and made an informal survey of antiquities on the island of Simi in 1981–82.[38] In 1988, he participated in the first season of the reopened Troy excavations.

Lucy Talcott (1899–1970) returned to the Agora excavations in 1946 and continued as registrar until 1958, when she focused on her own research on ancient Greek pottery. In 1947, she worked with Oscar Broneer on *Triumph over Time*. Like Crosby, Talcott was decorated by King Paul in 1956. She copublished a volume of the Agora excavation series in 1970.

Rodney Stuart Young "RSY" (1907–74) left UNRRA in November 1945. He was awarded a bronze star for "extremely valuable service in the Africa and Middle East Theatre of Operations and in direct support of the U.S. Army Forces in the Middle East and . . . an accurate and voluminous flow of valuable intelligence."[39] From 1946 to 1948, Young worked on the Agora excavations. In December 1948, he succeeded Daniel as curator of the Mediterranean Section of the University Museum and professor of Classical archaeology at the University of Pennsylvania. He directed its excavations at the site of Gordion in Turkey, assisted by Dorothy Cox, an association that lasted for decades and included an archaeological expedition to Balkh, Afghanistan, in 1953. In 1964, Young helped found the American Research Institute in Turkey (ARIT), an institution first suggested in 1942 and worked toward by Daniel in 1948. In 1969, Young was elected president of the AIA, serving until 1972. He taught at Penn, served on the board of ARIT, and excavated at Gordion until his untimely death in 1974.

In the postwar landscape, the United States was vitally interested in the eastern Mediterranean and eager to establish permanent intelligence networks not only in Greece, but also in the other countries where the archaeologists had served. In Greece, although the OSS undoubtedly used the U.S. embassy as a cover for operatives, according to MacVeagh's wishes, and from 1947 onward the CIA housed the likes of Thomas Karamessines and Valerie Plame, it is interesting to note that the chief institutions continually recommended by the wartime intelligence agents for cover were the American School of Classical Studies at Athens, Athens College, Anatolia College, the American Farm School, and other American cultural institutions or businesses in Greece.

Considering that the American School of Oriental Research (now the Albright Institute of Archaeological Research) in Jerusalem was the hub of American intelligence for the OSS in Palestine and American School personnel were the hub for the OSS in Greece, it cannot be coincidental that after World War II American research institutions were founded in Turkey, Egypt (American Research Center in Egypt-ARCE), and Cyprus (the Cyprus American Archaeological Research Institute).[40] The American Research Institute in Turkey (ARIT) is strikingly similar to what the Istanbul SI chief proposed in 1944 as deep cover for a permanent intelligence operative in Turkey. OSS had been seeking future SI agents whose cover would be established in America and maintained implicitly. For those agents who would be "completely under cover with absolutely no contact with the office and only most guarded and secret contact" with middlemen, they recommended "students and professors on leave doing research in Turkey." He continued, "The establishment of an American Archaeological Institute or Oriental Institute in Turkey would open possibilities to work in the domain. Even preliminary soundings on this subject could be utilized for getting people in and out of Turkey. . . . [and] be of service to the organization."[41]

From the Cold War to the present, some American archaeologists engaged in area studies have conducted espionage for the United States in the eastern Mediterranean. The Pentagon's Minerva Project and Human Terrain System (which embeds anthropologists in Iraq) have sparked passionate debates about what association, if any, social scientists should have with the military.[42] The AIA has chosen to educate American soldiers about the cultural property in the areas where they will serve, evoking comparisons with William Dinsmoor's "monuments men" who single-handedly protected the cultural treasures of Europe while embedded with American troops in World War II.[43] Although ethicists today debate the pros and cons of such activities and the possibility of their tainting the profession by using archaeology or anthropology as covers, it is important to note that in the heat of war and its immediate aftermath, the Greek Desk of the OSS did not.

APPENDIXES

Internal Assessment

AS THE ARCHAEOLOGISTS WERE DEBRIEFED at OSS Cairo or Area F, the Congressional Country Club outside Washington, they wrote histories of their operations and evaluated their experiences. From radio operators and field agents to Else and Edson, they chronicled similar problems. Penrose evaluated each report and excerpted its salient messages for Shepardson: lack of communication from Washington; inadequate briefing, training in reporting, and direction in selecting what to cover; insufficient staff; lack of clerical support resulting in decreased efficiency; friction with British allies; unsatisfactory supply and transportation; and interbranch rivalries and divided authority necessitating a solitary commander at each base to manage the branches involved.[1]

Penrose, who evaluated Crosby's final report, noted that

> The unfortunate fact with regard to the entire Greek Desk was that, although intelligence coverage was excellent and complete, there was actually very little American interest in the Greek scene. Our Greek Section was in the position of a man all dressed up and no place to go.[2]

Many problems stemmed from the quick growth of OSS and were common to operations in other regions. The need to get personnel into the field necessitated a short catchall training that would hopefully give a smattering of preparation for any espionage situation encountered abroad but, in fact, left SI agents ill prepared to gather and transmit secret intelligence. De-Bardeleben admitted, "Difficulties in command, supply and training were due to inexperience and the necessity of improvising and shortcutting because of our late start." Donovan's "inept vertical organization" of OSS bu-reaucracy into branches arranged by function rather than by area caused other difficulties. This "inflexible departmentalization of OSS . . . had an ad-verse effect on operations" and required continuous liaison uniting branches operating in or connected with the same countries or regions.[3] The lack thereof resulted in divided authority and lack of cooperation and communication between them.

Security was another issue. Else mentioned that the archaeologists were "excessively spooky—concerned with mystery and intrigue." Excessive con-cern for security hampered Dow's ability to communicate. Georgiades complained of Sperling's byzantine security measures. Meanwhile, the lack thereof in the Supply branch endangered Greek Desk operations in Izmir.

The historian of OSS Cairo wrote, "The SI Greek section was in the very odd position of an American intelligence source almost all of whose re-ports, except political and economic ones, were of use only to the British. As curious to the British as would be to the Americans a British intention to procure intelligence from Panama or the Philippines." It is true that Britain was far more interested in its product and that the archaeologists' intent cleaved with Britain's military strategy (the invasion of Greece); however to compare Greece to Panama is a misnomer since, though long dependent on the Great Powers, Greece was a sovereign nation. Although its intelligence had mainly been of use to its British allies (of whom it was highly critical), the Greek Desk's SI also proved valuable to U.S. agencies concerned with Balkan political and economic matters. MacVeagh regarded it as of "pre-cious assistance" in giving him the "benefit of an overall view," and Laird Archer, in charge of relief and rehabilitation efforts, credited SI as his "quickest channel of communication" of "precise and most useful intelli-gence."[4] And that was before liberation.

From Amoss on down, the Greek Desk suffered from insufficient ad-ministrative experience. Not "bureaucratically minded," Rodney Young proved a poor administrator. John Calvocoressi, who worked in Cairo and as field agent on Evvia, claimed that Young

> proved incapable of reaching any decision as to future operations. . . . The Greek desk in Cairo suffered from a lack of proper organization and ad-ministrative talent, . . . a lack of planning . . . personnel being obtained for one purpose and used for another [Calvo's own situation] or being found useless; sharp fluctuations between comparative idleness and too heavy

work; avoidable last-minute rushes; vagueness concerning functions; terms of employment.

DeBardeleben noted, "While bases were in desperate need of qualified personnel, Cairo had individuals whose missions had been cancelled 'with no profitable work to do.'" Things improved when Else arrived in November 1943 and assumed much of the burden for new operations, including all those dispatched from Bari.[5]

Young interfaced poorly with other branches that dovetailed with SI at every point. They should have been most closely coordinated with it, but instead maintained a guild like attitude, as did Young. Using Greek nationals as agents exacerbated the interbranch disorganization and made recruiting, preparing, and servicing the missions and processing their reports extremely difficult. A Greek-speaking OSS officer always had to be on hand, and they were scarce. Personnel from other branches (Maritime, Supply, and Services) did not speak Greek and could not interact with the agents. The Labor Desk could not read Couvaras's reports. Only SI had a reservoir of Greek knowledge, experience, and personnel. Therefore, everyone relied on Young, the "nerve centre" and "effective head of all Greek operations." "When he moved, the centre of gravity moved with him." But as charismatic and strong as Young was, he was spread too thin. Moreover, although he was tacitly regarded as the OSS Middle East chief on Greek matters, he did not control the entire scope of Greek affairs. Leadership without authority plagued every SI base in the Aegean and east Mediterranean. It caused resentment between SI and the other OSS branches. The faulty vertical structure of OSS only complicated Young's problems. Although he clearly cooperated with the Labor Desk, Maritime, and Special Operations, Else claimed that the Greek Desk held the virtually undisputed title of the Most Hated Branch of OSS ME" and "Young was not the man to pour oil on the waters or waste his precious time in diplomacy."[6]

For Young and Caskey, the most serious obstacles were jurisdictional disputes internal to OSS. Caskey's "chief disappointments[,] discouragement, and exhaustion came not from the difficulty of opposing the enemy, but from profitless and wasteful antagonism and inefficiencies among the Allies, between American agencies, and within the OSS itself," which needed to focus on "eliminating rather than prolonging the conflict." Among these problems were "confused policy in Cairo" and "time wasted" with Maritime, which was given the authority to organize and maintain the caique service and to establish bases in Turkey . . . [without] the personnel to operate the service, or an understanding of its purpose . . . Maritime did not measure up to the job . . . it undertook. . . . [Its] representatives never seemed to have assumed responsibility for performance. . . . [They] could not serve simultaneously as officer in charge of a base as big as Boston.[7]

For base officers and agents, the most critical shortfall was in Supply, stemming in part from a lack of communication between Young and the Services Branch in Cairo. Early on, Young had to supply everything himself. Later Young failed to delegate authority and rely on the services of the OSS Supply Officer. Each thought the other was supplying Izmir, but frequently neither was doing the job. The archaeologists at the satellite offices blamed Washington when, in fact, supplies had never been properly requisitioned in Cairo. For this, Young needed a services officer, but even when he had access to one, Young usually insisted on doing the work himself ("one of Mr. Young's peculiarities") with the result of slow delivery of supplies to the field.[8] Meanwhile, the theater commander (through whom all requests were funneled) often neglected Young's requests.

Beyond OSS interbranch problems, Else lamented the lack of cooperation within the American intelligence community in Cairo, which regarded certain archaeologists as "primadonnas."[9] And the Americans on the Joint Committee for Allied Intelligence seemed "not to be convinced that they were fighting the same war."[10]

Washington could have obviated some of the trouble by communicating substantively with the Greek Desk. To improve understanding, OSS generally rotated personnel between their hubs and Washington, but the only member of the Greek Desk who did so was Sterling Dow, "whose efficiency was not of the best" and who quit shortly after he returned from Cairo.[11] As a result, Washington never got an adequate understanding of the enormous operational difficulties involved and could not imagine the byzantine complexity inherent in the smallest operations. Communication could also have been improved by base personnel meeting regularly, but because of insufficient backup staff, the archaeologists could not get away, so that even between the bases and Cairo there was no rotation. Although Cox, Sperling, and Daniel made it to Cairo at least once during their tenure, Caskey did not see Cairo for over a year and a half while he was in Izmir.[12] The lack of rotation, however, was somewhat ameliorated by the strength of their long-standing relationships and their willingness to work together.

For most of its life, the Greek Desk remained hopelessly undermanned with insufficient personnel to maintain and service its missions. "Not having been advised on the number of desk men needed to service field missions, they got ambitious and sent in too many teams. Once they were operational, the desk men were overwhelmed with the flood of intelligence that they generated."[13] DeBardeleben noted that "Additional personnel . . . services men, briefing officers, conducting officers . . . would have relieved the confusion immensely."[14]

Without clerical personnel, the archaeologists spent much of their time deskbound—typing, copying, and filing reports. Virginia Grace decried the lack of secretaries.

> [It was] foolish not to include an American girl with secretarial and book-keeping training to handle the mechanical with mechanical skill and detachment . . . special background desirable . . . [OSS could have sent] Caskey's own graduate students to free Caskey for badly needed supervision and consultation at the bases, and intelligence work greatly understaffed . . . the whole office worked seven days a week except when they dropped . . . Code clerks, finance officers and security officers were also in short supply. . . . the code clerk sent by Cairo did not speak Greek . . . could not type and would not make his own copies.[15]

Because they had no support personnel, intelligence analysts ran the show rather than participating in it. They devoted themselves to operational matters, such as finding agents and boats, infiltrating and maintaining the field missions, servicing the secret harbors, and a "frantic round of problems . . . recruiting, training, discipline, personal adjustments, finance, equipping, transportation, requests and complaints." Intelligence gathering was to be their main focus, but Grace claimed that "by June 2, 1944 Izmir had ceased to produce any intelligence reports at all because Cox was fully occupied with clerical work."[16] Else later wrote that "from the beginning the Greek Section of SI has been busy with anything and everything but intelligence. The job of getting these teams in the field, and maintaining them after they were there, took all the time."[17] The archaeologists *could* generate intelligence and often did under their bird monikers, for instance Young's "Pigeon eggs" on the wrangling of Greek politicians in Cairo. More often, however, that critical responsibility was left to the Greek field agents whose work they translated and processed for Cairo and Washington.

Else criticized their training at "the Farm," whose instruction was impractical for Greek Desk operations. The archaeologists' SI training, the direction of intelligence and thorough training in reporting, was woefully inadequate. They were "given no idea which kinds of intelligence had priority over others, how they might be used, where to lay emphasis and where not. . . . no real idea who would use our product, or for what purpose." They replicated the lack at their own training school, which Else described as "laughable." This was not lost on several of the agents trained there, and Calvo noted that "The Greek *Desk* personnel was unacquainted with both actual field conditions and intelligence operations." Else blamed the lack of intelligence direction and vagueness that SI passed on to their field agents on the lack of a clear U.S. policy toward Greece and the fact that American forces had never planned or conducted any operations there. As a result, in addition to highly important information, SI collected masses of trivia.[18]

Lack of direction from Washington stemmed from inexperience and disinterest. Georgiades noted that OSS was "cooking fish with the wrong oil" and wasting time on objectives that did not interest Washington.[19] The Greek Desk SI and R&A in Cairo were constantly trying to get Washington to pay attention and found demoralizing their "gnawing suspicion . . . that nobody paid attention to their reports."[20] It was true. Crosby reported the feeling of "working in a vacuum" and the need for greater contact with and from Washington. Having worked on the Greek Desk in Washington, Cairo, Athens, and Caserta, Crosby had a unique perspective. Although her complaint was a common one, the fact that Crosby made it after months of service during a bloody civil war when OSS Athens was virtually isolated and confined to its headquarters made it particularly poignant. She also noted the difficulties inherent in the arbitrary division of staff at small offices into SI and R&A.[21]

For Oliver, the chief external bogie was their hostile British allies.

> Members of the Allied Military Mission to Greece viewed SI agents in their areas with disapproval as potential enemies who might make unfavorable reports about them. . . . they considered the existence of an Intelligence System, extending into their area but independent of their control, as superfluous and invidious. . . . the local British feel that the Americans are there merely on sufferance and that they (the British) are being generous in fulfilling obligations undertaken by their distant superiors. . . . As the war,

moreover, nears an end, the British may subordinate the common interest of defeating the Germans to what they consider is to the interest of the post-war British Empire. The British upper class is convinced that what is to the interest of the British Empire is to the interest of the world. . . . [This class,] while individually honourable, may resort, where the Empire is concerned, to the most dishonest and ruthless behavior on the highest moral principle. . . . "To safeguard the British Empire we must control the Mediterranean, and to control the Mediterranean, we must control (1) Italy, (2) Greece." As the end of the German Occupation approached the American Intelligence Service became an embarrassment . . . [to them]: . . . it did not regard the interests of the British Empire as the criterion and hence it would represent certain things in an unfavorable light. . . . the presence of Americans or of supplies from an American source tended to encourage the Greeks to assume an attitude of less dependence upon the British.[22]

In spite of all its obstacles, the Greek Desk succeeded in carrying out most of its goals. Izmir was the most critical base. "The success of all SI operations was entirely dependent on its successful performance." Fortunately, Caskey was, according to Virginia Grace, an excellent administrator whose grasp was comprehensive and objective. Like Young, Caskey induced cooperation between incompatibles and exacted performance from assistants ill matched to their tasks by virtue of administrative power and his own willingness to do any job. He delegated without jealousy, unlike some of his fellows who were described as "unduly stiff-necked."[23]

Edson credited an

> enormous debt to . . . Young. His deep knowledge of Greece and the Greek character, the esteem in which he was held by the Greeks of every political party and social class, his extraordinary memory, tireless stamina, forthright and uncompromising character and meticulous honesty were the foundation on which the Greek Section was built.[24]

Young was a good judge of men and women, and his choices panned out. Young employed civilian women in Washington, Cairo, Istanbul, and Izmir and gave them responsibility, generally as reports officers, whereas elsewhere in OSS, the majority of women worked at menial tasks as secretaries or clerks.[25] Good at communicating with his fellow archaeologists in the field and sending long handwritten or single-spaced typed letters to them, he kept them motivated to get the job done. Young was extremely attentive and loyal to a fault. He worked hard and was willing to do all aspects of the job. "The chief factor in its success was Young's tireless energy, but each of the others contributed his share."[26]

"All had an intense interest in the liberation of the country . . . The Section learned as it went along." Virginia Grace wrote that "Cooperative spirit was so obviously urgent that it felt like passing the ammunition (as indeed it often was) . . . We worked hard and wanted to do nothing else. . . . [Young inspired in SI] a devotion more usually found in amateurs than professionals doing technically excellent work." Even Calvo, who was highly critical, commended the archaeologists for their complete conscientiousness and devoted energy.[27]

The successes of the Greek Desk can be attributed to the trust and working relationships forged long before the war in the archaeological fieldwork. The job needed to be done, and they did it. Aside from their area studies expertise, their chief qualifications were tireless energy and passion, powers of observation, and ability to describe and analyze what they saw. They were armed with a personal sense of duty in time of crisis. Young wrote that each played "his part in a communal enterprise shared with colleagues to whom he bore loyalty and with whom he wanted to get the job done in spite of every damn difficulty that arose."[28]

> The outstanding impression of the SI Greek Desk was the prevailing friendly spirit and desire to do the job for the job's sake. This was made possible by a nucleus of men who had been friends before the war, respected each other's abilities, and were deeply interested in Greece. Newcomers were indoctrinated with a feeling of mutual loyalty and whether it was Cairo, Cyprus, Izmir, or Athens the spirit was catching.[29]

Young's own analysis of the Greek Desk as well as the internal assessment by the United States intelligence community of the archaeologists' contributions to the period of the Dekemvriana and the Cold War in Greece have not yet been made available. They remain classified, as do personnel files for several of the archaeologists and many documents relating to the end of the war in Greece. The contributions of Else and Edson in spearheading the post-liberation Athens station clearly merited greater responsibility in Washington. Sperling's and Daniel's accounts of their dangerous espionage expeditions in the permeable northern border regions of Greece were among the last documents declassified by the Central Intelligence Agency. No doubt that is where the next chapters of the story lie.

Who's Who

Note: The numbers preceded by "X-" indicate Cairo agents. The other numbers are internal OSS designations that were often used in place of names for security in letters and cabled intelligence.

WASHINGTON AND THE UNITED STATES

William Donovan, 109, director of OSS, Washington
General John Magruder, OSS deputy director of intelligence overseeing SI
David Bruce, first chief of OSS, SI, then head of OSS London
Whitney Shepardson, 154, OSS, chief of SI
Florimund Duke, 110, OSS, Southeastern Europe SI
William Bell Dinsmoor, Monuments Commission, ASCSA archaeologist, Columbia
Thomas Karamessines, (X-2) in Turkey, then U.S. embassy, Athens, CIA

FOREIGN NATIONALITIES BRANCH OF OSS

DeWitt Clinton Poole, assistant chief; Princeton University, Institute for Advanced Study
Benjamin Meritt, chief of chancery division, Princeton and Washington; ASCSA, Agora, Institute for Advanced Study
T. Leslie Shear, chief of volunteer readers, Princeton and Washington; ASCSA, director of Agora Excavations, Princeton professor

Carl Blegen, chief of chancery division, Washington; ASCSA, Yale, University of Cincinnati professor, director of Troy excavations

Alison Frantz, political analyst, chancery division, Washington; Smith College; Columbia Ph.D., ASCSA, Agora photographer

Lucy Talcott, social science analyst, chancery division, Washington; Radcliffe; ASCSA, Agora registrar; Yale Classics Department staff

GREEK DESK

Ulius L. Amoss, lieutenant colonel, AUS, chief COI/OSS Greek Operations; GIP; chief of Cairo Operations, March–July 1943

Rodney S. Young, 765, 4224; ("Roger") Pigeon; chief Greek Desk SI Cairo; Dove, chief of NIKI I, founder of Young Plan; and OSS Athens Base October–November 1944; ASCSA, Agora, Princeton, University of Pennsylvania professor

James "Jim" ("O'Neal") Oliver, Jr., major, AUS, Owl, instructor, Area A, Greek Desk SI Cairo; Rhinoceros, chief, Greek Desk SI Bari 1943–44; ASCSA; Agora; Yale; Barnard College professor

John L. "Jack" (Cronin) Caskey, major, AUS, 607, Chickadee, chief, Izmir SI, 1943–44; chief, SI Munich, 1945–46; Yale University; Troy, director of Lerna and Kea excavations; University of Cincinnati professor

Dorothy Hanna Cox (Hiram), Thrush, 718; reports officer, GWRA Izmir; Bryn Mawr and Columbia; Colophon, Troy, Kourion, Lapithos, Tarsus ASCSA excavations; Yale Classics staff

John Franklin "Pete" Daniel III, major, AUS, Duck, Cyprus chief, Greek Desk SI, 1943–44; "Havana" chief 1944; Young Plan SI operative (Florina); ASCSA; Agora; Kourion; University of Pennsylvania professor

Jerome L. "Jerry" Sperling, major, AUS; 174 Cairo, Sparrow, Sapsucker, OWI, Istanbul, Basil, head of Greek SI, Istanbul, liaison with Emniyet; Cairo Young Plan; June–October 1944; Young Plan SI operative Central Macedonia SI Salonika, 1944–45; chief SI, Young Plan, 1945–46, University of Cincinnati; Yale professor; Troy excavations

Sterling Dow ("Silver"), chief of Washington Greek Desk SI; Cairo, September 20–December 18, 1943, temporary chief of Cairo Greek Desk SI, November 1943, ASCSA, Agora; Harvard professor

Alekko Georgiades, X-5, Cairo's Gander and Istanbul's Aster, Edirne chief

Charles Edson, lieutenant, AUS, Eagle, Greek Desk SI Cairo October 28,

1943, Reports; chief OSS Athens, January–July 1945; Harvard, ASCSA, University of Wisconsin professor

Gerald Else, captain, USMC, Greek Desk SI Cairo SI, November 1943–44; chief OSS Athens, November 5, 1944–January 9, 1945. Harvard; ASCSA, State University of Iowa and University of Michigan professor

Margaret Crosby (Missy), reports officer Washington, Cairo, June–November 1944, Athens, November 1944–May 1945; Bryn Mawr, Yale Ph.D.; ASCSA; Agora excavations

Virginia Grace (Tiggie), reporting, translation, Greek Desk Istanbul February–June 1944; Izmir reporting, translation, cipher, clerk and secretary; Bryn Mawr Ph.D.; ASCSA; Agora, Kourion, Lapithos, and Tarsus excavations

Richard Treat Bruère, lieutenant, USN, ONI. Seconded to OSS Greek Desk SI Bari, Black Camel; ASCSA, University of Chicago professor

Sherman Wallace, chief of Greek Desk SI, Washington, ASCSA; 1944–46, historian of OSS SI

Margaret ("Miggy") Hill Wittmann, Reports, Greek Desk Washington; ASCSA

Clio Philippidou Adossides, lieutenant RHAF, ("Colonel"), assistant section officer; March 15, 1943, Cairo; Translation, cipher, cables, personnel; OSS Athens November 1944–46

Demetrios Petrou, Penguin, early 1943, former British agent in ME; Cairo Greek Desk liaison, personnel, interrogation, contacts, Greek civilian

Constantine Yavis, Bushtit, OSS Athens

Frederick Tunnell, Greek Desk SI, Cairo, ASCSA

Christian Freer, G2 Cairo; acting head of Greek Desk Cairo; executive officer OSS Athens; chief OSS Athens July 1945–September 1946

LABOR DESK, CAIRO

Mort Kollender, Carl Devoe, Costas ("Gus") Couvaras

OSS CAIRO

Col. John Toulmin, head of OSS Cairo, September 1943–August 1944

Gen. Harry S. Aldrich, general, head of OSS Cairo, from August 1944 on

Stephen Penrose, chief, Near East SI, then chief, SI

Moses Hadas, chief, R&A, Greek Section, Cairo; Athens Base; ASCSA

George Emanuel, Ibis when interrogator; Egret when producing intelligence

Panos Morphopoulos

SPECIAL OPERATIONS AND MARITIME

George H. McFadden, lieutenant, USNR, 746, Daffy; ONI seconded to OSS owner of the *Samothrace;* Princeton alumnus; patron of University of Pennsylvania's Kourion excavations

Christ J. Petrow, lieutenant, junior grade, USNR, Petrel, chief of Alexandria and "Elba" (MU) Greek-American, Harvard Law School, July 1943

Everett J. (Johnny) Athens, ensign then lieutenant, Albatross, (MU) chief, "Boston," then SO mission to Euboea EAM and Chicago mission

George Vournas, Vulture, GIP, Greek-American, New York lawyer, AHEPA president

Gerald K. Wines, SO, Allied Military Mission, arrived in Greece via Tochra in December 1943, departed in May 1944, returned in October 1944

Robert Moyers, lieutenant SO, established hospital for Allied Military Mission in Greece

Spiro Kapponis (Cappony), Chicago mission

NON-OSS AMERICANS

Cairo

Laird Archer, chief, Near East Foundation in Greece, U.S. Office of Foreign Relief and Rehabilitation, and UNRRA mission to Greece

Ralph Kent, Athens College, ONI, JICAME, Cairo

Arthur Parsons, ASCSA, Agora, U.S. embassy, political analyst, UNSCOB

Istanbul Consulate

Burton Berry, U.S. consul general; secretary to the U.S. embassy in Athens; secretary to the U.S. embassy in Ankara, Turkey

Gladys Davidson Weinberg, Corinth excavations, special assistant for Greece, State Department

Lanning MacFarland, 550, (Packy), Juniper, chief OSS Istanbul; replaced by Frank Wisner

Frank Wisner, reports chief, OSS Istanbul; OSS Germany; chief of plans, CIA

Izmir, U.S. Consulate

Ellis A. Johnson, U.S. consul
H. Lanning Williams, lieutenant, junior grade, USNR, shipping advisor, ONI
Homer Davis, special assistant for Greece, State Department
Nick Kyrtatos

Izmir, British Consulate

Noel Rees, 106, ("Hadzis"), head of MI-6, replaced by Dudley Bennett
David Pawson, 107, head of SOE, replaced by A. Payton
Michael Parish, 114, MI-9
Morrison Bell, MI-5

British in Istanbul

Harold Gibson, MI-6 chief
Lt. Col. Antony Simmonds
Heather, MI-6 handouts

GREEKS IN IZMIR AND GREECE

Miliaressis, Greek consul, Izmir[1]
Athenasios Zangas, 701, RHN, working with the British, then the OSS Greek Desk
Alexander Levides, 102, RHN, HIS working with the British
Capt. Orestes Valasakis, 705, RHN, HIS working with the British
Comm. Stamboulis, RHN, Greek shipping advisor and harbormaster, Greek consulate, Izmir
Boyotas, 101, Pawson's man at Cheshme, Greek consulate, Izmir
Broom, previous cell of Greek agents in Evros, found by OSS to be unsatisfactory
Euripides Bakirdzis, colonel, president and secretary of foreign affairs of PEEA
Dimitrios Psarros, head of EKKA, republican resistance group in Greece

Stefanos Sarafis, ELAS chief
Nikolas Zervas, chief, EDES
Ares Veloukhiotes, ELAS
Laurel, Evros guerrillas
Odysseas, chief ELAS guerrilla in Evros until February 1944
Telemachos, head of Odysseas's death battalion in Evros
Kriton, ELAS leader who succeeded Odysseas in Evros
Athinodoros, EAM political commissar in Salonika
Lykourgos, leader of the Evros guerrillas

TURKISH AGENTS OF MILLI EMNIYET MÜFETTISLIGI (EMNIYET) (TURKISH SECURITY, INTELLIGENCE, AND SECRET POLICE)

Naci Bey, "Aunt Jane," high chief, Ankara
Recai Bey, 113, Grosbeak, head of Aegean area, colonel, Turkish Army
Tahsin Bey, 114, representative in Kusadasi, lieutenant, Turkish Army
Celal Bey, Savory, counterintelligence chief in Istanbul 1943, colonel, Turkish army
Tevfik Bey, Paprika, military intelligence chief, Istanbul
Saim Bey, Poppy, agent near Edirne, lieutenant colonel, Turkish army
Shevket Bey, Lavender, chief, Cheshme and Reshadiye, *caymacam* of Bergama
"Mint," agent in Canakkale
Halil Bey, agent in Marmaris
Hamdy Bey, agent in Marmaris

YOUNG PLAN PERSONNEL IN ATHENS, SALONIKA, FLORINA, AND THROUGHOUT GREECE

SI: Rodney Young (Dove), Jerome Sperling (Sparrow), Gerald Else, John Franklin Daniel (Duck), Alekko Georgiades (Gander), Costas Couvaras (Plover), George Emanuel (Egret when producing SI; Ibis when interrogating), Tom Stix (also transportation officer)
Reports: Margaret Crosby, Pauline Manos (also office manager), Elias Pepper, and Tom Bartholomay (temporary)
Security: Lt. H. G. Nickles
Finance: Lt. William Peratino

Communications: Capt. George Chrysostomas, Joseph Rudas, Sgt. William
  Gross, Cpl. Tom Lantzas, and Cpl. Martin Dickson
Services: Sgt. Chris Meledones
R&A: Jay Seeley and Constantine Yavis (Bushtit), Charles Edson (Eagle),
  and Moses Hadas
Greek Liaison: Petrou (also SI)

OSS Greek Desk Missions

Mission	Location(s)	Dates	Rating	Agent(s)	Wireless Operator(s)	Sub Sources/Other
Settler	Athens	8/16/43–12/44	"excellent"	X-3, Grackle, George Gerakakis aka Apostolides, Greek Army private	X-6, Hummingbird, Yannis Theodoros aka Ted Theotokis, Greek air force sgt. / X-33, Spyros (Spencer) Mouhas, Greek	Cardinal, Evros guerrilla
Sorcery	Evros/Edirne	7/43–10/44	"worthy of highest praise"	X-5, Gander, Aster, Alexander (Alekko) Georgiades, agent-operator, Greek-American, U.S. Army lt.	X-5, Nick Kantaras aka Nick IV	
				George Tsarparas	"Giorgio"	Goose, aka Manoli II, Greek, cipher, secretarial
				Gosling, Haralambos Lavras, aka Marty, Greek gendarmerie sgt.	"Vassili II," American	Broom, Anglo-Greek intelligence organization / Laurel, Evros guerrilla
untitled	Samos	9/1–18/43		Zisinos Karakristodoulou, 110, Izmir's first agent, veteran of HIS and British services, recruited by Manoudis		
Brigand	Athens	10/43–	"complete failure"	X-8, Falcon, Manousos (Fass) Fasoulakis, aka Christos Papayannis, RHN lt., worked with EAM and Zangas, moved	X-11, Stavros Michalopoulos, Greek Army 2nd lt.	X-8A, George (Leo) Leodis, RHN

to Evvia in 1944

						X-10, aka Sid, Greek
Crayon	Mytilene/ Tinos/ Cyclades	10/43– 10/44	"qualified success" "useful"	X-7, Vassilios (Vasili) Koskinas, Greek Army lt, veteran of HIS, Seagull Tern, subagent	X-12, Dimitrios (Nick II) Karapatakis, Greek Army private from Samos Yanni Koukou, Greek X-45, Michael Zervas, Greek refugee recruited in Izmir X-10, aka Sid, Greek	X-43 set up subagents on the islands
Gasoline	Chalkidiki/ Salonika	12/43– 12/44	"striking success"	X-39, Roadrunner, Kosmas Yapitsoglou, RHN ensign veteran HIS caique captain	X-54, Elias Doundolakis aka Kando or Nikolaou, repatriated, Greek-American, U.S. Army private, brother of X-53	Mockingbird
Phalanx	Salonika	12/30/43– 11/44	"best mission"	X-17, Broiled Pheasant, Anargyros (Bill) Ballas, Greek Army capt., worked for Kanellopoulos, knew Young in Albania X-16, Stewed Pheasant, Photios (Steve) Stavreas, Greek Army capt., prewar intelligence agent	X-21, Pheasant, Yannis (John or John I) Moraitis, Greek Air Force sgt., radio operator for Tsigantes mission in 1942	
Oracle	Parnassus/ Lamia/ Amphissa	4/44	"useful" "moderately successful"	X-26, Loon, Yannis (Lefty) Lagouranis, aka Yannis Eleftheriou, Greek Army lt. X-27, Jay, Yannis Sorokos,	X-44, "Jackson," Greek, Izmir-trained for Skyros, replaced X-12 X-14, Nicholas Aletras, "Nick	

Mission	Location(s)	Dates	Rating	Agent(s)	Wireless Operator(s)	Sub Sources/Other
				"Jack I," aka Yannis Politis, Greek Army lt.	"II," Greek Army corp.	
Despot	Evvia/Athens	12/43	"one of most successful missions"	X-24, Pelican, George Persakis, aka George I, Greek Air Force private, worked in Bishop of Karystos's escape organization, disappeared	X-19, Dodo, Polydoros (Doros) Mouzourakis, Greek Army 1st lt., refused SI training, but prolific intelligence producer	Stewed Dodo Fried Dodo
Kore	Athens	canceled	compromised by politics	Markos (Marko) Kladakis, Greek Army major, leftist, role in March 1944 mutiny, McBaine's man	X-29, Duckling, Diogenes (Dios) Fanourakis, Greek Army capt., later with Helios	Harry (Harold) Savaides, American
untitled	Mytilene/ Lemnos	11/11/43		Recruited by Cox, reports processed under Thrush or Chickadee		
Emerald	Samos stay-behind	11/43– 10/44	Not rated	X-40? Antonios Michalainas aka Miltiades, American X-37, Nikolaos Hadzidimitriou, "Simo," agent/courier/wireless operator, recruited by Izmir	"Dimitrios III," Greek from Tigani	
Enfant	Patras	canceled	"failed due to poor handling in Bari"	George Sakelleris, "George II," Greek Army capt., refused to go in	Harry (Harold) Savaides, American	
Apple	Florina	canceled	Not rated			

Code name	Location	Date	Evaluation	Personnel		
(MO)	Crete	6/3/44		Starling, Grady McGlassen, U.S. Army lt. col. John Moatsos		Nicholas Lampathakis, lt. Jack
Chicago (SO)	Evros	12/43–8/31/44		Terfi, James Kellis, U.S. Air Corps capt., arrived in Istanbul 12/43, in Evros 3/29/44 E. J. (Johnny) Athens, USNR lt. Thomas Curtis (MU), U.S. Marines gunnery sgt.		Greek-Americans X-33, Vern, Spyridon (Gus) Kapponis (Spiro Cappony), USNR X-61, George Psoinos, USNR Michael Angelos, USNR
Floka	Florina/Salonika area	2/27/44		X-50, Hawk, Dimitrios Koronaios, aka Dimitrios II, agent-operator, Greek Army lt., Young recruit		
Dago	North Dodecanese	3–6/44	"very creditable"	Binelli, Italian capt., recruited by Caskey		Capon, reports of Italian origin
	Rhodes, Leros, Kos	6/44		A-11, Curlew, Sabato Carotenuto, lt.	X-36, Franco Merlo, sgt. major	A-2, Gabriel Fabrini and Francisco Fossati, sgt.
Horse-breeders	Volos/Pelion	5/44	"superb" "most efficient" "finest of the missions . . . by SI"	X-53, Stork, George Doundoulakis, aka George Papadakis or George IV, repatriated Greek-American from Crete, U.S. Army sgt., brother of X-54, worked with Patrick Leigh Fermor (SOE),		X-47, Aristotelis (Telis, Aristotle) Hadzidakis, Greek Army, veteran of Cretan resistance

Mission	Location(s)	Dates	Rating	Agent(s)	Wireless Operator(s)	Sub Sources/Other
				awarded Legion of Merit		
Alcinoos	Corfu, Ionian islands	3/25/44		George Kaloudes, recruited by Bari; George Targakis	Scudder Georgia "the American Lord Byron"	
Pericles (Labor Desk) SI	Karpenisi Special Mission to EAM Central Committee	4/8/44–10/44	"outstandingly successful"	X-75, Plover, Costas Couvaras Greek-American	Constantine Papadopoulos, aka Alex	John Kakossaios ("George Kardiakis"), Greek Seaman's Union, liaison with the EAM; Zeno, EAM source
Gold	West Thrace/ Sidherokastro	4/4/44		X-28, Peacock, Panayiotis Kalfas, aka Panos I, from Ferrai (Evros), recruited by Kladakis and Georgiades	X-34 "Nick IV" Greek Army private, from Alexandroupolis	
Byzantine	Athens	4/3/44	recalled en route because of politics	X-86, Cormorant, Yannis Komninos aka John V	X-90, "Mario", Greek-American, U.S. Army private, refused to go in	
Ali Pasha/ Molossos	Epirus	6/44			X-67, "Panos II"	
Iron	Chalkidiki/ Salonika	6/44	"failed," "never reached ultimate destination"	X-28, Partridge, Panayiotis Kalfas, "Panos I," Evros cloth merchant	X-34, backed out	

Operation	Location	Date	Rating	Personnel	Additional personnel
Helios	South Dodecanese	6/24/44	Sunk by British Raiding Forces	X-29, Duckling, Diogenes (Dios) Fanourakis, Greek Army capt., originally to serve with Kladakis on Kore, died on Chalki, 11/1/44	X-90, "Mario," Greek-American, U.S. Army private, refused to go in; X-49, "Jack II" Greek Army lt, refused to go
Archangel	Dodecanese/ Tilos	8/44	canceled	Duckling Mike, Michael Katsaras, aka Mike II, American	Michael Panayiotakis, "Michael," Cyprus recruit, former SBS guide on Tilos
Lucian	Leros, Patmos	6/20/44	"useful"	A-12, Little Thrush, Luciano Meazza, recruited in Izmir	
	Lisso	8/44		Little Thrush, Michele and Giovanni Veneto Franco Merlo, sgt. major	
Ulysses (MO)	Volos/Pelion	4/44	Not rated	Knapp, briefed and infiltrated into Evvia Shambos	
Helot	South Peloponnese	6/25/44– 10/44	"most creditable"	A-21, Finch, John Fatseas, aka John IV, Greek-American	A-21, Chanticleer, "Charles," Greek-American, U.S. Army corp.

Mission	Location(s)	Dates	Rating	Agent(s)	Wireless Operator(s)	Sub Sources/Other
				A-21, Phoebe, "Panos IV" Lapwing, aka Larry of Athletes		
Vlach	Parnes/Attica	7/44	Not rated	X-6, Toucan, Theophanis Christophes, Greek	X-6, Ted, from Settler	
Stygia	Evvia	7–10/44	"unqualified success"	Tomtit, Tom Stix, U.S. Army 1st lt. Flamingo, John Calvocoressi, aka Grover, Greek-American	X-90, Marios, Greek-American, U.S. Army private	
Ellas	Kardhitsa, Thessaly	9/1/44	Not rated	Kingfisher, Christopher Kantianis, "Kandy," Greek-American, USNR lt. jg. (Archie or Chris) Argyris, Greek-American, capt.	Kachiroubas "Jacky" A-35, "Evarestos," "Eugene," Greek	
Ajax	Aetolia, Agrinion to Gulf of Arta	8/44	"disappointing"	A-26, Marty, Greek	A-26, Antonis, Greek	
Athletes	West Peloponnese Elasson, Katerini, Kozani, Larissa	7/44	"unsuccessful"	A-21, Lapwing, "Larry" A-25, Linnet, "Leon," Greek	A-25, Achilleas, Greek	
Fleece		8/44	Not rated	Mountain Canary, "Monty" Nightingale, "Manty"	X-49, "Jack II," Greek Army lt.	

Operation	Location	Date	Rating	Members		
Elephant	Epirus Zervas/ EDES Headquarters	7/44	"useful"	A-24, Black Bustard, Milton Stavis, Greek-American, U.S. Army capt. Swan, Stathakos, Greek-American, U.S. Army lt.	A-24, "George VI," Greek radio operator	Sidney Stokos, Greek-American, U.S. Army corp.
Simmons (Special Projects)	Salonika	10/2–16/44	Delayed waiting for Bulgarian-speaking wireless operator	John Russell, aka Jean, 2nd lt.	A-28, Lt. Nikolaos Sotiriou "Neil," Greek Sacred Brigade (squadron)	George Skouras
Gorgon	Lamia, Evvia Straits Stilis, Domokos Pass	8/44	"successful"	Condor, "Sophoklis," Greek	A-27, Cormorant, Charalambos, Greek	
Bankers		6/44	Not rated			
Niki I Young Plan	Evvia/Athens	9–10/44	Not rated	X-100, Dove, Rodney Young, previously Pigeon	George Chrysostomas, U.S. Army capt.	Charles Meledones, U.S. Army sgt.
Niki II	Athens/ Salonika	10/44	Not rated	Sparrow, Jerome Sperling George Skouras Petrel, Chris Petrow (MU), USNR lt. jg. Penguin, Dimitris Petrou		

Mission	Location(s)	Dates	Rating	Agent(s)	Wireless Operator(s)	Sub Sources/Other
Smokey			Not rated			
Lyric	Mytilene/ Lemnos	8/44	Not rated		"Niko," American	
Salaminia	Mytilene/ Lemnos	9/14– 16/44	Not rated	Thrush, Dorothy Cox		Virginia Grace
Mastic	Chios	9/21– 23/44	Not rated	Thrush, Dorothy Cox		

Notes: Ratings recorded in History of OSS Cairo. NARA 226/99 and 226/92A/3/36.

OSS Bases and Secret Harbors or Coded Targets

Rodney Young, chief, Greek Desk SI, June 1942–March 1943
Sterling Dow, chief, Greek Desk SI, 1943–February 1944
Sherman Wallace, chief, Greek Desk SI, February 1944–on
Margaret Crosby, Reports
Gerald Else, Reports
Charles Edson, R&A
Milton Anastos, Recruiting
Margaret (Miggy) Hill Wittmann, Reports

TURKEY

Izmir

Capt. J. L. Caskey, U.S. Army, SI, chief, code name Chickadee
Capon, intelligence from Italians under Lieutenant Colonel Del Balzo and Binelli
Dorothy Cox, SI, code name Thrush, Reports, GWR, interrogation
Virginia Grace, clerical, ciphers, reports, June–November 1944
Dimitrios Stamatopoulos, 703, Comm. RHN, "Stopson," Caskey's shipping adviser and assistant chief, veteran of British service, under 102, OSS, July 22–November 30, 1943
Sgt. Romeo Soucy, radio operator

Lt. Comm. A. Koutisikopoulos, RHN, code name Kite, chief Greek adjutant, maritime expert, translator, intelligence officer, replaced Stamatopoulos in December 1943

Theochares Stavrides, Athens College; supply, interrogation, reports, translation, arrived May 25, 1944; GWRA cover

Vassilios Koskinas, X-7, Greek consulate, Izmir, code name Seagull

Taxakis, X-9, Lt. RHN, Caskey's first radio operator, replaced by Romeo Soucy

X-56, "Tom"

"Panos III"

"Miami" or "Nea Efessos": Kushadasi, fifty miles south of Izmir; in June 1943; first caique arrived in late September 1943

George Manoudis, 704, chief, code name Bittern; warrant officer Greek gendarmerie and formerly with Greek service

Karnambitsa: anchorage at Mykale, near Dip Burnu on Dilek Peninsula at Straits

"Key West": at Arslan Burnu, approximately three miles south of Kushadasi

George Manoudis, chief, July 1943–November 1944

Evanthia Manoudis, wife of above, typing and translations, supply, June 1944

"Boston": Rasadia (Reshadiye) near Chandarli, forty to fifty miles northwest of Izmir

Lt. Jg. Everett "Johnny" Athens (MU), chief

Lt. John Savage (MU), chief (August 1944). Shrike, 2nd Lt. Ord. adjutant, supply officer, former chemistry teacher at Athens College; arrived Izmir September 1943; cover consular employee

Marion J. Spence

Richard S. Buchholz, Communications

"Nick VII," Nick Kyrtatos

"Portland": Aivalik

"Norfolk": Plati, island off coast between Aivalik and Chandarli

"Dover": Istanbul

Jerome Sperling, code name Basil Sparrow, chief of Greek Desk

Virginia Grace, clerk

Therapia/Tarabya: OSS safe house on the shores of the Bosphorus

"Cardiff": Kum Kale

"Pittsburgh": Edirne (Adrianople); established September 1943
    Alekko Georgiades, code name Gander, Aster, chief

"Ottawa": Chorlu in Turkish Thrace

"Detroit": Ipsala Evros crossing in Turkish Thrace

"New Orleans": Enos, on the Evros delta in Turkish Thrace

"Plymouth": Gallipoli Peninsula

"Bristol": Tenedos/Bozceada

"Dublin" (Imbros/Imroz) never opened
    Curtis, Mossidus to be chief
    George Psoinos, X-61, radio operator

"Havana": initially Kastellorizo, then Miliontes on the Knidian Peninsula
    John Franklin Daniel, SI, code name Duck, chief
    Petros Kritikos (Symi), Miaoulis Miaoulis (Khalki), Emmanuel
        Avtas
    Michael Katsaras (Tilos), code name Duckling Mike
    "Nick VIII"

CYPRUS

    John Franklin Daniel, SI, chief

Episkopi/Kourion: University of Pennsylvania excavations, McFadden's villa

"Cincinnati": Pissouri harbor on the southwest coast

Karavostasi: maritime caique repair base

Metamorphosis Farm: "the cooler"

EGYPT

Cairo
    Rodney Young, Charles Edson, Gerald Else, Clio Adossides,

Dimitrios Petrou, Greek Desk liaison, personnel, interrogation, contacts

Alexandria: OSS Maritime caique base
Chris Petrow, chief, January 1944

"Area A": Ras el Kanayas (Schools and Training) Camp in Western Desert
Major Koch, Major John Vassos, chief; Jim Oliver, George "Chris" Chrysostomas, trained radio operators

GREECE

Athens
Rodney Young, Gerald Else, Margaret Crosby, Dimitrios Petrou (code name Penguin), Tom Stix, Clio Adossides, Charles Edson

"Cuba": Vathi, Samos September–November 1943
Founded by Caskey, chief
Dimitrios Stamatopoulos, 703, Comm. RHN, "Stopson," July 22–November 30, 1943
Andreas Koutsikopoulos, code name Kite, former harbormaster at Vathi
John Savage succeeded Caskey
X-12, Karapatakis, radio operator

"Halifax": Krouso, Kassandra. Mail drop for Gasoline, Floka, and Phalanx; blown and replaced by Olympia on the Struma Gulf in June 1944

"New Orleans": (?) Evros delta

"Lisbon": Kalamos, Evvia

"Elba": Kea
Chris Petrow (MU), chief; Marion Spence, Richard Buchholz, Dodson

"Bermuda": Syra

Salonika
Jerry Sperling

CHICAGO MISSION TARGETS

"Milwaukee," bridge over Evros at Svilengrad in Bulgaria

"Joliet," bridge over Evros at Antheia, east of Alexandroupolis

"Chicago," bridge over Evros at Marasia

"Cicero," bridge over Evros at Karaagatch, Greece

ITALY

Bari: sent Alcinoos mission to Corfu and Molossos/Ali Pasha missions to Epirus
James Oliver, chief
Lt. Richard Bruère, assistant

BRITISH BASES

Levant: Beirut: British Royal Navy Base: Haifa: SOE base used by U.S. caiques

Cyprus: Famagusta, Paphos

Turkey: Khioste MI-6 and MI-9; Cheshme MI-6 and MI-9
Rees chief

Egrilar/Eritrea: SOE; Rees owned the island

Port Deremen: SOE, LSF, LRDG

Notes

PROLOGUE

1. Several books by key players treated the Cicero affair, but none uncovered Caskey's full role: Bazna 1962; Moysich 1950; Kahn 1978, 69, 345n; Rubin 1989; Heatts 1995, 48; Wires 1999; Breuer 1989, 176.

2. Lodwick 1947; Seligman 1996; Moss 1950; Myers 1955; Casson 1941; Hamson 1947; Hammond 1983; Fielding 1953, 1954; Parish 1993; Sweet-Escott 1965; Woodhouse 1948, 1976, 1982; Elliott 1991; Clive 1985; Grundon 2007; Waugh 1955; Hamson 1989; Byford-Jones 1945; Wallace 1982; Ward 1992; Windmill 2006. John Cook's unpublished wartime memoir is housed at the British School at Athens.

3. Hinsley 1990; Howard 1990; Foot and Langley 1979; Murphy 2006; Gerolymatos 1992 and 2004; Rees 2003; Hawkes 1982; Hunt 1989; Sweet-Escott 1975; Cooper 1989; Beevor 1991; Haag 2004; Clogg 2000; Wylie 2007; Jakub 1999; Goulter-Zervoudakis 1998, 165–94; Foot 1992, 295–300.

4. Koliopoulos 1977; Malakasses 1980; Zannas 1964; Konstas 1955; Levides 1975; Paspati 2009. For Turkey, see Ozkan 2001. Ladas 2010 gives a fictionalized account of the Levant Schooner Flotilla.

5. Vasilis Petrakos has investigated the work of the Greek Archaeological Service during the war and German occupation. At a colloquium, "Archaeology, Politics, and War: Italy, Greece, and Germany in World War II," held at the 2010 AIA annual meeting, C. Jansen delivered "The German Archaeological Institute during the Age of Extremities: National Socialism, World War II, and Reconstruction under Democratic Auspices," and G. Salmieri spoke on "Archaeology and Fascism in Italy: The Role of Institutions and the Emergence of Local Initiative." Kahn 1978 and Breuer 1989 deal globally with German intelligence.

6. Ellen Kohler, interview by the author, May 2008. Also interview with Gareth Darbyshire, March 2009.

7. Journalist Vlanton investigated the Foreign Nationalities Branch of the OSS

(1982a, 31–84; 1982b (2) 36–104, (3) 65–132, (4) 63–110). David Price (2007) investigated the role of cultural anthropologists in intelligence services in southeast Asia during World War II, but no one has treated the archaeologists in the Mediterranean basin.

CHAPTER ONE

1. Hamilakis 2007, 169–204; Sakka 2002, 39; Hamilakis 2008; Markatou 2008; Mazower 2008; and Plantzos 2008.

2. German archaeologists had even infiltrated the hinterland of Corinth, which the Americans regarded as their own "turf." G. P. Stevens to Louis Lord, February 14, 1940, Admin 804/2/6, ASCSA.

3. Young to "Old Horse" (Alison Frantz), no date, Agora Excavation Archives. Agora, Young, ASCSA.

4. Metaxas's speech in Macris 1979, 343. Karamanos 1943 provides a different translation. Proclamation of the Prime Minister to the Greek People, October 28, 1940, no. 181, p. 15. Vatikhiotis 1998, 164–81. M 3-258-59.

5. For eyewitness accounts, see Homer Davis, "Greek War Relief and the Greek Spirit," in H. Davis 1942, 27; Stowe 1942, 90–91; Archer 1944; and Casson 1941. All references to NARA are cited by NARA Record Group, entry, and folder with each separated by /. Young, "The War," NARA 226/100/AD 2–9, 51–54.

6. Stowe 1942, 90–96.

7. Young to "Old Horse," no date.

8. This account is based on numerous letters and administrative files in the collection of the University Archives of the University of Cincinnati (UAUC), the Frantz Papers, Rare Books and Manuscripts Collection, Firestone Library, Princeton University (Frantz/PU), the University of Pennsylvania University Museum Archives (UPUMA), Bryn Mawr College, the Institute for Advanced Study (IAS), the American School of Classical Studies at Athens (ASCSA), the National Archives Records Administration in College Park, MD (NARA) and the American Philosophical Society (APS). Meritt 1984, 1. Stevens to Lord, October 28, 1940. Shirley Weber to Lord, February 6, 1941, Admin 310/5/4, ASCSA. Young's account of the Hymettus excavations is preserved in his notebooks in the ASCSA Archives and Young 1940. Langdon 1976, 1, accepts Young's interpretations.

9. Hamilakis 2008; Sakka 2008, 111–24. The American Socony Vacuum Oil Company (later Standard Oil of New Jersey) funded several American excavations. Admin 804/1/ 8, ASCSA.

10. For four years Young and Vanderpool shared the same room at Princeton and before that at St. Paul's School in New Hampshire. Their fathers and grandfathers had been friends and colleagues in Newark for decades. Young's father was on the board of Vanderpool's bank, and both were devout Episcopalians: Vanderpool's grandfather, Wynant, had been rector of Grace Church, and Young's father was on the vestry of the Episcopal cathedral, Trinity Church.

John Franklin "Pete" Daniel III of Berkeley worked briefly at the Agora for a season. Crosby worked on pottery; Grace launched her legendary career reconstructing ancient trading networks through the stamped handles of clay amphorae; Young became devoted to the Iron Age; and Meritt published the *Athenian Tribute Lists*. Homer Thompson to Ruth Washburn, May 8, 1974, and his ms. "Margaret Crosby as an Archaeologist," courtesy Mary Parker.

11. Daniel to Edith Dohan, April 26, 1939 (UPUMA).

12. Blegen fretted lest European hostilities "affect feelings in the [University of Cincinnati Classics] tearoom." To Caskey, April 17, 1939, UCUA. Hamilakis 2007, 195. Sakka 2002 and Hamilakis 2007, 169–73, 204, explored the archaeologists who used their discipline to promote nationalist ends of the Metaxas regime, such as Spyridon Marinatos, who within a month of Mussolini's invasion of Albania, undertook an excavation of Thermopylae to uncover the remains of the ancient Spartan defenders of Greek soil from the barbarians in 1939.

13. Instructions advised on food and fuel shortages, gas mask purchases, and bomb shelters. They disseminated news to the Near East Foundation's U.S. staff, Athens College, Monks Ulen, American Express, Hellenic College for Girls, American Tobacco Company, and American School. April 24, 1939. Admin 804/4 and 5/1, ASCSA.

14. APS Meritt. Jansen, presentation at the 2010 AIA annual meeting (see note 5 to the prologue).

15. After Germany's *Anschluss* with Austria, Meritt moved the printing of the School's publication, *Hesperia*, from Vienna to America. Meritt rescued Jewish archaeologists in Austria, Germany, and Italy who had lost their university and museum posts or were threatened with internment in concentration camps and found them temporary asylum at the Institute. He wrote, "I was in the last war as an enlisted infantryman. I did not like it, and I don't want to go again. I have two sons, and I don't want them to go. But I would fight and I would be glad to see my sons fight to preserve our American way of living. . . . we must become a militarized nation to defend ourselves. In plain self-interest . . . we ought to ship to England and France all the supplies they need to help them win." Meritt to Warren Barbour (U.S. senator from New Jersey), October 19, 1939. APS Meritt, Box 5/Barbour.

16. Jansen, presentation at the 2010 AIA annual meeting (see note 5 to the prologue).

17. Frantz to her mother, August 27 and September 9, 17, 19, and 28 and October 12, 15, 25, 1939, Frantz/PU. Stevens to Lord, September 6, 1939, Admin 310/5/2, ASCSA. They dug the shelter under the colonnade of the Gennadius Library across the street from the School. Yet Louis Lord, chair of the School's managing committee, wrote naively, "Next year war may collapse long before that . . . doesn't seem to be much enthusiasm for fighting on the German side. Of course, the English don't need to fight. They can win without it." Lord to Parsons, October 24, 1939. MacVeagh to Roosevelt, December 3, 1939, in Iatrides 1980, 178–80. "The students are getting much more out of their work than usual, for there are fewer of them." Shirley Weber to Lord, January 30, 1940, Admin 804/2/3 and 5 and 4/2, ASCSA.

18. Wace had conducted research in the Pindus Mountains at Samarina in

1911–12 and wryly commented in 1912, the year of the First Balkan War, that the "annual disturbance" in Albania had begun "earlier than usual." Wace and Thompson 1914, 12–13. In Athens British archaeologists conducted military intelligence on Turkey under the cover of the British Refugee Relief Commission and Passport Control, which granted visas, under the Foreign Office and under MI-5. John Travlos worked at the Bureau of Information annex to the British Legation; Compton Mackenzie worked in the legation; and Ellis Waterhouse worked at the British School. Gerolymatos 1992, 85; Mackenzie 1932; 1940, 253; Clogg 2000, 172 n. 29; Waterhouse 1986, 22–24.

19. Clogg 2000, 33. Others, such as A. R. Burn, worked in intelligence at the British Council. Parish 1993, 172; Gerolymatos 1992, 84–85. Wace's Cambridge student, archaeologist Frank Stubbings, was his assistant. Thomas Dunbabin was assistant director of the British School and later served British intelligence on Crete.

20. The well-respected excavator H. H. von der Osten coordinated Germany's espionage activities in Turkey until his arrest in Istanbul, and Walter Wrede, director of the DAI in Athens, doubled as local Nazi Party leader. Mazower 2008, 35.

21. Frantz to her mother, October 25, 1939, Frantz/PU.

22. Frantz to her mother, November 5 and December 8, 1939, and January 24, February 2, 18, and 27, 1940, Frantz/PU. Young tried to learn touch-typing, while others played cards to pass the time. Young to Homer and Dorothy Thompson, Wednesday 28 (February 1940). Agora, Young, ASCSA.

23. Wilhelm Dörpfeld, a bridge between the German and American excavators, died on April 26, 1940, and despite the Nazi provocations, the School sent a wreath to the German Archaeological Institute in his memory. Carpenter to Lord, April 25, and Shear to Lord, June 20, 1940, Admin 310/4/6 and 804/5/2, ASCSA. MacVeagh to Roosevelt May 4, 1940, in Iatrides 1980, 199–200.

24. Dinsmoor to the president of the DAI, May 10, 1940. U.S. State Department 1983, 525–31. Meritt went further. "After last week's invasion of three more neutral countries . . . Germany has placed herself in a position where mere convention would no longer play a part even in our dealing with that country. . . . incongruous that we should tolerate longer the hospitality of the aggressors and extend our hospitality to them . . . the only self-respecting thing for us now to do is to recall our diplomatic representatives to Germany and to invite the Germans to remove their diplomatic representatives from this country. . . . As a citizen of the United States I am ashamed that we keep up even a pretense of friendly relations." Meritt to Sumner Welles, May 13 and to Cordell Hull, May 17, 1940, APS Meritt, Box 17/W Gen. Hill and Stevens refused to resign from the DAI even if the United States entered the war.

25. After suffering over 60,000 casualties at Dunkirk, the Royal Navy had to evacuate in one week. *New York Post,* June 7, 1940. MacVeagh to Roosevelt, May 24 and 28, 1940, in Iatrides 1980, 206.

26. The Canadians took six weeks to reach Baghdad alone. Shirley Weber to Lord, July 28, 1940, Admin 804/5/2, ASCSA.

27. Henry Robinson left on the *Exminster* and Margaret Thompson on the *Ex-*

mouth. She arrived six weeks later in July, as her New York–bound ship fetched cargo 650 miles east in Turkey before braving Gibraltar and the Atlantic. Meanwhile, the French signed the armistice with Germany on June 21, 1940.

28. Frantz to Mary Frantz, April 4, 1940, June 2 and 13, 1940, Frantz/PU.

29. MacVeagh to Roosevelt, June 20, 1940, in Iatrides 1980, 208. Shirley Weber sent his manuscript of Schliemann's 1841–53 diary with Talcott and Frantz. Helen Wace and daughter Lisa spent the war outside Chicago.

30. Blegen, Report on Greece with Young Annotations "The War," NARA 226/100, p. 36. Crown Prince Paul, a Princeton alumnus, regularly joined the outings and appears in Clio Sperling's photographs.

31. Meritt pressured his congressman to advocate total preparedness and went "on record as being in favor of all necessary aid to Britain to make sure that Germany is defeated on the other side of the Atlantic." He urged all haste: "Our trouble is that we take so long to let our policies become effective that those who are our declared enemies can make almost any move they desire and leave us holding the bag." He commended Cordell Hull on his tough rhetoric, but demanded action. Meritt to Lane Powers (U.S. Congressman, NJ), September 17 and 24 and to Hull September 24, 1940, APS Meritt, Boxes 12/P Gen and 9/H Gen.

32. Young, Grace, and Vanderpool were in Athens, Hill and Peggy MacVeagh at Corinth, and John and Suzanne Young (no relation to Rodney) at Sounion. Rumanians, Serbs, Poles, Italians, and Greeks continued to use the Gennadius Library. Stevens to Lord, September 30 and October 9, 1940, Admin 310/5, ASCSA. MacVeagh diary, September 6, 1940, in Iatrides 1980. American School refugee scholar Heinrich Immerwahr secured a berth on an overcrowded boat with inedible food and undrinkable water. Meritt to Immerwahr, October 17, 1940, APS Meritt, Box 9/I Gen.

33. Hill to Meritt, October 25, 1940, APS Meritt, Box 9/Hill.

34. Young applied for the permit in September. Stevens to Lord, September 30, 1940. Meritt to Lord, October 7, 1940. Admin 310/4/6, ASCSA. MacVeagh diary, October 14, 1940, in Iatrides 1980, 230–31. Lord to Cordell Hull, October 7, 1940, NARA 59/Central Decimal File (hereafter CDF)/1306/368.115. Leslie E. Reed, the U.S. consul general, sent out State Department brochures entitled "When you must be your own Health Officer." September 18, 1940. Still around the School were Hill, Rodney Young, the Parsonses, the Stevenses, the Webers, the Vanderpools, and the John Youngs. September 30, 1940. Admin 804/1/10 and 5/1, ASCSA. MacVeagh diary, October 25 and 26, 1940, in Iatrides 1980, 233. On October 28, Mussolini and Hitler met in Florence as the invasion of Greece proceeded.

35. After Congress passed the Espionage Act in 1917, the ONI and the Military Intelligence Division placed naval and military attachés at U.S. legations in several European capitals through which the Bureau of Secret Intelligence (later the FBI) reported to the State Department. NARA 165/65/55/10039–11233.

36. Mussolini's elite Julia division, the Third Alpine with its fierce Wolf battalions and armored Centaurs, had led the way.

37. Markoyianni 1940 diary, in Hadjipateras and Fafalios 1995, 37–40. Stevens to

Lord, November 1, 1940, Admin 804/2/6 and 310/4/6, ASCSA. The *New York Times* (*NYT*) published its October 29 account on October 30, 1940.

38. Thanassis Voulgaropoulos remembers how as an eight-year-old boy he watched Italian planes, masquerading as Greek, bomb cinemas and schools before he fled to Khalkidiki with his mother and siblings. One plane dropped a bomb near the flatbed wagon carrying his family's provisions and blew the leg off a young girl in their entourage. Such deception is recorded in a November 3, 1940, account of a raid published in the *Los Angeles Times* on November 4, 1940. NARA 84/2694A/ 44–60.

39. MacVeagh in Iatrides 1980, 238. Peggy MacVeagh worked with Hill in Corinth and returned to Athens with Parsons on the morning of October 28. Stevens to Lord, November 1, 1940, Admin 310/4/6 and 804/2/6, ASCSA. October 31 Athens report in *NYT,* November 1, 1940.

40. The British minister Michael Palairet wrote that the Greeks would not appreciate a token military mission without troops and would "particularly resent our sending people whom they know to be Archaeologists and not soldiers." November 23, 1940. Higham 1986, 41; and AIR 8/514.

41. Archer noted in his diary that Greeks' spontaneous demonstrations of esteem and gratitude toward America ended his own neutrality. November 2, 1940. Archer 1944, 130–33. MacVeagh diary, October 31, 1940, in Iatrides 1980, 238. October 31 Athens report in *NYT,* November 1, 1940.

CHAPTER TWO

1. Lewis Jones, assistant commercial attaché, located the chassis November 2 and 7, 1940, in Archer 1944, 130, 136.

2. *Princeton Alumni Weekly,* April 28, 1941. Hetty Goldman also engaged in Greek relief during the Balkan Wars and World War I. Americans poured into the Near East Foundation (NEF) wanting to know how they could help. Stevens to Shear, December 13, 1940, and Stevens (age sixty-four) to Lord, January 20, 1941. Since the post office no longer accepted letters for the United States, MacVeagh forwarded School correspondence in the diplomatic pouch. Stevens to Lord, October 30 and November 1, 1940, Admin 804/4/3, 4 and 2/6, ASCSA. Quote from Meverette Smith, NEF relief worker in Salonika. NARA 84/2694A.

3. When teaching at the University of Michigan, Meritt wrote, "Greece is my second home. I respect and admire her past, her present, and her future. If I can do anything to give others my own point of view, I am always happy to do it." To Heracles Gazepis, secretary of GAPA, Ann Arbor, April 15, 1930, APS Meritt, Box 8/G Gen 2.

4. Meritt to Lane Powers, November 12, and to Cordell Hull, October, 28, 1940, and emendation. APS Meritt, Boxes 12/P Gen and 9/H Gen.

5. Capps to Lord, November 7 and 9, 1940, the latter of which quoted Rodman Peabody's cable. A. Winsor Weld to Lord, November 9, 1940. Peabody to Capps, November 9, 1940, and to Shear, November 15, 1940. MacVeagh to Peabody, November

12, 1940. NARA 84/2694A. Shear to Peabody, November 9 and 13, 1940. Shear wrote, "the $3,000 for the purchase of the ambulance was sent to Rodney Young as an individual." Stevens to Peabody, November 16, 1940; Peabody to Lord, November 20, 1940. Lord was affronted that Young had not consulted him. Lord to Stevens, January 10, 1941, and Stevens to Lord, February 24, 1941. Admin 804/2/7 and 4/3, 310/4/6 and 5/4, and 1001/2/2, ASCSA.

6. Athena Motorworks to Young, November 8, 1940, Admin 1001/2/2, ASCSA.

7. Meritt attended the School from 1920 to 1922, served as associate director from 1926 to 1928 and visiting professor from 1932 to 1933, and presided over its first Alumni Association meeting in December 1940. Basil Vlavianos, editor of the *National Herald*, wrote Meritt, "Your characteristically American stand . . . your eloquent and heart-stirring letter . . . will be published today" (November 9) and Meritt to Vlavianos, November 12, 1940. "It is a glorious achievement of the Greeks that they have been able to inflict punishing reverses in land operations on the axis powers. . . . facilitate the showing of moving pictures of these operations in the north in the newsreels of our cinema theatres." Capps to Greek ambassador Kimon Diamantopoulos, November 15, 1940. After November 21, checks poured in for the School's hospital unit, and Spyros Skouras invited Meritt to become a sponsor of Greek War Relief Association (GWRA). Greek colleagues deeply appreciated his support. Professor George P. Oikonomos, University of Athens and Academy of Athens, to Meritt, December 9, 1940: "friend, devoted entirely to Greece. . . . I thank you for your voice, raised so nobly." APS Meritt, Box 12/O Gen and 8/G Relief.

8. H. Davis to Meritt, December 16, 1940, newspaper clipping. Basil Vlavianos, M. J. Politis to Meritt, January 20, and D. Callimachos to Meritt, January 22, 1941. APS Meritt, Boxes 6/D Gen and 8/G Relief.

9. Prince Peter (Prinkipos Petros 1997) wrote the definitive history of the Albanian Campaign. See also Koridis 2003.

10. The British bombed the Italian naval base at Taranto and engaged in sea battles off Corfu. November 10, 1940, in Archer 1944, 137. The Greeks took 5,000 Italian prisoners and fed, shaved, deloused, and corralled them into POW camps outside Athens and in the Peloponnese. Casson 1941.

11. Tirana is the Albanian capital. Stowe 1942, 90–96. November 10 and 22, 1940, in Archer 1944, 137, 141; Casson 1941.

12. Spyros and George Skouras emigrated to the United States in 1908 and joined the U.S. Army Air Corps in World War I. Spyros became president of the National Theatres Corporation with 563 theaters and head of Twentieth Century Fox in 1942. He raised $10,000,000 (90 percent of which came from Greek-Americans) at charity balls and theater parties and, with AHEPA's help, created 300 committees to organize 2,000 Greek clubs and organizations. By late February 1941, the GWRA had 964 chapters and collected $5,263,000 for ambulances, bomb shelters, soup kitchens, refugee workshops, and assistance to veterans' widows and children since the soldiers were unpaid and their families received next to no compensation. See Saloutos 1964, 348; McNeill 1957; Munkman 1958; M. Davis 1942, 88–89; and Kyrou 1991, 111–28; Kyrou 2001.

13. The American Friends of Greece (with three Princetonian trustees and seven archaeologists—three from the Agora) assisted the GWRA, published *Greece 1821–1941* (American Friends of Greece 1941), *Greece Fights: The People behind the Front* (H. Davis 1942) and *Lest we Forget* (Karamanos 1943) and helped to plan for the postwar reconstruction of Greece.

14. *Time,* November 11, 1940; *Time* and *Fort Wayne News Sentinel,* December 7, 1940; and *Life* and *Time,* December 16, 1940. Greece responded by issuing a stamp with Roosevelt's image. The United States appropriated $50,000,000,000 of which $31,000,000 went to Britain, $11,000,000,000 to the USSR, and the remainder to other countries, such as Greece.

Meritt aided Britain and Greece financially and raved about the Greeks. "When I wrote to you I was pretty enthusiastic about the Greeks. . . . that's mild compared to what I am feeling now. What a people!" Meritt to Paul Mills, November 26, 1940, and Meritt to Dinsmoor, December 13, 1940. After Meritt spoke to the Dodecanesian National Council on November 30, its leader, Dr. N. G. Mavris, called America "that true heir of the most genuine democratic heritage of our ancestors." December 5 and 18, 1940. Meritt to Warren Barbour (U.S. senator from NJ), December 5, 23, 28, 1940; Meritt telegram to Lane Powers, December 16, 1940, and Meritt to FDR, December 18, 1940, APS Meritt, Boxes 5/Barbour, Box 6/Dinsmoor, 8/G Relief, 11/M Gen, and 12/P Gen.

15. The Greeks took Delvino and Himara on the twenty-second. December 25, 1940, in Archer 1944, 150. MacVeagh to Roosevelt, December 7, 1940, in Iatrides 2001, 32.

16. PRO FO 371/29818.

17. The tiny Royal Hellenic Air Force fought back, but was ill equipped with thirty-eight outdated planes and thirty-four officers to defend all of Greece and push back the Italians. One of four fighter squadrons supported the Greeks in Albania. The other three defended Athens, Piraeus, Central Greece, and Salonika. Mostly they attacked enemy bombers in the north and engaged in dogfights over Athens to protect the overcrowded refugee neighborhoods near Piraeus. December 15, 1940, in Archer 1944, 147.

18. Ann House to family, December 15, 1940, Memoirs, 165, 168, American Farm School; Marder 2004, 193.

19. Alexandra Zannas founded the Eleventh Greek Military Hospital at Athens College, an elite boys' prep school outside Athens, founded by her grandfather, Alexandrian Greek Emmanuel Benaki, and others, including Bert Hill, and equipped it with girls' dowry linens. Parmelee and Willms 1942, 47; M. Davis 1942, 84–89; December 15, 1940, in Archer 1944, 146, 147.

20. The School raised $20,000. With it, they reimbursed Young's father for the first ambulance and Shear cabled $3,500 to Athens on December 6, 1940, but it got delayed for three critical weeks. They canceled the second ambulance, named *Nike* and intended for Vanderpool. Before heading north, Young raided Frantz's, Crosby's, and the Thompsons' supplies for sheets, blankets, and thermos for the

ambulance and canteens. Admin 804/4/5 and Young to "Old Horse," no date (Agora, Young, ASCSA).

21. The Clio Sperling Collection has a photograph of Elli Adossides administering relief in Salonika during World War I. *The Philhellene* II: 3–4, March–April 1943, 3–5. Stevens cable to Lord December 3, 1940, Admin 804/3 and 1001, ASCSA.

22. Clio Adossides was an athlete, hiking and racing in ski competitions on Mt. Parnes. She had been skiing in Italy when Germany invaded France.

23. Dimitri Mitropoulos, later conductor of the New York Philharmonic, mentored her.

24. While the Greek fleet lay at anchor in Corfu's harbor, Clio had performed with a girlfriend. When they opened the shutters on the morning of October 28, 1940, the fleet had fled. The women jumped on an Australian ship bound for Athens, but because it was too big to squeeze through the Corinth Canal, it took three days to round the Peloponnese and get home. This story could not have been written without the testimony and archives of Clio Adossides Sperling.

25. Initially, the American School Committee provided all support, but later Greek funds joined the American dollars. The Bandage Circle included Peggy MacVeagh and her mother, Mrs. Lewis Jones, Mrs. Foy Kohler, and Mrs. Leslie Reed, wife of the chargé d'affaires, and Stevens's wife. John and Suzanne Young handled the broadcasts. MacVeagh 1942, 71–74. Stevens to Lord, October 31, 1940, and to Shear, January 13, 1941, Admin 804/2 and 1001, ASCSA.

26. Metaxas to MacVeagh. January 4, 1941. "The ambulance, although it looks empty . . . , is . . . filled . . . with the good wishes of the donors." Admin 804/1/4 and 310/5, ASCSA. Maniadakis later became the head of the dreaded security battalions, or Rallides. See chapters 9 and 11.

27. MacVeagh to King George II, December 18, 1940. Stevens to Shear, December 30, 1940, and January 6, 1941. MacVeagh to Metaxas, January 3, 1941, and Stevens to Lord, January 5 and 7, 1941, ASCSA.

28. *NYT,* January 7, 1941. Young brought rubber hospital sheeting, hospital supplies, blankets, medicines, forty pairs of socks, and milk from the Greek Red Cross and a large bale of woolen goods from the British community. Stevens to Shear, January 6 and February 8, 1941, Admin 804/1/4, ASCSA.

29. The bombardments destroyed Larisa on February 2, just after an earthquake had devastated it.

30. Metaxas secretly asked England to augment the tiny Greek air force. Initially, the British only gave planes, but these needed all-weather airfields and runways (available only near Athens) as well as antiaircraft defenses to protect them on the ground. This lack of landing fields west of Larisa limited their time near the front. Meanwhile, fog and bad weather in the mountains hampered flights and craft, and crews abandoned most of the planes that crash-landed. RAF personnel began to operate secretly in Greece in November, but until December 29 Metaxas refused to allow them build or augment airports south of Olympus. Wavell had opposed getting embroiled in Greece and evacuated planes from Greece to defend

Alexandria from Italian advances just 250 miles away in Cyrenaica, but Churchill insisted, convinced that the Germans would invade on January 20, 1941.

31. West 1998.

32. Frank Knox, secretary of the U.S. Navy, suggested Donovan to Roosevelt.

33. MacVeagh to Hull, February 3, 1941, NARA 84/2694A; Smith 1983, 48.

34. Meanwhile, MacVeagh wrote Roosevelt that "neither bad weather nor difficult terrain, nor enemy reinforcements, nor inferiority of equipment, nor deficiency in transport, nor lack of airplanes has yet halted the Greek advance." January 19, 1941, in Iatrides 2001, 32–33.

35. In spite of British insistence that Donovan's visit be given no publicity, newspapers chronicled how he traveled under the alias "Donald Williams." In Sofia, Donovan tried to persuade the Bulgarian king, Czar Boris III, not to join the Axis. In Belgrade on January 23, he tried to enlist the support of Prince Paul, the pro-German co-regent of Yugoslavia who later left with the defense minister to confer with Hitler. Meanwhile, Donovan met with General Dušan Simović, commander of the Yugoslav air force, and showed him a telegram from FDR, stating that "any nation which tamely submits on the grounds of being quickly overrun would receive less sympathy from the world than the nation which resists, even if this resistance can be continued only a few weeks." Simović replied that "Yugoslavia would not permit the passage of German troops through its territory" and assured Donovan that they would fight the Germans if they invaded either Yugoslavia or Bulgaria or made a move against Greece. Then Donovan advised MacVeagh that the United States should give gestures of encouragement to British sympathizers, i.e., supply the Greeks (MacVeagh to State, February 3, 1941, NARA 84/2694A). Donovan's attempt to persuade the Balkan heads of state to resist the Axis delayed Hitler's invasion of Greece for eight days. "Highlights of Conversation between Col. Wm. Donovan and the Chief of Aviation, Army General Simović," January 24, 1941, Balkans Trip, vol. 1, CIA Collection. Seen and noted by Cave Brown 1982, 157 and 843 n10. Telegram FDR to Donovan, January 20, 1941, and Donovan radio address to NBC and CBS, March 26, 1941, Donovan Miscellaneous Papers, Army War College (AWC), Box 1; Smith 1983, 47–48; and Danchev 1990.

36. The GWRA in Greece was known as the Vanderbilt Committee and involved a number of Americans, including Dr. Ruth Parmelee, the director of American Women's Hospitals in Greece, who accompanied House and Korizis. *Newark Star Ledger,* November 20, 1941.

37. NARA 84/2694A/56 121.8.

38. Young 1942, 22–26. See photographs of Clio Adossides Sperling.

39. MacVeagh to Roosevelt, February 23, 1941, in Iatrides 2001, 33.

40. Then Donovan visited British military, diplomatic, and secret intelligence outposts in Turkey, Cyprus, and Palestine with quick trips to Baghdad and Benghazi from Cairo and stops in Malta, Gibraltar, Lisbon, Madrid, London, and Dublin before returning to Washington. AWC Donovan Box 1.

41. Clio's friend—dancer Ralo Manou—opened the fourth. When casualties overwhelmed them, Tsolakoglou asked that more triage stations be opened. Mean-

while, American-trained Greek nurses worked at Florina, Verria, and Salonika. Young to Lucy Shoe, November 19, 1941, in Shoe's letter to School alumni, December 12, 1941 (Agora, Young, ASCSA). NARA 84/2694A.

42. Young 1942, 22–26.

43. Ibid.

44. Young, "The War," NARA 226/100/AD 2–9, 51–54; and Young 1942, 22–26.

45. Personal communication to the author from Clio Adossides Sperling.

46. All supplies were obtained by School employees, such as Arthur Parsons and Anastasios Adossides. Archaeologist and refugee scholar Karl Lehmann of New York University's Samothrace excavations contributed sleeping bags to the canteens. Stevens to Lord, March 3, 1941, Admin 804/4, ASCSA. Young to Lucy Shoe, November 19, 1941.

47. Personal communication to the author from Clio Adossides Sperling. Young to "Old Horse," no date (Agora, Young, ASCSA).

48. On February 13, Cretans broke the Albanian stalemate and pushed past Pogradets to take the heights northwest of the city at Trebenischte, Medjigorani, and Sen Deli, but were stopped by heavy snows.

49. Young to Lucy Shoe, November 19, 1941.

50. The Committee and the AIA sent money to the Society and the Greek Archaeological Service to safeguard ancient Athenian monuments and to the beleaguered Societies for the Promotion of Hellenic and Roman Studies in England. Stevens to Lord, February 1, 1941, Admin 804 and 310, ASCSA.

51. Stevens quoted an extract from Elli's postcard to Adossides in his letter to Shear. Stevens to Lord and Shear, February 15 and 22, 1941, Admin 310/5/4, ASCSA.

52. Prince Paul of Yugoslavia reproached the U.S. minister, Arthur Lane, "You big nations . . . talk of our honor, but you are far away." War Cabinet Minutes, PRO, February 24, 1941.

53. April 9, 1941, in Archer 1944, 170. Although British troops pushed the Italians back to Tobruk in mid-February, Field Marshall Erwin Rommel arrived in North Africa and, before the end of the month, was pushing east. Wilson, who had been military governor of Cyrenaica until the British lost it, established his headquarters at the Hotel Acropole opposite the National Museum, while the Bletchley Park code officers set up at the RAF Headquarters in the Marasleion School, just down the street from the American and British Schools.

54. Laird Archer records the wrong date in his diary (1944, 160). The *Newark Star Ledger* published the story in "Young Tells Experiences in Greece" on November 20, 1941. Testimony of Clio Adossides Sperling.

55. Charles House to U.S. legation May 31, 1941, NARA 59/CDF 1306/368.115–1164. *Estia* carried the story on March 28, 1941. "Bomb Injures American," *NYT,* March 29, 1941. "Greeks Decorate Young," *NYT,* March 31, 1941, based on a story in *Eleftheron Vema.* Stevens cabled Lord, "Rodney seriously wounded condition now much improved Parsons with him Telegraph Rodneys [*sic*] father." April 1, 1941, Admin 310/5/4 and 804/5/4, ASCSA.

CHAPTER THREE

1. Meverette Smith, a teacher who worked for the NEF, took care of soldiers in Salonika until the night before the city fell. Smith 1942, 76–79. I thank Clio Adossides Sperling for sharing her memories, which I contextualized with archival sources from the ASCSA, records dating to 1940–41 from the Athens legation NARA 84/2694A/44–60, UPUMA, and published accounts.

2. The Adolf Hitler Division of proven Teutonic ancestry (with whom the Führer had spent Christmas) took Monastir. April 14, 1940, in Archer 1944, 175. To the conquest of Greece Hitler devoted fourteen infantry as well as four mountain, six panzer, and two motorized divisions, and over 1,000 aircraft, including fighters, bombers, and transport planes.

3. Peter Fleming, brother of James Bond's creator, blew up bridges in the north while David Pawson (later chief of SOE, Izmir) blew up others around Thebes and left a wireless transmitter with Col. Euripides Bakirdzis, aka "Prometheus." Sweet-Escott 1965, 26, and 1975, 7.

4. The Vanderbilt Committee, included Harry Hill, Edward Capps's British son-in-law and head of American Express, and others. (See chap. 2.) American School couple John and Suzanne Young fled through Thrace to Turkey. Lankton 1942, 37–40.

5. Gerolymatos 1992, 158; April 8, 1941, in Archer 1944, 168. Those in Fort Rupel volunteered to remain. Calvocoressi 1989, 179; Haritonitis 2002; and George Weller, *Boston Evening Transcript*, April 14, 1941, 1.

6. Stevens to Lord, April 1 and May 10, 1941, and Shear to Lord, April 9, 1941, Admin 310/5/2, ASCSA.

7. Phylactopoulos 1991, 15.

8. Report on the Occupation with Young Notations by Carl Blegen, NARA 226/100/3.

9. *NYT,* March 29 and 31, April 9 and 15, 1941.

10. Weber to Lord, April 14, 1941. Later Stevens again cabled Lord, "Rodney here in Greek Red Cross Hospital," April 20, 1941, and House to American legation, May 31, 1941. Admin 310/5/ 2 and 4 and 804/5/4, ASCSA; NARA 59/CDF 1306/368.115–1164. November 18, 1938, January 19, and December 10, 1940, and April 1 and 9, 1941. Later notices appeared on April 26, May 5, and October 5, 1941.

11. Stevens to Lord, April 20 and May 10, 1941; MacVeagh 1942, 73–74; Weber to Shear, April 4, 1941, Admin 310/5/ 2 and 4, ASCSA.

12. In Athens, drunken youths sang anti-Mussolini songs and bragged of the Greek flag flying over Rome. Young, "The War," in NARA 226/100/AD 2–9, p. 71. April 10, 1941, in Archer 1944, 171.

13. Phylactopoulos 1991, 15–16. The desperate retreat resembled that from Anatolia in August 1922. Beevor 1991, 37, 39. St. John 1942, 242–326. MacVeagh diary, April 14, 1941, in Iatrides 2001, 34.

14. Stevens to Lord, April 12, 13, 19, 1941; Stevens to Shear, April 12, 19, 1941; Weber to Shear, April 14, 1941. Admin 804/4 and 310/5/4, HAT Shear, ASCSA. NARA 59/CDF 1306/368.115.

15. Parmelee and Willms 1942, 50.

16. Agora architect John Travlos, one of the last out of Albania, was with a unit responsible for blowing up bridges and roads to cover the retreat. The Italians were furious that Tsolakoglou had not surrendered to them. To pacify the Italians, the Germans made him surrender a second time two days later in Salonika.

17. MacVeagh diary, April 9, 1941, in Iatrides 2001, 34.

18. April 18, 1941, in Archer 1944, 180–81. Admiral Sakellariou, navy minister, and stepfather of Clio's friend on Corfu, became vice president of the cabinet on April 21, 1941.

19. February 22, 1940, in Archer 1944, 160. Both women were awarded medals by the Greek Red Cross. According to Clio, Young quipped that he would prefer hamburger, steak, or ouzo. Clio Adossides Sperling's personal communication. Young's student, William Biers, said that Young had lost his teeth in the bombing. Later Young had the shrapnel fashioned into a talismanic watch fob that he wore. Clio and Young both knew the crown prince from the Royal Alpine Club.

20. Sam Rayburn, Speaker of the House, read Roosevelt's statement to Greek-American delegates at the Pan Hellenic Congress of April 25, 1941. Saloutos 1964, 348. The Vanderbilt Committee ended when Harry Hill evacuated to Egypt just before the Germans reached Athens. Later Hill's office, American Express, became one of the main evacuation centers for smuggling the British out of Greece. MacVeagh diary, April 24, 1941, in Iatrides 2001, 35. May 1, 1941, in Archer 1944, 208. Stevens to Lord, April 26 and June 24, 1941, Admin 804/4, ASCSA.

21. NARA, T1-120/1174/468908 Hitler to Mussolini, August 6, 1942.

22. Mazower 1995, 1–7, and 2008.

23. MacVeagh to Cordell Hull, May 15, 1941, NARA 59/CDF 1306/368.115.

24. *NYT,* September 26, 1941; and Parmelee and Willms 1942, 46–54. The diplomat was Nicholas Mavroudis.

25. H. Davis 1942, 30. Priscilla Hill gave them raw materials provided by the Near East Foundation.

26. New Zealand troops disembarked in Greece on April 25, 1941, the twenty-sixth anniversary of ANZAC Day marking the ill-starred Gallipoli landings.

27. Some towed smaller gliders "like young vultures following the parent bird." May 20, 1941, in Archer 1944, 217. Beevor 1991, 106, 110.

28. That night the British still controlled the airfield, but within two days they were shelling it from the sea.

29. Pendlebury arrived in June 1940. Beevor 1991, 70–71; Grundon 2007.

30. *NYT,* May 26 and 27, 1941.

31. Waugh 1955, 231.

32. As they climbed the foothills above Maleme, a colonel passed a dressing station that reminded him of the Atlanta hospital in *Gone with the Wind.* Beevor 1991, 205.

33. Clio Adossides Sperling.

34. First the Italians captured Sidi Barrani; then the British regained it in December 1940.

35. Clio Adossides Sperling.

36. The Zannas family were conservative Venizelist republicans. Alexandros was active in pioneer aviation in Greece, cabinet ministries, law, the Greek Red Cross, relief and resistance work, and favored installing a stable middle-class republican regime in order to forestall the leftists' comprehensive social and economic reforms. He was also a close friend of the Adossideses since they served together in Venizelos's Salonika government during World War I. He was the principal contact in Athens for Major Robert Menzies, SOE operative in the north and helped set up the escape route that the British later used from Athens, to Anavysos on the south coast of Attica, and by submarine to Antiparos and Egypt. Leftists accused him of being a British agent and royalists of being a partisan. A trustee of the American Farm School, he was arrested by the Germans in 1942 and served his sentence in Italy. Sotiris was in Section D of SOE—also known as MO-4 and under the War Office, hiding British soldiers and helping prisoners of war escape as part of Alexandros Levides' organization, Maleas, before he was forced to evacuate. He arrived in Cairo at the end of 1941. Zannas Papers (Benaki Museum); Zannas 1964, 74ff.; Zannas in Clogg 2008, 113–24; Malakasses 1980, 49; Gerolymatos 1992, 224–25, 234–36; and NARA 59/CDF 868.01/365 PS/LF, p. 13. Murphy 2006 and Wylie 2007. (See n36 chapter 6 in this volume.)

37. Only five men out of three British squadrons in Athens reached Cairo from the Phaleron airfield. Adossides commanded the Thirteenth Hellenic (Anson) squadron.

38. *NYT,* May 28, 1941.

39. Crete fell on May 30. Destroyers picked up over 3,000 British from Iraklion in fewer than twenty-four hours and ferried them to offshore cruisers, but one-fifth died from relentless German bombing. After surrendering, thousands of British were stranded at Sphakia and forced by the Germans to reverse their trek, past their dead comrades, back over the mountains to Khania. Beevor 1991, 207, 210.

40. MacVeagh evacuated on June 5, 1941. Stevens to Lord, May 7, 1941, Admin 804/4, ASCSA. Meritt 1984, 10. NARA 84/2694A/44–60.

41. Young report, April 10, 1942, NARA 226/100.

42. Young report, pp. 6 and 55, April 10, 1942, NARA 226/100. F. van den Arend, Acting Assistant Chief, Special Division, Department of State to Lord, June 3, 1941, Admin 310/5, ASCSA.

43. Ruth Parmelee, *NYT,* September 7, 1941, *Washington Post,* July 21, 1941.

44. *Newark Star Ledger,* November 20, 1941. Churchill set the policy of blockading occupied Europe on August 20, 1940. Ralph Kent (principal of Athens College) 1942, 60–66. Young report, p. 63, April 10, 1942, NARA 226/100.

45. Adossides to Parsons, July 28, 1941, Admin 804/5/4, ASCSA; Archer 1944, 237–42; and *NYT, Chicago Daily Tribune, Washington Post, Los Angeles Times,* July 16–20, 1941.

46. *NYT,* July 15, 1941; *Chicago Daily Tribune,* July 16, 1941; *Washington Post,* July 15, 1941; *Los Angeles Times,* July 16, 1941.

47. Industrialists sponsored other soup kitchens in the greater Athens area.

Zannas 1964, 19–21; Henderson 1988; Iatrides 1980, 374, Hionidou 2006; and Clogg 2008. On June 10, 1941, Joan Vanderpool had written her brother Tom Jeffery, Wellesley College professor, to send "medicine (inoculations of all kinds and serums) and food rich in fats and sugar," malted milk tablets and liver extract, "even though it may not arrive and even though it is expensive." Archer to G. W. Wadsworth, June 21, 1941, and Wynant V. Vanderpool to Hon. Breckenridge Long, Assistant Secretary of State, May 28, 1941. NARA 59/CDF 1306/368.1163–64 and May 1, July 20, 1941, in Archer 1944, 207, 243. Stevens to Lord, February 1 and 4 and August 9, 1941, Admin 804/4, ASCSA.

48. *Chicago Daily Tribune* and *NYT,* August 11, 1941. The Americans were given five seats on each of three weekly flights. Figures varied from 100 to 150 on the total stranded. July 20, 1941, Archer 1944, 242–44.

49. Parsons had left with his mother-in-law and wife on the thirty-first. Lord to Stevens September 8, 1941, Stevens to Lord, September 9, 1941, Admin 804/7/3 and 4/5 and 310/5, ASCSA. Cordell Hull to the NEF, August 9, 1941. NARA 59/CDF 1306/368.1163–64. For the Atlantic Charter, see http://avalon.law.yale.edu/wwii/at10.asp.

CHAPTER FOUR

1. Vanderpool, September 10, 1941, quoted in Young to Lucy Shoe, November 19, 1941, ibid. *NYT,* August 31 and September 7, 21, and 26 and October 8, 1941. With the help of the GWRA and the American Red Cross, Turkish ships managed to bring $2,250,000 worth of food purchased in Turkey through the British UK Commercial Corporation and the British embassy to the starving nation between October 1941 and August 1942. Kazamias 1992, 293–307. Later the GWRA, using Swedish ships, managed to bring $100 million worth of aid—700 tons of food, medicine and clothing as the "Gift of the American people," thereby saving more than a third of the population. Saloutos 1964, 349, Hionidou 2006, and Clogg 2008.

2. *NYT* and the *Washington Post,* July 10 and 12 and *NYT,* September 11, 12 and 14, 1941. The Foreign Information Service (FIS), under playwright Robert Sherwood, prepared and disseminated propaganda in the Eastern Hemisphere while its translators' unit created radio scripts in Greek and Turkish. Archibald MacLeish, Librarian of Congress, helped form Research and Analysis (R&A), which interviewed the refugees with others from Oral Intelligence (OI). Military intelligence was under Army General George Strong, G-2, and Rear-Admiral J. H. Godfrey (ONI).

3. In March 1941, prominent Anglophiles from the Committee to Defend America (CDA) formed the Fight for Freedom Committee (FFFC), which advocated American intervention and whose members were Donovan, David Bruce, Whitney Shepardson, and New York lawyer Allen Dulles.

4. Lord to Young, October 14, 1941, Admin 310/5/4, ASCSA. Homer Davis, president of Athens College; Laird Archer (Office of Foreign Relief and Rehabilitation) and others from the Near East Foundation; Foy Kohler of the American legation in Athens; and Arthur Parsons (later with the State Department in Washington

and Cairo) wrote for the *Nation, Saturday Evening Post,* and *NYT* and lectured across the country. Davis (1942) collected their testimony. Others, such as Helen Wace, lectured to benefit the GWRA.

For the Grand Central Palace induction center, see *Life Magazine,* November 16, 1942, 51–58.

Young spoke to the Essex Club on November 13, *Newark Star Ledger,* November 20, 1941. Parsons to Lord and Lord to Stevens, September 1 and 8, 1941, Admin 804/5/2 ASCSA. Blegen also wanted to return to Greece. Blegen to Hill, January 24, 1942, UAUC.

5. German archaeologist Frank Brommer led the raid on Corinth. German planes machine-gunned the village of Old Corinth, but not the excavations, which soldiers had left intact. Young to Shoe, November 19, 1941, ibid.

6. Ralph Smiley to Poole, January 2, 1942; FNB Manual and History, May 1944. NARA 226/100.

7. Meritt had already supplied the British Library of Information with a list of Americans sympathetic to the Britain. COI initially paid Meritt as a consultant with a $10 per diem and expenses, but from April 17 onward, as chancery chief with a State Department clearance of P-7, he earned $6,500 annually. Meritt interviewed refugees as R&A's, FIS's, and OI's Greek expert. In February, he learned how Greek resistance kept in touch with the British via a caique from Turkey. Poole's memorandum to Wiley, December 26, 1941, and "Memorandum for Volunteer Helpers," April 24, 1942, NARA 226/86.

8. Edward Mead Earle, Princeton historian and member of the Institute, 1940, 490, 487. Katz 1989, 6.

9. Young to Homer Thompson, "Sunday 15th" [February 1942]. Agora, Young, ASCSA.

10. Young wrote his report in three weeks and still managed to address audiences at Bryn Mawr and in Toronto. Young to H. Thompson, "Sunday 15th" and "26" (February 1942) (Agora, Young, ASCSA). Meritt to Poole, February 21, 1942. Young report, p. 63, April 10, 1942, NARA 226/100.

11. A joint SOE-MI-9 mission under Atkinson penetrated Greece in November 1941. In January 1942, Italian police surprised Atkinson, who shot the Italian commander and was captured along with his incriminating lists, endangering the network built up by Alexandros Zannas, Amoss's "grapevine intelligence system." Later British evacuees brought out code with which Greek officers hoped to establish radio communication with the British in Cairo to coordinate activities in Greece. Clogg 2000, 73; Gerolymatos 1992, 223–29, 264.

12. At Christmas 1941, Costas Adossides' sister Bessie and her husband George Trypanis left by caique with Col. Frank Mackaskie (MI-6 and MI-9) and other escapees. In January 1942 (independent of Atkinson), they had engine trouble near Kythnos, where they were arrested, separated, and imprisoned, then moved to the Cycladic island of Syra (Syros). Trypanis was placed in a twelve-foot by twelve-foot cell with forty other men. Every three days they got drinking water. The men huddled together, devoured by lice. Each day they found one, two, or as many as

five or six dead. Bessie was locked in a flooded bathroom for three months, contracted pneumonia and pleurisy, and required hospitalization. Elli Adossides hired a boat for a three-day journey in order to see her, but got only twenty minutes before Bessie was transported to Rhodes in chains and put on trial, where she "behaved with great courage." Later they sent her to Samos and released her on parole. After the liberation of Greece, Bessie was decorated by the British. Elli had two other sons, Andreas, exiled in London since Metaxas came to power, and the youngest, Alekko, who had remained at home. Andreas Adossides to Marjorie Davis, November 7, 1942, HAT Shear; Adossides diary, Agora, ASCSA; Paspati 2009.

13. Out of a total of 1,900 to 2,000 dying daily, 700 to 800 were children. Others suffered from pneumonia, typhus, typhoid, malaria, cholera, and tuberculosis. *NYT,* January 15 and February 5, 7, and 15, 1942.

14. Adossides had sent letters to Lord through Burton Berry, former counselor to the U.S. legation in Athens who had been posted to the legation in Rome, but made occasional trips to Greece. For nine months Lord ignored Adossides, and no American aid arrived. Weber to Lord, April 11, 1942, Admin 310/5/3, ASCSA.

15. Adossides to Lord, October 15, 1941, Admin 804/5/2 and 5, ASCSA.

16. Hill to Adossides, July 5, 1942, Admin 804/4 and 5/2, ASCSA. Adossides wrote that the suffering of fictional characters in *Gone with the Wind* could not compare to the Athenians' misery. Adossides to Lord, March 1942, Admin 804/5/5, ASCSA. NARA 59/CDF/368.1163–64.

17. Shoe to School alumni, September 15, 1942, Admin 804/1/4, ASCSA.

18. Adossides to Shear, March 9, 1942, HAT Shear, ASCSA. Adossides to Lord, April 8, 1942, Admin 804/5/5, ASCSA. NARA 59/CDF 1306/368.1163–64. Burton Berry, Athenian Legation, PRO FO 371/32467. Mazower 1995, 23. Hionidou 2006. E. Adossides, excerpts from diary, Agora (A), ASCSA.

19. The *NYT,* March 1, 1942, reported that sweets peddled in Athens were made of ersatz cream whitened with marble dust and a bean paste that caused 500 new cases of stomach ulcers daily, while vendors sold dog, cat, and rat sausages, cutlets, and giblets, prompting a rise in ptomaine poisonings. Sulzberger's fiancé was Marina Ladas, whose brother Alexi was imprisoned on Samos with Paspati and Bessie Adossides for helping Mackaskie escape. See n. 12. Their mother, Dora, lived with Joan Vanderpool during the war. Sulzberger 1969 and *NYT,* February 20, 1942.

20. Twenty-nine were rescued. *NYT,* April 10, 1942.

21. Meritt, Shear, Frantz and Talcott, Panofsky, and Hetty Goldman lived within a five-block radius centered on Battle Road near the Institute for Advanced Study. Elderkin, Capps, and Weber also lived close by. Meritt recruited Frantz, Weber, and Helen Wace in April; Elderkin in June; Talcott, Oscar Broneer, Goldman, and Dinsmoor in July; Ida Thallon Hill and Raphael Demos in August; and Elizabeth Blegen in October. The Harvard scholars reported from the Fogg Museum of Art, the Museum of Comparative Zoology, and Wellesley College until December 1943. Stephen Ladas, New York lawyer and secretary of the American Friends of Greece, ran security checks for Shear. HAT Shear, ASCSA.

22. In February Kenneth McKenzie of Princeton scanned the Italian press. Later Meritt recruited Dorothy Schullian (Albion), George McCracken (Otterbein), Dominic Rotunda (Mills College), Mary Pearl (Sweetbriar), Dagmar LaBreton (Tulane), Roy Alan Cox and Howard Comfort (Haverford), Edwin D'Arms (University of Colorado, Boulder), W. E. Gwatkin (Columbia), Lewis Gordon (Hamilton), and Aline Boyce. He also recruited Teodorescu of the Institute. Lily Ross Taylor and Meriwether Stuart (Bryn Mawr), replaced Oliver in June and July.

23. Roosevelt 1976, 63–66 and 200.

24. In all, FNB monitored 20,350 individuals, 3,550 organizations, and 2,053 publications. FNB Manual, NARA 226/100. Young to Thompsons, "Tuesday 28th" (April 1942) (Agora, Young, ASCSA).

25. Meritt wrote Poole on March 31, 1942. Carl Dean Wittke, quoted in FNB History, NARA 226/100, p. 25. Poole to Newark native James C. Dunn, April 2, 1942. C. W. Cannon, European Affairs, memo April 18, 1942, NARA 59/CDF/868.00/1143 ½.

26. Amoss was recruited on December 16 and met with Donovan on December 31, 1941. A church deacon before he became regional chief and director of the YMCA in Adrianople (Edirne), Amoss administered relief in the Greek Thrace and later directed the YMCA in Salonika, then flooded with refugees following the Smyrna disaster. As executive secretary for the Anglo-American Relief Committee, he billeted the vanquished Greek army in tents at the Salonika YMCA and organized refugee shelter and relief, directing a hospital for them and schools for their children. King George II came to the throne after the defeat of the Greek army in Asia Minor and subsequent armed insurrection led by General Nikolaos Plastiras and General Stylianos Gonatas that executed six royalist leaders and dethroned the king's father in autumn 1922. King George II made Amoss a Knight and Officer of the Savior, but after Venizelos negotiated the peace, the king went into exile in London in 1923. For his relief work, the British foreign secretary commended Amoss, and he was honored with the Order of the Holy Savior, the Order of the Phoenix, the Order of the Holy Sepulchre, the Medal of Military Merit with Golden Palm, the Military Victory Medal, and other awards. Later he worked for Near East Relief, Save the Children, and the Red Cross. YMCA Archives, Salonika. University of Minnesota, Anderson Library, YMCA biographical 1853–2004 Box 2. FNB History. NARA 226/100/INT GR 2 and 226/A1–224/13.

27. Theofanides, an Asia Minor Greek and Robert College graduate, served in the Turkish army in World War I as Greek and English interpreter and worked in British intelligence general headquarters in Smyrna in 1918–19 and for the Smyrna YMCA before relocating to Athens, where he earned a reputation as a Greek liberal and American expert. Theofanides wanted a constitutional monarchy without Metaxists.

28. Tsouderos's man was Gonatas, the Secret Governing Committee's liaison officer. Theofanides met with Donovan on January 25, 1942, intending to send Amoss to Istanbul or Alexandria to establish communication between Greece and the United States. Amoss to Poole, January 6, 1942; to Bruce, January 28, 1942; and

to Donovan, "Greece: Political," October 19, 1943, NARA 226/210/57/1; 378/3; 401; 402/2; 226/100.

29. He drew up "The Greek Project I." Bruce to Donovan, January 15, 1942, NARA 226/210/378.

30. Amoss Report to Bruce, January 28, 1942, NARA 226/210/378/7 and 402/2.

31. Theofanides provided Amoss with an assistant, Leon Melas. "The Comprehensive Greek Project (*CGP*)," April 24, 1942, NARA 226/210/378/4 and 226/92A/112/24.

32. Young thought Tsolakoglou a shrewd and clever opportunist, but a "very capable and efficient strategist and general." Young also knew Generals Panagiotis Demestichas at Klisura, S. Mantouzis, who had held the sector north and west of Pogradets, and Bakos, the pro-Nazi military governor of Salonika. CGP, NARA 226/210/378, 226/100/15, and Young report, p. 63, April 10, 1942, 226/100. 226/59/CDF 868.00/1143 ½.

33. Amoss to Ellery Huntington, Jr. and Robert Cresswell, April 22, 1942. The New York Special Reports Division of FIS wanted Young. Amoss to Huntington, May 6, 1942. Young to Amoss, May 3, 1942. Amoss hired Young by May 7. Young earned $4,000 a year with a $7.00 per diem abroad. NARA 226/211/1, 226/92A/5/57, and 226/210/378/4, 226/A1-224/860.

34. Poole, Meritt, and Talcott worked in the old National Institute of Health at Twenty-fifth and E, NW, then COI's headquarters. Meritt was discussing working with a clandestine Jewish army when Young joined him in the Chevy Chase house of Homer Davis, who left to head up the New York office of Greek War Relief when Skouras took charge of Twentieth Century Fox. Meanwhile, Margaret Crosby worked in navy cryptography, and Ralph Kent (former principal of Athens College and also navy) was two houses away. Charles Morgan was with the Army Air "Corpse." Young to H. Thompson, May 21, 1942 (Agora, Young, ASCSA). Meritt to Lord, May 16, 1942, Admin 310 ASCSA. When Meritt left, Jim Oliver moved in.

35. COI moved continually, from the State Department's APEX Building at Seventh and Pennsylvania, to the old National Institute of Health (until June 13, 1942) as well as the Administration, South and North Buildings on Lafayette Square near the Cosmos Club by September 1941. By late 1941, it also acquired two buildings in the Naval Hospital grounds at Pennsylvania Avenue SE between 9th and 10th Streets SE.

In New York, the topography of intelligence was more complex. COI/OSS offices clustered in midtown within a two-block radius. The Foreign Information Service (FIS) had its covert office at 270 Madison Avenue near Bryant Park, within a block of the headquarters of the CDA and the American Hellenic Society and a short walk to the Century Club. COI's principal offices were at 270 Madison Avenue, under the cover of the Mohawk Trading Company; Oral Intelligence (OI), under Ned Buxton, originally with FIS, was at 21 E. 40th St. by December 1941. In February 1942 Secret Intelligence (SI) established its own office with OI, FNB, and almost a third of all SI staff, although FNB also had several cover and hideaway offices, such as the Oversees Press Service. COI's Ship Observer Unit, located at 42 Broadway, interviewed seamen from the merchant marine. The Foreign Language Division was at 224 W. 57th St. The BSC used OI, which interviewed refugees in September 1941, as its first point of contact with COI, and SI data were the medium of exchange. The 270 Madison Avenue address became overt later when it was used by the OWI. SI, SO, FNB, and R&A leased additional space at 55 West 42nd and other offices. There were other offices for SI, FNB, and counterintelligence (X-2) recruiting and confidential work while the Labor Desk recruited and liaised with the parallel services in the UN, and Special Operations opened its own office in April 1942.

SI's office was located in the International Building at Rockefeller Center at 630 Fifth Avenue. The Greek consul general; the Greek Ministry of Information; the Coordinating Committee of American Agencies in Greece, headed by Laird Archer, Leslie Shear, and Stephen Ladas; the National Committee for the Restitution of Greece, headed by Dr. Nicholas Mavris; BSC; and the British Library of Information, headed by Stephenson, were in the same complex at 30 Rockefeller Plaza between Fifth and Sixth on W. 49th Street, immediately over the UK Commercial Corporation. All other organizations connected with Greece clustered nearby: the American School Committee for Aid to Greece, American Friends of Greece, American Hellenic Student Committee for Medical Aid to Greece, and GWRA at 730 Fifth Avenue, just five blocks away.

36. The FIS became the OWI under Elmer Davis with journalists, broadcasters, and writers in press, radio, motion pictures, and general propaganda, including Merion Cooper, the director of *King Kong,* while Sherwood focused on its *Voice of America* at 224 W. 57th Street in New York.

37. Roosevelt 1976, xii. X-2 was created in 1943 as a liaison with the British concerning ULTRA, the British designation for decrypted German signal intelligence, largely encrypted on the Enigma machine.

38. The same day Young addressed a luncheon at the Cosmopolitan Club in New York attended by Frantz, Talcott, and the Olivers. Young to Thompsons, "Friday 27th" (March 1942) (Agora, Young, ASCSA). *NYT,* March 25 and 26, 1942. The plebiscite protocol was dated March 31, 1942. Richard Howland, George Mylonas, and Alexander Robinson also interviewed. Meritt to Shear, May 25, 1942. Frantz, "The Visit of King George II of Greece," FNB Rep. 38, June 8, 1942, NARA 226/100, INT GR 33 11–24. Frantz recalled her work on "political movements of exiles in the U.S. . . . sometimes little embryonic movements that would burst into full-fledged revolutions or something less violent. . . . I used to see a lot of statesmen and politicians who came and find out just what they thought was going on." Taped interview for Smith College Centennial by Jacqueline van Voris with M. Alison Frantz on December 4, 1971. Frantz/PU, 416.

39. Meritt's luncheon was on Friday the twelfth, followed by the Columbia dinner on the seventeenth, and the American Educational Institutions of the Near East dinner—at which Foreign Service officer and American School trustee Thomas Lamont, spoke—on June 22.

40. Tsouderos confirmed that resistance existed on Crete and in Macedonia

and that landings could be made on the Attic coast between Marathon and Karystos, but that they needed money from the OSS to keep their escape service running. CGP, NARA 226/210/378/15.

41. Sources disagree as to the death date of Costas Adossides. Archer 1944 has it occurring before July 6, 1941, but is wrong on several other dates. One OSS document also refers to 1941; however Clio Adossides Sperling recorded it as May 13, 1942. Elsewhere she inscribed a photograph of Costas as taken on May 18, 1942. Condolence letters date from the summer of 1942 and support that as the correct date. Andreas Adossides to Marjorie Davis, November 7, 1942, HAT Shear. After Costas's death, his brother wrote, "Now that the first member of the family has been killed I have a feeling of impending catastrophe." Andreas to Clio Adossides, August 2, 1942, archives and personal communication of Clio Adossides Sperling. After the war, Costas's remains were transported from the war cemetery in Palestine to a crypt and monument to celebrity war dead at the entrance to the first cemetery in Athens.

42. The king and prime minister waited when Donovan returned from London, Amoss introduced them, and the king signed the L-L agreement on July 10, 1942, pledging that his government would transport American food shipped from Canada and elsewhere, support the refugees, and provide two submarines.

43. Amoss, Young, Miles, McBaine, D. G. Stampados, and Arthur Reed wrote reports compiled in the CGP. Young prepared "Greece: War against the Axis," "Proposed Bases of Operation," "Amplification of the Greek Project," "Memo of the Meeting with Prime Minister Tsouderos," and the "File of names of Greek Americans with special abilities, compiled from the Archbishop's Lists." CGP, 6, 9, 11, and 12. April 24 and June 25, 1942, NARA 226/210/378/4 and 6 and 226/190/3/29.

44. Amoss to Bruce, January 28, 1942, NARA 226/210/378 and 402/2. McBaine had been the prewar general counsel for Standard Oil of California. He came to Cairo for COI in April 1942 and found that Alexander Kirk, U.S. minister to Egypt and the Greek government-in-exile, distrusted "cloak and dagger" men since McBaine's COI predecessor Frank Mauran had signed agreements "on behalf of the U.S. government" without informing him. Donovan had met all-American Yale quarterback Huntington in law school, and he had been a major fund-raiser for Donovan's gubernatorial campaign. Lt. Com. Joseph Leete arrived that May under Foreign Economic Administration (FEA) cover.

45. See above. Kanellopoulos became vice prime minister by May 1942. NARA 226/210/402/4.

46. OSS hoped the *Protos* or head at Mt. Athos would "enrobe" its agents. The British wanted OSS to penetrate areas where they had no presence or where Greek resistance had died out. Instead OSS often replicated British efforts in Crete, Macedonia, Mani, and Olympus.

47. Amoss, "Project: Eastern European Section Preamble," June 25, 1942, NARA 226/210/402/4.

48. There were 60,000 Greek-Americans in Chicago alone in the 1930s. Saloutos 1964, 328. For Hartford, see NARA 226/92/14/203.

49. They recommended carrier pigeons, forbidden since the Albanian campaign, for communication between Cyprus and Alexandria. Young to Amoss, July 18, 1942, NARA 226/210/378/15.

CHAPTER FIVE

1. Oliver studied in Bonn from 1927 to 1928 and for two years as a fellow at the American Academy in Rome (1928–30), but spent most of his time at the School in 1932–33 and as a fellow and later staff member at the Agora, where he worked from 1932 to 1936 and 1939–40. He was one of a decreasing number of scholars of both Greek and Latin, served on the managing committees of both institutions, and taught at Barnard from 1937 to 1942. Oliver to Young, May 27 and 31, 1942, Young to Oliver, May 26, 1942, Van Halsey to Amoss, June 5, 1942, NARA 226/92A/57/1, 2; Engagement Letter, 226/A1-224/571; "Proposed Bases of Operation," Young to Amoss, May 27, and "Amplification of the Greek Project," June 8, 1942, 226/190/2/29. Recollections by Diskin Clay and Oliver's students, Herbert Benario and Kevin Clinton.

2. Sperling ranked seventh on Young's list. He explored Elis in 1939 and published the results before joining OSS. Young to Sperling, May 27 and June 3, 1942; Sperling to Young, May 31 and June 6 and 9, 1942; Amoss to W. Lane Rehm, July 11, 1942, Amoss to William Kimbel, January 6, 1943, NARA 226/92A/13/198 and 14/199; Young to Amoss, May 27 and June 8, 1942, 226/190/2/29; Engagement Sheet, 226/A1-224/732.

3. Izmir-born Arthur Reed supplied the information on Izmir, but OSS rejected him as too young. Homer Davis suggested that the GWRA position be voluntary. A Red Cross report claimed that Turks had interned 4,200 Greek refugees in a camp at Cheshme near Izmir, and that the British had interned another 2,000 in Cyprus and more in Syria and Palestine. Up to this point, British secret intelligence (MI-6) handled all Greek refugees, claiming that they were Cypriots and therefore British subjects.

4. Initially, Young considered George Mylonas, an Izmir-born Greek archaeologist and naturalized U.S. citizen. German archaeologists Theodore Wiegand and Georg Karo had apparently operated there as secret agents during World War I. Young to Amoss, May 27 and June 8, 1942, NARA 226/190/2/29.

5. Daniel ranked second, backed up by John H. Young (ranked sixth) who had worked at Kourion in Cyprus and been at the School during the Albanian campaign. In April 1942, Daniel sent Meritt information on American firms in the Near East. His boss at the University Museum, George Vaillant, also joined OSS. NARA 226/92A/17/253, 254; Young to Amoss, May 27, 1942, 226/190/2/29; and 226/A1-224/166. Recollections by Sara Anderson Immerwahr and Ellen Kohler. Wilson taught English at the American University of Beirut, then from 1931 to 1936 he taught Egyptology and later became the director of the Oriental Institute, for which he had excavated at Luxor from 1926 to 1931. Initially, he supervised and administered COI research in the gathering and analyzing of wartime material at a Pay Grade of P-8 and $8,000 salary. Later, he became the principal R&A research analyst at a rank of P-6 and salary of $5,600. NARA 226/A1-224/844.

6. Boas 1919 Letter. *The Nation.* David W. King to Col. Smith, February 14, 1941, NARA 51-20512, MID. Harris and Sadler 2003.

7. Each had a draft status of 3-A with a salary of $4,000 a year and a per diem abroad of $7.00.

8. Cooper 1989, 171–72; Haag 2004, 190. Nelson Glueck, May 7, 1942, newsletter #9 to ASOR. NARA 226/169A/10/462. J. Y. Brinton, Memoirs, Alternative XIII, 1.

9. Haag 2004, 198.

10. Personal communication from Clio Adossides Sperling. Her friend was Nina Athenagenos.

11. See Cooper 1989, 195. Wace also evacuated to Jerusalem.

12. On July 5, New York City was totally blacked out. Meanwhile, six Germans, who had previously lived in the States, came ashore for the purpose of sabotaging ALCOA and the Chesapeake and Ohio and Pennsylvania Railroads. Russia was bearing the full brunt of the German army and air force, and Anglo-American forces were losing on every battlefield while Japan swallowed up the Pacific, and Axis armies again threatened the Middle East. *NYT,* July 5, 6 and *Washington Post,* July 20, 26, and 31, 1942. Amoss to David Bruce, the head of SI, "Primary Blueprint for the Creation and Functioning of Eastern European Section's Secret Intelligence," June 25, 1942, NARA 226/190/2/29. The punishment for passing intelligence to the enemy was court martial or death. A signed oath can be found in 226/A1-224/268.

13. Temporary Q Building was at 2340 E Street within sight of the Lincoln Memorial on the site of the later Kennedy Center. It and buildings on the Naval Hospital grounds at Pennsylvania Avenue SE between Ninth and Tenth Streets SE were OSS's Washington headquarters throughout the war. The relief-based group formed the Coordinating Committee of American Agencies in Greece.

14. Application. Registrant #894, July 6, 1942, NARA 226/92A/19/283. Caskey entered service on July 23, 1942. Amoss to W. Lane Rehm, July 31, 1942. 226/A1-224/112. Amoss to Robert Oerswell, July 10, 1942, 226/92A/137/25. Caskey to Carl Blegen, July 29, 1942, UCUA. Caskey's wife, classicist Elizabeth Gwynn Caskey, taught his classes.

15. NARA 226/A1-224/150, and Young to Cox, July 16, 1942, 226/92A/120/301.

16. Young to Amoss, June 15, 1942, Edson to Lt. Comm. W. H. Vanderbilt, July 24, 1942. Edson was the protégé of W. S. Ferguson and Arthur Darby Nock. For six months, Langer labored to free him for R&A. December 28, 1942, NARA 226/A1-224/15/223.

17. Daniel was commissioned on August 11, Caskey and Sperling on the sixteenth, and Oliver on the seventeenth. Major Gen. J. A. Ulia, Adjutant Gen. to Caskey, August 11, 1942, NARA 226/92A/283/14050-42 War Dept.

18. In Clinton, MD, near present location of Andrews Air Force Base. See Chambers 2008, 358.

19. Sperling and Oliver entered camp on July 10, Young and Pearce on July 28, Caskey and Daniel on August 10, and Cox on August 24, 1942, NARA 226/190/511/167. See chap. 6 for other camps.

20. Kenneth H. Baker to Amoss, September 23, 1942, and Pearce to Baker, August 1942. A. Van Buren to Amoss, November 16, 1942, NARA 226/92A/20/301.

21. Baker to Amoss, August 12 and 13, September 2, 16, and 23, 1942, NARA 226/92A/5/69, 13/198, 19/283, and 20/301.

22. Sperling would go first to the U.S. consulate in Alexandretta and thence to Ankara and Izmir. Sperling to Amoss, November 3, 1942, NARA 226/92A/14. Edward R Stettinius, Jr., to Donovan, November 19, and Amoss to Donovan, November 30, 1942, NARA 226/92A/283/9242.1119 and 226/211/1/47. Smith 1983, 272, 353–354, 381, 384, 396, 399, 402, 461 n. 52.

23. The Greek government-in-exile received 82 percent of GWRA funds. Harry Hill, Capps's son-in-law, was executive vice president, succeeded by Homer Davis in January 1943, and Oscar Broneer in 1944. PRO FO 188/438. Summary statement of the Greek Relief Program, August 1942–March 1944. Hionidou 2006, 135. Subsequent Americans with the State Department also had GWRA covers: Homer and Marjorie Davis and archaeologist Gladys Davidson in 1944.

24. "Situation in Cyprus: Prospect 1942," December 24, 1942, transcription of conversation between Dow and Daniel, NARA 226/92A/17.

25. SOE wanted to sabotage a bridge near Lamia and needed a Greek liaison. Kanellopoulos recommended Colonel Ioannis Tsigantes to blow up bridges to disrupt Rommel's supply lines in July 1942 and set up the Anglo-Greek Committee to coordinate resistance and oversee and direct intelligence and guerrilla warfare in Greece that would be loyal to the government-in-exile. Through the efforts of MI-6, MI-5, SOE, and HIS, Tsigantes' mission, Midas 614, reached Mani in the southern Peloponnese on August 1, 1942, but while he was awaiting orders and supplies, the British switched their allegiance from him to their own team, and he engaged in sabotage in Athens. A struggle ensued between Kanellopoulos and SOE, which had not anticipated the complex guerrilla politics (see chap. 6 n. 36). Gerolymatos 1992, 135, 212, 264, 283, 290–97, Myers 1955.

26. HIS was commanded by Captain Nikolaos Tsangaris of the Royal Hellenic Navy, a former employee of Greek munitions manufacturer and industrialist Bodosakis-Athanasiades.

27. The former Greek Military Intelligence was the Diefthinsis Eidikon Ypiresion Polemou, the Directorate of Special War Services (*DYE* or Ypsilon Pi in Greek records). NARA 226/190/2/29. Before the war, its "the second bureau" had handled domestic and foreign information, acted as a liaison with and coordinated the Bureau of Foreign Intelligence of the Ministry of Foreign Affairs, Air and Naval Intelligence, and controlled the counterespionage activities of the departments of national security, the police, and the gendarmerie. It had also monitored intelligence training, morale and security in the military, and had an office of Anti-Communist Defense. Later the Special Security (Eidiki Asfalia) was established with offices nationwide in those of the city police or gendarmerie, but reporting directly to Athens. It was under the vice-admiral and the Home Service connected with the army.

28. The only other swimmer was the wife of the Chinese ambassador. At three in the afternoon, the pool opened to soldiers, and every night Arabs emptied and scrubbed it clean. Bernard Spencer and Robin Fedden of classicist Robert Graves's English Department at Fuad University were among the British poets of Cairo.

29. The soldier was L. Coromilas. The colonial governor of Palestine and his staff occupied the two top floors of the King David, but the back had cots for anyone who needed them.

30 Clio Adossides Sperling, personal communication.

31. In September 1942, Meritt became FNB's associate director, moved to the Apex Building at Seventh and Pennsylvania, and oversaw both Chancery and Field Study divisions, maintaining contact with foreign leaders and the State Department.

32. Duke was a former college football player and advertising executive for *Fortune, Time,* and *Life.* Caskey and Sperling honed the drafts for their bases. In New York, Daniel worked with OSS's British SI liaison at BSC. At Theofanides' suggestion that there might still be "some fishing" in the Dodecanese and Crete, Daniel broadened his plans. NARA 226/92A/17. Daniel's ostensible purpose was to correct the army's military map of Greece. Daniel to Amoss, December 23, 1942. Amoss to Bruce, October 23, 1942, NARA 226/92A/13/198 and 226/92A/17. Duke and Swaart 1969. Sperling to Amoss, November 17 and 25, 1942, and Sperling to Huntington, October 22, 1942, NARA 226/190. During this time, Caskey became Amoss's adjutant, and U.S. Army intelligence recruited Daniel as its "observer" and liaison with the British on Cyprus on whom they wanted him to spy.

33. They budgeted a million dollars for the first three months with one tenth for personnel and the rest for equipment and supplies. The actual cost is not known. Sperling to Amoss, November 17 and 25, 1942, and Sperling to Huntington, November 2 and 27, 1942, NARA 226/190/1.

34. Under Metaxas, all Greek intelligence services and Metaxas's minister of police had reported to Xenos. Young vetted Xenos with Lt. Col. Bickham Sweet-Escott of British intelligence, who vouched for his unquestioned loyalty to the Allies. Although Xenos claimed to be "non-political and disinterested," the royalist scorned Kanellopoulos and HIS and wanted to set up his own intelligence and sabotage organization in Greece, offering OSS a different list of names. Young worried that his contacts in the gendarmerie and among army officers might sway OSS to the royalist camp and suggested using both Xenos and HIS. Young to Amoss, October 13, 1942; Amoss to Bruce, December 15, 1942, NARA 226/210/401/6.

35. Melas, the son of one of Tsouderos's secret contacts, liberal republican Commodore Constantine Melas, had worked with Archer at the NEF in Athens, fought in Albania, and come to the United States to procure military equipment. He was employed by the Greek Consulate and then by Theofanides. American architect Ronald Pearce ran the GIP's New York office under the cover of Amoss's company Gramtrade International in Room 1514 of 30 Rockefeller Plaza, which also housed the Greek consul general, the Greek Ministry of Information, and the British Library of Information. Pearce was to establish centers in Lisbon, Buenos Aires, Bern,

Egypt, Turkey, Durban, Capetown, and neutral Portuguese East Africa. Melas to Whitney Shepardson (part-time spy in World War I and OSS's head of SI), July 11, 1944. D. G. Stampados, chief of Air Section, Middle East, was Amoss's assistant in Washington. Amoss hired Vournas (rated 1A) in October 1942. Melas to Amoss, August 12, 1942, NARA 226/210/389; 401/2, 4, and 6; and 402/2 and 226/92A/324.

36. In New York Amoss used two highly sensitive Greeks for special missions. Munitions magnate Bodosakis-Athanasiades (GIP agent 173) had a private espionage system in Greece and elsewhere that Amoss coveted, although Young reported that it was under investigation. Amoss thought that Sophocles Venizelos, Admiral Voulgaris, and Karapaniotis took his orders, and he was connected with businessman John Mermingas. Later Bodosakis-Athanasiades was interned for allegedly inciting the Greeks to riot in Egypt. Document from AG/000 to SAINT in Washington and London, September 25, 1944, NARA 226/216/9/41. Amoss "Project: Eastern European Section" and "Preamble" dated June 25, 1942. Pelt 1998.

37. Formerly Alexander Melas had worked with the SOE under Kafandaris, who resented British support of the king and distrusted SOE's security after January's Italian capture of Atkinson. Melas worked for OSS until March 1943 (chap. 6). The Evvian guerrillas were under Major Elias, Melas's political lieutenant and a GIP agent, later "on ice" in Cairo. GIP agent 379 monitored the communists. BSC made Daniel its OSS liaison with the Combined Service Detailed Interrogation Centre (CSDIC), set up in 1939 under MI-9 to interrogate refugees, POWs, and escaped prisoners for irregular warfare. Amoss to Donovan, October 14, 1943, and Amoss, "Greece," October 19, 1943, NARA 226/210/401/2.

38. Boyotas facilitated Amoss's GIP operations from the British consulate at Izmir and from Cheshme. Copy from Brereton via Zangas to Boyotas. Original to Jadwin, Guenther from Amoss and Brereton, March 17, 1943. Amoss to Donovan, October 14, 1943. Amoss to Duke, March 12, 1943, NARA 226/210/401/2.

39. Tsouderos's aide-mémoire, August 5, 1942, to the British Foreign Office. NARA 226/210/511/7.

40. Adossides died thinking that Costas was still fighting in Egypt because Clio refused to deprive his parents of hope. Of his other children, one son had stayed in Greece; another was exiled in England; and his daughter and son-in-law remained in prison. The School paid for his funeral. While interned, Vanderpool read Pausanias, taught fellow internees Greek, and roomed with Charles House. Dow joined OSS on November 16, 1942. Andreas Adossides to Clio, August 12, 1942, and to Marjorie Davis, November 7, 1942, HAT Shear. Farm School Archives. NARA 226/A1-224.

41. *AIA Annual Report* 33 (1942) 5.

42. Blegen's State Department clearance was P-7 while Frantz's was P-4. When Langer, head of R & A, asked Meritt to write a general political survey of Greece in December 1942, he moved back to the Institute, where Shear continued to direct the Princeton Group.

43. Gen. George Strong wished to hobble Donovan so that he himself could be the postwar intelligence chief. Cave Brown 1982, 304–11. "History of OSS Cairo." NARA 226/99/50.

CHAPTER SIX

1. The Casablanca Conference lasted from January 14 to January 24, 1943.

2. By early 1943, OSS reshuffled. Bruce became chief of OSS London and Magruder deputy director of intelligence overseeing SI. Winks 1992, 27. Amoss to Donovan and Duke, Acting Chief of Southeast Europe, Bruce, and R. D. Halliwell. January 19, 20, 22, 26, 28, 29, 30, and February 1, 1943, NARA 226/190/247/690.

3. NARA 226/190/1. See chap. 5. Early in 1943, Tsigantes tried to form a national council of resistance including a number of Venizelists. On January 15, he was betrayed. Amoss told Donovan that he was either killed by Italians resisting arrest or executed by Greek patriots, but others believe that he was set up and deserted by the SOE, and the murder remains unsolved. January 25, 1943, NARA 226/190/247/690. Gerolymatos 1992, 264–84. Fleischer 1988, 304.

4. In March 1943, Stefanos Sarafis became ELAS commander in chief, supported by SOE, while EDES swore allegiance to the British. Woodhouse 1975, 117, and Gerolymatos 1992, 212, 293–94.

5. Leete had taken over Cairo for OSS in September when McBaine returned to Washington. Leete was the liaison with the Greek king and his government. OSS History of Cairo. NARA 226/99/50 and 226/A1-224/496. Cave Brown 1982, 286.

6. Amoss alerted Donovan that the Russian insistence on a second front in the west indicated that it was reserving the eastern front for itself and wanted to know U.S. policy. If Washington planned to allow Stalin to create a series of new Soviet states in southeastern Europe, Amoss did not want to encourage suicidal resistance to the Axis only to be "check-mated" by Communists. Instead, he proposed to leave a stay-behind network (to inform on the Soviets with political intelligence on Communist activities in occupied Europe). Amoss to Donovan, March 10, and to Duke, March 12, 1943, NARA 226/190/3/29 and 226/210/401/2.

7. Amoss's field organizer or "liaison," James B. Underwood, was also liaison with the Ninth Air Force under Brereton and GIP chief in enemy-occupied territory as group captain in the RHAF, but answering directly and only to Amoss. He organized and supervised agents, directed landing parties in hostile territory, and provided crucial intelligence.

8. Amoss only let Brereton, Guenther, and Brig. Gen. Victor Strahm, acting chief of staff, USAFIME, know of the GIP, which was not to interfere with the archaeologists. Major Valerian Lada-Mocarski was Amoss's executive officer of SO Cairo until Guenther sent the White Russian to Jerusalem. Amoss joined Capt. George White, former Federal Bureau of Narcotics undercover agent coordinating COI counterintelligence in North Africa since November 1942, and Col. Harold Hoskins, chief of operations, OSS Middle East. "Charlie" was otherwise known only to the Cairo MI-6 chief and Strahm. Amoss was unaware that he himself was being tailed by a British agent whom he later married. Memorandum, February 9, 1943, NARA 226/210/410/7. Amoss to Miss Sieber for Huntington, Shepardson, Duke, Pearce, Wes Howland, James Murphy, and Lane Rehm, February 24, and Amoss to Duke, March 12, 1943, 226/210/401/2.

9. Caskey to Dow, February 14, 1943. NARA 226/190/1 and 226/92/19/283.

10. By March, over one hundred German submarines prowled the Atlantic, dogging Allied troop carriers and supply ships. David Bruce had wanted Young in Cairo earlier, but not until late February was he cleared to serve on Colonel Guenther's staff. Bruce to James W. Kirk, January 11 and February 24, 1943, NARA 226/211/1 and 226/92A/5/71; and MacVeagh to Dow April 27, 1943, NARA 226/190/1. Daniel went as military observer.

11. Tsouderos planned to have Bodosakis-Athanasiades control the army, navy and air force. Amoss to Miss Sieber for Duke and Shepardson and Amoss to Donovan, March 20, 1943, and Amoss, "Greece: Political," October 19, 1943, NARA 226/210/401/2.

12. The Pittsburgh electrical engineer had just completed three months' drill in Fairbane close combat, field work, demolitions, wireless, and physical training at secret camps south and east of Washington for two weeks each at Special Operations (SO) facilities at Areas A, E (a secret SI/SO camp), and the "Farm," and six weeks at Area C. Area A and Area C were located in 5,000 wooded acres between Joplin and Hickory Ridge west of Quantico, Virginia, in Prince William Forest Park. The CCC had built the camps as a nature retreat for underprivileged youth before the OSS took over, fenced them with barbed wire, and policed them with guard dogs. One hundred recruits were processed in groups of ten, lived under false names in tents or bugged cabins, ate in dining halls, attended classes in craft buildings, and used weapons ranges and abandoned homes for target and demolition practice. In Area A recruits concealed their identities and discovered those of their fellows as preparation for SO missions behind enemy lines. They learned to fire weapons, use codes and radios, make and disarm booby traps, and jump from planes. Area C taught communications: Morse code and ciphers, covert radio practices, weapons, and martial arts. They also took field trip/missions to the Norfolk and Washington navy yards, Gravelly Point and Boiling Field (now Washington National Airport), and nearby cities. Georgiades arrived by way of Ascension Island, Accra, and Khartoum on April 28, 1943. Georgiades "Report on Field Conditions Evros mission," October 30, 1945, NARA 226/210/358, and Georgiades to John O. Iatrides, February 7, 1973 (courtesy of Iatrides). See Chambers 2008.

13. Amoss to Donovan, March 22, 1943, NARA 226/99/43/212.

14. Huntington and Charles Hambro (SOE chief) agreed that American SO could be "independent and coordinated" with SOE, but SOE Cairo boss Lord Glenconner resisted. Guenther informed Donovan that the British "field groups are no longer free to present unbiased intelligence. We would be making a great mistake to accept blindly the well moulded statements which obviously are issued to us with definite intent to retain us within their orbits in certain very important fields." Huntington to McBaine and V. Lada Mocarski, March 28, 1943, "OSS History of Cairo," and Guenther to Donovan, April 29, 1943, NARA 226/99/50 and 226/99/43/212.

15. The consulate was at 24 Sharia Nabatat. Major Louis Huot, a liberal journalist with the Paris edition of the *Chicago Tribune,* was in charge of Greek and Yugoslav SO until September, when he established SO in Italy and was replaced by Col.

Paul West. On Guenther's staff were Dimitri Petrou, Romeo Soucy, administrative officer Major Charles Edwards, a Johns Hopkins archaeology Ph.D., and Josie Brinton, Tennessee socialite whose husband John was assistant military attaché and father-in-law was Philadelphian expatriate Judge Jasper Brinton, George McFadden's uncle. NARA 226/211/7/93.

16. Amoss, May 1943, and Amoss to Caskey, May 30, 1943, NARA 226/92/137/25 and 226/190/1/4.

17. This narrative is drawn from Caskey's letters to Amoss (April 26 and May 9), Stettinius (May 13), Duke (May 12), Dow (May 25), his wife, Elizabeth Caskey (May 12), and G. P. Williams in Washington (May 12). NARA 226/92A/19/283. Rameses II passed through 3,244 years earlier.

18. NARA 226/190/1/G160.

19. *AIA Annual Report* 34 (1942) 5–7. Caskey met a Dane employed by the American Eastern Trading Corporation in Alexandria who traveled all over the Middle East and reported that the Russians were in control in Persia and would dominate it after the war. Caskey to G. P. [Williams], June 22, 1943, NARA 226/92A/19/283. Young to Amoss, May 27 and June 8, 1942, NARA 226/190/2/29. Campbell was "Stallion." 226/210/63/58–59.

20. Michael Rostovtzeff excavated Dura Europus on the Euphrates.

21. He shipped the jeep to Ankara for Steinhardt.

22. A British official from the Aleppo consulate took the Americans as far west as the Syrian border and showed them a more direct route. Then American archaeologist W. S. (Bill) Smith, the ONI "shipping agent," picked them up on the Turkish side at Alexandretta.

23. The flat was managed by assistant military attaché Major Edwin O. Brown.

24. Miles, who knew Cox from the American Numismatic Society, forwarded her mail and reports to Washington. In the 1970s, his son-in-law James McCredie became director of the ASCSA. Caskey's boss, Mike Cardozo, Lend-Lease chief in Turkey, warned him that the British-American Coordinating Committee controlled Lend-Lease in Turkey (since Britain and Turkey had a military alliance), but it also took credit for U.S.-supplied goods. Caskey would work with them and economic branches of the State Department. Caskey to Dow, May 25, 1943, NARA 226/92A/19.

25. Cedric, Ewart, and John Seager were from Bebek in Istanbul. Cedric had served as a coal broker and Cunard agent. NARA 226/92/116/18. Following advice, Caskey duly sent for his gun and uniform, which he had left with their brother in Aleppo.

26. Caskey to Stettinius, May 13, 1943. NARA 226/92A/19.

27. Gnade had risen from junior clerk (1940); to vice consul (1941); to third secretary and vice consul, Baghdad (1942); and third secretary, Ankara (March 2, 1944). Walter Birge was vice consul, and Capt. Webb Trammell (naval) and Earle Taylor (commercial) were attachés. Caskey to Amoss, April 26, May 9, 1943, NARA 226/210/195/5.

28. The two-day trip took forty hours by boat or train. Caskey plunged into

trade negotiations to substantiate his Lend-Lease cover, writing on the "fascinating" topic of citronella tails, figs, raisins, and tobacco. Caskey to Duke, May 12, 1943, NARA 226/92A/19/283. Caskey to Dow, August 10, 1943, 226/92/19. The archaeologists all used the Greek "Smyrna," rather than Izmir, the city's Turkish name. Blegen had excavated not far from Izmir in the summer of 1922 only months before the disastrous war between the Greeks and Turks had left "infidel Smyrna" a heap of ashes known as *ta kammena*. The subsequent population exchange had purged the Orthodox Christians from Turkey and rent the rich multiethnic brocade of Izmir and its hinterland. Since then the Greeks lived in permanent exile in America or crowded into shantytowns outside Athens and Salonika, on offshore islands in sight of their old villages and farms crumbling to ruin just out of reach on Anatolian hills sloping down to the Aegean.

29. The British consul general was Mr. Hole of the Foreign Office whose assistant was Charles Edwards. Morrison-Bell represented internal security or MI-5 under Colonel Thompson, Istanbul. Among MI-5's tasks were interrogations and the vetting of all foreign personnel. Murphy 2006, 52. MI-5 fell under the Home Office. Izmir D-55-1109, Caskey to OSS Washington, November 1, 1943. NARA 226/92A/19.

30. Rees lived from 1902 to 1947. The Reeses lived in the Alexandrian suburb Ramleh, near King Farouk and Judge Jasper Brinton. Rees's sister had married an Egyptian prince, and his elder brother was with British intelligence in Cairo. Rees 2003, 200–203.

31. MI-9 fell under the War Office, handled services for and interrogations of British prisoners, gathered their intelligence, and managed their escapes and evasion. Foot and Langley 1979, 35. The Royal Navy had requisitioned all boats belonging to British subjects, including Rees's yacht, *Branwen*. Frank Macaskie, friend of Bessie Adossides, worked with MI-6 and MI-9, which linked up through Rees. Before it was requisitioned by the Royal Navy, the *Lilias* had belonged to Levantine industrialist William Giraud (Alain's father), son of Harold Giraud.

32. MacFarland to Amoss, May 23, 1943, NARA 226/210/195/5.

33. Boyotas removed the files. Amoss to Duke, March 12, 1943, and Brereton/ Zangas to Boyotas in Amoss/Brereton to U.S. military attaché to Turkey Col. C. C. Jadwin/Guenther in Ankara, March 17, 1943, NARA 226/210/410/2.

34. Levides, who had lost his commission in 1932, postdated Zangas. He founded the "Maleas" organization and an escape route for MI-9 and SOE and was told to get on with Rees and avoid "the Zangos troubles."

Admiral Panagiotis Konstas was head of HIS in Cairo. Later Rees directed the Turkish operations of N section as lieutenant commander Turkish Operations, RVNR, charged with organizing the escape service under Lt. Col. Antony Simonds, Cairo, formerly SOE, and Commander Wolfson, assistant naval attaché, Istanbul. Under Simonds, MI-9 and A Force, Wavell's special unit, both dealt with the escape service, though for A Force, it was partly a cover.

35. In World War I, Kastellorizo was shelled from Turkey near the Roman site of Patara and its fleet sold to the British for the Gallipoli Campaign. In December 1940, 50 Middle East Commando, directed by Pendlebury and assisted by classicist Terence

Bruce-Mitford (lecturer in classics at St. Andrews) and Levantine Englishman Jack Hamson, took part in a botched moonlit raid on the island of Kasos, "past the Venetian fort and down to the water . . . we went in silence with equipment and rifles and bombs and knives through the ruins of other wars: a scene in a boy's story-book" (Hamson 1989). Later, a handful of special forces arrived on Kastellorizo, including Ian Pirie, C. M. Woodhouse, and Patrick Leigh Fermor, provoking a German bombardment of exceptional severity in which a quarter of the main town was razed.

36. Pawson, who had worked for a British company in Greece since 1933, employed Alain's uncle, Eldon Giraud. At Pawson's request in April 1942, long before Tsigantes' sabotage and that of the Gorgopotamos Bridge, Levides conveyed to Athens the SOE codebook, transmitter, and agent Gerasimos Alexatos ("Odysseus," a smuggler who, like Pawson, sympathized with the Left). He set up a meeting with senior republican officers in Athens as well as one from EAM/ELAS and tried to interest them in appointing a republican officer to join EAM/ELAS, but they refused. Then he set up a meeting with Zervas, who agreed to establish a guerrilla base in Epirus and later western Greece as well. Alexatos was to divide 2,000 gold sovereigns between EAM and EDES, who agreed to work with the British. SOE Section D had two cells: one under (conservative republican) Alexandros Zannas, in the north, the other consisting of more liberal republicans under Colonel Bakirdzis, who was not interested in espionage in Athens and believed all partisan forces would be under his control (chap. 3, chap. 4, and chap. 5). Eventually, Zannas gave up sabotage and focused on A Force work. His brother Sotiris had worked with the British in 1940–41, but had to evacuate in 1943 because of his work with Levides. Zannas 1964. Later Psarros (of a smaller resistance group) was given central Greece, Sarafis Thessaly, and Bakirdzis Macedonia. Rees instructed Levides to stay away from the guerrillas and focus on MI-9 work. Levides 1975, 23, 26ff. Bakirdzis informed the British about EDES and EAM/ELAS while Alexatos was with the Communists (KKE). Gerolymatos 1992, 213–15. In Greece, SOE boasted many classicists and archaeologists, including Antony Andrewes, Nicholas Hammond, A. W. Lawrence, David Hunt, Peter Fraser, John M. Cook, Stanley Casson, Thomas Dunbabin, C. M. Woodhouse, Eric Gray, David Talbot Rice, Mitford, and Pendlebury. *Report on SOE Activities in Greece and the Islands of the Aegean Sea*, appendix I, "Origins and Constitution." Gerolymatos 1992, 134–35. After September 1943, SOE was known as Force 133. Ward 1992, 173, 175.

37. Cox needed the maps to identify unfamiliar place-names, which she later discovered were refugee communities in Attica. When Dow finally wrote, he told her to get whatever she could from whatever source. Communication improved when Margaret Crosby joined the team as reports officer in July 1943. Washington treated Cox as an anomaly. Dow to Cox, May 28, 1943, NARA 226/92A/20/301. J. C. Young to Thomas F. Bland and Cox to J. C. Young: accounts, October 18, 1944, 226/219/1/26964, 26966, 651. "Cox Report on Field Conditions," January 12, 1945, 226/210/64/4.

38. PRO WO 208/3253; "Cox Report on Field Conditions," January 12, 1945;

MacFarland to Caskey, July 22, 1943, NARA 226/190/1/5; and Cox to Dow, June 18, 1943, 226/92A/20/301.

39. Cox to Dow, June 18, 1943, NARA 226/92A/20. Cox "What I Did in the Field" January 11, 1945, 226/250/64/4.

40. "Rankling with the Greeks is that the British are not willing to bring out members of all political parties. And when it comes to sending men back in, it is feared that they will again be partisan. The Greeks feel that there are only one or two men who are strong and big enough to be trusted by all parties, so that if they went back they would be able to unite the various factions and convince them that they must work together to get rid of the Axis, but that after that, no matter who is in command now, they will be able to choose the sort of government the majority wants. They doubt very much that the British will choose those men." Cox to Dow April 20, 1943. By July 1943, the Turks threatened to close down the MI-9 operation because of the high number of Greek soldiers passing through Turkey. Again the British, told to "lie low," pledged to use a smaller fleet and not bring their "exports" through Turkey. Instead Rees kept them at Cheshme and from there sent them direct to Cyprus by sea. Caskey to Young, July 14, 1943, NARA 226/92A/20/301.

41. Later Young denounced Rees as an "unpleasant Franko Levantine beast." Cox to Dow and Young, July 6, Cox to Dow, March 30 and July 15, Young to Dow, July 16, Cox to Dow, July 21 and August 10, 1943, NARA 226/92A/5/71.

42. "However illegal it is to land men in Turkey, we shall have to land some." Cox to Dow, July 21, 1943, and Young to Caskey, August 6, 1943, NARA 226/92A/5/71.

43. Cox reported that Rees was "not much liked by anyone except his underlings." HIS agents complained to Cox that, through high-handed carelessness, the British (SOE) had sacrificed three good agents and the British consul general of Izmir referred to SOE as "ignorant whipper-snappers" and said that "straightening out the messes made by the Intelligence" took up most of his time. U.S. commander George Earle had had a run-in with Rees and the head of the IRC in an exchange of prisoners in the second week of April. Cox worried that consul Miliaressis might blow her cover with the British, for he talked and was too pro-British. She threw off all pretense when she interrogated Christos Gonatas, a pro-British Greek and former British consul of Mytilene, who was high up in the British service in Izmir. Cox to Dow April 20, June 23 addendum to June 18, and July 1, 1943, NARA 226/92A/20/301 and 226/92A/5/71.

44. Cox to Dow, June 18, 1943. Nilsson, the Swede, was on the side of the Allies, but young and intimidated by the Swiss. Cox to Dow, August 10 and July 16, 1943, NARA 226/92A/20/301.

45. Blegen had introduced Caskey to the Levantines: British, French, Austrian, Italian, and Dutch who had for centuries lived and worked in Izmir while reinforcing their nationalities by sending their children home to be educated and married. They welcomed Caskey with legendary hospitality. MacFarland to Caskey, July 15 and 17, 1943, NARA 226/190/1/5.

46. MacFarland wanted Sperling, a base radio station, and ten portable wirelesses immediately. He wanted to bring agents out of Bulgaria, Rumania, Macedo-

nia, and Hungary to train and send back. MacFarland to Amoss, May 23, 1943, NARA 226/210/195/5.

47. For Amoss, see chap. 7. Amoss, May 1943, and Amoss to Caskey, May 30, 1943. Caskey had been recommended for a promotion before the others arrived, but it was thought improper to promote just one of the four captains. NARA 226/92/137/25 and 226/190/1/4.

48. In the autumn of 1942, OWI had caused the Joint Intelligence Committee to repeatedly block Donovan and the OSS in Washington, and now OWI obstructed OSS agents in Turkey.

49. Caskey, U.S. Embassy, to G. P. Williams, June 22, 1943. Caskey to Dow in Washington and Young in Cairo, June 17, 1943, NARA 226/92A/20/301; Amoss (to G. F. Else), May 1943, 226/92/137/25; and Amoss to Caskey, May 30, 1943, 226/190/1/4.

50. C. Kantianis, "Report on the Secret Activities of the Ellas Mission." NARA 226/210/64/5.

51. In 2004 the British wartime vice consul's daughter, Gwynneth Edwards Giraud, still remembered being called from her bed in Bournabat to decode cables in that tower room. Caskey's first radio man, Lieutenant Taxakis (X-9), was trained in Cairo and showed up in midsummer 1943, but was replaced because of sloth.

CHAPTER SEVEN

1. Young bore a letter of introduction from the Coordinating Committee of Greek Reconstruction. It worked with the Lehman Organization, later the United Nations Relief and Rescue Administration (UNRRA).

2. Penrose was prewar assistant director of the Near East College Association, whose board member, Allen Dulles, had recruited him for COI.

3. Petrou had escaped from the Battle of Crete, run a clandestine radio station in Palestine, and resigned from British service to work for McBaine, and later became Young's most valuable source for political intelligence of the extreme Left and Right.

4. Venizelos, a family friend, sent Clio Adossides light blue material for a Greek air force cap in honor of Costas. "OSS History of Cairo SI." NARA 226/99.

5. Amoss to Donovan, October 14, 1943, NARA 226/210/410/2.

6. Each American had an OSS number; commissioned officers had a serial number; and field agents sent from Cairo, an X number. Cable codes: Sterling Dow SILVER = DC. HURBE = Istanbul. GUSTAV = Cairo, HECTOR = Izmir. See appendix for complete roster. Georgiades to Iatrides, February 7, 1973, courtesy of Iatrides. Young to Dow, May 30, June 6 and 18, and August 30, 1943, NARA 226/92/5/71. Frank Mauran, Special Assistant to the Coordinator, had already tried to secure the yacht in Suez. McFadden learned code and helped with translation, interviewing refugees, and curating maps.

7. Young to Dow, June 18, and Caskey to Young July 14, 1943, NARA 226/92A/20. See chapter 6.

8. Young's friend, Lt. Ralph Kent, worked with JICAME.

9. Also at the British embassy was Frank Stubbings, Wace's student of Mycenaean pottery. From February 1944, Young sat on Kanellopoulos's Anglo-Greek Committee where Tsangaris (HIS) presided.

10. Dow reported that Washington had appreciated Amoss's cables about the March riots, Oliver's on "the silphion area" (code for Cyrenaica, based on its extinct ancient abortifacient), and Cox's, but that he had heard nothing from Sperling. Caskey to Betty Caskey, May 13, and Cox to Young and Dow, July 6, 1943; Dow to Cox, May 28, and Caskey to Dow, May 25, 1943, NARA 226/92A/19/and 20/301. Dow to colleagues, July 29, 1943, 226/92A/5/71. Dow sent letters with George Vournas and Robert Koch, later head of Young's Area A, who arrived in late July and August. See below.

11. Else studied at the University of Nebraska before earning a doctorate in classics at Harvard University. After teaching at Harvard, Else took a job at the State University of Iowa, where three out of five classics professors had already left for war service. Else would be the fourth. Although he was married with a newborn, he felt the job "was really important" and something that he was "fitted to do." He wrote, "I am not afraid of being drafted, but if I am going to war, I am sure I can pull more weight in the boat in the job I have been offered than as a private in the army." Else to Mr. Foerster, March 27, 1943, Special Collections, University Archives, University of Iowa. Else spoke German, French, and Italian and had traveled widely. His trainer noted that he was a good organizer, accepted responsibility naturally, got on well with others, and possessed "a very keen mind." He joined the OSS in June and was commissioned captain in the marines in August. NARA 226/A1-224/218; 226/92A/54/361.

12. Dow had known Crosby for ten years. Crosby had dug at Dura Europus in the Syrian Desert and knew French, Greek, Italian, and German. After working as a navy cryptanalyst, she joined OSS on July 19, 1943. Dow had known Edson for fifteen years. Colleagues recommended Edson as "industrious, careful, and thorough." NARA 226/A1-224/156; 226/92A/70.

13. Hamit Kosay was Sperling's former colleague, and Benno Lansberger and Irwin Rohde were the German archaeologists. Sperling to Young, June 9 and 23, 1943, NARA 226/190/1/12.

14. Grace to Shear, June 29, 1942, Agora, Grace, ASCSA. Grace had earned a Bryn Mawr Ph.D. and spent years in the eastern Mediterranean, but earned two-thirds the salary of her male predecessor.

15. It was "rare and a precious thing at our age to find a crying need for exactly oneself." Grace to Talcott, November 26, 1942. Agora, Grace, ASCSA. Her only brother had died in the war earlier that month. NARA CDF 1940–44, 123/18. Rubin 1989, 102, 129.

16. Sperling to Young, June 6 and 9, 1943; Patsy Sperling to Dow, April 27, 1943; and Dow to Lieutenant Lucas, October 13, 1943, NARA 226/92A/13/198, 226/92A/14/199, and 226/A1-224/732.

17. Sperling to Young, June 9, 23, and 30, 1943, NARA 226/190/1/12.

18. Sperling and Joseph Toy Curtiss, newly arrived Yale assistant professor, and

later Istanbul X-2 chief, lived at Robert College, the American missionary school on the Bosphorus where OSS agents like David Garwood, Yale '38, taught English. Winks 1987, 133. On July 1, 1943, OSS Istanbul moved to 471 Istiklal Caddesi. In September, it moved to adjoining top-floor apartments at Necip Apartimani Mesrutiyet with a penthouse for radio transmission and a guard on twenty-four-hour duty. It used apartments for rendezvous, Arch Coleman's house in Bebek for training, and a SI safe house in Tarabya.

19. Oliver to Dow, July 5, 1943, NARA 226/92A/57/1 and 2. U.S. archaeologists dug Cyrene in 1910.

20. Daniel to Young, July 2, 1943, NARA 226/190/1/8 and Hinsley 1990, 35–36. Foot and Langley 1979, 76–85.

21. LeFroy was with the Twenty-fifth Corps of the Mediterranean Expeditionary Force, Cyprus. A branch of MI-5, SIME (Security Intelligence Middle East) handled counterintelligence, security, and secret domestic intelligence outside England, in British Cyprus, Palestine, and Egypt. The Combined Service Interrogation Centers (CSDIC), which Daniel would work with, were set up in 1939 under MI-9a to interrogate POWs and refugees and escaped prisoners for irregular warfare, the most useful of whom were flown to its interrogation centers outside Cairo in Maadi or Helwan.

22. The British nixed McFadden "for indiscretion and poor former associations," some of whom were then interned in detention camps, and would not even permit him to be "allowed to wander at large over the island." Young to Dow, July 22, 1943; Daniel to Young, July 2 and 6, 1943, and Daniel to Guenther, July 24, 1943, NARA 226/190/1/8 and 6. Young to Sterling Dow, July 16, 1943, 226/92A/5/71.

23. Daniel to Guenther, July 24, 1943. The farm was in the village of Ayios Nikolaos ("Ay Nik" to the British), twelve miles north of Evdhimou and approximately five miles southwest of Platres on the Mandria Road on the northeastern edge of the Paphos District. Goodwin 1976, 127, 128, 452.

24. Kolossi had controlled vast sugar plantations whose cane was distilled for Commanderia, a sweet, heavy Cypriot port.

25. Daniel to Young, July 2, 1943, NARA 226/190/1/8.

26. Hill, Talcott, Grace, and Cox had dug at Lapithos in 1931–32.

27. Founded in the 1920s by Harvey Mudd (1888–1955), the CMC supplied copper to Nazi Germany until the start of the World War II. Lavender 1962.

28. Young to Dow, July 16, 1943, NARA 226/92A/5/71.

29. Cox to Dow, June 18, 1943, NARA 226/92A/20; Iatrides 1972, 36.

30. In May and June, the BMM blew up the bridge over the Asopus River. Myers brokered the National Bands Agreement on July 4, 1943. Hondros 1983, 150–51, 160–62.

31. They also leaked a complete defense plan and order of battle in Cairo. Howard 1990, 35–36; Hunt 1989.

32. Cox to Dow, July 8, 1943, NARA 226/92A/20/301. Clearly Caskey was a romantic, and relief and rescue were critical to his plan. To Caskey, the resort of Lidja (near Khioste) was like Marblehead or Duxbury to Boston. Caskey to Young, July 8, 1943, 226/190/2/14.

33. Caskey to Young, July 14, 1943, NARA 226/92A/20/301.

34. Young to Dow, July 13 and 16, 1943, NARA 226/92A/71/5.

35. Sperling to Young, July 20, 1943, NARA 226/190/1/12.

36. Caskey "Cronin" was 100, 109 or 123, "Pete" Daniel 300s, Oliver "O'Neal" 400s, Young "Roger" 700, 765, or 789, "Daffy" McFadden 746, Sperling "Stewart" 600s, Cox "Hiram" or "Hannah" 200s, Meverette Smith "Melvin" 500s. "Packy" MacFarland (#550) was Juniper, Chrysostomas "Chris, Grace "Tiggie," Dow "Silver" 000s. He also gave Greeks, Turks, and British numbers and nicknames. Sperling, "Sparrow," changed to "Sapsucker," and Caskey was Harry to Washington, Incir in Algiers, Green to Cairo and Istanbul. Caskey to Young August 26, 1943.

37. Georgiades regarded Greek army captain Demertzis (MI-6) as a "British stooge." Young "To colleagues," August 30, 1943, NARA 226/92A/5/71. Georgiades to Iatrides, February 7, 1973. Courtesy Iatrides.

38. OSS exchanged tools and equipment for storage and use of the Emniyet's marine repair area.

39. MacFarland to Caskey, July 15 and 17, 1943, NARA 226/190/1/5. Bribing Tahsin Bey would cost would cost 1,000 Turkish lire a month. Caskey to Young, July 14 and August 25, 1943, NARA 226/92A/20/301. The British had less trouble with their Emniyet representative because they had a military alliance with Turkey, a larger and more powerful organization, and a more secluded port. Caskey to Young, October 12, 1943, 226/210/277/2.

40. Settler aka Propompe also had to prepare the way for another called Oracle. They would rent small apartments in large buildings between which the wireless operators would alternate to avoid detection, hoping that the city's overcrowding would help hide them. Young to Oliver, August 5, 1943, NARA 226/190/78/96.

41. Smith left for Cairo in September 1943.

42. Mussolini spent July 19, 1943, with Hitler in Rimini while the United States bombed Rome's railroads and airport.

43. To placate Washington and retain control in Cairo, Amoss revised the GIP as "Project II," but Robert Delaney, OSS Security, purged Amoss for importing "an ex-convict from the United States for the purposes of expert assassination." Meanwhile, Stampados replaced GIP agent Underwood as SI liaison with the Ninth Air Force. Valentine 2004, 44–45. "Rough Draft of Regular Greek Project," unsigned, July 31, 1943, and revised version; and Melas to Shepardson, July 11, 1944, NARA 226/210/389. "Greece: Political," October 19, 1943, 226/210/401/4 and 2.

44. A document "dated 10/9/99 and . . . stamped EYES ONLY and DO NOT COPY" states that while in Cairo in 1943, Amoss "recruited, trained and launched numerous teams of assassins that carried out hits on various targets all over North Africa, Southern Europe, Switzerland, Spain and Portugal." Officially Donovan fired Amoss, but kept him on the OSS payroll in an undercover capacity while he worked as a colonel in the Ninth Air Force under Brereton, who left Cairo in September 1943 and recommended him as a freelancer for CIA projects in the 1950s. See appendix.

45. Under AHEPA cover, Vournas and Petrow sold war bonds coast to coast to Greek-American communities and the Serbs for FNB in January 1943. Petrow,

twenty-eight, a graduate of Swarthmore and Harvard Law School, was born of naturalized Greek parents. Vournas planned to serve on Project Z with guerrilla Kapetanios "Y," but Washington ordered Young to drop "Z" as "too risky." March 17, 1943, Amoss/Brereton letter to Jadwin and Guenther. Florimund Duke to R. Oliver, March 22, 1943; W. A. Kimbel to Shepardson, June 26, 1943; Lt. D. V. Mc-Granahan to McBaine, July 23, 1943; McBaine to Shepardson, August 28, 1943, NARA 226/92/326. Young to colleagues, August 30, 1943, 226/92/5/71. See chapters 5 and 6.

46. Else thought the Washington staff should include "at least one person who knows Greece, at least one person who knows Greek, and others who, though not entirely ignorant of Greece or Greek, are outstanding for their ability in research." Dow to Young, July 29, 1943, NARA 226/92A/5/71.

47. Young to Dow, July 2, 16, and 22, 1943, NARA 226/92A/5/71.

48. Young to Oliver, August 5, 1943, NARA 226/190/78/96; Young to Dow, July 22, 1943, NARA 226/92A/5/71; Young to Caskey, August 6, 1943. By the end of July, the British were also on to Cox.

49. Caskey to Dow, July 29, 1943, NARA 226/92A/19/283.

50. Caskey to Young, August 25, 1943, NARA 226/190/2/14.

51. Young to Dow, May 30 and July 22, 1943. McBaine, July 21, 1943, cable. Dow to Young, July 29, 1943. Young to Caskey, August 6, 1943. Else to colleagues, August 26, 1943, NARA 226/92A/5/71. Milton Anastos of Dumbarton Oaks began working for Dow in August 1943. He and Sherman Wallace replaced Edson and Else.

52. Taylor was to open a Maritime base in the Western Harbor of Alexandria. Else to "colleagues," August 9, 1943; unsigned to "colleagues," August 26, 1943, NARA 226/92A/20; Dow to Young, July 29, 1943, 226/92A/5/71.

53. Caskey to Young, July 14, 1943, NARA 226/190/2/14. Cairo weekly report, August 1–8, 1943, 226/199/198.

54. X-3 was George Gerakakis "Apostolidis," and radio operator John Theodorou "Ted Theotokis" was X-6. NARA 226/190/7 and Cairo weekly report, August 1–8, 1943, 226/199/198/96. Doundoulakis 2008.

55. In August, an OSS caique brought "most secret" battle orders and codes for the Dodecanese invasion from LeFroy to SIME in Alexandria. (British Force 292 on Cyprus planned the operation, and assault Force 100 led by General Anderson was to take Rhodes.)

56. Wilson to Churchill, September 9, 1943. From August 1943 to the end of the war, they conducted 381 raids over seventy islands.

57. See chapter 8. Windmill 2006, Doundoulakis 2008, and Paspati 2009.

58. Air Force Lieutenant Chrysostomas was educated in Greece until 1939. Doundoulakis 2008.

59. Oliver Report to Donovan, January 12, 1945, NARA 226/92A/57/1 and 2, and Cairo weekly report, September 13–20, 1943, 226/199/198.

60. The first OSS trainees at SOE's camp (where Costas Adossides died) jumped day and night from August 29 to September 3, 1943. Doundoulakis (2008) recounts jumping from 2,000, 750, and 500 feet. He also attended the commando

360 · Notes to Pages 135–40

training there. By the time the school closed in April 1944, sixty-eight American Special Operations agents had trained at Area A, including Gerald Wines, Elias Doundoulakis, and Spiro Cappony.

61. Supplies included gasoline, diesel and lubricating oil, oakum, cable, rope, tar, and spare engine parts.

62. McFadden's cook worked at Metamorphosis until October, when Daniel abandoned the farm. Daniel to Guenther, July 24, 1943, and to Young August 25 and 28, 1943, NARA 226/190/1/8; and Young to "colleagues," August 26, 1943, and to Crosby, October 15, 1943, 226/92A/5/71.

63. Briton Charles Cowan (Gwynne's lover) skippered it from Mombasa. By late July, McFadden was seconded to the OSS. Chaney 1998, 163, 165; Cooper 1999, 89, 106, 117; and Haag 2004, 270–75. Young to Dow, NARA 226/92A/5/71, and Cairo weekly report, August 1–8, 1943, 226/199/198.

64. Young to Dow, July 2, 1943, NARA 226/92A/5/71.

65. 16th Cairo weekly report, August 1–8, 1943, NARA 226/199/198.

66. See Leeper 1950, 31; Churchill 1951, 536; Iatrides 1972, 37; Gerolymatos 1992, 302; and Clogg 2000, 91–94.

67. When Lt. Col. Paul West of Morale Operations dumped Vournas for being "too politically minded," Young proposed to send him to Greece on the postliberation Project G, but he replied that he was too old and too prominent for such a job and backed out. Then Young and McBaine decided that Vournas was not a good "Greek Desk man," and Guenther and West sent him back to the United States. McBaine's agent, Kladakis was also removed for meddling in politics. Young to colleagues, August 30, and McBaine to W. Shepardson, September 14, 1943, NARA 226/92/326. Clogg 2000, 91–94, 138, 160.

68. Young to colleagues, August 30, 1943, NARA 226/92A/5/71.

69. Metamorphosis was in a highly malarial area, but everyone remained healthy. Young apologized for sending Cowan without warning, but had to since McFadden could not captain the yacht. The British also questioned using Cowan, for the engineer, when drunk, claimed that British intelligence had asked him to report back on Cowan. Daniel to Young, September 3 and 9, 1943, NARA 223/190/1/8.

CHAPTER EIGHT

The phrase "Entering the danger zone" in the chapter's title comes from a Daniel cable to Young, October 10, 1943. Caskey and Young often referred to the liberation of Samos and Caskey's organization there as the "Samos Show."

1. Caskey to Young, July 8 and 14 and August 25, 1943, and Young to Caskey, August 8, 1943, NARA 226/190/2/14. Dow left on August 13 and arrived on September 18.

2. Caskey to Young, August 25, 1943, NARA 226/190/2/14.

3. Caskey's first agent was Zizinos Karakristodoulou. Manoudis report on Nea Efessos (henceforth Manoudis), January 20, 1944, NARA 226/210/277.

4. They moored at Karnambitsa. Caskey to Young September 7, with post-

script of September 9 and Caskey to Dow, November 11, 1943, NARA 226/190/2/14. Manoudis.

5. Young to colleagues, September 8, 1943, NARA 226/190/2.

6. Churchill 1951, 182, 203, 205.

7. Young to Caskey, September 15, 1943, NARA 226/190/1. MacFarland to Caskey September 9, 1943, 226/92A/283. Caskey to Young, September 29, 1943, NARA 226/190/2/14.

8. After remaining neutral for two days, the Italians declared war on Germany on September 10.

9. Manoudis; Papelas 2005.

10. The waterless island's main harbor was small but sheltered and protected by crusader forts perched above it that had good views of the Anatolian coast and deep cisterns.

11. Windmill 2006, 69–80. Another SBS commander took Simi on the seventeenth. See below and chap. 9.

12. Theokritos wrote his Seventh Idyll here. Kos had long been dominated by foreigners. Roman conquerors were succeeded by the Byzantines, the Saracens, the Genoese, and the Knights, who fortified it in 1391–96. It fell to the Turks in 1522 and to the Italians in 1912.

13. Gaudioso Costo and Cavour (Parish 1993, 209; Pawson Reports of September 16 Smyrna Office to M.E. MO 4 (SOE). PRO. (Henceforth, Pawson Reports).

14. Caskey to Young, September 29, 1943, NARA 226/190/2/14. Papelas 2005.

15. Daniel to Young, October 1; and December 16, 1943, NARA 226/190/1/6.

16. Daniel to Young, October 1, 1943, NARA 226/190/1/6.

17. NARA 226/210/283, and Daniel to Young, October 10, 1943, 226/190/1/6.

18. Young to Daniel, September 19, 1943, and Young cable to Daniel, September 25, 1943, NARA 226/190/1.

19. Pawson Reports.

20. Pawson report SITREPS Smyrna to M.E., September 15, 1943.

21. Pawson Reports.

22. MacFarland to Caskey, September 9, 11, 14, 1943, and Sperling to Young, September 18, 1943. The intelligence log is in NARA 226/190.

23. Parish 1993, 194–226.

24. MacFarland to Caskey, September 9, 11, 14, 1943; Caskey, "Report on the Conditions in Samos since the fall of Italy," September 29, 1943, NARA 226/92A/19/283; 226/190/1/5.

25. Only one month earlier, Stamatopoulos had been on SOE's payroll. August 8, SITREP Smyrna-Cairo, PRO FO. The base is described in the Maritime Unit (MU) "Report on Turkish Maritime Bases," July 25, 1944, NARA 226/99. (Henceforth Maritime).

26. Rees had tried unsuccessfully to appropriate the caique *Taxiarchis* for MI-9. The Persian sack was in 479 BC, and Admiral Kanaris had attacked the Turkish navy in 1824.

27. *The Histories*. Polykrates' architects had erected the largest temple in the Greek world to the goddess Hera, wife of Zeus, on a promontory west of Tigani harbor, near her legendary birthplace. As one of the seven sages of Archaic Greece, and friend to Egyptian pharaohs, Polykrates welcomed poets, such as Anakreon, at court. Perhaps echoing his patron's centrality to the Aegean, the philosopher Aristarkos placed the sun at the center of the universe 2,000 years before Galileo. Young to Toulmin, Cairo Weekly Report, October 27, 1943, NARA 226/199/198.

28. Nazi archaeologist Theodor Wiegand had been excavating on Samos for decades.

29. Caskey to Young, September 29, 1943, and Caskey to Cox and Cairo, September 15, 1943, and Caskey to Young, October 12, 1943, NARA 226/190/2/14.

30. Young to Margaret Crosby, Reports Officer for the Greek Desk in Washington, October 15, 1943, NARA 226/92A/5/71. Papalas 2005, 220 n. 95.

31. The Germans treated Levides as a double agent (SOE and HIS). They shot regular Italian soldiers and "rolled them" over the pier and into the water off the main quay. They gave the British a bucket and placed them in seven-by-seven-foot cells and then flew them to Belgrade and on to the Wehrmacht's Interrogation Center at Lukenwald in Germany. Parish 1993, 194–226.

32. Caskey to Cox and Cairo, September 15, 1943, NARA 226/190/2 /14. Later SOE lent him a submachine gun with two clips. Caskey to Young, September 29, 1943, 226/190/2/14.

33. So Jim Oliver, weakened by dysentery at Area A, outfitted them, but could not get other critical equipment: cameras, small pistols, first-aid kits, field glasses, three-color flashlights, etc. September 29, 1943, report, NARA 226/190/2/14.

34. Caskey requested twenty pistols, tommy guns, machine guns, and Mills grenades by diplomatic pouch, which contained everything from gold to radio equipment. Young cable to Daniel, September 25, 1943.

35. The Greeks wanted the Dodecanese as a reward, but would have to wait until 1947.

36. Caskey to Young, September 29, 1943, NARA 226/190/2/14.

37. Young to Caskey, October 1, 1943, NARA 226/190/1.

38. FDR supported Churchill. U.S. Dept. of State, 1964, 150–51. SOE was in turmoil. As a result of the fiasco, the SOE heads in London and Cairo were replaced, as was Myers by C. M. Woodhouse. The four EAM and one EDES and EKKA representatives went back to Salonika with Peltekis, Bakirdzis, David Wallace (SOE) and U.S. Army Captain Wilson Ehrgott of Special Operations, who gave the United States its earliest American-reported intelligence on ELAS. The AMM dealt with POWs and supported espionage, intelligence, and anti-ELAS activities. (British classicist Lt. Col. Nicholas Hammond was in charge of the Pieria/Salonika region [Hammond 1983, 1991, 1995], and British archaeologist John Cook served nearby.) The Americans depended on the British for communication and supply. In early December, Woodhouse rejected Ehrgott as too supportive of EAM/ELAS and got him replaced by Major Gerald Wines, who never opposed him. Woodhouse claimed that Wines's "good sense" prevented schism with the British. Col. Stefanos Sarafis,

head of ELAS, thought Wines understood and communicated the situation, but kept quiet with the British (Sarafis 1980).

39. Caskey put up the Kushadasi Emniyet's agent George Tsarparas at "Key West." Later Manoudis's wife took care of the men at the base. It served as a food and fuel dump, and, after November 1943, all the munitions from the Vathi base were hidden in its attic. Manoudis and Maritime.

40. Brigand arrived safely on October 6. Caskey to Dow, November 11, 1943, NARA 226/190/2/14. Koskinas headed to Mytilene.

41. Allied officers found safe refuge, hot tea, cheese, and dried bread and received first aid there. Manoudis. September 29, 1943, report, NARA 226/190/2/14.

42. They arrived almost a month and a half later. Caskey to Young, October 2, 1943, and Caskey to Sperling, November 13, 1943, NARA 226/210/277/2.

43. MacFarland to Caskey, September 9, 1943, and Sperling to Young, NARA 226/92A/283. Young to Caskey, October 1, 1943, 226/92A/283.

44. Young to Caskey, October 11, 1943, NARA 226/92A/283. Penrose was connected with Allen Dulles through the Near East College Association before the war and arrived in Cairo before Young.

45. Young to Daniel, September 19, 1943, NARA 226/190/1.

46. In 1943 Albert Speer, Hitler's minister of munitions and armaments, wrote that "should supplies of chromium from Turkey be cut off, the manufacture of tanks, U-boats and other war machines would cease, the current reserve would be sufficient only for 6 months." 1970, 316–17.

47. Transshipment in Cyprus proved not only difficult to administer, but also costly to run. The Greek Desk needed to streamline operations. Daniel recommended dispensing with the inefficient *Samothrace* and replacing it with caiques, using three on each run. Henceforth, they would only go to Alexandria for bodies, food, and medical items. For fuel, oil and naval supplies, they would go between Samos and Haifa. Daniel to Young, September 15 and 24, 1943, and Daniel to Dow, November 20, 1943, NARA 226/190/1/6.

48. As of September 28, the beaches had not been mined, and tanks were concealed under the olive trees at the port of Rhodes town. Daniel interrogated the Greeks at the Allied Interrogation Centre and Italian military personnel for the CS-DIC until its interrogators moved up to Cyprus. Daniel to Young, September 9, 15, 20 and 25; October 1, 10, with postscript October 12, and cable on October 13, 1943, NARA 226/190/1/6.

49. Among the Greeks in British employ who helped Caskey and Cox were Koskinas (X-7), Caskey's translator, assistant, and "ear-to-the-ground man," and Boyotas, who left Rees for SOE. Caskey to Young, August 25, 1943, NARA 226/92A/20/301; Caskey to Dow, November 11, 1943, 226/190/2/14.

50. GWRA had appropriated $10,000 for island relief, but its funds, administered by Sterling Dow, arrived only at the time of the British evacuation. Young to Caskey, October 11, 1943, NARA 226/92A/283.

51. See Denniston 1997, 107.

52. The Twenty-second Infantry Division was under Friedrich Wilhelm Müller,

who later led the invasion of Leros. As commandant of Crete, he inhabited Sir Arthur Evans's home, the Villa Ariadne at Knossos. Later, SOE officer Patrick Leigh Fermor planned to kidnap him. Moss 1950.

53. Other sources claim 1,388 British and 3,145 Italians taken prisoner.

54. Savage was twenty-six. The Stanford graduate worked in Ordnance at an OSS chemistry lab (Camp Huckstep) before transferring to Caskey. Taylor began as Daniel's assistant, victualing crews and servicing caiques. Caskey to Young, October 7, 1943, NARA 226/190/2/14. Taylor Report 226/144/7.

55. Caskey to Young, October 7, 1943, NARA 226/190/2/14.

56. Young cables to Daniel, October 9 and 12, 1943, NARA 226/190/1.

57. Roosevelt to Churchill, October 9, 1943, and Churchill to Roosevelt to Churchill, October 9, 1943, in Churchill 1951, 214.

58. Wilson to Churchill, October 10, 1943, cable from the meeting of the Joint Chiefs of Staff at Tunis on October 9, 1943, Churchill to Roosevelt, cable, October 10, 1943. He cabled General Alexander to remove the LRDG from the other islands to avoid their being taken as POWs. Churchill 1951, 217–18, 219.

59. Young to Crosby, October 15, 1943, NARA 226/92A/5/71.

60. McFadden had left on the *Samothrace's* second run on September 24. Its third run was delayed because of enemy submarines on September 27, the British shipping freeze, engine trouble on October 10, and renewed submarine activity on the twelfth. It finally left Alexandria for Cyprus on the eighteenth.

61. Yapitzoglou (X-39) was the advance agent for Gasoline, whose mission was to set up ports in Khalkidiki and later an underground organization in Salonika. Caskey to Dow, November 11, 1943, NARA 226/190/2/14. Daniel Cables to Dow, October 20 and 25, 1943, 226/190/1/8 and 226/144/76. McFadden was eventually sent home to be indoctrinated in naval procedure.

62. After this, OSS recognized the need for a Turkish Desk in Washington and representation in Cairo because of the intensification of work from Turkey and the field problems there. Crosby to colleagues, October 29, 1943, NARA 226/92A/5/71.

63. MacFarland to Caskey, October 27, 1943, NARA 226/92A/283.

64. Daniel to Young, October 10 and 20, 1943, NARA 226/190/1/6; and Cairo weekly report, October 11–18, 1943, 226/199/198. See chap. 10.

65. OSS caiques brought British personnel, refugees, and others from points north to Cyprus. In November OSS caiques took Major LeFroy's batman and personal gear to Alexandria. MI-9 requested that they take two MI-6 agents to SIME Alexandria along with a box from LeFroy marked "most secret," and, according to Daniel, so important that "they didn't trust the RAF with it." Then Daniel cabled Dow that LeFroy was arming all his boats before heading to Egypt. Daniel to Young, October 10 and 20, and to Dow, November 1, 1943, NARA 226/190/1/6.

66. Toulmin placed Taylor in full charge of the bases that SI had founded and then decided that SI would handle the bases and Maritime the boats. To placate Daniel, Maritime promised to send him Ensign E. J. Athens, but instead Athens took charge of "Boston." Young to Daniel, October 22 and 26, 1943, NARA 226/190/1.

67. Else was under OWI cover.

68. Young to Caskey, October 16, 1943, Young cable to Daniel October 26, 1943, and Caskey on October 29, 1943, NARA 226/92A/283. Daniel to Young, October 20, 1943, 226/190/1/6. Caskey heard that Brigand was known to the Germans. Rees became outraged thinking that they might blow entire agent chains, as Atkinson had done in 1942.

69. See chaps. 9 and 10.

70. October 10, 1943. Churchill 1951, 218.

71. Churchill 1951, 286.

72. Caskey to Dow, November 11, 1943, NARA 226/190/2/14.

73. Caskey to Sperling, November 13, 1943, NARA 226/210/277/2 and 3.

74. Holland 1988; Hinsley 1984, 133; Seligman 1996, 72; and Lodwick 1947, 92.

75. Bradford 1963, 224–25; Lodwick 1947.

76. Savage's radio operator was Romeo Soucy, X-40. Caskey railed at the possibility of having to clear out of Vathi without leaving a working wireless contact behind because Cairo had given him an insufficiently powerful wireless transmitter and an insensitive receiver. Caskey to Dow, November 14, 1943, NARA 226/190/2/14.

77. Dead were 520 Germans, 187 British (including a lieutenant colonel), 164 Italians, 168 Greeks of the Royal Hellenic Navy, and twenty civilians. Lt. Commander L. F. Ramseyer, RNVR, took charge of the evacuation with Levant Schooner Patrol 2. Jellicoe and his surviving SBS and LRDG troops escaped from Pandeli to the island of Lipsos, and thence to Turkey. Denniston 1997, 123.

78. Caskey to Sperling, November 3, 1943, NARA 226/210/277/2 and 3. Seligman 1996, 119–21.

79. The Sacred Brigade was divided into three commando groups, the first of which had parachuted to Samos on October 30; the others had arrived by caique. Arnold to Caskey, November 19, 1943, NARA 226/92A/19/283.

80. Daniel continued dashing between Nicosia and Famagusta in ignorance, "hopelessly screaming for information and supplies and get[ting] neither." Daniel to Young, November 1, 1943. Daniel recommended a simplified cipher to quicken communications between the four bases: Alexandria, Cyprus, Vathi, and "Miami," not knowing that one, Vathi, was, at that moment, being evacuated. Daniel to Dow, November 20, 1943, NARA 226/190/1/6. While the lucky left, others ransacked British stores and dined on bacon and marmalade before the Germans arrived by hydroplane at Tigani and confiscated everything. Papelas 2005, 201 n. 116.

81. Steinhardt to Secretary of State, December 8, 1943, and Steinhardt to General Wilson, December 8, 1943. Wilson to Steinhardt November 22, 1943; Arnold to Tindall, November 23, 1943, NARA 226/92A/19/283. Churchill 1951, 223.

82. Rhodes, Leros, and Crete would not be liberated until the spring of 1945.

83. Wilson cable to Churchill, November 17, Churchill to Wilson, November 18, and Churchill to Anthony Eden and Chiefs of Staff, November 21, 1943. Churchill 1951, 222, 223, 331.

84. See Churchill's minute of December 6, 1943.

CHAPTER NINE

1. Hondros 1983, 204.

2. Roosevelt and Churchill had a postmortem at Giza December 2–6, 1943. Stalin and Roosevelt disagreed over the future of the Turkish straits. Stalin wanted to control them, reversing the Treaty of Sèvres; but FDR thought they should be free for world commerce. Churchill 1951, 370.

3. MacVeagh Reports, Diary entry for December 3, 1943, in Iatrides 1980, 397.

4. Iatrides 1972, 99. King George conferred with MacVeagh on December 3. MacVeagh strongly urged FDR to see the king before he left for the United States. Iatrides 1980, 395–404. After their meeting, FDR communicated the gist of his conversation in a memorandum to MacVeagh received on the eighth. FDR departed on the second anniversary of Pearl Harbor.

5. Despot would arrive on Evvia on December 20.

6. The CMC had offered them four bungalows for a mess, an office, and radio shack, Greeks and storage, and enlisted men as well as various sheds, warehouses, a shipyard for caique repair, and a jetty with two berths.

7. Fighting between resistance factions in Greece added to the Cyprus troubles. Across the island, the British hushed up barroom brawls between Cypriot soldiers of the Cyprus Volunteer Force and British soldiers in Nicosia and Famagusta. The Cypriots came prepared, armed with knives and clubs. Outsiders suspected the "EAMish" AKEL (the Reform Party of the Working People), which had gained control in Limassol and Famagusta in 1943. Daniel, however, thought that rowdy elements in the Cyprus Volunteer Force, who had a score to settle with some British noncommissioned officer or the British generally, had "organized a knifing party." Both sides were well represented. Still the British intended to use Cypriot Greeks as their interpreters in Greece, to avoid political pitfalls with the Greek armed services and "hope thereby to avoid being given distorted views of the facts by the politically-minded Greeks." Daniel to Dow, November 20, 1943, and Daniel to Young, February 4, 1944, NARA 226/190/1/6.

8. Young departed on December 4 and Caskey on the fifth. The freeze was announced the day after Caskey left Cyprus. Calvert, with British intelligence in Mersin, was the nephew of Frank Calvert (Allen 1999). Caskey passed Inönü's entourage at Adana and reported from Ankara that Virginia Grace was still angling for a transfer. Caskey spent the tenth and eleventh in Istanbul with Sperling and then continued to Izmir, where he found the missions Gasoline and Oracle were still waiting to leave Izmir as of December 28, 1943.

9. Hamilton had trained for Special Operations and Communications with Spiro Cappony of the Chicago mission; see below.

10. Oliver left on November 19, 1943, after Major John Vassos, the new director of Area A, finally appeared.

11. Southern 2002.

12. Young to colleagues, January 4, 1944, NARA 226/190.

13. Information from Frank Clover.

14. When Alcinoos agent George Kaloudes finally was able to return to Greece in March, Oliver and Bruère acted as reports officers, translating and editing his intelligence. Soon Ali Pasha and Molossos agents would head to Yaninna and Argyrokastro.

15. Radio instruction improved. In January, the new director, Vassos, fell ill and the school suffered. McBaine report "School Operational Analysis," NARA 226/190/75/43.

16. At the end of the war, Clio had one coin left.

17. Sperling to Caskey, January 8, 1944, NARA 226/190/1/4. For Sperling's bases, see the appendix.

18. Donovan to MacFarland, November 27, 1943. In December 1943, OSS Istanbul included Felix Guepin, "Jumps" Gordon, Berry, Homer and Marjorie Davis, and Balkans men: Frank Stevens, Beeler, and Brown. Sperling to Young November 27, 1943, NARA 226/190/1/12. Clio Sperling.

19. Young to Sperling, December 28, 1943. Sperling wrote to Caskey of "Dublin" and the missions to Mt. Pangaion, Khalkidiki, Pelion, Olympus, and Evvia on January 13 and 29, 1944, and February 7, 1944, NARA 226/190/1/8 and 4. Caskey to Sperling, January 13, 1944, 226/210/277.

20. Frank Mackaskie was the officer. Hondros 1983, 173, and 1988, 36–37; and Gerolymatos 2004, 92–93.

21. Young also wanted military intelligence on troops, numbers, regiments, newspapers, official decrees, changes in identity papers, travel permits, hours of circulation, etc. Economic questions concerned the Marathon Dam, electric and telephone companies, the flour mills, the Piraeus harbor works; theft of machinery from large factories; the supplies of raw materials, labor, fuel; the state of warehouses in Piraeus and unloading facilities; the status of mines; the sabotage of railroads, roads, and bridges; the number of functioning locomotives, freight cars, autos, horses and mules, etc., ships and caiques; the staff of the Red Cross and the number, location, and quality of its doctors and nurses; the diseases present; the usable hospitals and available medicines; the German atrocities and villages affected; the kind and percentage of crops sown; and presence of seeds, fertilizer, work animals. Young to Caskey, January 27, 1944, and Young to George (Apostolidis), March 6 and 12, 1944, NARA 226/190/1 and 226/190/78/96.

22. Count Del Balzo served until March 1944. Three artillery lieutenants were mission leaders, a sergeant major of signals was a radio operator, a corporal was a mission guide and courier, and others were the caique crew. A Milanese artillery captain led an Izmir SI operational group with two privates as orderly and boatman. NARA 226/210/277/2. In time, Caskey had a part-time radio operator as well. Eventually, Caskey would employ Greeks from Athens College. In addition, army, navy, and civilian personnel arrived without written orders. Caskey to Thomas Bland, Cairo, August 16, 1944, NARA 226/202/1/3.

23. Young to Caskey, January 13 and February 29, 1944, NARA 226/190/1.

24. As early as September 13, Taylor recommended disposing of the *Samothrace*. Daniel seconded his opinion on December 1, 1943. Maritime.

25. Petrow's villa was east of the harbor at Sidi Haber with a car and a supply of liquor.

26. Kanapitsa (Karnambitsa) was a fairly well sheltered small harbor opposite Samos where six uniformed Turkish officers were stationed, and British caiques with Greek crews moored.

27. Caskey valued Manoudis for his fluency in Turkish.

28. Debriefing of W. Ehrgott (AMM and Maritime). NARA 226/99.

29. Cox left on December 17 and arrived on December 23. Cox protested the Allied bombing of Piraeus and Salonika, which in Piraeus alone had sunk a Red Cross ship, left countless refugees, and killed 12,000. Cox to Dow January 21, 1944, NARA 226/215/1/25887. Devastated by the snafus encountered in delivering the food and clothing to Samos, she conferred with George White, GWRA chief in Cairo. Sperling to Caskey, January 1, 1944, NARA 226/190/1/4. Later she was advised to stockpile them in Cyprus, where they could be better controlled, shipped up to Izmir Bay, and offloaded to smaller caiques, thus avoiding Turkish customs and other difficulties. Cox to Donovan, March 13, 1944; Donovan to Steinhardt, January 8, 1944, 226/215/1/25887. By March 15, Cox recommended that the supplies be warehoused on Cyprus. The plan was approved by Davis and Harry Hill by April 26, 1944.

30. Cox "Report on Field Conditions," January 12, 1945. Cox to Dow, February 23, 1944, NARA 226/219/1/26828 and 26872.

31. Cox to Sherman Wallace, August 16, 1944. Cox to Dow, February 23, 1944, NARA 226/219/1/26828 and 26872.

32. Sperling to Caskey January 29 and February 24, 1944, NARA 226/190/1/4. Sperling thought Howard Reed, an Izmir-born American, could work at "Dublin," but Young did not want to waste a good SI man there and instead assigned George Psoinos (Special Operations) and Mossidus (Maritime). Sperling to Young, February 2, 5, 9 and 12, 1944. Young to Sperling February 8 and 15, 1944, 226/190/1/12.

33. Young to colleagues, January 4, 1944; Cairo weekly report, February 5–12, 1944; Young to Caskey, March 10, 1944, NARA 226/190/1 and 3. Her Beirut post had been filled and her cover given to another.

34. In 1941, the Turks threatened to go to war if the Germans occupied its border with Bulgaria. The Turks and Germans signed the nonaggression pact on June 18, 1941, three days before the Germans invaded the Soviet Union, and the trade agreement in October 1941, but tension did not subside for months. In November 1943 Georgiades apprised Young that chrome was being barged to Varna, Bulgaria and copper ore was traveling by train. Young to Paul [West], November 12, 1943, NARA 226/99/54 and 35/4.

35. Kellis had been at Cairo since May 1943. Young to Lada Mocarski, February 13 and 28 and March 7, 1944, NARA 226/199/198. "Preclusive Operations in the Neutral Countries in World War II," March 20, 1947, 169/159/1 BL 6522 "Production of Chrome in Turkey," September 16, 1943, 169/159/5. Agreements concluded between Turkish and German negotiators stipulated that Turkey would sell Germany a maximum of 90,000 tons of chrome in 1943 and 45,000 tons in 1944 in exchange for mil-

itary equipment. See Deringil 1989, 129. Although the Montreux Convention of 1936 stipulated that the Bosphorus be considered neutral waters, Turkey interpreted its responsibilities to monitor and enforce neutrality of the straits liberally and allowed German merchant ships carrying war matériel and ore access to the Black Sea. Much of the diplomatic correspondence and negotiations between the countries focused on this issue. OSS Inter-working Group (IWG) Files of George Wood, alias Fritz Kolbe, NARA 226/Boxes 440–42. Box 440: 1–3: February 1944; 137: Turkish American Affairs, March 1944; 169: Turkey's relations with Bulgaria and Russia, March 1944; 229: Anglo-American Demands made of Turkey, January 1944; 257: Turkish Foreign Affairs, April 1944; 258 Turkish Chrome shipments to Germany, April 1944; 302: Turkish negotiations with Germany, Box 441: Box 442: 1178: German Chrome Negotiations, September 1943; 1179: German Chromium Ore Project. Spiro Cappony, personal communication, January 3, 2008.

36. The Emniyet cooperated with Georgiades because he had informed on Turks who were spying for the Bulgarians, twelve of whom they executed. Except Marty ("Gosling") and his original courier, George Valassiades, his four or five sub-agents were unknown to OSS because of fear of betrayal from both sides. NARA 226/190/1/13. Georgiades to Iatrides, February 7, 1973, courtesy Iatrides. Georgiades scotched the plan to use "Chicago," the longest bridge (over 450 yards) at Marasia, and "Cicero," at Karaagatch, because they both originated in Turkey and destroying them would do the same to OSS posts in Turkey. So they decided to focus on those that passed only through Greek and Bulgarian territory instead. Young to Paul [West], November 12, 1943, ibid. The Germans had totally purged the Greeks in the town of Marasia earlier that year.

37. There was a change in leadership of guerrillas with arrival on February 17 of Athinodorus, EAM political commissar, and others arrived in Evros from the KKE central headquarters. Kriton became the ELAS leader in Evros and Lykourgos the leader of the Evros guerrillas.

38. Leslie Boyd described Cairo as being "the dog that wags the tail and Istanbul was the tail." Boyd to MacFarland, January 26, 1944. Young to Sperling, February 8 and 15, Penrose to Wickam, February 19, 1944, and Sperling to Young, March 11, 1944, NARA 226/190/1/10.

39. Von Papen's source was "Cicero." See chap. 10.

40. Sperling Report, February 24–March 1 and March 2–8, 1944, NARA 226/210/277/2 and 3. Sperling to Caskey, February 16, 17, and 27, 1944, 226/190/1/5; Young to Sperling, February 24 and March 21, 1944, 226/190/1/8.

41. Young to Caskey and to Lada Mocarski, weekly report, February 13, 1944. Young to Caskey, March 21, 1944, NARA 226/199/198.

42. Manolis Alnakidis was the imprisoned agent. Caskey to Young, February 10, 1944. NARA 226/190/2/14.

43. Caskey to Young, January 30, 1944. Athens was to return by March 6, but instead returned on the nineteenth—almost two weeks late. Eventually, Lt. John Savage took over on July 25, 1944. NARA 226/190/2/14.

44. C. M. Woodhouse and G. Wines convened the conference, which took place

from February 11 to February 22. On March 3, 1944, they reached an agreement. After Wines was recalled, Sarafis sent him copies of all correspondence since he got nothing from the British. Iatrides 1972, 43–44. Wines earned the Legion of Merit award for his labors.

45. Sterling Hayden infiltrated him, and Taylor (and Oliver) brought him out. Afterward, a Greek whose dory was named "the United States of America" transported all of Oliver's agents back and forth through the Strait of Otranto.

46. This dwarfed the autumn squabble over "Havana" between Taylor (Maritime) and Daniel over control of the caique service when Taylor rightly maintained that the archaeologists were wasting their time on Maritime matters when they should have been focusing on intelligence. The divided authority between SI and Maritime on Cyprus sacrificed its efficiency. Daniel to Dow, cable of November 8, 9, 14, and 20, 1943, NARA 226/190/1/6 and 226/144/76. Long after Taylor had left for Italy, Daniel was still trying "to put in a couple of punches in the battle of Cairo" over Maritime issues, and his behavior temporarily cost him a promotion. See chap. 8.

47. Caskey to Toulmin, March 22, 1944, NARA 226/210/277.

48. Penrose to Shepardson, March 11; McBaine to Toulmin, March 13; and Young to colleagues March 26, 1944, NARA 226/190/1 and 226/211/1.

49. MacFarland hired Lt. Subi Saadi to handle his Greek Desk matters in Cairo, but he did not speak Greek. Young to Caskey, March 10, 1944, NARA 226/190/1. Young to colleagues, March 26 and Caskey to Young April 9, 1944, 226/211/1. OSS Cairo History. Young, History of the Greek Desk, April 10, 1944, NARA 226/216/9/41. Young, "S.I. Greek Desk, Cairo, Historical Outline" April 10, 1944, NARA 226/216/9/44.

50. On March 16, 1944, Else met with Cox's friends at an EAM conference with MI-6, SOE, and A Force in Haifa. Later they appointed republican General Euripides Bakirdzis president and minister of foreign affairs while Communists led the ministries of interior, justice, and agriculture. Iatrides 1972, 43–45.

51. Iatrides 1972, 53–54. MacVeagh blamed both Greeks and British for the failure. Stavrianos 1950, 302–11.

CHAPTER TEN

1. Young to Caskey, April 3, 1944, received by Caskey on April 21. NARA 226/190/1.

2. The notes in this chapter are for those who would like to try to unravel the myth of "Cicero" and his denouement. Much has been written on the spy and quite a lot of misinformation put forth, not least by the protagonists themselves.

3. Nele Kapp was born on July 31, 1919. Case Western Reserve University Records, courtesy Don Laing. Bazna's autobiographical account of his alter ego, Cicero, included snatches of interviews, conducted in the early 1960s by journalist G. Thomas Beyl with Kapp, whose taped transcriptions Bazna used (1962, 107, 114–15, 145, 178–80) and by Hans Schwartz with Moysich's friend and colleague at the German embassy (Seiler Bazna OSS agent, 1962, 137–43, 152) henceforth (Kapp, Beyl)

and (Seiler, Schwartz). Heatts published W. Ewart Seager's report on "Operation Honeymoon" (henceforth Seager) in Heatts 1995, 48.

4. *Cleveland Plain Dealer,* April 24, 1944, 1. Karl Kapp led the Cleveland Germans in *Sieg Heils* and the national anthem and, in 1940, assured them of Hitler's victory. Kahn 1978, 69, 590 n. 345; Breuer 1989, 176. *Auswärtiges Amt. Politisches Archiv. Inland II Geheim* vol. 106: January 26, 1944, PRO FO. According to Farago, who mined the Abwehr archives, in 1938 the Abwehr, Germany's military intelligence service, gave Kapp a list of what *Oberkommando der Wehrmacht* wanted information on: factories of "special military significance," which manufactured "aluminum, magnesium, and rubber, essential for the production of aircraft." He complied, hiring agents whom he set up in Canada after helping them transit the border at Detroit. They furnished "a great number of up-to-date Canadian newspapers, the careful reading of which yielded important information, and also original material that could not be published because of censorship." In the summer of 1944, Kapp produced "invaluable information that was not otherwise or normally available about new factories and older ones in the process of being converted to the production of engines, tanks, ammunition, chemicals, machines, and machine tools." Apparently, Kapp tried to infiltrate the Cleveland civil defense system as well as that for chemical warfare and had one of his agents procure the latest GI gas mask. He sent his materials to Major General Friedrich von Bötticher, German military attaché in Washington, who forwarded them via diplomatic pouch to Berlin (Farago 1971, 489). By contrast, Seager maintained that Kapp detested the Führer silently, as did his daughter. Heatts 1995, 49.

5. She graduated from the Laurel School in Shaker Heights and attended the Flora Stone Mather College at Case Western Reserve University for three years. *Cleveland Plain Dealer,* April 24, 1944, 1 and September 21, 1972, 7E, by Robert Stock. See also the Case Western Reserve Archives. (Kapp, Beyl) in Bazna 1962, 107.

6. (Kapp, Beyl) in Bazna 1962, 107.

7. According to Caskey's report of April 19, 1944, to OSS Headquarters, Cairo, NARA 226/210/277/2 (henceforth, Caskey). (Kapp, Beyl) in Bazna 1962, 107. Wires (1999), who never saw Caskey's account, offers a conflicting version.

8. Kapp claimed that this was after the assassination of the Bulgarian king. Bazna (1962, 112) charged that it was Roosevelt's friend George H. Earle III who recruited her. Earle was a Philadelphia Main Liner and former governor of Pennsylvania whom the president personally commissioned lieutenant commander to serve as assistant naval attaché in Istanbul. Earle was American envoy to Vienna in 1933–34, and the U.S. ambassador to Bulgaria until December 27, 1941. Farago 1971, 572–75. Cave Brown 1975, 446, claimed that Kapp met and fell in love with an American on Earle's staff who had followed him to Turkey as an OSS agent, and subsequently married him. While intriguing, this has not been corroborated and there are many inaccuracies in Cave Brown's narrative. Seager mentioned nothing about her espionage work in Sofia. Heatts 1995.

9. They stayed at the Bulgari Hotel. (Seiler, Schwartz) in Bazna 1962, 141.

10. (Kapp, Beyl) in Bazna 1962, 107–8.

11. According to Seiler, "There was a general impression among German diplomatists in Sofia that things were going to get unpleasant there." This knowledge had been acquired by the agent Cicero. (Seiler, Schwartz) in Bazna 1962, 141.

12. Moysich 1950, 202.

13. Caskey. Seiler, the attaché, noted that she was quiet.

14. Moysich 1950 and (Seiler, Schwartz) in Bazna 1962, 141–43. Cave Brown (1975, 146) claimed that she arrived with an OSS agent as her bodyguard.

15. (Kapp, Beyl) in Bazna 1962, 145.

16. Under the *Reichssicherheitshauptamt,* the RSHA, or Reich Security Department VI.

17. Moysich 1950, 145.

18. Caskey.

19. Rubin (1989) alleged that it was an anti-Hitler Austrian friend. He claimed, without citing his sources, that they met at the Austrian's apartment near the Iranian embassy as late as March 17. Gnade was there.

20. When he was contacted, Gnade was completing a report, "British Military Controls in Iraq," for the U.S. State Department. NARA 165.

21. (Kapp, Beyl) in Bazna 1962, 108, 176. This would have been Richard Gnade or Ewart Seager. She may have fantasized about the friendship with the American and conflated it with that with her later German lover in Ankara.

22. Heatts, using Seager 1995, 49.

23. Rubin 1989, 242. Accounts vary concerning this man; he was one of two pilots who claimed to have crash-landed in the Black Sea and were lionized by the German community in Turkey before being discovered as deserters. Moysich 1950, 19–22, 144, 171, 173. According to another source, they worked for MI–6.

24. Seager in Heatts 1995, 49.

25. Since October 26, 1943. Bazna 1962, 46, 50–51. Cicero's first delivery was on October 30, the last day of the Moscow Conference, when they had met at ten that night in a toolshed on the grounds of the German embassy.

26. The film included the telegrams to the ambassador concerning decisions reached at the Moscow conference. Moysich 1950, 59.

27. The bombing raid was planned at the Tehran Conference, and plans circulated by telegram to all ambassadors, including the British ambassador in Turkey, Sir Hughe Knatchbull-Hugesen.

28. (Kapp, Beyl) in Bazna 1962, 108, 145. Kapp alleged that the meeting happened right away, but Rubin (1989, 241) claimed that this meeting did not take place until more than two months after her arrival in Turkey, that is, on March 17. Her reports began in mid-January. Because of OSS friction with MI-6, the Americans kept the knowledge to themselves. Wires 1999, 132.

29. (Kapp, Beyl) in Bazna 1962, 109.

30. Bazna (1962, 109) thought she had recognized him on the first day.

31. Seager in Heatts 1995, 49.

32. Kolbe passed documents from the German Foreign Ministry to Dulles be-

ginning in August 1943. One Foreign Office document of October 7 contained British long-range policy toward Turkey. By January 19, 1944, the British had begun an official inquiry and cabled Ankara. Wires 1999, 130–31.

33. Count Vanden Huyvel was the head of Berne MI-6, responsible for security at all diplomatic missions, whose counterespionage section was to protect it from incursions and spies.

34. Bazna 1962, 102–5.

35. This conflicts with Wires's statement that the Americans, knowing by February that there was a spy in the British embassy, chose not to reveal this to their British "cousins." Wires 1999, 167–68, 194–95.

36. They were Sir John Dashwood, head of security, and detective Chief Inspector Cochrane. Lt. Col. Montague Chidson, the assistant military attaché working for MI-6, barely spoke to Knatchbull-Hugesen, according to Nicholas Elliott of MI-6 Cairo. Elliott 1991, 135.

37. In Berlin, the foreign minister, Joachim von Ribbentrop, who had received the celluloid gold, distrusted the documents' authenticity and thought the valet a British plant, "too good to be true." Moysich 1950; Bazna 1962, 111; and Elliott 1991, 133. The British could not see that the Germans were actually using the intelligence.

38. Sperling to Young February 16, 1944, NARA 226/190/1.

39. The woman who translated the documents in Berlin recorded the exact number. After the first payment in bona fide pounds sterling, the Germans duped Cicero with counterfeit bills produced in Sachsenhausen concentration camp outside Berlin. Moysich 1950, 203.

40. Rubin 1989, 242.

41. (Kapp, Beyl) in Bazna 1962, 109. When her boss returned from Istanbul, she inquired about Pierre's identity. Moysich 1950.

42. Moysich 1950, 17–18, 142.

43. Bazna 1962, 109 and (Kapp, Beyl) in Bazna 1962, 178–79.

44. According to her own report. Rubin 1989, 243.

45. Taking a fiercely patriotic line to mask her own sympathies, she discussed recent defections of German agents to the Americans. (Seiler, Schwartz) in Bazna 1962, 153. Moysich 1950, 176.

46. In the third week of March. (Seiler, Schwartz) in Bazna 1962, 154.

47. Moysich 1950, 170.

48. Bazna 1962, 178.

49. (Seiler, Schwartz) in Bazna 1962, 155, 175; (Kapp, Beyl) in Bazna 1962, 170, 179; Moysich (1950, 177) insisted that she contacted the Americans on April 3. Rubin (1989, 243) claimed that she phoned Gnade on April 6.

50. (Kapp, Beyl) in Bazna 1962; and Moysich 1950, 169–71. (Seiler, Schwartz) in Bazna 1962, 155, does not mention the date.

51. Moysich 1950, 177–78.

52. In mid-December. (Kapp, Beyl) in Bazna 1962, 109. Bazna (1962, 160–61) thought the individual was named "Sears."

53. Bazna systematically excised all incriminating evidence. He moved the banknotes hidden under the carpet of his room to a hiding place under the basement steps of the embassy, packed them in a suitcase, and took them to the house of his mistress. He smashed his Leica, lightbulb, and quadripod and threw them into the river. The next day, he had his mistress bring the suitcase to the embassy by taxi. Then they deposited the British banknotes in his private safe deposit box at the bank and never returned to the house, to which he had once referred as "Villa Cicero" in the Kavaklidere neighborhood of Ankara. Bazna 1962, 116, 156–57, 162–68.

54. Caskey.

55. (Seiler, Schwartz) in Bazna 1962, 176–77.

56. Rubin 1989, 244.

57. Moysich 1950, 181–83. (Seiler, Schwartz) in Bazna 1962, 177.

58. Rubin 1989, 244. There was no mention of this by Moysich or Bazna.

59. (Kapp, Beyl) in Bazna 1962, 179. There had been leaks in OSS Istanbul and they may have wanted to show that they were able to conduct work with absolute discretion.

60. OSS X-2 or counterintelligence claimed that they had interrogated her through Gnade. John Maxson, X-2 Branch History Report, September 1944; Cairo X-2 Branch Report, April 22, 1944, NARA 226/210/503/6 and 294/5.When a date appeared during her captivity, she was shoved under the bed. Her picture with hennaed hair appeared in the *Cleveland Plain Dealer,* April 24, 1944, 1.

61. His story about spotting her has not been corroborated. Wires 1999, 167. Brigadier General Tindall (U.S. military attaché) requested that the special mission "Operation Honeymoon" be undertaken because Kapp had defected to his office. April 1944 report. NARA 226/99/122/3.

62. Rubin (1989, 244) confused the two and gave the wrong brother credit. He also gave the wrong day, April 6, for the phone call to the Americans (1989, 243).

63. Seager in Heatts 1995, 52.

64. Seager in Heatts 1995, 52. Rees had cancer.

65. Major Christian and Morrison-Bell. Seager had planned for her to stay with his relatives, but it proved impossible. He probably suggested his friend Caskey as an alternative. His older brother had been one of Caskey's first contacts in Turkey, and Caskey frequently bunked with him in Ankara.

66. The archaeologist later confessed that he was unsure of what to do if someone had actually shown up to kidnap her. Rubin (1989, 244) mistakenly claimed that she stayed "with an American couple."

67. Tindall to Toulmin, April 25, 1944, NARA 226/92A/19/283.

68. Gonatas (MI-6) notified the Emniyet. Caskey. See chap. 6 n. 43.

69. This was the second marine escape that Caskey had masterminded. See chap. 8.

70. Captain Olivey. Caskey.

71. Thomas Curtis and George Psoinos of the Chicago mission and Costas Couvaras of Pericles were at "Boston" when Kapp passed through and remembered the big black sedan pulling up and Kapp getting out and sailing off. Another Greek

who knew Turkish and French volunteered to accompany the party. Again Rubin wrongly (1989, 244) claimed that on April 13 she fled with Seager by ship to Cairo, where she was interrogated for two months. She had not even arrived in Izmir by that date, and Seager never left Turkey. Wires (1999) mistakenly claimed that she was flown to Cairo for questioning and returned in disguise to Ankara.

72. Seager thanked Caskey for the "endless courtesies" extended by Caskey to him and his "ward." Ewart Seager to Caskey, April 26, 1944, NARA 226/190/1/10; and Caskey.

73. To Selcuk and Kushadasi. *Auswärtiges Amt. Politisches Archiv. Inland II Geheim* vol. 106: 8, April 18, 1944, PRO FO.

74. Caskey's April 20–26, 1944, weekly report to OSS Cairo, NARA 226/210/277/2.

75. *Times* (London), April 21, 1944, 3: 3, 2; Associated Press, Ankara, April 23, 1944; and *Cleveland Plain Dealer,* April 24, 1944, 1. To protect her parents and himself, von Papen had local doctors report that she was mentally imbalanced.

76. *Cleveland Plain Dealer,* April 24, 1944, 1, wrongly reported that Kapp had been taken to Syria. Diplomatic intercepts also concerned chrome: on the Turks ceasing the shipment of chrome to Germany on April 29, 1944, and between Ankara and Tokyo, May 4, 1944, NARA RG 457 Boxes 410 VI-11 and 412 VI-12. Turkish Chrome Shipments to Bulgaria, March–April 1944, 447/2, and Operation Royal Flush supplies and Turkish Chrome to Germany, May 1944, 447/8, and Cutting off ties to Turkey, July 1944, Reel 168, British Cabinet Papers PREM 3, Series 1 Parts 1 and 2 Turkey III.

77. NARA 226/210/277/2.

78. Daniel to Caskey, May 17, 1944, NARA 226/190/1.

79. Seager to Caskey, April 26, 1944, NARA 226/190/1/10. Seager wrote Kapp, "You have been elected a charter and original member of the 'Blue Gentian' Society which consists solely of persons like yourself who have undergone similar experiences. . . . It was such a disappointment that I wasn't able to collect the reward for you—the idea was fascinating." Rubin 1989, 248. His letter was seized and he was investigated for corresponding with an enemy alien.

80. Sadly, they did just that. As a result, it took years of sleuthing to find the document.

81. Although Moysich was said to have been reduced to "a state of nervous incompetence" and to have been "ripe for defection" after Kapp, Washington virtually prohibited future defections. Its lack of support for those, like Kapp, who did defect was a great disappointment to X-2. The Americans were junior partners who had to submit to British oversight in almost everything, including the interrogation of defectors, specifically Kapp. Carl Packer, "X-2 History from its Inception to 31 August, 1944," NARA 226/210/64/4. Caskey could not have imagined what would happen to Kapp. She was flown to Cairo and interned in a POW camp in Egypt. There she was "presented" to the British, who, judging by the expressionless faces of her British interrogators in Cairo, she gathered had never heard of Cicero. For them she was "a slap in the face." Kapp wrote Seager from Cairo protesting her incarceration. "The

British still minimize the whole thing to avoid losing face." Long after the Cicero affair had been disclosed, General Sir Stewart Menzies, the head of MI-6, snapped, "Of course Cicero was under our control." Cave Brown 1975, 404. Meanwhile, the unrepentant Moysich, frequently approached to switch sides, was interned on the grounds of the German embassy with his family until late April 1945, by which time Hitler was dead.

82. Seager to Caskey, April 26, 1944, NARA 226/190/1/10.

83. Tindall to Toulmin, April 25, 1944, NARA 226/92A/19/283. Shepardson to Toulmin for Young, June 2, 1944.

CHAPTER ELEVEN

1. Anne Fuller, an archaeologist who had spent six years in Syria and Palestine on archaeological and sociological work, also reported to Cairo as a reports officer for Near East SI in June 1944. She began with COI R&A in September 1941. To go abroad she had to be commissioned, so she enlisted, was commissioned a second lieutenant in the Women's Army Corps.

2. In early June, Cox alleged that Greek government services in Izmir were fabricating reports on EAM atrocities on Skyros. July 20, 1944, G4365 NARA 226/108. Young to Caskey, June 1, 1944, 226/190/1.

3. Sperling, March 30–April 5, April 6–12, April 27–May 3, May 18–31, 1944, Reports NARA 226/210/277/2 and 3.

4. On April 19, Athens left Cyprus on a caique loaded with high explosives and machine guns to join the Chicago mission in Evros. At Egrilar, he piled on 800 pounds of warehoused OSS ammunition and supplies as well as navigation intelligence for the northern Aegean. On the twenty-fourth, he reached "Boston." There he picked up Maritime Gunnery Sergeant Thomas Curtis and a radio operator who had been shunted off to "Boston" after the operator brought a whore to Cox's flat. They established recognition signals with Kellis and appointed April 30 for their rendezvous in Evros, but ran aground and were delayed by storms for almost two weeks. They hid on the Turkish coast several miles south of the appointed spot and, on the night of May 11, finally contacted Kellis and the guerrillas, who offloaded men and supplies and carried the munitions to their mountain hideout and stashed them with others dropped by U.S. planes from Bari. Once all were safe, Kellis gave the guerrillas a five-day training in the use of American weapons, selected twenty for further training in explosives and sabotage, and assigned groups to different target areas. On May 23, Kellis led an advance party north, and Athens squired the rest of the 170 guerrillas with 1,400 pounds of plastic explosives (C-2). After two days of mountain hiking, they descended into the Evros Valley, where they traveled only at night, zigzagging to confuse trackers. Only three people knew the destination and purpose for the trip. The saboteurs had no idea that the rear guard carried explosives, and the rear guard did not know that saboteurs were part of the group. Kellis and Athens left the main body in the Evros triangle and canvassed the bridges from Edirne to Bulgaria with two

guerrillas. On the twenty-ninth, they returned and apprised the others of the plan. Then they divided them into four groups. One group would eliminate interference from German and Bulgarian guards. A diversionary screen would prevent reinforcements from reaching the area. A third would cut communications while Athens, Kellis, and the demolition squad set the charges. As luck would have it, they caught the Germans napping. They had spent an hour and twenty minutes mining the bridge before a sentry finally noticed activity and began firing, but it was too late. Kellis lit the five-minute delay fuse, and it went off. Curtis blew up "Joliet." Caskey to Young, May 3, 1944, NARA 226/190/1. James Kellis, "Report on the Evros Mission" (Kellis), 226/215/54. MEDTO pouch for June 19, 1944, 226/99/35/4. Cappony interview, January 7, 2008 (Cappony).

5. Kellis. MEDTO pouch for June 19, 1944, 226/99/35/4.

6. Brigadier General R. A. Osmun, Memo of Information for the Joint Chiefs of Staff, 8–13, NARA Modern Military Division, 1.

7. Mort Kollender to V. Lada-Mocarski, Chief Cairo SI, December 12, 1943, NARA 226/190/74/34.

8. Young to Caskey, April 3, May 11, and June 15, 1944, NARA 226/190/1.

9. Pericles left Cairo on March 13 and Alexandria five days later. They reached Karavostasi on the twenty-fifth and departed for Izmir on April 5. On the thirteenth they arrived in "Boston," whence they departed on the twenty-third.

10. "Tomtit," Tom Stix, was a wealthy liberal who had graduated Phi Beta Kappa and gotten a law degree from Yale. He had served with the American Field Service in 1941 in England, the West Indies, and Panama, and left for Greece on May 28, 1944. NARA 226/190/1/4.

11. Stix to Young, May 31, 1944; Young to Caskey, May 11 and 24, 1944, NARA 226/190/1/4.

12. Couvaras to Kollender, May 28, 1944, NARA 226/190/74/34.

13. Frank Wisner to Young, June 14–22 Report, NARA 226/211/187/5. Sperling to Young, June 19, 1944; Sperling to Penrose, July 29, 1944, 226/190/1/13.

14. Elli Adossides, who had continued her relief work during the Occupation, was one of the first witnesses fewer than six days after the massacre. She reported to Cairo 200 dead, 80 percent of whom were children and infants. In their killing spree they had not spared mules, cats, and dogs. Agora, A, ASCSA.

15. Couvaras to Kollender, Pericles radio dispatches, June 5, 12, 13, 14, 19, 27, and 28; July 1 and 2, 1944. Courtesy Iatrides.

16. Stix to Young, May 31 and June 15, 1944, and Couvaras to Kollender, Pericles radio dispatches, June 5, 12, 13, 14, 19, 27, and 28; July 1 and 2, 1944. Courtesy Iatrides.

17. Iatrides 1972, 71–72.

18. Couvaras to Kollender, May 1, 4, and 28; June 16, and July 14, 1944, and to George, June 1, 1944 NARA 226/190/74/34 and 36.

19. In late February, MI-6 sent Demertzis (in cahoots with the Greek vice consul in Istanbul) and a Jewish intelligence agent under relief cover from Moses into Thrace. Previously the Bulgarians had protected their own Jews and sent off to concentration camps only those from Greek Thrace, but now the Germans pressured

the Bulgarians to surrender their Jews. Col. Edward Buxton to Toulmin April 22, and Caskey to Young, May 1, 1944, NARA.

20. Cable 694, Istanbul Cairo.

21. Because the refugees had to be landed near Cheshme, they became a British responsibility. When Berry asked about using the British escape service, Caskey said he was not at liberty to discuss it, but volunteered to engineer a meeting with Berry and the British. Cable 444, Izmir Cairo.

22. 109 (Donovan) to Toulmin and Penrose, July 26, 1944, asked Izmir to help the WRB find boats. Caskey affirmed his desire for harmony and mutual assistance among American agencies, but said that he could not divulge information about the British without their consent. He was "willing and eager to carry out directives issued by competent authority," but believed that the Jews could not be brought out without danger to security, unfair burden on the British, and extreme danger to delicate relationships with the Emniyet. Young volunteered to transfer WRB money to Athens for Jews hiding there, but refused to evacuate Jews from Greece without clearance from the Turkish Government, which he had not received. In August, MacFarland asked Caskey to release a base to the WRB, but Caskey refused. Instead, he agreed to speak to the Izmir Emniyet and provide technical help once Ankara (the U.S. embassy, the Turkish Foreign Office, General Staff, and Emniyet) had approved the scheme. He held three caiques for the WRB, but it did not respond. Cable 3339, Cairo to Washington, July 9, 1944; MacFarland to Caskey, August 4, 1944; Caskey to MacFarland, August 4, 14, and 21, 1944; Young to Caskey, July 6, 20, and 27, August 25, 1944, NARA 226/190/1.

23. Kollender to Toulmin, July 3, 1944, postscript. Penrose, the former head of Near East SI, succeeded Lada-Mocarski.

24. There is no record of Young, Penrose, or McBaine disapproving the plan, but Young did not like Couvaras. Kollender to 109 (Donovan), July 8, 1944, #33244; Toulmin to 109, Wolf, and 154 (Shepardson), July 8, 1944, #33254; and Donovan and Shepardson to Toulmin #37364. July Reports contained in pouch for July 10, 1944. Couvaras was notified by cable on July 12, 1944. MEDTO Daily Report of Cables, NARA 226/99/35/4 and 5.

25. Couvaras, radio dispatch to Kollender, July 14, 1944. Courtesy Iatrides.

26. On May 29 Else left with Helot's agents and arrived after a fortnight in Bari, where they trained in parachutes with SOE. They dropped at Monemvasia on June 26 and by the thirtieth were in radio contact. They documented the economic toll: houses bare of furniture, crops ruined or taken, atrocities and the liberation of Kalamata, during which John Fatseas saved lives. Reports of August 17 and September 9, 1944, NARA 226/190/178/89.

27. Gasoline agent "Roadrunner" opened three bases on Khalkidiki, at Kassandra, Krouso, and Olympia on the Struma Gulf (to be used only for black market caiques), and traveled by pirate caiques, by caiques carrying coal and charcoal to Stavros, and by train or car to Salonika. After its first base was betrayed, Gasoline's endangered agent survived in hiding from December 10, 1943, to February 1944 (see chap. 9). He returned with a radio operator in April 1944 and from that time was based in Salonika. Although the Germans occupied the house and seized its wire-

less, arrested a subagent, imprisoned him in a Greek concentration camp, and shipped him to Germany, and its radio contact did not begin until May, by June Phalanx was productive. NARA 226/92A/3/36.

28. Emerald was headquartered in Vathi and organized, directed, and supplied by Izmir from December 1943 to November 1944.

29. Helios (originally Gold for Siderokastro [East Macedonia], Mt. Pangaion, and western Thrace in March 1944) was canceled and renamed Helios and restaffed in June 1944 with agent Capt. Dios Fanourakis ("Duckling").

30. Lieutenant Colonel del Balzo organized Dago with Italians, later replaced by Greeks. It returned on March 20, 1944, and made a good report. Caskey's Lucian operated on different Dodecanese islands. It paid operatives in food: meat, rice, cigarettes, and sugar. They placed an agent and operator in Porto Lago on June 18–19, 1944, after the daytime blockade was lifted, volunteered to save buildings and factories, and delivered saboteurs to OSS Samos. They visited Pharmako-Gaidharo on August 26, Lisso from August 27 to August 31, Leros from September 1 to September 3 to provide military and shipping intelligence, Patmos from October 24 to November 5, and Lipsos from November 5 to November 7, 1944. Their stay-behind agents on Leros reported that 5,000 Germans were still in Leros on October 2. Daniel canceled his Archangel to Tilos on September 11, 1944.

31. It had reached the field in April after five months en route.

32. Roosevelt 1976, 121.

33. Young to Toulmin, April 22, 1944, NARA 226/210/168/9.

34. "Plan for SI Action in Greece. Statement of the Problem," August 29, 1944. NARA 226/154/34/518.

35. The AML was represented by Lieutenant Colonel Breckenridge and Bellm, UNRRA by Laird Archer and Kelsey, the American legation by MacVeagh, Arthur Parsons, and Harry Hill, the FEA by Wilson and Landis, and OWI by Snedeker and Grimbalis. Young to Toulmin, February 10, 1944, "Project for Activities in Greece after Liberation," March 23, 1944, NARA 226/194/34/518 and 226/211/1.

36. Reworded version in memorandum, Sperling to Toulmin, July 28, 1944, NARA 226/211/1.

37. The archaeologists had their own ideas for divvying up postliberation Greece. Any or all of the Peloponnese looked good to Young, who assumed that Sperling would be stationed in the western part of the Peloponnese where he had conducted archaeological work. Young to Caskey, March 1, 1944, and to Sperling, February 15, 1944, NARA 226/190/1/12 and 10 and 226/154/34/518. "Cruising around the islands" appealed to Caskey, and he focused on the military job of defeating the enemy. Before he opened the island base at Syra, he had to close the Turkish bases. Caskey to Young, March 15 and August 2, 1944, NARA 226/190/1.

38. Young to Toulmin, "Project for Activities in Greece after Liberation," March 23, 1944, in NARA 226/211/1. Later he added Volos, Mytilene, Messolonghi, Corinth, Naxos, and Samos to the list of sites for their intelligence network. "Hellenic Project," Young to Toulmin, April 22, 1944, 226/210/168/9.

39. Sperling memorandum, July 28, 1944, NARA 226/M1642/83. Microfilm M1642 contains correspondence to and from Donovan.

40. Young included the American College at Psychiko, Girls' School at Elleniko, and Farm School. Young to Toulmin, March 23, 1944, and April 22, 1944, NARA 226/211/1/88 and 226/210/168/9.

41. Donovan to J. Edgar Hoover, February 28, 1942, NARA 226/A1-224/717. Penrose and Young to SASAC 154 and Toulmin, April 22 and 23, 1944, NARA 226/211/1 and 226/211/7/88. 226/210/168/9. Young to Caskey, May 11, 1944. Penrose to Shepardson, May 5, 1944. Toulmin maintained that Skouras was not fit for Greek undercover work, and others voiced concern that, like his lawyer, George Vournas, he "planned to participate in Greek internal politics." 226/211/187/5. Scribner and Doering to Donovan, June 5 and 7, 1944. Toulmin to Doering and Scribner, June 7, 1944, NARA 226/99/35/4.

42. Cairo to "Plover," June 22, 1944. Carl Devoe, "Report on the Pericles Mission," August 25, 1944. See chap. 12. George Skouras to John Shaheen, August 4, 1944, and Report on Simmons Mission, December 13, 1944, 226/190/78/98.

43. Young to Caskey, July 6, 1944, NARA 226/190/1. "OSS History of Cairo," 226/99/53 doc p. 34.

44. "Duck," June 19–24 report received July 28, 1944, G4307, NARA 226/108. The agent, Fanourakis (Duckling), survived the sinking and returned to his island, Chalki. He turned himself in to prevent reprisals and committed suicide on November 1, 1944. Raiding Forces made 381 raids on seventy islands with 400 men by July 1944. By September, the SBS, now the Special Boat Squadron, left the Aegean.

45. Sperling, "Progress Report #1," "Project for SI Activities in Greece after Liberation," July 1, 1944, NARA 226/199/78/96. Sperling to Caskey and Daniel, July 24, 1944. State Department to Donovan, July 25, 1944, 226/M1642/83.

46. #4580, July 28, 1944, and #4620, August 1, 1944. Courtesy Iatrides.

47. Reports contained in MEDTO pouch for June 19, 1944, NARA 226/99/35/4.

48. Young and Else would take over Athens and Attica, Daniel Larissa, and Sperling Salonika.

49. Major General Hughes, AML.

50. Stavrides had taught at Athens College. Caskey to Young, May 3, 18, June 8, and August 2, 1944, and Young to Caskey July 25, 1944, NARA 226/190/1 and 226/190/2/14.

51. Young to Caskey, August 1, 1944, NARA 226/190/1. Col. J. G. O'Connor to Shepardson, May 23, 1944, 226/210/294/5. MacFarland switched to the Yugoslavia desk.

52. Zervas took Paramythia as his reward. Only in July 1944 did the British denounce them. PRO FO 371/43706.

53. "Plover" (Couvaras), Pericles radio dispatches and letters to Cairo, July 14, 17, 20, 23, 24, 26, 27, and 28 and August 1, 4, 6, 8 13, 15, 17, 24, and 27, 1944, NARA 226/90/74/34 and 36.

54. "Tomtit" (Stix) to Young, July 24 and 27, 1944, NARA 226/190/78/100.

55. Stix to Young, August 15, 1944, NARA 226/190/78/100.

56. The next voyage of the *Ayios Ioannis* brought 30,000 rounds of ammunition and machine guns for Kellis's second mission and then evacuated Curtis.

57. To be sure there would be no reprisals, Athens and Kapponis took all the prisoners' dog tags and wrote a letter to the commanding officer, threatening to give the prisoners to the partisans if atrocities continued. All summer long, they survived behind enemy lines in caves. To keep away from wild animals, they slept in trees. Thanks to the Bari supply drops, they had plenty of ammunition. With the guerrillas, they attacked isolated garrisons and interrupted enemy communications, cutting telephone lines, wrenching up railroad ties, putting up roadblocks on important highways, and ambushing them. Volunteers flocked to join, and eventually the group swelled to about 3,500 regulars and 25,000 reservists. The guerrillas would enter a town in the afternoon, be sheltered by the resistance, and then assemble at night, draw their weapons, and attack their targets. Meanwhile, the German garrisons surrendered or withdrew toward Salonika, or occasionally fought to the last man.

58. On the night of August 2, Kapponis was shot in the arm. Like a mantra, he kept repeating Ralph Waldo Emerson, "Do what you fear to do and the fear will die." Cappony. Britain recalled Knatchbull-Hugesen whose lax security had enabled Cicero's coup.

59. Penrose to Shepardson, Chief, SI, OSS in Washington, August 12, 1944, NARA 226/M1642/83. Young to Caskey, August 8 and 17, 1944; Sperling to Caskey and Cox, August 11, 1944, 226/190/1.

60. Cairo to Donovan in London and Toulmin at Bari, August 19, 1944. Cairo to Donovan August 18 and 22, 1944, NARA 226/M1642/83.

61. "OSS History of Cairo," p. 34. NARA 226/99. Donovan, Buxton, Rodrigo and Magruder stressed the need for evaluation by personnel outside Greece. Perfect cover for officers was not necessary. EXDET ALGIERS to Cairo, August 30, 1944, NARA 226/M1642/83.

CHAPTER TWELVE

1. OSS promised honorable terms, and more than 250 surrendered. Of the 1,500 Germans garrisoned there, 300 were captured and the rest fled into Turkey or were killed. The Greeks imprisoned the German POWs in a village schoolhouse and made off with 900 rifles and several mortars and submachine guns. The people went out with carts and collected the captured material, which they used to rip up train tracks and tear down bridges. Kapponis kept awake all night sending, receiving, coding, and decoding, with his uninjured hand. Lieutenant Athens and Kapponis made their way south as the Germans were passing north and westward. Athens stopped to collect the POWs' letters home as a German plane strafed villages and troops set them on fire. The Bulgarians allowed hundreds of Germans to escape from Alexandroupolis. Ferrai changed hands several times, and fighting continued on August 31, but Alexandroupolis was the only town in Thrace still held by the Germans. Then six guerrillas rowed Athens and Kapponis across the mouth of the Evros to an isolated stretch of beach on the Turkish shore where they waited for Kellis, who had brought up three more tons of plastic explosives, ammunition, and

other demolition devices as well as shoes, clothing, and food from the OSS supplies on Cyprus. After making contact, offloading the supplies onto guerrilla boats, and evacuating Athens and Kapponis, Kellis departed and brought them to recuperate at "Boston" before the long voyage to Egypt. Kellis, NARA 226/215/54. Reports contained in MEDTO pouch for June 19, 1944, 226/99/35/4. Cappony. SO History 226/99/55 and Wood to Scribner cable, June 16, 1944, 226/99/55; MEDTO daily report, 226/99/35/4.

2. *NYT,* August 19, 1944.

3. He came across with Captain George Chrysostomas and Sgt. Charles Meledones. Young to Else, September 8, 1944, NARA 226/190/9/79.

4. C. Kantianis (Kingfisher) "Report on the Secret Activities of the ELLAS Mission," NARA 226/210/64/5.

5. Hadas to Langer, September 13, 1944, NARA 226/M1642/83.

6. Papalas 2008, 205, Caskey to Aldrich, October 2, and to Else, October 3, 1944. October 5, 1944, semimonthly report of OSS-ME for September 16–30, 1944, NARA 226/99/52/4.

7. Aldrich and Glavin to Donovan, October 8, 19, 1944, from Caserta. Young to colleagues October 29, 1944, NARA 226/99/35/3.

8. Pili was one of three ports for OSS on Evvia that Athens arranged in March. Young to Else, September 22, 1944, NARA 226/190/9/79. Calvocoressi Final Report, November 15, 1944.

9. Young to colleagues, October 1, and to Else, September 22, 1944, NARA 226/190/9/79.

10. Young to colleagues, October 1, 1944, and to Else, October 3, 1944, NARA 226/190/9/79.

11. Cable, October 13, 1944.

12. Report of October 1–15, 1944, OSS-ME to Donovan, October 20, 1944, NARA 226/210/410/2. Aldrich to OSS SI Washington from Cairo, September 8, 1944. Else to Young and Caskey, October 6, 1944, 226/190/1.

13. Cox to the GWRA Executive Committee, May 19, 1944. Weinberg worked under Berry and Davis, and Crosby was to be the reports officer for the Athens base. Sperling to Caskey and Cox, August 11 and 15, 1944, NARA 226/190/1, 226/92A/5. Else to colleagues, September 9, 1944. Else report, September 16–30, 1944. Cox to Frank Curtis, GWRA, Cairo, September 26, 1944. 226/190/2/17. Cox went to Mytilene from September 14 to 16 and to Chios from September 21 to 23. She was disgusted with the preferential treatment received on Chios, thanks to British presence there. Her hero was an aristocratic Greek who had joined EAM. Cox to Else, September 26 and October 3, 1944.

14. Young to Caskey, September 19, 1944, cable. Else to Cox, cable of October 27, 1944, NARA 226/211/7/60. Else advised Penrose to avoid UNRRA and AML. September 30, 1944, 226/99/35/3. Else to Young and Caskey, October 6, 1944, 226/190/1. Toulmin to Donovan from Cairo, September 2, 1944. Penrose to W. T. M. Beale, Executive officer SI Washington, October 14, 1944, 226/M1642/83.

15. Else to Caskey, September 21 and 28, 1944, NARA226/190/1/9.

16. Petrow and Savage would be free to circulate in the islands and conduct intelligence activities, time permitting, but Petrow had to find a supply terminus on the mainland near Athens, repair facilities, etc. Aldrich to Petrow, October 8, 1944. Else to Caskey and Young October 6, 1944, NARA 226/210/277 and 226/190/1. After closing the propaganda broadcasting station at "Boston" just after the liberation of Athens, Savage closed "Boston" by October 30 and left for "Elba" on November 2.

17. Meeting held in Cairo with Maritime, Services, Communications, and SI September 24, 1944, NARA 226/250/1/5. Else to Caskey, September 28, 1944, 226/190/1. Savage and Dodson reconnoitered Tinos on September 30, 1944. Caskey to Aldrich, October 2, 1944, 226/190/1/9. But Aldrich was in Italy for conferences and did not receive his letter.

18. Donovan to the U.S. Joint Chiefs of Staff, October 9, 1944, NARA 226/M1642/83. G 6005 October 2, 1944, 226/108.

19. Pericles agent Plover (Costas Couvaras) joined them on the fifteenth. Wisner was a Wall Street lawyer.

20. Churchill 1953, 227–28.

21. G 5964 of October 2; G 5979 of October 4; G 5916 of October 1; G 5917 of October 2; G 5996 of October 5; G 6019 of October 6; G 5965, G 5925 and 6 of October 2; G 5980 of October 4, 1944; G 6021 of October 6, 1944. NARA 226/108.

22. On November 6, OSS Captain Andrew Rogers, whose chief concern was to negotiate a peace and keep EAM and Zervas's EDES forces from fighting, reported that EDES had occupied Corfu and discovered that the Germans had gone. Theater pouch review including November 6, 1944, report. His assistant, George Ghicas, was very unfavorable about the British delays. December 2 report on the liberation of Corfu in the December 9, 1944, MEDTO pouch, NARA 226/99/35/3.

23. A week later, Jellicoe of the SBS returned to Greece, secured the Patras airfield without bloodshed, and paved the way for Kanellopoulos.

24. En route, Young's bag with his special passport, 100 gold sovereigns, and cipher books was stolen. Sgt. Meledones, Theochares Stavrides, and a courier brought the vehicles. November 25, 1944, "Thirteenth semimonthly report of OSS-ME for October 31 through November 15, 1944," NARA 226/99/52/4.

25. Young to colleagues, October 19, 1944, NARA 226/190/9/79.

26. Loon's report on the day's events was filed on the fourteenth and rated B2. Dodo's was rated A2. NARA 226/108.

27. Young's report (6026) was rated A1 and circulated to Washington, Bari, and Caserta. NARA 226/108.

28. On October 2, Stevens reported to Lord, "no fighting . . . in Old Corinth" where Blegen's chauffeur, Athanasi, watched over School property. Meritt 1984, 25.

29. Young to Shear, November 3, and to Else, October 22, 1944, in HAT Shear, ASCSA, and NARA 226/190.

30. MacVeagh to Roosevelt, October 15, 1944, in Iatrides 1980, 397.

31. Rees's brother was also on Scobie's staff and already ensconced at the Grande Bretagne. Immediately after October 15, the entire Greek section of MI-6

moved to Allied Forces Headquarters in Naples. October 20, 1944, semimonthly report of OSS-ME for October 1–15, 1944, NARA 226/99/52/4. Iatrides 1972.

32. Young to colleagues, October 29, 1944, NARA 226/99/35/3.

33. Young to colleagues, October 29, 1944, NARA 226/99/35/3. Young to Shear November 3, 1944, in HAT Shear, ASCSA.

34. Evacuating Germans had trucked away hundreds of crates and trunks from their school. Young to colleagues "Athens, Sunday, [Nov.] 29th," NARA 226/190. Aldrich and Glavin to Donovan, October 8, 19, 1944, from Caserta. 226/M1642/53, Young to Meritt, February 7, 1945, APS Meritt. Keramopoullos was most bitter against Von Schoenbeck, Hampe, Kraiker, Welter, Jansen, and Wrede. One, Gebauer, was killed in an air crash. Young to Shear, November 3, 1944, HAT Shear. On February 8, 1943, Arthur Vining Davis asked Lord "what the German School has which the American School would like to get. . . . if the American School could get possession of the library and collections of the German school then there would be centered in the American school practically all the material of that character which is now or ever likely to be in Athens or Greece." Lord responded that "measures be taken to turn over to the American School of Classical Studies at Athens the library and the photographs and other scientific property of the institution . . . to be held in trust . . . or . . . confiscated. . . . they would nowhere be so useful as in our possession. . . . With the addition of the German library and the photographs belonging to the German School, the American School would become the center for all archaeological work in Greece." February 17, 1943. This matter was revisited after the end of the war. Stevens to Lord, November 30, 1945, Admin 310 and 804/2/8, ASCSA. "Thirteenth semimonthly report of OSS-ME for October 31 to November 15, 1944," to Director of Strategic Services NARA 226/99/52/4.

35. Report to Donovan on OSS-ME to USAFIME, October 31–November 15, 1944, NARA 226/99/52/4.

36. Aldrich traveled with Lieutenant Atwater, the new head of Maritime. Daniel's agent closed Cyprus while Daniel filed reports on traitors and collaborators in the Dodecanese and ceased SI coverage there on October 30.

37. Sailing via Syros, Delos, and Tinos on the twenty-fifth, Caskey arrived at "Key West" the next day. Then Savage proceeded to "Boston" on the twenty-eighth and returned to "Elba" on the thirty-first.

38. Three packs of American cigarettes purchased twelve to fifteen pounds of fresh fish. Laborers worked all day for a two-pound tin of corned beef hash and a few ounces of evaporated milk. "History of the OSS Maritime Unit in the Middle East, July 1943 to March 1945." "Elba" report, NARA 226/99 and 226/144/76.

39. Maritime report October 16–31, 1944, NARA 226/99/35/3.

40. According to plans laid by Lieutenant Percy Wood, Special Operations chief in Cairo. With the approval of Glavin and Davis at Caserta and Toulmin at Bari. Aldrich to 109 (Donovan), October 24, 1944, in November 17 Report on OSS-ME to USAFIME, October 1–15, 1944, NARA 226/210/410/2.

41. MacVeagh report. October 28, 1944, NARA 226/M1642/83. MEDTO daily report for November 1, 1944, NARA 226/99/35/6.

42. Oliver to CO, October 11, 1944, NARA 226/A1 224/571.

43. Penrose to W. T. M. Beale, Executive officer SI Washington, October 14; Penrose to Maddox, SI chief for MEDTO in Caserta, October 27, 1944, NARA 226/190.

44. With John Fatseas of Helot.

45. Skouras report, "The Peloponnese," January 27, 1945, NARA 226/210/484/2.

46. Caskey wrote Aldrich, "I had devoted my whole mind to the Elba Project and was surprised and, frankly, disappointed when I was suddenly removed from it without warning or consultation. . . . I realize that I have had the prize plum of all the Greek operations (except the men inside) for a long time." Then he continued bitterly, "You said . . . I was wanted in Athens. I was glad to have the opportunity of spending a day there and talking with Young, but . . . Young . . . could give me little hint of what I was supposed to do when I arrived, other than odd jobs of administration that he wants to be rid of . . . Send Else to Athens . . . or . . . appoint a deputy for him as real and authentic chief of the mission for Greece." November 2, 1944, NARA 226/210/277. Bailey replaced Else as acting chief of the Greek Desk in Cairo. November 25, 1944, "Thirteenth semimonthly report of OSS-ME for October 31 through November 15, 1944," 226/99/52/4.

47. Bailey sent the first report (GA-1) on November 8, 1944. Aldrich to Donovan November 7, 1944, NARA 226/M1642/83. He was there November 12–14, 1944. Cairo to Donovan, November 12, 1944. Captain Cain of Caserta was in Athens with Colonel Van Flack, General Sadler's medical officer, to discuss medical relief and to see Moyer's unit.

48. Crosby to Wallace, November 11, 1944. Crosby came with Young's former secretary, Pauline Manos, Ensign Constantine (X-2) Levathes, and Sgt. Wm. Gross. Roy Macridis and John Poulicos's secretary brought over mail, four typewriters, and a jeep and trailer for Moyers. Penrose semimonthly report for late November, 1944, NARA 226/99/52.

49. Aldrich had Petrow meet the British naval chief of staff for Piraeus, who agreed to supply him with oil from the British stocks and coordinated with the Piraeus shipping transport officer the protocol for the arrival of OSS supplies from Egypt. "New Elba" was one mile from the airport at Hassani. "Thirteenth semimonthly report of OSS ME, for October 31–November 15, 1944," NARA 226/99/52/4.

50. After depositing Caskey on November 13, Savage returned to close the Turkish bases while his assistant discharged caiques on Chios.

51. Report of October 1–15, 1944, OSS-ME to Donovan, October 20, 1944, NARA 226/210/410/2. E. G. Wilson to Glavin, December 9, 1944, 226/M1642/83.

52. On November 16, Clio flew with repatriated Greeks in an RAF bomber from Tobruk to a small military airfield near Parnes. At the end of life, she still remembered "the wonder and joy of flying over Taygetus," for just as they approached the Peloponnese, the clouds parted, revealing Mt. Taygetus covered in snow.

53. Young to colleagues Athens, "Sunday, 29th." November 25, 1944, "Thirteenth semimonthly report of OSS-ME for October 31 through November 15, 1944," NARA 226/99/52/4.

54. Aside from Else, Young Plan personnel were SI—Couvaras, Emanuel, Stix (also transportation officer), Reports—Crosby, Pauline Manos (also office manager), Pepper and Bartholomay (temporary); Security—Nickles; Finance—Lt. William Peratino; Communications—Chrysostomas, Rudas, Gross, Lantzas, Dickson, and Meledones (also Services); R&A—Seeley and Yavis; and Greek Liaison—Petrou (also SI). "Thirteenth semimonthly report of OSS ME for October 31–November 15, 1944," NARA 226/99/52/4.

55. "Dove" number 6362, October 18 reported on October 21, 1944, "B2" rating. NARA 226/108/60.

56. November 12 and 17 cables in MEDTO dailies, November 14 and 20, 1944, NARA 226/99/35/3.

57. The Simmons agents were 2nd Lt. John P. Russell "Jean" and Bulgarian-speaking radio operator from Salonika Lt. Nikolaos (Neil) Sotiriou (Greek Sacred Brigade and trained on codes and signals at the OSS school in Cairo). Skouras had bribed General Tsigantes of the Sacred Brigade to participate by saying that the mission's heroics would make a great movie. Skouras to Lt. Comm. John L. Shaheen, August 4, 1944. But this would not be a heroic narrative.

The two men left Alexandria on July 29 and arrived at "Boston" two weeks later. Khalkidiki was infested with security battalions and "very insecure" since the crew of the previous voyage had been beaten and robbed after landing an agent on the Kassandra Peninsula. Caskey and Savage recommended going via Pelion, but Young disagreed. Eighteen days passed while they waited at "Boston" for contacts, pin points, and details about their receiving party. They finally left on September 1, anchoring at Aivalik since they could not sail at night. At dusk on the second, they were machine-gunned by Turks on the coast of the Troad, but suffered no casualties and the next day reached the mouth of the Evros. From there, they sailed all night, reaching Pelion where they met Colonel Bakeless (junior military attaché, U.S. Embassy, Ankara), stayed with Lieutenant Downey, and waited for the guerrillas to issue a permit to travel. On September 14, it arrived, and Sotiriou proceeded north. On the twenty-fifth, he hired a rowboat with three black marketers, but after three days a storm forced them to shore near Tempi. Harassed by a German coast watcher, they reached a town three kilometers from Salonika on October 2 and looked for agents from Phalanx. To do so, he went to the Alcazar Cinema in Salonika, his left thumb bandaged, wearing glasses, and ready with rehearsed phrases. He found them, but too late. Although Sotiriou searched the airfields three times (as a shepherd, farmer, and fisherman) all were empty and the bombs gone. After the mission was canceled on October 16, Sotiriou joined Phalanx. Skouras report, January 27, 1945, NARA 226/210/484.

58. Skouras report, January 27, 1945, NARA 226/210/484. Khortiatis was destroyed on September 2, 1944. Waldheim was later UN secretary-general and elected president of Austria.

59. Skouras report, January 27, 1945, NARA 226/210/484.

60. A month later Skouras had met Lieutenant Russell in Volos. On November 21, they had found Sotiriou in Salonika and, for two days, also searched the airfields,

but found them destroyed, with only one upright wall. On November 23 they left for Athens, where Sotiriou met them on the twenty-ninth, and disbanded on December 4 while Sotiriou submitted his report. Skouras to OSS, December 1 and 6, 1944; Russell to OSS, December 13, 1944, NARA 226/190/78/98. Skouras report, January 27, 1945, 226/210/484.

61. Aldrich memorandum to Shepardson, December 18, 1944, NARA 226/92A/19/283.

62. Virginia Grace reports for November 7–13 and 20–23, 1944, NARA 226/210/277, and "Report," January 10, 1945, 226/190/3/35.

63. Petrow established an eight-man local committee with representatives from EDES, EAM, and the gendarmerie using Red Cross lists to make sure the distribution was equitable and based on need.

64. It remained open until February 4, 1945, when X-2 moved into its quarters. Penrose semimonthly report for late November, 1944, NARA 226/99/52.

65. On November 3, fire erupted in the OSS Cairo office at 8 Rustum Pasha, destroying the projection theater on the roof and flooding all the lower offices that two months earlier had undergone a massive reorganization, including R&A's library and SI's Central Intelligence Files, which had been united as the Central Intelligence Division of OSS Cairo under Virginia Rathbun. October 5, 1944, semimonthly report of OSS-ME for September 16–30, 1944, NARA 226/99/52/4. Women had their own apartments near headquarters or in the Zamalek neighborhood on Gezira, while male officers stayed at the Moffit-Astoria Hotel in downtown Cairo.

66. Penrose to Shepardson, November 27, 1944, NARA 226/190.

67. Penrose to W. T. M. Beale, Executive officer SI Washington, October 14 and November 1, 1944, and to Shepardson, November 22 and 28, 1944, NARA 226/190 and 226/99/35/3.

68. NARA 226/A1-224/249 and 61. James Murphy (the X-2 chief in Washington) tried to recruit Blegen and Alison Frantz for counterintelligence in 1944, NARA 226/92A/81. Murphy to Poole.

69. Wilson to Magruder, Aldrich, and Donovan, November 22, 1944, NARA 226/M1642/83. Penrose to Shepardson, November 22 and 28, 1944, 226/99/35/3. Robert P. Joyce, SI chief, Rear Zone, in Caserta to Glavin, November 28, 1944. Cables from Glavin and Joyce to Donovan, November 28 and 29, 1944, 226/210/285/4.

70. Meanwhile, M. R. Royce, embedded with SOE on Crete to encourage German surrender, reported that by November 16 the Germans had evacuated most of the island. December 14, 1944, report on Morale Operations activities on Crete in MEDTO pouch review for December 22, 1944, NARA 226/99/35/3.

CHAPTER THIRTEEN

1. Kirk in Caserta to Donovan in Washington. "Greece: EAM Crisis on the wane." November 23, 1944, NARA 226/M1642/83.

2. On November 30, Aldrich informed General Wilson that Caskey was returning to Washington and released him on the thirteenth. MEDTO daily report,

December 2, 1944, NARA 226/99/35/3. After discussing the matter with Shepardson and De Bardeleben, Aldrich recommended on December 18 that Caskey's services be terminated and that he be returned to the army. In a report on Caskey's work, Aldrich wrote that he considered Caskey a bad administrator who treated U.S. enlisted men no better than Greek seamen, and championing Greek-Americans who "were 90% Greek and 10% American." This "loss of balance" had greatly lowered American morale at his bases. Memorandum to Shepardson, December 18, 1944. On December 19, Caskey departed for the United States. He arrived on December 26. List of personnel SI Branch, Greece, January 18, 1945, Else to Lewis Leary, NARA 226/211/1/46.

3. Sperling's ("Sparrow") assistant Papadopoulos ("Raven") reported that German stay-behind agents were present in Salonika. A German naval officer in Salonika claimed to be a meteorologist, but he had no instruments. He had joined ELAS and led a group of German communist deserters in harassing the German withdrawals. But every night more Germans got away, avoiding British arrest, heading for Russia.

4. Glavin and Robert P. Joyce (Caserta) to 109 (Donovan), 154 (Shepardson), and Aldrich, December 3, 1944, NARA 226/M1642/83.

5. Penrose was replaced by Lewis Leary as head of Cairo SI, and Bailey, the acting head of the Greek Desk, who moved to Caserta as chief of Balkan SI, was replaced by Lt. Christian Freer (G2 or U.S. Army Intelligence). Glavin and Joyce cabled Else's request to Donovan. December 3, 1944, NARA 226/M1642/83. After the war, Penrose became head of the American University in Beirut until his premature death there in 1954.

6. "Plover" GA-146, December 3, 1944. Couvaras's report was marked "TO BE SHOWN U.S. ARMY and NAVY OFFICALS ONLY," evaluated as A-2, highest value, and circulated to Washington, London, Cairo, Caserta, AEG, and OSS files. NARA 226/108/68.

7. Assistant military attaché Captain William McNeill (G2) was with them. For photographs of the events, see Kessel 1994; Delavorrias 2006; and unpublished photographs taken by Couvaras in the Tsakopoulos Collection of the California State University, Sacramento (Couvaras CSUS). McNeill, personal communication.

8. "Chickadee" and "Tom-tit." This was the OSS reference report GA-149 of the December 3, 1944, events, filed a day later on December 4, 1944. It was evaluated A-2, the highest value, and circulated to Washington (Military Intelligence Division [MID]), ONI, and the State Department, as well as London, Cairo, Caserta, ISLO, AEG, and Files. NARA 226/108/68.

9. "Constitution Square events Dec. 3 1944." Draft. Couvaras CSUS.

10. "Plover" GA-181, filed on December 7, 1944, to supplement GA-149. Like Caskey's, Couvaras's report was evaluated as A-2, the highest value and circulated to Washington, London, Cairo, Caserta, ISLO, AEG, and to OSS files. NARA 226/108/68.

11. "Constitution Square events Dec. 3 1944." Draft. Couvaras CSUS.

12. "Plover" GA-181, filed on December 7, 1944, NARA 226/108/68.

13. Crosby, December 3, 1944, GA-038-3 to Leslie C. Houck in Washington. MEDTO daily report, December 20, 1944, NARA 226/99/35/3. Wines ms. p. 225.

14. MacVeagh Diary, December 5, 1944, in Iatrides 1980, 657.

15. Lt. Edward G. Wilson, Acting Chief, OSS Cairo, cable to Donovan and Aldrich, December 5, 1944, NARA 226/M1642/83.

16. Cpl. Constantine George, a courier forced to remain a month in Athens because of conditions, doubled as a code clerk.

17. On December 12, 1944. In MEDTO daily report for December 13, 1944, NARA 226/99/35/6. Else fortnightly report December 1–15 to Donovan, 226/M1642/83.

18. Else to E. G. Wilson, December 10, 1944, NARA 226/M1642/83.

19. Donovan and Lowman cable to Glavin in Caserta, December 6, 1944, NARA 226/99/35/6 and 226/M1642/82. Any changes in the relations with MacVeagh would come only from Donovan.

20. Glavin and Joyce cable to Else, December 6, 1944, in MEDTO daily report of December 9, 1944, NARA 226/99/35/6.

21. Unsettled conditions in Greece and bad weather at sea stretched the seven- to nine-day trip to Alexandria into three to four weeks.

22. E. G. Wilson cable to Donovan and Aldrich, December 5, 1944, NARA 226/M1642/83. Else to E. G. Wilson, December 10, 1944, ibid.

23. Else fortnightly report December 1–15 to Donovan. ISLD-B section. NARA 226/M1642/83.

24. SI cable for Donovan, Magruder, Secretariat, Bigelow, MEDTO and X-2, December 7, 1944.

25. Churchill 1953, 289–91.

26. Donovan cable to Else on December 10, 1944, in MEDTO daily report of December 12, 1944, NARA 226/99/35/6; MacVeagh to Franklin, December 8, 1944; Iatrides 1980, 660.

27. Without money or supplies, John Fatseas, based at Tripoli, covered also Kalamata, Kythera, Gythion, and Sparta; Skokos was at Patras; Captains Milton and James Stathakos "Stack" were in Yannina; George Doundoulakis covered Volos; and Kantianis handled Larissa. Else to E. G. Wilson, December 10, 1944, NARA 226/M1642/83.

28. Ibid.

29. Crosby to Luida Wendell "Wendy," December 9, 1944, NARA 226/190/8/61.

30. Else to E. G. Wilson, December 10, 1944, NARA 226/M1642/83.

31. Else to E. G. Wilson and Penrose, December 10, 1944. Else fortnightly report December 1–15 to Donovan. Else to Lt. E. G. Wilson, December 10, 1944. E. G. Wilson to Donovan, December 14, 1944, NARA 226/M1642/83.

32. E. G. Wilson in Cairo to Glavin, December 9, 1944. Cc'd to Else, Donovan, Aldrich, and Joyce. NARA 226/M1642/83. Doundoulakis 2008.

33. Else fortnightly report December 1–15 to Donovan. NARA 226/M1642/83.

34. E. G. Wilson to Glavin, December 9, 1944. The Athens office had twelve different kinds of currency on hand and kept records of every transaction, in dollars

or drachmae. Else fortnightly report December 1–15 to Donovan. NARA 226/99/52 and 226/M1642/83.

35. E. G. Wilson semimonthly report, November 30–December 15, 1944, to Donovan, NARA 226/99/52.

36. Else to E. G. Wilson, December 10, 1944, NARA 226/M1642/83.

37. Ibid.

38. Ibid.

39. Ibid.

40. Churchill 1953, 291–304.

41. E. G. Wilson Cairo cable to Donovan and Aldrich, December 5, 1944, and Crosby to Wendell, December 9, 1944, NARA 226/190 and 226/M1642/83.

42. Else to E. G. Wilson, December 10, 1944, NARA 226/M1642/83.

43. Else to C. M. Freer, December 11 and 14, 1944. Else fortnightly report December 1–15 to Donovan. Edson to Aldrich, February 19, 1945. NARA 226/190/7/57 and 226/M1642/83.

44. UNARMS UNRRA Greek Mission: Office of the Chief PAG-4/3.0.12.0.0. Box 1, 5 0527-0531. PAG-4/3.0.12.3.1.0.3. Thanks to Shelley Lightburn, UN Archives New York.

45. Freer to Else, December 17, 1944, NARA 226/190/7/57.

46. Jay Seeley was a thirty-five-year-old who had an M.A. from the University of Chicago and taught cartography and geography at Anatolia College. In Athens, he also took charge of translators, interviewers, and the motor pool. Seeley worked with Constantine Yavis of R&A.

47. MEDTO daily report, December 12, 1944, cable 0287 to R&A. NARA 226/99/35/6.

48. Churchill 1953, 304–324. Among the British troops was John Campbell, who became a pioneer anthropologist in Greece and had a long and distinguished teaching career at Oxford.

49. Freer to Else, December 17, 1944, NARA 226/190/7/57.

50. Savage escorted Rudas's body back to Cairo, where he was given a military funeral and buried in the American Military Cemetery near Heliopolis on the Suez road. A memorial service was held in Athens on the thirtieth, and Rudas was replaced by Thomas Lantzas. Couvaras 1978.

51. Churchill 1953, 304–24.

52. Crosby to Wallace, January 5, 1945 NARA 226/215/1.

53. Young to Thompson, January 21, 1945, Agora, Thompson, ASCSA.

54. Young to Thompson, January 13, 15, and 21, 1945, Agora, Thompson, ASCSA.

55. Wallace to George White, February 14, 1945. Cox to Young, January 22, 1945. "Notice to Members of the Institute," AIA Archives Box 9 File 7.

56. E. G. Wilson and Penrose cable for Aldrich to Donovan, Shepardson, and Magruder, December 8, 1944. Glavin, Joyce, and Maddox to Donovan and Aldrich, January 1, 1945, NARA 226/M1642/83. They recommended as Else's successor Lieutenant Colonel Van der Hoef, who had just arrived at Caserta.

57. Else to Freer, January 3, 1945. Edson June 1945 NARA 226/190/8/61 and RG 84.

58. While Else was in Cairo, Savage was honored with a Purple Heart and Silver Star for his help in the evacuation of Samos, and Horsebreeders agent George Doundoulakis was awarded the Legion of Merit.

59. He reflected on the last month's events "hardly very accurately described in Churchill's shocking speech to Parliament." Young to Thompson, January 21, 1945. Agora, Thompson, ASCSA.

60. Caserta wished to control X-2, Moyers, and Petrow. When Else departed, Clio Adossides was recalled to Cairo. Leary Cairo Reports to Washington, January 1–15, 1945, NARA 226/99/52/4. Else to Commanding Officer, January 31, 1945, 226/210/286/1.

61. Else to R. P. Joyce, Chief of Intelligence, Rear Zone, February 4, 1945, NARA 226/210/285/4, 226/M1642/83.

62. Else to Joyce, February 4, 1945, NARA 226/210/285/4.

63. Ibid.

64. Iatrides 1980, 669.

65. Freer arrived to assist Edson as executive officer, and Stathakos (Elephant) replaced him in Cairo.

66. Edson to Leary, March 11, 1945. Crosby "Field Report," May 14, 1945, NARA 226/99/57/4. Wallace had tried to interest Virginia Grace in the position for Blegen, but she considered it "beneath her dignity." They also considered Gladys Weinberg, librarian at the Athens embassy.

67. Daniel to Edson, February 1, 1945, NARA 226/190/8/61.

68. Young to Blegen, March 19, 1945. UCUA.

69. Petrou and Adossides were the oldest continuous Greek employees of OSS ME who served in Athens. For his labors, Petrou earned American citizenship, sponsored by George Skouras.

70. Freer replaced her, and a new executive officer arrived. Edson report, NARA 226/99/52/6.

CHAPTER FOURTEEN

1. Stevens to Lord, "Informal Report of April, May, June 1945," July 1, 1945, Admin/804/2/8, ASCSA.

2. Edson to Lawrence Houston, Acting SSO/NETO Cairo, June 22, 1945, NARA 226/190/8/61.

3. Wallace to Freer, April 24, 1945, and DeBardeleben to Edson, April 27, 1945, NARA 226/190/8/61. Ironically, R&A admitted that they could not produce their summaries without SI's reports.

4. Edson to Penrose, Divisional Deputy, Europe SI, May 30, 1945, NARA 226/215/1, and Edson, "Review of Greek Mission as of 20 June 1945," June 21, 1945, 226/190/8/61.

5. Shepardson to Aldrich, July 3, 1945, NARA 226/190/8/61.

6. The reports contributed by all of the archaeologists in 1943–44 (Owl, 1; Sparrow, 1; Pigeon, 4; Chickadee, 25; Duck, 0; and Thrush, 100), did not equal those of Gander, 193. NARA 226/190/8/61.

7. Sperling to Edson, January 31, 1945, NARA 226/190/211/8/33 and 190/8/61.

8. OSS History of Cairo, NARA 226/99/44/215.

9. Sperling to MacVeagh, May 14, 1945, NARA 226/165/1/3. Report of December to February 1945 SAINT Athens to SAINTS Cairo, Washington, London, April 21, 1945, 226/211/45/6. Control Cables from Daniel to Else, March 1, 1945, and Sperling to Edson April 6 and 9, 1945, 226/211/8/33.

10. Control Cables from Daniel to Else, March 1, 1945, and Sperling to Edson, March 28 and April 3, 6 and 9, 1945, NARA 226/211/8/33. Sperling to MacVeagh, May 14, 1945, 226/165/1/3.

11. Sperling to MacVeagh, May 14, 1945, NARA 226/165/1/3. Control Cables from Daniel to Else, March 1, 1945, and Sperling to Edson, March 28 and April 3, 6 and 9, 1945, 226/211/8/33. For Okhrana, see references in Mazower 2000, 58 n. 9.

12. Edson to Lawrence Houston, Acting SSO/NETO Cairo, June 22, 1945, NARA 226/190/8/61.

13. Edson to Penrose, Divisional Deputy, Europe SI, May 30, 1945, NARA 226/215/1; Edson, "Review of Greek Mission as of 20 June 1945," June 21, 1945; and Freer to Aldrich August 13, 1945, 226/190/8/61.

14. British and Greek attempts to replace ELAS in Evros did not stop. They infiltrated agents, but used the wrong courier, the secretary of the local Communist Party. Eventually, ELAS purged all pro-British leaders. Edson to Houston, June 18, 1945, NARA 226/211/2/3 and 226/190/8/61.

15. Edson to Penrose, Divisional Deputy, Europe SI, May 30, 1945, NARA 226/215/1. Edson report to Donovan, June 16–30, 1945, sent July 12, 1945, NARA 226/99/52/6.

16. Edson to Houston, June 16, 19, and 22, and Wallace to Edson, June 23, 1945, NARA 84 and 226/190/8/61.

17. Freer focused on "Safe Haven"—flight of Axis capital. Shepardson to Aldrich, July 3, 1945. Penrose to Edson, July 16, 1945. NARA 84.

18. Daniel and Georgiades helped W. McNeill and third secretary Leonard Cromie in Greek Macedonia.

19. Reports Officer Report for July 1945, August 18, 1945, NARA 226/99/52/6. Daniel to Edson, June 12, 1945, 226/190/2/22.

20. Aldrich to CO AMET, November 16, 1945, NARA 226/A1 224/166.

21. Progress Report, July 1–31, London Reports and Registry Office. De-Bardeleben to Sperling, October 16, 1945. Freer to DeBardeleben, October 6, 1945. NARA 226/190/8/61. Louis Frechtling IRIS chief to Moses Hadas, November 5, 1945. By December, Hadas's output represented the bulk of the information from the Greek Desk. Robert L. Wolff (RLU) to Hadas, December 4, 1945, 226/250/1. Sperling to DeBardeleben, October 20 and 24, 1945, and DeBardeleben to Sperling, October 24 and 25, 1945, 226/190/8/61.

22. George Emanuel (fig. 23) (previously X-2) and Constantinos "Gus" Peristianis came to Athens to work for Sperling in SSU with the latter circulating between Salonika and Athens. Emanuel worked on Safe Haven and Peristianis and Corporal Frederick Tunnell on the biographies, reviewing press. Both engaged in SI: Tunnell on Evvia and Peristianis in Central Macedonia and Western Thrace. Sperling to

Wallace, May 29 and June 12, 1946, Weekly Letter, NARA 226/215/1. Young to Thompson. Agora, ASCSA.

23. One was Jay Seeley, former R&A man from the Athens OSS office.

24. Report of Allied Mission to Observe the Greek Elections, April 1946. Department of State Publication 2522.

25. Sperling to Sherman Wallace, Chief SI, Southeastern Europe, SSU, War Department, March 14 and May 8, 1946. Sperling also discussed John Poulicos, in Cairo. Freer to Wallace, April 3, 1946, Wallace to Sperling, April 3 and 26, 1946, NARA 226/215/1.

26. Wallace to Sperling, July 9, 1946, NARA 226/215/1.

27. Sperling to Wallace, May 22, 1946, NARA 226/215/1.

EPILOGUE

1. MacVeagh to Roosevelt, February 17, 1944, in Iatrides 1980, 454.

2. Leighton 1963, 919–37. Jones 1996; 1997, 27–48; 2007, 93.

3. MacVeagh diary, December 3, 1943, in Iatrides 1980, 395–98.

4. Cox "Report on Field Conditions," January 11, 1945, NARA 226/250/64/4 and 226/210/64/4.

5. Donovan, memorandum to the Joint Chiefs of Staff, July 27, 1945, NARA 226/M1642/83.

6. Wallace to Edson, April 24, 1945, NARA 226/190.

7. Else.

8. Archives, ASCSA

9. Frantz to her mother, August 24 and September 2, 1946, Frantz/PU.

10. Named for General George Marshall, U.S. secretary of state.

11. Meritt 1984, 182.

12. Recently digitized and rereleased by the ASCSA.

13. The U.S. and Greece," pp. 256–60, Blegen Papers 25/3, Archives, ASCSA.

14. Keeley 1989.

15. Telegram from Marshall to Athens Embassy of June 10, 1948, for Winston Burdett of CBS from William Davidson Taylor. Donovan arrived on June 10. NARA 59/CDF 811.912/6 1048.

16. Costas Hadjiargyris to Stringer, May 24, 1948, NARA 59/CDF 811.91268/6-1048.

17. Admin 705/1, Archives, ASCSA.

18. Freer to DeDardeleben, December 3, 1945. In a letter recommending Sperling for the Legion of Merit Freer further noted that Sperling "frequently exposed himself to personal hardships and to physical danger from anti-American elements." He had demonstrated himself "to be the most conscientious, the most responsible and the most security conscious officer known to the undersigned. His highly intelligent and inquiring mind, his capacity for objectivity, his painstaking thoroughness, his alertness, and resourcefulness, his energy and enthusiasm have all combined to make him an example of the best type of intelligence operative produced by the United States in the course of the recent war." Freer to director of SSU, August 25, 1946, NARA 226/A1-224/732.

19. Weiner 2007. Helms led the CIA from 1966 to 1973.

20. Froehlich Rainey, the new director of the University of Pennsylvania's University Museum, boasted of recent hires: "Most of the new men who will join us in July of this year expect to work in foreign countries which are storm centres of political conflict. . . . They are for the most part young men who have been engaged in war service and presumably will return to such service if the present threat of a third world war materializes." Rainey, "From the Director," *UPMB* 13, no. 3: 3–5.

21. A portion of the diary appears in the A file of the Agora Archives, ASCSA. Meritt 1984, 189, 191.

22. University of Oregon Libraries, Special Collections and University Archives, Amoss Papers, Collection 005/2/5, 005/2/7, 005/2/11–13, and 005/8/4–5.
www.homelandsecurity.org/journal/Articles/displayarticle.asp?article=72-70k.
http://educationforum.ipbhost.com/index.php?showtopic=7171.

23. Meritt 1984, 182.

24. Helms to Lt. Col. William E. Walker, OSS Personnel, January 31, 1945, NARA 226/92A/19/283 and 226/A1-224/112.

25. Caskey to Dick, May 11, 1946. Helms to Walker, January 31, 1945. NARA 226/92A/19/283 and 226/A1-224/112. Srode 1999, 310; Cutler 2004.

26. Caskey to Dick, May 11, 1946, NARA 226/92A/19/283 and NARA 226/A1-224.

27. Harvard anthropologist and army major Carleton Coon (OSS Algiers, "Special Assistant in the U.S. Department of State," who had seen active service and was severely wounded in the North Africa campaign) had been appointed curator of ethnology for the museum's Africa and Oceania Section.

28. Daniel to J. M. Steeves, Division Near East and Africa Office of Information and Educational Exchange, Department of State, April 29 and August 5, 1948. Daniel to Gordon Bowles, National Research Council, May 21, 1948. Daniel to Blegen, June 22 and July 9 and 21, 1948, includes Young in the plan, but because the Turks had not signed pertinent legislation, considered excavating in the Dodecanese instead. Blegen to Daniel, July 17, 1948 (UPUMA). NARA 226/A1-224/166.

29. Daniel to Dow, May 11, 1948 (UPUMA). As a coda, Daniel recounted his Kourion achievements and published future plans. Benson 1972. Roger Edwards, the ASCSA student who accompanied Young to Delphi in 1946, accompanied them to Turkey. Edwards, personal communication.

30. *Annual Report of the AIA* 37 (1946), 49.

31. Dow to Rainey, November 20, 1947, Rainey to Dow, December 10, 1947, Daniel to Dow, May 11, 1948, concerning the establishment of the Fulbright Foundation and American School in Turkey (UPUMA). Young to Davis Goddard, November 25, 1963 (Turkey File, UPUMA).

32. Rubin 1989, 248–49.

33. Kapp wrote to Harold H. Burton, the former mayor of Cleveland and U.S. senator from Ohio who had become an associate justice of the U.S. Supreme Court. Burton correspondence, Library of Congress Manuscript Division, MSS14472/62, Miscellaneous Correspondence for 1945–1946.

34. Violet Kyle statement in Bazna 1962, 203. Kahn interviewed Gorman in May 1977, Kahn 1978, 591, 629.

35. Ruth Coutandin statement in Bazna 1962, 204–5.

36. It is not known whether McFadden funded Young's position. Daniel, then still doing intelligence work in Greece, was not McFadden's first choice. January 9, 1946, Kourion Correspondence—1946 (UPUMA).

37. Parsons served again from February to April 1947. To Stevens, July 8, 1946, Admin 804/2/11; HAT, Parsons correspondence, ASCSA.

38. Freer to DeBardeleben, December 3, 1945, NARA 226/A1-224/732; and Sperling's resume, Clio Sperling collection.

39. Magruder to Donovan, August 10, 1945, NARA 226/A1-224/595.

40. In this study, I have not scrutinized this line of questioning as it falls outside the chronological scope of the book. However, it is a profitable area of research for those postwar historians examining the role of American cultural institutions in U.S. relations with Greece.

41. "S.I. in Turkey," NARA 226/215/1/WN 25870. X-2 Turkey would establish substations in Izmir and the Adana-Iskenderun region, expand the substation in Ankara, and enlarge the Istanbul office. "Whatever may happen to the OSS Mission in Istanbul, it appears certain that X-2 should maintain a base office and base personnel in Istanbul. Istanbul will remain a most important center for espionage and counter espionage throughout the duration of the war and throughout the following peace. It affords a base of operations for X-2 activities which is reasonably secure and which can adequately be supplied." NARA 226/M1642/83, doc p. 9; and X-2 report, November 15, 1944, Cairo, 226/99/35/3.

42. Price 2003, 29–48; 2006, 12.

43. Brian Rose, former AIA president, has spearheaded this initiative and carried it out largely single-handedly.

INTERNAL ASSESSMENT

1. These reports are among the more sensitive materials, and many have yet to be declassified. These include the final reports of Rodney Young, Jerome Sperling, John Franklin Daniel, Carl Blegen, Alison Frantz, Benjamin Meritt, and Sterling Dow, several of whom continued their intelligence work after the war.

2. Crosby to Executive Officer, SI, May 14, 1945, "Field Report," NARA 226/92A/ 70/1303. Penrose to Shepardson, May 29, 1945, 226/99/57/3.

3. DeBardeleben, "Report on Field Conditions Transmitted by Major John L. Caskey," January 23, 1945, NARA 226/92A/19/283 and 226/210/64/4. Henceforth DeBardeleben. Edson to Donovan, through Shepardson, September 7, 1945, 226/190. "History of OSS Cairo," p. 109, 226/99.

4. "History of OSS Cairo," p. 109. MacVeagh to Edson, October 14, 1944. Archer to Edson, October 20, 1944, NARA 226/99.

5. Oliver "Report on Field Conditions," NARA 226/92/57/1 and 2 (henceforth Oliver). DeBardeleben. Calvocoressi "Report on Field Conditions," January 10, 1945, NARA 226/99/57/1 (henceforth Calvocoressi). Else, "Report on Field Conditions: Cairo and Greece," June 6, 1945, 226/92A/54/361, and Else to CO, "Report on Activities of OSS, Greece," January 31, 1945 (henceforth Else), 226/210/286/1. Penrose to Chief, SI, March 12, 1945, 226/M1642/83. DeBardeleben.

6. Calvocoressi. Else, "Report on Field Conditions: Cairo and Greece," June 6, 1945.

7. Caskey, "Report on Izmir Base January 23, 1945," NARA 226/210/277/2. Calvocoressi and DeBardeleben reiterated its inefficiency. DeBardeleben. Grace, "Report," January 10, 1945, NARA 226/190/3/35 (henceforth Grace).

8. Penrose to Chief, SI, "Report on Field Conditions by John L. Calvocoressi," March 2, 1945, NARA 226/99/57/1. DeBardeleben.

9. "OSS History," NARA 226/99, p. 94. Grace.

10. Else, "Report on Field Conditions: Cairo and Greece," June 6, 1945.

11. Penrose noted, with respect to Dow, that rotation should not be for "rest and relaxation only," to Shepardson, March 12, 1945, NARA 226/99/57/3. 226/M1642/83.

12. Oliver.

13. Penrose, "Report on Field Conditions Transmitted by Major John L. Caskey," February 2, 1945, NARA 226/92A/19/283. Georgiades to Young, February 21, 1944, 226/190/77/87.

14. Grace.

15. Penrose to Chief, SI, "Report on Field Conditions by John L. Calvocoressi," March 2, 1945, NARA 226/99/57/1. DeBardeleben.

16. Grace.

17. Grace.

18. Else, "Report on Field Conditions: Cairo and Greece," June 6, 1945, NARA 226/92A/54/361, and Else.

19. Calvocoressi. Else, "Report on Field Conditions: Cairo and Greece," June 6, 1945, NARA 226/92A/54/361.

20. Else, "Report on Field Conditions: Cairo and Greece," NARA 226/92A/54/361.

21. Crosby to Executive Officer, SI, "Field Report," May 14, 1945, NARA 226/92A/70/1303. Penrose to Shepardson, May 29, 1945, NARA 226/99/57/3.

22. Oliver.

23. "OSS History," NARA 226/99, p. 94. Grace.

24. "OSS History of Cairo SI," NARA 226/99.

25. Julia Child is a case in point. Anne Fuller was hired as a reports officer in Cairo in the summer of 1944.

26. Else.

27. Grace.

28. Calvocoressi. Grace. Young to colleagues, March 26, 1944, NARA 226/211/1.

29. 1st Lt. Tom Stix, "Report *Stygia* Mission," NARA 226/190/78/100.

WHO'S WHO

1. The Greeks and Turks were also given agent numbers and nicknames. All of the available agents had already worked for either the Emniyet or the British or Greek intelligence services and often all three.

Bibliography

ARCHIVES AND UNPUBLISHED SOURCES

Universities, Institutes, Colleges, and Scholarly Societies

American Farm School Ann K. House Papers. Memoirs.

American Philosophical Society (APS): Meritt Papers

American School of Classical Studies at Athens (ASCSA): Papers of C. W. Blegen, O. Broneer, W. B. Dinsmoor, B. H. Hill, R. H. Howland, G. D. Weinberg, H. A. Thompson (HAT) (includes papers of T. Leslie Shear [HAT Shear]), Administrative (Admin), Series 300, 800, and 1001, and Agora Archives

Archaeological Institute of America (AIA)

Benaki Museum, Department of Historical Archives, Zannas Papers, 542 and 562

British School at Athens (BSA)

California State University, Sacramento, Tsakopoulos Collection, Couvaras Papers (CSUS)

Greek Ministry of Foreign Affairs, Historical Archives

Institute for Advanced Study (IAS): Meritt Papers

Princeton University Rare Books and Manuscripts, Firestone Library: Mary Alison Frantz Papers CO772 (Frantz, PU); Archives, Mudd Library: Departmental, Student and Faculty files

University of Cincinnati, University Archives (UAUC): Papers of Carl Blegen, John L. Caskey

University of Iowa: University Archives, Special Collections, Papers of Gerald Else

University of Minnesota, Elmer Anderson Library: Kautz Family YMCA Archives, YMCA biographical files 1853–2004, Box 2.

University of Oregon Libraries: Special Collections and University Archives: Ulius Amoss Papers Collection 005.

University of Pennsylvania, University Museum Archives (UPUMA): Papers of

Dorothy Cox, John Franklin Daniel, Edith Hall Dohan, Gordion, Kourion, George McFadden, Rodney S. Young

Private Collections

Jasper Yeates Brinton. "East and Near East: Memoirs of a Philadelphia Lawyer." Typescript; XIV, 2. Memoirs Alternative XIII, 1, Diary, "Stanley Bay," "Burg el Arab," and correspondence. Geneva "War Chronicles." Josie Diary and correspondence. Nancy B. Turck 1972 interview typescript for the *Philadelphia Bulletin*.
Miriam Caskey
Clio Adossides Sperling

Public Record Office (PRO)

Foreign Office (FO) FO 371
War Office (WO) WO 106, 201, 202, and 208
Pawson SITREPS Reports of Smyrna Office to M.E. MO 4

National Archives (NARA)

RG 38 Correspondence with Naval Attaches 1930–1948, Boxes 1–5, 8
RG 59 U.S. Dept. of State Central Files, Central Decimal File (CDF) 1940–1944, 1945–
RG 84 U.S. Dept. of State Foreign Service Post Files, Diplomatic and Consular Posts
Entry 2694A Athens Legation General Records 1936–1945: Boxes 66–67
RG 129 Records of the Bureau of Prisons
RG 165 Records of the War Department General and Special Staff
RG 169 Records of the Foreign Economic Administration (FEA), Box 5
RG 319 Records of Army Staff Intelligence Command (G2) 1942–64 atrocities in Greece
RG 226 Records of the Coordinator of Information (COI) and the Office of Strategic Services (OSS): cited Record Group, Entry, Box, File 226/A1 224/518/1
Entry A1-224 Personnel Files: Boxes 13, 15, 29, 61, 112, 149, 150, 156, 166, 212, 218, 249, 250, 255, 268, 277, 286, 302, 391, 472, 496, 516, 518, 571, 592, 595, 611, 636, 717, 732, 736, 764, 794, 844, 860
Entry 92 COI/OSS Central Files: Boxes 1, 3, 5, 13, 14, 19, 22–28, 47, 49, 50, 57, 109, 112, 116, 132, 137, 312, 326
Entry 92A COI/OSS Central Files: Boxes 5, 13–20, 24, 54, 57, 67, 70, 71, 81, 120, 204, 283
Entry 99 OSS History Office Collection: Boxes 14, 35, 40–41, 45, 50, 52–57, 60, 63, 74, 94, 115, 286
Entry 100 Foreign Nationalities Branch: Boxes 1–9, 50–54, 95, 108–13, 115–31
Entry 108 Washington Registry SI Intelligence Files Field: Boxes 44–59, 60, 62–75, 410–31

Entry 108A Washington Registry SI Intelligence Files Field
Entry 124 Field Station Files
Entry 139 Washington Field Station Files: Box 147
Entry 144 Field Station Files
Entry 165 Records of OSS Operations, Mediterranean and Burma: Boxes 1–4
Entry 165A Records of OSS Operations
Entry 169A Records of Washington and London Special Funds: Box 5
Entry 190 Field Stations Files: Boxes 1–9, 71–78, 247, 471–72, 480, 511
Entry 190A Field Stations Files
Entry 194 Washington and Field Station Files: Athens, Cairo, Istanbul: Boxes 2 and 4
Entry 199 Field Station Special Funds Files: Boxes 78, 132, 198
Entries 202–19: Previously Withdrawn Documents: Entry 202: Box 1
Entry 210: Boxes 3, 5, 7, 8, 52, 57–58, 63–64, 168, 195, 198, 275, 277, 283, 285–86, 294, 313, 345, 358, 378, 389, 393, 401, 402, 410, 420, 422, 437, 470, 477, 484, 503, 510, 511
Entry 211: Boxes 1–2, 7, 14, 33, 45, 133, 187
Entry 215: Boxes 1, 54; Entry 216: Boxes 9, 484; Entry 219: Box 1
M1642 Microfilm Director's Office: Roll 83
United Nations Archives, Records Management Section (ARMS) UNRRA Collection, Greece Mission, 1944–1947
United States Army Military History Institute, Carlisle, PA, Papers of William J. Donovan Boxes 1–2, 16–19, 24, 34, 39–40, 51, 67–68, 71–75, 79, 81, 94, 104, 119, 121, 124–26, 359

PUBLISHED SOURCES AND DISSERTATIONS

Adam, P. 1987. Alexandria Revisited. *Twentieth Century Literature* 33 (3): 395–410.
AIA *Annual Reports* 1939–48 vols. 31–39.
Allen, S. H. 1999. *Finding the Walls of Troy: Frank Culvert and Heinrich Schliemann at Hisarlik.* Berkeley: University of California Press.
Alsop, S., and T. Braden. 1946. *Sub Rosa: The OSS and American Espionage.* New York: Reynal and Hitchcock.
American Friends of Greece. 1941. *Greece, 1821–1941.* New York: American Friends of Greece.
Archer, L. 1944. *Balkan Journal: An Unofficial Observer in Greece.* New York: W. W. Norton.
Auty, P., and R. Clogg, eds. 1975. *British Policy towards Wartime Resistance in Yugoslavia and Greece.* London: MacMillan.
Baerentzen, L., ed. 1982. *British Reports on Greece, 1943–4.* Copenhagen: Museum Tusculanum Press.
Baerentzen, L. J. O., J. O. Iatrides, and O. L. Smith. 1987. *Studies in the History of the Greek Civil War 1945–1949.* Copenhagen: Museum Tusculanum Press.
Bazna, E. 1962. *I Was Cicero.* New York: Harper and Row.

Beevor, A. 1991. *Crete: The Battle and the Resistance.* London: John Murray.

Benson, J. L. 1972. *Bamboula at Kourion: The Necropolis and the Finds Excavated by J. F. Daniel.* Philadelphia: University of Pennsylvania Press.

Blegen, C. W. 1943. Foreign Nationality Groups in the United States: The Greeks. Unpublished.

Boas, F. 1919. Scientists as Spies. *The Nation.*

Bradford, E. 1963. *The Greek Islands: A Travel Guide.* New York: Harper and Row.

Breuer, W. B. 1989. *Hitler's Undercover War: The Nazi Espionage of the U.S.A.* New York: St. Martin's.

Buckley, C. 1984. *Greece and Crete 1941.* Athens: Efstathiadis Group.

Byford-Jones, W. 1945. *The Greek Trilogy.* New York: Huntington.

Calvocoressi, P. 1989. *Total War: Causes and Courses of the Second World War.* Rev. ed. New York: Penguin-Putnam.

Carlile, E., and G. Scott. 2008. 1948 to 2008: ARCE Reflects on Its Past and Looks to Its Future. *Bulletin of the American Research Center in Egypt* 193 (Summer–Fall): 1–7.

Cassidy, W. L. 1983. *History of the Schools and Training Branch, Office of Strategic Services.* San Francisco: Kingfisher.

Cassimatis, L. 1988. *American Influence in Greece 1917–1929.* Kent, OH: Kent State University Press.

Casson, S. 1941. *Greece against the Axis.* London: Hamish Hamilton.

Cave Brown, A. 1975. *Bodyguard of Lies.* New York: Harper and Row.

Cave Brown, A. 1976. *The Secret War Report of the OSS.* New York: Berkeley Medallion.

Cave Brown, A. 1982. *The Last Hero: Wild Bill Donovan.* New York: Times Books.

Chalou, G. C., ed. 1992. *The Secrets War: The Office of Strategic Services in World War II.* Washington, DC: National Archives and Records Administration.

Chambers, J. W. 2008. *OSS Training in the National Parks and Service Abroad in World War II.* Washington, DC: National Parks Service.

Chaney, L. 1998. *Elizabeth David: A Biography.* London.

Churchill, W. 1950. *Hinge of Fate.* Vol. 4 of *The Second World War.* Boston: Houghton Mifflin.

Churchill, W. 1951. *Closing the Ring.* Vol. 5 of *The Second World War.* Boston: Houghton Mifflin.

Churchill, W. 1953. *Triumph and Tragedy.* Vol. 6 of *The Second World War.* Boston: Houghton Mifflin.

Clark, B. 2006. *Twice Strangers: The Mass Expulsions That Forged Modern Greece and Turkey.* Cambridge: Harvard University Press.

Clive, N. 1985. *A Greek Experience 1943–1948.* Wiltshire: Michael Russell.

Clogg, R. 2000. *Anglo-Greek Attitudes: Studies in History.* London: St. Martin's.

Clogg, R., ed. 2002. *Greece 1940–1949: Occupation, Resistance, Civil War. A Documentary History.* London: Palgrave.

Clogg, R., ed. 2008. *Bearing Gifts to Greeks: Humanitarian Aid to Greece in the 1940s.* New York: Palgrave Macmillan.

Close, D. H. 1995. *The Origins of the Greek Civil War.* London: Longman.

Close, D. H. 2002. *Greece since 1945.* London: Longman.

Constantinides, G. C. 1992. The OSS: A Brief Review of Literature. In *The Secrets War: The Office of Strategic Services in World War II,* ed. G. C. Chalou, 109–17. Washington, DC: National Archives and Records Administration.

Coon, C. S. 1980. *A North Africa Story: The Anthropologist as OSS Agent, 1941–43.* Ipswich, MA: Gambit.

Cooper, A. 1989. *Cairo in the War 1939–1945.* London: Hamish Hamilton.

Cooper, A. 1999. *Writing at the Kitchen Table: The Authorized Biography of Elizabeth David.* London: ECCO Press.

Cossaboom, R., and G. Leiser. 1998. Adana Station 1943–45: Prelude to the Post-War American Military Presence in Turkey. *Middle Eastern Studies* 34, no. 1: 73–86.

Couvaras, C. 1976. *OSS Me thn Kentrikh Tou EAM.* (OSS with the EAM Central Committee). Athens: Exantas.

Couvaras, C. 1978. *Photo Album of the Greek Resistance.* San Francisco: Wire Press.

Cowan, C. G. 1946. *The Voyage of the Evelyn Hope.* London: Cresset Press.

Cox, D. H. 1959. *Coins from the Excavations at Curium, 1932–1953.* Numismatic Notes and Monographs 145. New York: American Numismatic Society.

Cutler, R. 2004. *Counterspy: Memoirs of a Counterintelligence Officer in World War II and the Cold War.* Washington: Brassey's.

Damaskos, D., and D. Plantzos, eds. 2008. *A Singular Antiquity: Archaeology and Hellenic Identity in Twentieth-Century Greece.* Athens: Benaki Museum.

Danchev, A., ed. 1990. *Establishing the Anglo-American Alliance: The Second World War Diaries of Brigadier Vivian Dykes.* London: Brassey's.

Daniel, J. F. 1941. Prolegomena to the Cypro-Minoan Script. *American Journal of Archaeology* 45:249–82.

Davis, H., ed. 1942. *Greece Fights: The People Behind the Front.* New York: American Friends of Greece.

Davis, H., ed. 1991. *The Story of Athens College: The First 35 Years.* Athens: Athens College Press.

Davis, M. 1942. A Glimpse of the Total War Effort of the Greeks. In *Greece Fights: The People Behind the Front,* ed. H. Davis, 84–89. New York: American Friends of Greece.

Davis, T. W. 1989. A History of American Archaeology on Cyprus. *Biblical Archaeologist* 49:163–69.

Delavorrias, A. 2006. *H Photographos Voula Papaioannou apo photographiko arkhio to Mouseiou Benaki.* Kaiseriani: Ekdoseis Agra M. B.

De Loverdo, C. 1968. *Le battaillon sacré, 1942–1945.* Paris: Stock.

Denniston, R. 1997. *Churchill's Secret War: Diplomatic Decrypts, the Foreign Office, and Turkey 1942–44.* New York: St. Martin's.

Deringil, S. 1989. *Turkish Foreign Policy during the Second World War: An Active Neutrality.* Cambridge: Cambridge University Press.

Doundoulakis, H. 2008. *I Was Trained to Be a Spy: A True Story.* New York: X Libris.

Duke, F., and C. M. Swaart. 1969. *Name, Rank, and Serial Number.* New York: Meredith Press.

Durrell, L. 1971. *The Spirit of Place: Letters and Essays on Travel.* Ed. A. G. Thomas. New York: E. P. Dutton.

Durrell, L. 1973. *The Greek Islands.* New York: Viking Press.

Earle, E. M. 1940. National Defense and Political Science. *Political Science Quarterly* 55:481–95.

Edson, C. F. 1967. Greece during the Second World War. *Balkan Studies* 8:225–38.

Elliott, N. 1991. *Never Judge a Man by His Umbrella.* Wilton: Michael Russell.

Eudes, D. 1972. *The Kapetanios: Partisans and Civil War in Greece 1943–49.* New York: New Left Books.

Farago, L. 1971. *The Game of the Foxes: The Untold Story of German Espionage in the United States and Great Britain during World War II.* New York: David McKay.

Fayard, Fakhry, A. 1973. *Oases of Egypt.* Vol. 1. Cairo: American University in Cairo Press.

Fermor, P. L. 2003. *Words of Mercury.* Ed. A. Cooper. London: John Murray.

Fielding, X. 1953. *The Stronghold.* London: Secker and Warburg.

Fielding, X. 1954. *Hide and Seek: The Story of a War-Time Agent.* London: Secker and Warburg.

Fleischer, H. 1988. *Stemma kai Swastika: I Elladatis Kato chis kai tis Antistasis, 1941–1944* (Crown and Swastika: The Greece of the Occupation and Resistance, 1941–1944). Athens: Papazis.

Foot, M. R. D. 1984. *SOE: The Special Operations Executive, 1940–1946.* London.

Foot, M. R. D. 1992. The OSS and SOE: An Equal Partnership? In *The Secrets War: The Office of Strategic Services in World War II,* ed. G. C. Chalou, 295–300. Washington, DC: National Archives and Records Administration.

Foot, M. R. D., and J. M. Langley. 1979. *MI 9: Escape and Evasion, 1939–1945.* Boston: Little, Brown.

Ford, C., and A. MacBain. 1945. *Cloak and Dagger: The Secret Story of the OSS.* New York: Random House.

Forster, E. M. 1938. *Alexandria: A History and a Guide.* 2nd ed. Alexandria: Whitehead Morris.

Frazier, R. 1991. *Anglo-American Relations with Greece: The Coming of the Cold War 1942–1947.* London: Macmillan.

Friend, A. M., Jr. 1954. George H. McFadden. *American Journal of Archaeology* 58:154.

Galaty, M. L., and C. Watkinson, eds. 2004. *Archaeology under Dictatorship.* New York: Kluwer/Plenum.

Gerolymatos, A. 1992. *Guerrilla Warfare and Espionage in Greece, 1940–1944.* New York: Pella.

Gerolymatos, A. 2001. Greek War Time Actions: From the Albanian War to the Battle of Crete and National Resistance. In *Greece's Pivotal Role in World War II and its Importance to the U.S. Today,* ed. E. Rossides, 37–56. Washington, DC: American Hellenic Institute Foundation.

Gerolymatos, A. 2004. *Red Acropolis Black Terror.* New York: Basic Books.

Goodwin, J. 1976. *A Toponymy of Cyprus*. Nicosia: Cyprus College.

Goulter-Zervoudakis, C. 1998. The Politicization of Intelligence: The British Experience in Greece 1941–44. *Intelligence & National Security* 13, no. 1: 165–94.

Graftey-Smith, L. 2002. *Bright Levant*. London: Stacey International.

Grundon, I. 2007. *Rash Adventurer: A Life of John Pendlebury*. London: Libri.

Gyphtopoulos. 1990. *Mystikes Apostoles sten Echthrokratoumene Hellada, 1941–1944*. Athens: Ekdoseis Dodona.

Haag, M. 2004. *Alexandria: City of Memory*. New Haven: Yale University Press.

Hadjipateras, C., and M. Fafalios, eds. 1989. *Crete 1941 Eyewitnessed*. Athens: Efstathiadis.

Hadjipateras, C., and M. Fafalios, eds. 1995. *Greece 1940–41 Eyewitnessed*. Athens: Efstathiadis.

Hamilakis, Y. 2007. *The Nation and Its Ruins: Antiquity, Archaeology, and National Imagination*. Oxford: Oxford University Press.

Hamilakis, Y. 2008. Decolonizing Greek Archaeology: Indigenous Archaeologies, Modernist Archaeology, and the Post-colonialist Critique. In *A Singular Antiquity: Archaeology and Hellenic Identity in Twentieth-Century Greece*, ed. D. Damaskos and D. Plantzos, 273–86. Athens: Benaki Museum.

Hammond, N. G. L. 1983. *Venture into Greece: With the Guerrillas, 1943–1944*. London: William Kimber.

Hammond, N. G. L. 1991. The Allied Military Mission in Northwest Macedonia 1943–1944. *Balkon Studies* 32 (Winter): 107–44.

Hammond, N. G. L. 1995. *The Allied Military Mission and the Resistance in West Macedonia*. Thessaloniki: Institute for Balkan Studies.

Hamson, C. J. 1989. *Liber in Vinculis: or, The Mock Turtle's Adventures*. Trinity College Cambridge.

Hamson, D. 1947. *We Fell among Greeks*. London: Jonathan Cape.

Harakopos, G. E. 1998. *The Forgotten Debt*. Athens: Airjet.

Haritonitis, G. 2002. *Roupel: Aprilios 1941. Elliniko Logotechniko kai Istoriko*. Athens: Archeio.

Harris, C. H., and L. R. Sadler. 2003. *The Archaeologist Was a Spy*. Albuquerque: University of New Mexico Press.

Hawkes, J. 1982. *Adventurer in Archaeology: The Biography of Sir Mortimer Wheeler*. New York: St. Martin's.

Heatts, D. J. 1995. Footnote to Cicero. *CIA Historical Review Program*. September 18. https://www.cia.gov/library/center_for_the_study_of_intelligence/kent_csi/vol 1no4/html/v01i4a06p_0001.

Heinrichs, W. 1988. *Threshold of War: Franklin D. Roosevelt and American Entry into World War II*. New York: Oxford University Press.

Heinrichs, W. 1992. The United States Prepares for War. In *The Secrets War: The Office of Strategic Services in World War II*, ed. G. C. Chalou, 8–18. Washington, DC: National Archives and Records Administration.

Hellenic Army General Staff. 1997. *An Abridged History of the Greek-Italian and Greek-German War 1940–1941 (Land Operations)*. Athens: Army History Directorate Editions.

Hemingway, E. 1929. *A Farewell to Arms.* New York: Charles Scribner's Sons.

Henderson, M. 1988. *Xenia—a Memoir: Greece, 1919–1949.* London: Weidenfeld.

Herbert, K. 1998. Introduction: The Classics and Military Service. *Classical Bulletin* 74:1.

Higham, R. 1986. *Diary of a Disaster: British Aid to Greece, 1940–41.* Lexington: University of Kentucky Press.

Higham, R. 2001. Elements of Confusion: Britain and Greece, 1940–41. In *Greece's Pivotal Role in World War II and Its Importance to the U.S. Today,* ed. E. Rossides, 57–72. Washington, DC: American Hellenic Institute Foundation.

Hinsley, F. H. 1984. *British Intelligence in the Second World War.* Vol. 3:2, *Its Influence on Strategy and Operations.* New York: Cambridge University Press.

Hinsley, F. H. 1990. *British Intelligence in the Second World War.* Vol. 4, *Security and Counterintelligence.* New York: Cambridge University Press.

Hionidou, V. 2006. *Famine and Death in Occupied Greece, 1941–1944.* Cambridge: Cambridge University Press.

Hogan, D. W., Jr. 1991. *U.S. Army Special Operations in World War II.* Washington, DC: Center of Military History, Department of the Army.

Hogarth, P. 1988. *The Mediterranean Shore: Travels in Lawrence Durrell Country.* London: Pavilion.

Holland, J. 1988. *The Aegean Mission: Allied Operations in the Dodecanese, 1943.* Westport, CT: Greenwood Press.

Hondros, J. L. 1983. *Occupation and Resistance: The Greek Agony, 1941–44.* New York: Pella.

Hondros, J. L. 1988. Too Weighty a Weapon: Britain and the Greek Security Battalions. *Journal of the Hellenic Diaspora* 15, nos. 1–2: 36–37.

Hood, R. 1998. *Faces of Archaeology in Greece: Caricatures by Piet de Jong.* London: Leopard's Head Press.

Howard, M. 1968. *Mediterranean Strategy in the Second World War.* New York: Cambridge University Press.

Howard, M. 1990. *British Intelligence in the Second World War.* Vol. 5, *Strategic Deception.* Cambridge: Cambridge University Press.

Hunt, Sir D. 1989. The Intelligence Colonel's Tale. In *Trojan Horses,* ed. M. Young and R. Stump. London: Bodley Head.

Huot, L. 1945. *Guns for Tito.* New York: L. B. Fischer.

Iatrides, J. O. 1972. *Revolt in Athens: The Greek Communist "Second Round," 1944–1945.* Princeton: Princeton University Press.

Iatrides, J. O. 1980. *The Ambassador MacVeagh Reports: Greece, 1933–1947.* Princeton: Princeton University Press.

Iatrides, J. O. 1981. *Greece in the 1940s: A Nation in Crisis.* Hanover, NH: University Press of New England.

Iatrides, J. O. 2001. The Greek-Italian War: The View from the US Embassy in Athens. In *Greece's Pivotal Role in World War II and Its Importance to the U.S. Today,* ed. E. Rossides, 27–36. Washington, DC: American Hellenic Institute Foundation.

Iatrides, J. O., and L. Wrigley, eds. 1995. *Greece at the Crossroads: The Civil War and Its Legacy.* University Park: Pennsylvania State University Press.

Jakub, J. 1999. *Spies and Saboteurs: Anglo-American Collaboration and Rivalry in Human Intelligence Collection and Special Operations, 1940–45.* London: Macmillan.

Jones, M. 1996. *Britain, the United States and the Mediterranean War 1942–44.* London: MacMillan.

Jones, M. 1997. Macmillan, Eden, the War in the Mediterranean and Anglo-American Relations. *Twentieth Century British History* 8, no. 1: 27–48.

Jones, M. 2007. "Kipling and All That": American Perceptions of SOE and British Imperial Intrigue in the Balkans, 1939–1945. In *The Politics and Strategy of Clandestine War: Special Operations Executive 1940–1946,* ed. N. Wylie, 90–108. New York: Routledge.

Kahn, D. 1978. *Hitler's Spies: German Military Intelligence in World War II.* New York: Da Capo Press.

Kanellopoulos, P. 1964. *The Years of the Great War (1939–1944).* 2nd ed. Athens.

Kanellopoulos, P. 1977. *Imerologia, 31 Martiou 1942–4 Ianouaríou 1945* (Journal: 31 March 1942–1944–January 1945). Athens: Kedros.

Karamanolakis, V. 2008. University of Athens and Archaeological Studies: The Contribution of Archaeology to the Creation of a National Past (1911–1932). In *A Singular Antiquity: Archaeology and Hellenic Identity in Twentieth-Century Greece,* ed. D. Damaskos and D. Plantzos, 185–96. Athens: Benaki Museum.

Karamanos, G. 1943. *Lest We Forget That Noble and Immortal Nation . . . Greece.* New York: Athenian Press.

Kasapis, V. (Kriton). 1977. *Stan Korfo tis Gkymprenas: Chroniko tis Ethnikis Antistasis Stan Evro* (On the Summit of Gibrena: Chronicle of the National Resistance in Evros). 2 vols. Athens: Kalvos.

Katz, B. 1989. *Foreign Intelligence: Research and Analysis in the Office of Strategic Services, 1942–1945.* Cambridge: Harvard University Press.

Kazamias, G. A. 1992. Turks, Swedes, and Greeks: Some Aspects of Famine Relief in Occupied Greece, 1941–1944. *Balkan Studies* 33, no. 2: 293–307.

Keeley, E. 1989. *The Salonika Bay Murder: Cold War Politics and the Polk Affair.* Princeton: Princeton University Press.

Kent, R. 1942. I Saw Greece Looted. In *Greece Fights: The People Behind the Front,* ed. H. Davis, 60–66. New York: American Friends of Greece.

Kessel, D. 1994. *Ellada tou '44.* Athens: Aminos.

Kimball, W. F. 1984. *Churchill and Roosevelt: The Complete Correspondence.* Princeton: Princeton University Press.

King, P. 1983. *American Archaeology in the Mideast: A History of the American Schools of Oriental Research.* Philadelphia: American Schools of Oriental Research.

Kitroeff, A. 1989. *The Greeks in Egypt, 1919–1937: Ethnicity and Class.* London: Published for the Middle East Centre, St. Anthony's College, Oxford by Ithaca Press.

Kitroeff, A. 1982. A Divided Land: Greece in the Nineteen Forties. *Journal of the Hellenic Diaspora* 9, no. 2: 118–36.

Koliopoulos, J. 1977. *Greece and the British Connection 1935–1941*. Oxford: Clarendon Press.

Konstas, Admiral P. 1955. *I Ellas tis Dekaetias 1940–1950*. Athens.

Koridis, Y. 2003. *To Albaniko Epos 1940–41 Photographies: Arxeio Kouli Zampatha Keimena-Epilogi Yiannis*. Iolkos.

Kyrou, A. 1991. The Greek-American Relief Campaign for Occupied Greece, 1941–1944. In *New Directions in Greek-American Studies,* ed. D. Georgaka and C. Moskos, 111–27. New York: Pella.

Kyrou, A. 2001. Operation Blockade: Greek-American Humanitarianism during World War II. In *Greece's Pivotal Role in World War II and Its Importance to the U.S. Today,* ed. E. Rossides, 109–28. Washington, DC: American Hellenic Institute Foundation.

Ladas, A. 2010. *Falconera*. Athens: Lycabettas Press.

Laiou, A. 1984. The Resistance in Evros. *Journal of the Hellenic Diaspora* 11 (Fall): 33–38.

Langdon, M. 1976. *A Sanctuary of Zeus on Mount Hymettos*. Princeton, NJ: American School of Classical Studies at Athens.

Lankton, A. 1942. On the Eve of the Nazi Invasion. In *Greece Fights: The People Behind the Front,* ed. H. Davis, 37–40. New York: American Friends of Greece.

Lavender, D. S. 1962. *The Story of the Cyprus Mines Corporation*. San Marino, CA: Huntington Library.

Leeper, R. 1950. *When Greek Meets Greek: On the War in Greece, 1943–1945*. London: Chatto & Windus.

Leighton, R. 1963. Overlord Revisited: An Interpretation of American Strategy in the European War 1942–1944. *American Historical Review* 68:919–37.

Levides, A. 1975. Gia Hare tis Alithias: Intelligence kai Andistasi. Unpublished manuscript, Athens.

Lodwick, J. 1947. *Raiders from the Sea: The Story of the Special Boat Service in WWII*. Annapolis, MD: Naval Institute Press.

Lord, L. 1947. *A History of the American School of Classical Studies at Athens: 1882–1942*. Cambridge: Harvard University Press.

MacDonald, L. H. 1992. The OSS and its Records. In *The Secrets War: The Office of Strategic Services in World War II,* ed. G. C. Chalou, 78–102. Washington, DC: National Archives and Records Administration.

Mackenzie, C. 1931. *First Athenian Memories*. London: Cassell.

Mackenzie, C. 1932. *Greek Memories*. London: Cassell.

Mackenzie, C. 1940. *Aegean Memories*. London: Chatto and Windus.

Macris, B. J. 1979. The Foreign Policy of Ioannis Metaxas, 1936–1941. Ph.D. diss., Indiana University.

MacVeagh, M. 1942. The American Bandage Circle. In *Greece Fights: The People Behind the Front,* ed. H. Davis, 71–74. New York: American Friends of Greece.

Malakasses, J. T. 1980. *British American Conflict over the Question of Monarchy in Greece*. Ioannina: Ioannina University.

Marder, B. 2004. *Stewards of the Land: The American Farm School and Greece in the Twentieth Century.* Macon, GA: Mercer University Press.

Markatou, D. 2008. Archaeology and Greekness in the Centenary Celebrations of the Greek State. In *A Singular Antiquity: Archaeology and Hellenic Identity in Twentieth-Century Greece,* ed. D. Damaskos and D. Plantzos, 309–20. Athens: Benaki Museum.

Markoyianni, M. 1940. Diary. In *Greece 1940–41 Eyewitnessed,* ed. C. Hadjipateras, and M. Fafalios, 37–40. Athens: Efstathiadis.

Mauzy, C. 2006. *Agora Excavations, 1931–46: A Pictorial History.* Princeton, NJ: American School of Classical Studies at Athens.

Mazower, M. 1995. *Inside Hitler's Greece.* New Haven: Yale University Press.

Mazower, M. 2000. *After the War Was Over: Reconstructing the Family, Nation, and State in Greece, 1943–1960.* Princeton: Princeton University Press.

Mazower, M. 2006. *Salonica, City of Ghosts: Christians, Muslims, and Jews.* New York: Vintage.

Mazower, M. 2008. Archaeology, Nationalism and the Land in Modern Greece. In *A Singular Antiquity: Archaeology and Hellenic Identity in Twentieth-Century Greece,* ed. D. Damaskos and D. Plantzos, 33–42. Athens: Benaki Museum.

McClymont, W. G. 1959. *To Greece.* Wellington, New Zealand: War History Branch, Department of Internal Affairs.

McFadden, G. 1940. The Sanctuary of Apollo at Kourion. *UPMB* 8, no. 1: 2–21.

McNeill, W. H. 1947. *The Greek Dilemma: War and Aftermath.* Philadelphia: J. B. Lippincott.

McNeill, W. H. 1957. *Greece: American Aid in Action 1947–1956.* New York: The Twentieth Century Fund.

Meritt, L. S. 1984. *History of the American School of Classical Studies at Athens, 1939–1980.* Princeton, NJ: American School of Classical Studies at Athens.

Michalopoulos, A. 1943. *Greek Fire.* London: Michael Joseph.

Moss, W. S. 1950. *Ill Met by Moonlight.* New York: Macmillan.

Moysich, L. C. 1950. *Operation Cicero.* New York: Coward-McCann.

Munkman, C. A. 1958. *American Aid to Greece.* New York: Methuen.

Murphy, C. J. 2006. *Security and Special Operations: SOE and MI5 in the Second World War.* New York: Palgrave Macmillian.

Myers, E. C. M. 1955. *Greek Entanglement.* London: Alan Sutton.

Myres, J. L., and W. R. Paton. 1896. Karian Sites and Inscriptions. *Journal of Hellenic Studies* 16:188–271.

Myres, J. L. N. 1980. *The Blackbeard of the Aegean.* London: Leopard's Head Press.

O'Donnell, P. 2004. *Operatives, Spies, and Saboteurs: The Unknown Story of the Men and Women of World War II's OSS.* New York: Free Press.

Oikonomou, K. 1996. *H Mesanatolikh Allhnikh Tragodia 1941–1945.* Athens.

Owen, E. R. J. 1969. *Cotton and the Egyptian Economy.* Oxford: Oxford University Press.

Ozkan, T. 2001. *Bir Gizle Servisin Tarihi Milli Istibarat Teskilat* (The History of a Secret Service). Istanbul: National Intelligence Organization, N. D. Milliyet Yayinlari.

Papalas, A. J. 2005. *Rebels and Radicals: Icaria, 1600–2000.* Wauconda, IL: Bolchazy-Carducci.

Papayiannakis, E. 2004. *O Ellhnoikos Polemos 1940–41.* Iolkos.

Parish, M. 1993. *Aegean Adventures, 1940–43, and the End of Churchill's Dreams.* Lewes: Book Guild.

Parmelee, R., and E. Willms. 1942. Three Times "No." In *Greece Fights: The People Behind the Front,* ed. H. Davis, 46–52. New York: American Friends of Greece.

Paspati, G. 2009. *Dead Reckoning: A Memoir of World War II in the Aegean.* Privately printed.

Pelt, M. 1998. *Tobacco, Arms, Politics.* Copenhagen: Museum Tusculanum Press.

The Philhellene: Bulletin of the American Friends of Greece 1–9 (1940–50).

Phylactopoulos, G. S. 1991. Memoirs of a Witness: The German Occupation of Athens College (1941–1944). In *Athens College: The First 35 Years,* ed. H. Davis. Athens.

Plantzos, D. 2008. Archaeology and Hellenic Identity, 1896–2004: The Frustrated Vision. In *A Singular Antiquity: Archaeology and Hellenic Identity in Twentieth-Century Greece,* ed. D. Damaskos and D. Plantzos, 11–30. Athens: Benaki Museum.

Price, D. H. 2000. Anthropologists as Spies. *The Nation,* November 20, 24–27.

Price, D. H. 2003. Anthropology Sub Rosa: The CIA, AAA, and Ethical Problems Inherent in Secret Research. In *Ethics and the Profession of Anthropology: Dialogues for Ethically Conscious Practice,* ed. C. Fluehr-Lobban, 29–48. Walnut Creek, CA: Alta Mira.

Price, D. H. 2006. The Osthoff Affair. *Archaeology Magazine,* March–April, 12.

Price, D. H. 2007. *Anthropological Intelligence: The Deployment and Neglect of American Anthropology in the Second World War.* Durham, NC: Duke University Press.

Prinkipos Petros. 1997. *Hmerologia Polemou 1940–1941 A'.* Athens: Idryma Goulandri-Khorh.

Rainey, F. 1948. From the Director. *UPMB* 13, no. 3: 3–5.

Ranfurly, Countess of. 1955. *To War with Whitaker: The Wartime Diaries of the Countess of Ranfurly 1935–45.* London: Mandarin.

Rees, T. 2003. *Merchant Adventurers in the Levant: Two British Families of Privateers, Consuls, and Traders, 1700–1950.* London: Talbot.

Reimer, M. J. 1997. *Colonial Bridgehead: Government and Society in Alexandria, 1807–1882.* Boulder: Westview Press.

Roosevelt, K. 1976. *The Overseas Targets: War Report of the O.S.S.* New York: Walker.

Rossides, E., ed. 2001. *Greece's Pivotal Role in World War II and Its Importance to the U.S. Today.* Washington, DC: American Hellenic Institute Foundation.

Rubin, B. 1989. *Istanbul Intrigues.* New York: McGraw Hill.

Sakka, N. 2002. Archaeological Activities in Greece (1928–1940): Political and Ideological Dimensions. Ph.D. diss., University of Rethymno.

Sakka, N. 2008. The Excavation of the Ancient Agora of Athens: The Politics of Commissioning and Managing the Project. In *A Singular Antiquity: Archaeology and Hellenic Identity in Twentieth-Century Greece,* ed. D. Damaskos and D. Plantzos, 111–24. Athens: Benaki Museum.

Saloutos, T. 1964. *The Greeks in the United States.* Cambridge, MA: Harvard University Press.

Sarafis, S. 1980. *ELAS: Greek Resistance Army.* London: Merlin Press.

Seligman, A. 1996. *War in the Islands: Undercover Operations in the Aegean, 1942–4 Recalled by the Men of the Levant Schooner Flotilla, the Greek Sacred Company and Aegean Raiding Forces.* London: Sutton.

Sherman, A. J. 1998. *Mandate Days: British Lives in Palestine, 1918–1948.* New York: Thames and Hudson.

Shirer, W. L. 1941. *Berlin Diary: The Journal of a Foreign Correspondent, 1934–1941.* New York: Knopf.

Smith, B. F. 1983. *The Shadow Warriors: O.S.S. and the Origins of the C.I.A.* New York: Basic Books.

Smith, M. 1942. Unbeaten Greece. In *Greece Fights: The People Behind the Front,* ed. H. Davis, 76–79. New York: American Friends of Greece.

Smith, O. 1984. The Memoirs and Reports of the British Liaison Officers in Greece, 1942–1944: Problems of Source Value. *Journal of the Hellenic Diaspora* 11 (Fall): 9–32.

Smith, R. H. 1972. OSS: *The Secret History of America's First Central Intelligence Agency.* New York: Dell.

Southern, G. 2002. *Poisonous Inferno: World War II Tragedy at Bari Harbour.* Shrewsbury, UK: Airlife.

Speer, A. 1970. *Inside the Third Reich: Memoirs.* Trans. Richard and Clara Winston. New York: Simon and Schuster.

Sperling, J. 1942. Explorations in Elis. *American Journal of Archaeology* 46:77–89.

Srodes, J. 1999. *Allen Dulles: Master of Spies.* Washington: Regnery.

St. John, R. 1942. *From the Land of the Silent People.* Garden City: Doubleday, Doran & Co.

Stavrianos, L. S. 1950. The Munity in the Greek Armed Forces, April, 1944. *American Slavic and East European Review* 9 (December): 302–11.

Stoler, M. A. 1977. *The Politics of the Second Front: American Military Planning and Diplomacy in Coalition Warfare, 1941–1943.* Westport, CT: Greenwood Press.

Stoler, M. A. 2000. *Allies and Adversaries: The Joint Chiefs of Staff, the Grand Alliance, and U.S. Strategy in World War II.* Chapel Hill: University of North Carolina Press.

Stowe, L. 1942. No Other Road to Freedom. In *Greece Fights: The People Behind the Front,* ed. H. Davis, 90–96. New York: American Friends of Greece.

Sulzberger, C. 1969. *A Long Row of Candles: Memoirs and Diaries.* New York Macmillan.

Sweet-Escott, B. 1965. *Baker Street Irregular.* London: Methuen.

Sweet-Escott, B. 1975. SOE in the Balkans. In *British Policy towards Wartime Resistance in Yugoslavia and Greece,* ed. P. Auty and R. Clogg, 3–21. London: Macmillan.

Swindler, M. H. 1948. John Franklin Daniel III 1910–1948. *American Journal of Archaeology* 52:4 (2 unnumbered pages).

Theotokas, G. 1982. *Tetradia Imerologia (1939–1953)* (Pages from a Diary, 1939–1953). Athens: Estia.

To Albanikos Epos 1940–41. 2003. Photographies Arkehio Koulh Zampatha Keimena-Epilogh Iolkos: Yiannhs Koridis.

Troy, T. 1980. *Donovan and the CIA.* Washington, DC: Central Intelligence Agency.

Troy, T., ed. 1987. *Wartime Washington: The Secret OSS Journal of James Grafton Rogers.* Frederick, MD: University Publications of America.

Turk, H. *Milli Istihbarat Teskilati* (National Intelligence Organization). Akademi TV Programcilik.

U.S. Department of State. 1964. *Foreign Relations of the United States. The Conferences at Washington and Quebec. 1943.* Vol. 4 (FRUS). Washington, DC.

U.S. Department of State. 1983. *Peace and War: United States Foreign Policy, 1931–1941.* Washington, DC: U.S. Government Printing Office.

U.S. War Department, Secret Service Unit. 1976a. *War Report of the OSS (Office of Strategic Services).* New York: Walker.

U.S. War Department, Secret Service Unit. 1976b. *The Overseas Targets: War Report of the OSS.* Vol. 2. New York: Walker.

Valentine, D. 2004. *The Strength of the Wolf: The Secret History of America's War on Drugs.* London: Verso.

Vatikhiotis, P. J. 1998. *Popular Autocracy in Greece, 1936–41: A Political Biography of General Ioannis Metaxas.* London: Frank Cass.

Vivian, C. 2000. *The Western Desert of Egypt: An Explorer's Handbook.* Cairo: American University in Cairo Press.

Vlanton, E. 1982a. The O.S.S. and Greek-Americans: An Introduction. *Journal of Hellenic Diaspora* 9, no. 1: 31–84.

Vlanton, E. 1982b. Documents: The O.S.S. and Greek-Americans. *Journal of Hellenic Diaspora* 9, no. 2: 36–104; 9, no. 3: 65–132; and 9, no. 4: 63–110.

Wace, A. J. B., and M. S. Thompson. 1914. *Nomads of the Balkans: An Account of Life and Customs.* New York: E. P. Dutton.

Wallace, D. 1982. Conditions in Zervas-Held Territory in Greece. In *British Reports on Greece 1943–44,* ed. L. Baerentzen, 119–40. Copenhagen: Museum Tusculum Press.

Ward, M. 1992. *Greek Assignments: SOE 1943–1948 UNSCOB.* Athens: Lycabettus Press.

Waterhouse, H. 1986. *The British School at Athens: The First Hundred Years.* London: Thames and Hudson.

Waugh, E. 1955. *Officers and Gentlemen.* Boston: Little, Brown.

Weiner, T. 2007. *Legacy of Ashes: The History of the CIA.* New York: Doubleday.

West, N. 1998. *British Security Coordination: The Secret History of British Intelligence in the Americas, 1940–45.* London: St. Ermin's Press.

Windmill, L. A. 2006. *A British Achilles: The Story of George, 2nd Earl Jellicoe KBE DSO MC FRS, Soldier, Diplomat, Politician.* Barnsley: Pen and Sword.

Winks, R. W. 1987. *Cloak & Gown: Scholars in the Secret War, 1939–1961.* New York: Morrow.

Winks, R. W. 1992. Getting the Right Stuff: FDR, Donovan, and the American Quest for Professional Intelligence. In *The Secrets War: The Office of Strategic Services in World War II,* ed. G. C. Chalou, 19–38. Washington, DC: National Archives and Records Administration.

Wires, R. 1999. *The Cicero Spy Affair.* Westport, CT: Praeger.

Woodhouse, C. M. 1948. *Apple of Discord.* London: Hutchinson.

Woodhouse, C. M. 1975. Summer 1943: The Critical Months. In *British Policy towards Wartime Resistance in Yugoslavia and Greece,* ed. P. Auty and R. Clogg, 117–46. London: Macmillan.

Woodhouse, C. M. 1976. *The Struggle for Greece, 1941–1949.* Chicago: Ivan R. Dee.

Woodhouse, C. M. 1982. *Something Ventured.* London: Granada.

Wylie, N., ed. 2007. *The Politics and Strategy of Clandestine War: Special Operations Executive, 1940–1946.* New York: Routledge.

Young, R. 1940. Archaeological Notes: Excavation on Mount Hymettos, 1939. *American Journal of Archaeology* 44:1–9.

Young, R. 1942. In Lesnitza. In *Greece Fights: The People Behind the Front,* ed. H. Davis, 22–26. New York: American Friends of Greece.

Zannas, A. 1964. *I Katochi: Anamniseis-Epistoles* (The Occupation: Memories-Letters). Athens: Estia.

Zannas, A. P. 2008. Ce que j'ai vu dans la Grèce d'aujourd'hui: Alexandros Zannas and the Greek Red Cross. In *Bearing Gifts to Greeks: Humanitarian Aid to Greece in the 1940s,* ed. R. Clogg, 113–24. New York: Palgrave Macmillan.

Index

Adana, Turkey, 102, 108, 187, 188, 189, 366n8, 395n41
Adossides, Anastasios, 5, 16, 23, 36, 39, 41, 50, 54, 66, 72–73, 100, 339n14, 339n16, 348n41
Adossides, Bessie, 37, 72, 256, 333n46, 338n12, 339n14, 339n16, 339n19, 348n41, 352n31
Adossides, Clio Philippidou. *See* Clio
Adossides, Costas, 5, 36, 38, 58, 60, 62, 79–80, 336n37, 338n12, 343n41, 348n4, 359n60
Adossides, Elli, 36–37, 39, 41, 43, 44, 49, 50–51, 58, 80, 231, 256, 281, 331n21, 333n51, 335n19, 336n36, 339n12, 377n14
AFHQ (Allied Forces Headquarters), xi, Algiers, 96
See also Caserta
AHEPA (American Hellenic Educational Progressive Association), 32, 78, 99, 130, 174, 304, 358n45
AIA. *See* Archaeological Institute of America
Aivalik, 127, 139, 318, 331n21, 386n57
Ajax mission (Aetolia: Agrinion to Gulf of Arta), 202, 237, 314
Albania, 5, 11, 18–19, 23, 27, 34–35, 40, 47, 51, 54, 73, 98, 134, 164, 166, 212, 214,
234, 263–65, 267, 277, 279, 309, 326, 329n11, 330n17, 333n48, 335n16, 347n36
Albanian Campaign (Greco-Italian War), 14, 20, 23, 27–59, 73, 329n9
Albright Institute of Archaeological Research. *See* American School of Oriental Research
Alcinoos mission (Corfu, Fano, Erikousa), 165, 177, 203, 234, 312
Aldrich, Harry S., 212, 215, 218–20, 226–27, 229–33, 235–36, 257, 262–63, 303, 384n36, 385n46, 385n49, 387n2
Alexandretta (Iskenderun), Turkey, 27, 107, 346n22, 351n22, 395n41
Alexandria, Egypt, 2, 62–63; Greek Desk base at, 85, 88–90, 96–97, 105, 110, 122, 124, 127, 134–37, 151, 154, 156, 161, 164, 169–70, 196, 213, 218, 275, 284, 304, 320, 332n30, 344n49, 352n30, 359n55, 363n47, 364n60, 364n65, 365n80, 386n57, 389n21
Allied Forces Headquarters. *See* AFHQ
Allied Military Mission (AMM), 150, 165, 176, 211, 212, 226, 284, 298, 304, 362n38, 368n28
ambulance
    Iaso, 31–33, 36, 39–41, 46, 48, 54, 69, 74, 329n5, 330n20, 331n26

413